D1435505

Geological Conservation Review

Quaternary of Wales

S Campbell and D Q Bowen

W A Wimbledon
Editor in Chief

NCC catalogue number **A4.1**

Contents

Preface

General preface to the Geological Conservation Review series

The British Isles, a comparatively small land area, contains an unrivalled sequence of rocks, rich and varied mineral and fossil deposits, and landforms spanning much of the Earth's long history, including most of that since the appearance of life. Well documented ancient volcanic episodes, famous fossil sites, and sedimentary rock sections used as comparative standards around the world, have given these islands an importance out of all proportion to their small size. The fact that these long sequences of strata and their organic and inorganic contents, evidencing enormous periods of time, have been studied by generations of leading geologists gives Britain a unique status in the development of the science. Many of the divisions of geological time used throughout the world are named after British sites or areas, for instance the Cambrian, Devonian, and Ordovician systems, the Ludlow Series or the Kimmeridgian and Portlandian stages.

The Geological Conservation Review (GCR) was initiated in late 1977 to assess, document and ultimately publish descriptions of the most important parts of this rich heritage. The GCR is intended as a review of the current state of knowledge of the key earth-science sites in Great Britain. It provides a firm factual basis on which site conservation will be founded in coming years. Each of the volumes of the GCR series describes and assesses key sites in the context of a portion of the geological column, or a geological, palaeontological or mineralogical topic. Each site description and assessment is a justification of a particular scientific interest at a locality, of its importance in a British or international setting, and ultimately, by implication, of its worthiness for conservation.

The aim of the Geological Conservation Review series is to inform landowners and occupiers of land, geologists and other scientists, planners and members of a wider public of special features of interest in sites being considered for notification as Sites of Special Scientific Interest (SSSIs). It is written to the highest scientific standards but in such a way that the assessment and conservation value of the sites is clear. It is a public statement of the value set on our geological heritage by the earth-science community which has participated in its production, and it will be used by the Nature Conservancy Council (NCC) in carrying out its conservation functions.

All the sites described in this volume have been proposed for notification as SSSIs by NCC staff, the final decision to notify or renotify is made by the Council itself.

Preface to the Quaternary of Wales

This volume, the first in the Geological Conservation Review series, describes the Quaternary rocks and landforms of Wales. It covers the evidence in the rock record for Pleistocene glaciations, fluctuating sea-levels during and between these catastrophic cold phases, and the presence of ancient flora and fauna, including early Man. The severe climatic decline that characterises the last part of the Cenozoic Era ends with the present (Holocene) interglacial, a period of rapid vegetational change reflecting the climatic improvement which has come with the last ten thousand years of geological time (West 1968).

British geologists were relatively slow to accept the full glacial origins of landscapes and deposits as they had been expounded by Alpine workers such as Venetz and Charpentier in the 1820s and 1830s (North 1943). As late as 1852, Ramsay was systematically documenting and interpreting the evidence for the land-based nature of Britain's ice-masses (Ramsay 1852, 1860; Zittel 1901). The spectacularly glaciated terrain of Wales, particularly Snowdonia, was of the greatest importance in the establishment and acceptance of the Glacial Theory. It was in Wales and the Welsh borderlands that it was for the first time demonstrated that the 'Ice Age' was in fact not a single event, but a sequence of cold events separated by temperate phases. The ice-carved Welsh uplands still form classic ground for the student of Pleistocene glacial history and geomorphology. They and the coastal fringe have been at the forefront of research in recent years (Lowe and Walker 1984).

The layout of this volume reflects a dual need: to demonstrate adequately the scientific and conservation interest of the localities it describes, and to elucidate the significance of sites in the context of the volume and of the Quaternary of Britain. The first chapter, written by Professor D Q Bowen, is a general account of the Quaternary, and this combined with the simplified conclusion section of each site description is intended for the less specialist reader. Chapter 2 and all other descriptive and interpretive material in the volume is written in language consistent with that in publications on the Pleistocene and Holocene, and is intended for a readership in the earth-sciences and related fields.

Each account of a site in this volume is given in the context of an area, the geology and geomorphology

4

of which is described in a chapter introduction. Each locality is described in detail in a self-contained account, consisting of highlights (a précis of the specific interest of the site), an introduction (with a concise history of previous work), a description, an interpretation (assessing the fundamentals of the site's scientific interest and importance), and a conclusion (written in simpler terms for the non-specialist).

The terminology employed in the text is conservative; we do not attempt any radical refinement of what is in some cases a confused nomenclature. The Pleistocene Series/Epoch has had a basal stratotype defined, and this has received international recognition – we follow this usage. The Holocene is variously regarded as a sub-division of the Pleistocene (very reasonably because it includes the present interglacial) which would give it a status equivalent to a stage, or as a series separate from the Pleistocene. The Pleistocene Series is widely regarded by geologists as a series of the Neogene System, along with the earlier Miocene and Pliocene series. Quaternary is here used in a somewhat loose sense, following its traditional usage for the last part of Cenozoic time, and as a less precise alternative to a combined Pleistocene and Holocene. The final decision on whether Quaternary is to be retained and what its hierarchical status and definition will then be, are matters presently being considered by the International Commission on Stratigraphy.

Special note

This volume is not intended for use as a field guide. The description or mention of any site should not be taken as an indication that access to a site is open or that a right of way exists. Most sites described are in private ownership, and their inclusion herein is solely for the purpose of justifying their conservation. Their description or appearance on a map in this work should in no way be construed as an invitation to visit. Prior consent for visits should always be obtained from the landowner and/or occupier. Information on ownership of particular sites may be available from the appropriate NCC regional office – see next page.

Acknowledgements

Acknowledgements

Work started on this volume with the preliminary compilation of a site coverage by Dr Wishart Mitchell. This early work was incorporated into a final list, and documentation and draft writing was undertaken by Dr Stewart Campbell between 1983 and 1986. A full first draft of this volume was completed by him in May 1988. Drafts of the first two chapters were completed in January 1989 by Professor D Q Bowen, who jointly edited the remainder of the volume.

We would like to acknowledge the many colleagues who have made an invaluable contribution to the production of this volume and the site coverage which it describes. In particular, we thank the following for detailed discussion and information: Dr M J C Walker, Dr P D Moore, Dr J M Gray, Dr D F Ball, Dr A J Sutcliffe, Dr F M Chambers, Dr B S John, Dr G E Saunders, Professor J A Taylor, Professor J Rose, Dr Y Battiau-Queney, Dr A J Stuart, Dr H S Green, Mr J G Rutter, Mr M Davies, Dr N F MacMillan and Dr R C Preece.

Further useful information was provided by Professor A G Smith, Dr K Simpkins, Professor J B Whittow, Dr C Harris, Dr I D Ellis-Gruffydd, Dr C A Lewis, Dr R A Shakesby, Mr I C Thompson, Mr M D Wright, Dr R Donnelly, Mr P S Wright, Dr G S P Thomas and Brother J van Nedervelde. S Campbell thanks Dr G P Black and Dr J E Gordon for their enthusiastic encouragement in the early stages of the project.

Professor N Stephens kindly provided facilities in the Department of Geography at University College, Swansea during the field assessment phase of the project.

It is also a pleasure to acknowledge the contribution made to this work by Mrs Shirley Drake, who typed early versions of the text, by Miss Kathleen Harrison, who typed the final draft, and by Mr Paul Butler who drafted the figures. The work on the volume bibliography and on bibliographic searching by Mr Peter Cann and Mr Kevin Hayward is also acknowledged with thanks.

Lastly, we would like to acknowledge Professor Nicholas Stephens for his constructive comments on the typescript in his capacity as referee.

Information

Information on conservation matters relating to Sites of Special Scientific Interest (SSSIs) or National Nature Reserves (NNRs) in particular counties or districts may be obtained from the relevant Nature Conservancy Council Regional Officer as listed below –

Regional Officer
Dyfed – Powys Region
Plas Gogerddan
Aberystwyth
Dyfed
SY23 3EE

Regional Officer
North Region
Plas Penrhos
Ffordd Penrhos
Bangor
Gwynedd
LL57 2LQ

Regional Officer
South Region
43 The Parade
Roath
Cardiff
CF2 3UH

An introduction to the Quaternary

1

The geologically recent ice ages opened some 2.4 million years ago and they include the 'geological present' (Zagwijn 1974; Ruddiman and Raymo 1988). To some the Quaternary is synonymous with the Ice Age. The reality is, however, that there have been many ice ages (glacials), each separated by interglacials, when the climate of the Earth was similar to the present. Quaternary Science seeks to understand the way in which the various interactive systems of the planet Earth have functioned in the past, to explain the present, and thereby to predict the future.

During the Quaternary (the Pleistocene Series and Holocene combined), erosional agencies, particularly those of rivers and glaciers, fashioned the British landscape. The rock debris that this produced was deposited in a variety of environments and became the parent material for soils.

Repeated climatic change subjected the flora and fauna of northern lands to stress. Populations of plants and animals were forced to migrate southward or northward in response to, respectively, worsening or improving climate. Little evolution of the flora occurred and the majority of Quaternary plant species are still with us today. Many former vegetational environments, however, lack modern counterparts; therefore, the geological dictum that 'the present is the key to the past' is not always applicable. Interglacial environments in the British Isles were characterised by a mixed deciduous oak forest (the climax vegetation). This was replaced by tundra and polar desert during the ice ages, when extensive ice-sheets sometimes developed. The last time the British Isles experienced conditions similar to the present was about 125,000 years ago, when the interglacial (part of the Ipswichian Stage) lasted some 10,000 years. Because the present (Holocene) interglacial has already lasted 10,000 years, a geological perspective would indicate that the present flora and fauna consists of rare and endangered species.

Unlike the flora, some elements of the fauna did evolve. The evolution of Man and his increasing capacity for modifying his environment, both deliberately and inadvertently, has been an outstanding characteristic of the Quaternary. Indeed a Russian view is that the period should be called the Anthropogene. Some large mammal types evolved, but they are of limited value in trying to sub-divide the Pleistocene and Holocene. The major extinctions of certain large species (for instance, the mammoth) at the end of the Pleistocene may be in part, if not mostly, attributable to Man.

The succession of ice ages (glacial) and interglacials has occurred at known frequencies, and one of the goals of Quaternary Science is to predict future changes in climate, for example global warming, and to reveal whether Man's activities are sufficient to override natural tendencies in the Earth's climatic patterns.

The Geological Conservation Review sites described in this volume are the building blocks from which the Pleistocene and Holocene evolution of Wales may be determined. They include some unique evidence for the timing of glacier advances and retreats, major changes in sea-level, and movements of the Earth's crust. These sites are important in a wider context, because Wales lies on the margin of the North Atlantic, where climatic change is translated, through the dynamic coupling of atmosphere, oceans and biosphere, into rapid environmental changes. These changes have been exceptionally rapid by comparison with the geological timescale, and their implications are potentially relevant to society. Thus, the Quaternary history of Wales assumes a disproportionate importance in the wider context of research in our hemisphere into why and how environments change through time.

The history of the ice ages

Evidence from planktonic fossils in North Atlantic ocean sediments shows that sea temperatures fell at the beginning of the Quaternary, as polar ice-sheets grew and launched ice-floes into the surrounding seas (Ruddiman and Wright 1987; Ruddiman and Raymo 1988).

Changes in the global climate were driven by two principal controlling (forcing) agencies. First, by movements in the Earth's crust; changes which created and modified continents and oceans, especially mountain ranges and seaways, and which in turn have influenced ocean currents. Second, by changes in the Earth's orbit around the Sun, which have led to variability in the amount of solar radiation received at the outer edge of the atmosphere at different latitudes. Together, these two effects have altered interactions between the atmosphere, the oceans and the continents, notably in bringing about changes in continental and oceanic biomass and chemistry. Such effects have in turn led to climatic change.

Northern hemisphere glaciation began with the closure of the Straits of Panama and the creation of the Isthmus of Panama by crustal upheaval, at about 3.1 million years ago. This ended the latitudinal movement of surface waters between the Atlantic and Pacific Oceans, and replaced it with a meridional flow in the North Atlantic. Thus, warmer waters reached higher latitudes, and created a potential for the increased precipitation necessary for ice growth. Shortly afterwards, glaciers developed in Iceland (Einarsson and Albertson 1988). It was not until about 2.4 million years ago, however, that large ice-sheets spread in middle latitudes (Shackleton *et al.* 1984).

Evidence for long-term climatic change throughout the Quaternary is not readily available on the continents. This is because the continental (land) environment is largely one of net erosion, and evidence for earlier events has been, and is being, continually destroyed. On the other hand, long sequences of sediments build up, more or less continuously, on the floor of the deep open ocean. Investigation of these undisturbed sediments has provided an historical (stratigraphic) framework unequalled in its detail (Shackleton and Opdyke 1973).

Such ocean sediments have provided three principal lines of evidence, all of which indicate simultaneous changes in environmental conditions. These are –

1   Oxygen isotope analysis of the $^{18}O/^{16}O$ ratio in planktonic and benthonic organisms (foraminifera) provides a signal for the variability of the isotopic composition of the global ocean. Because this composition is controlled principally by the volume of ice, it is also a signal of warm and cold events, and of ice growth and decay. It therefore, provides a framework of global significance and applicability (Shackleton and Opdyke 1973).

2   Past sea-surface temperatures (SSTs) may be calculated from assemblages of fossil planktonic organisms in the sea bed sediments.

3   Ice-rafting episodes during colder periods caused the input of coarse sediment to the ocean floor sequence. These periods of clastic sedimentation alternated with episodes of high calcium carbonate ($CaCo_3$) productivity which occurred during warmer times.

The location in cores of the deep-sea sediments of a major reversal in the Earth's magnetic field, the Matuyama-Brunhes reversal at 730,000 years BP (before the present), provides a yardstick with which to estimate the duration and timing of the ice ages. This reversal can be detected in Pleistocene rocks around the world.

Cycles of changing ice volumes, and hence climatic variability as shown by deep-sea cores, have been matched with the changes in the pattern of the Earth's orbital rhythms; its cycles of eccentricity (with a periodicity of 100,000 years), tilt (41,000 years) and precession (23,000 and 19,000 years) (Hayes *et al.* 1976; Imbrie and Imbrie 1979). These

strong similarities show that orbital forcing (changing orbital patterns) has almost certainly been responsible for the succession of Quaternary ice ages. However, it does not show how climatic change actually occurs. Orbital fluctuations probably act to trigger interactions between atmosphere, oceans, biosphere and cryosphere (the realm of snow and ice). In these, the role of atmospheric carbon dioxide appears to be of major importance, because it has been shown that orbital changes precede changes in atmospheric carbon dioxide and, in turn, ice volume (climatic) changes (Shackleton *et al.* 1983).

The deep-sea sediment pile has been sub-divided on the basis of its changing oxygen isotope chemistry into a number of successive oxygen isotope stages. These can be recognised on a global basis. Because the mixing time of the global ocean is only about 1,000 years, correlation within the ocean is accurate to within that length of time. These stages (running counter to normal geological practice) are numbered backwards in time and down through the column. Low ice volume stages (interglacials) are given odd numbers, and so the latest, the Holocene, is Stage 1. Times of high ice volume (ice ages) are given even numbers, and thus the last glacial phase is Stage 2. Stages may be sub-divided into sub-stages, for example, Stage 5 into Sub-stages 5a, 5c and 5e.

The age of oxygen isotope stage boundaries is based on their positions relative to the Matuyama-Brunhes magnetic reversal in each sea bed core, and on calculations of thickness founded on an assumption of constant sedimentation rates. The original age calculations (Shackleton and Opdyke 1973) have been refined by means of 'orbital tuning', that is, they have been adjusted using known orbital frequencies (Imbrie *et al.* 1984; Martinson *et al.* 1987).

With these data it is possible to trace the history of the ice ages. The earliest ice-sheets, between 2.4 million and 900,000 years ago, fluctuated on a scale of 41,000 years, which is the rhythm of orbital obliquity (the tilt of the Earth's axis). After about 900,000 years ago, ice-sheets grew to maximum volumes twice their previous size, and fluctuated with a 100,000 year rhythm, namely that of the orbital eccentricity. Other fluctuations in ice volume, superimposed on the longer term patterns, occurred at frequencies of 41,000 and 23,000 years.

The cause of change in the pattern of ice age rhythms at about 900,000 years ago is not known. One theory suggests that it was caused by a change in the behaviour of the ice-sheets; after that time marine-based ice-sheets developed on continental shelf areas such as Hudson's Bay, the Baltic and the Irish Sea. They were able to grow rapidly and to reach considerable thicknesses; their collapse and disappearance was also probably catastrophic. Another theory attributes the change in scale and intensity of glaciation to changes in atmospheric circulation caused by renewed uplift of high mountain and plateau areas; for example, the Sierra Nevada in North America, and the Himalayas and Tibetan Plateau in Asia were uplifted to such elevations that caused waves in the circulation of the upper atmosphere. This brought cold air to lower middle latitudes and produced the cooling necessary for glaciation. Evidence exists to support both of these theories, which may not be mutually exclusive.

Wales in the Quaternary

Because of its maritime position adjacent to the warm North Atlantic, it is probable that ice in Wales accumulated rapidly in response to orbital changes which cooled the land. A conventional text-book view would be that, initially, ice thickened in upland hollows enlarging them into cirques. The ice then flowed out from these into valleys, over-deepening and over-steepening their slopes as it moved. Converging valley glaciers coalesced on lowlands where they formed piedmont lobes which eventually grew in size to form an ice-sheet (for example, Flint 1943). An alternative theory proposed that ice developed more or less everywhere across the landscape (instantaneous glacierisation) (Ives *et al.* 1975), especially on upland plateaux that were partially surrounded by higher ground. For example, it is clear that the thickest ice mass in Wales lay on plateau areas such as that between the Rhinog and the Arenig Mountains, and that there it far exceeded ice thicknesses farther north in Snowdonia (Greenly 1919; Foster 1968). Another theory proposed that marine-based ice-sheets grew on shallow water continental shelf areas (Denton and Hughes 1981), such as the Irish Sea (Bowen 1981c).

Different ancient rock types carried by the ice can be used to trace the sources and directions of ice movement. These erratics, together with landforms streamlined in the direction of flow, provide a good indication of the pattern of such movement, even over very large areas. Wales was glaciated on a number of occasions by ice from several sources. An Irish Sea ice-sheet invaded the margins of Wales; its Cheshire-Shropshire-Staffordshire lobe moved into the Welsh Borderlands, and another glaciated Llŷn and parts of west Wales. At one time this Irish Sea ice crossed south-west Dyfed and penetrated into Carmarthen Bay. Its maximum extent is unknown, but it probably filled the Bristol Channel and reached the Isles of Scilly. The sources of the Irish Sea ice lay in Ireland and as far afield as the Lake District and southern Scotland. Alternatively, Welsh ice was dispersed from a central Welsh ice cap, the axis of which lay east of the Rhinog Mountains and west of Rhobell Fawr and Arenig Fawr. Northern Snowdonia, Cadair Idris, and the Brecon Beacons (especially the dip-slope of Fforest Fawr) all nourished their own ice caps; and a smaller ice centre lay on Pumlumon – see Figure 1.

Glacial erosion

Glacial erosion was not uniform. Three characteristic landforms show that this was the case. These are – (i) cirques (corries), (ii) troughs (U-shaped valleys) and rock basins, and (iii) streamlined forms such as ridge tops and roches moutonées. The distribution of such features shows that glacial erosion was most intense in north-west Wales – see Figure 1. There is a clear relationship between areas of high precipitation today and areas of intense glacial erosion which, if 'the present is the key to the past', shows how precipitation was important in initiating and nourishing Pleistocene ice caps. Important glacial erosional features do, however, occur well outside the main areas – see Figure 1. For example, the deep rock basins of the lower Neath and Teifi Valleys. These may have been formed during early glaciations for which little other evidence remains.

Glacial deposition

The products of glacial erosion were transported, then deposited by a variety of means. Till (boulder clay) was deposited beneath ice as lodgement till, from within the ice as englacial till (melt-out till), and from the surface of melting ice as supra-glacial and flow till. These deposits often have colours characteristic of the rocks from which they were derived, and they contain erratics showing over what terrains and rock formations the ice had travelled. In general, till forms a blanket-cover over the landscape. Landforms composed of till, such as moraines, either mark the maximum extent of an ice advance, such as the Llanfihangel-Crucorney (Crocornau) moraine, or they prove still-stands and minor readvances of the ice margin during deglaciation (ice wastage), as, for example, at Glais in the Swansea Valley. Drumlins, streamlined mounds of till, were formed by rapid glacier flow; they occur on the Denbighshire Moors and at Hirwaun, south of Fforest Fawr and also at lower altitudes, for example, in Anglesey – see Figure 1.

Fluvioglacial deposition and erosion

During deglaciation (ice wastage) the ice margins 'retreat', shrinking towards their centres of origin. Evidence for pauses in this retreat are marked by the end-moraines such as those in the South Wales valleys, the Wye Valley, and at Tregaron in the Teifi Valley. In the upper Clwyd, glacier thinning led to the detachment of masses of stagnant ice: for example, in the Alun and Wheeler Valleys where eskers and kettle holes developed. Similar ice wastage phenomena developed south of the Pennant Measures Scarp in Glamorgan east of the Ewenny Valley, and where the Nantlle, Glaslyn and Ffestiniog glaciers combined in eastern Llŷn.

Impressive numbers of glacial meltwater channels occur in Wales. The majority appear to have been fashioned by subglacial erosion (that is erosion by streams below the ice); the pattern of some, such as the Fishguard channels, allows the course of deglaciation to be reconstructed. Initially, glacial drainage in Preseli was directed southwards and south-westwards, but with ice retreat in Cardigan

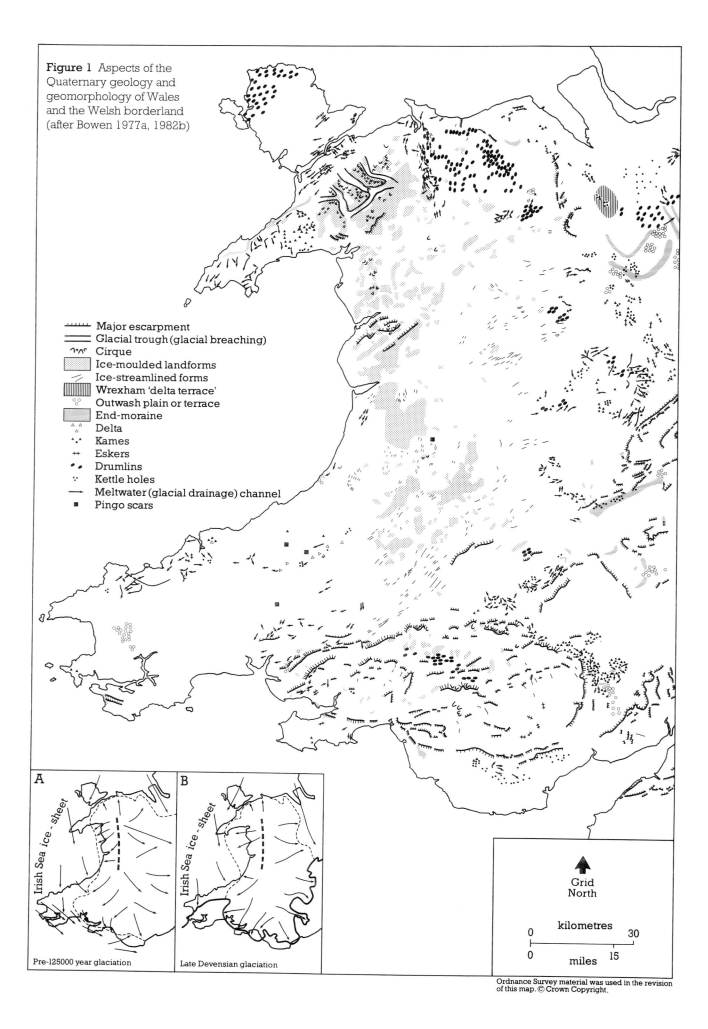

Figure 1 Aspects of the Quaternary geology and geomorphology of Wales and the Welsh borderland (after Bowen 1977a, 1982b)

Major escarpment
Glacial trough (glacial breaching)
Cirque
Ice-moulded landforms
Ice-streamlined forms
Wrexham 'delta terrace'
Outwash plain or terrace
End-moraine
Delta
Kames
Eskers
Drumlins
Kettle holes
Meltwater (glacial drainage) channel
Pingo scars

A

Irish Sea ice-sheet

Pre-125000 year glaciation

B

Irish Sea ice-sheet

Late Devensian glaciation

Grid North

kilometres
0   30

miles
0   15

Ordnance Survey material was used in the revision of this map. © Crown Copyright.

10

Bay, rivers were able to flow to the north. In the Arfon foothills, glacial drainage channels run from north-east to south-west, and probably formed beneath and just inside the ice margin. Some of the most spectacular subglacial channels in Wales occur in the lower Teifi Valley at, for example, Cilgeran and Cenarth, the gorges through which the Teifi flows today.

Formerly, many glacial drainage channels were interpreted as having been fashioned by proglacial lake water spilling over watersheds or spurs. It is difficult, however, to ascribe any channel unequivocally to such an origin, although independent evidence (such as shoreline features and delta deposits) sometimes shows the existence of a former proglacial lake, such as Lake Teifi – see Chapter 2.

Principles of classification

One of the main challenges of Quaternary research is to correlate events on the land with the oxygen isotope stratigraphy derived from the ocean floor. This is not easy to accomplish because the continents are areas of net erosion. The record is, therefore, often fragmentary, and only rarely do deposits at any one site show evidence for more than a single ice age or interglacial event. The reconstructed rock sequence, therefore, is built up from place to place – see Table 1. A further problem is that successive ice ages produce similar evidence, that is, comparable rock types and fossils. They are homotaxial and appear to be the same, but are of different ages, so it is not always easy to determine the correct position of a given deposit in time. Thus, dating techniques are important although, unfortunately, these are not uniformly applicable in all areas and in all parts of the Pleistocene sequence. Moreover, all dating techniques have their own inherent problems and sources of error.

Quaternary events on the continents are recognised from the actualities of the rocks. Thus, a till is evidence for a glaciation, and stratified sands and gravels may relate to a period of ice wastage (deglaciation). Head deposits (scree or solifluction sediments) indicate a cold climate. A peat or lake deposit containing fossil pollen grains could show a temperate (interglacial) event. Classification of Quaternary events has in recent years been based on the establishment of stages, recognised on the evidence of either ice age or interglacial events. These have been founded on a typical section (type section or stratotype) that demonstrates such an event, a standard to act as a yardstick with which other sites may be compared or correlated.

Before continental (onshore) sections can be correlated in time with the global oxygen isotope framework, it is first necessary to 1) examine and describe them, 2) correlate between such onshore sections, and 3) classify the evidence available in the sections.

Lithostratigraphy

Lithostratigraphy (rock stratigraphy) is concerned with the description and organisation of rocks into lithological units (beds, members and formations) based on their intrinsic characteristics. The lithostratigraphic succession of Pleistocene deposits in Wales has been determined mainly along the coastline, where good exposures have been created by marine erosion. These exposures are important because they show both marine and terrestrial deposits – see Table 1. Marine deposits consist, for example, of raised beach (former shoreline) deposits, marine muds, sands and gravels. Continental deposits include till, fluvioglacial sands and gravels, several varieties of head deposits (for example, scree), loess (cold climate wind-blown silt) and wind-blown sand.

Drawing inferences about the origin of Quaternary sediments is not always straightforward, and deposits are often interpreted in a variety of ways by different workers. Three examples have figured prominently in the history of investigations in Wales.

1   In Gower, a deposit containing erratic pebbles was once interpreted as a glacial sediment (George 1932, 1933a). Now, however, it is regarded as a cold climate periglacial deposit, formed by the downslope movement of materials including sediments derived from older, truly glacial deposits (for example, Bowen 1971a).

2   In Mid Wales and along the Cardigan Bay coastline, a characteristically blue diamict (a poorly sorted, pebbly clay deposit) consisting almost entirely of local rock types, has been interpreted variously as a till (Wood 1959; Potts 1971), as a recycled till (Potts 1971; Bowen 1973a, 1974) or as a periglacial slope deposit (Watson and Watson 1967; Watson 1970).

3   The dark blue-purple calcareous clay, often containing marine shells or shell fragments, called Irish Sea till has, at some localities, recently been reinterpreted as a glacio-marine mud; that is, it was deposited in the sea when plumes of trapped sediment were released from floating or grounded ice. Such differences of opinion about the depositional origins of sediments have led to radically different environmental reconstructions and of the precise sequence of events.

Additional information about the nature and the sequence of events may be provided by depositional and erosional landforms: for example, subglacial eskers and kettle holes demonstrate the former presence of stagnating ice that had lost all forward motion.

A Pleistocene correlation chart for Wales

Irish Sea Province	Welsh Province	South Gower	Gower Caves	Chronostratigraphy		Oxygen Isotope Stage	Age (in thousands of years BP)
loess head solifluction deposits	North Wales, Mid Wales and Brecon Beacons cirque moraines and protalus ramparts	Horton loess	Cat Hole breccia	Younger Dryas			10
Cwm yr Eglwys peat	Traeth Mawr peat			Allerød		2	11
	Glanllynnau basal clay		Bacon Hole stalagmite	Older Dryas	Late Devensian		12 13
Abermawr Till, Trevor Till, Banc-y-Warren sands and gravels, Moel Tryfan shelly drift	Langland Bay and Broughton Bay Tills, Llanystumdwy Till	head	Minchin Hole Outer Talus Cone, Bacon Hole breccia				14 17
remanié molluscan fauna in overlying beds	Glanllynnau: weathered surface and frost cracking of Criccieth Till?		Long Hole breccia	Middle Devensian		3	24
	Criccieth Till, Langland Bay head	Western Slade redeposited glacial sediments	Bacon Hole breccia			4	59
Red Wharf Bay, Porth Oer, Abermawr lower heads			Bacon Hole stalagmite	Early Devensian		5a	71 80
		Colluvial beds				5b	
			Bacon Hole temperate fauna			5c	105
Red Wharf Bay, Porth Oer and Poppit raised beaches?	Langland and Broughton raised beaches	Hunts Bay Beach	Minchin Hole Outer Beach	Ipswichian (Pennard D/L Stage)		5d 5e	122
		Horton head?	Minchin Hole Lower Red Cave Earth			6	128
Pontnewydd Cave Intermediate Complex		Horton (Upper), Butterslade and Overton raised beaches	Minchin Hole Inner Beach	Minchin Hole D/L Stage		7	186 245
						8	
		Hunts Bay Beach marine fauna		Hoxnian Stage ?		9	303 339
						10	
						11	
		Paviland Till		Anglian		12	423 478
Kenn Freshwater Beds				Cromerian		13	
						14 15	524
West Angle and Kenn Tills, South Wales Irish Sea drifts?		Irish Sea remanié drifts		Elster 1		16	620
						17	659

Table 1 Geochronology (age) of Oxygen Isotope Stage boundaries is from Martinson *et al.* (1987) [back to stage 7], and Imbrie *et al.* (1984). Specific events are radiocarbon dated at 10, 11, 12, 13, 14 and 17,000 years BP (details in text).
The Pennard and Minchin Hole D/L Stages are from Bowen *et al.* (1985). For chronostratigraphic correlations see Bowen and Sykes (1988), Behre (1989) and Bowen *et al.* (1989). Sites outside Wales are correlated with Oxygen Isotope Stages as follows – Upton Warren, St Germain II and Odderade (Sub-stage 5a), Chelford, Brörup and St Germain I (Sub-stage 5c) and Stanton Harcourt and Aveley (Stage 7).

Formal classification of the Pleistocene and Holocene rocks of Wales by recognising formations (the fundamental mappable lithostratigraphic unit) has not occurred widely (for example, Henry 1984a), and description has been largely at the level of beds.

Biostratigraphy

Biostratigraphy is concerned with the organisation of the rock column into units on the basis of their fossil content, and the correlation of these units in often widely separated sections. The fossil record of the Quaternary of Wales is discontinuous, but it does provide important information.

Fossil marine molluscs (snails and bivalves) are found in the interglacial raised beaches which formed when global sea-level was relatively high. Others were incorporated from the sea floor into ice-sheets, and they now occur in glacial and fluvioglacial sediments. Hitherto, marine fossils have only provided a limited amount of palaeoecological and stratigraphic information. Non-marine snails have been more widely used for biostratigraphy, but not so much in Wales. They also provide better palaeoecological information, and have been used for amino acid dating.

Large and small fossil mammals are found in the Welsh cave deposits, notably in Gower, South Pembrokeshire and the Elwy Valley of Clwyd, and these have allowed important palaeoecological inferences to be drawn. They have, however, proved to be of limited use for long range biostratigraphic correlation.

Pollen analytical investigations of sediments are important because they allow a reconstruction of the former vegetation, and this in turn allows inferences to be drawn about the prevailing climate at the time the sediments were formed. Deposits containing pollen usually only occur plentifully in the rocks of the last 13,000 years or so. However, they allow precise biozonation of the younger sedimentary sequences, with characteristic floras being used to define pollen assemblage zones (biozones).

Correlation

Correlation should be pursued by all possible means. Unlike many pre-Quaternary rocks, however, the greater variability in lithology and the discontinuous nature of Quaternary rocks makes correlation difficult. Furthermore, the cyclical nature of climatic events has formed repetitive, homotaxial rock sequences, which make correlation and dating difficult. For example, it is known that interglacial raised beaches of different ages lie at similar elevations around our coasts. Likewise, repetitive glaciation from similar ice centres could have produced more or less identical deposits.

The correlation of most Pleistocene rocks in Wales is based on telecorrelation, which is a method founded on the assumption that repetitive sequences of rocks are of broadly similar age. To some extent, independent geochronometric age determinations have confirmed such correlation, but in some cases, absolute age determinations have revealed a greater complexity in the rock record than had been inferred from the rock sequences alone.

As the climate improved towards the close of the last glacial phase (Devensian Stage), after about 15,000 years ago, Wales was progressively colonised by vegetation. The pollen assemblage zones which represent the vegetation at particular times have been used for correlation. These biozones are the representatives in the fossil record of migrating, and therefore time-transgressive (diachronous), floras. Radiocarbon dating of significant changes in vegetational history, is a better basis for attempting a time correlation.

Classification

The classification of Pleistocene rocks, and thus of events, has by custom been based on climatic change: that is, by defining ice ages (glacials) and the relatively warmer periods between (interglacials). In addition, 'interstadials', episodes of climatic improvement within a glacial, and separate episodes of cold 'stadial' ice advances have been recognised. In Britain and North-West Europe, interglacials have been defined on the basis of their vegetational history. By definition, these must show a climate at least as warm as the Holocene (present interglacial). This is inferred from pollen assemblages showing a mixed oak deciduous forest. Specific interglacials are recognised by their vegetational 'signatures', although these were not based on the appearance of new species, acme development, nor extinctions, but rather on floral assemblages which consist of species still in existence. In other words, the definitive assemblage floras were controlled not by evolution but by the prevailing climate. It has been argued (Bowen 1978) that this is not a satisfactory means for sub-dividing the time represented in the rock record. Glacials have been recognised and defined by the identification of cold climate deposits such as till and periglacial scree.

Definition and classification on such a basis is at best informal and, at worst, potentially misleading. This is all the more so because the record is fragmentary and must be arranged in proper sequence by adding and overlapping the available surviving fragments – see Table 1.

Stratigraphical procedure for classifying rocks is based on chronostratigraphy and the recognition and definition of chronostratigraphic units (time-rock units), such as stages, series and periods. These are made up of sequences of rock that accumulated during a particular span of time, and are defined in a chosen, type section (stratotype). The age of such units, in years before the present, may be determined by geochronology. The distinction between chronostratigraphy and geochronology is an important one, but it has frequently been overlooked by expert writers and editors alike. Hedburg (1976) uses the analogy of an hour glass to explain the distinction. The sand in the glass represents the chronostratigraphic unit (that is the tangible or physical unit), and the time taken for the sand to pass from the upper to the lower half of the glass is the time interval or geochronological unit, an abstract concept which measures the passage of time.

One of the goals in reconstructing Quaternary history is to arrange the rocks into their original order and into chronostratigraphic units. If it is possible to determine their actual ages by geochronological means, so much the better. Most rocks, however, cannot be so readily dated, and correlation is attempted by other means.*

An attempt to classify the Quaternary rocks of the British Isles by defining chronostratigraphic units was made by Mitchell *et al.* (1973). They defined a sequence of temperate and cold stages. 'Fixed points in time' were provided by the temperate stages, which were defined from their vegetational history (from pollen analysis). This method has been criticised (see above): its standard sequence of stages was not based on the demonstrable, direct superposition of rock units; for it is generally rare to see representatives of one stage above those of another at one locality. The classification has been criticised, mostly because it oversimplified the sequence of events and because it cannot accommodate additional events. A multiple approach to these problems has led to the recognition of a much more complex pattern, and a chronostratigraphy which reflects this sequence of events.

The emergence of techniques for dating rocks, especially for those older than the range of radiocarbon dating, has not only demonstrated greater complexity and allowed precise correlation, but has also provided the means of relating Pleistocene rocks to the global oxygen isotope framework (Kukla 1977; Bowen 1978). The oxygen isotope stages of the deep-sea record (for example, Shackleton and Opdyke 1973; Sibrava *et al.* 1986) provide the standard stratigraphical scale with which continental sequences are now routinely correlated.

In Wales, a chronology based on the concepts of 'Older' and 'Newer Drifts' (Wright 1914; Charlesworth 1929; George 1932) dominated classification for more than fifty years. It was replaced by a scheme based on sections in East Anglia and Ireland (Mitchell 1960, 1972). A classification based on the superposition of actual rock sequences had started to emerge by 1970 (for example, Bowen 1970a, 1973a, 1973b). Progressive amplification of this lithostratigraphy in subsequent years led to the rejection of the East Anglian and Irish models in Wales. In parallel, a global oxygen isotope stratigraphy was also emerging (Bowen 1973a, 1973b, 1977a, 1981a; Bowen (*in* Jenkins *et al.* 1985); Bowen *et al.* 1985;

1986; Bowen and Sykes 1988). These advances have been underpinned by the coastal exposures of Gower, which thus comprise a type area, and supplement the regional stratotype sections now proposed at Minchin Hole and Bacon Hole Caves (Bowen *et al.* 1985; Stringer *et al.* 1986).

In the Gower rock sequence it has been possible to recognise the global events of the last 250,000 years or so. These include correlatives of Oxygen Isotope Stages 1, 2, 3, 4, 5 (including its sub-stages), 6 and 7, with some evidence for a Stage 9 high sea-level event. Other evidence in Gower permits recognition of the oldest glaciations in Wales, the earliest of which may be more than half a million years old.

*Editor in Chief's note

In an attempt at achieving a common international approach to correlation and a common chronostratigraphic language, geologists have chosen a stratotype for the base of the Pleistocene Series at Vrica, in southern Italy. There, the lower boundary of the Pleistocene (boundary stratotype) has been placed in a sequence of marine rocks, defining the base of the series (and of the Quaternary) at a level that has been dated geochronologically at 1.6 million years before the present.

The Quaternary rocks and landforms of Wales

2

The sequence of events

No known evidence has survived from that part of the Quaternary when glacial phases were dominated by the 41,000 year rhythm, and the earliest evidence only dates to sometime before half a million years ago, about two thirds of the way through the Pleistocene; but even this is not securely dated.

It seems likely, however, that the earlier ice ages in Wales witnessed repetitive glaciation of the uplands, but it is unlikely that large ice-sheets comparable to those of the last 900,000 years developed. The principal legacy of these early glaciations would have been the modification of the topography of upland Wales. During interglacials it is probable that the coastline was successively reoccupied by the sea, when the great coastal slope, which dominates many stretches of the Welsh coastline and immediate hinterland, was repeatedly fashioned.

Glaciation of the Celtic Sea and Bristol Channel

The evidence for this, the earliest known Quaternary event in Wales, consists of highly fragmented outcrops of till and sands and gravels in south-west Dyfed, together with scattered erratics in Gower and the Vale of Glamorgan. This glaciation has been called the Irish Sea glaciation, or the 'Older Drift' glaciation, at which time the Irish Sea and Welsh ice-sheets coalesced in South Wales. The direction of Irish Sea ice movement, from north-west to south-east across south-west Dyfed, has been inferred from the distribution of erratic rocks. No other clear indications of this glaciation occur elsewhere in Wales.

The field relationships of these glacial deposits show that they antedate the raised beaches of south-west Dyfed and Gower, because the latter are not overlain by glacial deposits *in situ*. The glaciation is, therefore, older than Oxygen Isotope Stage 9, to which the oldest raised beach faunas have been ascribed (Bowen *et al.* 1985). The basal till at West Angle Bay (Dixon 1921; Bowen 1977b), which underlies marine deposits, may date from this event.

If, as seems likely, the glacial deposits of the Bristol district are the same age (Hawkins and Kellaway 1971), it may be possible to date this glaciation with more precision. At Yew Tree Farm and at Kenn, near Bristol, till is overlain by freshwater beds containing *Corbicula fluminalis* (Müller). These have amino acid ratios (Andrews *et al.* 1984) which have been correlated with those of the Cromerian Stage of East Anglia (Bowen 1989b) and ascribed to Oxygen Isotope Stage 13 (Bowen and Sykes 1988;

Bowen 1989b; Bowen *et al.* 1989); so that the early Irish Sea glaciation may be time-equivalent to Stage 14, or older. As such it could correlate with the Elster 1 glaciation of Europe (Bowen *et al.* 1985; Bowen and Sykes 1988). A Stage 16 age is thought to be probable because the oxygen isotope record indicates a major glaciation at this time (Shackleton 1987).

The geomorphological position of the glacial deposits in the Bristol district, together with those of West Angle Bay, at the entrance to Milford Haven, and to a lesser extent the highly dissected deposits on the coastal plateaux of south-west Dyfed, show that the geomorphology of the coastal fringe was similar to that of the present.

Although this is the oldest glaciation for which there is still evidence in Wales, it is probable that an earlier one may have occurred. This is based on the evidence of igneous erratics from eastern Snowdonia and Mynydd Berwyn, which have been discovered in the high level gravels of the Middle Thames, and the Kesgrave Formation of East Anglia (Bowen *et al.* 1985). The fact that erratics from Wales were introduced into the Thames drainage system, suggests that the geomorphology of the Vale of Gloucester and the Lower Severn readily allowed ice from Wales to pass and to surmount the Cotswolds. On the other hand, the evidence adduced here for glaciation of the Celtic Sea and Bristol Channel lowlands, indicates a topography not greatly dissimilar to that of the present. It seems likely that the onset of the 100,000 year ice age rhythm and the incidence of the earliest major glaciations of middle latitude Britain, coincided with major changes in topography.

The Paviland glaciation

Recognition of the Paviland glaciation is based on the Paviland end-moraine in Gower, and the glacial deposits lying between it and the margin of the Late Devensian glaciation – see Figure 2. The Paviland moraine was recognised in 1985 and, although greatly degraded, it forms a major landform. The end-moraine represents the maximum extent of an ice-sheet which moved from north to south. The principal erratic constituent of the Paviland glaciation is Namurian 'quartzite' derived from the North Crop of the South Wales Coalfield, notably from Mynydd-y-garreg, in south-east Dyfed. It is possible that it transported the great block of 'quartzite' known as Arthur's Stone, which forms the capstone to a Megalithic tomb on Cefn Bryn, in Gower. Some large boulders of this Namurian sandstone lie beyond the Paviland moraine on the foreshore at Western Slade. These could indicate a more extensive advance than that marked by the end-moraine, but equally, they may have been derived from the periglacial deposits, including recycled glacial material, which infill the valleys of Eastern Slade and Western Slade.

Local field relationships in south-west Gower show that this glaciation antedated the oldest local raised beaches (at Horton and Butterslade), which have been ascribed to the Minchin Hole Stage (Oxygen Isotope Stage 7). On these considerations, therefore, the Paviland glaciation is provisionally ascribed to some time before this stage. One possibility is that it is time-equivalent to part of the Anglian Stage, when extensive glaciation occurred in the Midlands and eastern England, which has been correlated with Oxygen Isotope Stage 12 (Bowen and Sykes 1988; Bowen 1989b).

The Minchin Hole Stage

Minchin Hole Cave, Gower, contains the proposed stratotype for this stage (Bowen *et al.* 1985) in the sand bed which has been named the Inner Beach. On the basis of its amino acid geochronology it has been ascribed to Oxygen Isotope Stage 7. The Inner Beach deposits contain two populations of marine molluscs, recognised on the basis of their different amino acid ratios, 0.18 and 0.14, which probably represent the respective faunas of Oxygen Isotope Sub-stages 7c and 7a. Hitherto, there has been no formally defined stage to which these could be chronostratigraphically related in Britain. It does, however, correspond with the Stanton Harcourt interglacial event previously recognised from non-marine evidence, and, later, dated by amino acid methods (Bowen 1989b; Bowen *et al.* 1989).

Because the critical rock unit lies in a cave, it is difficult to relate it to deposits over a wider area. Amino acid geochronology, however, has enabled wider correlation with other marine deposits. The raised beach at nearby Horton contains shells with amino acid ratios ascribed to the Minchin Hole Stage.

Uranium-series, thermoluminescence and electron spin resonance dating methods show that cave sediments of Oxygen Isotope Stage 7 age also occur at Pontnewydd Cave in Clwyd (Green 1984). It is not possible, however, to relate these to Pleistocene deposits outside the cave.

A cold climate event between the Minchin Hole and Pennard Stages

Between the marine beds of the Minchin Hole Stage (Oxygen Isotope Stage 7) and the Pennard Stage (Oxygen Isotope Stage 5, Sub-stage 5e; see below), there occurs at Minchin Hole the Lower Red Cave Earth (head). This bed is proof of a cold climate event. It has, therefore, been ascribed to Oxygen Isotope Stage 6. A large form of the northern vole *Microtus oeconomus* (Pallas), now found living in northernmost Scandinavia, was discovered in it, showing an extremely cold Arctic environment for the deposit. Bowen *et al.* (1985) drew attention to the likelihood that similar aged

deposits could overlie Minchin Hole Stage raised beach sediments elsewhere.

Raised beaches of the Minchin Hole Stage crop out at Butterslade, Overton Cliff and Horton in Gower. At Horton, this beach is overlain by two lithofacies of limestone head. A short distance below, and away from it, a younger beach of Pennard Stage age occurs in a gully. It would seem on this evidence that the head deposits overlying the higher beach may, at least in part, antedate the younger beach. Similar stratigraphical relationships are clearly displayed in sections in northern France (Lautridou 1982). The majority of sites, however, shows that the Pennard Stage marine transgression removed pre-existing deposits.

The Pennard (Ipswichian) Stage

The proposed stratotype for the Pennard Stage is the Outer Beach bed at Minchin Hole Cave (Bowen *et al.* 1985). This bed has been ascribed to Oxygen Isotope Sub-stage 5e on the basis of its amino acid geochronology, calibrated by Uranium-Thorium age determinations on speleothem (stalagmitic tufa) collected at Minchin Hole and at nearby Bacon Hole (Bowen *et al.* 1985; Stringer *et al.* 1986; Bowen and Sykes 1988). The Pennard Stage is, in age terms, synonymous with the Ipswichian Stage of England, and the Eemian Stage of the Netherlands.

Terrestrial beds overlying the Ipswichian Stage raised beaches at both Minchin Hole and Bacon Hole are also probably of Ipswichian age. Bacon Hole contains one of the best known mammal faunas of this age.

The Ipswichian Stage (Pennard) raised beach is extensive in Gower, at Marros and Ragwen Point in Carmarthen Bay, and at points throughout south-west Dyfed. It may also be represented by the Porth Oer and Red Wharf Bay raised beaches in Gwynedd and Anglesey, respectively. The former raised beaches show that the platforms and abandoned cliffs of the Welsh coastline were re-occupied by the sea about 122,000 years ago. Since that time they have been degraded by subaerial slope processes, and some of them have been glaciated by Devensian ice. Only in geologically recent times have some been stripped of their sediment cover for the sea to attack the cliff base again – for example, at Morfa-bychan and in Cardigan Bay between Llan-non and Aberarth.

On the assumption that a widely recorded British interglacial fauna with hippopotamus is everywhere of Ipswichian age (Sutcliffe 1981), the fossiliferous cave sediments at the Cefn Caves in the Elwy Valley of Clwyd should also probably date, at least in part, from the Ipswichian Stage.

Other sediments which have been ascribed to the Ipswichian are – (i) the Llansantffraid Soil described by Mitchell (1962), (ii) an ancient brown earth soil at Hunts Bay, Gower (Clayden 1977a) and, (iii) numerous pockets of red clays south of the limit of the Late Devensian ice-sheet in the Vale of

Glamorgan (for example, Crampton 1966c, Bowen 1970a).

The Devensian (Weichselian) Stage

In the British Isles the Devensian (Weichselian) Stage is sub-divided into three sub-stages as follows (Mitchell *et al.* 1973) –

Upper (Late) Devensian	26,000 to 10,000 BP
Middle (Mid) Devensian	50,000 to 26,000 BP
Lower (Early) Devensian	before 50,000 BP

Broadly, these divisions correspond with Oxygen Isotope Stage 2 (Late Devensian), Stage 3 (Middle Devensian), Stages 4, 5a to 5d (Early Devensian). The inclusion of Sub-stages 5a to 5d in the Devensian corresponds with international usage (Sibrava *et al.* 1986).

The Devensian stratotype is at Four Ashes, near Wolverhampton; and it shows Late Devensian Irish Sea till overlying gravels of the Early and Middle Devensian.

Early and Middle Devensian Sub-stages

Bacon Hole Cave, Gower, contains the only potentially complete and demonstrable lithostratigraphic, biostratigraphic and geochronological record of Early Devensian time in Britain (Stringer *et al.* 1986). Bracketing Uranium-Thorium age determinations on the rock sequence show that a major part of Oxygen Isotope Stage 5 is represented here. The post Sub-stage 5e sediments are fossiliferous, and their mammalian fauna demonstrates a warmer interval between the deposition of marine sediment (representing Sub-stage 5e) and the speleothem ('Stalagmite Floor') dated to 81,000 ± 18,000 BP (Stringer *et al.* 1986). It is probable that this warmer interval corresponds to Oxygen Isotope Sub-stage 5c (*c.* 105,000 BP), and that the speleothem and overlying head deposits accumulated throughout the remainder of Devensian time. Other Uranium-series dates potentially allow further division of the cold period and the scree units.

The Devensian fossiliferous sequence of cave deposits overlying the Pennard raised beach at Minchin Hole (Sutcliffe 1981) has been correlated with beds at Bacon Hole (Bowen *et al.* 1985). It is probable that the lower beds of the Outer Talus at Minchin Hole (Sutcliffe and Bowen 1973) are also of Early Devensian age.

Because they lie between the Pennard (Ipswichian Stage/Oxygen Isotope Sub-stage 5e) raised beach and glacial and glacio-marine beds of proposed Late Devensian age, head deposits in Gower, south-west Dyfed, Llŷn and Anglesey, are ascribed to Early and Middle Devensian time. In Gower, the succession of Devensian head deposits consists of basal colluvial (red) beds, limestone scree and redistributed older (pre-Devensian) glacial deposits. Western Slade has been proposed as the standard section for this redistributed older glacial

material in South Wales and south-west England. Their recognition as recycled glacial deposits, not glacial beds *in situ* (Bowen 1966, 1970a, 1971a, 1973b), has helped in settling the controversy on the glacial sequence in Wales that has continued since the discussion of the issue by Prestwich (1892) and Tiddeman (1900).

With the exception of Long Hole Cave, it has not proved possible, hitherto, to identify discrete deposits of Middle Devensian age in Wales. Deposits of that age, however, are probably represented in the head units referred to above.

Possible Early Devensian glaciation in Wales

Evidence for Early Devensian glaciation in Europe and North America has long been the subject of debate and speculation. The ability to discriminate, using amino acid geochronology, between shelly deposits of Early and Late Devensian age has made it possible, however, for the first time, to demonstrate Early Devensian glaciation in Britain (Bowen *et al.* 1985; Bowen and Sykes 1988; Bowen 1989b). Hitherto, presumed Early Devensian glacial and glacio-marine deposits have only been identified in Orkney, Caithness and in Ulster. In comparison with the Late Devensian, this earlier British ice-sheet was displaced farther north, which is probably related to the position of the zone of effective precipitation for ice-sheet growth (Bowen 1989b). No unequivocal evidence for this Early Devensian glaciation is yet available from Wales, although it seems unlikely that the Welsh mountains were ice-free at that time.

In north-west Wales, Whittow and Ball (1970) recognised two 'stadial' events or ice cap advances. In the Criccieth district these are represented respectively by the Criccieth Till and the Llanystumdwy Till (Simpkins 1968).

The significance of the multi-till sequence in south-east Llŷn has caused much debate – see Chapter 7. The sequence of deposits there might further be interpreted as consisting of – (1) Criccieth Till deposited by Snowdonian ice (Early Devensian), (2) zone of weathering and ice-wedges (Middle Devensian), (3) Llanystumdwy Till deposited by Snowdonian ice (Late Devensian) – see Table 1. This hypothesis is additional to the existing ones.

The Late Devensian

The Late Devensian glaciation of Wales was effected by ice coming from Welsh centres of dispersal and from the Irish Sea Basin – see Figure 1. The extent of both ice-sheets has been the subject of debate (Bowen 1973a, 1973b). The dimensions and nature of the ice-sheets and the timing of their growth and shrinkage are still poorly understood.

The distribution of distinctive erratics, however, enables the relative strength and dimensions of some Welsh ice-streams to be estimated. For example, in the South Wales Coalfield, the Vale of

Neath ice was sufficiently powerful to cross its south-east interfluve and deposit typical Brecknockshire drift at heights above 300 metres near Pen Moelgrochlef (Bowen 1970a). Therefore, in a downstream direction the Vale of Neath ice was at least 300m thick. Upstream, however, the Fforest Fawr ice failed to cross the Pennant Measures escarpment at Craig-y-llyn. In Gwynedd, ice from the main ice cap crossed the Rhinog Mountains of the Harlech Dome. The Wye glacier was at least 300m thick where it impinged on the Black Mountains in Gwent (Dwerryhouse and Miller 1930). Given the known extent of ice (Figure 14), it is difficult to escape the conclusion that most of the Welsh upland was submerged at the maximum of the Late Devensian glaciation.

Estimating the extent of the Irish Sea ice is more difficult, because the nature and the dimensions of this ice-sheet are controversial. Irish Sea ice deposits, of presumed Late Devensian age, lie at elevations of over 300m in the north and middle Welsh Borderland, at over 400m in north-west Wales (Moel Tryfan), and at over 180m in Preseli: from which the relative thicknesses of the ice can be estimated.

The traditional view is that the Irish Sea ice-sheet was land-based (for example, Thomas 1976) and that it advanced across a dry sea-floor, exposed as a consequence of the global lowering of sea-level. A reinterpretation of the glacial deposits of the Isle of Man as glacio-marine in origin (Eyles and Eyles 1984), suggests that the Irish Sea ice-sheet in that region was marine-based (Bowen 1981c; Denton and Hughes 1981).

A marine-based Irish Sea ice-sheet would, in places, have been grounded on an isostatically depressed crust. Its distal margin would have been controlled by sea-level (not climate) and, given the evidence for its maximum extent in Preseli and Wexford, it is clear that these areas would have functioned as pinning points which prevented surging and collapse of the ice domes (Eyles and McCabe 1989).

The timing of Late Devensian glaciation in Wales and the Irish Sea is difficult to establish. Radiocarbon analyses from the Cheshire-Shropshire-Staffordshire lowland give dates which are too early to be useful in fixing the onset of glaciation. The date of 18,000 years obtained on a woolly rhinoceros bone from one of the Tremeirchion Caves, may provide critical evidence. However, some doubt must attach to its reliability, the sample being of unknown stratigraphic provenance. Furthermore, the enhanced radiocarbon content of the atmosphere before 17,000 years ago (Shackleton *et al.* 1988) may point to a somewhat older true age for this sample.

Radiocarbon dates from basal organic samples in kettle holes show that Late Devensian deglaciation was locally complete in the lowlands of north-west Wales by 14,468 BP, and in the Isle of Man by 19,000 BP. The Isle of Man dates, however, are almost certainly too old. Indications of somewhat earlier deglaciation of the Irish Sea ice-sheet are available from a combination of radiocarbon and amino acid dates. The radiocarbon dated age of shells (*Macoma calcarea* Gruelin) collected from glacio-marine deltas in Ireland is about 17,000 BP; and these have amino acid ratios of 0.07. Similar ratios occur in shells from proposed glacio-marine deposits in County Cork, Waterford, south-west Dyfed and the Isle of Man. These show that deglaciation had occurred in these areas by 17,000 BP, and that glacio-marine conditions obtained at that time in the southern Irish Sea Basin. From these considerations it is reasonable to assume that Late Devensian glaciation reached its greatest extent not long before, and the conventional date of 20,000 to 18,000 BP is, therefore, retained here.

The sequence of deglaciation

If, as has been suggested, the Irish Sea ice-sheet were marine-based and the Welsh ice-sheet land-based, their modes of deglaciation were probably different. It is likely that both reached their maximum extent at about the same time. The proposal that the Irish Sea ice-sheet was marine-based has helped towards the construction of an integrated model of glaciation and deglaciation. The Irish Sea ice terminus in the St George's Channel has been located along a zone crossing from south-west Dyfed to Wexford; this is marked by a thickening of the drift on the sea floor. To some extent the ice was probably 'pinned' between the Pembrokeshire peninsula and Wexford. Beyond the ice margin, the crust would have been depressed for a considerable distance. It is proposed that glacio-marine muds of this age occur at Fremington, North Devon, and possibly at Broughton Bay, in Gower.

Initial deglaciation of Late Devensian Irish Sea ice was probably rapid, as is shown by widespread deposition of glacio-marine muds. De-stabilisation of the ice margin would have led to rapid calving of the ice and marine downdraw. The fluvioglacial deposits and landforms of Preseli, for example, probably developed rapidly. These include the Fishguard glacial drainage channels which may have been cut by catastrophic discharges.

Glacio-marine muds in south-west Dyfed and in the Llŷn Peninsula contain a shell fauna with amino acid ratios which indicate an age of approximately 17,000 BP. Their deposition was diachronous, from south to north. During deglaciation, the Irish sea ice margin may have stabilised through 'pinning' against the Llŷn peninsula. In such an interpretation, the lake terraces described by Matley (1936) might be reinterpreted as glacio-marine deltas? In north-east Wales, the origin of the Wrexham 'delta terrace' may well be re-evaluated in the context of the marine-based ice-sheet paradigm. Eventual disintegration of the Irish Sea ice in Liverpool Bay may have allowed outflow of Welsh ice from North Wales, with fast glacier flow streamlining the drumlins of the Denbighshire

Moors, a similar origin to that proposed for the drumlins of the 'Drumlin Readvance' in Ireland (McCabe 1987).

Glacio-marine deposition may have transgressed onshore along major valleys. Thick deposits occur in the Lower Teifi Valley (Nunn and Boztas 1977), where the Llechryd Formation is widespread (Bowen and Lear 1982). Deltas which occur between Cardigan and Lampeter have previously been interpreted as deposits formed in part of proglacial Lake Teifi (Charlesworth 1929), but it is significant that satisfactory evidence for an ice-margin for the alleged ice dam which impounded that lake has never been identified. The same is true in the Ewenny Valley, where laminated sediments recovered from boreholes drilled by the British Geological Survey could also be glacio-marine. This might also explain the anomalous discovery of Irish Sea erratics and shell fragments at Pencoed (Strahan and Cantrill 1904).

This model of rapid, even catastrophic, deglaciation is not consistent with an hypothesis of Late Devensian ice readvance in North Wales, but it is consistent with the oxygen isotope signal of deglaciation in North Atlantic deep-sea cores (Ruddiman 1987). Its timing, however, with the retreating ice-margin stabilised at the 'Drumlin Readvance' limit in north-east Ireland at 17,000 BP, is earlier than the commencement of significant deglaciation identified by Ruddiman (1987), largely for the Laurentide ice-sheet of North America. Evidence for later deglaciation of the marine-based Barents Shelf ice-sheet at 15,000 BP (Jones and Keigwin 1988) shows that global deglaciation was not synchronous. Earlier deglaciation of the marine-based Irish Sea ice-sheet, at about 17,000 BP, may not be inconsistent with its more southerly position.

The Devensian late-glacial

Latest Devensian Stage events which occurred between the deglaciation of the main Late Devensian ice and the commencement of the Holocene ('post-glacial') fall within Devensian late-glacial time. These, however, have not been defined in an entirely satisfactory way. To some extent this is because in the late-glacial, geological-climatic (climatostratigraphic), chronostratigraphic and geochronological terminology has been used, incorrectly, in an interchangeable and synonymous fashion.

A threefold sub-division of south Scandinavian Late Weichselian (Devensian) deposits was originally proposed using macroscopic plant remains, evidence which corresponded with lithostratigraphic sub-divisions. These showed a sequence of cold-temperate-cold environments. Pollen analysis became the basis for precise identification of the temperate event, based on the stratotype at Allerød (in Denmark). The Allerød event is recognised by means of identification of Pollen Zone II which shows a flora with maximum percentages of arboreal pollen (mostly Betula).

This is the middle of the three late-glacial pollen zones; the earlier Pollen Zone I was equated with the cold Older Dryas, and the later Pollen Zone III with the cold Younger Dryas, both named after the arctic-alpine plant Dryas octopetala L. Greater resolution sub-divided the Older Dryas to make possible the recognition of a further temperate event, the Bølling Interstadial.

Late-glacial pollen diagrams have customarily been zoned on this basis (Mitchell et al. 1973). It became evident, however, that the Scandinavian sequence of events was not precisely comparable with those proven in the British Isles, and that a considerable regional diversity occurred in Britain's vegetational history.

A simpler interpretation of the late-glacial is to regard it as a period of gradual climatic warming during and after deglacation of the main Late Devensian ice-sheet. This warming was interrupted latterly by a deterioration in climate leading to the establishment of glaciers in upland Britain between 11,000 and 10,000 years ago, that is during the Younger Dryas (Watts 1980).

Notwithstanding the considerable variation in regional vegetational history in Britain, the broad pattern of events is clear. The evidence shows that there was a continuous development of soils and plant communities from before 14,500 BP.

A widespread increase in Juniperus pollen, at about 13,000 years ago, is believed to be one of the consequences of climatic improvement. This rapid expansion of Juniperus has been used to define the base of the Windermere Interstadial (Pennington 1977; Coope and Pennington 1977), based on a stratotype at Low Wray Bay, Windermere, Cumbria. In the latter part of the Windermere event, the fluctuating amounts of Betula and Juniperus pollen indicate probably declining, albeit fluctuating, temperatures (Coope and Brophy 1972; Pennington 1977). The fossil coleoptera (beetles) indicate a warming earlier here than elsewhere, at about 14,600 BP, and thus indicate an earlier beginning for the Windermere Interstadial (Coope 1977; Coope and Pennington 1977) than the general warming indicated by Juniperus. The term 'late-glacial interstadial' has been used synonymously, more or less, with the Windermere Interstadial.

In Wales, the Younger Dryas is characterised by glacier growth in the uplands and the development of large permanent snow patches. It was a time when discontinuous permafrost obtained and when an extensive, frequently spectacular, periglacial inheritance was fashioned.

The timing of glacier growth in Snowdonia and in the Brecon Beacons has, to some extent, been constrained by radiocarbon dating. It is doubtful, however, that this is sufficiently precise to allow comparison with the detail of glacier growth discernible elsewhere, for example in Scotland, and certainly not for purposes of precise geochronological definition of the event.

Periglacial modification of the land surface was extensive and, in places, radical during the Younger Dryas. Glacial deposits were subject to reworking and solifluction downslope, often forming large terraces, and alluvial redeposition as stream gravels and alluvial fans. The occurrence of permafrost is shown by ice-wedge pseudomorphs (casts) and open-system pingo scars. Overall, the degree of landscape modification during less than a thousand years of Younger Dryas time was considerable, confirming notions that geomorphological activity is essentially episodic.

The Holocene

By international agreement the commencement of the Holocene is deemed to be 10,000 BP. The warming at the close of the Late Devensian, briefly interrupted by the Younger Dryas event, continued. Pollen analysis has shown that the Holocene in Wales was a time of development of temperate deciduous mixed oak forest and its progressive modification by Man (Taylor 1980). Regional variation in the vegetational history occurred, but the main course of development is clear.

Along the coastline of Wales, the Holocene rise in sea-level culminated about 5,000 years ago, and this is recorded by the alternation of coastal peat beds and marine clay in Swansea Bay (Godwin 1940b), at Clarach (Heyworth *et al.* 1985) and Ynyslas (Taylor 1973) in Cardigan Bay, and along the coast of Clwyd (Tooley 1974).

Inland, colluvial materials were deposited on hillslopes, and, on flood plains, gravel accumulations were subject to terracing as streams changed their courses in response to hydrological variations. Landslips occurred in several Welsh valleys, especially in the South Wales Coalfield where the removal of ice support from over-steepened valley sides caused collapse (Woodland and Evans 1964).

Throughout Devensian late-glacial time, and into the Holocene, the earth's crust recovered from its depression beneath the ice. Rates of relative land/sea-level change due to the interplay between ice retreat (during deglaciation), rising global sea-level and crustal recovery, were subject to wide variation. Because deglaciation of the Welsh coastlands occurred earlier, and crustal rebound was advanced before the rise in global sea-level was able to influence the coastline, spectacular Holocene raised beaches do not occur. The only features attributable to such coastal recovery are the slightly raised Holocene beaches of Anglesey (Môn) just above present sea-level, which compare with the 'Main Postglacial' shorelines farther north, such as those in Scotland.

There is, however, an extensive inheritance of raised, possible glacio-marine deposits and deltas, which have considerable potential for determining the extent and course of isostatic recovery in Wales. These may point to a considerable crustal depression in the Late Devensian and equally to a rapid and elastic recovery, largely completed before *c.* 13,000 BP, when the earliest of the Scottish late-glacial rebound beaches, for instance those in East Fife, was fashioned. It is possible that the thickness of the Late Devensian Irish Sea ice-sheet exceeded that in Scotland, a proposal not inconsistent with the asymmetrical nature of the Late Devensian ice-sheet as compared with the proposed Early Devensian ice-sheet, which may have expanded to the north of Scotland across areas which remained ice-free during the Late Devensian.

Introduction

Over many years, Gower has assumed considerable importance in Quaternary investigations, and stratigraphic sequences around the south and west coasts have yielded important evidence for the marine and terrestrial Pleistocene records.

Early interest in the cave sequences and their mammalian remains was followed by attempts to sub-divide the local rock sequences to provide a chronology of Pleistocene events for the area. The precepts established from lithostratigraphic sequences around Gower have been applied elsewhere for regional stratigraphic correlations. Studies of the coastal and cave sequences and their calibration and correlation by dating methods, have further shown the importance of Gower as a reference area.

The caves

The large number of caves on Gower and their fossil remains first attracted attention. Discoveries of fossil mammals during the 1830s led to major excavations by Colonel E R Wood in many of the caves. These excavations were documented by Benson (1852), Falconer (1860, 1868), Vivian (1887) and Roberts (1887-8), and they were important in establishing Gower for Pleistocene investigations. Indeed, evidence from the caves shaped scientific thought when fierce debates obtained between the 'glacialist' and 'diluvialist' schools. In particular, Gower caves such as Paviland and Long Hole provided evidence to demonstrate the association between extinct Pleistocene mammals and the development of Man (Lyell 1873). The Gower caves figure prominently in modern studies, and their continuing importance is reflected in the GCR site coverage.

Early sub-division of Pleistocene sequences

Gower was used in one of the earliest Pleistocene classifications in Britain. This attempted to establish the relationship between the well developed raised beach deposits and local glacial and cave sediments. Prestwich (1892) suggested that the raised beach deposits were younger than the local glacial drift, and that the caves had been filled with mammalian remains since deposition of the local till. These conclusions were reversed by the Geological Survey: Tiddeman (1900) and Strahan (1907a, 1907b) suggested that the raised beach deposits were pre-glacial or interglacial in age, and were probably penecontemporaenous with bone beds found in some of the caves, such as Minchin Hole. The raised beach and associated bone beds were thus considered to pre-date the glaciation of the area.

The South Wales end-moraine

Charlesworth (1929) ushered in an important phase of investigations and reconstructed a limit for the 'Newer Drift' glaciation in South Wales. He believed that this most recent ice-sheet had impinged only on the easternmost fringe of Gower and was of Magdalenian age (Creswellian-Cheddarian). He considered that the raised beaches pre-dated both the 'Older' and 'Newer Drift' glaciations in the area.

T N George (1932, 1933a, 1933b) set new standards in the investigation of Pleistocene stratigraphy in South Wales in his work on the raised beaches, head and glacial deposits of Gower (Bowen 1984). George (1932, 1933a) synthesised the evidence of earlier workers (for example, Tiddeman 1900; Strahan 1907a, 1907b; Charlesworth 1929) and showed that Gower had been covered by two ice masses of different origin. One had a northerly source and deposited largely local, Welsh rock types; the other had a source to the west and brought erratics from the Irish Sea Basin. George upheld Charlesworth's 'Newer Drift' ice limit in the area and concluded that south of that limit, and covering much of Gower, there were 'Older Drift' glacial deposits of mixed Irish Sea and Welsh provenance; the former deposits being more widespread on the south and, particularly, the western margins of the peninsula. The mixing of the lithologies was used as evidence by George for the contemporaneity of the Irish Sea and Welsh ice masses during the 'Older Drift' glaciation.

George integrated evidence from the coastal sections into a sequence of events; in this sequence, the raised beaches form key marker beds – Table 2. This chronology represents the first sub-division of Pleistocene deposits in Wales, subsequent to the tripartite schemes of earlier workers.

Table 2 Gower chronology (T N George 1932)

9	Modern beach platform – coincident with Heatherslade Beach
8	Submerged forest (Late Neolithic)
7	Heatherslade Beach and platform (Early Neolithic)
6	Newer Drift glaciation – deposits present only along the eastern fringe of Gower, to the north of Mumbles Head (Magdalenian)
5	Cave deposits of Paviland and blown sand

(Aurignacian – possibly latest Mousterian to Early Solutrean)

4   Older Drift glaciation and associated head deposits (Mousterian)

3   Blown sands and the *Neritoides* Beach, containing *Neritoides obtusata* (L.) and ossiferous breccia of Minchin Hole (Late Acheulian to Early Mousterian)

2   *Patella* Beach, containing *Patella vulgata* (L.) formed during a cold period – an interpretation based on erratics in the *Patella* Beach which George considered had been ice-rafted

1   Intense cliff erosion

Griffiths (1937, 1939, 1940) used heavy mineral analysis to ascertain the origins of the ice-sheets and the provenances of the drifts. He defined the limits and directions of movement of the Irish Sea and Welsh ice masses over the region; and suggested that the deposits in Gower showed two significant variations. The deposits in west Gower contained a high chlorite constituent, suggesting that southward moving ice from the Tywi Valley, with a dominant Lower Palaeozoic mineral assemblage, had invaded the area. The deposits on the west side of Langland Bay in east Gower contained a basal heavy mineral suite of Irish Sea provenance ('Older Drift') and an upper suite of heavy minerals from the South Wales Coalfield ('Newer Drift'), both younger than the raised beach.

Correlations

Gower has been incorporated into stratigraphic correlations over wider areas. Zeuner (1945, 1959), for example, argued that the last glaciation consisted of two discrete advances ('Older Drift' and 'Newer Drift') because he assumed the *Patella* Beach was of Monastirian (last interglacial) [Ipswichian Stage] age (Bowen 1984). Wirtz (1953) and Mitchell (1960), however, argued that the *Patella* Beach was older and of Hoxnian age, and was overlain by 'Older Drift' glacial deposits and 'Newer Drift' (Devensian Stage) periglacial sediments, except in east Gower. Subsequently, Mitchell (1972) modified this scheme and suggested that two interglacial beaches occurred in Gower: an erratic-free deposit of Hoxnian age, and an erratic-rich deposit of Ipswichian age. Furthermore he suggested that two head deposits occurred, one erratic-free (Wolstonian) and one erratic-rich (Devensian). This interpretation implied that the Ipswichian Stage was lost in a notional unconformity within some head sequences (Bowen 1973a, 1973b).

Lithostratigraphy

Although George (1932, 1933a) described a lithostratigraphy, Gower has become increasingly important as the result of work by Bowen (1965, 1966, 1970a, 1970b, 1973a, 1973b, 1973c, 1974, 1977a, 1977b, 1977c) who reinterpreted the origins and relationships of stratigraphic units. This work led to a revision of the chronology proposed by

earlier workers. The lithostratigraphy of Gower was subsequently correlated with that of the Irish Sea Basin (Bowen 1973a, 1973b).

Central to Bowen's chronostratigraphical model was the assumption that the raised beaches of Gower were Ipswichian in age. This view was based largely on the association of raised marine (interglacial) sediments and faunal remains of apparently Ipswichian age in Minchin Hole Cave (for example, Bowen 1973c; Sutcliffe and Bowen 1973). This led to the use of the raised beach as a stratigraphic marker in the coastal sequences. It followed from this precept that deposits overlying the raised beach in Gower were Devensian in age. Bowen (1970a, 1971a, 1974) demonstrated that only in south-east Gower do unequivocal glacial beds overlie the Ipswichian (*Patella*) raised beach. Elsewhere along the south Gower coast, sediments overlying the raised beach consist of a series of aeolian, colluvial, head of different lithofacies and redeposited glacial sediments. The redeposited glacial sediments were originally deposited during a pre-Devensian ('Older Drift') glaciation and were subsequently redeposited by solifluction and alluviation during the Devensian. The 'Older Drift' glaciation thus antedated the deposition of the interglacial raised beach, for which its deposits provided erratics for incorporation into the beaches, but its precise age was indeterminate (Bowen 1970a, 1984).

Using the proposed Ipswichian raised beach as a marker, Bowen (for example, 1970a, 1971a) distinguished between glaciated and unglaciated areas in Gower. This approach has also been important in ascertaining the age of glacial sediments elsewhere around the coast of South and west Wales, and thereby in delimiting the extent of Late Devensian ice, particularly in respect of the lack of clear terminal features associated with the ice-sheet in many places (Bowen 1973a, 1973b, 1974). This approach is independent of both morphological indicators for estimating the age of the glacial deposits, such as 'freshness of form' and 'degree of dissection', and the now redundant radiocarbon timescale proposed for south-west Wales (for example, John 1970a).

Geochronology

Research during the last decade can be considered under three categories. First, the raised beaches have been dated. Much of this work has been based on the internationally important cave sites at Minchin Hole and Bacon Hole, and is centred on amino acid geochronology and Uranium-series dating (for example, Andrews *et al.* 1979; Bowen 1981a; Campbell *et al.* 1982; Davies 1983; Bowen 1984; Bowen *et al.* 1984; Bowen *et al.* 1985; Stringer *et al.* 1986; Bowen and Sykes 1988).

Second, advances have been made in detailed studies of the Gower cave sequences with new stratigraphic, mammalian, and archaeological evidence (for example, Stringer 1975, 1977a, 1977b; Campbell 1977; Sutcliffe 1981; Currant *et al.*

1984; Henry 1984a; Sutcliffe and Currant 1984; Stringer *et al.* 1986).

Third, detailed sedimentological and quantitative methods have amplified lithostratigraphic description of the coastal sequences (for example, Case 1983; Campbell 1984; Henry 1984a).

These investigations collectively have led to new discoveries on the nature and timing of Late Pleistocene events in Gower. Andrews *et al.* (1979) concluded, from (isoleucine-alloisoleucine) amino acid ratios measured from fossil protein in molluscs from the raised beaches, that two or possibly three separate sea-level events are represented by raised beaches in south-west Britain. The separate identity of two high sea-level events shown by the Outer (*Patella*) and Inner Beaches at Minchin Hole Cave was discussed by Sutcliffe and Bowen (1973) and was confirmed by amino acid ratios (Bowen *et al.* 1985), and ascribed to deep-sea Oxygen Isotope Stage 7 (Inner Beach) and Sub-stage 5e (Outer Beach) (Bowen and Sykes 1988).

Campbell *et al.* (1982) presented amino acid ratios from the raised beach at Broughton Bay, west Gower, showing a correlation with beach remnants regarded as Ipswichian (Sub-stage 5e) age in south-west Britain (Andrews *et al.* 1979). Davies (1983) identified two principal groups of amino acid ratios from raised beaches in southern Britain which she ascribed to Stage 7 and Sub-stage 5e of the deep-sea oxygen isotope scale. These data showed that although most of the raised beach remnants around the south and west coasts of Gower were ascribed to Sub-stage 5e, other older elements were present, for example, the Inner Beach at Minchin Hole and uncemented beach deposits at Horton. These older beach remnants were ascribed to Oxygen Isotope Stage 7 of the marine record (Davies 1983), one of the possible correlations discussed by Bowen (1973c).

Amino acid measurements published before 1985 (and including Davies 1983) were based on samples prepared by a method no longer used because it gave isoleucine-alloisoleucine ratios that were too low, and also because it involved an uncertain, but potentially unacceptable high level of variability (Miller 1985). Since 1983, a modified sample preparation has been used. Although it may appear reasonable to regard the earlier data as internally consistent, and potentially convertible, subsequent analyses which are sufficiently numerous for statistical evaluation, show that the earlier preparation methods (there were several variations on the basic procedure) show large variability, and, moreover, were not sufficiently sensitive to detect additional sea-level events.

Four separate marine/raised beach events have now been detected in Gower (Bowen *et al.* 1985; Bowen and Sykes 1988). The two main ones have been tied to a lithostratigraphy, and used as a basis for the erection of chronostratigraphic stages – the Minchin Hole D/L * Stage, and the Pennard D/L Stage. These have been defined in rock sequences which have characteristic D/L ratios. Two other sea-level events were recognised – one from D/L values from discrete outcrops of raised beach, although, unlike Minchin Hole, not in a stratigraphic sequence. These beach fragments are now believed to be a sub-stage of the Minchin Hole Stage (Bowen and Sykes 1988). The presence of the earliest event is founded on the identification of a mixed molluscan population in raised beach deposits at Hunts Bay, but correlated with deposits elsewhere (Bowen *et al.* 1985). Using a separate geochronologically calibrated amino acid framework for North-West Europe, these stages have been correlated with the oxygen isotope record as follows (Bowen and Sykes 1988; Bowen 1989b) –

Oxygen Isotope Stage	Chronostratigraphic Stage	**
Sub-stage 5e	Pennard Stage	0.1
Stage 7	Minchin Hole Stage	(0.14 (0.17
Stage 9	Unnamed	0.22

*Ratios of D-alloisoleucine to L-isoleucine

**Mean amino acid ratios for *Littorina* sp. and other chemically comparable species.

Conclusions

Some problems remain. The long held belief that the raised beaches around Gower are of Ipswichian age and overlain by Devensian Stage glacial and periglacial sediments, offered an economical model for interpreting the coastal sequences. Amino acid data show that raised beaches of different ages exist, some antedating the Ipswichian Stage. Potentially, this complicates interpreting the age of the overlying sediments (Bowen *et al.* 1985). The age of the pre-Devensian glaciations of the region is only fixed within broad limits – see Chapter 2. Glacial deposits belonging to three distinct glaciations are probably present on the peninsula (Bowen *et al.* 1985). In the absence of terminal features associated with the Late Devensian ice-sheet, the maximum extent of ice was delimited by Bowen (1970a) mostly using lithostratigraphical evidence from the coastal exposures – see Figure 2. A revised and extended ice limit was proposed by Bowen (1984) (Figure 2) for south-west Gower. However, the results of recent drilling and geophysical work show that glacial sediments in this area are older. An earlier glaciation of Irish Sea origin is inferred from erratics and heavy minerals, but a later one of Welsh provenance is represented by deposits dominated by Namurian 'quartzite', and which appear to terminate at the Paviland Moraine (Bowen *et al.* 1985; Bowen, Jenkins and Catt, unpublished – see Figure 2). Remains of glacial sediments from both Welsh and Irish Sea sources are found in the coastal exposures but have been

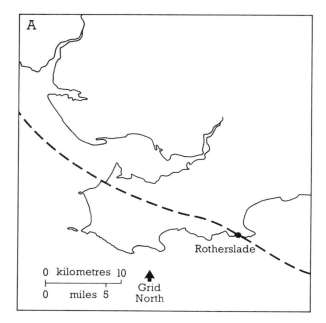

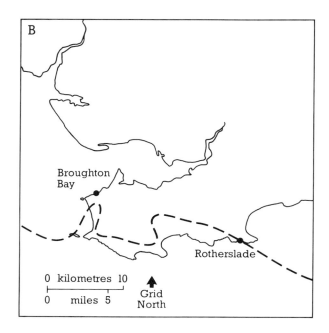

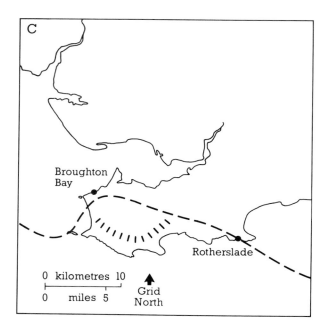

Late Devensian maximum ice limit

A   after Bowen (1970a)

B   after Bowen (1981a, 1981b)

C   after Campbell (1984)

Proposed limit of Paviland moraine
(pre-Devensian) glaciation from
Bowen et al (1985)

Figure 2 Some proposed ice limits on Gower (from Bowen 1970a; Bowen 1981a, 1981b; Campbell 1984; Bowen et al. 1985)

redeposited. Bowen et al. (1985) ascribed the earlier Irish Sea glaciation to Oxygen Isotope Stage 10 or earlier, and the Welsh, Paviland Moraine glaciation to Oxygen Isotope Stage 8 or earlier – see Chapter 2.

Finally, although a Late Devensian age for the last glaciation of Gower is evident, its precise timing is as indeterminate as elsewhere in Britain. The recently exposed Pleistocene sediments at Broughton Bay in north-west Gower may be of considerable importance in this context: the site shows Late Devensian shelly glacial deposits overlying an Ipswichian fossiliferous raised beach (Campbell et al. 1982; Campbell 1984). A combination of amino acid and radiocarbon dated evidence from the site was recently presented, and was thought to show a Late Devensian age of c. 17,000 BP for the emplacement of the glacial sediments (Bowen et al. 1985; Bowen et al. 1986; Bowen and Sykes 1988).

The selected GCR sites in Gower reflect many of the themes discussed, and in particular, illustrate many of the latest developments in research on the Pleistocene, its sub-division and dating.

Rotherslade (Langland Bay)

Highlights

This locality is a rare site proving the position of the maximum extent of the ice front during the last, Devensian, glaciation. Although the rest of south Gower was unaffected by Welsh ice, lying in the periglacial zone, this area was overrun.

Introduction

The exposures at Rotherslade demonstrate Devensian glaciation in Gower post-dating the raised beach ascribed to Oxygen Isotope Sub-stage 5e. The site provides contrasting evidence to nearby sites at Hunts Bay, Slade and Horton, which demonstrate ice-free conditions throughout the Devensian. The site has a long-standing history of research commencing with the work of Strahan (1907a). It was later studied by George (1932, 1933a, 1933b), Griffiths (1939), Bowen (1966, 1969a, 1970a, 1971a, 1973a, 1973b, 1974, 1977a, 1977b, 1984), Campbell (1984) and Bowen *et al.* (1985). The site has also been mentioned in studies by Stephens and Shakesby (1982), Davies (1983), Shakesby and Campbell (1985) and Bridges (1985).

Description

The following generalised sequence occurs at Rotherslade (SS613872) –

5	Modern soil}	(1.0m)
4	Colluvium }	
3	Glacial deposits (14.0m)	
2	Limestone head with red silty sand matrix (3.5m)	
1	Raised beach deposits (0.6m)	

Maximum bed thicknesses after Bowen (1971a)

The raised beach deposits lie on a Carboniferous Limestone shore platform at 10m OD, which is dissected by relict potholes and gullies (Bowen 1971a, 1984). In places, the beach sediments adhere to the walls of these gullies and form a tough cemented conglomerate of limestone pebbles, although erratics from the South Wales Coalfield and Irish Sea Basin are also present (George 1932). The raised beach contains numerous marine shells and shell fragments. The thickest sediments are glacial deposits which are often crudely stratified, well imbricated, and contain an erratic suite typical of Breconshire drift (Bowen 1970a).

Interpretation

The sections at Rotherslade were first described and interpreted by Strahan (1907a). The relationship between the raised beach deposits and the overlying glacial beds was used as critical evidence by Strahan to suggest a 'pre-glacial' or possibly 'interglacial' age for the raised beach sediments at the site and elsewhere around the Gower coast.

George (1932, 1933a, 1933b), who also suggested a 'pre-glacial' age for the *Patella* raised beach, considered that a sand, interpreted by Strahan (1907a) as aeolian, was a fluvioglacial deposit, overlain by a sequence of interdigitating limestone head and glacial sediments representing glacial deposition at an oscillating ice margin. It was unclear if the glacial sediments belonged to the 'Older' or 'Newer Drift' glaciations (George 1933a, 1933b), but he subsequently favoured that this part of east Gower had been overrun by the 'Newer Drift' ice-sheet (George 1970).

Griffiths (1939) identified the heavy minerals from the deposits on the west side of Langland Bay as part of his analysis of South Wales drifts. He considered that the drift at Langland consisted of basal layers rich in Irish Sea minerals as well as containing a few Irish Sea erratics. Higher, only a few 'foreign minerals' occurred while the uppermost layers and overlying gravels contained only 'local' (South Wales Coalfield) erratics and minerals. He concluded that the lower part was ground moraine deposited by combined Irish Sea and local Welsh ice of 'Older Drift' age. The overlying drift showed that some of the underlying material had been incorporated by the succeeding advance of 'Newer Drift' Welsh ice (the Tawe glacier). The coarse upper gravel represented the 'outwash fan' of the retreating 'Newer Drift' Tawe glacier (Griffiths 1939). He therefore believed that "..... at this exposure a complete sequence of deposits representative of both glaciations can be traced in the correct chronological and spatial order"; namely that both post-dated the raised beach.

The exposures at Rotherslade were also studied in a series of papers by Bowen (1966, 1969a, 1970a, 1971a, 1973a, 1973b, 1974, 1977a, 1977b, 1984). He originally suggested that the raised beach at Rotherslade could be Hoxnian, with the overlying deposits consisting of periglacial and redeposited glacial sediments (Bowen 1966). Subsequently, he revised this interpretation, and ascribed the raised beach sediments to the Ipswichian Stage and the overlying deposits, which consisted of head and glacial deposits *in situ*, to the Devensian Stage.

From the evidence at Rotherslade, Bowen (1969a, 1970a, 1984) reconstructed the following sequence of events. During temperate, high sea-level conditions, raised beach sediments accumulated on a limestone shore platform. Erratics from the South Wales Coalfield and the Irish Sea Basin present in the raised beach deposits were considered to have been reworked from glacial sediments of pre-Ipswichian age. As environmental conditions worsened with the onset of the Devensian Stage, locally derived limestone head began to accumulate on the raised beach, and was mixed with colluvial sediments washed from a sparsely vegetated landscape. At the same time, sea-level began to fall and sand from the exposed shore was incorporated into the head deposits (Bowen 1969a, 1971a, 1977a, 1977b, 1984). These head deposits were thought by Bowen (1971a) to have accumulated during the Early and Middle Devensian, under cold but not necessarily continuous periglacial conditions. During the Late Devensian glacial maximum (*c.* 20,000-18,000 BP), Welsh ice crossed the eastern tip of Gower, depositing a sequence of glacial sediments up to 14m thick; lodgement till at the base overlain by crudely stratified and imbricated ablation till (Bowen 1970a) and fluvioglacial sands and gravels (Bowen 1971a). Lenses of till occur in the gravels, the entire deposit having probably formed in the rapidly changing depositional conditions at an ice margin. Imbrication in the gravel layers indicated that part of the sequence had been subjected to redeposition, partly by solifluction and partly by water. A minimum age of *c.* 14,000 BP (Bowen 1969a, 1970a, 1971a) for the glacial deposits was indicated by Devensian late-glacial sediments occupying a kettle hole (now destroyed) in the same lithostratigraphic formation at nearby Derwen Fawr, Swansea (Trotman 1963). Bowen (1969a) suggested that the imbrication and fabric of the glacial sediments at Rotherslade also showed that they had been derived from the north-east. Finally, towards the close of the Late Devensian and into the Devensian late-glacial, loess (Case 1984) and colluvial (slope wash) sediments were deposited as a capping to the sequence. Bowen (1977b) considered the site allowed the extent of the post-*Patella* Beach glaciation (Late Devensian) to be established in east Gower. Bowen's interpretation of the sequence at Rotherslade was supported by Peake *et al.* (1973), Stephens and Shakesby (1982), Shakesby and Campbell (1985) and Bridges (1985).

Amino acid dating and correlation by both older and current preparation methods led to the raised beach being ascribed to Oxygen Isotope Sub-stage 5e (Davies 1983; Bowen *et al.* 1985), and the Ipswichian (Bowen and Sykes 1988).

Campbell (1984) applied a range of techniques including Scanning Electron Microscopy of quartz sand grains, clast lithology, fabric and roundness analyses to the interpretation of the Rotherslade sequence. An absence of Carboniferous Limestone clasts in the glacial sediments (also noted by Strahan (1907a)) suggested deposition by ice moving south-west from the Nedd (Neath) and Tawe Valleys rather than south across the extensive limestone terrain of south Gower. The glacial deposits at Rotherslade were thus considered to represent the south-westward extension of a piedmont ice-lobe in Swansea Bay. This interpretation was also supported by clast fabric analysis which showed a strongly preferred north-east to south-west orientation. Campbell (1984), however, noted that this fabric 'trend' could also have resulted from subsequent redeposition of the glacial sediments by solifluction.

Rotherslade has an important stratigraphic record

showing changing environmental conditions in central South Wales during the Late Pleistocene, with evidence for a transition from the high sea-level conditions of the Ipswichian Stage, to cold and eventually full glacial conditions during the Devensian Stage, when east Gower was overrun by south-west moving Welsh ice.

The ascription of the raised beach deposits at Rotherslade (Langland Bay) to Oxygen Isotope Sub-stage 5e (Bowen *et al.* 1985; Bowen and Sykes 1988) (*c.* 125,000 BP) and the pollen analysis of deposits lying in a kettle hole in glacial sediments nearby (Trotman 1963), provide evidence for the ages of these respective deposits. The evidence from Rotherslade is similar to that at Broughton Bay in north-west Gower (Campbell *et al.* 1982; Campbell 1984), and both provide constraints for the extent of Late Devensian ice. Both are dissimilar to the evidence from Hunts Bay, Western Slade, Eastern Slade and Horton, which show ice-free conditions throughout the Devensian (Bowen 1970a).

Rotherslade is important for interpreting Late Pleistocene events in central South Wales; showing a sequence of raised beach sediments overlain by head and glacial deposits. The raised beach has been correlated by amino acid geochronology with Oxygen Isotope Sub-stage 5e of the deep-sea record. This shows that the overlying sediments must be Devensian. Local pollen evidence provides a minimum late-glacial age for the glacial deposits at Rotherslade and shows that the last glaciation of eastern Gower was Late Devensian in age. As such it is important evidence for establishing the maximum extent of Late Devensian ice from the uplands of South Wales.

Conclusions

Rotherslade (Langland Bay) displays a sequence of deposits which represents the entire last glacial cycle. The site is also exceptional because it shows evidence for the last time Britain enjoyed conditions similar to the present, about 125,000 years ago. Then global sea-level was some metres higher than it is today (shown by the raised beach). Glacial deposits were laid down by the last great Welsh ice-sheet.

Hunts Bay

Highlights

A locality which shows outstanding sections of head, colluvium and reworked till deposited during the Devensian when this part of Gower was not glaciated. Devensian rocks overlie raised beach deposits and platform which may indicate at least three episodes of earlier Pleistocene temperate climate.

Introduction

Hunts Bay (SS565867) shows a Pleistocene sequence of marine deposits and terrestrial periglacial sediments, proving that south Gower was not glaciated during the Late Devensian. The site has a long history of research, commencing with the work of Strahan (1907a). It has been studied by George (1932, 1933a, 1933b), Bowen (1970a, 1971a, 1973a, 1973b, 1974, 1977a, 1977b) and Harris (1973). The site was also mentioned by Mitchell (1972), Peake et al. (1973), Stephens and Shakesby (1982), Davies (1983), Shakesby and Campbell (1985) and Bridges (1985). Henry (1984a, 1984b) provided descriptions of the exposures, and the raised beaches were dated by amino acid geochronology (Bowen et al. 1985; Bowen and Sykes 1988).

Description

The sequence of colluvial and periglacial sediments overlying raised beach deposits can be traced along much of the south Gower coast, but it is extensive and well exposed at Hunts Bay (Deep Slade), where the following generalised sequence (not necessarily in stratigraphic order at any one exposure) occurs overlying a Carboniferous Limestone shore platform. (Stratigraphic terminology of Henry (1984a, 1984b) in parenthesis) –

7   Colluvium and blown sand (Port-Eynon Silt)

6   Limestone head with erratics (Hunts West Breccia and Erratics)

5   Redeposited glacial sediments (Western Slade Diamicton)

4   Fine angular limestone head (Hunts Breccia)

3   Coarse blocky limestone head with red silt matrix (Hunts East Breccia)

2   Colluvial silts (Pwll Du Red Beds)

1   Raised beach deposits (Hunts Bay Beach)

The sequence is laterally variable (Figure 3) and a number of important exposures has been described (named by Bowen (1971a)). These are, a) Hunts Bay East Cove (SS566866); b) Hunts Bay East (SS565867); c) Hunts Bay Centre (SS564868); and d) Hunts Bay West (SS562868).

Interpretation

The Pleistocene sections at Hunts Bay were first described by Strahan (1907a), who noted a sequence of glacial deposits containing Old Red Sandstone, grey sandstones and quartz conglomerates, resting on raised beach deposits which were largely devoid of 'travelled' rock types. The absence of such rocks indicated a 'pre-glacial' or possibly 'interglacial' age for the raised beach (Strahan 1907a).

George (1932, 1933a, 1933b) recorded a sequence of –

4   Head with pockets of glacial sediment

3   Fox red sand and loam

2   *Patella* raised beach

1   *Patella* beach platform

He considered that the raised beach had been deposited before the 'Older Drift' glaciation of the area because it contained very few erratics, and he regarded the overlying head as a typical solifluction deposit. The fox red sand and loam was believed to be fluvioglacial in origin, and pockets of glacial sediments, originally deposited by ice of 'Older Drift' age, had later been incorporated into the head deposits (George 1933a). George showed that the majority of rocks in the glacial gravel had been derived from the South Wales Coalfield to the north, but others of a more distant origin were also present. These included Triassic conglomerate, soda-felsite from Llŷn and other rocks from North Wales and northern Pembrokeshire. The mixture of foreign and local rock types indicated to him the possible confluence between the Irish Sea and Welsh ice masses during the 'Older Drift' glaciation.

The nature and origin of the sequence at Hunts Bay, which makes up a large solifluction terrace, was discussed by Bowen (1970a, 1971a, 1973a, 1973b, 1974, 1977a, 1977b). From the evidence at Hunts Bay and elsewhere in Gower, he reconstructed the following sequence of events. The raised beach (bed 1) was of probable Ipswichian age, and represented a period of high sea-level conditions. With the onset of colder conditions during the Devensian Stage, colluvial silts (bed 2) and blocky limestone head (bed 3) were deposited. The colluvial silts were the product of sheet washing and soil erosion, and much of the material in beds 2 and 3 had been subjected to chemical weathering during the previous temperate (Ipswichian) event (Bowen 1970a, 1971a). This view was supported by Clayden (1977a), who described a possible pre-Devensian weathered profile in situ on the plateau above Hunts Bay (SS563873). Unlike the blocky head (bed 3) which was attributed to frost-action on chemically prepared regolith, the finer calibre head (bed 4) was attributed to frost-action on fresh unweathered bedrock, during the later Devensian (Bowen 1971a). Contemporaneously, 'Older Drift' glacial deposits mantling the plateau above Hunts Bay were reworked and redeposited (bed 5) by alluvial and solifluction processes along the valley of Deep Slade (cf. Eastern Slade, Western Slade), and head (bed 6), also continued to form at Hunts Bay. Finally, during the Devensian late-glacial, the colluvium and blown sand (bed 7) were deposited.

Mitchell (1972), however, argued that the Hunts Bay raised beach was erratic-free and was probably Hoxnian (not Ipswichian) in age, and that the overlying lower blocky head and upper fine calibre head (Bowen 1971a) represented the Saalian and Devensian Stages, respectively.

In marked contrast to Mitchell (1972), Bowen therefore regarded sediments overlying the raised

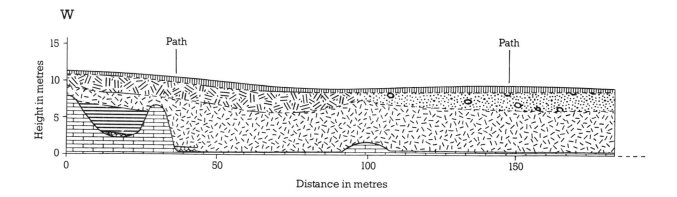

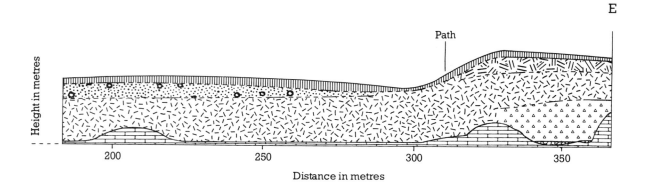

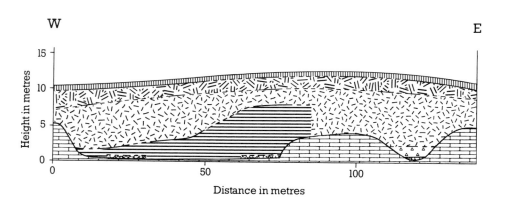

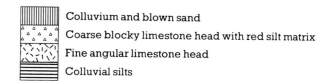

Colluvium and blown sand	Redeposited glacial sediments
Coarse blocky limestone head with red silt matrix	Hunts Bay Beach
Fine angular limestone head	Limestone head with erratics
Colluvial silts	Carboniferous Limestone bedrock

Figure 3 Quaternary sequence at Hunts Bay (after Bowen and Henry 1984)

beach at Hunts Bay as the result of a single depositional cycle during the Devensian. He also noted that the erratic content of the raised beach was highly variable, thus making the basis of Mitchell's interpretation of its age even more untenable. Moreover, interpretation of the sequence as the result of a single depositional cycle did not necessitate loss of the Ipswichian Stage in a notional unconformity within the sequence (Bowen 1970a).

A detailed study of clast fabrics in the head

deposits by Harris (1973) tended to confirm the origin of the sediments as solifluction deposits, with head having moved down the valley and from the sides.

From amino acid analysis of fossil marine molluscs Davies (1983) ascribed the raised beach deposits at Hunts Bay West (Site d) to Oxygen Isotope Sub-stage 5e of the deep-sea record, the Ipswichian Stage (*c.* 125,000 BP), as proposed earlier by Bowen (1977b). Raised beach deposits at Hunts Bay East (Site b) also date from this time, although they contain some older shells, probably reworked from deposits of Oxygen Isotope Stage 7 age (*c.* 210,000 BP) (Davies 1983). Amino acid data with greater precision and less variability, show that a fauna of Oxygen Isotope Stage 9 also occurs in this beach (Bowen *et al.* 1985; Bowen and Sykes 1988).

Henry (1984a, 1984b) provided a detailed description of the deposits at Hunts Bay, and gave them formal stratigraphic names (see site description). She showed that the raised beach at Hunts Bay contained a fossil assemblage of marine molluscs characteristic of the middle shore zone of rocky coasts. Foraminiferal and ostracod assemblages indicate temperate, shallow water marine conditions, and Henry concluded that the beach had been deposited during a temperate interglacial episode with sea-level similar to or a few metres higher than at present; amino acid ratios confirmed this as an Ipswichian event (Oxygen Isotope Sub-stage 5e) (Davies 1983; Bowen *et al.* 1985; Bowen and Sykes 1988).

Amino acid geochronology has established that raised beach sediments at the site are Ipswichian in age (Bowen *et al.* 1985; Bowen and Sykes 1988). Deposits overlying these Sub-stage 5e marine beds demonstrate a deterioration of conditions during the Devensian Stage, when sheet-washing and soil erosion was followed by the accumulation of frost-shattered bedrock; at the same time, glacial deposits from an earlier pre-Devensian glaciation were recycled and redeposited by alluvial and solifluction processes. This exceptionally detailed sequence of head deposits is significant in illustrating in a single section some of the range of periglacial sediments and processes associated with the Devensian Stage (Bowen 1971a). Hunts Bay has been proposed as a reference site for limestone head deposits in Gower (Henry 1984a), and together with several other sites, is notable in demonstrating that parts of south Gower were not glaciated during the Late Devensian ice maximum.

Hunts Bay is a classic site for Quaternary research. It shows a sequence of raised marine deposits overlain by colluvial, head and redeposited glacial sediments. The raised beach sediments have been ascribed by amino acid geochronology to Oxygen Isotope Sub-stage 5e of the deep-sea record, although elements of an older reworked fauna are also present in the deposits. Together with the raised marine shore platform, the site therefore provides evidence for three high sea-level stands, at least, during the Pleistocene. Detailed

sedimentary evidence has shown that the overlying terrestrial sequence is the product of a single Devensian depositional cycle during both cold and periglacial conditions. This evidence suggests the south Gower coast was not overrun by Late Devensian ice, unlike Rotherslade (Langland Bay) in the east and Broughton in the north-west.

Conclusions

Hunts Bay contains a sequence of deposits representing the last glacial cycle. When the global sea-level was high, about 125,000 years ago, the Hunts Bay raised beach was formed, and represents the last time Britain enjoyed conditions similar to the present. The last ice age is represented at Hunts Bay by cold climate (periglacial) deposits. These show that this site was not covered by an ice-sheet during the last ice age. As such, the evidence is important in establishing the maximum dimensions of the last ice-sheet in Wales.

Bosco's Den

Highlights

A key site yielding a rich Late Pleistocene mammal fauna. This consists of typical cold stage (glacial) species with, in particular, a remarkable accumulation of deer antlers.

Introduction

Bosco's Den (SS559868) is a large fissure cave containing fossiliferous deposits. The site was originally excavated in the mid-nineteenth century and it yielded prolific mammalian remains, which would appear to date from the Devensian Stage. Falconer (1868) concluded that "...On the whole, Bosco's Den of all the Gower Caves, furnishes the more complete succession of marine, brecciated and alluvial deposits disposed in a section of no less than 47 feet". The site was originally excavated by Wood in 1858 (see Falconer 1860, 1868), and was subsequently described by Prestwich (1892), Strahan (1907a), George (1933b, 1970), Allen and Rutter (1944, 1948), and Stringer and Currant (1981).

Description and interpretation

Bosco's Den, once known as Bacon's Eye, and situated only 150m west of Bacon Hole, is on two levels. The lower, which is unfossiliferous, reaches 25 ft (7.6m) above the modern beach, and extends inwards for some 30 ft (9.1m); the upper reaches about 70 ft (21m) above the modern beach and penetrates the limestone cliff for about 75 ft (23m) (Allen and Rutter 1944, 1948). The dividing floor comprises a thick sequence of raised beach deposits overlain by a sequence of fossiliferous cave earth and head deposits.
The first excavations at Bosco's Den were carried

out by Wood in 1858, and these were subsequently documented by Falconer (1860, 1868). Falconer recorded the following generalised sequence –

8   Sandy peat*
7   Stalagmitic floor (<0.3m)
6   Sandy loam (0.4m)
5   Sand (0.7m)
4   Loose breccia (1.2m)
3   Cave earth (2.0m)
2   Cemented breccia*
1   Raised marine sands and gravels*

(* bed thicknesses not recorded)

Bones of ox, wolf and shed antlers of deer (species allied to the reindeer) were recovered from the sandy peat (bed 8), and the remains of cave bear *Ursus spelaeus* (Rosenmüller & Heinroth), wolf *Canis lupus* L., fox *Vulpes vulpes* (L.), *Bos* sp., *Cervus* sp. and *Arvicola* sp. were recovered from the cave earth (bed 3). Falconer (1860) remarked that – "The most remarkable circumstance about these remains was the great excess of deers antlers above the others. Upwards of one thousand antlers, mostly shed and of young animals belonging chiefly to *Cervus guetardi* were collected."

Traces of marine sand and patches of cemented raised beach at Bosco's Den were also noted by Prestwich (1892), Strahan (1907a) and George (1933b). George (1933b) considered the raised marine deposits at Bosco's Den to be related to the *Patella* raised beach found elsewhere around the Gower coast. As such, it was considered to pre-date the 'Older Drift' glaciation of Gower, and its position beneath the cave deposits was used as evidence by George that the cave fauna was of considerable antiquity. He noted that the bones had accumulated *in situ*. Precise interpretations of the age and significance of the finds were not, however, forthcoming, although Strahan had noted that thermophilous taxa such as elephant, rhino, hyaena and cave lion were absent. Strahan emphasised that the precise stratigraphic context of many of Wood's and Falconer's finds was not clear.

Bosco's Den was later described in some detail by Allen and Rutter (1944, 1948) in their survey of the Gower caves, although no new finds were recorded. They noted that the cave was particularly significant for the considerable collection of antlers. Such an accumulation of a single species may be compared with caves at Kuhloch in Germany and San Ciro in Sicily where the remains of 2,500 cave bears and at least 2,000 hippopotamuses, respectively, had been found. (Allen and Rutter 1944, 1948).

Bosco's Den was cited by Stringer and Currant (1981) as an example of a cave where abundant mammalian remains had been recovered, but where there was little evidence for hyaena, or

human, activity to account for the accumulations. This, they considered discounted Turner's (1981a) suggestion that the presence and activity of hyaena were prerequisites for such large accumulations, although Turner (1981b) later stressed that it was possible for the bones to have accumulated by other means. The dating and palaeoenvironmental significance of the remains from Bosco's Den have not yet been established, but the fauna can probably be ascribed to the Devensian Stage. Hitherto, no species with distinct warm climate preferences have been recorded. The site is particularly significant in containing deposits that may provide a comprehensive fauna for comparison with the records from adjacent sites at Minchin Hole and Bacon Hole. Well developed interglacial marine sediments also occur.

Bosco's Den's sequence of raised marine deposits and terrestrial sediments are important for interpreting Late Pleistocene events in South Wales. Mammalian remains recovered during early excavations appear to form a 'cold' fauna probably dating from the Devensian Stage, although their precise stratigraphic context is debatable. The site is unusual in having yielded prolific remains of a single species, but their mode of accumulation has not been established.

Conclusions

Bosco's Den contains marine and cave deposits which have yielded important mammalian fossil remains. Over a thousand deer antlers have been recovered from this site.

Bacon Hole Cave

Highlights

This site shows an outstanding sequence of cold and temperate interglacial rocks and faunas. It has yielded the most complete faunal record for the Ipswichian and Early Devensian in Wales from a complex section.

Introduction

Bacon Hole (SS559868) is an important cave in Gower, preserving a sequence of deposits and faunal assemblages important for understanding Late Pleistocene events in Britain. The site contains one of the most detailed records of faunal change recorded at any Ipswichian Stage site in Britain. Bacon Hole has an unusually long history of research which commenced with the work of Wood (see Benson 1852; Falconer 1860, 1868). It was also mentioned by Prestwich (1892), Tiddeman (1900), Strahan (1907a) and George (1932, 1933b). The site became the focus of a controversy concerning possible Palaeolithic cave paintings (Sollas and Breuil 1912; R E Morgan 1913; W L Morgan 1913; Sollas 1924; Wheeler 1925; Garrod 1926). Archaeological finds were described by

Williams (1939, 1941) and the site was partially re-excavated in 1943 by Allen and Rutter (1948). More recently, evidence has been discussed by Bowen (1970a, 1977a, 1977b, 1980a, 1981a), George (1970), Griffiths (1972), Sutcliffe (1976, 1981), Houlder (1977), Stringer and Currant (1981) and Turner (1981a, 1981b). Detailed studies have been carried out by Stringer (1975, 1977a, 1977b), Harrison (1977), Bowen et al. (1984), Currant et al. (1984) and Henry (1984a). Most recently Stringer et al. (1986) have provided a detailed interpretation of the age and significance of the sequence at Bacon Hole. Bacon Hole is an important site for the correlation and classification of the marine sequences of western and southern Britain using amino acid geochronology (Bowen et al. 1985; Bowen and Sykes 1988).

Description

Bacon Hole is a large terrestrial cave formed along a near vertical fault in Carboniferous Limestone. The cave opens onto a sloping rock platform at c. 11.5m OD (Stringer et al. 1986) upon which a sequence of marine and terrestrial sediments occurs. There is little evidence for channelling or reworking of the deposits, and the boundaries between units are unusually clear for cave deposits (Currant et al. 1984). In addition there is a remarkable consistency of deposition across the platform into the cave, which assists correlation and interpretation. The following units are recognised (Currant et al. 1984; Stringer et al. 1986) –

10	Cemented Breccias
9	Upper Cave Earth
8	Upper Sands
7	Grey Clays, Silts and Sands
6	Shelly Sand
5	Sandy Cave Earth
4	Sandy Breccio-Conglomerate
3	Coarse Orange Sands
2	Coarse Grey Sands
1	Basal Pebbles

Schematic sections through the platform and cave sequences are shown in Figure 4.

The first excavation at Bacon Hole by Wood was subsequently documented by Benson (1852) and Falconer (1860, 1868). These workers noted a sequence of –

9	Dark superficial earth (with *Bos* sp., *Cervus* sp., *Vulpes vulpes*, reindeer antlers, roebuck, a variety of littoral molluscs and pieces of pottery)
8	Stalagmite (with *Ursus* sp.)
7	Limestone breccia and stalagmite (with bones of *Ursus* and *Bos*)
6	Stalagmite (enveloping an elephant tusk)
5	Ochreous cave earth and limestone breccia (with *Palaeoloxodon antiquus* Falconer &

Cautley, *Dicerorhinus hemitoechus* (Falconer), *Crocuta* sp., *Canis lupus*, *Ursus spelaeus*, *Bos* sp. and *Cervus* sp.)

4	Blackish sand (with bones of *Palaeoloxodon antiquus*, *Meles meles* (L.) and *Mustela putorius* (L.)
3	Stalagmite
2	Marine sand (with *Littorina* sp. shells, bones of *Arvicola* sp. and birds)
1	Limestone floor

Interpretation

Prestwich (1892) noted cemented fragments of raised beach near the entrance to the cave but was unclear about the relative ages of the Pleistocene deposits concluding "..... that the Gower caves have probably been filled up with their mammalian remains since the deposition of the boulder clay". Such a conclusion was reversed by Tiddeman (1900) and Strahan (1907a) who suggested that the raised beach was probably pre-glacial or interglacial and that the overlying bone beds were of similar age; both formations pre-dating deposition of glacial drift in the local area. Strahan (1907a) observed that such an interglacial age corresponded well with the 'warm' fauna recovered from the beds, and alluded to the possibility that the 'colder' fauna excavated by Wood, might have occurred in significantly younger beds not associated with the interglacial phase. Similarly, George (1932, 1933b) maintained that the raised beach at Bacon Hole was of pre-glacial age, and correlated it with the *Patella* Beach.

During the early part of the twentieth century, Bacon Hole featured in a controversy concerning the possible existence of Palaeolithic paintings within the cave. Sollas and Breuil (1912) had claimed that ten red bands on the wall of the cave were painted by Aurignacian Man, and that they were the oldest of their kind in Britain. Some workers, however, claimed that the markings had been formed naturally from oxides within the rock (R E Morgan 1913; W L Morgan 1913; Wheeler 1925; Allen and Rutter 1948), and Garrod (1926) discussed the possibility that they had been produced fraudulently during more recent years. Sollas (1924) maintained, however, that the painted bands were genuine. The status of the cave markings remains obscure, although some authors (for example, Bowen 1970a) allude to the possibility that they are genuine. The archaeological interest of the site was further enhanced by Williams' (1939, 1941) descriptions of finds of Iron Age pottery from the cave floor.

In 1943, Allen and Rutter excavated a small mound outside the cave as part of a comprehensive survey of the Gower caves (Allen and Rutter 1948). They discovered teeth, bones and coprolites; the coprolites they attributed to hyaenas, and their restricted occurrence was seen as evidence that the species may have been relatively rare in Bacon Hole. Their study confirmed the stratigraphical observations of Wood and Benson, and produced

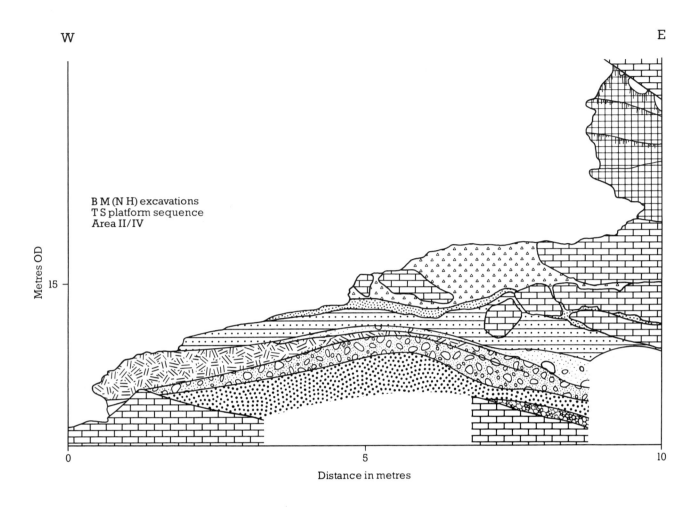

W   E

B M (N H) excavations
T S platform sequence
Area II/IV

Metres OD

15

Distance in metres

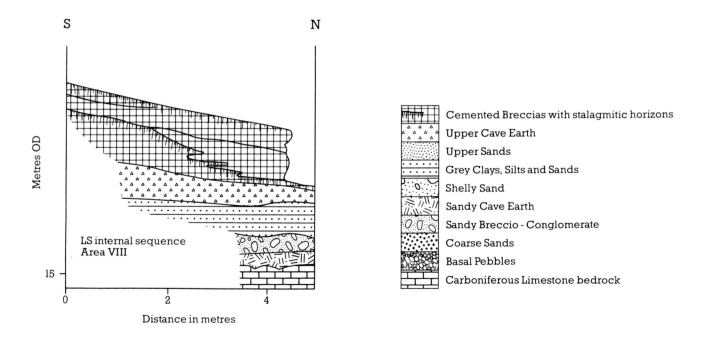

S   N

Metres OD

LS internal sequence
Area VIII

15

Distance in metres

Cemented Breccias with stalagmitic horizons
Upper Cave Earth
Upper Sands
Grey Clays, Silts and Sands
Shelly Sand
Sandy Cave Earth
Sandy Breccio - Conglomerate
Coarse Sands
Basal Pebbles
Carboniferous Limestone bedrock

Figure 4 Pleistocene sequence at Bacon Hole Cave (from Currant *et al.* 1984)

additional fossil specimens further suggesting an interglacial age for the older deposits in the cave.

Work in Gower by Bowen, since 1965, has further established the importance of the area for sub-dividing and classifying the Pleistocene stratigraphy of Wales and the Irish Sea Basin. From a re-examination of the Pleistocene stratigraphy in coastal sections and caves around the Gower coast, Bowen (1970a) suggested that the simplest interpretation of the sequences at Bacon Hole (and Minchin Hole), was to regard the 'warm' beds as Ipswichian in age, and the overlying 'cold' beds as Devensian. Such an interpretation has largely been substantiated by more recent detailed examinations of the site (for example, Stringer 1977b; Bowen *et al.* 1984; Henry 1984a; Stringer *et al.* 1986).

In addition to recovering numerous fossils including bison or giant ox, cave hyaena, bank or field vole and various marine and terrestrial molluscs from deposits on the shore platform just outside the cave, Griffiths (1972) made a notable discovery of pieces of fossil ivory (mammoth?) which, he considered, had been shaped by Palaeolithic Man. As a result of this excavation, he attributed the recovered remains to an interstadial phase within a glaciation, presumably during the Devensian Stage.

Excavations in 1974 and 1975 in superficial deposits on the rock platform outside the cave, yielded abundant remains of interglacial fossil mammals, possibly representing the early, middle and late parts of an interglacial (Ipswichian) climatic cycle (Stringer 1975).

Further excavation and additional information led Stringer (1977a, 1977b) to revise the established stratigraphy of the site. He recorded a sequence of –

8   Cemented Breccias (not then excavated)
7   Upper Cave Earth
6   Upper Sands
5   Coarse Brown Sands
4   Grey Clays, Silts and Sands
3   Sandy Cave earth
2   Sandy Breccio-Conglomerate
1   Basal Sands

Stringer demonstrated that the Basal Sands were probably marine in origin, especially towards the base where they contained rounded pebbles and marine molluscs. Scanning Electron Microscopy (SEM) showed that the beach also contained reworked sand from glacial sources. Faunal elements such as horse and northern vole were indicative of open-country, boreal conditions; and a restricted fauna of land snails suggested an environment of bare cliff faces and scree slopes. The presence of fox (Stringer 1977b) and razorbill (Harrison 1977), however, paint a slightly less bleak picture. Stringer concluded that the Basal Sands (his bed 1) represented a period of high sea-

level, perhaps during the early part of an interglacial cycle. The overlying Sandy Breccio-Conglomerate (bed 2) generally indicated more typical 'fully' interglacial conditions with mammals of mixed temperate oak forest (for instance, red deer, wood mouse, field vole and bank vole). The succeeding Sandy Cave Earth (bed 3) was considered to represent a more typical cave entrance deposit, but still with a high proportion of marine characteristics. The mammal, fish and bird faunas, the latter with curlew, dunlin, starling and Cory's shearwater (Harrison 1977), were indicative of generally warm conditions during deposition of the bed. Cory's shearwater was displaced at least 10° north of its present range, possibly indicating warmer conditions than at present.

The Grey Clay, Silts and Sands (bed 4) provided rich fossil material including over 100 coprolites, probably of hyaena. Stringer confirmed the presence of giant ox and bison from this bed and also noted the occurrence of northern vole and bean goose (Harrison 1977) which he argued showed a return to more boreal conditions, although several temperate species such as badger, shrew and woodmouse were also recorded. Stringer noted that this bed had contained the 'polished' bones which he suggested had been used to dress animal skins. Houlder (1977) believed these 'tools' represented the oldest evidence (then available) of Man's presence in Wales.

The succeeding Coarse Brown Sands (bed 5) contained (Stringer 1977b) a 'distinct small mammal assemblage', although the significance and nature of the bed was not established. The ivory artefact described by Griffiths (1972) was thought to have originated from this bed (Stringer 1977b). The overlying Upper Sands (bed 6) contained a mixture of marine-derived and wind-blown sand grains, with a foraminiferal assemblage typical of modern British coastal waters.

Stringer also described new finds from the Upper Cave Earth (bed 7), including wolf and hyaena. The faunal assemblage showed a mixture of temperate (for instance, red deer and straight-tusked elephant) and more boreal (for instance, northern vole) species, although the land snail fauna was typically interglacial and indicated an environment of local woodland and scrub. Beds 1-7 were traced under a series of cemented breccias (bed 8) which Stringer considered to be thermoclastic screes, accumulated at the cave mouth during the coldest phases of the Devensian Stage. Subsequent work (Currant *et al.* 1984; Stringer *et al.* 1986) recorded a fauna from the screes including reindeer, brown bear and a new record of glutton (*Gulo gulo* (L.)). Stringer (1977b) concluded that the deposits at the cave entrance were of Ipswichian age and that their fossil fauna was evidence for environmental changes during that stage.

Following a paper (Turner 1981a) on the importance of hyaena (*Crocuta crocuta* Erxleben),

Table 3 Uranium-series age determinations on stalagmite samples from Bacon Hole

Sample No.		Age	Corrected Age	Stratigraphic significance
1978–801	:01	14,000 ± 2,000	13,000 ± 3,000	Broken block of surface
	:02	18,600 ± 1,999	12,800 ± 1,700	stalagmite giving minimum age for Devensian fauna
1981–250		81,000 ± 18,000	–	Minimum age for the interglacial elements in Upper Cave Earth (bed 9)
1981–212	:01 (top)	129,000 ± 16,000	–	All are broken blocks of
	:02 (middle)	136,000 ± 23,000	125,000 ± 26,000	stalagmite floor incorporated
	:03 (bottom)	142,000 ± 27,000	129,000 ± 30,000	into Shelly Sand (bed 6)
1981–252	:02	116,000 ± 18,000	107,000 ± 21,000	This stalagmite probably
	:01	122,000 ± 11,000	–	formed on the underlying Sandy Cave earth (bed 5)
Mean of last 5 determinations		127,000 +9,000 −8,000	122,000 ± 9,000	These dates relate to the main interglacial fauna and the last major Pleistocene marine transgression at the site

as a bone accumulating agent during the Ipswichian in Britain, Stringer and Currant (1981) used the faunal evidence from Bacon Hole to refute Turner's claims. They noted that hyaena was absent or poorly represented in a fauna of otherwise Ipswichian character at the site, but that it is associated later in the sequence with deposits considered to post-date the warmest part of that stage. This, they believed, refuted Turner's hypothesis on the 'unique' role of hyaenas in producing bone accumulations in caves, and the restricted occurrence of *Crocuta crocuta* in Britain during the Ipswichian Stage. In reply, Turner (1981b) noted that other animals could have been responsible for the bone accumulations at some sites (for instance, wolf or bear), but emphasised the overwhelming evidence pointing to hyaena as the most probable and important single agent.

Following Stringer's (1975, 1977a, 1977b) interpretation of the sequence at Bacon Hole, considerable efforts were made to establish a more precise chronological framework for the deposits. Bowen *et al.* (1984) obtained amino acid ratios from shells of *Patella vulgata* and *Littorina* found in – a) the Basal Sands, b) the Sandy Breccio-Conglomerate, c) the Sandy Cave Earth and d) the Grey Clays, Silts and Sands. Their results confirmed that all the stratigraphic units up to and including the Grey Clays, Silts and Sands were of Ipswichian age.

Currant *et al.* (1984) and Stringer *et al.* (1986) presented a comprehensive series of Uranium-series age determinations (Table 3) from Bacon Hole, which place the interglacial fauna at the site between *c.* 130,000 and 80,000 BP. They adopted a slightly revised site stratigraphy and recognised a coarse lag deposit at the base of the succession (the Basal Pebbles) and an additional bed (the

Shelly Sand) between the Sandy Cave Earth and the Grey Clays, Silts and Sands – see site description.

By combining all the available data, especially from Henry (1984a) and Stringer *et al.* (1986), the following sequence of Pleistocene events at Bacon Hole can be reconstructed. Deposits accumulated before Oxygen Isotope Sub-stage 5e, as shown by a Uranium-series age determination of 175,000 ± 19,000 BP on a stalagmite layer capping altered sediments in a cleft in the cave floor. These sediments only occur at one location in the cave and appear to have been largely removed elsewhere by marine scouring during a period of pre-Oxygen Isotope Sub-stage 5e high sea-level (perhaps represented by the Basal Pebbles (bed 1); Bowen *et al.* 1985). The succeeding Coarse Grey and Orange Sands (beds 2 and 3) were deposited during a period of cool dry climate with relatively open vegetation. A rise in relative sea-level accompanied by a rise in temperature and humidity saw deposition of the Sandy Breccio-Conglomerate (bed 4), the Sandy Cave Earth (bed 5) and the Shelly Sand (bed 6). The Sandy Breccio-Conglomerate may represent a storm beach, marginally higher than its modern day equivalent, and closely related on altitudinal, lithological, aminostratigraphic and faunal grounds with the +2m *Patella* Beach in the nearby Minchin Hole. Stringer *et al.* (1986) provided a date of *c.* 122,000 BP (from broken stalagmite fragments, not *in situ*, from the top of bed 5) for this marine transgression, which they claimed was the first direct correlation of a British Ipswichian fauna with the high sea-level of Oxygen Isotope Sub-stage 5e. Amino acid ratios from the terrestrial snail *Cepaea nemoralis* (L.), allowed correlation of the Sandy Cave Earth (bed 5) at Bacon Hole with the interglacial deposit at Tattershall, Lincolnshire (Hughes 1984). Stringer *et al.* (1986) considered that the Grey

Clays, Silts and Sands (bed 7) marked a change in the environment, with falling sea-level and temperature. Mammoth *Mammuthus primigenius* (Blumenbach) is recorded for the first time in this bed, and temperate birds of the preceding beds are replaced by species now only known as winter visitors to Britain. The Upper Sands (bed 8) indicate a drier phase, with deposition of marine-derived wind-blown sediments. Stringer *et al.* (1986) concluded that the Upper Cave Earth (bed 9) was deposited during a period of lower sea-level than the superficially similar Sandy Cave Earth (bed 5). The former (bed 9) contains a restricted mammal fauna of interglacial character, a minimum age for which is indicated by a Uranium-series date of *c.* 81,000 BP obtained from stalagmite enclosing a tusk of *Palaeoloxodon*. This phase probably represents an Early Devensian interstadial, time-equivalent to Oxygen Isotope Sub-stage 5a. Stringer *et al.* (1986) noted that *Palaeoloxodon* and *Dicerorhinus* continued to be unusually abundant in this Early Devensian fauna. A date of *c.* 13,000 BP for broken stalagmite from the uppermost part of the Cemented Breccia (bed 10), provides a minimum age for the more typically cold Devensian fauna within these sediments.

The faunal sequence at Bacon Hole, therefore, would appear to record a number of cycles similar to those in the deep-sea oxygen isotope record (Sub-stages 5a, 5c and 5e). A boreal environment with relatively low sea-level was followed by warmer conditions in Oxygen Isotope Sub-stage 5e; this phase, with sea-level close to that of the present day, has been dated at *c.* 122,000 BP. The following deposits, containing less typically interglacial faunas, are associated with lower sea-levels until around 80,000 BP (Oxygen Isotope Stage 5a?). Subsequently, breccias with a 'cold' fauna were deposited (Stringer *et al.* 1986).

The sequence at Bacon Hole Cave (and nearby Minchin Hole Cave) presents a unique opportunity in Britain to correlate sea-level and palaeotemperature data with the deep-sea oxygen isotope record. The amino acid data and lithostratigraphy are more complete at Minchin Hole Cave, but the faunal evidence from Bacon Hole is more detailed, and it has provided unique information concerning the nature and complexity of the Ipswichian-Devensian transition. The dating of specific beds in the sequence by amino acid and Uranium-series techniques, has contributed towards a geochronological framework for British evidence during the Ipswichian and Devensian Stages (Bowen and Sykes 1988; Bowen 1989b).

Conclusions

Bacon Hole Cave is one of the most important sites in Europe. It is the only site in Britain which contains evidence for sub-dividing the important period of time between 130,000 and 70,000 years ago. That time period is important because it led directly to the last major ice age. It provides important evidence showing how the world moves from an interglacial into an ice age. As such it may be used as an analogue for future changes in climate. A full range of modern techniques has been applied at Bacon Hole Cave. The evidence is of high quality, it is plentiful and well preserved, and is exceptional by international standards.

Minchin Hole Cave

Highlights

The complex story of changing Pleistocene sea-levels is nowhere better seen than in the rocks and mammal faunas of this site. Its detailed evidence for Ipswichian and earlier interglacial events is unrivalled, and forms one of the most important Pleistocene sites in Wales.

Introduction

Minchin Hole Cave (SS555869) has been studied for over a century and is noted for the diverse faunal remains contained in its sequence of marginal marine and terrestrial sediments. The sequence provides an opportunity to study the simultaneous effect of climatic change on sea-levels and local terrestrial environments. The site was chosen by George (1932) as the type locality for the *Patella* raised beach. The first major excavations at the site were carried out by Wood in 1850 (see Falconer 1860, 1868). It was also noted by Prestwich (1892), Strahan (1907a) and Baden-Powell (1933) and was partially re-excavated by George (1932, 1933b). From the early 1940s to 1957, further extensive investigations were conducted by Allen and Rutter (1948) and Rutter and Mason (Rutter 1948, 1949, 1950, 1952, 1953, 1955, 1956, 1957), and its stratigraphical significance in the context of the Pleistocene history of the Irish Sea Basin discussed (Bowen 1966, 1969a, 1970a, 1971a, 1973a, 1973b). Minchin Hole was further excavated in the 1970s and the initial results and implications presented by Sutcliffe and Bowen (1973) and Bowen (1973c). The site has also been mentioned by Williams (1941), Bowen (1973d, 1974, 1977a, 1977b, 1980a, 1984), Peake *et al.* (1973), Sutcliffe (1976), Harrison (1977), Campbell *et al.* (1982) and Campbell (1984). A geochronology has been based on the epimerization of isoleucine in fossil shell protein from the raised beaches (Andrews *et al.* 1979; Bowen 1981a; Davies 1983; Bowen *et al.* 1984; Bowen *et al.* 1985; Bowen and Sykes 1988). Detailed biostratigraphical descriptions have been given by Sutcliffe (1981), Sutcliffe and Currant (1984) and Henry (1984a).

Description

Minchin Hole is the largest of the Gower caves. It is a single chambered fissure cave cut in Carboniferous Limestone; it opens onto a narrow gully entered by the sea at high tides. William Buckland visited Minchin Hole in July 1831, but there is no record of any excavation (Sutcliffe 1981). Falconer (1860, 1868) documented Wood's excavations in 1850 and recorded a sequence of sands with extant marine shell species, overlain by bone-bearing beds containing remains of narrow-nosed rhinoceros *Dicerorhinus hemitoechus* and straight-tusked elephant *Palaeoloxodon antiquus*. He noted that the Gower caves contained two apparently distinct faunal assemblages: one with the above temperate species, and another with woolly mammoth *Mammuthus primigenius* and woolly rhinoceros *Coelodonta antiquitatis* Blumenbach, indicating colder conditions (Sutcliffe 1981). *Hippopotamus* was not recorded from the deposits at either Minchin Hole or Bacon Hole, but Falconer did record it as a member of a comparable 'warm' fauna at nearby Ravenscliff Cave.

George (1932) provided the first detailed description of the stratigraphic succession near the cave entrance –

4   Wind-blown sand

3   Coarse gritty sand with common remains of *Neritoides obtusata* (L.) – the *Neritoides* Beach

2   Ossiferous breccia with remains of a temperate mammal fauna

1   Pebbly beach with common remains of *Patella vulgata* (L.) – the *Patella* Beach

Allen and Rutter (1948) and Rutter (1948, 1949, 1950, 1952, 1953, 1955, 1956, 1957) recorded

additional Pleistocene mammalian specimens, the stratigraphic context of which is uncertain, and evidence of human occupation (Iron Age, Roman and Saxon) from the upper levels. Details of the Iron Age B and Roman remains were given by Williams (1941). This series of excavations exposed, for the first time, an earlier raised beach deposit, subsequently rediscovered and called the Inner Beach (Sutcliffe and Bowen 1973) which was not encountered by George at the cave entrance.

Recent excavations have described a more detailed sequence (Sutcliffe 1981; Henry 1984a; Sutcliffe and Currant 1984) –

12   Flowstone floor**

11   Breccia**

10   Flowstone floor**

9   Upper Red Cave Earth**

8   Earthy Breccias

7   *Neritoides* Beach*

6   Fallen flowstone block

5   *Patella* Beach*

4   Flowstone floor

3   Lower Red Cave Earth

2   White layer (incipient stalagmite?)

1   Inner Beach

* These beds make up the Outer Beach
** Inner and Outer Talus Cones
This sequence is shown schematically in Figure 5.

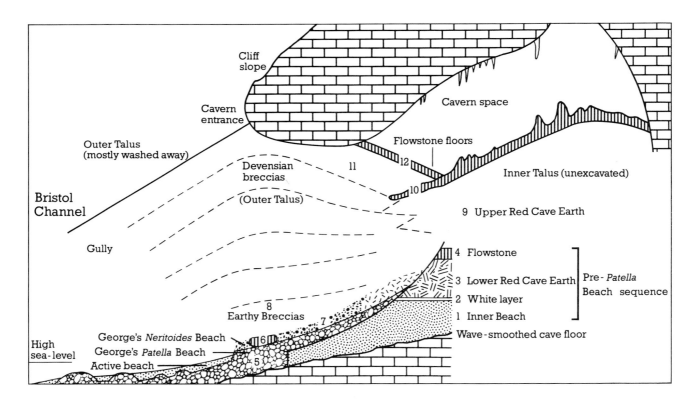

Figure 5 Pleistocene sequence at Minchin Hole (from Sutcliffe and Currant 1984)

Interpretation

In discussing the evidence from the Gower caves, in particular, the relationship between the glacial deposits and breccias of the area, Prestwich (1892) concluded that the caves had probably been filled with their mammalian remains after deposition of the local boulder clay. Strahan (1907a), however, considered that the bone-bearing beds were related to and were similar in age to, the raised beach deposits of Gower, which he believed to be of pre-glacial or interglacial age. He believed that the bone-beds pre-dated the earliest glaciation of Gower.

This relationship was confirmed by George (1932, 1933b). By recognising two distinct marine units (his beds 1 and 3) separated by terrestrial deposits (bed 2), George (1932) concluded that "..... the stratigraphical distinction that can be made between the *Patella* Beach and the *Neritoides* Beach thus represents a time interval of not inconsiderable dimensions". He regarded both beaches as being older than the first ('Older Drift') glaciation of the area, and considered the *Patella* Beach to have been deposited under conditions of incipient glaciation. The latter claim was refuted by Baden-Powell (1933) who observed that the fauna of the *Patella* Beach could easily be found in the area today. George (1970) maintained, however, that distantly-derived igneous erratics in the *Patella* Beach of South Wales may have been carried by drifting ice at the onset of arctic conditions.

The Pleistocene chronology of Minchin Hole was discussed in the context of a wider region by Bowen (1966, 1969a, 1970a, 1971a, 1973a, 1973b). Originally, he accepted Mitchell's (1960) proposal that the *Patella* Beach (bed 5) at Minchin Hole was Hoxnian, and from this, argued that the Ossiferous Breccia (bed 2 of George 1932) was Saalian, the *Neritoides* Beach was Ipswichian Stage and the overlying breccias (beds 9-12) were Devensian Stage (Bowen 1966). Subsequently, however, Bowen (1969a, 1970a, 1971a, 1973b) after establishing a lithostratigraphy for the coastal Pleistocene deposits around Gower, argued that the marine and bone-bearing beds were Ipswichian, and the overlying deposits were Devensian. Bowen (1971a) noted that the evidence from Minchin Hole could be used to support Zeuner's (1959) claim that the 'last interglacial' was characterised by two discrete high sea-level events (Main and Late Monastirian).

New excavations (Bowen 1973c; Sutcliffe and Bowen 1973) revealed an 'Inner Beach' (bed 1) as well as a *Patella* (Outer) Beach recorded by George. George considered the *Neritoides* deposit to be a transitional marine and terrestrial lithofacies. Sutcliffe and Bowen reconstructed the following sequence of events – the Inner Beach (bed 1) was deposited during a sea-level stand higher than at present. With a fall of sea-level, the surface of the Inner Beach became cemented (unit 2) and the Lower Red Cave Earth (bed 3) accumulated with its contained bones. A

subsequent rise of sea-level to just above the present level cut a cliff in the Inner Beach and Red Cave Earth. The Outer Beach (consisting of the *Patella* (bed 5) and *Neritoides* (bed 7) Beaches combined) was deposited unconformably on the earlier sediments. As sea-level fell again, sand from the exposed sea floor was blown into the cave. Environmental conditions deteriorated during the Devensian, and the Outer and Inner Talus Cones (beds 9-12), made up of frost-shattered scree, accumulated, with the Outer Talus Cone blocking the cave entrance. This was all but completely removed during the Holocene.

Sutcliffe and Bowen (1973) proposed that both the Inner and Outer Beaches, together with the intervening ossiferous deposits, were Ipswichian, although Bowen (1973c) noted the possibility that the two beaches could represent separate interglacials (the Hoxnian and the Ipswichian), with the intervening cave earth perhaps representing a cold interval (the Wolstonian?), or with the Inner Beach representing an interglacial between the Hoxnian and Ipswichian (Oxygen Isotope Stage 7). Bowen noted that if the beaches were Hoxnian and Ipswichian respectively, then the Red Cave Earth must have formed over a period of 200,000 years which is unlikely. He therefore regarded the two high sea-level phases as two events in the Ipswichian Stage. The *Neritoides* Beach was grouped as part of a *Patella* Beach sequence (see also Bowen 1973d, 1974, 1977a, 1977b; Peake *et al.* 1973).

In a study of the bird fauna, Harrison (1977) recorded dunlin *Calidris alpina* (L.) and razorbill *Alca torda* (L.) from the lower beds of the sequence at Minchin Hole, tending to confirm their interglacial character. He noted that the dunlin bones had probably been introduced in owl pellets, but that the razorbill may have nested within the cave.

Recent work at Minchin Hole has provided a more precise chronological framework for the sequence, with the application of amino acid geochronology and Uranium-series techniques (for example, Andrews *et al.* 1979; Davies 1983; Bowen *et al.* 1985; Bowen and Sykes 1988). Further amplification of the lithostratigraphy and biostratigraphy have also been provided (Sutcliffe 1981; Sutcliffe and Currant 1984; Henry 1984a).

Andrews *et al.* (1979) used amino acid ratios from *Patella vulgata* to correlate the Outer (*Patella*) Beach at Minchin Hole with raised beach remnants elsewhere in south-west Britain and suggested that it was Ipswichian in age. Following this, Bowen (1980a) suggested that the *Neritoides,* the *Patella* and the Inner Beaches at Minchin Hole might correspond with the high sea-level stands of Oxygen Isotope Sub-stages 5e, 5c and 5a. The amino acid ratio derived from the Inner Beach (Bowen 1981a), indicated a greater age than that obtained from the *Patella* Beach; but both were still considered to belong to the Ipswichian.

Following the earlier amino acid work (Andrews *et*

al. 1979; Davies 1983), and using Uranium-series age determinations from broken stalagmite at Bacon Hole, the current amino acid dating (Bowen *et al.* 1985) shows that the Outer Beach *(Patella)* is probably time-equivalent to Oxygen Isotope Sub-stage 5e, and the Inner Beach contains faunal elements of Oxygen Isotope Sub-stages 7a and 7c (Bowen and Sykes 1988).

Work at Minchin Hole by Sutcliffe (1981), Henry (1984a) and Sutcliffe and Currant (1984) allows the following generalised sequence of events to be reconstructed. 1) The Inner Beach (bed 1) probably formed during temperate conditions with relative sea-level from 3 to 5m higher than at present (Sutcliffe 1981; Sutcliffe and Currant 1984). Its mixed molluscan fauna has been ascribed to sub-stages of Oxygen Isotope Stage 7 (Bowen and Sykes 1988). An erratic of volcanic tuff (perhaps from south Pembrokeshire or Anglesey) may derive from an Irish Sea glaciation which pre-dates Stage 7 (Bowen 1984; Henry 1984a). Following partial cementation and cracking of the Inner Beach, the Lower Red Cave Earth (bed 3) was deposited. This indicates a fall in relative sea-level when frost-shattered and colluviated material accumulated during colder conditions. The fauna from the Lower Red Cave Earth contains a large form of northern vole, *Microtus oeconomus* (Pallas), which led Sutcliffe (1981) to correlate the bed with the Basal Sands horizon at Bacon Hole, where similar remains were recovered (Stringer 1977b).

The Inner Beach and Lower Red Cave Earth were cliffed by the sea when the Outer Beach was deposited. The Outer Beach is a storm beach facies, and is best developed at the cave mouth where it comprises a mixture of boulders, shingle and shell fragments (Sutcliffe 1981). It has an altitudinal range of about 6m within the cave and is ascribed to Oxygen Isotope Sub-stage 5e by aminostratigraphic correlations with Bacon Hole Cave (Bowen *et al.* 1985; Bowen and Sykes 1988). Uranium-series determinations of 127,000 ± 21,000 to 107,000 ± 10,000 BP on a fragment of flowstone (unit 6) resting on the surface of the Outer *(Patella)* Beach (bed 5) precludes a later age for the Outer Beach (Sutcliffe and Currant 1984). The *Patella* Beach is overlain by the *Neritoides* deposit, (bed 7) and although George (1932) described a breccia between the two units, more recent excavations have not yet confirmed this relationship, although in places the *Neritoides* Beach does merge with brecciated limestone. For the most part, the *Neritoides* Beach is a sandy deposit containing the remains of rodents, other small mammals and many small littoral gastropods. The deposit formed during a fall in relative sea-level after the *Patella* Beach event (Sutcliffe 1981; Henry, 1984a). It is thought to be a transitional deposit between the fully marine *Patella* Beach and the overlying terrestrial sediments (the Earthy Breccias).

The Earthy Breccias (bed 8) contain the remains of birds (Harrison 1977; Sutcliffe and Currant 1984) and relatively abundant mammalian remains including – spotted hyaena *Crocuta crocuta,* lion *Panthera leo* (L.), bear *Ursus* sp., narrow-nosed rhinoceros *Dicerorhinus hemitoechus,* red deer *Cervus elaphus* L., fallow deer *Dama dama* (L.), field vole *Microtus gregalis* Pallas and wood mouse *Apodemus sylvaticus* (L.). A previous record of horse (Sutcliffe 1981) was erroneous (Sutcliffe and Currant 1984). This fauna is typical of the Ipswichian Stage, though it lacks *Hippopotamus* (Sutcliffe and Currant 1984). The Earthy Breccias were deposited at a time of relatively lower sea-level than that of today.

As environmental conditions deteriorated after the Ipswichian Stage, sea-level continued to fall and the Outer and Inner Talus Cones formed at Minchin Hole. Cemented sand in the Outer Talus deposits was probably deflated from the exposed shore as sea-level fell. The uppermost layers of the talus are thermoclastic in origin and are of presumed (Late) Devensian age.

The Inner Talus is capped with a thick flowstone, and this is overlain by some Holocene deposits, including Romano-British occupation debris (Sutcliffe and Currant 1984). Finally, the continuing rise of the Holocene sea to its present level removed most of the Outer Talus deposits from the cave entrance.

Minchin Hole provides one of the longest Pleistocene records in Wales. Of particular importance is the existence of two distinct marine deposits (Inner and Outer Beaches), both representing former relative high sea-level stands. A composite single interglacial age for these beaches was once proposed, but recent evidence suggests that the Outer *(Patella)* Beach is Ipswichian (Oxygen Isotope Sub-stage 5e), while the Inner Beach has been ascribed to Oxygen Isotope Stage 7. The intervening Lower Red Cave Earth, therefore, represents a period of lowered sea-level later in age than the Inner Beach, but earlier than the Outer *(Patella)* Beach. The *Neritoides* Beach represents a transition between the fully marine Outer *(Patella)* Beach and the overlying terrestrial sediments. Faunal, amino acid ratio and Uranium-series evidence points strongly to an Ipswichian age for the Outer Beach, *Neritoides* Beach, and the overlying Earthy Breccias. All succeeding deposits are interpreted as having accumulated when sea-level was lower than at present during the Devensian Stage.

Although Bacon Hole provides the more complete faunal record for the Ipswichian and Early Devensian (Stringer *et al.* 1986), Minchin Hole provides a longer record of sea-level changes.

Conclusions

Minchin Hole Cave contains the longest record of ice age time in Wales. Of European significance, is evidence at the site for two high global sea-level events, one at 200,000 years ago, the other 125,000 years ago. It proves a period of severe climate between about 200,000 and 130,000 years ago, and evidence for the last ice age. Because Minchin Hole was beyond the extent of the last ice-sheets, such evidence from that time relates to cold climate processes and events. The changeover from the last interglacial (125,000 years ago) to the last ice age is of some significance. This may contain important pointers for future climate. The full range of modern techniques has been applied at Minchin Hole Cave, and its scientific status is international in importance.

Cat Hole Cave

Highlights

This site has yielded a 'cold' Pleistocene mammal fauna and Upper Palaeolithic artefacts from periglacial climate screes. These have been assigned to the Devensian late-glacial, indicating the possibility that many such screes in Wales date from this final glacial phase.

Introduction

Cat Hole Cave (SS538900) contains artefacts and fossils that can be dated towards the close of the Devensian Stage (Late Devensian late-glacial). Numerous flint artefacts of Creswellian type have been recovered in association with a 'cold' fauna including mammoth, woolly rhinoceros, horse, reindeer, arctic fox and arctic lemming taken to be typical of the Devensian Stage. The site was first excavated by Wood in 1864 and was mentioned by Vivian (1887), Roberts (1887-8), Morgan (1919), Garrod (1926) and Allen and Rutter (1948), but it was not re-excavated until the late fifties (McBurney 1959). Campbell (1977) provided a detailed description and interpretation of the site, supported by accounts of the pollen (Campbell 1977), the land snails (Evans 1977b) and the bird faunas (Bramwell 1977). The site has also been referred to by McBurney (1965), Houlder (1977) and Bowen (1974, 1980a).

Description

Archaeologically Cat Hole is the most important of the inland caves of Gower. It is formed in a crag of Carboniferous Limestone at a level c. 10m above the floor of the dry valley of Parkmill at about 30m OD (Campbell 1977). It has two main entrances and chambers, the largest chamber reaching some 40 ft (12m) maximum width. The cave lies only about 250m from the megalithic tomb of Parc le Breos. The limestone platform outside the cave supports a sequence of terrestrial sediments that was excavated by McBurney (1959) and Campbell (1977) and that can be generalised as follows –

4	Modern soil
3	Weathered scree
2	Scree
1	Silt and sand

A more detailed sub-division of the sequence was provided by Campbell (1977). Substantial deposits remain *in situ*, both in the cave and on the platform outside.

Interpretation

The first known excavations at Cat Hole were carried out mainly inside the cave and at the mouth to the larger entrance by Wood in 1864, but the results were not recorded in Falconer's (1860, 1868) work on the Gower caves. A brief mention of the remains was, however, made by Vivian (1887), and Wood's finds which were housed in the British Museum (Natural History), were itemised by Roberts (1887-8). These included – two human skulls, numerous flint cores and flakes, a stone hammer, a bronze celt, pottery, shells of limpet, oyster and whelk and remains of bear, fox, hyaena, wild cat, Irish deer, reindeer, red deer, horse, woolly rhinoceros, vole, mammoth, sheep or goat and pig (Roberts 1887-8). Two of Wood's other finds, a gnawed bone and a worked bone, were housed in the Museum of the Royal Institution of South Wales, Swansea (Morgan 1919). Although Wood did not record the stratigraphy, his collection of flint artefacts was assigned by Garrod (1926) to the Upper Palaeolithic, either to the Upper Aurignacian or Magdalenian, and a close resemblance was noted between these artefacts and those recovered from Paviland Cave in south Gower (Sollas 1913). Wood's finds from Cat Hole were also discussed by Allen and Rutter (1948), who noted that although the faunal list contained some recent species, it was essentially a 'cold' Pleistocene assemblage. They observed that the human remains had been unearthed near the surface in the cave and were, therefore, not likely to be of an early date.

Further excavations at Cat Hole were conducted by McBurney in 1958 and 1959 (McBurney 1959). The results of the 1959 season have not been published, although Campbell (1977) refers to some of McBurney's unpublished data. McBurney excavated outside the larger cave entrance, recording details of stratigraphy and find locations. Most of the 280 flint artefacts, and many of the faunal remains were recovered by McBurney from the scree and weathered scree (beds 2 and 3). McBurney considered that most of the implements were of Creswellian-type culture and described several artefacts not previously recorded from Creswellian assemblages. A small, finely worked needle and bone awl were also recovered. Most of the flints were scattered vertically throughout the scree (bed 2) but were the result of a single occupation. McBurney accounted for the vertical scattering by solifluction or other natural re-sorting. In addition to many of the species recovered by Wood, he discovered the remains of aurochs *Bos*, arctic fox *Alopex lagopus* (L.), mountain hare *Lepus timidus* L., badger *Meles meles*, Norway lemming

Lemmus lemmus (L.), and a number of unidentified rodents and birds. He considered the fauna to be typically Devensian late-glacial, although Campbell (1977) noted that the list was mixed, with species such as goat, sheep and aurochs more likely to be Holocene in age.

The third excavation was conducted by Campbell in 1968 (Campbell 1977). He excavated adjacent to McBurney's trenches and at the entrance to the smaller cave. The latter site proved unrewarding and was abandoned. Campbell recognised the same basic stratigraphy as McBurney, but he sub-divided the sequence in greater detail, and discovered additional mammal, artefact, granulometric and pollen evidence. Land snails were analysed from the sequence (Evans *in* Campbell 1977), and a bird fauna was described (Bramwell *in* Campbell 1977).

Campbell observed that the artefacts from Cat Hole showed surprising typological variation and that they occurred at three of four separate levels, rather than scattered more or less randomly as McBurney (1959) had suggested. Although McBurney had interpreted the scattered artefacts as a result of natural re-sorting by, for example solifluction, Campbell suggested that their vertical distribution reflected a number of distinct occupations; two perhaps of later Upper Palaeolithic age and two of Mesolithic age.

From pollen analysis Campbell interpreted systematic changes in the flora which spanned the Devensian Stage and Holocene. He observed that Devensian late-glacial Pollen Zones I, II and III were well represented in the pollen spectra, but that the record of the remainder of the Devensian and the Holocene was compressed. This reflected that the greatest thickness of deposits at Cat Hole is of Devensian late-glacial age. In relating the archaeological evidence to the pollen record, he concluded that the later Palaeolithic artefacts belonged entirely to Devensian late-glacial Pollen Zone I, and that the Mesolithic artefacts were associated with the early part of the Holocene. The Creswellian artefacts described by McBurney were believed by Campbell to have originated from a horizon time-equivalent to Pollen Zone III (the Younger Dryas). Bowen (1980a) noted that some of the pollen in Campbell's reconstruction might be derived.

Campbell also presented detailed faunal analyses and plotted the vertical distribution of all undisturbed teeth, bones and bone fragments found during his excavations. He concluded that the fauna associated with the later Upper Palaeolithic artefacts of Devensian late-glacial/Pollen Zone I age, would probably have included red fox *Vulpes vulpes*, arctic fox *Alopex lagopus*, brown bear *Ursus arctos* L., woolly rhinoceros *Coelodonta antiquitatis*, horse *Equus przewalski*, red deer *Cervus elaphus*, giant deer *Megaceros giganteus* Blumenbach, reindeer *Rangifer tarandus* L. and mountain hare *Lepus timidus*. Smaller mammals, such as arctic lemming

Dicrostonyx torquatus (Pallas), Norway lemming *Lemmus lemmus* and tundra vole *Microtus gregalis* were also associated with the Devensian late-glacial sediments at Cat Hole. Campbell demonstrated that faunal elements such as goat, sheep and aurochs were clearly associated with the Holocene sediments at the site, and were not part of a 'mixed' single fauna described by earlier workers. Small mammals such as the woodmouse, water vole and mole were also associated with more temperate conditions during the Holocene. Similarly, Campbell noted that Wood's record of mammoth *Mammuthus primigenius* may have been associated with Devensian sediments of pre-Devensian late-glacial age at the site. This general interpretation of deposits according to the included fauna was also supported by analysis of the bird faunas from Cat Hole (Bramwell 1977).

Detailed analysis of the land snail faunas by Evans (1977b) *(in* Campbell 1977) did not reveal a Late Pleistocene 'cold' fauna but rather one of Holocene age that occurred within the older Devensian late-glacial sediments as an intrusive element; the snails had exploited the cavities of the loose rock rubble which comprised the bulk of the deposits (Evans 1977b). This was particularly well shown by the fauna found in the scree (bed 2). The lithology, pollen, small and large mammal fauna of this complex layer all indicated a cold climate, an open-country landscape and a Devensian late-glacial age; only the molluscan fauna was unequivocally of a warm temperate Holocene character (Evans 1977b).

The deposits at Cat Hole therefore reveal a sequence of changes during cold climate open-country (tundra) conditions when frost-shattered scree accumulated together with a generally 'cold' fauna including, for example, reindeer, arctic fox, arctic and Norway lemming. The site is also notable for a record of mammoth. The deposits also contain pollen indicating a pattern of floral changes characteristic of the Devensian late-glacial. The presence of Upper Palaeolithic Man at this time is indicated by numerous artefacts believed to be of Creswellian-type, and the site shows that variants of this culture extended into Wales. Faunal and pollen analyses clearly reveal the change from the generally cold conditions of the Devensian late-glacial to the Holocene, the latter being characterised by more temperate conditions and the presence of Mesolithic Man. The relative dating of the screes at Cat Hole by faunal, archaeological and pollen analytical means, provides evidence to suggest that scree found at many coastal sections around south Gower, may also have accumulated, at least in part, during the Devensian late-glacial.

Mammal, tools, pollen and sedimentary evidence from Cat Hole Cave have allowed the reconstruction of a detailed sequence of Devensian late-glacial and Holocene conditions. A 'cold' mammal fauna, found in association with Creswellian 'type' culture artefacts, provides the principal basis for dating most of the sediment sequence to the Devensian late-glacial. Pollen evidence also strongly suggests that most of the deposits at Cat Hole date from this time.

Conclusions

Cat Hole has yielded an exceptional combination of evidence for the fauna, flora and archaeology of the last 13,000 years, and is thus an important site for the period following the last major ice age.

Eastern Slade and Western Slade

Highlights

This site provides evidence, in the form of reworked glacial sediments, that this part of South Wales was glaciated by Irish Sea ice during a pre-Ipswichian glaciation. Its colluvial sediments and redeposited drift are proof that Devensian ice did not reach this part of Gower.

Introduction

Coastal exposures between Eastern Slade (SS489854) and Western Slade (SS484855) show evidence for the late Middle and Late Pleistocene history of south Gower. The locality is a reference site for redeposited pre-Devensian glacial sediments. It demonstrates that south Gower was free of glacier ice during the Late Devensian. The site was first described by Strahan (1907b) and later featured in studies by George (1932, 1933a, 1933b). The sequence was described and interpreted by Bowen (1966, 1969a, 1970a, 1971a, 1973b, 1974, 1977a, 1977b, 1984), and mentioned by Peake *et al.* (1973), Stephens and Shakesby (1982) and Bridges (1985).

Description

Between Oxwich Point and Horton, a fossil sea-cliff is buried by superficial deposits which were trimmed by the sea during the Holocene. At Western Slade, Eastern Slade and Horton, fault-guided dry valleys run inland to a plateau which is

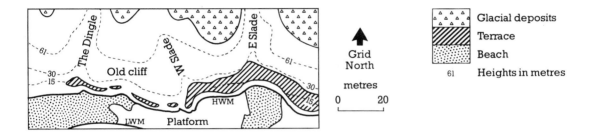

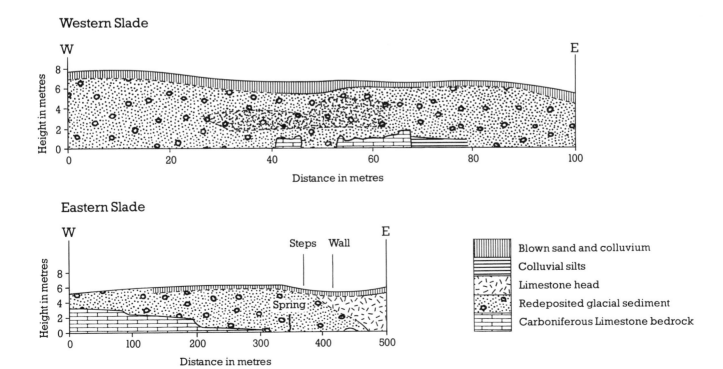

Figure 6 Quaternary sequence at Eastern Slade and Western Slade (after Bowen and Henry 1984)

mantled with glacial deposits. These valleys are infilled with Late Pleistocene sediments that extend onto the coastal margin as an apron or terrace. The following sequence overlies a Carboniferous Limestone shore platform.
(Stratigraphic terminology of Henry (1984a, 1984b) in parenthesis) –

3   Blown sand and colluvium (Port-Eynon Silt)
2   Redeposited glacial drift (Western Slade Diamicton) and limestone head (Hunts Breccia)
1   Colluvial silts (Pwll Du Red Beds)

This sequence is shown in Figure 6. Raised beach sediments may occur towards the base of the sections (Strahan 1907b; George 1932; Bowen 1970a) but are not usually exposed.

The sections at Eastern Slade and Western Slade were first described by Strahan (1907b) who recorded a sequence of –

4   Loam (3.0m)
3   Till (6.0m)
2   Blown sand (0.10m)
1   Raised beach deposits

In some places, the loam was described as filling pipes in an earlier head deposit, and the glacial sediments (bed 3) were considered to have found their way to the coast via the small valleys at Eastern Slade and Western Slade.

Interpretation

George (1932, 1933a, 1933b), described the sections and observed that the deposits consisted very largely of glacial sand and gravel with head and loam, although *Patella* raised beach deposits occurred at the base of the sections near Eastern Slade. He noted that the glacial gravel contained a mixture of rocks from the South Wales Coalfield with a smaller number of Precambrian and igneous types which included examples from Llŷn, Anglesey, Skomer and Scotland. Ailsa Craig microgranite was also recorded by George. These far-travelled rock types were mixed randomly amongst the Upper Carboniferous pebbles, and George concluded that the deposits had resulted from "..... the outpourings of a tiny valley glacier" during the 'Older Drift' glaciation, when, he believed, Gower was affected by confluent Irish Sea and Welsh ice masses. Towards the base of the sections near Eastern Slade, he noted that the normally chaotic glacial gravels were replaced by 8 ft (2.4m) of stratified sands and gravels which he considered were of fluvioglacial origin. He noted that glacial sediments were replaced eastwards by limestone head and loam, regarding the limestone head as a solifluction deposit, and interpreting small lenses of finer-grained material within the head as seasonal meltwater deposits. The capping loam was derived from older superficial deposits

by wind action. The entire sequence of deposits had been trimmed flat by the sea sometime after deposition of the 'Older Drift'. George (1932) termed the upper surface of the terrace the 'Post Older Drift Platform', and considered it to be equivalent in age and origin to similar features in Rhosili and Hunts Bays.

Bowen (1966, 1969a, 1970a, 1971a, 1973b, 1974, 1977a, 1977b, 1984) recorded the sequence given in the site description of this report. He noted that colluvial silts (bed 1) were exposed in the lee of a large limestone buttress at Western Slade, and that they showed bedding indicating derivation from the north-west – see Figure 6. The unit was considered to post-date glaciation in the area because it contained derived erratics and was nowhere overlain by glacial deposits *in situ* (Bowen 1970a). The colluvial silts were overlain by slope deposits consisting of limestone head and redeposited glacial sediments (bed 2) or a mixture of both, with the proportion of head being greatest near limestone outcrops. Bowen (1970a, 1971a, 1984) noted that the redeposited till was confined to the middle of the bay at Western Slade and was replaced on its flanks by limestone head. This, together with the fabric of the sediment (Bowen 1969a, 1970a, 1971a, 1984), demonstrated that the deposit had been reworked down the Western Slade Valley from pre-existing inland glacial sediments. In addition to the mixture of South Wales and Irish Sea erratics recorded by George (1933a) from the redeposited glacial sediments, Bowen (1984) also noted that colluvial silts at the site contained staurolite, kyanite and zoisite, three minerals characteristic of an Irish Sea provenance (Griffiths 1939), in addition to possible Triassic components. The fluvioglacial sediments described by George (1933a) were reinterpreted by Bowen (1971a) as alluvially re-sorted and redeposited glacial sediments.

From the evidence in the coastal sections at this site and from elsewhere in Gower, Bowen (1971a) proposed the following sequence of events. 1) During an earlier pre-Devensian glaciation, sediments were deposited in Gower from sources in Wales and the Irish Sea Basin. 2) This glaciation was followed by a period of temperate interglacial conditions, probably during the Ipswichian Stage. The rock cliffs and platform at Eastern Slade and Western Slade were modified, and raised beach sediments accumulated at nearby Horton and elsewhere around the south Gower coast. 3) As conditions deteriorated with the onset of the Devensian Stage, sea-level fell and vegetation cover was reduced, promoting surface sheet-wash and the accumulation of bedded colluvial silts. 4) With a further deterioration of climate towards full periglacial conditions during the Late Devensian, limestone talus from local bedrock accumulated, and pre-Devensian glacial sediments were redeposited by solifluction and alluvial processes from inland, along the Slade and Horton Valleys. 5) Finally, towards the end of the Late Devensian, loess and colluvial sediments (bed 3) were deposited as a capping to the sequence (Bowen 1971a).

The sequence of sediments at Eastern Slade and Western Slade therefore provides an important record of environmental and geomorphological changes in Gower. The site shows particularly important evidence for the pre-Devensian glacial history of Gower, and is a reference site for redeposited glacial and other sediments of pre-Devensian age. During an 'early' glaciation, Gower was affected by ice, not only from the South Wales Coalfield, but also from the Irish Sea Basin. The sections also provide stratigraphic evidence to show that this part of south Gower lay outside the maximum limit of the Late Devensian ice-sheet.

Eastern Slade and Western Slade demonstrate the combined effects of topographic control and sedimentary processes on the accumulation and distribution of different sediment types. The site provides evidence with which to interpret coastal drift exposures elsewhere along the south Gower coast, and forms an integral part of a network of sites in Gower that constrain the position of the maximum limit of Late Devensian ice across the peninsula.

Eastern Slade and Western Slade provide a rock record of changing conditions in south Gower during the Late Pleistocene. The occurrence of igneous erratics from the Irish Sea Basin in redistributed till, provides evidence that Gower was once glaciated by ice from the Irish Sea Basin. The mixing of Irish Sea and Welsh rock types was used by T N George to show that Gower was glaciated by confluent Irish Sea and Welsh ice during the 'Older Drift' glaciation. The site is notable in recording the sole occurrence in Gower of Ailsa Craig microgranite from the Firth of Clyde. It is also important for establishing the limit of Late Devensian ice across Gower.

Conclusions

These localities are important as reference sites for a particular deposit which is nowhere else developed in such detail. This consists of a massive unsorted deposit (that is ranging from clay particles to large boulders) which was originally interpreted as a glacial deposit. That is, it was used as evidence to demonstrate a glaciation of Gower at a particular time. It is now known, however, that the deposit is not, in its present position, a product of an ice-sheet. Instead, it was formed by soil creep and other processes down the two valleys from older glacial deposits lying on the plateau surface above the cliffs. Recognition of the true origin of these deposits revolutionised the knowledge of ice age history in South Wales.

Horton

Highlights

This is a key site for the study of periglacial head, colluvial and loessic sediments dating from the Devensian Stage. Below these occur remnants of marine raised beaches probably formed in two separate interglacial periods, allowing the elucidation of a long and complex climatic and sea-level record.

Introduction

Exposures of superficial deposits near Horton (SS482856) show evidence of changing environmental conditions in south Gower. Until recently, it was held that head and colluvial deposits of Devensian age overlay raised beach deposits of Ipswichian age at Horton. Recent work, however, indicates that the raised beach deposits date from two separate sea-level events, which poses a question about the age of the sediment overlying the earlier beach (Bowen *et al.* 1985). Loessic deposits which are common around the South Wales coast are particularly well exposed at Horton. The site was first described by George (1933a), and subsequently by Wirtz (1953). The interpretation is attributed to Bowen (1966, 1969a, 1970a, 1971a, 1973a, 1973b, 1974, 1977a, 1977b), and references to the site have also been made by Mitchell (1972), Peake *et al.* (1973), Stephens and Shakesby (1982) and Case (1977). More recently, detailed studies at Horton were undertaken by Case (1983, 1984), Davies (1983), Henry (1984a, 1984b) and Bowen *et al.* (1984, 1985).

Description

The 200 ft (61m) coastal platform between Port-Eynon and Oxwich is terminated seawards by a fossil cliff, partly buried by superficial deposits which were marine trimmed during the Holocene. At Horton (SS479856), Western Slade (SS483856) and Eastern Slade (SS487857) fault-guided dry valleys run inland to a plateau which is mantled by glacial deposits. The valleys are infilled with Pleistocene sediments which form terraces at the foot of the old cliffs (Bowen 1971a, 1977a; Henry 1984b). At Horton, the exposures are laterally variable (Figure 7), but they show the following generalised sequence above a Carboniferous Limestone shore platform at *c.* 10m OD. (Stratigraphic terminology of Henry (1984a, 1984b) and Bowen *et al.* (1985) in parenthesis) –

5	Colluvium, blown sand and silt (Port-Eynon Silt)
4	Limestone head (Hunts Breccia)
3	Colluvial silts and boulders (Horton Boulder Bed)
2	Colluvial silts (Pwll Du Red Beds)
1	Raised beach deposits, largely uncemented with red silt (Horton Upper Beach)

Fragments of cemented raised beach, lithologically distinct from bed 1, occur in patches cemented on the walls of gullies in the exposed limestone shore platform (Horton Lower Beach; Davies (1983), Bowen *et al.* (1985)).

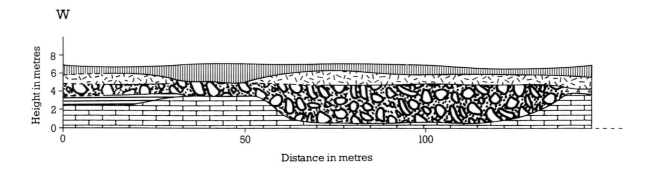

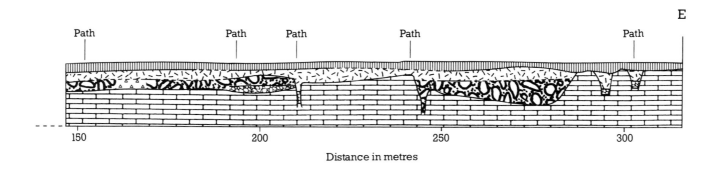

Horton Upper Beach
Limestone head
Blocky limestone head with red silt matrix
Colluvium, blown sand and loess

Colluvial silts and boulders
Colluvial silts
Carboniferous Limestone bedrock

Figure 7 Quaternary sequence at Horton (after Bowen and Henry 1984)

Interpretation

The Pleistocene deposits at Horton were first described and interpreted by George (1933a) who noted a coarse breccia containing massive limestone blocks overlying bedrock. Pockets of glacial material and solitary erratics, including several igneous rock types from outside the local area, were scattered through the breccia. He therefore concluded that the deposit was 'not merely a local talus' and 'had undergone some measure of transportation by ice' (George 1933a).

Wirtz (1953) referred to raised beach deposits at Horton, which he considered to be of Holstein age (Hoxnian Stage). These were overlain by cold-climate 'frost-shattered rubble' attributable to one or more phases of glacial climate. In a series of papers, Bowen (1966, 1969a, 1970a, 1971a, 1973a, 1973b, 1974, 1977a, 1977b) described and interpreted the stratigraphy at Horton. The raised beach (bed 1) differed from the typical *Patella* Beach (George 1932) around Gower in its uncemented character, its matrix of colluvial material and its high erratic content, both from South Wales and the Irish Sea Basin sources. He

suggested that the anomalous matrix may have been translocated downwards or accumulated contemporaneously with the beach. He referred to the boulder bed described by Wirtz (1953) as 'frost-shattered rubble', and noted that the boulders did not have the angular edges characteristic of periglacial material. Rather, they were subrounded and compared with 'joint-bounded weathered limestone' from 'the fossil cliff at the rear of the exposure'.

From the evidence at Horton, Bowen (1969a, 1970a, 1971a, 1977a, 1977b) proposed the following sequence of events –

1   During the 'Older Drift' glaciation, glacial sediments were deposited in Gower. Erratic and stratigraphic evidence from South and west Wales suggested that this 'early' glaciation was probably multiple in nature and from both Irish Sea Basin and local Welsh sources.

2   During high relative sea-levels in the succeeding Ipswichian Stage, raised beach deposits (bed 1) accumulated at Horton, and erratics became incorporated into the beach

from the earlier 'Older Drift' glacial deposits. During this interglacial phase, temperate soils formed locally and weathering occurred on the limestone cliffs. The red, probably colluvial matrix of the raised beach shows that it may have accumulated late in the Ipswichian. Bowen (1970a) tentatively correlated this phase of formation with the Neritoides Beach at nearby Minchin Hole Cave.

3   As sea-level began to fall and climate deteriorated in the succeeding cold Devensian Stage, reduced vegetation cover promoted sheet-wash and colluviation. Soils from the plateau and weathered limestone from the local cliffs moved downslope to form the colluvial silts (bed 2) and boulder beds (bed 3) at Horton. The dominance of weathered limestone blocks in the latter bed and the lack of appreciably angular material strongly suggests that these deposits did not form under periglacial conditions (Bowen 1971a, 1974).

4   However, probably during the Late Devensian, periglacial conditions were experienced at the site, limestone head (bed 4) accumulated and elsewhere, for example, Western Slade, 'Older Drift' glacial deposits were reworked from the plateau, along fault-guided valleys to the coast.

5   Case (1977, 1983) suggested that head formation at Horton was succeeded, without hiatus, by deposition of sand and silt (bed 5). This largely wind-blown deposit formed at the end of the Devensian, with proglacial outwash from the Late Devensian ice-sheets as a source for the aeolian silt (Case 1977, 1983). Cryoturbation of the upper head deposits (bed 4) at Horton may also have occurred at this time (Bowen 1966) and loess and colluvial deposits (bed 5) may well have continued to form into the Holocene (Bowen 1971a). The entire sequence of cold-climate and periglacial deposits (Beds 2-5) at Horton was thus considered by Bowen (1973b) to represent the whole of the Devensian Stage (but see Bowen et al. 1985). During the Holocene, the drift sequence was marine trimmed.

In addition to the sequence described by Bowen (1970a), Stephens and Shakesby (1982) noted a sub-horizontal bed of well rounded limestone cobbles in the head sequence at Horton, the origin of which was uncertain. One possible interpretation, however, is that the limestone pebbles are from reworked (that is soliflucted) raised beach sediments.

Case (1983, 1984) examined the Port-Eynon Silt (bed 5) as part of a detailed study of Quaternary airfall and coversand deposits in South Wales. He confirmed the origin of the sediment as a loess and concluded that it had accumulated during dry, cold and windy conditions at the end of the Devensian Stage. The mineralogy of the deposit, however,

showed that the loessic silt had probably been derived from Irish Sea glacial deposits to the west, and not from proglacial Welsh outwash as he had previously suggested (Case 1977). A thin layer of sand capping the loess at Horton was also described (Case 1983, 1984) and was considered to be the product of Holocene dune formation.

Henry (1984a, 1984b) described the lithological characteristics of the deposits at Horton and proposed formal lithostratigraphic units (see site description). She showed that two raised beaches at Horton (Horton Upper Beach (bed 1) and Horton Lower Beach (isolated on the limestone platform); Bowen et al. 1985) could be distinguished on lithology, texture, clast roundness and foraminiferal assemblage. She concluded, however, that in both beaches, the forams indicated temperate shallow marine conditions, and that the beaches represented sea-level stands at least as high as at present.

Davies (1983) had already, in an amino acid geochronological study of the raised beaches of Gower, presented data which suggested that the two raised beach deposits at Horton were of different ages. She suggested that the largely uncemented raised beach deposits (bed 1; Horton Upper Beach) could be correlated with Oxygen Isotope Stage 7 of the deep-sea record (c. 210,000 BP). The Horton Lower Beach, only found cemented to the limestone bedrock and not in a stratigraphic context, was correlated with Oxygen Isotope Sub-stage 5e (c. 125,000 BP): in common with many other raised beach deposits in Gower. Bowen et al. (1985) and Bowen and Sykes (1988) presented further amino acid geochronological data for the raised beach deposits at Horton, using an improved measurement technique. The ascription of the beaches, however, remains unchanged, but fauna from two separate events is contained in the Upper Beach.

The occurrence at Horton of raised beach sediments of different ages, causes problems in interpreting the overlying beds (Henry 1984a, 1984b; Bowen et al. 1985). The Horton Lower Beach was deposited during Oxygen Isotope Sub-stage 5e. The terrestrial deposits overlying the Horton Upper Beach (bed 1), however, are all thought to have been deposited in the Devensian Stage. Henry (1984a, 1984b) proposed that the colluvial silts (bed 2) and colluvial silts with boulders (bed 3) accumulated during the Early and Middle Devensian: as sea-level fell and climate deteriorated, vegetation cover was reduced and sheet washing of previously weathered deposits occurred. During ensuing periglacial conditions in the Late Devensian frost-shattered limestone head (bed 4) accumulated (cf. Bowen 1970a, 1971a). Case (1977, 1983, 1984) has shown that head formation was followed without a break by deposition of wind-blown sand and loess (bed 5).

Horton is, therefore, an integral member of a network of sites in Gower that shows evidence for changing conditions during the Late Pleistocene.

The occurrence of raised beach deposits of different ages makes the site especially important, but causes problems in interpreting the ages of the deposits which overlie the oldest beach. Horton is a reference site for the colluvial deposits and associated boulder beds. It may be regarded as a standard section for the loess in South Wales.

Conclusions

Horton displays two adjacent raised beaches of different ages. One is about 200,000 years, and the other 125,000 years old. It is also important because it is the type-site for loess in South Wales. Loess is a wind-blown silt which was deposited from large dust storms towards the end of the ice age. Loess is extensive in South Wales, but rarely is it seen to such advantage as at Horton. Loess is an important element in South Wales soils, and provides the loamy character of many of the most productive soils in the region.

Long Hole Cave

Highlights

A site with rich Pleistocene mammal remains and human artefacts dating from the Ipswichian and Devensian Stages. 'Cold' and 'warm' mammal faunas and pollen indicate several phases of marked climatic and vegetational change, varying from temperate interglacial and interstadial conditions to arctic desert.

Introduction

Long Hole Cave (SS452851) is important for deposits which have yielded faunal remains, artefacts and pollen. Excavations at the site during the last century produced what could be identified as 'warm' and 'cold' mammal faunas. More recent excavations have revealed a series of well stratified sediments together with fossils and artefacts from mainly pre-late-glacial times in the Devensian Stage. The site was first excavated by Wood in 1861 (see Falconer 1868). Evidence from the site was subsequently discussed by Lyell (1873), Roberts (1887-8), Garrod (1926), Allen and Rutter (1948) and Bowen (1980a). Campbell (1977) provided a detailed account of the sequence and its interpretation, and Evans (1977b) (*in* Campbell 1977) analysed the land snail fauna.

Description

Long Hole Cave is situated in cliffs of Carboniferous Limestone in south-west Gower. The cave lies at *c.* 55m OD and from a SSE-facing entrance, opens directly into a single passage some 15m long. A sequence of terrestrial sediments comprising cave earths, scree, weathered scree and fine-grained wind-blown sediment up to 3m thick rests on a limestone floor. Substantial deposits are thought to remain *in situ*. Full details of the stratigraphy are

provided by Campbell (1977).

The first known excavations at Long Hole by Wood were largely within the cave, and they were later documented by Falconer (1868). Initially, the cave was blocked by a talus cone, but after this had been removed, Falconer recorded a single layer of ferruginous cave earth mixed with angular limestone fragments overlying the limestone floor. The 'cave earth' was noted as being about 7 ft (2.1m) thick, but there was no trace of marine sand or shingle, like that found at nearby Minchin Hole and Bacon Hole. Falconer recorded a mixture of 'warm' and 'cold' Pleistocene faunas, with – cave bear *Ursus spelaeus*, badger *Meles meles*, polecat *Mustela putorius*, marten *Martes* sp., otter *Lutra lutra* L., red fox *Vulpes vulpes*, wolf *Canis lupus*, spotted hyaena *Crocuta crocuta*, wild cat *Felis sylvestris* Schreber, lion *Panthera leo*, Irish elk *Megaceros giganteus*, reindeer *Rangifer tarandus*, red deer *Cervus elaphus*, bison *Bison priscus*, wild boar *Sus scrofa* L., horse *Equus ferus* Bodaert, and European wild ass *Equus asinus*, narrow-nosed rhinoceros *Dicerorhinus hemitoechus*, woolly rhinoceros *Coelodonta antiquitatis*, straight-tusked elephant *Palaeoloxodon antiquus*, mammoth *Mammuthus primigenius*, mountain hare *Lepus timidus*, rabbit *Oryctolagus cuniculus* (L.) and water vole *Arvicola terrestris* (Hinton). Flint and chert artefacts associated with the fauna were also unearthed (Falconer 1868). These finds were regarded with considerable interest because, according to Sir Charles Lyell (1873), they provided "the first well authenticated example of the occurrence of *D. hemitoechus* in connection with human implements". The finds were therefore used as evidence for the 'antiquity of Man', clearly showing the relationship between the handiwork of Man and the remains of animals, many of which were extinct (Roberts 1887-8).

Interpretation

The stone implements found by Wood were fully described by Garrod (1926), who suggested that the artefact assemblage was probably of Middle or Upper Aurignacian age. She noted, however, that the fauna associated with it was mixed, some of the mammals being of known interglacial ('warm') and others of glacial ('cold') character. This indicated that there had been either some disturbance of the cave earth or that two levels were present but that they had not been detected. For the same reasons, Allen and Rutter (1948) thought that the contemporaneity of Palaeolithic Man with *Dicerorhinus hemitoechus* was questionable.

Campbell in 1969 (Campbell 1977) cut a trench adjacent to Wood's at the cave entrance. He presented detailed stratigraphic, granulometric, faunal, artefact and pollen evidence in his analysis of the sequence. Land snails found in the older deposits were present, but as at Cat Hole, only as an intrusive Holocene element (Evans 1977b).

Campbell reconstructed the following sequence of events. The earliest stage recorded is the

Ipswichian when a temperate woodland environment prevailed, with a thermophilous flora and a fauna including *Bison* or *Bos.* Several of Falconer's species such as *Palaeoloxodon antiquus* and *Dicerorhinus hemitoechus* may also have originated from this temperate phase or even earlier (Campbell 1977). A prolonged period of arctic tundra development is then indicated by the pollen record. This phase is interrupted early in the sedimentary sequence by deposits with pollen that indicate the development of boreal coniferous forest with *Picea, Pinus* and *Betula,* and which allow a correlation tentatively with the Early Devensian Chelford Interstadial at *c.* 65,000 BP. The lithology of the bed containing the Chelford pollen is dominantly weathered scree, and Campbell observed that Palaeolithic artefacts (of presumably Mousterian culture (Bowen 1980a)) were associated with it. A Chelford Interstadial age was supported by a fauna including elk and marten. This phase was followed by a protracted period of steppe and tundra conditions during which screes accumulated. These were believed to have been deposited during the Middle Devensian; they were characterised by a comparative abundance of *Juniperus* and *Salix* pollen, and by a fauna including hyaena, mammoth, woolly rhinoceros, horse, giant deer, reindeer and mountain hare (Campbell 1977). Artefacts indicating the presence of Upper Palaeolithic Man are associated with these deposits. Bowen (1980a) agreed that the pollen record from these sediments was consistent with the Middle Devensian, perhaps reflecting conditions during the Upton Warren Interstadial.

According to Campbell, the Late Devensian ice maximum was indicated in the Long Hole sequence by the apparent minimum of tree and shrub pollen, accompanied by deposition of fine-grained wind-blown sediment. This severely cold phase was associated with a fauna of arctic fox, horse and reindeer. Devensian late-glacial Pollen Zones I, II and III and Holocene Pollen Zones IV-VIII were also distinguished in the sequence at Long Hole (Campbell 1977).

Thus, Campbell's work showed that at least four separate faunal assemblages ranging from the late Ipswichian Stage through the Devensian Stage, and clearly associated with climatically related changes in lithology and pollen, occurred within Long Hole Cave. Falconer's original species list is considered to be a mixture of Ipswichian ('warm') and Devensian ('cold') mammal faunas.

The evidence from Long Hole, particularly the pollen record, was discussed by Bowen (1980a). He noted that except for the event referred to the Chelford Interstadial, and the rise in *Juniperus* and *Salix* pollen, no other indications of Early and Middle Devensian interstadial conditions were then known from Wales. Bowen stressed, however, that Campbell's pollen analysis had been carried out on sediments that were technically head and colluvium and there was therefore a distinct possibility that some of the pollen was derived. This was probably true, especially for the basal layers. The Chelford pollen might easily be reworked pollen of Ipswichian age. Equally, both events recorded could be equivalent to Oxygen Isotope Sub-stages 5e and 5c (Bowen 1980a).

The record of elk *Alces alces* (L.) from Long Hole was of particular interest, as this species was extremely rare in Britain prior to the Late Devensian Allerød. The antler base, found in 1969, is now preserved at the Baden-Powell Museum, Oxford. Re-examination of the specimen, however, indicates that it should almost certainly not be referred to *Alces alces* but to reindeer *Rangifer tarandus* (Lister 1984).

With the reservations noted earlier, the pollen record is perhaps the best so far available in Wales for the whole of the Devensian Stage, showing possible evidence for a brief temperate interlude correlated tentatively with the Chelford Interstadial. The site thus covers an important part of the Pleistocene record that is not well represented at other sites; for instance, it contrasts with Minchin Hole where the sequence shows strong evidence for changing marine and terrestrial conditions during the Ipswichian Stage and earlier. The Long Hole sequence also contrasts with those at Bacon Hole and Cat Hole Caves where particularly detailed palaeoenvironmental evidence for the Ipswichian and Early Devensian stages and the Devensian late-glacial are represented, respectively.

Long Hole Cave contains an important record of changing conditions from the Ipswichian Stage through the Devensian Stage into the Devensian late-glacial. The site is particularly important for its pollen record which covers the Devensian Stage. This record shows that a period of arctic conditions was interrupted by the development of boreal coniferous forest. This warmer phase has been correlated with the Early Devensian Chelford Interstadial; as such, the site provides the only evidence in Wales for this event. Long Hole Cave is therefore the only known Welsh site with fossil, implement, rock, pollen and spore evidence for changing climatic conditions in Wales during the Early and Middle Devensian.

Conclusions

Long Hole Cave contains deposits representing all of the last ice age: from about 80,000 years ago to 10,000 years ago. It contains archaeological evidence for the earlier part of the last ice age. In addition, some of the deposits contain pollen which show the former existence of boreal (northern) forest. It is an important site because of the range of evidence it contains.

Worm's Head

Highlights

This site provides an important record of climatic change from the last, Ipswichian, interglacial through the cold and periglacial phases of the Devensian. Evidence presented for the presence of an interglacial soil has provoked much research interest.

Introduction

Worm's Head (SS396874) records important information for changing conditions in central South Wales during the Late Pleistocene. Its raised marine sediments, periglacial head and glacigenic sediments have long been recognised (George 1932), but the site has gained further importance through the description of a possible interglacial soil (Ball 1960). The site was first mentioned by Strahan (1907b) and was subsequently described by George (1932, 1933a, 1933b). It has featured in studies by Ball (1960), Bowen (1965, 1966, 1969a, 1970a, 1974, 1977b), and more recently was mentioned by Stephens and Shakesby (1982). Aspects of the Pleistocene deposits were also studied by Tindall (1983) and Campbell (1984).

Description

Raised beach, glacigenic and periglacial head and colluvial sediments are widely distributed on the 'outer', 'middle' and 'inner' heads that make up Worm's Head, and they were mapped by George (1932). These deposits, however, are best developed on the south and west flanks of the inner head overlying a Carboniferous Limestone shore platform, where the following sequence occurs (Ball 1960) –

5   Dull grey-brown sandy loam, almost stoneless (0.75m)
4   Dull grey-brown, stony sandy loam, with common Devonian and Carboniferous sandstones (glacial sediment) (1.0-2.0m)
3   Brown loam with abundant angular limestone clasts (head) (3.0m)
2   Red sandy-clay loam, with rare limestone pebbles (0.25-0.45m)
1   Cemented *Patella* raised beach deposits

Most beds from this sequence are well displayed on a small knoll or terrace separated from the inner head (SS396874), although sections through the raised beach, head and glacial deposits also occur on the west side of the inner head (SS392877).

Interpretation

The Pleistocene sequence was first described by Strahan (1907b) who recorded a succession of raised beach, head and sand bordering the inner head of Worm's Head. George (1932) mapped these deposits, and considered that the distribution of the glacial gravels was particularly significant (George 1933a). He noted that a drift terrace bordered much of the Worm, but that, on the south side of the main upstanding hills, locally derived limestone head was preserved above the *Patella* raised beach but no glacial sediments. This contrasted to the east and west margins of the hills where mixed lithology gravel occurred; which could only satisfactorily be explained, George (1933a) suggested, on the assumption that the inner, middle and outer heads had formed three buttresses protecting ground to the south from the onslaught of the ice. George (1932, 1933a, 1933b) envisaged that the *Patella* Beach had formed before the 'Older Drift' glaciation of South Wales. He noted the similarity between the glacial gravels on Worm's Head and those at Rhosili, and suggested that they had been derived from the north and north-east during the 'Older Drift' glaciation, when confluent Welsh and Irish Sea ice masses may have affected the south and west coasts of Gower.

George (1933a) also described the upper loam (bed 5) as a loess-like deposit which had probably been derived from the underlying glacial sediments, and which had accumulated under aeolian conditions. He noted, however, that this loess-like sediment provided a flat capping to many of the sections along the Gower coast, and suggested that, like the drift terrace at Rhosili, these sediments had finally been fashioned by marine agencies. The platform was tentatively referred to as the 'Post Older Drift Platform', although its specific age was uncertain (George 1932).

Ball (1960) described what he believed to be an *in situ* interglacial soil (bed 2). The micro-fabric and mineralogy of this deposit suggested that it was transitional between *terra fusca* and *terra rossa* soils commonly found on limestone around the Mediterranean today (Ball 1960). He concluded that the soil had formed under slightly warmer summer conditions than at present, and postulated that it was *in situ* relict material, formed during interglacial (Ipswichian) conditions; moreover that together with other similar deposits, it had only survived locally in areas not glaciated by Late Devensian ice.

Accepting that the sediment described by Ball (1960) might contain elements of an interglacial soil, Bowen (1965, 1966) considered that the bed had been reworked by solifluction. Subsequently, Bowen (1969a, 1970a, 1971a, 1974, 1977b) suggested that such sediments had formed by soil erosion and sheet-washing. He classified them as colluvial silts and compared them to the 'limon rouges' of the Mediterranean. Bowen (1970a) noted that such sediments were widespread in south Gower, and that they formed an important stratigraphic unit, suggesting that they had been deposited by colluviation at the foot of the coastal cliffs, as sea-level fell towards the end of the Ipswichian Stage. At that time, an ever increasing area of sea-bed was exposed, and deflated sand from this source may also have been mixed with the colluviated remnants of interglacial soil, perhaps even with residual Keuper Marl and the fines washed from glacial deposits of pre-Ipswichian ('Older Drift') age (Bowen 1969a, 1970a). The mixed lithology drift (bed 4) on Worm's Head, and at Rhosili, had been deposited as outwash from the Late Devensian ice-sheet which may have reached its southern limit where Whitford Point now lies (Bowen 1970a). Stephens and Shakesby (1982) suggested that drift overlying Ball's (1960) interglacial soil, might be redistributed pre-Devensian glacial sediment, or, alternatively (for example, Bowen 1970a), Late Devensian outwash.

Tindall (1983), in an examination of diagnostic sedimentary properties of the deposits on Worm's Head, noted that the fabric of bed 4 (the outwash sediments of Bowen (1970a)) showed a marked downslope orientation, and she concluded that the glacial sediments were not *in situ*, but had been soliflucted into position. She also recorded that elsewhere (for example, at SS396874) these beds were disrupted by periglacial convolutions.

Campbell (1984) concluded from Scanning Electron Microscopy studies of sediments that there was no evidence for a protracted period of *in situ* interglacial weathering as proposed by Ball (1960), and the presence of many well rounded marine-type quartz sand grains supported Bowen's view that the deposit (bed 2) contained deflated (wind-blown) marine sand. Ball (1985 - personal communication), now accepts that interglacial soil material on Worm's Head is probably not *in situ*. Campbell's (1984) SEM data, however, did not allow a palaeoenvironmental interpretation of the mixed lithology drift on Worm's Head, although he suggested that they were compatible with redeposited glacial material.

The raised beach deposits of both inner and outer Worm's Head (for example, bed 1) were formed during the Ipswichian Stage, as shown by amino acid geochronology (Bowen *et al.* 1985; Bowen and Sykes 1988). The colluvial sediments (bed 2) and head deposits of local lithology (bed 3) accumulated during the subsequent Devensian Stage. The origin of the gravels (bed 4), however, remains uncertain. They may represent soliflucted deposits from a glaciation that pre-dated the Ipswichian Stage, or they may have been deposited as outwash from the Late Devensian ice-sheet. The overlying silty sand (bed 5) is probably a mixture of wind-blown and colluvial sediments deposited towards the close of the Devensian Stage.

Worm's Head is important for sediments which show a sequence of changing conditions from the high sea-levels and temperate conditions of the Ipswichian Stage (Oxygen Isotope Sub-stage 5e) through cold, to fully periglacial conditions in the Devensian Stage. The site became particularly important following Ball's (1960) description of a possible interglacial soil. This has since been shown to be a colluvial deposit. Worm's Head remains important in understanding Late Pleistocene events in south-west Gower, particularly for establishing the precise limit of the Late Devensian ice-sheet.

Conclusions

Worm's Head displays a sequence of deposits representing the last glacial cycle. In particular, it contains a colluvial (slope wash) deposit previously interpreted as a soil profile, which is important evidence for showing how the last interglacial changed into the last ice age.

Rhosili Bay

Highlights

A key site where fluvioglacial sands and gravels, thick periglacial heads and possible till deposits provide vital evidence for reconstructing Devensian environments in west Gower, including possible evidence for a Late Devensian ice lobe in Carmarthen Bay.

Introduction

Rhosili Bay (SS414900) shows evidence for the glacial and periglacial history of west Gower. Thick head (periglacial) deposits are exposed in coastal cliffs for about 2km at the foot of Rhosili Down, and these form one of the finest examples of a solifluction terrace in Wales. Deposits at Rhosili also help to establish the maximum limit of the Late Devensian ice-sheet in west Gower. Site investigation commenced with Prestwich (1892). It was reinterpreted by Strahan (1907b) and was studied in detail by George (1932, 1933a). Aspects of the Pleistocene history of the site were also dealt with by George (1933b, 1938), Griffiths (1939), Bowen (1966, 1970a, 1973a, 1973d, 1974, 1977a, 1977b, 1980a), Peake *et al.* (1973), Green (1981b), Campbell and Shakesby (1982), Stephens and Shakesby (1982) and Bridges (1985). Campbell (1984) provided a detailed description.

Description

Rhosili Down is formed of Devonian Old Red Sandstone. It trends north-south, and rises steeply above the coastal plateau of Gower to a height of 193m OD. At several localities Old Red Sandstone sandstones and conglomerates crop out as tors. At the west side of Rhosili Down, a large solifluction terrace has been cliffed by the sea. Exposures in the terrace show that, for much of its length, it consists of head (periglacial) of local Old Red Sandstone sandstones and conglomerates. Towards the north end of the bay (SS414900), however, a more complex sequence is seen – see Figure 8; (Campbell 1984) –

5	Blown sand
4	Colluvium (0.5m)
3	Upper head (2.0-3.0m)

2   Gravel containing clasts of mixed lithology
     (6.0m)

1   Lower head (2.0-3.0m)

The gravel (bed 2) extends laterally for only 150m, and then lenses out to be replaced by head. It overlies the lower head (bed 1) with a sharp undulating boundary, and evidently corresponds with the 'glacial gravel' described by George (1933a) and the 'outwash' of Bowen (1970a). The boundary between beds 2 and 3, however, is gradational, and large pockets of sand and gravel from bed 2 are incorporated within the upper head. Till has also been described from the site, within the gravels of bed 2 (Campbell and Shakesby 1982; Campbell 1984).

Interpretation

Pleistocene deposits were first recorded at Rhosili Bay by Prestwich (1892), who described a bed of shelly sand and gravel (bed 2) between layers of Old Red Sandstone rubble in the coastal terrace. The presence of marine shell fragments in the gravelly drift led him provisionally to refer to the deposit as a 'raised beach'. Strahan (1907b), however, considered the gravel to be glacial in origin, noting the presence of many far-travelled Old Red Sandstone and South Wales Coalfield erratics. He concluded that the gravel had been derived from a northern source, and interpreted the upper and lower 'rubble' beds as strictly local talus deposits derived from the Old Red Sandstone hills above the bay. Strahan (1907b) could not locate shells similar to those described by

Prestwich (1892), but he speculated that the *Mya, Turitella* and *Nassa* shells had been derived from a sea-bed, probably in Carmarthen Bay. This implied a south-east flow of ice, which he suggested might also account for the presence of several igneous (Irish Sea) erratics in the gravel.

George (1932, 1933a) gave a comprehensive account of the deposits at Rhosili in his classic accounts of the raised beaches and glacial deposits of Gower. He suggested that the glacial gravel (bed 2) occurred as a large wedge which thinned to the south. Southwards, the upper and lower head deposits merged imperceptibly, and he considered that deposition of the glacial gravel had been merely "a brief interlude" in the formation of the head deposits. He recorded a number of far travelled rock types from the glacial gravel which included soda felsite (from Llŷn), perlitic-rhyolite (Pembrokeshire?), Llandovery mudstone (Haverfordwest?), horneblende-porphyrite (south Scotland), quartz-hyperite (south Scotland) and Precambrian slate. However, these rock types, thought to have been transported to Gower by Irish Sea ice, formed only a small proportion of the total assemblage so he was confident that the bulk of the gravel had been derived from the north; citing in particular, the presence of Millstone Grit from the North Crop, and Carboniferous Limestone traceable on its fossil content to north-west Gower. The shells described by Prestwich (1892) were considered to have been dredged from the floor of Carmarthen Bay as the Welsh ice moved southwards. The mixture of Welsh and Irish Sea erratics was used as evidence (George 1933a) to

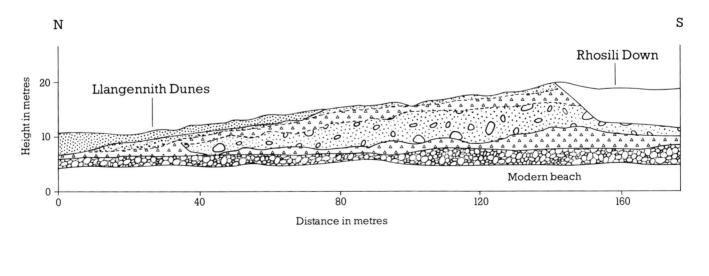

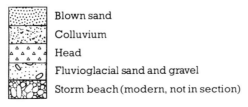

Figure 8 Quaternary sequence at Rhosili Bay (after Campbell 1984)

suggest that during the 'Older Drift' glaciation, Carmarthen Bay and the Loughor Estuary had been congested contemporaneously with ice masses both from the Welsh uplands and from the Irish Sea Basin. The mixed provenance of the drift deposits in west Gower in general, and Rhosili in particular, was later confirmed by heavy mineral analyses (Griffiths 1939).

George (1933a) considered that the Old Red Sandstone rubble horizons (beds 1 and 3) at Rhosili had been emplaced in a 'rigorous climate', and noted that the surface of the drift terrace was almost flat-topped, sloping gently seawards. Because this terrace and those elsewhere in Gower were cut across deposits of markedly different types (glacial gravel, cemented and uncemented heads, silts and sands), George (1932) remarked that they could not have been formed solely by subaerial processes, and he suggested that the final moulding of the features had taken place by planation during a short period of marine erosion, of unspecified age. He termed such features the 'Post Older Drift Platform'.

Bowen (1966) initially considered that the glacial gravels (bed 2) were of Saalian age, although he revised this in later papers. He accepted that shells in the gravels at Rhosili had been picked up by ice from the floor of Carmarthen Bay and the Loughor Estuary (Bowen 1970a). These shells were then incorporated into outwash from the margin of the Late Devensian ice-sheet which stood somewhere in the region of present day Whitford Point (Bowen 1970a). Gravels from this ice-sheet were deposited at Rhosili and on nearby Worm's Head. He considered that the Irish Sea erratics described by George had been reworked by the Devensian ice from earlier 'Older Drift' glacial deposits. Unlike George he did not believe that the sediments had been deposited by confluent Irish Sea and Welsh ice masses of 'Older Drift' age, citing the relatively undissected and fresh nature of the drifts as evidence for a Devensian age.

Following deglaciation of the Late Devensian ice-sheet, head deposits continued to form at Rhosili, covering the earlier outwash (Bowen 1970a, 1973a, 1973d, 1974, 1977a, 1977b, 1980a). Bowen noted that, as at Morfa-bychan (west Wales), local site conditions had been particularly favourable for the accumulation of solifluction deposits; a high slope of well jointed and well bedded Old Red Sandstone, and a westerly aspect which would have encouraged numerous freeze-thaw cycles, led to deposition of an upper head up to 15m thick. Bowen (1974, 1977a, 1980a) remarked that much of the upper head (bed 3) had probably accumulated during the Devensian late-glacial, and that the impressive solifluction terrace had formed over a period of, at most, 5,000 years. Rhosili Bay could be contrasted (Bowen 1973a, 1977a) with sequences at Glanllynnau in north-west Wales and Horton in south Gower where site conditions had not favoured head accumulation. At Horton, for example, the Devensian Stage was represented by only c. 2m of deposits (Bowen 1977a).

Winter storms in 1979-1980 revealed sediments at the base of the section that Campbell and Shakesby (1982) interpreted as till. Although the stratigraphic relationship of some of these deposits to those in the cliff behind was uncertain, others were interstratified with sands and gravels in bed 2. The clast lithologies and fabric pattern of the till indicated a north-west source, and this led to speculation (Campbell and Shakesby 1982; Stephens and Shakesby 1982) that Late Devensian ice may have reached farther south than others envisaged. They suggested that Carmarthen Bay may have been occupied by a large piedmont ice lobe, similar to that described in Swansea Bay (Charlesworth 1929; Bowen 1970a).

Following the discovery of the till, the site was re-investigated by Campbell (1984), who applied methods including Scanning Electron Microscopy, fabric analysis and clast lithological and roundness measurements to the interpretation of the sequence. From the evidence at Rhosili, Campbell (1984) proposed the following sequence of events. During the Late Devensian, around 18,000 years ago, Welsh ice moved southwards across Carmarthen Bay and on to west Gower to deposit shelly till at Broughton Bay. At that time, Rhosili Bay was probably in the periglacial zone, and the lower head may date from this time or even earlier in the Devensian Stage. The Late Devensian ice-sheet appears to have been near its maximum limit, and a mixture of fluvioglacial outwash and, perhaps, flow tills was deposited at the northern end of Rhosili Bay along the proglacial fringe of the ice-sheet. The lower head was truncated, possibly by glacial streams, before deposition of the glacial sands and gravels with their included marine shell fauna from Carmarthen Bay. The mixture of well rounded gravel clasts with large angular blocks of head, suggests that slope deposits may have been incorporated contemporaneously with fluvioglacial debris from the ice-sheet. Following melting of the ice-sheet, favourable site conditions promoted the accumulation of a thick upper head deposit (Bowen 1970a) which now forms the bulk of the solifluction terrace. Towards the end of this periglacial phase, sheet-washing formed a capping layer of colluvial sediments (bed 4). During the Holocene, dune sands (bed 5) were deposited at Llangennith and the northern end of Rhosili Down, and the whole terrace was trimmed by the rising sea.

Additional interest at the site was provided by Green's (1981b) discovery of a flint Palaeolithic handaxe from the foot of the terrace at the southern end of Rhosili Down (SS414088). He suggested that the handaxe, which on its form was of approximately Ipswichian age, had probably been incorporated into the solifluction deposits during the cold Devensian Stage; there was no evidence to suggest that the handaxe had been rolled or transported by fluvial agencies. This was only the second such 'stray' find of a Palaeolithic handaxe in Wales (Green 1981b).

The sequence, therefore, records evidence for two periglacial phases separated by an event when outwash and associated sediments from a nearby Late Devensian ice margin were deposited. The upper head, which forms much of the impressive terrace at Rhosili, is thought to have accumulated in about 5,000 years, following wastage of the Late Devensian ice-sheet and during the Devensian late-glacial. Irish Sea erratics in the glacial outwash gravel provide vital evidence for the enigmatic, possibly 'Older Drift' (pre-Devensian) Irish Sea ice-sheet, which is thought to have affected parts of south and west Gower. The site has also been used as important evidence for the location of the Late Devensian maximum ice margin in west Gower. The exposures provide contrasting evidence to nearby sites at Broughton Bay and Worm's Head.

Rhosili Bay provides a sequence of deposits which demonstrates two phases of periglacial climate in which a large terrace of solifluction deposits accumulated, and between which fluvioglacial sediments were deposited. The latter were deposited by Late Devensian ice and are interbedded with possible flow till, suggesting that the Late Devensian ice-sheet reached almost into Rhosili Bay. The solifluction terrace, associated bedrock slopes and tors are one of the finest landform assemblages of their kind in Britain and clearly show the relationship between bedrock lithology, site aspect and slope factors in the formation of solifluction terraces.

Conclusions

The drift terrace in Rhosili Bay is made up of a succession of deposits which may be used to delimit the maximum extent of the last Welsh ice-sheet. The terrace is also important because of the evidence it provides for the rates of operation of cold climate processes on hill slopes. It is unique in Wales because it can be shown that the majority of its deposits accumulated between the time of ice disappearance and the onset of post-glacial conditions 10,000 years ago.

Broughton Bay

Highlights

A remarkable Devensian multiple till sequence yields evidence of former ice limits. Raised beach sediments and derived faunal elements in the till provide evidence for an earlier temperate interglacial event in the Ipswichian.

Introduction

Broughton Bay (SS417930) is a site of considerable interest, for its deposits contain materials that have been used to date major geomorphological events and changing environmental conditions of regional significance since the Ipswichian Stage. Sedimentologically, the deposits are interesting because of their glaciotectonic structures. Holocene dune sands overlying the Pleistocene sediments also contain dateable horizons. Although the Pleistocene sequence has only been revealed by coastal erosion within the last 10 years, the site has attracted considerable interest, and it was first described by Campbell *et al.* (1982) when an amino acid analysis of molluscan shells was published. Further, similar dating was discussed by Davies (1983), Bowen (1984), Campbell (1984), Campbell and Shakesby (1985, 1986a, 1986b), Bowen *et al.* (1986) and Worsley (1986). The site

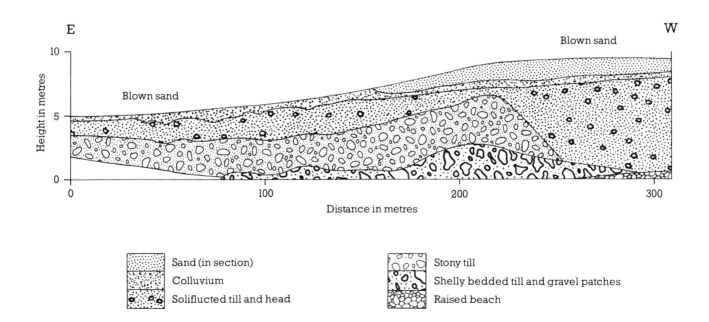

Figure 9 Quaternary sequence at Broughton Bay (after Campbell *et al.* 1982)

52

was also described by Campbell and Shakesby (1982, 1983), Stephens and Shakesby (1982), Bridges (1985) and Shakesby and Campbell (1985). Details of the Pleistocene and Holocene sequences can be found in Campbell (1984), and Lees (1982, 1983), respectively.

Description

The exposures run east from Twlc Point (SS417931) for about 300m and attain a maximum thickness of about 10m. The stratigraphy (Campbell 1984) is –

7   Holocene dune sand
6   Colluvium (1.5m)
5   Soliflucted till and head (5.0m)
4   Stony till (5.0m)
3   Bedded till containing marine shell fragments and pieces of wood (2.0m)
2   Limestone head (0.5m)
1   Raised beach conglomerate

The stratigraphy at the site is shown in Figure 9. The basal raised beach deposits are fragmentary and are only found near Twlc Point. They rest on a Carboniferous Limestone, probably marine-cut, platform and contain abundant marine shell fragments, principally of *Littorina littoralis* (L.). The raised beach grades upwards into limestone head, which is overlain by till units in which the bedding is often well defined, and from which an assemblage of 21 identifiable shell species has been recognised (MacMillan *in* Campbell *et al.* 1982; Campbell 1984). Wood fragments (Salicaceae) have also been recovered. Overlying the shelly tills (bed 3) and a thin discontinuous sand and gravel layer, is an unfossiliferous bed of stony till (bed 4), which is succeeded by redistributed till, head and colluvium. The colluvium fills well developed cracks which penetrate the stony till, and, in plan, form a polygonal pattern. Both the shelly and stony tills at Broughton Bay show glaciotectonically induced folds, most clearly displayed by close bedding in the shelly till. These structures are also seen, under favourable circumstances, in plan form on the foreshore. The structures appear as gentle anticlines and synclines in the sections and in an elliptical pattern elongated north to south on the beach (Campbell 1984).

Interpretation

The results of amino acid analysis of specimens of *Littorina littoralis* from the raised beach deposits indicated an Ipswichian Stage (Campbell *et al.* 1982) age, but shells from the till (bed 3) were of similar age or possibly slightly younger. However, faunal evidence suggested that the assemblage of shells in the till was fully interglacial, with several species found only at more southerly latitudes today. Campbell *et al.* (1982) concluded that it must have been ice of Devensian age and no older, which, moving southwards across the eastern part of Carmarthen Bay, incorporated shell litter that had accumulated during the preceding interglacial;

the fabric pattern and erratic content of the shelly till at Broughton Bay was consistent with this view. A study of amino acid ratios from raised beaches around Gower by Davies (1983), showed that most of the deposits were of the same age, and they were provisionally ascribed to the Ipswichian (Oxygen Isotope Sub-stage 5e). This study included further data from Broughton Bay. With an improved method of analysis, and using calibration provided by Uranium-series ages from Bacon Hole Cave, it was confirmed that the raised beach deposits at Broughton Bay could be ascribed to Sub-stage 5e (Bowen *et al.* 1985; Bowen and Sykes 1988).

The data of Campbell *et al.* (1982) did not, however, determine the point at which the Broughton Bay (shelly) Till was deposited during the Devensian, and attempts were made to establish the age more precisely by radiocarbon dating of Salicaceae fragments (Campbell and Shakesby 1985). An initial determination of >42,000 (HAR-5443) was obtained by radiocarbon dating. A second sample was dated using the isotopic enrichment method and yielded a date of 68,000 +13,000 -5,000 BP (GrN -12508). Campbell and Shakesby noted a relatively close correspondence between the Broughton Bay date (GrN -12508) and the date of 60,800 ± 1500 BP (GrN - 1475) (for example, Worsley 1980) for the Chelford Interstadial site in Cheshire. They concluded that the wood may therefore have been from a temperate willow species growing during the Chelford Interstadial but later incorporated into the Broughton Bay Till by ice of probable Late Devensian age. They had doubts about the radiocarbon date, however, and did not rule out an Ipswichian (or even earlier interglacial) or pre-Pleistocene age for the wood. Worsley (1986) noted that the date could be seriously misleading, and suggested that its apparent association with the Chelford Interstadial event was possibly the result of a radiocarbon assay on contaminated material, and this possibility was acknowledged by Campbell and Shakesby (1986b).

Bowen *et al.* (1986) recorded that the till at Broughton Bay contained shells of *Macoma balthica* (L.), the youngest of which (by amino acid and radiocarbon dating) could be shown to be Late Devensian (*c.* 17,000 BP) in age (see also Bowen and Sykes 1988) and therefore indigenous, unlike the derived Ipswichian elements. Although a Late Devensian age for the till was also favoured by Campbell and Shakesby (1986a), certain difficulties were noted in reconciling the new radiocarbon and amino acid dated evidence to existing data from the site. Amino acid ratios from *Macoma* correspond with ages of *c.* 17,000 BP elsewhere in the Irish Sea Basin, and could show that the shelly diamict is glacio-marine in origin – see Chapter 1.

Campbell (1984) applied a variety of detailed techniques, including Scanning Electron Microscopy, to interpret the following sequence of events at Broughton Bay. 1) During high sea-levels in the Ipswichian Stage, the raised beach deposits (bed 1) accumulated. 2) Towards the end of the Ipswichian, as climate deteriorated and sea-level fell, the Loughor Estuary and Carmarthen Bay became dry land. 3) During the Late Devensian, ice advanced southwards across the Loughor Estuary and Carmarthen Bay, incorporating marine shells, pieces of wood and estuarine sediments, and depositing tills (beds 3 and 4) at Broughton Bay. The stony upper till represents farther travelled debris within the ice-sediment profile, although it is believed to have been deposited contemporaneously with the lower till. 4) Following the wastage of Late Devensian ice, a phase of periglacial conditions occurred, and the upper layers of the till were rearranged by solifluction, and deposits of locally-derived head were formed (bed 5). Frost-cracking of the head and till deposits may have occurred during this periglacial phase, and surface washing of the unvegetated sediment surface may have given rise to the colluvial deposits (bed 6) which filled the cracks and capped the sequence.

The Quaternary sequence at Broughton Bay is completed by Holocene dune sands (bed 7) which run the full length of the bay, but which reach their maximum height west of Broughton Farm. The archaeology and depositional history of these dunes was studied by Lees (1982, 1983). The age of the dunes is not yet clear, but it appears that they were already in existence by the Roman period, with a renewed phase of sand mobility in late Mediaeval times when intense storms are known to have affected much of the South Wales coast (Lees 1982, 1983).

Considerable interest is provided by the glaciotectonic structures in the Pleistocene sequence at Broughton Bay. The origin of these structures has not yet been established, but various models of formation have been suggested (Campbell and Shakesby 1983; Campbell 1984). The Late Devensian ice-sheet may have been near its maximum extent locally, and the contortions in the till layers could have been caused by oscillations of this ice front. Alternatively, the structures may have formed as a result of differential ice or overburden loading. Campbell and Shakesby (1983) and Campbell (1984), however, thought that they resulted from horizontal stresses set up in the sediments as the constricted ice moved southwards between Burry Holms and Llanmadoc Hill.

Stratigraphic data from Broughton Bay and other Pleistocene sites in Gower, suggests that the Late Devensian ice-sheet was near its maximum southward limit at Broughton Bay. It is only at Broughton Bay, and east of Langland Bay (east Gower) that till *in situ* is seen to overlie raised beach sediments of Ipswichian age (Bowen 1984). This shows that the Late Devensian ice-sheet impinged upon the east and west margins of the peninsula where major valley glaciers emerged from the South Wales Coalfield. Broughton Bay is notable for being the only permanently exposed multiple till sequence in central South Wales, and

for being one of the first sites in Britain where both glacial and interglacial beds have been dated by amino acid geochronology.

Broughton Bay provides a record of Late Pleistocene environmental changes in central South Wales, and in particular, new evidence for the glacial and interglacial history of west Gower. Its raised beach conglomerate, deposited during Oxygen Isotope Sub-stage 5e (Ipswichian Stage) is overlain by a sequence of tills deposited during the Late Devensian. Glaciotectonic deformation structures in the till, and Holocene dune sands with archaeological and organic material, enhance the interest of the site.

Conclusions

Broughton Bay shows a sequence of deposits which span the last 125,000 years or so. It also provides an important constraint on the limit of the last Welsh ice-sheet. The shell fauna from some of the glacial deposits could be evidence that the earth's crust was depressed considerably in this area about 17,000 years ago.

Quaternary stratigraphy : west and south-west Wales

Introduction

Stratigraphic sites around the west and south-west coasts of Wales have been the basis for a variety of reconstructions in the Quaternary history of Wales. Some sequences display important evidence for the interplay of the Welsh and Irish Sea ice-sheets, while others illustrate the importance of periglacial conditions and processes to regional landscape evolution. A number of sites shows evidence for changes in relative sea-level during the Late Pleistocene and Holocene. The network of selected stratigraphical sites is essential in distinguishing between those areas glaciated or unglaciated during the Late Devensian. In this respect, the area is significant in its proximity to the Late Devensian maximum ice limit and thus may be compared with Gower – see Chapter 3.

Early sub-division

The area is historically important for early attempts to sub-divide the Quaternary sequences. Interest was first stimulated by the rich fossil contents of certain local caves, especially the Caldey and Tenby caves, including Little Hoyle and Hoyle's Mouth. Some of the first known excavations were made by Jervis and Pugett as early as the 1840s at the Hoyle Caves, although no accounts were left of their discoveries (Leach 1931). A series of excavations initiated by the Reverend G N Smith in the 1860s stimulated continued interest in these caves, culminating in the excavations led by Green of the National Museum of Wales (Green *et al.* 1986).

Following early interest in the bone caves, attempts were made to sub-divide the Pleistocene sediments of the coastal sequences (for example, Keeping 1882; Prestwich 1892; Hicks 1894; Reade 1896). Particularly important was the work of Jehu (1904) in northern Pembrokeshire (Preseli) and Williams (1927) in western Cardiganshire (Ceredigion). They used a tripartite scheme and proposed a sequence of Lower Boulder Clay, Intermediate Gravels and Sands and Upper Boulder Clay. Jehu believed that this tripartite sequence was evidence for two glacial episodes separated by an interglacial, but Williams suggested that the deposits could simply have accumulated at the margin of an ice-sheet during a single glaciation. This work, together with other observations on drift deposits and raised beaches by Strahan *et al.* (1909), Leach (1910, 1911), Cantrill *et al.* (1916) and Dixon (1921), were important in the first elucidation of Quaternary events in the region. Collectively, they showed that parts of the west Wales coast had been glaciated by Welsh ice from the uplands, but that parts of Pembrokeshire and Cardiganshire had been inundated by ice from the

north-west, that is, from the Irish Sea Basin.

The South Wales end-moraine

Following Wright's (1914) formal division of British glacial deposits into an 'Older Drift' and 'Newer Drift', Charlesworth (1929) traced what he considered was the maximum limit of the 'Newer Drift' ice-sheet of 'Magdalenian' age across South Wales. He distinguished between areas glaciated in 'Newer Drift' times and those previously glaciated during an 'Older Drift' glaciation. He established that south-west Wales had been glaciated on two occasions by ice from the Irish Sea Basin. Charlesworth used both stratigraphical and morphological evidence to delimit the extent of the 'Newer Drift' ice-sheet across Pembrokeshire (south-west Dyfed). With the tripartite division still much in vogue, he proposed that the maximum limit of the 'Newer Drift' coincided with the extent of the Upper Boulder Clay. Two other lines of evidence were also used to establish this limit. First, sands and gravels, forming hummocky topography, were regarded as terminal accumulations marking the maximum ice limit. Second, at the height of the 'Newer Drift' glaciation, he believed that Irish Sea ice in Cardigan Bay blocked the drainage from surrounding ice-free areas and resulted in the development of a series of extra-glacial lakes that were connected by ice marginal stream channels and 'direct' overflow channels. As the ice margin retreated, water spilled from one lake to another cutting a spectacular series of channels (the Gwaun-Jordanston system – see Figure 15, Chapter 5). The distribution of the sands and gravels, the Upper Boulder Clay and the meltwater channels was therefore used by Charlesworth to establish the area of south-west Wales affected by 'Newer Drift' ice. His hypothesis, relating the channels to overflows from glacial lakes, has since been shown to be partly untenable: the channels have now been interpreted as subglacial meltwater channels, indicating a far greater coverage of Late Devensian ice in the area than previously anticipated (Bowen and Gregory 1965; Gregory and Bowen 1966). The sand and gravel accumulations have also been reinterpreted to show that they did not accumulate at an ice margin (for example, Gregory and Bowen 1966; Bowen 1971b, 1981a, 1982a; Helm and Roberts 1975; Allen 1982; Bowen and Lear 1982).

Stratigraphical correlations

In common with north-west Wales and Gower, the coastal Pleistocene deposits of west and south-west Wales have been important in regional stratigraphical syntheses. Following Wirtz's (1953) delimitation of the maximum extent of Late

Late Devensian, and used as evidence for the maximum offshore limit of this Irish Sea ice-sheet (Garrard and Dobson 1974; Garrard 1977). Problems still remain in correlating offshore data with the stratigraphical record of the coastal exposures. The offshore reconstruction of Late Devensian maximum ice limits may also not take into account marine erosion at the distal end of the till sheet during the Holocene transgression (Bowen 1977c). The prominent sarns along the west Wales coast (for instance, Sarn Badrig) also have important implications for Late Pleistocene glacial conditions (Foster 1970b; Bowen 1974). These are discussed more fully in Chapter 6.

Ynyslas and Borth Bog

Highlights

A site providing one of the most significant records of sea-level, environmental and vegetational change in the Holocene of Wales. Rock, pollen and radiocarbon evidence has provided a complex dated story of sea-level rise, forest and bog development.

Introduction

Ynyslas and Borth Bog provide a detailed record of coastal and environmental changes during the Holocene. Borth Bog is one of the largest and finest examples of a raised bog occurring near sea-level anywhere in Britain. The pollen biostratigraphy of the site was first studied by Campbell James (Godwin and Newton 1938). The site was also referred to in studies by Godwin (1940a, 1943), and Godwin and Willis (1961, 1964) provided radiocarbon age control. Foraminiferal studies have been carried out at the site by Adams and Haynes (1965) and Haynes and Dobson (1969). Moore (1963, 1966, 1968) studied the pollen biostratigraphy with particular reference to human influences, and the locality has been used in studies of sea-level changes by Churchill (1965), Wilks (1977, 1979) and Heyworth and Kidson (1982). Other accounts are given by Taylor (1973, 1980) and Turner (1977).

Description

Ynyslas and Borth Bog lie on Cardigan Bay just south of the Dyfi Estuary. The site comprises two main parts – the submerged forest and associated beds on the foreshore at Ynyslas (SN604927), and Borth Bog (SN630910) to the east. The submerged forest lies approximately halfway between high and low tide marks at about -1m OD. It was originally exposed by the building of sea defences at Borth, but these exposures are now largely obscured and the forest is best seen between c. SN604924 and SN604933. The best exposures occur in winter, especially after storms which reveal the stumps and trunks of the forest embedded in a peat which overlies clay. The upper surface of the forest bed is frequently riddled with borings of the common piddock, while the underlying clays contain shells of the burrowing bivalve *Scrobicularia*. The submerged forest beds continue inland, beneath a shingle and sand spit, to underlie the whole of Borth Bog at a level just below OD.

Borth Bog (Cors Fochno) occupies some 800 ha (2000 acres). It is bordered to the west by the River Leri which separates the main bog from the shingle and sand ridge and the submerged forest – see Figure 10. To the south and east of the bog lies high ground; to the north, the bog borders the flats and salt marshes of the Dyfi Estuary (Yapp *et al.* 1916, 1917). Several islands of higher ground also occur on the edges and in the centre of the bog.

The sequence over much of the bog consists of –

5   Fresh *Sphagnum* peat
4   Greasy peat interpreted as a *Grenzhorizont*
3   Highly humified *Sphagnum – Calluna* peat
2   Wood peat and submerged forest bed
1   Basal *Scrobicularia* clay

At the northern margin of the bog, the sequence is interrupted by a wedge of sand, clay and salt marsh clay that cuts across beds 1-4 and the lower part of bed 5, and is overlain by the upper part of the fresh *Sphagnum* peat (Godwin 1943) – see Figure 10.

At Ynyslas, Godwin and Newton (1938) described a sequence of –

5   *Sphagnum* peat
4   Fenwood peat containing a succession of *Alnus – Betula – Pinus* pollen
3   Alder-carr peat
2   *Phragmites* peat
1   Intertidal *(Scrobicularia)* clay

Interpretation

The submerged forest and basal blue-grey clay containing *Scrobicularia* at Ynyslas were first noted by Keeping (1878), and were discussed by Yapp *et al.* (1916, 1917). The first detailed study at the site was by Campbell James (Godwin and Newton 1938). Godwin and Newton suggested that the close correspondence between the sequences at Ynyslas and Borth Bog, indicated a parallel development of the areas from mid Pollen Zone VIIa of the Holocene. Godwin (1943) ran a line of borings from north to south across the bog as well as a line extending from east to west, linking the first sections to the beach exposures at Ynyslas foreshore – see Figure 10. These data confirmed that, over much of the area, the fossil forest and raised bog overlie the *Scrobicularia* clay. He suggested that the *Scrobicularia* clay was evidence for a marine transgression ending in mid Pollen Zone VIIa, followed by a long period of woodland and bog development that was unaffected by rising

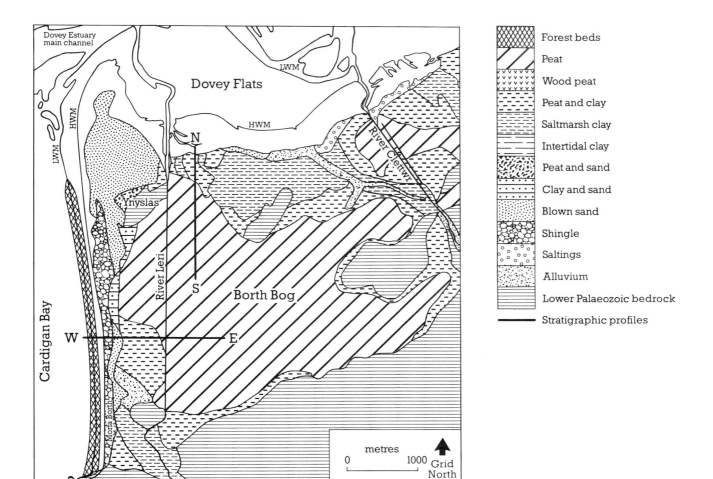

Key:
- Forest beds
- Peat
- Wood peat
- Peat and clay
- Saltmarsh clay
- Intertidal clay
- Peat and sand
- Clay and sand
- Blown sand
- Shingle
- Saltings
- Alluvium
- Lower Palaeozoic bedrock
- Stratigraphic profiles

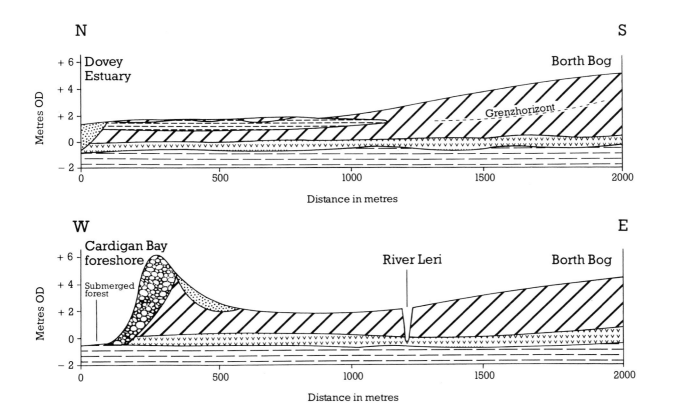

Figure 10 Quaternary deposits at Ynyslas and Borth Bog (after Godwin 1943)

sea-level. He proposed that a second marine transgression, shown by the clay within the upper part of the peat sequence along the northern margin of Borth Bog – see Figure 10, had occurred within early Pollen Zone VIII.

Godwin and Willis (1961) provided radiocarbon dates from the exposed forest bed near Ynyslas. Birch wood *in situ* near the base of the bed was dated to 6,026 ± 135 BP (Q-380), and a sample from the basal peat yielded a date of 5,898 ± 135 BP (Q-382). These dates show that an important change from marine to terrestrial conditions occurred in the area at about 6,000 BP. Subsequently, Godwin and Willis (1964) reported a date of 2,900 ± 110 BP (Q-712) from the base of the clay in the upper part of the peat sequence (bed 5) at the northern margin of the bog. Pollen evidence has shown that this later marine transgression occurred during the sub-Atlantic (Pollen Zone VIII), at the same time as the Romano-British transgression of the East Anglian Fens (Godwin 1943).

Churchill (1965) studied the relative displacement of deposits at sea-level at *c.* 6,500 BP at nine coastal sites in southern Britain, including Ynyslas. He proposed that the Ynyslas coast had been elevated by *c.* 3m since 6,500 BP by isostatic upwarping, a process which he considers has continued until the present day, except for a single interruption in the late Bronze Age, just before 2,700 BP. This, he suggested was too early to correspond to the marine event of the Romano-British transgression proposed at Borth (Godwin 1943; and subsequently Adams and Haynes 1965).

Adams and Haynes studied the foraminifera in the *Scrobicularia* clay and the later salt marsh clays around Ynyslas and Borth. The assemblages in the basal clay were shown to correspond closely with present day communities in the Dyfi Estuary, and they suggested that the assemblages showed a passage upwards from estuarine deposition through an open tidal flat, salt marsh and freshwater conditions. The *Scrobicularia* clay was believed to be the final deposit of the main Holocene transgression.

Moore (1963, 1966, 1968) studied the pollen stratigraphy of Borth Bog with particular reference to human influences in vegetation development during the Holocene. He showed that the forest peat contained a similar *Alnus-Betula-Pinus* succession to that reported by Godwin and Newton (1938) and Godwin (1943). He demonstrated that Man was a significant factor influencing the development and destruction of vegetation in the area: the times of most severe forest destruction appear to have been the Iron Age-Roman period and that between the fourteenth and eighteenth centuries (Moore 1968).

Recent studies by Wilks (1977, 1979) and Heyworth and Kidson (1982) have elaborated the sequence and the nature of the Holocene evolution of the area. Stratigraphic, microfaunal, pollen and comprehensive radiocarbon dating evidence show that, following glaciation by Late Devensian ice, a large basin in the Borth-Ynyslas-Dyfi area became progressively infilled with marine and estuarine sediments, as the Holocene sea rose. By about 6,500 BP the rate of sea-level rise had slowed, and coastline conditions stabilised, allowing the development of a sand and shingle spit which extended northwards from the cliffs near Borth (Wilks 1979). Estimates show that this spit or bar probably lay about 1 km seaward of the present shoreline. This protective barrier provided more stable and sheltered conditions on its landward side, and there vegetation began to develop. First a reed swamp grew, and, with continued sedimentation and drier conditions, vegetation successions from alder-carr to birch scrub and eventually to pine and oak forest. By about 6,000 BP, an oak and pine forest with alder, hazel and willow was well established.

Important changes in forest type and age have been noted between the southern and northern parts of the submerged forest beds, between Borth and Ynyslas (Wilks 1977, 1979; Campbell and Baxter 1979; Heyworth and Kidson 1982). First, remains of pine trees and reed swamp are prevalent in the northern part of the site, with oak more common in the south. Second, tree ring counts by Heyworth (see Wilks 1979) show the average age of large trunks in the south to range from 150-250 years, with some oaks up to 330 years. In the north, near Ynyslas, the average age of trunks was 80-120 years. Third, radiocarbon dating (76 dates) by Campbell and Baxter (1979) shows that the trees at Ynyslas died at *c.* 5,400 BP whereas those at the southern end died at *c.* 3,900 BP. These data show that the forest in the south near Borth was more mature, consisting mainly of oak trees, and longer-lived than the forest farther north near present day Ynyslas. In the north there was only sufficient time for the succession to reach the pine forest stage before tree growth was halted.

By about 4,700 BP, much of the forest growth had stopped. One exception was the northern flank of the present day Borth Bog where birch scrub developed (Wilks 1979). As peat developed in the wetter conditions over most of the area, tree stumps and fallen trunks were preserved by anaerobic conditions. Many fallen trunks show an orientation from WSW-ENE, suggesting an exposure to westerly winds (Taylor 1973).

By *c.* 4,500 BP, raised *Sphagnum* bog had developed over the site of present day Borth Bog, killing the forest as it extended southwards. Since *c.* 4,000 BP, as sea-level has continued to rise slowly, the cliffs south of Borth have been eroded gradually, maintaining the northwards development of the spit by longshore drift, and the spit has also pushed landwards to its present position. The spit has therefore migrated over the old land surface of the buried forest and peat, leaving them exposed on Ynyslas foreshore.

Ynyslas and Borth Bog provide a detailed record of coastal environmental changes in Wales during the Holocene. The sequence is especially significant in having been calibrated with a radiocarbon timescale (Godwin and Willis 1961, 1964; Campbell and Baxter 1979). Although the pattern of recorded changes is clear, the underlying causes are not yet fully understood. Stratigraphic, radiocarbon and pollen data provide convincing evidence that a coastal barrier had developed at the site by about 6,500 BP. By *c.* 6,000 BP, it is also clear that sedimentation was exceeding the rate of sea-level rise, and between *c.* 6,000-4,700 BP, a vegetation succession culminating in oak and pine forest developed on the prograding land surface behind the coastal barrier. Following this 'regressive overlap' (Shennan 1982, 1983) at about 4,700 BP, the forest was overwhelmed by *Sphagnum* peat bog as the result of a rising water table: a rising sea-level and increased rainfall, or a combination of the two may have been responsible. Any tendency towards impeded drainage and waterlogging would have been amplified by the flat surface of the *Scrobicularia* clay. Wilks (1977) suggested that the regressive overlap at Borth Bog and Ynyslas was, therefore, a consequence of local coastal geomorphological conditions.

Ynyslas and Borth Bog provide one of the most important records of Holocene coastal and environmental changes in Wales. The sequence shows evidence for a period of marine sedimentation followed by a phase in which a succession of terrestrial vegetation can be traced. The destruction of forest and the establishment of *Sphagnum* raised bog indicates wetter conditions. The causes of this are unclear, but a rise in sea-level and/or increased rainfall in the Holocene have been suggested. Whereas the sequence at nearby Clarach shows a balance between the rates of sea-level rise and terrestrial sedimentation, local coastal geomorphological conditions, in particular the development of a coastal barrier, appear to have been controlling factors at Ynyslas and Borth. The contrasting records serve to emphasise the need for a network of sites to trace former shorelines and to reconstruct past sea-levels. The Holocene pollen record from Borth Bog enhances the interest of the site, providing evidence of the influence of Man in vegetational development and destruction in west Wales.

Conclusions

Ynyslas and Borth Bog provide an important record of coastal, sea-level and environmental changes over the past 7,000 years. Part of this evidence is provided by the famous exposure of submerged forest. Such detailed records of sea-level change are important because they can be used to predict future changes.

Clarach

Highlights

This locality shows a complex record extending from the Late Devensian to the present. Its mainly organic sediments and forest beds, and the pollen and radiocarbon analyses have yielded evidence that prove reduced sea-levels in the latest Devensian and the subsequent drowning of the forests which developed around Cardigan Bay.

Introduction

Clarach is an important site with a sedimentary record extending from the start of the Late Devensian late-glacial to the present day. Pollen, diatoms and radiocarbon dates provide detailed evidence for environmental and sea-level changes (Taylor 1973; Heyworth *et al.* 1985).

Description

Clarach (SN588830) lies on the Cardigan Bay coast some 8km south of Ynyslas and Borth. The interest occurs around the mouth of the River Clarach and extends onto the modern day beach where a small area of submerged forest is occasionally exposed. The sequence and stratigraphy have been investigated by boreholes in the mainly organic sequence behind the modern beach, and by mechanically excavated sections in the submerged forest on the foreshore (Heyworth *et al.* 1985) – see Figure 11. The trench on the foreshore (Figure 11) showed a sequence of –

4	Shingle storm beach
3	Submerged forest
2	Grey clay
1	Gravel

Borings inland (Figure 11) showed a sequence of –

7	Silt and clay
6	Peats and peaty clays
5	Silt and clay
4	Limnic peat and organic mud
3	Gravel
2	Silt and clay
1	Gravel

Interpretation

The submerged forest beds at Clarach are rarely visible and are normally covered by sand and shingle. First described by Keeping in 1878, the beds were not recorded again until 1964 and 1965, following erosion of the overlying beach deposits (Taylor 1973). He described remains of *Pinus*, *Alnus*, *Corylus*, *Betula* and *Quercus* from the submerged forest which rested on a thin peat, overlying grey silty clay. He thought the clay corresponded with the *Scrobicularia* clay beneath the submerged forest at Ynyslas and Borth Bog

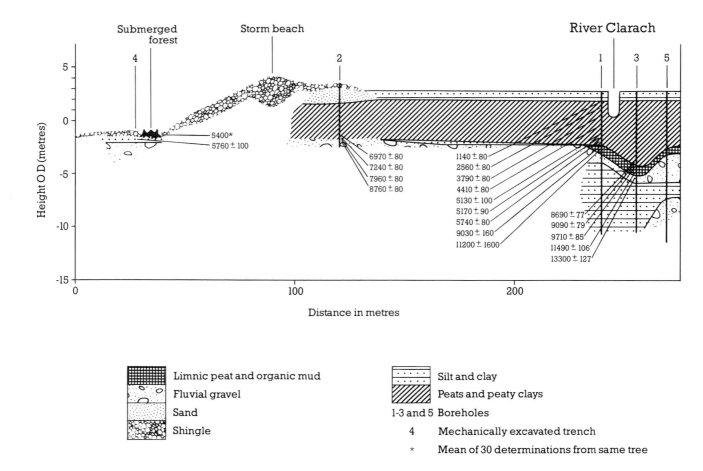

Figure 11 Quaternary sequence at Clarach (from Heyworth *et al.* 1985)

(Godwin and Newton 1938). A radiocarbon date of 5,970 ± 90 BP (NPL -113) was obtained from an *in situ* stump of *Pinus sylvestris* L., showing a close correspondence with the ages derived by Godwin and Willis (1961) from the submerged forest at Ynyslas and Borth.

Taylor investigated the pollen biostratigraphy of the deposits at Clarach in six boreholes. His preliminary study showed that a Devensian late-glacial sequence was present. The earliest evidence from these deposits suggested an environment characterised by local pine and birch woods, in an otherwise open landscape with marsh habitats. These communities were replaced by juniper at the end of late-glacial times, which was in turn replaced by extensive alder-carr with some birch at the beginning of Pollen Zone IV. The evidence indicates a rapid rise in temperature at this time along the coastal plain, leading to the early arrival of hazel *Corylus* and lime *Tilia* (Taylor 1973).

By Pollen Zone VIIa, pine had become established at Clarach and it was tolerant of the windy and salty conditions imposed by the proximity of the sea. The destruction of the forest at *c.* 6,000 BP was ultimately in response to inundation by the rising Holocene sea, influenced by strong tidal action under storm conditions and the wind funnelling effects of the lower Clarach Valley (Taylor 1973). Recently, the site has been re-investigated by

Heyworth *et al.* (1985), who drilled additional boreholes in the marshy area behind the storm ridge, and undertook pollen, diatom and radiocarbon analyses – see Figure 11. The earliest organic sediments (bed 4) were radiocarbon dated to about 13,600 BP. Pollen analysis of these deposits indicates a rapid amelioration of climate at this time, with an increase in tree and shrub pollen. However, the late-glacial and early Holocene sediments at Clarach have a pollen assemblage dominated by aquatic species, sedges and grasses, and little tree and shrub pollen is present even as late as 9,000 BP. Local pollen assemblages were reconstructed for this period, but zonation and correlation with other sites is difficult (Heyworth *et al.* 1985). The pollen diagram, however, reveals the start of a cold event (within bed 4) at about 10,900 BP, with the most severe conditions at *c.* 10,550 BP. This can probably be correlated with the climatic deterioration of the Younger Dryas, widely documented from Devensian late-glacial sites elsewhere. The end of this cold period, estimated at *c.* 10,100 BP, is not clearly marked in the pollen diagram (Heyworth *et al.* 1985). The late-glacial sequence, therefore, comprises freshwater fluviatile gravels (beds 1 and 3), silts and clays (bed 2) and organic (largely lacustrine) deposits (bed 4) which indicate that sea-level did not influence sedimentation during this period. Even by *c.* 7,000 BP, sea-level was still probably *c.* 10m below that of the present day. At the beginning of the late-glacial, sea-level was estimated to have been at least as low as 50m below present (Heyworth *et al.* 1985).

The lacustrine and peat deposits (bed 4) were deposited over a period of almost 5,000 years in the late-glacial and early Holocene. During this period, the Clarach Valley was probably occupied by lagoons or channels with current velocities too low to cause appreciable coarse sedimentation. Evidence from the submerged forest exposure on the beach suggests that freshwater silt and clay (bed 5) began to accumulate at *c.* 6,000 BP, its surface becoming rapidly colonised by *Alnus* and *Corylus*. By about 5,400 BP quite large oaks had become established. Shortly after 5,400 BP flooding occurred as sea-level rose, and stumps and trunks of trees were subsequently buried beneath alluvial deposits or by the landward-moving storm beach (Heyworth *et al.* 1985). From about 5,100 BP a succession of peats and clays (bed 6) provides evidence for a dynamic equilibrium between the rates of water table rise and sedimentation. Sea-level rise was clearly the underlying cause of water table rises and increased sedimentation (Heyworth *et al.* 1985). By 2,650 BP sedimentation was keeping pace with, or outstripping, sea-level rise, with sediment supplied by frequent flooding at times of high tide and high river discharge. This situation has persisted to the present day (Heyworth *et al.* 1985).

Pollen, diatom and radiocarbon studies have shown that the sedimentary record can be divided into two main parts: a lower late-glacial/early Holocene sequence of freshwater deposits; and a sequence of subsequent Holocene sediments in which the influences of changing sea-levels may be clearly detected. The site provides unique land-based evidence in west Wales for sea-level conditions during the late-glacial and early Holocene: sea-level, initially as low as -50m OD at *c.* 10,000 BP rose steadily to cause the demise of successive phases of vegetation as woodland developed on the coastal margins of Cardigan Bay. The most notable phase of this vegetation development appears to have occurred at *c.* 5,500 BP when substantial woodland, including pine and oak, became established approximately at ordnance datum, both at Clarach and farther north at Borth and Ynyslas. The destruction of this forest at both sites is believed to have been in response to the rising Holocene sea, although the site records show important differences. At Clarach, the succeeding marsh and alluvial sediments show a state of dynamic equilibrium between the rates of sea-level (and therefore water table) rise, and terrestrial sedimentation. In contrast, at Borth the submerged forest is succeeded by raised *Sphagnum* bog associated with wetter conditions, perhaps increased precipitation and rising sea-levels. The development of an extensive coastal barrier at Ynyslas and Borth appears to have minimised the direct effects of marine sedimentation during the period of Holocene bog formation, but at Clarach the influence of marine conditions during the same period of sedimentation is more clearly demonstrated.

Clarach is important in recording detailed information for changing sea-level and terrestrial conditions from the beginning of the Devensian late-glacial to the present day. It provides the most extended record of such conditions presently known from Wales. The sequence shows particularly detailed evidence for relative sea-levels during the Devensian late-glacial. It demonstrates successive phases of vegetation development on the margins of Cardigan Bay and the demise of pine and oak woodland at about 5,400 BP as Holocene sea-level rose. Marine influences are apparent in the remainder of the succession, which is therefore important in demonstrating that the extensive regressive overlap interpreted at Ynyslas and Borth is most probably the reflection of local coastal geomorphological changes, namely the development of a substantial coastal barrier.

Conclusions

Clarach provides detailed information on the nature and timing of changes in the relative level of land and sea over the past 13,000 years. It has the best record for this period in Wales.

Morfa-bychan

Highlights

Controversial periglacial and possible glacial sediments occur here in the finest sections of their kind in Wales. These sediments are important in interpreting the position of glacial and periglacial zones during the Late Devensian.

Introduction

The origin and age of the sediments at Morfa-bychan (SN562764) have been the subject of much debate. The site has a long history of research commencing with Keeping (1882) and Reade (1896). The sediments were interpreted by Watson and Watson (1967) and Watson (1977a, 1982) as slope deposits, accumulated under periglacial conditions during the Devensian Stage. Others, however, have suggested that at least part of the succession is glacial in origin (Wood 1959; Bowen 1974; Vincent 1976). Most workers agree that any glacial sediments do not rest *in situ*. The site is widely regarded as one of the best exposures of its kind in Wales.

Description

Pleistocene deposits exposed on the coast extend southwards from Morfa-bychan (SN565772) for over 1.5 km to beyond Ffos-Las (SN558757). The best exposures are found between Cwm-ceirw (SN563766) and Ffos-Las where, in places, the sediments reach up to 45 m in vertical section (Watson 1977a).

A Dip section

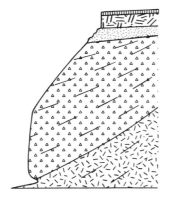

Loess-like silts
Brown head
Blue head interbedded with gravels
Blue head
Yellow head
Bedrock
▲ ▲ ▲ Large rock masses

B Strike section

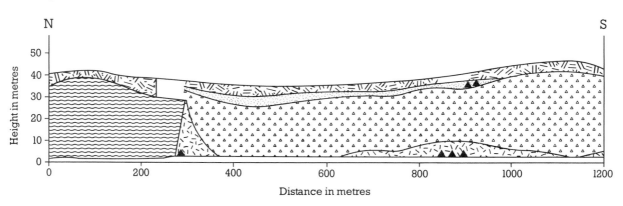

Figure 12 Pleistocene sequence at Morfa-bychan (after Watson and Watson 1967)

Watson (1977a) recognised a succession of –

5   Loess-like silts
4   Brown Head
3   Gravels
2   Blue Head
1   Yellow Head

The sequence is shown in Figure 12.

Interpretation

Early workers regarded the sequence as glacial in origin (Keeping 1882; Reade 1896; Williams 1927). Keeping noted that the sediments were composed entirely of local rock debris, and suggested that they had accumulated during a single glaciation of the area by ice coming from the Welsh uplands.

Wood (1959) reported that the drift at Morfa-bychan mantled a fossil coastline comprising a compound platform made up of a number of wave-cut benches. He described the relationship between the drift and the buried coastline, and believed that the former comprised Welsh till of Saalian age, rearranged by solifluction towards the end of the Devensian Stage.

Watson and Watson (1967) provided a detailed account of the deposits and stratigraphy. They showed that the beds dipped consistently towards the sea, and in strike section they appeared horizontal or very gently dipping – see Figure 12. Individual beds were concave, while the dip of individual beds decreased downslope, and the dips of a series of beds decreased upwards vertically, at any single point – see Figure 12. Detailed stone orientation analyses suggested that the beds, apart from the gravels and loess, had a fabric typical of solifluction deposits; in particular the azimuths of the stones' long axes were grouped tightly around the dip values of the beds (Watson and Watson 1967). Rock fragments in the drift deposits consisted entirely of the Aberystwyth Grits, greywackes and shales of Silurian age, derived from the local hinterland. Thus, in contrast to previous interpretations, they proposed that the sequence was typical of a coastal head, consisting of scree and solifluction deposits with subordinate rainwash gravels and a thin loess, all laid down under periglacial conditions during the Devensian Stage.

The periglacial origin of the entire drift sequence at Morfa-bychan has been restated in a number of papers by Watson (1968, 1970, 1976, 1977a, 1982). The periglacial origin of the Yellow Head, for example, has never been questioned, but the origin

64

of the Blue Head has been debated. Bowen (1977a) noted that many clasts in the Blue Head were striated. He concluded that the basal layers of the Blue Head, at least, might well include till, originally deposited upslope from its present position.

In an attempt to unravel the controversy concerning the origin of the deposits at Morfa-bychan, Vincent (1976) undertook an SEM study of quartz sand grain surface textures from the deposits. These surface textures indicated that the deposits could not be regarded solely as the products of periglacial slope activity (Watson and Watson 1967), and he showed that grains in the Blue Head had surface textures attributable to glacial abrasion.

The interpretation of these beds assumes considerable importance in establishing a sequence of Late Pleistocene events in west Wales. Much controversy has persisted concerning the nature, particularly, of the Blue Head. In arguing that it was periglacial in origin, although perhaps containing some material reworked from an earlier (Saalian?) glaciation, Watson and Watson envisaged that the local area would have been ice-free during the Late Devensian. They used the evidence from this site, and elsewhere in Wales, to propose an extremely restricted glaciation during the Late Devensian. Wood (1959) and Bowen (1973a, 1973b, 1974, 1977a, 1977b) argued that the Blue Head included glacial deposits of Welsh provenance redeposited downslope by solifluction. Wood, like the Watsons, considered that the periglacial conditions responsible for redeposition of the Morfa-bychan sequence had occurred during the Devensian Stage. Indeed, the Watsons suggested that the sequence at Morfa-bychan could be sub-divided to represent the whole of the Devensian Stage. In contrast, Bowen (1973a, 1973b, 1974, 1977a, 1977b) argued that the Morfa-bychan area had been glaciated by westward-moving Welsh ice during the Late Devensian. He cited Garrard and Dobson's (1974) evidence that Welsh till of a similar lithofacies, and up to 12m thick, extended offshore for some 8 km. Bowen (1977a) pointed out that the Morfa-bychan sequence was, therefore, somewhat anomalous in terms of regional stratigraphy, in that the clay-rich sediments had lent themselves to rearrangement by solifluction down the steep coastal slope, both during and after deglaciation of the Late Devensian ice-sheet. The latter view of an extensive Late Devensian glaciation in west Wales was also upheld by Peake *et al.* (1973). Bowen's view that at least part of the sequence at Morfa-bychan was formed of Late Devensian glacial deposits rearranged by periglacial processes is also supported by the work of Potts (1968, 1971) in central Wales, who showed that the majority of periglacial landforms and landscape features had probably formed during the Late Devensian and particularly during the Late Devensian late-glacial.

Morfa-bychan has an important stratigraphical record of environmental and geomorphological changes in west Wales. The interpretation of the sequence is important for understanding Late Pleistocene events and the extent of ice in west Wales. The stratigraphical detail and the extent of the exposures makes this an exceptional site for periglacial scree and solifluction deposits in Wales. The sections show clearly the importance and relationship of localised topographic and lithological controls on the accumulation of solifluction deposits.

Conclusions

Morfa-bychan has an internationally important sequence of ice age deposits. Their interpretation has proved controversial. One view is that they are glacial deposits, whereas another is that they are slope deposits which have sludged downwards from the high coastal slope at their rear. The details and internal structure of the deposits are exceptionally well exposed.

Llan-non

Highlights

This site demonstrates the complexities of glacial and periglacial events in western Mid Wales, showing Irish Sea and Welsh tills and some of the best multi-generation periglacial features in Britain. The site provides outstanding evidence for migrating ice fronts and polar desert during the Devensian Stage.

Introduction

The coastal sections at Llan-non display evidence for glacial and periglacial events and processes. The site is regarded as one of the finest exposures exhibiting periglacial involutions (festoons) and vertical stone structures in Great Britain (Watson and Watson 1971). Additional interest is provided by what some regard as a zone of interglacial weathering, the Llansantffraid Soil. The site was first noted by Williams (1927) and Mitchell (1960, 1962, 1972). The most detailed studies of the stratigraphy and periglacial structures were by Watson (1965b, 1970, 1976, 1977a, 1977b) and Watson and Watson (1971).

Description

The principal sections at Llan-non occur between the rivers Peris and Clydan, which flow west and dissect a low coastal terrace. The sections comprise a low cliff 3.5-4.5m high, almost entirely composed of alluvial gravels. Till deposits crop out to the north of the Peris and south of the Clydan, and the alluvial gravels occupy what is believed to be a fluvially excavated depression in the surface of the till. The following succession was recognised by Watson (1965b, 1976, 1977a) –

4   Fine gravels, sands and silts
3   Torrential alluvial boulder gravels
2   Irish Sea till
1   Welsh till

The sequence shows multi-generation periglacial involutions.

Interpretation

Williams (1927) noted that the drift deposits in the Llan-non area were banked up against what he interpreted as a fossil cliff of 'pre-glacial' age. Wood (1959) likewise described the relationship between the superficial deposits and the fossil cliff, and noted that the drift platform at Llan-non had resulted from the infilling of hollows on a till surface by water-washed, probably solifluction, debris.

Mitchell (1960, 1962, 1972) noted that the base of the exposures north of the Peris river (termed by him the "Llansantffraid sections") comprised a much cryoturbated stony till, which passed laterally southwards into a coarse gravel. The surface of the till and gravels was deeply weathered, frost-heaved and penetrated by vertical weathering cracks. This weathered surface was truncated and overlain by a younger series of gravels, also subsequently slightly disturbed by frost-heaving. The zone of weathering between the two gravels was termed by Mitchell the Llansantffraid Interglacial Soil, and was believed by him to have formed during the Ipswichian Stage. The underlying till was thus ascribed to the Gippingian glaciation (Saalian Stage), and the overlying gravels and subsequent phase of frost disturbance were ascribed to the Devensian. This evidence was used by Mitchell (1960, 1962, 1972) to support his concept of restricted glaciation in Wales in Late Devensian times, with much of the west Wales coast remaining ice-free.

Taylor (1973) noted that a deposit similar to the Llansantffraid Soil occurred to the south, along the coast at Aberaeron. There it contained a pollen assemblage with *Abies*, which he noted was otherwise rarely recorded in British Devensian late-glacial and Holocene pollen diagrams; he further considered that it supported Mitchell's view that the Llansantffraid bed was indeed an interglacial soil of pre-Holocene age. Other workers (Stewart 1961; Rudeforth 1970; Clayden 1977b) disputed that the bed was a soil at all, and doubted its inferred chronological significance. Stewart and Rudeforth suggested that the whole sequence could have resulted from fluctuating environmental conditions during the Devensian Stage, with the 'soil' simply representing a relict permafrost feature. Bowen (1973a, 1974) agreed, and classified it as part of the sequence of Devensian age.

From evidence in the coastal sections between Llan-non and Llansantffraid, Watson (1976, 1977a) proposed the following sequence of events. First,

till was deposited by local Welsh glaciers, and subsequently by Irish Sea ice moving southwards. Precursors of the Peris and Clydan rivers then dissected the resulting till surface, first truncating it and secondly, depositing coarse alluvial gravels in a large fan. Where undisturbed, the imbrication of the gravels shows that they were deposited by water moving from east to west. A period of intense cryoturbation under periglacial conditions led to the striking development of vertical stones and involutions in the gravels and in the upper horizons of the till. The lower limit of cryoturbation was interpreted by Watson as a fossil permafrost table, with intense freeze-thaw processes having occurred only in the active layer. A second period of erosion by the two rivers then removed part of the cryoturbated gravels and deposited beds of finer gravels, sands and silts. A renewed phase of cryoturbation, less intense than the first, produced smaller involutions in the later beds; Watson considered that this later episode could in fact be divided into two separate phases of fluvial deposition and cryoturbation. In view of the depth of weathering in the till and lower gravels, Watson (1976, 1977a), like Mitchell (1960, 1962, 1972), argued that they were probably Saalian in age, and attributed the upper alluvial gravels and frost structures to periglacial conditions in the Devensian Stage, when much of the west Wales coast was thought to have been free from glacier ice.

Although Watson provided the most detailed description and interpretation of the beds and structures at Llan-non, his classification has not been accepted by others. Bowen (1974, 1976), for example, argued that the till at Llan-non and Llansantffraid was the product of coeval Welsh and Irish Sea ice in the Late Devensian. Such a view is also supported by the work of Garrard and Dobson (1974) who showed that extensive Late Devensian glacial deposits occur offshore in Cardigan Bay. As such, Llan-non shows contrasting evidence to Morfa-bychan farther north where the deposits suggest the presence of Welsh ice only, and Traeth-y-Mwnt to the south, which clearly demonstrates the incursion of the Irish Sea ice-sheet into south-west Dyfed. Collectively, therefore, these sites demonstrate the complex interaction of the Welsh and Irish Sea ice masses along the west coast of Wales during the Late Pleistocene.

Although involutions and vertical stone structures can be seen at many sites along the Cardigan Bay coast, they are best developed between Llan-non and Llansantffraid; and they were probably formed in the active layer of former permafrost. The cryoturbated gravels and till at Llan-non provide exceptionally detailed evidence for a number of distinct periglacial phases, which have yet to be dated.

Llan-non is a rare exposure through a periglacial alluvial fan. The succession of till, alluvial gravels and associated periglacial structures has been used to reconstruct a sequence of Late Pleistocene events. The interpretation of one bed, the Llansantffraid Soil, however, has proved controversial. The multi-generation periglacial structures at the site are unparalleled in Wales, and they are amongst the finest of their kind in Britain. Glacial sediments at Llan-non are important for interpreting the complex interaction of the Irish Sea and Welsh ice masses along the west Wales coast during the Late Pleistocene.

Conclusions

The alluvial fan gravels at Llan-non are unique in Wales. They were deposited by the Peris and Clydan streams towards the end of the ice age. What makes the gravels exceptional, even by international standards, is the way in which they have been disturbed and arranged into distinctive structures by the former development of large ice lenses in the sub-soil. These have been used as examples in text-books.

Traeth-y-Mwnt

Highlights

This locality shows Irish Sea till and sand and gravels assigned to the Devensian, last, glaciation. The section is affected by enigmatic glaciotectonic folds.

Introduction

Traeth-y-Mwnt (SN194519) is an important exposure through glacial sediments which show large-scale glaciotectonic deformation structures. The sections provide important evidence for the incursion of Irish Sea ice into Ceredigion. The site featured in an early study by Williams (1927) and was described and discussed recently by Davies (1988).

Description

The sections at Traeth-y-Mwnt occupy the eastern part of the bay and extend laterally for about 100m. They reach about 15m in maximum height and comprise a sequence of –

3 Hillwash and blown sand

2 Shelly fluvioglacial sands and gravels

1 Shelly grey Irish Sea till

The principal glaciotectonic structure at Traeth-y-Mwnt is a large over-fold, about 15m across and 12m high. The feature is strongly accentuated by alternating bands of different textures and colours within the till sequence. Other parts of the till sequence also exhibit evidence of severe disturbance, in the form of near-vertical bedding. Further sedimentological interest is provided by fluvioglacial sands overlying the till, which show

well developed fault structures. The sands are in turn overlain by cryoturbated gravels.

Interpretation

Williams (1927) correlated the till at Traeth-y-Mwnt with the Lower Boulder Clay of his widely found tripartite sequence, for example, at Gwbert (SN163495). He noted the occurrence in the till of frequent Carboniferous Limestone clasts, many of which contained large radiating masses of *Lithostrotion*. Shell fragments, including *Cyprina* (*Arctica*) *islandica* L. and *Astarte* sp., were also noted, suggesting that the till had been deposited by ice moving onshore from the Irish Sea Basin. He regarded the overlying sands and gravels as fluvioglacial in origin and correlated them with the Middle Sands and Gravels of his tripartite classification. They had been deposited at the margin of a retreating ice-sheet, but no explanation was offered to account for the deformation structures in the underlying till (Williams 1927). The Irish Sea till at Traeth-y-Mwnt was also noted by Bowen (1977b).

Recently, Davies (1988) described and reinterpreted the sequence, arguing that it comprised a basal lodgement till overlain by varved glacio-lacustrine sediments, flow tills and fluvioglacial sands and gravels. The succession was believed to have accumulated during stagnation and deglaciation of the Irish Sea ice-sheet. Davies accounted for the glaciotectonic structures by a combination of subglacial deformation processes and post-depositional mass movements.

The position of Traeth-y-Mwnt in a regional Pleistocene chronology is not well established. In view of lithostratigraphical evidence elsewhere along the coast, it is likely that the glacial sediments at Traeth-y-Mwnt were deposited by southward moving Irish Sea ice (John 1968b; Bowen 1977b). In view of amino acid geochronological studies at nearby Banc-y-Warren and Abermawr (Bowen 1984), the deposits at Traeth-y-Mwnt are probably Late Devensian in age. It is interesting to note the similarity of the faulting structures in the sands at Traeth-y-Mwnt to those described at Banc-y-Warren (for example, Helm and Roberts 1975; Allen 1982; Worsley 1984), although they need not have formed in the same way(s).

The principal interest of the site lies in large deformation structures in the till. Although the scale of deformation is probably unparalleled elsewhere in Wales, no comprehensive and satisfactory explanation has yet been offered. The absence of an overlying till might imply that deformation was not caused by a readvance of ice, as has been proposed at, for example, Dinas Dinlle (Whittow and Ball 1970) – see Chapter 7. The till at Traeth-y-Mwnt occupies a deep and narrow coastal inlet which lies perpendicular to the inferred direction of ice movement. Although speculative, it is possible that deformation occurred as basal till was forced downwards into the tightly confined embayment.

Traeth-y-Mwnt provides an important section through Irish Sea glacial sediments which are probably the product of Late Devensian Irish Sea ice that moved generally south across the area. Traeth-y-Mwnt is, therefore, important for demonstrating the incursion of Irish Sea ice into Ceredigion and, with other reference sites, helps to show the complex interactions of Welsh and Irish Sea ice along the coast of west Wales. The site is also important for a series of spectacular large-scale glaciotectonic deformation structures. The precise environmental conditions for the sequence and structures, however, remain to be established.

Conclusions

The exposures at Traeth-y-Mwnt display large-scale deformation structures in glacial deposits. Although these structures have been interpreted as having formed on land, another view is that they developed through the process of submarine slumping in a cold climate sea, adjacent to marine-based glaciers.

Banc-y-Warren

Highlights

Complex fluvioglacial sediments here have afforded evidence of sedimentation during ice wastage at the end of the Devensian. A complex pattern of stream, lake and delta deposition, and collapse above melting entrapped ice has emerged.

Introduction

Banc-y-Warren (SN204475) is an important site in south-west Wales that has attracted interest for over sixty years. The site is geomorphologically striking, consisting of a group of steep-sided conical hills made up of sands and gravels that rise some 50m above the northern flank of the lower Teifi Valley. Banc-y-Warren is the most prominent of these hills. Both the origin and dating of the deposits have proved controversial. The Pleistocene deposits were first studied by Jehu (1904), and the sediments and their included fauna were described in some detail by Williams (1927). The site was mentioned by Charlesworth (1929), Wirtz (1953), Mitchell (1960, 1962, 1972), Synge (1963) and Jones (1965), and, in the late 1960s, much interest was stimulated by radiocarbon dates from the sediments (John 1967, 1968c, 1970a; Brown *et al.* 1967; Shotton 1967; Boulton 1968; John and Ellis-Gruffydd 1970). More recently, the site has been referred to by John (1969, 1973), Unwin (1969), Bowen (1971b, 1973a, 1974, 1977b) and Bowen and Lear (1982). Detailed accounts of the stratigraphy and sedimentology of the site were provided by Helm and Roberts (1975) and Allen (1982), and the available dating and sedimentological evidence from the site was reviewed by Worsley (1984). Amino acid ratios have been given by Bowen (1984).

Description

Glacigenic sands and gravels can be examined in pits at Cnwc-y-Seison and Cil-maenllwyd, and these constitute the Banc-y-Warren exposures referred to by early workers. The sediments form a continuous sheet that extends from Alma Grange (SN210460) through Banc-y-Warren to Aberporth (Helm and Roberts 1975). In detail, the succession varies laterally but may be generalised as one of fine current-bedded sands overlain by coarser sands and gravels exhibiting cross-bedding and slump structures. These in turn are overlain by very coarse, poorly stratified gravels. The gravels contain erratics from both Welsh and Irish Sea sources including Cambrian sandstones, Old Red Sandstone, flint, Chalk and a variety of igneous rock types. The finer grained, yellow sands yield whole marine shells and shell fragments, scattered nodules and layers of organic debris (Unwin 1969), and pollen and wood fragments (John 1969). The sediments exhibit complex patterns of small-scale faulting and the whole sand and gravel sequence is thought to overlie till (Williams 1927; Jones 1965). Fossil ice-wedge casts up to 1m deep were noted in the sands at Banc-y-Warren by John (1973). Williams (1927) mapped the extent of the sands and gravels. He also provided a general account of the sedimentology, noting the presence of cross-stratification, the water-worn appearance of the gravel clasts which included a mixture of Irish Sea and Welsh rock types, faunal details of the comminuted shallow marine molluscs and the presence of numerous small faults.

Interpretation

Although the deposits at Banc-y-Warren were mentioned by Jehu (1904), Williams (1927) made the first thorough description and interpretation of the succession as part of his synthesis of Pleistocene stratigraphy in western Cardiganshire. He classified the beds as part of the Intermediate Sands and Gravels division of his tripartite sequence. He concluded that the beds were deposited as fluvioglacial outwash from the margin of the Irish Sea ice-sheet, and interpreted the mounds as kames. The faults were believed to have been caused by the melting of buried ice masses (Williams 1927).

Shortly after, Charlesworth (1929) in his classic paper *The South Wales end-moraine*, briefly referred to the deposits at Banc-y-Warren. These he interpreted, largely on the basis of their external form, as end-moraines of the 'Newer Drift' ice-sheet, and constructed his 'Newer Drift' limit around them accordingly. Wirtz (1953) noted the fresh appearance of the beds at Banc-y-Warren, and also interpreted them as marking part of the 'Newer Drift' ice limit, although he envisaged that only a small tongue of the Irish Sea ice had impinged upon north Preseli and south Ceredigion in the area of the lower Teifi Valley.

The deposits at Banc-y-Warren were also noted by Mitchell (1960, 1962, 1972) who, unlike Charlesworth (1929), regarded the deposits as fluvioglacial outwash from a retreating Irish Sea ice-sheet of Gipping age.

Jones (1965) considered that the deposits had been laid down in a lake. He noted that the deposits were flat-topped, that they ended in steep south-west facing slopes and that the sequence coarsened upwards from fine sands to gravels. He interpreted the deposits as having been formed in a delta built into a deep proglacial Lake Teifi which, at that time, stood at the level of the postulated Llantood (Llantwyd) overflow. In the discussion following Jones' paper, however, Bowen argued that the supposed overflow channels were in fact subglacial in origin.

Banc-y-Warren attracted much attention in the late 1960s when radiocarbon determinations were attempted. Three radiocarbon assays were undertaken on organic material from the sands: and these gave dates of 31,800 +1,400 -1,200 BP (I-2559) (Brown *et al.* 1967); 33,750 +2,500, -1,900 BP (I-2564) (John 1967); and > 39,900 BP (I-2802) (John and Ellis-Gruffydd 1970). The radiocarbon determinations were used to support John's (1965b) and Bowen's (1966) earlier concept of an extensive Devensian glaciation in the Irish Sea Basin and Preseli. John (1967) suggested that pollen and radiocarbon evidence from Banc-y-Warren indicated a period of forest growth probably during a Middle Devensian interstadial, and that these organic remains had been incorporated into the kamiform deposits by fluvioglacial processes during the Late Devensian. However, he noted the occurrence of reworked Carboniferous and Mesozoic spores in the pollen assemblage, together with pieces of Tertiary lignite, acknowledging that the remains had most likely been reworked from a variety of older deposits. Indeed, strong reactions to the validity of the radiocarbon dates were forthcoming (Shotton 1967; Boulton 1968), but whereas certain difficulties in interpreting the organic remains and dates were acknowledged, the original interpretation was maintained by John (1968c, 1969, 1970a) and John and Ellis-Gruffydd (1970).

Subsequent reviews (for example, Unwin 1969; Bowen 1971b, 1973a, 1974, 1977b; Bowen and Lear 1982) have noted the equivocal nature of the faunal and radiocarbon dated evidence from the site. A Late Devensian age for the deposits, however, was still favoured by Bowen and Bowen and Lear on stratigraphical grounds. Recent amino acid ratios from fossil marine molluscs at Banc-y-Warren are consistent with the succession being of Late Devensian age (Bowen 1984), and show that the derived shell content of the deposits ranges in age from Early Pleistocene to Devensian; a discovery which invalidates all previous radiocarbon dates on bulk shell samples.

Helm and Roberts' (1975) detailed sedimentological account of the exposures interpreted the deposits as a complex of three large lake deltas formed in variable but substantial water depths, with thick cross-bedded gravels representing the foresets, and the sands the bottomset beds. Gravel channel fillings amongst the sand bottomsets were considered to have been cut and filled by turbidity currents which originated as slumps from the foresets. They discounted Williams' (1927) suggestion that faulting in the sequence had occurred from the melting of included ice masses, and, instead, they interpreted the faults as having been formed as a result of slope instability. Concurring with Jones (1965), Helm and Roberts associated one of their deltas with the Llantood (Llantwyd) overflow channel.

In a sedimentological study, Allen (1982) concluded from the lenticular gravels and the fault system at Banc-y-Warren that the deposits had accumulated as a fluvioglacial outwash spread on top of a downwasting ice-lobe in the Teifi Valley. He accepted the possible deltaic nature of the large gravel foresets but considered that they had probably been deposited in a restricted waterbody unrelated to a 'proglacial Lake Teifi'. He believed that extensive faulting of the sediments had occurred due to the downwasting of a single extensive prismatic wedge of ice beneath the entire sedimentary suite. Perhaps the most conclusive evidence in favour of a subaerial outwash origin for the sediments was the unlithified sand clasts described in some detail by Allen. Worsley (1984) considered that despite the enigmatic nature of much of the sedimentological data, it was difficult to resist the conclusion that these 'clasts' must have been frozen immediately prior to deposition, and that this evidence, in conjunction with the highly irregular form of the channel margins, suggested at least seasonal freezing of the aggrading sedimentary surface. He concluded that such a mechanism could not be reconciled with a deep water environment (Jones 1965; Helm and Roberts 1975).

A deltaic origin for part of the sequence at Banc-y-Warren seems possible, but the surviving evidence tends to support an origin as subaerial outwash for the bulk of the sequence. The site is also important for the developing Late Pleistocene chronology of south-west Wales, and is one of only very few sites where both radiocarbon and amino acid time-scales are available. Although the radiocarbon dates are misleading, amino acid ratios from the site provide strong evidence to suggest a Late Devensian age for the sequence. Banc-y-Warren forms part of an integral network of stratigraphic sites in south-west Wales that reveal major environmental variations during the Late Pleistocene. Although sequences associated with Late Pleistocene interglacial conditions (for instance, Poppit Sands, West Angle Bay, Porth Clais, Marros Sands), glacial conditions (for instance, Abermawr, Traeth-y-Mwnt, Druidston Haven) and periglacial conditions (for instance, Porth Clais, Marros Sands) are better developed elsewhere in south-west Wales, Banc-y-Warren is arguably the most important reference site for fluvioglacial processes and events in the region. The combination of excellent stratigraphic detail and the morphology of landforms, makes Banc-y-Warren of outstanding geomorphological interest. It is one of very few sites in Wales where detailed sedimentological techniques have been applied to interpret Pleistocene sequences. During the protracted history of investigations at the site, a number of radically different models of sedimentation has been proposed. The most recent evidence indicates that the majority of the succession was deposited as subaerial outwash with a subordinate proportion of the sequence originating as delta front sediments deposited in small, ephemeral water bodies. The site also provides important evidence for the dating of Late Pleistocene events in south-west Wales, particularly for establishing that the last glaciation of northern Preseli and southern Ceredigion occurred in the Late Devensian.

Conclusions

Banc-y-Warren is an outstanding site that has been subjected to the most detailed sedimentological investigations. It is generally agreed that there are elements in the internal composition of its landforms which suggest that some of the deposits were laid down in a lake during the last ice age, about 18,000 years ago.

Poppit Sands

Highlights

Poppit affords evidence of high sea-levels probably during the last, Ipswichian Stage, interglacial, followed by periglacial then glacial conditions. During the latter, Irish Sea ice deposited till in northern Preseli.

Introduction

Poppit Sands (Poppit) (SN146489) shows a sequence of deposits which provides evidence for marine, periglacial and glacial episodes in south-west Wales during the Late Pleistocene. The site is particularly important for a well developed shore platform overlain by raised beach sediments. The site was first noted by Jones (1965) and has been described by John (1968a, 1970a, 1971a), Bowen (1971b, 1973a, 1973b, 1974, 1977a, 1977b) and by Peake *et al.* (1973). The most detailed description and interpretation is provided by John (1970a, 1971a), Bowen (1977a, 1977b) and Bowen and Lear (1982).

Description

A raised shore platform overlain by raised beach sediments was first recorded at Poppit by Jones (1965). The succession was more fully described by John (1970a) as –

4	Irish Sea till (2.0m)
3	Blocky head (6.0m)
2	Raised beach sediments (1.7m)
1	Rock platform

The shore platform lies between 1.7 and 3m above high water mark; and can be traced along the coast between Cei-bach and Trwyn Careg-ddu for 1 km (John 1970a). The raised platform consists of a planed surface on tightly folded Lower Palaeozoic shale and sandstone beds, quite unlike the present shore platform which is being differentially eroded (Bowen 1977a, 1977b; Bowen and Lear 1982). The overlying raised beach deposits are characterised by a great deal of lateral variation in the size of pebbles and the nature of the matrix. In places, the beach deposits consist largely of shingle and small pebbles cemented with iron oxide and manganese oxide. Elsewhere it is made up entirely of boulders over 0.7m in diameter. It contains no shells (Bowen and Lear 1982). At the eastern end of the sections, the raised beach sediments are associated with up to 2m of stratified sand and silt (John 1970a; 1971a). Elsewhere, they are overlain directly by a blocky head, up to 6m thick, derived from the high local backslope which reaches 183m OD. The head is succeeded by up to 2.0m of Irish Sea till, although this is largely concealed by vegetation on the degraded surface of the drift terrace (Bowen 1977a). John (1970a) described the blocky head at Poppit as the lower head, the upper head being absent, although it occurred on the other side of the Teifi at Gwbert (Jones 1965; John 1970a). (The latter section no longer survives.)

Interpretation

From evidence at Poppit and elsewhere in the local area, John (1968a, 1970a, 1971a) proposed the following sequence of events. The rock platform was fashioned during an interglacial period when sea-level approached 15m (50 ft) OD. The raised beach sediments were believed to have been deposited during the Ipswichian Stage, when sea-level may have reached as high as 9m (30 ft) OD. John (1970a, 1971a) considered that the site fully deserved the status of type locality for the raised beaches of west Wales, and he accordingly named the period of their formation the Poppit Interglacial. The overlying head indicated a period of periglacial conditions in the succeeding Devensian Stage. He concluded that the head could be sub-divided into various facies; these reflecting a prolonged period of periglacial climate that was characterised by a number of distinct climatic fluctuations. The periglacial phase at Poppit was followed by deposition of till by ice moving southward from the Irish Sea Basin in the Late Devensian (locally named Dewisland) glaciation. The Irish Sea till at Poppit has not been studied in detail. John (1970a), however, believed that an equivalent till bed occurred at Gwbert on the opposite side of the Teifi Estuary. From the Gwbert till, MacDonald (1961) and Jones (1965) had recorded a wide range of erratics including granite from Ireland, Eskdale granite from the Lake District and a series of rock types from Llŷn and Meirionedd, confirming that it was ice from the Irish Sea Basin which had invaded the area around Gwbert and Poppit.

Such an interpretation was broadly followed by Bowen (1971b, 1973a, 1973b, 1974, 1977a, 1977b), who also regarded the Poppit raised beach sediments as being Ipswichian in age, with the overlying periglacial and glacial sediments attributable to the Devensian Stage.

Although the sequence at Poppit has not been dated, Bowen and Lear (1982) described a laminated clay, some 0.5m thick, interbedded with angular boulders and rounded cobbles from the raised beach near Trwyn Careg-ddu (SN148489). This clay contained a foraminiferal assemblage including *Elphidium crispum*, a species not present in the modern fauna of the bay. Since *E. crispum* had been shown to occur in sand and gravel sandwiched between till beds in the central part of Cardigan Bay, Bowen and Lear suggested that it was therefore of some use in correlating the upper till of Cardigan Bay, of believed Late Devensian age, with the till at Poppit.

Although Poppit is of interest primarily for its well developed shore platform and overlying raised beach deposits, the remainder of the succession also provides important information on changing environmental conditions in south-west Wales during the Late Pleistocene. The sequence shows that a period of high relative sea-level, probably during the Ipswichian Stage, was followed by a prolonged phase of periglacial climate when thick head deposits were formed. This was followed by fully glacial conditions when ice moved into northern Preseli from the Irish Sea Basin. Although Irish Sea till deposits are better exposed at Traeth-y-Mwnt and Abermawr, Poppit is a key reference site for raised beach deposits and, unlike the former sites, demonstrates the interaction of marine and terrestrial conditions in south-west Wales.

The shore platform and raised beach sediments at Poppit are amongst the finest features of their kind in Wales. The sections are particularly important in integrating both marine and terrestrial evidence in a single exposure. The sequence shows that high sea-levels, probably during the Ipswichian Stage, were followed by periglacial conditions when head accumulated. The succeeding till clearly demonstrates the onset of fully glacial conditions and provides important evidence for the movement of the Irish Sea ice-sheet into northern Preseli.

Conclusions

The raised shore platform and pre-last ice age (interglacial) raised beach deposits at Poppit are text-book examples of their kind. The raised beach was probably formed about 125,000 years ago. The sequence exposed here also shows the history of the last ice age.

Abermawr

Highlights

This site shows unrivalled evidence of two periglacial episodes and an intervening glacial event; all assigned to the Devensian Stage. These sediments lie within what may be a pre-Devensian meltwater channel.

Introduction

Abermawr (SM883346) shows one of the most detailed sequences of surface deposits in south-west Wales, and provides important information for changing environmental conditions in the region during the Late Pleistocene. The site has a long history of research commencing with the work of Jehu (1904). It has featured in studies by Synge (1963, 1969, 1970), John (1967, 1970a, 1971a, 1973), John and Ellis-Gruffydd (1970), Bowen (1971b, 1973a, 1973b, 1974, 1977a, 1977b, 1982, 1984) and Peake *et al.* (1973). Detailed descriptions were provided by John (1970a) and Bowen (1977a, 1977b, 1982, 1984).

Description

Exposures of Pleistocene sediments extend for about 300m at the northern end of Abermawr Bay. The following sequence can be given from the descriptions by John (1970a) and Bowen (1977a, 1977b, 1984) (maximum bed thickness in parenthesis) –

9   Sandy loam (0.6m)
8   Upper head – Jehu's (1904) 'rubble drift' (2m)
7   Fluvioglacial sands and gravels (4.5m)
6   Irish Sea till – Abermawr Till (2.4m)
5   Upper blocky head with scattered erratics (3.6m)
4   Water-worn gravels (3.6m)
3   Lower blocky head with scattered erratics (1.5m)
2   Green-grey clay – weathering horizon
1   Shale head (1-3m)

Raised beach sediments have not been recorded from Abermawr, but because the base of the succession has not been proved these may lie concealed beneath the modern shingle beach (Bowen 1971b, 1977a, 1977b). A further small section mainly through periglacial head, with intraformational fossil ice-wedge casts, is recorded at the southern end of the bay (John 1973).

Interpretation

The sections were first described by Jehu (1904), who considered that Abermawr was one of the best drift sections in north Pembrokeshire and regarded it as especially important for the fine development of the Upper Boulder Clay (bed 8) of his tripartite classification. Although this unit was taken to be primarily glacial in origin, Jehu noted that the deposit showed traces of bedding and contained many angular and subangular rocks derived from the local area. He concluded that the Upper Boulder Clay or 'rubble drift' might, therefore, represent a glacial deposit modified by subaerial agencies, rearranged and partially sorted by meltwater.

Jehu's Lower Boulder Clay is also present at Abermawr (bed 6), and he recognised a variety of rock types in the modern beach probably derived from it. These included Ailsa Craig microgranite, granite from Kirkcudbrightshire, and a variety of other igneous rocks from southern Scotland and the Lake District. Such an assemblage, together with marine shell fragments found in the till, provided strong evidence for the incursion of ice from the Irish Sea Basin into north Pembrokeshire (Jehu 1904).

Synge (1963, 1969 1970) also recognised the upper till at Abermawr, and further noted that the lower head deposits (bed 3) contained reworked glacial erratics. From this evidence, Synge postulated that the area had been glaciated on three separate occasions: he considered the redistributed glacial material in the lower head facies to be of Elster age, with the shelly Irish Sea till, and the more stony upper till being Saalian and Weichselian, respectively.

In contrast, other workers (for example, John 1970a; Bowen 1971b, 1974, 1977a, 1984) placed the entire sequence in the Devensian Stage, recognising only a single till (bed 6); the upper till of Jehu and Synge, being regarded as a head deposit, a mixture of local slope deposits and reworked glacial material (bed 8). John (1970a, 1971a) considered that the only true glacial deposits at Abermawr were therefore the Irish Sea till and its associated outwash (beds 6 and 7). These were underlain by a thick sequence of periglacial slope deposits (John 1973) and overlain by a thinner head which he suggested demonstrated that the Irish Sea glaciation had been preceded by a prolonged periglacial phase and succeeded by a shorter one. He noted a weathering horizon in the lower head, and suggested that it represented an amelioration of climatic conditions, possibly during an interstadial in the Devensian Stage. Complex bedding structures in the outwash sands and gravels showed they had been deposited in a dead-ice (stagnating) environment. The lower head and Irish Sea till were considered equivalent to corresponding horizons at Poppit (John 1970a).

John (1967, 1970a) and John and Ellis-Gruffydd (1970) noted abundant fragments of marine mollusca and pieces of carbonised wood in the till at Abermawr. Although *Pinus* was found, other fragments examined at Kew Gardens came from coniferous species not currently growing in North-West Europe. Radiocarbon dates from samples of the wood of >40,300 BP (NPL-98) and >54,300 BP

(GrN-5281) (John and Ellis-Gruffydd 1970) plus the presence in the samples of reworked pre-Pleistocene pollen and spores suggested that the wood was possibly Tertiary in age. The radiocarbon dates were therefore not taken to be significant for the development of a Late Pleistocene chronology at Abermawr (John and Ellis-Gruffydd 1970), but a Late Devensian age for the till was favoured on the basis of a radiocarbon timescale developed at other sites in Pembrokeshire (John 1965b, 1967, 1968c, 1970a; John and Ellis-Gruffydd 1970). It was, however, admitted that the Abermawr Till (bed 6) and associated fluvioglacial sediments (bed 7) could represent a pre-Devensian glaciation in north Pembrokeshire, as postulated by Wirtz (1953).

Bowen (1974) supported the single glaciation hypothesis for the Abermawr sequence (John 1970a). Both Bowen (1971b, 1974) and John, however, noted that erratic pebbles found in the lower head (bed 3) had been derived from a glaciation that pre-dated the Devensian Stage. Like John, Bowen considered that beds 1-5 were periglacial slope deposits, and suggested that although the significance of the gravels (bed 4) was unclear, they might have been deposited by fluvial action under conditions of climatic amelioration (Bowen 1977a, 1977b, 1982). Bowen also noted a weathering horizon (unit 2) in the lower head deposits. This was considered to be a seepage weathering horizon in which the shale had locally decomposed to a green-grey clay. The environmental and chronological significance of this horizon, however, was not discussed, although beds 1-5 were considered to have been deposited during periglacial conditions in Early and Middle Devensian times (Bowen 1973a).

In addition to the mixed assemblage of cold and warm molluscs recorded by John (1970a) from the Abermawr Till, Bowen (1982) further noted that it also contained a cold fauna of foraminifera, including *Elphidiella arctica* Parker & Jones. Amino acid epimerization studies of marine molluscs from Abermawr (Bowen 1984) showed that the derived shells in the till ranged in age from Early Pleistocene to Devensian. The youngest faunal elements present in the Abermawr Till, therefore, indicated that the shells had been derived from sediments deposited during a marine transgression in the Devensian, and transported to Abermawr by the Late Devensian ice-sheet.

The sands and gravels (bed 7) overlying the shelly till were regarded by Bowen (1971b, 1982) as the products of deglaciation of the Late Devensian ice-sheet, while the upper head was a periglacial scree deposit, representing cold conditions after melting of the ice (Bowen 1982).

The location of the Pleistocene deposits at Abermawr significantly enhances the geomorphological interest of the site: "..... the thick lower head shows every indication of being banked against the steep wall of a meltwater channel, and the rest of the drift fill similarly marks the channel wall for some hundreds of metres inland" (John 1970a). This evidence may therefore indicate that the channel, and perhaps others in the remarkable Gwaun-Jordanston system of channels, were probably first cut in pre-Devensian times. Bowen (1971b), however, regarded the 'channel' as a pre-diversion valley of the Western Cleddau. The sequence of deposits at Abermawr provides a key stratigraphic record of environmental and geomorphological changes in northern Preseli during the Late Pleistocene. It may occupy a meltwater channel possibly cut in pre-Devensian times, and provides evidence for the incursion of an ice-sheet from the Irish Sea Basin into northern Preseli. The sequence further demonstrates that periglacial conditions were prevalent both before and after the Irish Sea glaciation of the area. The sands and gravels are thought to represent outwash from the melting of the Irish Sea ice-sheet. Amino acid dating of the included fauna within the Irish Sea till provides evidence to suggest that the Irish Sea glaciation of northern Preseli occurred during the Late Devensian, and the site therefore helps to place constraints on the extent of the Late Devensian ice-sheet in south-west Wales. Raised beach sediments (such as those at Poppit Sands) are not exposed at Abermawr, but the glacial and periglacial sediments are better exposed than elsewhere in south-west Wales.

Abermawr has one of the most detailed stratigraphical sequences in south-west Wales. The Abermawr Till clearly demonstrates that northern Preseli was glaciated by Irish Sea ice, and amino acid ratios from the till provide convincing evidence that the glacial event was Late Devensian in age. The sequence also records important evidence for melting of the Late Devensian Irish Sea ice, and shows that periglacial conditions affected the area both before and after the glacial episode. The location of the sequence in a possible meltwater channel could have geomorphological and chronological implications for the interpretation and relative dating of similar landform features elsewhere in the region.

Conclusions

Abermawr provides one of the most detailed sequences of ice age deposits in south-west Wales. The sequence spans most of the last glacial cycle and shows evidence for an earlier period when scree accumulated under cold climatic conditions. Shell bearing clay deposits at Abermawr have been traditionally interpreted as the products of a land-based ice-sheet. It has recently been suggested that they are marine sediments, deposited in the ocean as the ice-sheets retreated towards the north.

Porth Clais

Highlights

A key site showing evidence in the St David's Head

area of a pre-Devensian glaciation, of high sea-levels with raised beach deposits during the Ipswichian, and glaciation and periglacial environments during the Devensian. Atypical till deposited during the Devensian by Irish Sea ice helps to define ice limits at that time.

Introduction

Porth Clais (SM741237) provides one of the most complete exposures of Late Pleistocene sediments in Preseli and has long been regarded as a classic locality for interpreting Late Pleistocene events in south-west Wales. The sequence provides evidence for a succession of marine, periglacial and glacial depositional episodes. Considerable controversy, however, has arisen concerning the interpretation of the sequence. Some regard part of the sequence as till, a 'land-facies' of the Irish Sea ice-sheet, while others maintain that the sediments have undergone substantial periglacial disturbance and are not in place. The site attracted much interest with early studies by Prestwich (1892), Hicks (1894) and Leach (1911). It has been discussed more recently by Zeuner (1959), Mitchell (1962), Synge (1963), Bowen (1966, 1973a, 1974, 1977b, 1984) and John (1965a, 1965b, 1968a, 1969, 1970a, 1970b, 1971a, 1973). The most detailed accounts were provided by Leach (1911) and John (1970b).

Description

The site is located close to a small cave, Ogof Golchfa (SM742237), about 90m west of Porth Clais harbour, and is sometimes referred to as Ogof Golchfa (John 1970b). The sections occur on a small headland which supports several raised shore platform remnants which vary in height from c. 3m to 9m OD (John 1970b). The exposures crop out around the margins of a small, 45m wide, vegetated terrace that slopes seawards at about 2°. John (1970b) noted the following sequence of deposits lying above the raised platform –

5	Sandy loam (0.75m)	
4	Upper head (0.6m)	
3	Non-calcareous local till (c. 2m)	
2	Lower head and beach pebbles (c. 2m)	
1	Raised beach shingle with erratics (c. 1m)	

The marine platform is cut across a fine-grained dolerite sill, intruded in near vertical Lower Cambrian shales and sandstones (Cox et al. 1930). Parts of the sill form slight ridges across the platform, and, in places, striae-bearing ice-smoothed surfaces have been preserved. Most of the striae trend north-west to south-east (John 1970b).

Both Leach (1911) and John (1970b) noted the presence of large, well-worn boulders on the rock platform, sometimes embedded within the raised beach shingle. Most of the boulders are not far-travelled although one large erratic boulder of 'diabase' (microgabbro) projects from the drift cliff

(Leach 1911). The platform bears few traces of the raised beach shingle, which is best developed above the entrance to Ogof Golchfa. The pebbles there are well rounded and comprise a mixture of local Cambrian rock types as well as Chalk flints, and igneous rocks from the St David's Head area. Leach noted that, in places, the shingle was cemented to the platform. The beach deposits grade up into a stratified head comprising a mixture of raised beach shingle set in a red-brown sandy matrix. Leach described the raised beach deposits as *c.* 3m thick, but John observed that this figure should include 2m of what he considered to be soliflucted beach material.

John (1970b) noted that the lower head was overlain by up to 2m of red-brown non-calcareous till, which, in places, lay directly on the striated shore platform. It contained a mixture of local rocks as well as farther-travelled igneous types.

Leach (1911) did not recognise an upper head overlying the till, unlike subsequent workers (for example, Mitchell 1962; Synge 1963; Bowen 1966; John 1970b). It is distinctly coloured as a result of a high concentration of purple Cambrian sandstone and shale fragments (John 1970b). To the west it is replaced by a 'rubble drift' of mixed local bedrock fragments and soliflucted till. It is succeeded by a thin veneer of sandy loam, often stoneless and silty, but also containing bands of flaky bedrock fragments and pebbles derived from the till.

Interpretation

Prestwich (1892) noted that the raised beach contained both local Cambrian rocks and more far-travelled igneous rocks and Chalk flints, but offered no explanation for the mixture. Hicks (1894) described large boulders of picrite and granite found on the cliff tops near Porth Clais and concluded that the area had been glaciated by ice from a northern source. From local evidence, such as striae and crag and tail features, he suggested that the northern ice had crossed the Porth Clais area from north-west to south-east.

The interpretation of the sequence was further elaborated by Leach (1911) who was the first to describe till at the site. He noted that the till overlay both the head and raised beach, and, in places, lay on the striated rock platform directly. He concluded that "Since this deposit rests in part on a striated surface and contains striated stones and erratic boulders, its glacial origin is clear". The Porth Clais section was thus comparable with sections in Gower, and because the raised beach at these sites always occurred beneath the glacial sediments, a 'pre-glacial' age for the bed was favoured by Leach. The large erratics associated with the rock platform were considered by him to have been deposited by floating ice both before and during accumulation of the raised beach shingle, he concluded that the shingle must have been deposited during a period of cold climate.

From the evidence at Porth Clais, Mitchell (1962)

and Synge (1963) developed a Late Pleistocene chronology of events for south-west Wales, based on stratigraphical analogies with sites on both sides of the Irish Sea Basin. Erratics found in the Porth Clais raised beach were considered to have been derived from deposits, now destroyed, of Lowestoft (Anglian) age, while the beach itself was considered to have accumulated during the Hoxnian Stage. The lower head and till were ascribed to the Saalian Stage. Both authors envisaged that the Porth Clais area had not been affected directly by Weichselian (Devensian) ice. Subsequently, however, it has been more simply suggested that the Porth Clais area was glaciated by Devensian ice, and that the raised beach deposits are of Ipswichian age (Bowen 1973a, 1974, 1977b, 1984; John 1965a, 1965b, 1968a, 1970a, 1970b). Despite such broad agreement, major differences have arisen in interpreting the evidence at Porth Clais.

According to John (1970b), the raised shore platform was fashioned during temperate interglacial conditions. Its age was uncertain, although it was probably Hoxnian or older, and possibly of composite age. Erratics found in the raised beach were considered to represent an early glaciation, of probable Saalian age. John disagreed with Leach's suggestion that large erratic boulders could have been ice-rafted during formation of the raised beach, particularly in view of the widely accepted correlation between Late Pleistocene glacial stages and low stands of the sea. He accepted that the boulders were both rounded and foreign but considered, in view of the slumped face of the exposure, that they could have fallen from the till. He placed the raised beach deposits in the Ipswichian Stage, and the overlying lower head (including soliflucted elements of the raised beach) at the beginning of the Devensian Stage, believing it to mark the onset of cold, periglacial conditions. The overlying non-calcareous till was considered to have been deposited as a 'land-facies' of the north-west to south-east moving Irish Sea ice-sheet. Fabric data from the till, although equivocal, suggested that the till had not been deposited beneath a powerful ice stream but in an ice wastage environment as flow or ablation till. The till has not been dated, but radiocarbon dates from fluvioglacial sediments at Mullock Bridge, south of Porth Clais, indicated that the Porth Clais till was of probable Late Devensian age (John 1965b). It was therefore comparable to equivalent horizons at Druidston Haven, Abermawr and Poppit Sands. Further, the upper head was attributed to a short periglacial phase towards the end of the Late Devensian, and the upper sandy loam was considered to represent a mixture of aeolian and colluvial (hillwash) sediments, formed possibly during an ensuing cold-temperate, arid phase.

Bowen (1977b) suggested that glacial sediments at the site were neither *in situ* nor representative of a 'land-facies' of the Irish Sea glacier (John 1970b), and he argued that the distance of glacial transport across the St David's Head area was too small for the Irish Sea till to have lost its usual characteristics.

He suggested that the considerable coastal slopes around Porth Clais had promoted redeposition of the glacial sediments, and he contrasted the site with Druidston Haven to the south, where the glacial sediments had been extensively preserved at the base of a steep-sided coastal valley. Porth Clais had therefore been glaciated by Late Devensian ice, but local site factors had led to substantial re-sorting of the sediments.

Porth Clais demonstrates that a period of high interglacial sea-levels, probably during the Ipswichian Stage, was followed by a phase of periglacial conditions. There is evidence to suggest that this periglacial phase was succeeded by a period of fully glacial conditions. The precise dating of events at Porth Clais has not been established, although most recent workers prefer an Ipswichian age for the raised beach sediments with the periglacial and glacial sediments belonging to the Devensian Stage. A Late Devensian age has been suggested for the till at Porth Clais, but the interpretation of these sediments is debatable. The glacial deposits lack the marine shell fragments commonly found at other sites in the region where Irish Sea ice moved onshore (for instance, Traeth-y-Mwnt, Abermawr, Poppit Sands and Druidston Haven). Its interpretation as a 'land-facies' of the Irish Sea ice-sheet (John 1970b) has been seen as unsatisfactory, and the till may have been redeposited under periglacial conditions (Bowen 1977b).

Porth Clais provides a sequence that can be used to reconstruct changing environmental conditions in south-west Wales during the Late Pleistocene. It provides one of the finest examples of raised beach sediments in the region and shows marine and terrestrial beds in a single section. Although the interpretation of till at the site is controversial, it is important for establishing regional patterns of ice movement: it demonstrates that St David's Head was glaciated by Irish Sea ice during the Late Devensian, and helps to constrain the maximum limit for this ice-sheet in south-west Wales.

Conclusions

Porth Clais shows a succession of ice age deposits which represent the history of the last glacial cycle in south-west Wales. The till (boulder clay) shows that the St David's Head area was glaciated by an Irish Sea ice-sheet which moved from north-west to south-east.

Druidston Haven

Highlights

This site shows the best exposure of Devensian Irish Sea till in southern Preseli, at a position taken to be close to the southern limit of ice during the last glaciation. The till and periglacial sediments lie within a channel interpreted as evidence of an even earlier glaciation.

Introduction

Druidston Haven (Druidston) (SM862172) on the west-facing shore of St Brides Bay, contains one of the most extensive and best exposed sections through Irish Sea glacial sediments in south-west Wales. The sequence of deposits shows a succession of marine, periglacial and glacial episodes during the Late Pleistocene. Although dating of the sequence has proved difficult, some regard the site as the southernmost occurrence of Late Devensian till *in situ* in the area. The site was first investigated by Cantrill *et al.* (1916) and has featured in studies by Bowen (1966, 1973a, 1973b, 1974, 1977b, 1984), John (1965a, 1967, 1968a, 1969, 1970a, 1971a) and John and Ellis-Gruffydd (1970). Detailed accounts of the sequence and its interpretation are provided by John (1965a, 1970a).

Description

The exposures extend laterally for about 150m and comprise a sequence of –

6   Sandy loam (0.3m)
5   Upper head
4   Irish Sea fluvioglacial sands
3   Irish Sea till (*c.* 15m)
2   Lower head (up to 2m)
1   Raised beach deposits

The sediments occupy a deeply-cut rock channel, interpreted by John (1965a, 1970a) as a glacial meltwater channel.

The raised beach sediments recorded at Druidston (for example, Bowen 1973a, 1973b, 1974, 1977b, 1984; John 1968a, 1970a, 1971a) occur at the base of the section. This gravel, stained and cemented, has not been relocated in recent years. John recorded that this bed was overlain by blocky quartz sandstone head, also stained with iron oxide. These head deposits are succeeded by highly calcareous Irish Sea till containing northern erratics, numerous fragments of marine molluscs (sixteen species from both cold and warm environments recorded) and pieces of carbonised wood, including *Pinus* sp. (John 1967). The till is decalcified to a depth of *c.*1.3m at the top and in a thin layer at its base. The upper layers of till contain a high proportion of sand and gravel, and these grade upwards into interbedded outwash sands (bed 4), layers of till and, finally, solifluction deposits (bed 5) (John 1970a).

Interpretation

Dating of the sequence at Druidston has proved difficult. A Late Devensian age for the till was suggested by John (1970a) for two main reasons. First, the glacial and periglacial sediments were considered to overlie raised beach deposits of presumed Ipswichian age. Second, a series of radiocarbon dates from sites in south-west Wales was used as evidence (John 1965b, 1967, 1968c) for a Middle Würm (Devensian) interstadial in the region. He argued that the subsequent ice advance, which incorporated the organic remains, must therefore have been of Main Würm (Late Devensian) age. A date of >36,300 BP (I-1687) from a bulk sample of marine mollusc fragments from the till, however, did not help to establish its age any more precisely (John and Ellis-Gruffydd 1970). The faunal assemblage was, however, similar to that at other sites in the region (where finite dates indicating a Late Devensian age for the sediments had been obtained), but John and Ellis-Gruffydd admitted the possibility that the till at Druidston could be pre-Devensian.

Bowen (1966) originally suggested that the till was of pre-Devensian age and that it had been rearranged by solifluction onto a Hoxnian raised beach during the Devensian. John (1965a, 1970a), however, maintained that fabric analysis of the till showed that it was *in situ,* and this was agreed by Bowen (1973a, 1973b, 1974, 1977b, 1984) who regarded the site as an important stratigraphic locality for the association of Ipswichian (not Hoxnian) raised beach sediments and Late Devensian Irish Sea glacial sediments. Druidston is the southernmost limit of the raised beach overlain by till in this part of south-west Wales (Bowen 1974, 1977b). At localities to the south, for example at Milford Haven, the beach is succeeded by periglacial head deposits only. The evidence was therefore seen to place important restrictions on the maximum limit of the Late Devensian ice-sheet in south-west Wales. In contrast to Porth Clais, to the north, where site conditions had promoted redeposition of glacial sediments during the Devensian, the till at Druidston is substantially *in situ,* preserved within the steep walls of a coastal valley (Bowen 1977b).

Also using evidence from the adjacent area, John (1965a, 1970a) interpreted the following sequence of events. During high relative sea-levels in the Ipswichian Stage, raised beach sediments (bed 1) were deposited. This was followed by the accumulation of autochthonous head deposits (bed 2) during a prolonged period of periglacial climate in the Early and Middle Devensian. During the Late Devensian, Irish Sea ice moved onshore from the north-west (John 1971a) depositing shelly Irish Sea till (bed 3). The wasting phase of the ice-sheet was marked by the deposition of fluvioglacial sediment (bed 4). The upper head (bed 5) formed in a later, shorter periglacial phase, probably during Pollen Zones I-III of the Late Devensian late-glacial (John 1969).

As at Abermawr, John (1970a) argued that the sediments occurred within the walls of a glacial meltwater channel. Following his premise that the sequence at Druidston consisted of an Ipswichian raised beach overlain by a series of cold-climate Devensian sediments, he considered that the channel must therefore be pre-Devensian, and probably Saalian in age.

Although dating of the sequence has proved controversial, Druidston provides an important record of changing environmental conditions during the Late Pleistocene. In several respects, it is comparable with other stratigraphic sites in the region; it demonstrates a period of high interglacial sea-levels, probably during the Ipswichian Stage, followed by periglacial and glacial conditions in the Devensian Stage. However, whereas raised beach deposits are better developed at Poppit Sands and Porth Clais, and the glacial succession at Abermawr more firmly established within the regional Pleistocene chronology, Druidston can be regarded as a reference site for the Irish Sea till in south-west Wales, and it helps to establish former patterns of ice movement in the region. Its position, as the southernmost exposure of unequivocal undisturbed till in southern Preseli, provides a crucial reference point for the maximum limit of Late Devensian ice in this part of Wales.

Druidston provides the best exposure through Irish Sea till in southern Preseli. The sequence is important for demonstrating a succession of marine, periglacial and glacial episodes in a single section. It is particularly valuable as the southernmost occurrence of Irish Sea till *in situ* in the region, and therefore helps to establish the maximum extent of Late Devensian ice in south-west Wales.

Conclusions

Druidston Haven shows a thick sequence of last ice age deposits. The deposits which have traditionally been interpreted as glacial in origin, could also have dropped into a sea from floating or grounded ice. The extensive exposures in these deposits makes Druidston an important site for future work.

West Angle Bay

Highlights

A unique site showing glacial sediments perhaps attributable to more than one glaciation. A pre-Devensian till may underlie Ipswichian raised beach deposits, and both overlie a rock platform which is thus not attributable to the last, Ipswichian, interglacial.

Introduction

West Angle Bay (West Angle) (SM853031) is important because it shows a sequence of marine and terrestrial sediments that record major changes in environmental and geomorphological conditions in south-west Wales during the Late Pleistocene. Although dating of the beds exposed has been controversial, the site is potentially one of the most important in Wales. The interpretation of the sediments at West Angle is also relevant to the establishment of local ice limits. The site attracted early studies by Cantrill *et al.* (1916), Dixon (1921) and Leach (1933) and since by John (1965a, 1968a, 1969, 1970a, 1971a, 1974), John and Ellis-Gruffydd (1970), Mitchell (1972), Bowen (1973a, 1973b, 1973d, 1974, 1977b, 1980a, 1981a, 1984), Peake *et al.* (1973) and Shotton and Williams (1973). The palynology of the site was studied in detail by Stevenson and Moore (1982).

Description

Pleistocene sediments are well exposed for about 100m at the head of West Angle Bay. The following generalised sequence occurs above a bedrock platform –

5   Sandy loam

4   Red gravel

3   Sands, silts, loams and peat

2   Cemented raised beach deposits

1   Irish Sea till

The sequence is laterally variable, and the exposures are subject to change through erosion; this has resulted in difficulties in comparing the sequences described by different workers (Stevenson and Moore 1982). A comparable sequence to that above was also noted in an old, and now infilled, brick pit behind the main cliff line (Dixon 1921).

Interpretation

At West Angle, Dixon (1921) interpreted the sequence as till overlain by raised beach sands and gravels, and head deposits. The till contained scratched clasts, including igneous rock types, in a stiff purplish clay. He suggested that the site was unique in showing raised beach deposits overlying glacial sediments; for at other localities on the Welsh coast the relationship was reversed. This indicated an interglacial rather than pre-glacial age for the raised beach deposits. Dixon noted that the till in this section was underlain by a black clay with debris of silicified Carboniferous shells. This bed, he concluded, could be Lower Limestone Shales rotted *in situ,* but was more likely an ancient estuarine mud because it contained nests of pyrite and selenite.

Although till beneath raised beach deposits was also recorded by Leach (1933), it was not subsequently seen by John (for example, 1965a, 1968a, 1969, 1974) who recognised stained and cemented raised beach deposits (bed 2) conformably overlain by a sequence of sands, silts and clays (bed 3) containing organic debris. A sharp unconformity was noted separating these sediments from an overlying red gravelly deposit (bed 4). According to John, the red gravel was glacial in origin, being either fluvioglacial outwash or a gravelly 'land facies' of the Irish Sea ice-sheet (John 1968a, 1971a). On stratigraphic grounds, and from radiocarbon dates obtained from elsewhere in south-west Wales, he considered the till here to be Late Devensian in age; proving that the Late

Devensian ice-sheet reached at least as far south as West Angle and the Milford Haven area (John 1971a).

John (1969) suggested that there had been no hiatus in deposition between the raised beach sediments and the overlying sands, silts and clays. The sediments were therefore closely related in age (John 1968a). The raised beach had been deposited close to present day high water mark, and the overlying sediments had been deposited under estuarine conditions. The site recorded a relatively comprehensive marine transgression during which the sea may have risen to 6m (20 ft) OD. The sands and silts contained abundant organic remains, including small wood fragments, leaves and marine shell fragments. A preliminary study (Field 1968) of pollen from these beds showed that the vegetation of the area probably comprised a mixed oak and alder forest with pine and hazel and salt-tolerant plants – the latter probably living close to the water's edge. John (1968a) considered that the cemented raised beach at West Angle probably dated from an early phase of an interglacial and that the overlying deposits were estuarine, representing a marine transgression towards the peak of the same interglacial. A temperate interglacial phase is clearly indicated, but the pollen data do not allow it to be correlated with the pollen sequence of any standard interglacial stage elsewhere. The raised beach sequence was, however, tentatively assigned to the Ipswichian Stage, although some pollen known to occur in Hoxnian deposits elsewhere was noted (Field 1968; John 1969; John and Ellis-Gruffydd 1970).

Bowen (for example, 1973a, 1973b, 1974, 1977b) also supported an Ipswichian age for the interglacial succession at West Angle Bay, noting, however, that the palynological evidence was equivocal.

A radiocarbon date of >35,000 BP (Birm 327) was obtained from *Alnus* wood collected by Ribbon and Bowen from the base of a peat bed at 3.6 - 3.9m OD in the interglacial succession (bed 3) (Shotton and Williams 1973). Although this age determination did not help to date the deposits any more precisely, it was important in precluding a Holocene age.

Like Dixon (1921), excavation allowed Bowen (1973a, 1973b, 1974, 1977b) to record an Irish Sea till (bed 1) at the base of the sections beneath the interglacial succession. According to Bowen, West Angle Bay provided important, if not unique, evidence for a pre-Devensian glaciation in South Wales; such a discovery was also of considerable importance because the interglacial deposits were separated from the underlying bedrock platform by till. The site demonstrated that at least one glacial period had occurred between planation of the rock platform and deposition of interglacial sediments; and therefore showed that the formation of the raised shore platform and raised beach sequence had not been contemporaneous. Bowen (1974) also suggested that the interglacial sequence (beds 2 and 3) showed clear evidence for two different stands of sea-level, probably during the Ipswichian Stage.

Bowen (1971b, 1974) reinterpreted the gravels (bed 4) at West Angle, previously described as till (John 1970a), as periglacial head deposits. Therefore, the Milford Haven and West Angle area had not been glaciated during the Late Devensian, but lay in the 'extra-glacial' zone (Bowen 1974). The red periglacial gravels were considered to have accumulated during Early and Middle Devensian times (Bowen 1977b).

An Ipswichian age for the raised beach deposits was also favoured by Mitchell (1972). The upper red gravel, however, was regarded by Mitchell as solifluced till of Saalian age; the equivalent of the till described by Dixon (1921), but moved down into its present position by freeze-thaw processes in the Devensian Stage.

In view of the controversy and considerable interest surrounding the interglacial succession, a detailed re-investigation of the palynology of the site was undertaken by Stevenson and Moore (1982). Four pollen assemblage zones were defined (from bed 3), all dominated by temperate forest taxa, thus confirming a temperate environment during deposition. However, they were unable to correlate the sequence precisely with other British and Irish interglacial sites, although certain features of the West Angle pollen diagram, they suggested, correlated most closely with some Hoxnian pollen diagrams from eastern England. Periods of forest disturbance were noted in the profile and were considered to have been caused by local flood catastrophes. The red gravels overlying the interglacial sequence were considered to be head (periglacial).

The sequence of glacial, interglacial and periglacial sediments at West Angle Bay provides a key stratigraphic Late Pleistocene record. The nature and dating of the sediments have proved controversial and the sequence has been interpreted in a number of ways. The simplest of these interpretations recognises a sequence of Ipswichian Stage sediments overlain by Devensian glacial and periglacial sediments (for example, John 1968a). However, recent work suggests that the interglacial sediments have Hoxnian affinities (Stevenson and Moore 1982) and that they overlie an Irish Sea till (Bowen 1974, 1977b).

West Angle Bay also provides important evidence for a succession of different sea-level stands, and evidence to suggest that the shore platforms and raised beach deposits found commonly around the coast of south-west Britain are not necessarily contemporaneous: at West Angle, the raised beach is separated from a rock platform by glacial sediments.

The controversy regarding the interpretation of the sediments which overlie the interglacial sequence at West Angle has led to different interpretations of the maximum extent of the Late Devensian ice-sheet in the region. Some authors have regarded the red gravel as glacial in origin, envisaging that Late Devensian ice reached at least as far south as Milford Haven. Others, however, argued that the same deposits had a periglacial origin, placing the maximum limit of the Late Devensian ice-sheet somewhat farther to the north.

West Angle Bay displays one of the most complete Pleistocene sequences in Wales. It is important for showing what is believed to be the only known example of pre-Devensian till in Wales. Because this till rests on a presumably interglacial rock shore platform and is overlain by interglacial raised beach deposits, the evidence is important for demonstrating that the platform and raised marine sediments here and probably, therefore, elsewhere in Wales, are not contemporaneous. Although the succession shows a number of clear environmental and geomorphological changes in the region during the Late Pleistocene, dating of the sequence has proved controversial; and an Ipswichian age for the raised beach sequence is not firmly established. The disputed origin of deposits overlying the raised beach sediments, has a major bearing on reconstructing the maximum limit for Late Devensian ice in this part of south-west Wales.

Conclusions

West Angle Bay contains one of the longest sequences of ice age deposits in Wales. The lowest bed (normally only found below beach level) may be evidence for the oldest known glaciation of Wales. It is overlain by marine deposits which are thought to be 125,000 years old. The origin of the red gravel deposit overlying the marine beds is controversial.

Hoyle's Mouth and Little Hoyle Caves

Highlights

These localities show sediments which span the last 50,000 years, including the Late Devensian ice maximum and the Devensian late-glacial. These contain rich fossil mammal faunas typical of a glacial period, together with human artefacts.

Introduction

The Little Hoyle and Hoyle's Mouth Caves are important for sequences of deposits which have yielded rich faunas and artefacts dated towards the end of the Late Devensian. Environmental and geochronological evidence from recent excavations at Little Hoyle Cave show that the deposits probably span 50,000 years, although the principal mammal finds (which include bear, red fox, reindeer and collared lemming), are thought to date from the Late Devensian glacial maximum (*c.* 18,000 BP) and the Late Devensian late-glacial. Faunal evidence from nearby Hoyle's Mouth Cave has also been ascribed to the latter period on the basis of archaeological finds. Both caves have a longstanding history of research.

Hoyle's Mouth Cave

Description

Hoyle's Mouth Cave (SN112003) or 'the Hoyle' is a winding tunnel cave formed in Carboniferous Limestone. The large entrance at 21m (70 ft) OD opens northwards onto marshy land of the Ritec Valley, and must once have overlooked a long inlet of the sea. According to Garrod (1926) its various passages and chambers run for a total length of about 130 ft (39.6m). The deposits in the cave have been much disturbed, although it appears that in places up to 1m of ossiferous cave earth and breccia was originally sealed by a layer of stalagmite 0.09m thick (Leach 1931). More recently, Savory (1973) described a sequence near the cave entrance of –

4   Disturbed layer with Creswellian culture flints, early Iron Age, Roman and post-Mediaeval potsherds, recent animal bones, shells, iron-slag, charcoal and several hearths

3   Powdery yellow earth with bones of hyaena, cave bear and bison? and occasional flints

2   Sandy yellow silt

1   Sticky brown earth with stones

Continuing excavations by the National Museum of Wales (H S Green) have shown that deposits *in situ* remain at the site.

Interpretation

The first exploration of the cave was made in the 1840s by Colonel Jervis and Major Pugett, although no account is left of their discoveries (Leach 1931). However, according to the Reverend G N Smith, they dug up three Celt axes, two of flint and one of bronze. In 1860, Smith himself began to dig, although no plans nor stratigraphic details accompanied his brief reports read before the British Association at Oxford (1860), Cambridge (1862), the Cambrian Archaeological Association at Haverfordwest (1864), and the Naturalists' Association at Bristol (1866). The 1860 paper was also republished as a local pamphlet *On the Tenby Bone Caves*. Smith recorded that the Hoyle had contained a stalagmite floor overlying a stony cave earth. The stalagmite and cave earth had been much intermixed and he was therefore never satisfied that the flints and human bones that he found had originated beneath the stalagmite floor. By 1866, Smith had recovered about 200 flint flakes, and others of 'chert' together with bones of bear,

sheep, pig, dog and fish, and shells (limpet, mussel, periwinkle, cockle). According to Smith the artefacts had been fashioned by Neolithic Man, who he also considered had raised the tumuli on the nearby 'Ridgeway'.

The Hoyle was explored again in 1865 by Winwood and Sanford in conjunction with Smith (Winwood 1865). This excavation revealed an undisturbed breccia in the farthest part of the cave which yielded the remains of cave bear, hyaena, fox, deer, ox, the bones of a large bird and flint. Winwood thought that recent shells and rolled pebbles within the cave indicated occupation by the sea on at least two occasions. He also excavated at the cave entrance where he found a large quantity of artefacts in association with Irish elk, ox and horse. He noted that some of the tools were not flint, but a non-local vitrified igneous rock, later designated by J F N Green as 'adinole' (Leach 1931). Human remains, probably associated with the artefacts, were also found below the level of the stalagmite floor.

The Hoyle was visited by W Boyd Dawkins in 1872, gathering materials for his book on cave hunting (Dawkins 1874). The flints he found were considered by him to be of Palaeolithic age.

Laws (1877-8) recorded mammal remains of species already described from the cave. He noted that their significance was limited, as the deposits in which they were found were mixed and disturbed. At approximately the same time, Rolleston *et al.* (1878) explored the cave, noting that there were 'no objects of special interest'. Their investigation at Hoyle's Mouth was therefore concluded at an early stage and attention diverted to nearby Little Hoyle or Longbury Bank Cave.

Around 1878, Jones began to dig at Hoyle's Mouth and an account of the deposits and a plan of the cave was published (Jones 1882). From disturbed deposits in the innermost chamber, he recorded bones of many of the species described earlier, and flint chips. Nearer to the cave entrance, and beneath unbroken stalagmite, he recovered remains of brown bear and a single flint flake, and at the cave entrance bones of reindeer, wild boar, recent animals, humans and a variety of flint and adinole artefacts. Jones was sceptical about the earlier records of hyaena, cave bear and Irish elk and suggested that the cave had been a dwelling and burial place during the Neolithic, and not the Palaeolithic as Dawkins had suggested. Laws (1888), however, suggested that the cave had probably been a hyaena den in Palaeolithic times, but that Neolithic Man had subsequently used it as a dwelling place and cemetery.

Hoyle's Mouth was next visited by Prestwich (1892) who found evidence of Neolithic flints and flakes only. In contrast, Dixon (1921) discerned the presence of Aurignacian and Magdalenian cultures of the Palaeolithic age, with flint implements representing the Aurignacian culture, and those of adinole the Magdalenian. Garrod (1926), however, while supporting a broadly Palaeolithic age for the industries, saw no basis for such a sub-division.

Leach (1913, 1918b, 1931, 1945) provided reviews of the early excavations and finds from Hoyle's Mouth. He thought that the cave had probably been a bear and hyaena den during Palaeolithic times, and inhabited periodically by Man in Neolithic, Bronze Age, Iron Age and early historic times.

With the belief expressed by Leach (1931) that few undisturbed deposits remained at the Hoyle, interest in the site subsequently dwindled. However, a threat to exploit the cave commercially led to a rescue dig by the National Museum of Wales in 1968 (Savory 1973). Savory dug trenches at the cave entrance and immediately inside the cave recording details of the stratigraphy (see site description). He noted that although the deposits were largely unstratified, there could be little doubt that most of the flints discovered by earlier workers had been derived from deposits in the cave, originally sealed by a stalagmite layer. He suggested that these artefacts represented occupation in the Late Devensian late-glacial or early Holocene, and that they were of broadly Creswellian culture. He was particularly influenced by Webley's report on the silty sand at Hoyle's Mouth which was compared to a similar deposit in Nanna's Cave, Caldey which Cornwall (in Lacaille and Grimes 1955) considered had been deposited during the Boreal period of the Holocene. Savory, therefore, argued that the silty sand at Hoyle's Mouth also dated from the Boreal, c. 8000-6000 BC, although he noted that this did not agree with the late-glacial (or earlier) fauna. He considered it possible that the cave had been occupied by Man before the end of the Devensian Stage, with occupation lasting into the Boreal and Atlantic periods of the Holocene. This suggestion was supported by some of the flint artefacts which had a markedly microlithic tendency, and whose Mesolithic character was also consistent with this later Holocene phase. In contrast, ApSimon (1976) suggested that Savory's (1973) correlations were very loosely based; placing the Creswellian industries at the Hoyle into the late-glacial rather than the early Holocene, a practice also followed by Houlder (1977).

The site has also been mentioned by George (1970) and Bowen (1974) in a regional context, and continuing excavations by the National Museum of Wales (H S Green) are expected to elaborate the sequence.

Little Hoyle Cave

Description

Little Hoyle Cave (SS112999), sometimes known as Longbury Bank Cave, is situated in a narrow Carboniferous Limestone ridge. Three entrances open on the north side of the ridge, one on the south side. The centre of the cave is connected to the surface via a large chimney. The cave lies at c. 20m OD, around 7m above the floors of the narrow valleys on either side. It would probably have been within the range of the Ipswichian sea-level (Green et al. 1986). The stratigraphic succession is complex, and it varies at different locations within the cave (Green et al. 1986). Green et al. opened trenches within the cave, adjacent to the chimney and on platforms at the northern and southern entrances. On the north platform they recorded the following sequence –

10	Soil
9	Orange-brown clay with stones
8	Upper scree
7	Buff-grey silt
6	Stony silt
5	Pink clay
4	Middle scree
3	Orange and black clay
2	Lower scree
1	Bedrock

Interpretation

The first known exploration of Little Hoyle Cave was made by Winwood in 1866 who partly excavated a kitchen midden in the north chamber (Laws 1888; Leach 1931). His discoveries included bones of *Bos,* goat, badger and dog, shells of marine molluscs, pottery fragments, flints and human bones. Many of these remains were probably of post-Pleistocene age (Green et al. 1986). The cave was also cursorily examined around 1870 by Smith, although no records of his discoveries were made (Laws 1888; Leach 1945). Excavations in 1877 by Power and Laws (Laws 1878), revealed breccia cemented to the cave walls and overlying deposits on the cave floor as 'brackets' or 'shelves'; beneath these cemented breccias, they discovered a variety of mostly historic and one or two pre-historic remains. According to Green et al. (1986) no certain Pleistocene fauna was recovered.

Between 1877 and 1878 the cave was examined by Laws and a committee comprising Rolleston, Lane Fox (better known as General Pitt Rivers), Busk, Dawkins, Evans and Hilton-Price; accounts of their findings were published by Laws (1878) and Rolleston et al. (1878). This phase of excavations was centred largely upon emptying the central chimney of deposits, from which were recovered the human remains of some 9-11 individuals associated with Roman and later finds, flints and other implements, bones of domestic animals and shellfish. From the northern cave, Rolleston and his team recorded some 160 fragments of bone and teeth including remains of rhinoceros or elephant, mammoth, bear, red deer, eagle and black grouse, some of which had apparently been gnawed by hyaenas. In all, some 500 fragments of human bone were recovered from Little Hoyle, but Rolleston *et al.* considered there was no evidence for Man having been contemporary with the extinct Pleistocene mammals: although there was some evidence to suggest that the northern cave had been occupied by Man, perhaps in Bronze Age times, most of the remains had entered the cave via the chimney and were of possibly relatively recent age. Rolleston *et al.* also noted that the cave had at some time probably been invaded by the sea, although Dixon (1921) considered this unlikely. From this phase of excavations is an important watercolour, now preserved in Tenby Museum, and entitled *Longbury Bank cave near Penally, explored by Prof. Rolleston and E Laws.* This painting is important in allowing a comparison of the early accounts of the cave with more recent excavations (Green *et al.* 1986).

Laws in 1888, in his book *The history of Little England beyond Wales ...* , concluded that the cave had been exhausted by earlier work, remarking that the accumulated evidence indicated that the cave had been a hyaena den during the Pleistocene, while he also considered the site to be "... the most instructive Neolithic find in Pembrokeshire". Reviews of the early excavations and finds from the Little Hoyle were provided by Leach (1913, 1918b, 1931, 1945).

More recently, three seasons of excavations (1958 - 1963) have been undertaken by McBurney (McBurney 1959). He described a sequence which included two principal scree beds, the lower and upper screes. From the upper scree he recovered a number of bones including those of reindeer, bear and fox, charcoal, and a single, large, typically Creswellian culture, pen-knife blade. The lower scree yielded one identifiable bone, that of *Lepus* cf. *timidus.* He tentatively suggested a Late Devensian late-glacial rather than Holocene age for the Creswellian artefact. More recently, Bowen (1974) used McBurney's evidence in support of a Devensian age for the scree.

Recently, Little Hoyle was selected by the National Museum of Wales as the Upper Palaeolithic representative in a programme of excavations intended to elaborate the Palaeolithic settlement of Wales. One aim of this programme was the definitive publication of McBurney's work; this and the preliminary results of the excavations at Little Hoyle carried out by Green and his colleagues during 1984 and 1986 were published by Green *et al.* (1986).

Detailed geochronological and environmental evidence presented by Green and his team has shown that the surviving deposits at Little Hoyle span some 50,000 years. A Uranium-series age determination of 47,500 +9,500 -8,500 BP on a wall stalagmite capping provides a minimum age for the underlying deposits. Bone remains including *Ursus* and *Rangifer,* in the cemented breccia beneath such capping material, would therefore appear to be Early or Middle Devensian in age, coming from the oldest deposits so far known from the cave.

Most of the cave deposits were formed fluvially or as thermoclastic scree, and appear to date from the Late Devensian. Uranium-series and radiocarbon dates from bones in a red sandy silt in the north cave, are closely grouped at around 18,000 BP. This shows that the included fauna of brown bear *Ursus arctos,* reindeer *Rangifer tarandus,* fox *Vulpes vulpes,* arctic lemming *Dicrostonyx torquatus,* water vole *Arvicola terrestris,* tundra vole *Microtus gregalis,* hare *Lepus* sp. and some large birds dates, at least in part, from the Late Devensian glacial maximum. Currant *(in* Green *et al.* 1986) suggested that elements of a Pleistocene fauna including large mammalian herbivores such as woolly rhinoceros and mammoth, recovered by earlier workers, also probably dates from this phase, as such species did not survive in Britain after the retreat of the Late Devensian ice-sheet.

The succeeding deposit contains a fauna including reindeer, arctic lemming, Norway lemming *Lemmus lemmus,* water vole, northern vole *Microtus oeconomus,* shrew *Sorex* sp., and is dominated by bones identified by C Harrison (BMNH) as those of barnacle goose *Branta leucopsis* (Bechstein). It seems likely that this fauna dates from the Late Devensian late-glacial (Green *et al.* 1986).

The 'platform sequence' recorded by Green *et al.*, although not yet dated, would also appear to be Late Devensian late-glacial (*c.* 13,000-10,000 BP) in age. Preliminary pollen evidence shows a period of fluctuating climate with three successively more severe cold phases, separated by successively less mild phases. Green *et al.* noted that the exact chronological position of the Upper Palaeolithic settlement of the Little Hoyle could not yet be finally resolved, but they suggested that the upper scree of the platform sequence (bed 8), with its included Creswellian artefact (McBurney 1959), might date from Late Devensian late-glacial Pollen Zone III.

Further work at Little Hoyle by Green *et al.* is expected to provide dating of the platform sequences, which would seem to offer the best possibility for correlation with the sequence inside the cave. Bones from the site have also been used in a comparative dating study using amino acid, radiocarbon and Uranium-series techniques (Rae *et al.* 1987).

Hoyle's Mouth and the Little Hoyle Caves provide some of the most detailed evidence currently available from the Upper Palaeolithic period in Wales. Recent excavations show that the deposits at Little Hoyle cover about 50,000 years. Faunal remains dated to *c.* 18,000 BP show that the area attracted both a varied large and small mammal fauna during the Late Devensian. This dated evidence is particularly important for it lends support to the views of Oakley (1968), Bowen (1970b) and Molleson and Burleigh (1978) that parts of South Wales may have been inhabited by Man even at the peak of the Late Devensian glaciation, and also suggests that the area was free from glacier ice at this time. Much of the sequence and its included fauna at Little Hoyle, however, would appear to date from the Late Devensian late-glacial, and it is believed that the upper scree from the platform sequence, together with McBurney's Creswellian artefact, may date from as late as Pollen Zone III of the late-glacial. The vertebrate fauna from that period is dominated by the bones of the barnacle goose, which appears to have been present at the site as a breeding population. This is the first such record from Pleistocene Britain. Faunal evidence from Hoyle's Mouth has also been dated, archaeologically, to approximately the same time.

These caves provide contrasting records to the more extensive sequences at Minchin and Bacon Hole Caves, Gower, and, together with Cat Hole Cave, provide a detailed record of environmental changes towards the end of the Devensian.

The Hoyles Caves provide an important record of environmental conditions in the Devensian Stage. Little Hoyle, in particular, is important for showing detailed faunal, archaeological, pollen and other palaeoenvironmental evidence that can be related to a radiometrically dated timescale. This evidence establishes that the principal faunal remains and artefacts date from both the late-glacial and the earlier glacial maximum of the Late Devensian. The evidence also supports the belief that parts of South Wales were inhabited by Man at the peak of the Late Devensian glaciation.

Conclusions

The caves of Little Hoyle and Hoyle's Mouth, contain an important sequence of deposits representing the last ice age. In particular, they contain fossils of the ice age fauna, together with archaeological remains showing that Man was active in the area at that time. Dating techniques have shown that the deposits represent some 50,000 years, and the principal fossil and archaeological remains date from the maximum of the last ice age, about 18,000 years ago, and from the period between about 14,000 years and 10,000 years.

Marros Sands

Highlights

This site shows deposits spanning the Ipswichian-Holocene interval, and including Ipswichian raised shoreline deposits, Devensian periglacial sediments which indicate that the area lay south of the Devensian ice limit, and Holocene submerged forest.

Introduction

Marros Sands (Marros) (SS210073) is important for its Late Pleistocene sequence of raised beach and head deposits which represents a succession from interglacial marine to periglacial conditions. Palaeobotanical and stratigraphical evidence indicates that the marine sequence was probably formed during the Ipswichian Stage, and the site records possible evidence for a number of high sea-level stands during this time. Head deposits at the site probably accumulated during the subsequent Devensian Stage when it lay in the periglacial zone. The geomorphological interest of the site is enhanced by extensively developed submerged forest and associated beds which occur along Marros Sands (Leach 1918a). The site was first described by Strahan *et al.* (1909) and was also mentioned by Leach (1910). More recently it has been described by John (1968a, 1971a, 1973), Bowen (1970a, 1973a, 1973b, 1974, 1977b) and Peake *et al.* (1973).

Description

The Pleistocene sequence is well exposed in coastal cliffs between Marros (SS201071) and Ragwen Point (SS219072). Cemented and stratified head deposits are also well exposed near Gilman Point (SS227075). Holocene submerged forest and associated beds occur along much of the shore at Marros Sands, and they are particularly well developed between SS200074 and SS214072.

The sequence is laterally variable, but along much of the coastal cliff comprises –

4	Hillwash sediments
3	Head
2	Raised beach shingle and sand (often mixed with head)
1	Rock shore platform

At Ragwen Point the sequence is (Bowen 1970a) –

8	Hillwash sediments
7	Head
6	Colluvial silts
5	Cemented sand
4	Raised beach sediments
3	Cemented sand
2	Raised beach sediments
1	Rock shore platform

Beds 2 to 6 and the lower part of bed 7, at Ragwen Point, are partly cemented by iron and manganese oxides (John 1971a). The head, of angular shale and quartzite blocks, reaches about 12m maximum thickness. It was sub-divided into at least four facies by John, but only two by Bowen (1974) – a lower blue shale head and an overlying brown sandstone head. Cryoturbation structures occur in the head deposits (John 1973), and well developed fossil ice-wedge casts penetrate the brown head (Bowen 1974). Polygonal fossil ice-cracks are also exposed in periglacial deposits near Marros Mill (Bowen 1974).

Interpretation

The raised beach deposit at Ragwen Point was first described by A Strahan (*in* Strahan *et al.* 1909) as a concreted sand with small pebbles, just above HWM, and beneath a small cliff of 'boulder clay'. No shells were observed in the raised beach deposit, which was correlated with the raised beaches in Gower, of believed 'pre-glacial' or 'inter-glacial' age (Tiddeman *in* Strahan 1907a). Leach noted the drift deposits in the coastal cliffs at Marros, and described a sequence of glacial drift and local talus deposits farther west along the coast, near Amroth.

Subsequently, in 1965, Bowen discovered the raised beach at Marros Sands (Bowen 1966) and gave an account of the sediments and stratigraphy in the coastal cliffs between Marros and Gilman Point (Bowen 1970a).

At Marros, the raised beach is succeeded by a sandy, silty mud which lies below the head deposits (Bowen 1970a). This bed yielded various seeds and fruits, moss stems and beetle fragments, together with pollen (Mitchell *et al.* in Bowen 1970a). The palaeobotanical data indicated that trees and bushes were rare at the time of deposition, but that there was a rich herbaceous flora with a strong calcicole element. Bowen (1970a) considered that this environment was probably very similar to the Allerød phase of the Devensian late-glacial, with open countryside, young soils and rich meadows. From the stratigraphic and palaeobotanical evidence, he interpreted the following sequence of Late Pleistocene events at Marros. During high interglacial sea-levels, in the Ipswichian Stage, raised beach sediments were deposited. The fossiliferous, sandy silty mud probably accumulated in a dune slack during temperate conditions towards the end of this interglacial phase, and it marks a transition between fully interglacial and periglacial conditions. The upper beds of raised beach shingle and sand at Ragwen Point (beds 4 and 5) may represent a further high sea-level stand during an Ipswichian Stage interglacial, and this Bowen tentatively correlated with the *Neritoides* sand at the key interglacial site of Minchin Hole, Gower (Bowen 1970a). He otherwise considered all deposits overlying the raised beach and dune slack sediments at Marros to be unquestionable periglacial slope deposits derived from the interglacial cliff line behind the sections; concluding that the absence of even a single erratic proved the non-glacial origin of the sediments. He argued that the head deposits had accumulated during the Devensian Stage when Marros lay in the periglacial zone, an interpretation followed by John (1971a, 1973). John also suggested that huge quartzite blocks weighing several tons, in the head, showed a high degree of instability on the coastal cliffs during these periglacial conditions. Occasional catastrophic collapses of huge blocks had interrupted the otherwise slower, but dominant, process of solifluction. The evidence was used by Bowen

(1970a) to demonstrate that the area was south of the Late Devensian (Welsh) ice-sheet which did not reach this part of south Dyfed and the Carmarthen Bay area. The head deposits contained no trace of erratic material, but Bowen (1977b) noted that the plateaux adjacent to the coastline bore unmistakable boulder trains and outliers of till and fluvioglacial sediments: these deposits, he suggested, demonstrated a pre-Devensian glaciation of the area by an Irish Sea ice-sheet moving NNW to SSE. Similar interpretations of the sequence were followed by Bowen (1973a, 1973b, 1974) and Peake *et al.* (1973).

A fine example of a cemented and stratified scree occurs at Gilman Point. Bowen (1977b) noted that a considerable thickness of limestone head mantles the former cliff here. The deposit consists of colluvium with boulders. This is overlain by a blocky, calcite-cemented head that fines upwards into scree beds which dip off the limestone outcrop. Cementation of similar screes elsewhere in Britain is thought to have occurred during discontinuous permafrost conditions in the Late Devensian (Prentice and Morris 1959).

The geomorphological interest at Marros is enhanced by well developed submerged forest and peat beds which crop out along the modern beach. Leach (1918a) noted that the beds extended from near HWM to the lowest levels of the shore uncovered by Spring tides, and stretched almost continuously for a mile along Marros Sands. Leach described a sequence of –

4   Peat and submerged forest
3   Peaty soil with roots and leaves of aquatic plants
2   Blue 'slime'
1   Unstratified rubble (head)

Leach noted that the peat and submerged forest bed contained abundant leaves, twigs, branches and trunks of trees; stems, leaves and roots of marsh plants; mosses; hazel nuts, oak cupules, alder catkins; seeds and seed capsules of small plants and a large quantity of other disintegrated plant tissues. A Holocene age for the beds was suggested by Leach (1918a).

The sequence of deposits at Marros provides an important record of Late Pleistocene and Holocene environmental conditions and changes. The site demonstrates evidence for periods of high sea-level, probably during the Ipswichian, when raised beach sediments accumulated. Several facies of raised beach shingle separated by cemented sand are present at Ragwen Point, and the sequence may therefore provide rare evidence for marked climatic and sea-level fluctuations during this stage. These horizons have been correlated tentatively with raised beach deposits at Minchin Hole Cave, Gower (Bowen 1970a). The period of raised beach sedimentation came to an end with deteriorating climatic conditions, revealed by palaeobotanical evidence. Thick head deposits and colluvial sediments accumulated at Marros, probably during the Devensian Stage, and the site therefore sets a limit for the maximum extent of Late Devensian ice of Welsh provenance in the west Carmarthen Bay area. Marros is also notable for the fine development of infilled crack and polygonal structures that occur in the head deposits. These have not been dated, although similar cracks were noted in Late Devensian glacial sediments in west Gower: these features were considered to be either frost or desiccation cracks of Late Devensian late-glacial age (Campbell 1984). The submerged forest beds at Marros extend the stratigraphic record into the Holocene. These deposits have not been studied in detail and the site therefore has potential for Holocene sea-level studies.

Marros provides a rock record containing marine and terrestrial evidence. It demonstrates rare evidence for fluctuating sea-levels, probably in the Ipswichian Stage. Pollen evidence records the transition from these temperate interglacial conditions to periglacial conditions in the Devensian Stage, when substantial colluvial and head deposits accumulated. The association of marine deposits overlain by periglacial sediments establishes that Marros lay in the extra-glacial zone during the Late Devensian.

Conclusions

Marros Sands shows extensive exposures of marine and periglacial (cold climate) deposits. This is an important site, because it shows that ice-sheets did not cross this area after 125,000 years ago. It, therefore, provides important evidence for the reconstruction of the last Welsh ice-sheet; and proves that although it covered most of Wales and crossed west Gower, it did not cover this area.

Introduction

Studies of coastal and cave stratigraphic sequences particularly in Gower (Chapter 3) and south-west Wales (Chapter 4) have provided the most detailed evidence about the Middle and Late Pleistocene and its sub-division in southern Wales (for example, Bowen 1970a, 1973a, 1973b, 1974, 1984). Elsewhere in Dyfed, the Brecon Beacons, Black Mountains, the South Wales Coalfield and the Vale of Glamorgan particular details of the Late Pleistocene and Holocene history provide further complementary evidence. A prominent theme of past studies has been attempts to delimit the maximum extent of the Late Devensian ice-sheet. Another theme relates to the upland areas of South Wales, particularly the Brecon Beacons, which exhibit a range of glacial and periglacial landforms that provide evidence for Late Devensian and especially Devensian late-glacial environmental events and conditions. A number of sites within the region has also yielded important data for reconstructing Holocene palaeoenvironments.

Events pre-dating the Ipswichian Stage

With the exception of landforms such as erosion surfaces and tors, which have evolved in response to processes operating over long timescales (Brown 1960; George 1974; Battiau-Queney 1980, 1984), the oldest evidence for the Pleistocene in South Wales is generally held to be the deposits of the 'Older Drift' (Bowen 1970a, 1974). It has long been believed that glacial deposits of the 'Older Drift' were younger than the *Patella* Beach of Gower (George 1932), but in recent years it has been demonstrated that the raised beach in fact post-dates the 'Older Drift' (Bowen 1970a, 1973a, 1973b, 1974, 1984). Bowen (1973a, 1973b) argued that only derived, redistributed 'Older Drift' glacial sediments overlie the raised beach, having been reworked into this position by periglacial processes during the Devensian Stage.

'Older Drift' glacial deposits occur, for example, in west Gower and in the Vale of Glamorgan. These consist of both Irish Sea and Welsh glacial deposits, and they exist in areas outside the limit of the Late Devensian ('Newer Drift') glaciation (Charlesworth 1929; Bowen 1970a, 1973a, 1973b, 1981a, 1981b). They are sometimes characterised by considerable dissection in comparison with more coherent deposits of the Late Devensian, although those in west Gower cannot be distinguished in this way.

Much is owed to the work of the Geological Survey Officers (for example, Strahan and Gibson 1900; Strahan and Cantrill 1904; Strahan 1907a, 1907b, 1909; Strahan *et al.* 1907, 1909, 1914; Dixon 1921) who established the details of glaciation in South Wales. They showed that two ice-sheets had traversed the region: one from the Irish Sea Basin with erratics from as far afield as Scotland, the Lake District and North Wales, and another from the Welsh uplands. Strahan and his colleagues (and later T N George in Gower) demonstrated that 'Older Drift' ice crossed south-west Dyfed (Pembrokeshire) from the north-west, and moved in an easterly direction along the Bristol Channel, impinging on west Gower and parts of the Vale of Glamorgan. At Pencoed, in the Vale of Glamorgan, Strahan and Cantrill (1904) described shelly deposits with igneous Irish Sea erratics, underlying

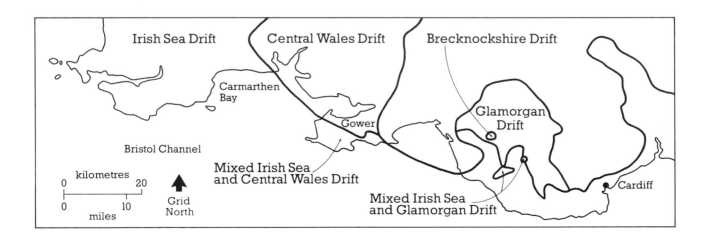

Figure 13 Drift provinces of South Wales (from Bowen 1970a)

Welsh glacial deposits. They demonstrated that this Irish Sea ice had carried erratic boulders to the Vale of Glamorgan as far east as Cowbridge and possibly beyond. Details of this extensive Irish Sea glaciation in the region were further elaborated by Griffiths (1937, 1939, 1940) who applied heavy mineral analyses and plotted erratics trains to ascertain the provenance of the drifts. He concluded that, over much of South Wales, the Irish Sea and Welsh ice masses had been coeval. Using similar evidence, Bowen (1970a) delimited six provinces of glacial drifts – Irish Sea, Central Wales, Brecknockshire, Glamorgan, mixed Irish Sea and Central Wales drift, and mixed Irish Sea and Glamorgan drift – see Figure 13. It is generally held that South Wales was entirely submerged beneath the Irish Sea and Welsh ice-sheets in 'Older Drift' times.

Bowen et al. (1985) and Bowen, Jenkins and Catt (unpublished) have shown that parts of the 'Older Drift' are of different ages in south-west Gower: with mixed provenance Irish Sea and Welsh drift succeeded by a Welsh drift delimited by a moraine at Paviland. Estimates of their ages in comparison with an oxygen isotope scale are made by Bowen et al. (1985).

Recent work in the Vale of Glamorgan and a re-examination of the 'Storrie erratic collection' from Pencoed (Strahan and Cantrill 1904) have confirmed the former presence of Irish Sea ice in the area (Donnelly 1988) – see also Chapter 2. Donnelly noted that the Irish Sea glacial sediments were probably extensively reworked by Welsh ice in the Late Devensian. Unfortunately, these drifts are no longer exposed in the Pencoed and Ewenny areas, although British Geological Survey boreholes record their presence.

The Ipswichian Stage

Other than for the coastal margins of South Wales, where raised marine and terrestrial cave sediments occur, evidence for temperate (interglacial) conditions is generally sparse. Possible evidence for the Ipswichian Stage comes from relict soils preserved in areas unaffected by the Late Devensian glaciation, on the ground previously glaciated by the 'Older Drift' ice-sheet (Bowen 1970a, 1973a, 1973b, 1974). Such soils have been described from the Vale of Glamorgan (Crampton 1960, 1961, 1964, 1966c), parts of south Gower (Ball 1960; Clayden 1977a, 1977b) and south Pembrokeshire. Such palaeosols are an important element of the coastal sequences around Gower, where they have been reworked as colluvial deposits, analogous to the 'limon rouges' of Mediterranean lands (Bowen 1966, 1970a). Where these palaeosols occur as surface features, they provide assistance in defining areas not glaciated by Devensian ice. They are represented in the GCR site coverage by the colluviated facies of coastal sections – see Chapter 3.

The Devensian Stage

Evidence for Early and Middle Devensian conditions is also confined to areas beyond the limit of the Late Devensian ice-sheet, and it is only represented by colluvial and head deposits widely exposed around the coast and in cave sequences (for example, at Long Hole and Bacon Hole Caves, Gower). It is reasonable to assume that comparable head and colluvial sequences also exist inland, but they have not yet been recognised. The long sequence described by Bull (1975, 1976) from Agen Allwedd Cave near Llangattock may cover much of the Devensian.

The South Wales end-moraine

An incidental but pre-eminent theme in investigations of the Late Pleistocene in South Wales is the delimitation of the extent of Late Devensian ice. Since Charlesworth (1929) first defined the 'Newer Drift' limit, the South Wales ice margin has been the subject of several revisions (Charlesworth 1929; Griffiths 1940; Wirtz 1953; Mitchell 1960, 1972; Lewis 1966b; Bowen 1970a, 1973a, 1973b, 1974, 1981a, 1981b; George 1970; John 1971a) – see Figure 14.

The most significant differences between these reconstructions have arisen from different methodology. For example, Mitchell (1960, 1972) used an East Anglian stratigraphical model amplified by work in Ireland and argued that the raised beaches around Wales were principally of Hoxnian age, thus making it implicit that they were overlain by deposits of both Saalian and Devensian age. Mitchell (1960) and Synge (1963, 1964) concluded that the majority of glacial sediments in Wales were of Saalian age, with Late Devensian Welsh ice only forming a limited ice cap in the uplands, and Irish Sea ice only impinging along the North Wales coastal margin. In contrast, faunal (Bowen 1970a, 1973a, 1973b, 1974) and amino acid evidence (Bowen et al. 1985; Bowen and Sykes 1988) suggests that most of the raised beach outcrops are probably of Ipswichian age. Principally on the basis of coastal lithostratigraphy, Bowen (1970a, 1973a, 1973b, 1974) and John (1970a) in Pembrokeshire, for example, have shown a more extensive Late Devensian glaciation in Wales than Mitchell (1960, 1972) – see Figure 14.

The Late Devensian ice limit: south-east Wales

In south-east Wales morphological evidence for the margin of the ice-sheet is well developed. Prominent moraines and areas of hummocky terrain were widely deposited by ice from Mid Wales and Breconshire, and Charlesworth's (1929) limit, drawn to coincide with the southern limit of continuous drift mapped by the Geological Survey, has been relatively little modified by subsequent workers. Lewis (1966a, 1966b) argued for little more than a Late Devensian cirque glaciation in the South Wales uplands, extending to valley glaciation in parts of the Usk Valley (the 'Breconshire end-moraine'), but it was subsequently demonstrated

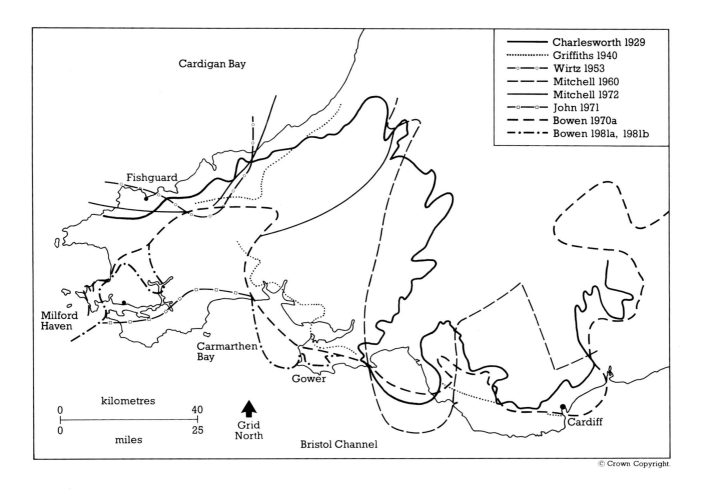

Legend:
- Charlesworth 1929
- Griffiths 1940
- Wirtz 1953
- Mitchell 1960
- Mitchell 1972
- John 1971
- Bowen 1970a
- Bowen 1981a, 1981b

Cardigan Bay

Fishguard

Milford Haven

Carmarthen Bay

Gower

kilometres
0 — 40
0 — 25
miles

Grid North

Bristol Channel

Cardiff

© Crown Copyright.

Figure 14 Some suggested Late Devensian ice limits in South Wales (from Bowen and Henry 1984; Campbell 1984)

that Late Devensian ice was extensive in the uplands. For example, Ellis-Gruffydd (1972, 1977) argued that glacial striae and erratics showed that the entire Old Red Sandstone escarpment had been submerged beneath the 'Breconshire ice-cap'. Ice from this dispersion centre flowed north into the Usk Valley (Williams 1968a); west through Cwm Dwr to join Mid Wales ice moving down the Tywi Valley; and south across the South Wales Coalfield, to the limits reconstructed by Bowen (1970a, 1973a, 1973b, 1974) (Ellis-Gruffydd 1977).

A powerful stream of ice from the uplands moved eastwards in the Brecon area; it bifurcated near present day Llangorse Lake, sending branches north-east into the Wye Valley and south-east into the Usk Valley (Williams 1968a; Lewis 1970b). Part of this Usk glacier probably coalesced with glaciers from the eastern Coalfield (Welch and Trotter 1961) to form a piedmont lobe extending offshore between Newport and Cardiff (Bowen 1970a). The relationship of Late Devensian ice to buried channels in the lower Usk region has been discussed by Williams (1968b). Ice moving north-east into the Wye Valley probably only over-topped the Black Mountains escarpment (Hay Bluff) locally, and the Usk glacier moved almost due east near Crickhowell to terminate near Llanfihangel-Crucorney where it formed a large moraine.

The Late Devensian ice limit: central South Wales

Farther west, a similar pattern is repeated, with Late Devensian Welsh ice from the Glamorgan uplands moving south and south-east into the Vale of Glamorgan. Although moraines associated with this ice were developed locally, the maximum limit is frequently marked in the Vale by extensive areas of hummocky terrain, for example, around Pyle, Margam and Llanilid (Bowen 1970a). Deposits in the Llanilid area were recently examined by Donnelly (1988) who upheld the established Late Devensian maximum limit (Bowen 1970a), and discussed the relationship of these deposits to the 'Older Drift' Irish Sea deposits of the Vale of Glamorgan. Late Devensian events near Pontypridd were discussed in detail by Harris and Wright (1980).

Evidence of Late Devensian glaciation in Swansea Bay is well established (for example, Strahan 1907a; Trueman 1924; Charlesworth 1929; Jones 1931a, 1931b; Griffiths 1939; Bowen 1970a; Al-Saadi and Brooks 1973; Culver 1976; Anderson 1977; Anderson and Owen 1979; Culver and Bull 1979). The Nedd (Neath), Tawe (Swansea) and Afan Valleys acted as major outlets for Welsh ice from the uplands. This ice coalesced to form a large piedmont lobe in Swansea Bay. Late

Devensian glacial sediments mark part of the western limit of this lobe in eastern Gower (for example, George 1933a; Bowen 1970a; Campbell 1984) – see Langland Bay (Rotherslade). Comparable glacial sediments occur in association with a series of over-deepened rock basins in the Neath and Swansea Valleys (Al-Saadi and Brooks 1973; Anderson and Owen 1979; Culver and Bull 1979). These basins may have formed by preferential ice erosion along major fault zones (for example, the Neath Disturbance) and pre-glacial river courses. Lacustrine deposits associated with wastage of the ice have been described from these basins and their offshore extensions (Culver and Bull 1979). They are truncated and succeeded, over large areas of Swansea Bay and its coastal fringes, by the marginal marine deposits of the Holocene transgression (Godwin 1940b; Culver and Bull 1979). Although the maximum Late Devensian ice limit lies offshore, the Neath, Swansea and Afan Valleys contain lacustrine deposits, kame terraces and halt-stage moraines; evidence for sequential ice wastage, as the ice-sheet thinned into individual valley glaciers (Charlesworth 1929; Hughes 1974; Anderson and Owen 1979; Culver and Bull 1979). A minimum age for the Late Devensian glaciation of the area is given by Pollen Zone I deposits recovered from a kettle hole (now destroyed) at Bryn House, Swansea (Trotman 1963).

In areas adjacent to Carmarthen Bay, some drifts contain both Irish Sea erratics and heavy minerals, but they are dominantly of Welsh origin (Griffiths 1940). Griffiths suggested that deposits in this region had lithological characteristics of the 'Older Drift' mixed Irish Sea and Welsh provinces, but had been substantially reshaped by 'Newer Drift' Welsh ice, which had only been weakly developed in the area. Subsequent workers (for instance, Bowen 1965, 1970a, 1980b; Campbell 1984) have discussed the evidence for Late Devensian ice streams moving into Carmarthen Bay from basal ice-sheds farther north, for example, in the Mynydd Sylen and Cross Hands areas (Cantrill in Strahan et al. 1907). This Welsh ice flowed along the valleys of the Tywi, Gwendraeth Fawr and Gwendraeth Fach. Upper layers of ice moved almost due south, providing important evidence for a considerable ice gradient and substantial central Wales ice cap in Late Devensian times (Strahan et al. 1907; Bowen 1970a; Campbell 1984). This evidence, together with important lithostratigraphic constraints provided by coastal sequences in west Gower (Chapter 3) and in the Carmarthen Bay coastlands (Chapter 4) have been used to revise Charlesworth's (1929) 'Newer Drift' limit in this area (Bowen 1970a) – see Figure 14.

The Late Devensian ice limit: south-west Wales

West of Carmarthen, the delimitation of the Late Devensian maximum ice limit has also been revised. Charlesworth (1929) restricted 'Newer Drift' Irish Sea ice to northern Pembrokeshire where he identified ice marginal overflow channels in the Fishguard district and end-moraine deposits

between Newport and Cardigan. Morphologically similar accumulations at Banc-y-Warren and near Tregaron were used to indicate large ice-free areas in Pembrokeshire and western Carmarthenshire (Dyfed) – see Figure 14. The Fishguard (Gwaun-Jordanston) meltwater channels have since been reinterpreted as subglacial in origin (Bowen and Gregory 1965; Bowen 1967), and they indicate a more extensive Late Devensian glaciation in the area than envisaged by Charlesworth (1929).

Remains of pingos are well developed in Wales (Figure 1) and numerous examples have been described – from Llangurig in Mid Wales (Pissart 1963, 1965; Trotman 1963), from the Cledlyn and Cletwr Valleys in south-west Wales (Watson 1971, 1972; Watson and Watson 1972, 1974; Handa and Moore 1976), and from northern Carmarthenshire, around Llanpumpsaint and Pontarsais (Bowen 1974). Their widespread occurrence in south-west Wales both inside and outside Charlesworth's (1929) 'Newer Drift' limit was believed by Watson (1972) to invalidate this limit. He argued that such features were only found in high densities outside the limit of the Late Devensian glaciation, by analogy with pingo densities in the Yukon. Their occurrence in south-west and Mid Wales together with other periglacial features, was used as an argument to substantiate ice-free areas during the Late Devensian – see Chapter 6. Others, however, have argued that the fossil pingos simply demonstrate the occurrence of areas of former permafrost subsequent to deglaciation of Late Devensian ice (Bowen 1973a, 1973b, 1974; Handa and Moore 1976).

The area also provides important evidence for geomorphological conditions in south-west Wales during the Late Devensian. Significant periglacial modification to the tors of Preseli and the Trefgarn area is thought to have occurred (John 1970a, 1973) when they lay close to, but south of, the maximum ice limit. The Preseli Hills are thought to have formed a barrier to Irish Sea ice in the area (Bowen 1973a, 1980a, 1984). The survival of tors as significant landscape features, particularly in glaciated areas, has been a longstanding geomorphological problem. Tors and other indicators of periglacial conditions at the Stiperstones in Shropshire have also been used as evidence in the argument that locally elevated areas escaped engulfment by Late Devensian ice in the Borderlands (Rowlands and Shotton 1971; Goudie and Piggott 1981). Sites with tors and associated weathering products, may provide useful information regarding the long term, pre-glacial evolution of the landscape of south-west Wales (Battiau-Queney 1980, 1984).

Upland landforms

Striking examples of landforms associated with glacial erosion and deposition have long been known from the South Wales uplands (Symonds 1872; David 1883; Reade 1894; Howard and Small 1901), and accounts of these features were given by the Geological Survey (for example, Robertson 1933). The distribution of the principal erosional and depositional landforms of the region was also given by Bowen (1970a) and Groom (1971); and the pre-Devensian late-glacial evolution of the uplands has been discussed widely (for example, Richardson 1910; Robertson 1933; North 1955; Thomas 1959; Lewis 1966a, 1966b, 1970a, 1970b; George 1970; Ellis-Gruffydd 1972, 1977). Cirques and Devensian late-glacial landforms including moraines and protalus ramparts are well developed in the Brecon Beacons, particularly at Cwm Llwch, Craig Cerrig-gleisiad and Mynydd Du (Black Mountain).

The significance of these landforms is that they show widespread cirque glaciation and snowpatch formation in the uplands during the Younger Dryas. The dating and interpretation of these features have been assisted by a number of pollen stratigraphic and radiocarbon dating studies (for example, Trotman 1963; Walker 1980, 1982a, 1982b).

Lewis (1966a, 1966b) gave the first detailed descriptions of the moraines and protalus ramparts of the Brecon Beacons. From their morphology, he inferred that their formation occurred during two separate periods in the Devensian late-glacial. On the basis of earlier pollen work in the region (Hyde 1940; Bartley 1960a; Trotman 1963) the older moraines and ramparts were assigned to Pollen Zone I (Older Dryas), and the newer ones to Pollen Zone III (the Younger Dryas) (Lewis 1966a, 1966b). Later studies of the moraines and protalus features in the Brecon Beacons by Ellis-Gruffydd (1972, 1977) and Walker (1980, 1982a, 1982b) showed that most of the features had formed during the Younger Dryas.

Ellis-Gruffydd (1977) mapped 27 moraines and protalus features of varying morphological complexity at 23 locations along the Old Red Sandstone escarpment. Recent pollen analytical studies in the Brecon Beacons by Walker (1980, 1982a, 1982b) have provided evidence to support a recrudescence of glacier ice in the region during the Younger Dryas.

Devensian late-glacial and Holocene environmental history

A major theme in South Wales has been the use of pollen assemblage biostratigraphy to reconstruct Devensian late-glacial and Holocene environmental conditions. Hyde's (1940) study at Ffos Ton Cenglau (on the Pennant Measures escarpment) produced one of the first pollen diagrams in Wales. About the same time, Godwin (1940b) integrated the earlier observations of Strahan (1896), von Post (1933), Hyde (1936), George (1936) and George and Griffiths (1938) into a comprehensive account of marine and related sediments in the Swansea Bay area. He established that the Holocene transgression in the bay occurred during the later part of the Boreal (Pollen Zone VI) and was interrupted by minor regressive phases when peat

beds formed. Many of these peat beds have been recorded at other sites around the coast as these were later correlated by radiocarbon dating (Godwin and Willis 1961).

The first Devensian late-glacial sequence described in South Wales was that at Rhosgoch Common (Bartley 1960a, 1960b). Subsequently, Trotman (1963) studied sequences at Bryn House (Swansea), Cwmllynfell (near Brynamman), and Waen Du (near Llangattock), and provided an outline of Devensian late-glacial and Holocene environmental history for the region. The sequence extending back to Pollen Zone I in a kettle hole at Bryn House (Trotman 1963) provided evidence for ascribing local glacial deposits to the Late Devensian (Bowen 1970a).

Further aspects of Holocene vegetational and environmental history have been widely discussed (for example, Seymour 1973; Moore 1975a; Handa and Moore 1976; Evans 1977a; Slater and Seymour 1977; Evans et al. 1978; Walker 1980, 1982a, 1982b; Chambers 1981, 1982a, 1982b, 1983; Smith and Cloutman 1984; Seymour 1985). Traeth Mawr, Craig Cerrig-gleisiad, Cwm yr Eglwys (Dinas) and Esgyrn Bottom, the Cledlyn Valley and Cwm Nash provide a framework for reconstructing and interpreting Holocene palaeoenvironments in the region.

Llanfihangel-Crucorney

Highlights

The finest example in South Wales of a terminal moraine formed at the extremity of the ice cap during the final (Devensian) phase of glaciation.

Introduction

The large arcuate moraine at Llanfihangel-Crucorney (SO316205), north of Abergavenny, provides some of the clearest evidence available for the terminus of the Late Devensian ice-sheet in South Wales. The moraine was formed by a branch of the Usk glacier. The site was first described by Strahan and Gibson (1900) who mapped the glacial deposits in the neighbourhood of Abergavenny. It was subsequently referred to by Grindley (1905) and Charlesworth (1929), and, more recently, Lewis (1970b) described the site in relation to the Late Pleistocene history of the region.

Description

The moraine runs west from Llanfihangel-Crucorney for about 1.5 km across the valley and rises about 20m on average above the general level of the valley floor. It has a steep, north-facing ice contact slope, best developed around Bridge Wood (SO320205). The moraine as a whole is characterised by the fine development of hummocky terrain, especially in its central portions. Sections through the moraine along a north-south railway line have been described (Strahan and Gibson 1900).

The site was first described by Strahan and Gibson (1900) who mapped an area of glacial sand and gravel (Abergavenny Sheet 232), extending some 1.2 km across the valley and for 1.6 km down its length. They noted that at Llangattoch, Llanfihangel and Clytha the gravels reached their northern and eastern margin, ending abruptly against a gently rising slope of Old Red Sandstone. The sand and gravel composition of these mounds was confirmed by exposures in the railway cutting at Llanfihangel. These exposures were also noted by Grindley (1905) who observed, in the deepest part of the cutting, solid rock capped by a considerable thickness of sand and what he considered to be coarse river drift. He noted that at its highest point the moraine lay about 127 ft (38m) above the level of the flood plain to the north, and that the feature was steep enough for it to be mistaken for an artificial embankment. To the south, the surface of the moraine sloped more gently, merging into an area of hummocky fluvioglacial terrain. Grindley considered that the moraine, the 'Llanfihangel dam', had caused a major diversion of Afon Honddu from a southerly course to its present north-east course, leaving the large valley south of the moraine occupied by a small misfit stream, the River Gavenny.

Interpretation

The Llanfihangel-Crucorney moraine was next referred to by Charlesworth (1929) who considered that during the 'Newer Drift' period a large glacier fed by ice from the Brecon Beacons had filled the Usk Valley. Part of this glacier had terminated near Llanfihangel, leaving extensive accumulations of outwash and morainic material.

More recently, Lewis (1966b, 1970b) concluded that, although a limited ice cap existed during the Late Devensian, the Usk Valley glacier was extensive. This bifurcated at Crickhowell, and the smaller of the two ice streams moved eastwards across the Lower Grwyne Fechan Valley to enter the Grwyne Fawr/Cwm Coed-y-cerrig trough at Llanbedr, and thence to the Vale of Ewyas where it formed the Llanfihangel-Crucorney terminal moraine (Lewis 1970b).

Charlesworth's (1929) 'Newer Drift' limit has been revised in many parts of Wales, but has been confirmed in south-east Wales (Bowen 1973b) where the morphological evidence of an ice-sheet terminus is well developed. The Llanfihangel moraine is probably the finest example of this morainic development in the area, and contrasts with that at Glais in the Swansea Valley, which is thought to represent a recessional rather than terminal feature of the Late Devensian ice-sheet. The moraine at Llanfihangel-Crucorney provides some of the finest evidence for an ice terminus in Wales and probably represents the maximum limit of the Late Devensian ice-sheet in the area. It was

formed by a branch of the Usk glacier and has caused a major diversion of drainage, in deflecting Afon Honddu from a southerly course to its present north-easterly route.

Conclusions

The Llanfihangel-Crucorney moraine accumulated at the margin of the last major ice-sheet in south-east Wales. It is an exceptional example of its kind and is important because it provides data for reconstructing the dimensions and nature of this last major ice-sheet in Wales. As such it adds to the information about the south-westernmost extension of the North-West European ice-sheet complex.

Glais

Highlights

The largest and most impressive of the South Wales valley moraines formed by a short-lived readvance of Late Devensian ice as it wasted and retreated up the Swansea Valley.

Introduction

The most spectacular of the South Wales valley moraines occurs at Glais (SN697004) in the Tawe (Swansea) Valley. It is thought to mark a still-stand of the Late Devensian ice. The site was first described by Strahan (1907a) and has featured in studies by Trueman (1924), Charlesworth (1929), Jones (1931a, 1931b), Griffiths (1939), Bowen (1970a) and Anderson (1977). The most detailed account of the feature was given by Jones (1942).

Description

The moraine extends westwards for a mile across the Swansea Valley from the hillside at Glais to the former Garth Farm. It reaches a height of 59m OD and rises up to c. 150 ft (45m) above the general level of the alluvial flat to the south. The northern slope of the moraine is gentle, but at its southern margin forms a steep slope, seen to advantage from the west side of the valley (at SO704000). Hummocky terrain is well developed over much of the moraine, especially towards Cefn-y-Garth (SN697004). Stream exposures through the moraine are visible at the northern and western margins especially at SN689006, where glaciotectonic structures are well displayed. Recent road excavations through the western part of the moraine have revealed the internal composition and structure of the moraine.

Interpretation

The moraine at Glais was first described by Strahan (1907a) who referred to the remarkable development of 'gravels' and the 'dam' across the Tawe Valley at Glais. He remarked that the surface of the moraine was diversified by a number of small ridges running parallel to the main mass, and concluded that the moraine had been produced by the advance and retreat of a valley glacier over sediments 'extruded' from the ice-front. A gravel flat to the south of the moraine, ending abruptly some 15 ft (4.5m) above the general level of the valley floor was also thought by Strahan to be associated with the moraine which had subsequently caused a major diversion of the River Tawe.

Charlesworth (1929) referred to the moraine and noted that moraines at intervals across the Tawe and Nedd (Neath) Valleys were recessional deposits associated with the 'Newer Drift' ice-sheet; the features in these valleys having formed as the ice-sheet thinned into two distinct valley glaciers. The interpretation of the Glais moraine and similar features in neighbouring valleys as halt-stage moraines of 'Newer Drift' age was also supported by R O Jones (1931a, 1931b) and Griffiths (1939).

The most detailed account of the Glais moraine was given by O T Jones (1942). He mapped the extent of the feature and the distribution of other Late Pleistocene and Holocene deposits in its vicinity. Using borehole and sedimentary evidence, he showed that a large buried channel, as deep as 146 ft (44.5m) below OD, occurred to the south-west of the moraine. He considered this channel had been excavated in either 'Glacial' or 'pre-Glacial' times and had then been filled with proglacial outwash sands and gravels associated with the glacier which formed the Glais moraine in 'Late-Glacial' times. Subsequently, the channel was further filled with lacustrine and alluvial deposits, the upper part of the sequence being cliffed by the Tawe in 'Post-Glacial' times. Jones estimated that during formation of the buried channel, sea-level must have been about 200 ft (60m) lower than at present.

Details of the Quaternary evolution of the Tawe drainage system have not yet been established, but studies by Al-Saadi and Brooks (1973), Anderson and Owen (1979) and Culver and Bull (1979) have confirmed the presence of deep buried rock basins in the area. A geophysical study by Al-Saadi and Brooks (1973) showed that a series of Pleistocene buried valleys was present in the lower Swansea and Neath Valleys. These, they suggested, had been over-deepened by preferential ice erosion along major fault zones and pre-glacial river courses. Lacustrine deposits were described from these basins and their offshore extensions in Swansea Bay (Culver and Bull 1979). These sediments were considered to be Devensian late-glacial and early Holocene in age although the precise relationship of these buried valleys and associated sediments to the Glais moraine was not established.

The Glais moraine is a classic glacial landform. Its exact age and significance within the Quaternary evolution of the Swansea Valley area is still indeterminate, but it is generally considered to represent an advance of ice during general

wastage of the Late Devensian ice-sheet (Bowen 1970a; Groom 1971; Anderson 1977). As such, the feature contrasts with the moraine at Llanfihangel-Crucorney in south-east Wales which probably marks the maximum extent of the Late Devensian ice-sheet.

Conclusions

The Glais moraine is a classic text-book example and is the best valley moraine in Wales. Its significance is not yet fully understood, but it may provide evidence for a minor and temporary readvance of a last ice age glacier as it wasted northwards.

Cwm yr Eglwys (Dinas) and Esgyrn Bottom

Highlights

This site shows fine examples of channels in one of the best and largest systems of meltwater channels in Wales. These features were formed by meltwater flowing under pressure beneath Late Pleistocene ice.

Introduction

Cwm yr Eglwys (Dinas) (SN010399) and Esgyrn Bottom (SM975346) are glacial meltwater channels in the well documented Gwaun-Jordanston system. This system is one of the largest and most spectacular in the British Isles, the interpretation of which has been important for determining the extent of Late Devensian ice in the area. The origin of the channels was first discussed by Charlesworth (1929). Since that time, numerous authors have investigated and described the features (for example, Jones 1946; Jones 1965; Bowen and Gregory 1965; Gregory and Bowen 1966; Bowen 1967, 1969a, 1971b, 1974, 1977a, 1981a, 1982, 1984; John 1965a; 1970a, 1971a, 1972, 1976; George 1970). The channels at Dinas and Esgyrn Bottom contain Devensian late-glacial and Holocene pollen sequences (Seymour 1973; Slater and Seymour 1977; Seymour 1985).

The Gwaun-Jordanston (Fishguard) meltwater channel system

The area to the north-west of Mynydd Preseli and immediately south of Fishguard contains a well developed network of glacial meltwater channels that has long been referred to as the Gwaun-Jordanston system. Detailed descriptions of the morphology and distribution of these features have been given, for example, by Bowen and Gregory (1965) and John (1970a) – see Figure 15. The largest channel is that of the modified Gwaun Valley, some 14 km long and passing between the Carn Ingli and Mynydd Preseli. Near its western end and its exit into Fishguard Bay, the Gwaun

Valley is joined from the north-east by the Cwmonnen Valley and, at this point, three major exits from the channel swing towards the south and west. This is the most complex part of the system comprising the spectacular channels of the Crinney Brook, Esgyrn Bottom, Nant-y-Bugail and numerous smaller and subsidiary channels. In addition to these interconnected channels, other examples have been described, particularly towards the west near Abermawr and Jordanston, and to the north-east where the Cwm yr Eglwys Channel all but separates Dinas Head from the mainland. The present day streams are small in relation to the channels they occupy; the Nant-y-Bugail, for example, is some 85m deep but contains a tiny stream (John 1970a). Some channels are cut through pre-existing watersheds, and they are steep-sided features with flat floors, the latter caused by substantial Devensian late-glacial and Holocene sedimentation and peat growth.

The Gwaun-Jordanston system was originally described by Charlesworth (1929). In defining his 'South Wales end-moraine' in Pembrokeshire, he interpreted the steep-sided channels as ice-marginal features produced by ice-dammed lake water overflow during the northward retreat of the Irish Sea ice-sheet – see Figure 15. These proglacial lakes were dammed by the Irish Sea ice margin in local valleys. Ice-marginal and direct overflow channels were formed as one lake spilled over into another. This glacial lake hypothesis was

subsequently accepted, albeit with minor modifications, by Griffiths (1940), M Jones (1946), O T Jones (1965) and Pringle and George (1948).

From a detailed survey of the channels, Bowen and Gregory (1965) reinterpreted their mode of formation. First, they showed that evidence for former extensive proglacial lakes such as shoreline features, delta or lake deposits was generally lacking in the area. Only in the Teifi Valley at, for example, Llechryd did laminated lake clays exist (Jones 1965; Bowen 1967, 1984; Bowen and Lear 1982), and these are widespread between Cardigan and Pentre Cwrt (Bowen and Lear 1982; Lear 1986). Second, the Fishguard channels show a range of characteristics incompatible with an ice-marginal hypothesis. Bowen and Gregory (1965) noted that many of these channels showed 'humped' long-profiles, and, on some valley sides, channels with V-shaped profiles were sharply incised along the lines of the steepest slopes. Bowen and Gregory suggested that such an assemblage of features was most readily interpreted as the result of subglacial stream erosion. Humps on some long-profiles, for example, could not have formed at an ice margin because subaerial meltwater could not have flowed upslope: these features were more easily explained by subglacial meltwater flowing under considerable hydrostatic pressure. The steeply incised, superimposed valley side channels showed a close correspondence to features

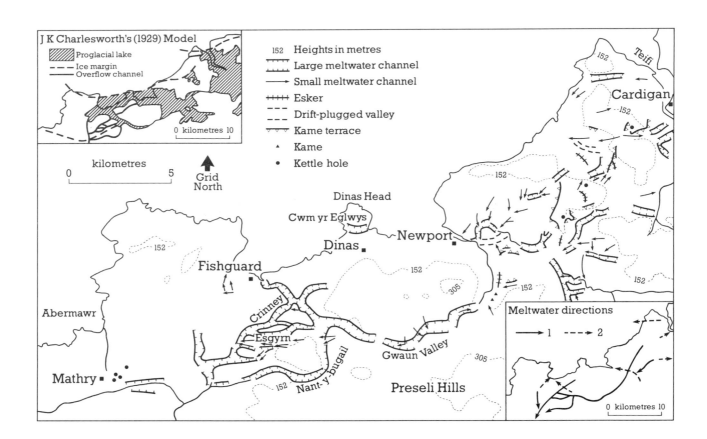

Figure 15 The Gwaun-Jordanston meltwater channel system (from Bowen and Henry 1984)

described as subglacial chutes by Mannerfelt (1945).

Thus, Bowen and Gregory and subsequently Gregory and Bowen (1966), and Bowen (1967, 1971b, 1974, 1977a, 1981a, 1982, 1984) have argued that the Gwaun-Jordanston system of channels had formed largely by processes of subglacial stream erosion, and that some channels may have developed following superimposition of englacial streams, and others as subglacial chutes. Bowen and Gregory also reconstructed a sequence of channel formation corresponding to various stages in the process of ice-sheet thinning – see Figure 15.

They considered that the fresh appearance of the channels probably indicated that they could be referred to glaciation in the Late Devensian, and observed that the re-evaluation of the channels as subglacial in origin necessitated a greater cover of ice than had been envisaged by Charlesworth (1929). This is consistent with the stratigraphic evidence from a wider area for Late Devensian glaciation (for example, Bowen 1973b, 1974).

The Gwaun-Jordanston channel system was also described and discussed by John (1970a, 1971a, 1972, 1976). He considered that the features had probably been cut by meltwater during a pre-Devensian (possibly Saalian) glaciation. Three main lines of evidence were put forward to support this contention –1) the large size of many of the channels; 2) many of the channels in Preseli are 'plugged' by thick sequences of periglacial and glacial sediments. These show that the channels existed prior to the depositional phase of the Late Devensian. Bowen (1966), however, argued that some of the tills were soliflucted, thus allowing for the possibility that both the channels and drift dated from the same (Late Devensian) glaciation. 3) The orientation of the channels was seen by John to have a bearing on their age, following the ideas of Mannerfelt (1945) who suggested that the orientation of subglacial meltwater channels, although influenced by bedrock relief, was controlled primarily by the direction of the ice surface gradient. Consequently, John observed that if the Gwaun-Jordanston channels dated from the Late Devensian, they would be expected to be aligned approximately north-west to south-east. In fact, the channels are generally oriented north-east to south-west; from which John concluded that it was more satisfactory to relate the channels to a pre-Devensian glaciation when there may have been a suitable ice gradient sloping from north-east to south-west on the flanks of Mynydd Preseli.

Such a conclusion is not, however, in keeping with prevailing opinion, which suggests that during the pre-Devensian glaciation of south-west Wales, Preseli was extensively invaded by north-west to south-east moving Irish Sea ice (for example, Griffiths 1940; Bowen 1973a, 1973b, 1974, 1977b). John (1970a) suggested that the 'fresh' appearance of the channels was satisfactorily explained if they

had again been utilised by meltwater during the Late Devensian glaciation.

Esgyrn Bottom

Esgyrn Bottom (SM975346) is a steep-sided, generally north-east to south-west oriented valley, lying approximately 80m above sea-level in the central 'interconnected' part of the Gwaun-Jordanston system – see Figure 15. Near Llanwern Farm (SM977349) a smaller channel enters the Esgyrn Bottom Channel. This runs west for a distance of about 0.5 km before joining the larger Crinney Brook Channel. The steep sides of Esgyrn Bottom are densely wooded, providing a contrast with the bog vegetation on the floor of the channel. The channel reaches a maximum width of some 180m, and the main raised peat area is some 800m in length.

The peat deposits have been described in detail by Seymour (1973) and Slater and Seymour (1977) who recorded the following generalised sequence –

8   *Eriophorum, Sphagnum, Eriophorum* and *Molinia*, and *Eriophorum* and *Sphagnum* peats
7   Well humified sedge peat
6   Well humified wood peat with *Betula, Calluna* and *Eriophorum* remains
5   Wood peat with *Betula* remains
4   Humified peat with some *Phragmites* remains
3   Grey clay with peat
2   Blue lake clay with shale fragments
1   Blue lake clay

Slater and Seymour (1977) zoned the pollen assemblages collected from the sequence into the standard Godwin Pollen Zones IV-VIII, and local pollen assemblage zones were also recognised; no radiocarbon calibration was, however, provided. They proposed the following sequence of vegetational and environmental changes based on the pollen and plant macrofossil evidence. Organic deposits first began to accumulate in an early Holocene lake at Esgyrn Bottom towards the close of the pre-Boreal (Pollen Zone IV of Godwin). They considered that a fairly typical hydroseral succession took place at the site; that is a succession from non-productive open-water through a submerged macrophyte stage, a floating-leaved macrophyte stage, a reed swamp, a sedge and grass dominated fen and finally to bog with ericaceous species and *Sphagnum.*

The pollen record preserved at Esgyrn Bottom shows many of the classic features of the Holocene vegetation succession recorded at other sites in Wales. The well documented 'elm decline' is clear in the record as are the effects of forest clearance and the agricultural activities of early Man. Although the preserved record of vegetational changes is unexceptional in itself, the extreme westerly position of the site makes the record important in terms of interpreting regional variations in vegetation development throughout Wales.

Cwm yr Eglwys (Dinas)

The Cwm yr Eglwys Channel (SN010399) is some 1,300m long and opens onto the sea at both ends. The floor of the channel lies at *c.* 5m OD, and virtually isolates the Dinas headland from northern Preseli.

Both ends of the channel are 'plugged' by blown sand, while the area between is waterlogged, and it contains an infill of up to 11m of Devensian late-glacial and Holocene deposits. Seymour (1985) constructed a series of twenty local pollen assemblage zones from the profile and provided nine radiocarbon dates. The sequence was assigned to part of the Allerød (the Devensian late-glacial interstadial), the Younger Dryas and most of the Holocene.

A radiocarbon age of 11,700 ± 250 BP (GU - 1267) from the basal organic sediments provides a date for increased slope stability and improving conditions in the channel during the Allerød (Devensian late-glacial interstadial), as well as providing a date for the local expansion of *Corylus* and other shrub taxa (Seymour 1985). A sample from the top of the organic sediments, underlying a thin inorganic horizon, gave a radiocarbon age of 11,100 ± 140 BP (GU-1275), and provided a date for the marked climatic deterioration at the onset of the Younger Dryas. This return to colder conditions is evident in the lithological and pollen records.

The palynological data from Dinas and other sites in the Preseli region were used by Seymour (1985) to demonstrate that the presently distinctive climatic character of Preseli was probably established in Devensian late-glacial times. *Corylus,* for example, was locally present during the Allerød, and probably expanded from refugia lying to the south and west. In contrast, birch was relatively uncommon during the Devensian late-glacial and early Holocene, suggesting that its eastwards migration across the Cambrian uplands was inhibited. Seymour (1985) suggested that the pollen data also confirmed the early establishment of mixed oak forest along the coastal plain.

Glacial meltwater channels form an important element of the landscape of South and west Wales. The Gwaun-Jordanston system of channels is one of the finest of its type in the British Isles. Cwm yr Eglwys and Esgyrn Bottom are outstanding examples of channels in this extensive system. Although the channels were originally interpreted as overflow features from glacially impounded lakes (Charlesworth 1929), many are now believed to have been formed by subglacial meltwaters (Bowen and Gregory 1965). The interpretation of the Gwaun-Jordanston channels as subglacial in origin and of Late Devensian age (for example, Bowen and Gregory 1965; Bowen 1984) has important repercussions for the extent of the Late

Devensian ice cover in south-west Wales and the manner of deglaciation: ice must have reached considerably farther south than envisaged by Charlesworth (1929), and ice wastage probably occurred by ice-thinning rather than by marginal retreat.

The channels are particularly noted for their large size and extent. This has led to some workers suggesting that they were occupied by meltwaters during more than one phase of ice wastage. As such, they contrast with the much more compact meltwater channel system near Carmarthen (at Maesyprior) of suggested Late Devensian age (Bowen 1967).

Cwm yr Eglwys and Esgyrn Bottom are both excellent and representative examples of glacial meltwater channels in the Gwaun-Jordanston system. This system is one of the largest and best documented in Britain, and is believed to have been formed largely by subglacial meltwaters. The scale and orientation of the channels are important factors in reconstructing and interpreting the sequence of Late Pleistocene events in south-west Wales; particularly for determining the extent of Late Devensian ice and the manner of ice wastage in the area. In addition, the channels at Cwm yr Eglwys and Esgyrn Bottom contain thick peat sequences with important Devensian late-glacial and Holocene pollen records.

Conclusions

The Cwm yr Eglwys and Esgyrn Bottom glacial drainage channels are thought to have been fashioned underneath an ice-sheet. They were probably formed at an early stage during the wastage of the last ice-sheet which occupied St George's Channel and Cardigan Bay. Because the disappearance of that ice-sheet may have been catastrophic, it means that these channels may well have been fashioned over a timescale that is brief even by human standards. The channels also contain thick deposits of peat that have yielded pollen grains which have been used for reconstructing climatic change since the ice age up to the present day.

Maesyprior

Highlights

This locality shows excellent evidence for the sub-ice-sheet formation of South Wales glacial meltwater channels. They were formed by water under great hydrostatic pressure beneath the ice, rather than as subaerial streams draining ice impounded lakes.

Introduction

At Maesyprior (SN361195), west of Carmarthen, a number of glacial meltwater channels provides evidence for the Late Devensian deglaciation of central South Wales. The channels are a rare example in South Wales of a meltwater channel system, and have been used to reconstruct a sequence of glacial drainage events as ice-thinning occurred. The distribution of the channels was mapped and described by Bowen (1965, 1967, 1969a, 1970a).

Description

The Maesyprior channel system occupies an area some 2.5 km² lying to the north of the major east-west trending valley now occupied by Llanllwch Bog (Thomas 1965). The distribution of Late Pleistocene deposits in the area was mapped by Strahan *et al.* (1909), and Bowen (1970a) demonstrated the relationship between these deposits and the channels – see Figure 16. The channels are, for the most part, cut in Ordovician shales, and they are dry and have steep sides; several channels commence and end abruptly, and one example demonstrates a humped (irregular up and down) profile.

Interpretation

Channel features associated with glacial meltwater were first noted in the Carmarthen area by Strahan *et al.* (1909) who described a 'glacial overflow-valley' at Cwm-du-hen, near Merthyr and interpreted it as having been formed by northward flowing, subaerial meltwater issuing from the large valley to the south which was filled with ice. The Merthyr channel has since been reinterpreted as a

subglacial chute (Bowen 1970a). Indeed, it was suggested for many years that meltwater channels in South Wales and elsewhere were associated with 'overflow' from postulated glacially impounded lakes. Workers, including Charlesworth (1929), Griffiths (1939), Driscoll (1953) and Crampton (1966c) have reconstructed such supposed ice-dammed lakes across South Wales, extrapolating Kendall's (1902) simple model.

Bowen (1967, 1970a) reviewed the evidence for such lakes in South Wales and observed that, in nearly all cases, shoreline features, bottom deposits and deltas – features that would normally be associated with such lakes – were conspicuously absent. Instead, he demonstrated that the majority of the channels had been formed by subglacial meltwater during ice-thinning, in the manner described by Flint (1929, 1942), Hoppe (1950, 1957) and Mannerfelt (1945). Bowen (1967) observed that patterns of meltwater channels, particularly around Carmarthen, confirmed this view. In all, he mapped some 370 such channels in central South Wales (Bowen 1965, 1980b), but noted that 'systems' of such channels were rare. One exception was the channel 'system' at Maesyprior, for which he reconstructed a sequence of channel development events.

First, the oldest channels at Maesyprior, which begin and end abruptly, were superimposed across the shale spurs by englacial streams flowing within the decaying ice. Alternatively, other channels demonstrating marked humped-profiles were cut later by subglacial meltwater flowing

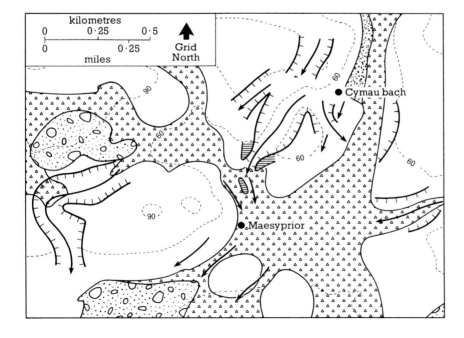
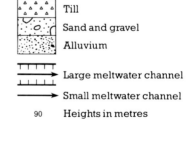

Figure 16 The Maesyprior meltwater channel system (after Bowen 1970a)

under considerable hydrostatic pressure. As the ice continued to thin, the channels became increasingly controlled by the underlying relief until, finally, meltwater flowed along the existing valley floor and sides. Bowen (1970a) considered that a Late Devensian age was likely in view of the freshness of the features.

The Maesyprior meltwater channels exhibit a number of features that cannot be reconciled with either an ice-marginal origin, nor an origin as direct overflow channels. The site therefore provides evidence to demonstrate the subglacial origin of the channels and to repudiate the long-held belief that similar channels throughout South Wales originated as overflows from major impounded glacial lakes.

Conclusions

The Maesyprior glacial drainage channels were probably fashioned underneath an ice-sheet. They are unusual because it is possible to infer stages in the process of ice-thinning from their mutual relationships. They also add to other evidence which shows that the last major ice-sheet to cover Wales extended at least as far south as this vicinity.

Mynydd Preseli

Highlights

One of the finest sets of tors in Britain, Mynydd Preseli shows evidence of tor formation in response to deep tropical weathering and later denudation during the Pleistocene. The balance between Devensian Stage periglacial action and earlier weathering has been the subject of controversy.

Introduction

Mynydd Preseli is important for an assemblage of summit and valley-side tors developed in Ordovician rhyolites and dolerites. The survival of tors as significant landscape features in the area is not fully understood, but the Preseli tors appear to have evolved, at least in part, under periglacial processes during the Late Devensian, when the area is thought to have been close to, but beyond, the maximum ice limit. Mynydd Preseli has been cited by Thomas (1923), Linton (1955) and Battiau-Queney (1980, 1984). It has also been mentioned in the wider context of the Pleistocene history of the region by Bowen (1970a, 1984), John (1971a, 1973) and Synge (1970). The debate concerning the Preseli 'bluestones' at Stonehenge was recently continued by Bowen (1980a).

Description

Mynydd Preseli forms a linear tract of elevated country that trends east to west for about 15 km near the northern coast of Preseli. The hills, which are the highest in south-west Wales, reach a maximum height of 536m OD, and rise above the adjacent plateaux, marking the outcrop of a series of Ordovician igneous rocks of a more resistant nature than the surrounding ancient sediments (Thomas 1923; Evans 1945). The most significant rocks in the range, from a geomorphological point of view, are the dolerites that form Marchogin and Carn Meini, and the rhyolites and felsites of Foel Trigarn and Carn Alw. The dolerites have been described as 'spotty' due to the occurrence of irregularly bounded white or pink patches of plagioclase feldspar (Thomas 1923), and they are quite distinctive. The generally smooth outline of the hills is punctuated by a series of summit and valley-side tors developed in these resistant intrusive and volcanic rocks.

Interpretation

The Preseli tors first attracted scientific attention in an archaeological context, as the possible source for the 'bluestones' at Stonehenge. Ramsay (1858) first alluded to the similarity of the 'Foreign Stones' at Stonehenge to certain igneous rocks in Pembrokeshire, and a possible Welsh source was also suggested by Moore (1865). It was not until the petrological study by Thomas (1923) that a conclusive geological connection was proved between Stonehenge and Mynydd Preseli.

In 1901, Judd put forward the theory that the 'Foreign Stones' of Stonehenge had been transported from Preseli to Salisbury Plain by ice. This mechanism found favour with subsequent workers, including, much later, Kellaway (1971) who proposed that the 'bluestones' had been transported eastwards up the Bristol Channel and onto Salisbury Plain by ice of Anglian age. Subsequently, Kellaway et al. (1975) used this hypothesis to invoke complete glaciation of southern England and the English Channel during an Anglian Stage glaciation, in marked contrast to the conventionally accepted extent of glacial limits proposed by other workers (for example, Kidson and Bowen 1976; West 1977; Bowen 1980a).

John (1976) also supported the agency of ice in transporting the 'bluestones' of Preseli, but Bowen (1980a) argued that the hypothesis is untenable for several reasons. First, the outcrops of dolerite are small and would not have furnished the quantity and size of material required. Second, the Irish Sea ice-sheet did not effect appreciable erosion in the area as is witnessed by the limited occurrence of dolerite erratics to the south: Griffiths (1940) showed that an erratic indicator fan of Preseli bluestone rocks could only be traced for a short distance to the Narbeth-Whitland district. Otherwise, these rock types are unknown from the glacial deposits of South Wales (Bowen 1980a). Bowen concluded that the geological evidence was thus inconsistent with "...... the scenario of liberally scattered Preseli dolerite pebbles in western England awaiting prehistoric man's collection for use at Stonehenge .....". Bowen (1984) proposed that during the Late Devensian, the Preselis formed a topographic barrier to ice from the Irish Sea Basin, whereas the previous 'Older Drift' glaciation had surmounted them, as shown by the train of dolerite erratics stretching south to Narbeth.

The question of the origin and survival of tors as significant landscape features has attracted considerable attention in the geomorphological literature. The Preseli tors were first described by Linton (1955). He proposed that tors were formed by a two-stage mechanism, involving deep tropical weathering (Tertiary) followed by mass wasting processes (probably during the Pleistocene) – see Trefgarn report. Others, however, have maintained that tors in Britain were formed principally under periglacial conditions (for example, Palmer and Radley 1961; Palmer and Nielson 1962), and in the case of the Preseli tors, John (1973) considered there could be no doubt that their present forms had evolved, above all, in response to periglacial processes. He noted that fossil scree slopes and lobate solifluction forms were widespread, citing large accumulations of scree and large frost-shattered blocks on the flanks of several of the upstanding summits at Carn Meini (Carnmenyn), Carngoedog and Carn Alw as examples (John 1973).

Battiau-Queney (1980, 1984) has recently suggested that tors in the Preseli and Trefgarn areas were, however, formed in response to two main factors. First, evidence, particularly from Trefgarn, showed that deep chemical weathering of the land surface had occurred in a hot humid environment (probably in Palaeogene times). Second, stripping of the weathered regolith and exhumation of the more resistant tors had occurred as the result of protracted uplift along old structural axes throughout the Cenozoic, and not solely as a result of changing climatic and environmental conditions. Therefore, Battiau-Queney suggested that the tors were formed in response to slow uplift where subaerial denudation had exceeded (perhaps only locally) the rate of chemical weathering. Consequently, a sharp deterioration of climate was not required to trigger stripping of the weathered regolith; rather a closely balanced relationship between persisting local uplift and erosion offered the most conducive conditions for tor formation (Battiau-Queney 1980, 1984).

Mynydd Preseli provides significant evidence for a range of geomorphological processes that have played a major role in the evolution of the south-west Wales landscape. Recent studies have shown that the tors may have formed in response to deep tropical weathering accompanied by subaerial denudation along a slowly uplifting axis. Significant modification of the tors is thought to have occurred especially during the Devensian Stage when the area lay close to the maximum ice limit. Hence the tors reflect a long history of landscape development.

Conclusions

The assemblage of tors on Mynydd Preseli is one of the finest in Britain. They provide important information about the history of landform evolution over long periods of time. Those at Carn Meini are famous because they provided the 'bluestones' for the Stonehenge monument.

Trefgarn

Highlights

Tors and profiles through weathered ancient bedrock and slope deposits have elucidated the processes behind tor formation. The site provides evidence for pre-Pleistocene deep tropical and Pleistocene periglacial weathering which combined to form the tors.

Introduction

Trefgarn is an important geomorphological site for the study of tors. It comprises two tors, Poll Carn and Maiden Castle, adjacent blockslopes and a quarry section showing deeply weathered bedrock overlain by superficial slope deposits. The site therefore displays several key elements that have featured in papers on the theory of tor formation. The tors were first investigated by Linton (1955) and the site has also featured in studies by Charlesworth (1929), Evans (in Jones 1965), George (1970) and John (1970a, 1971a, 1973). More recently, Battiau-Queney (1980, 1984) provided detailed accounts of the site.

Description

The site comprises three main geomorphological elements −1) the two spectacular low-level tors of Poll Carn (SM952245) and Maiden Castle (SM954248) developed in Precambrian rhyolite between 110m and 125m OD, with associated blockfield slopes; 2) the narrow gorge between Great Trefgarn and Little Trefgarn Rocks through which the modern Western Cleddau river runs at c. 25m OD and; 3) part of the disused quarry (SM958240) where deeply weathered Silurian andesites are truncated and overlain by possible alluvial (Battiau-Queney 1980, 1984) and slope deposits. The tor forms at Trefgarn are of the crestal type, but they are unusual in occurring on a rolling landscape at extremely low altitude.

Interpretation

Linton (1955) proposed a two-stage model for the formation of features such as the tors at Trefgarn. First, a period of deep weathering under warm humid conditions (probably during the Palaeogene) developed a thick regolith, with corestones occurring where joint planes were most widely-spaced. Second, the products of weathering (the regolith) were removed by mass-wasting processes, leaving the corestones as upstanding tors. Linton proposed that the tors had probably been exhumed under periglacial conditions during the Pleistocene when solifluction and meltwater would have been efficient agents in removing the regolith. During this period, periglacial activity may also have modified the tors (Linton 1955). Linton noted that at Trefgarn the rotting guided by joint planes had been so deep "as to produce masses of quite fantastic outline".

Since Linton's (1955) paper, however, others have maintained that tors elsewhere (Dartmoor and the Pennines) were formed essentially under Pleistocene periglacial conditions (Palmer and Radley 1961; Palmer and Nielson 1962). John (1971a) also noted that the present form of the tors at Trefgarn has evolved in response to periglacial processes. It is relevant to note that a considerable variety of tor morphology exists in both present and past periglacial regions (Embleton and King 1975b), and it would appear that no single hypothesis can satisfactorily cover all cases. Recent work in the Trefgarn area, however, has thrown additional light on the problem.

Battiau-Queney (1980, 1984) included Trefgarn in a study of the 'pre-glacial' evolution of Wales. She described exposures in a disused quarry downslope from the tors; the Silurian andesite (at SM959240) was weathered to a depth of several metres. This weathering profile was truncated and overlain by poorly sorted and weathered deposits of alluvial origin. She considered that the weathering horizon (saprolite) was of Tertiary age on the basis of both physical and chemical properties which included – the depth of weathering (several metres), the fine texture of the material with a high percentage of particles < 50 microns, the clay mineralogy of the deposits which included a high percentage of newly crystallised clay minerals in the profile, the appearance of quartz 'particles' and the massive loss of silica. She argued it was unlikely that the saprolite had developed during Pleistocene interglacial conditions because the weathering products were generally located on interfluves, indicating that their formation had preceded incision of the valley; and because the presence of kaolinite, produced by the hydrolysis of silicates and the solution of quartz, indicated that the chemical processes had been operative for a considerable duration – conditions most readily facilitated by a protracted hot and wet climate. She considered that the poorly sorted and weathered alluvial deposit capping the weathered profile had been laid down by a palaeo-Cleddau river flowing in a larger and higher valley than the present one. Detailed evidence to support the latter interpretation, however, was not presented, and the sediments can equally well be interpreted as slope deposits.

Battiau-Queney argued that the Trefgarn tors had formed in response to slow but prolonged uplift along an old structural axis developed in the Precambrian rocks. Where subaerial denudation had exceeded the rate of chemical weathering,

corestones were exhumed leaving tors at the land surface. Thus, a sharp deterioration of climate was not required to trigger the exposure of the tors (Battiau-Queney 1980, 1984). It is pertinent to note that the products of this 'tropical weathering', described at Trefgarn by Battiau-Queney, have survived in an area thought by most authors (for example, Griffiths 1940; John 1971a; Bowen 1974) to have been glaciated. This, Battiau-Queney suggested, indicated that Trefgarn had not been glaciated.

Trefgarn is also notable for the spectacular, deep, rocky gorge between Little and Great Trefgarn Rocks. Charlesworth (1929) considered that the Western Cleddau river had carried meltwater from a series of proglacial lakes impounded in north Pembrokeshire by the 'Newer Drift' ice-sheet, implying that the gorge had been used as a subaerial meltwater channel. This assertion was upheld by Evans (*in* Jones 1965) who suggested that quarrying operations within the gorge had revealed a complete lack of glacial sediments, therefore indicating that the gorge had probably been cut by large volumes of meltwater, a conclusion followed by John (1971a).

The geomorphological evolution of the landform assemblage at Trefgarn is the subject of some debate, but the site provides evidence for a range of geomorphological processes that have played an important role in the shaping of the south-west Wales landscape. In particular, the site exhibits several key elements that have featured in theories of tor formation, and the site shows evidence for probably pre-Pleistocene and Pleistocene geomorphological events and processes.

Conclusions

The landforms at Trefgarn provide evidence for the wide range of the erosional and weathering processes which have shaped the landscape of south-west Wales. The upstanding rock outcrops (tors) have been used as examples in developing theories on the formation of such landforms.

The Cledlyn Valley

Highlights

A locality showing the finest suite of fossil pingo features in Wales and some of the best examples in Britain. Formed in permafrost areas by the freezing of groundwater and the subsequent melting of sediment buried ice masses, their formation in relation to former ice-sheet limits has been the subject of controversy.

Introduction

Pingos are dome-shaped hills that occur in permafrost regions as a result of uplift of frozen ground by the growth of large convex masses of ground-ice in the substrate. Melting of the ice lens leads to a central depression or crater surrounded by a characteristic rampart of displaced substrate. Where permafrost conditions have ceased, the craters and surrounding ramparts are known as fossil pingos. The Cledlyn Valley contains probably the best preserved examples of pingo scars in Wales. The common occurrence of such features in northern Dyfed has been used as evidence for ice-free conditions in west Wales during the Late Devensian. The pingos were first described and mapped by Watson (1971) and the stratigraphy of the basin deposits investigated by Watson and Watson (1972). A detailed account of the Holocene pollen biostratigraphy from deposits infilling the pingo central depressions was provided by Handa and Moore (1976), and radiocarbon dates on the basal organic sediments by Shotton and Williams (1973) and Shotton et al. (1975). The site has also been referred to by Watson (1976, 1977c, 1982), Watson and Watson (1974, 1977) and Bowen (1977a).

Description

Widespread evidence for pingo development in the form of pronounced ramparts enclosing marshy tracts can be found in west Wales. The most notable groups of these features are near Llangurig (Pissart 1963, 1965; Trotman 1963), in the Cletwr Valley (Watson and Watson 1974; Handa and Moore 1976; Watson 1977c) and in the Cledlyn Valley (for example, Watson 1971; Watson and Watson 1972; Handa and Moore 1976).

The Cledlyn group of pingos – see Figure 17, is best developed in the more open part of the valley between 0.5 to 2.0 km above Cwrt Newydd. The features lie between 165m and 215m OD, particularly on long, low-angled north-facing slopes. They do not occur on slopes in excess of 8°. The altitude of the features rises with the valley since they are essentially valley bottom and valley side landforms (Watson 1971).

Characteristically, the tops of the ramparts are level and few of them completely surround the basins. Even in the case of isolated pingos, the upslope side of the rampart is frequently missing. Such 'mutually interfering' pingos (Watson 1971) show a range of forms; some are completely round or oval, others are more elongated with ramparts forming distinct linear ridges.

Although the steepest upper parts of some of the ramparts reach 23.5°, others have been ploughed and are therefore more subdued than they would have been in their natural state. The largest feature has a diameter of c. 200m, with ramparts up to 6m high enclosing a basin mire which is some 135m across.

The ramparts are formed in solifluction deposits consisting largely of unsorted gravelly clay (Watson 1971). The succession of deposits enclosed by the ramparts (up to 11m deep) appears to be

consistent across the group, comprising a series of organic deposits and grey clay and silt overlying the gravelly clay of the ramparts (Watson and Watson 1972). Full details of the morphology and distribution of the features, their precise dimensions, relationship to slopes and the local drifts can be found in Watson (1971), and details of the basin deposits, their stratigraphy and textural characteristics are to be found in Watson and Watson (1972).

Interpretation

Fossil pingos were first recognised in Britain by Pissart (1963, 1965) near Llangurig. A preliminary pollen study (Trotman 1963) established that the basin deposits they enclosed were of Holocene age. Subsequently, similar structures were described in the Cledlyn and Cletwr Valleys of west Wales (Watson 1971; Watson and Watson 1972, 1974; Handa and Moore 1976), in Ireland (Mitchell 1971, 1973), and in the Isle of Man (Watson 1971); and all were interpreted as fossil pingos. Comparable structures have also been described in East Anglia at, for example, East Walton Common (Bell 1969; Sparks et al. 1972). Sparks et al. (1972), however, preferred to describe the features using the non-committal term 'ground-ice depressions'.

The Cledlyn pingo remains are the most studied in Britain. Watson (1971) compared them with contemporary pingos in the Yukon and Alaska. The modern examples were considered to be of the 'open-system' type, formed by water under pressure coming from strata beneath the permafrost. He argued that ice lenses were formed repeatedly causing a complex pattern of intersecting ramparts from which it is difficult to distinguish individual pingos. Watson and Watson (1972) considered that the 'mutually interfering' form of the features in the Cledlyn Valley was highly indicative of the open-system type of pingo. Similarly, ramparts which were open on their upslope sides, were also extremely characteristic of this type of pingo. The restricted distribution of the features, to valley side and valley bottom locations on gentle slopes, reflected the requirements for the growth of open-system pingos stressed by Müller (1959), Sinclair (1963) and Holmes et al. (1968): namely, that the water flowing below or within the permafrost should be small in amount as well as close to freezing point.

Watson (1972) argued that pingos were widespread in west Wales, both inside and outside the maximum limit of the 'Newer Drift' (Late Devensian) ice-sheet mapped by Charlesworth (1929). He observed that because pingos in the Yukon were only found in high densities outside the limit of the last (Late Wisconsinian) glaciation, and that they required a long time to develop, Charlesworth's reconstructed ice limit in south-west Wales was therefore incorrect. More recent work around the coast of Wales (for example, Bowen 1974) has shown that this area of south-west Wales was glaciated during the Late Devensian.

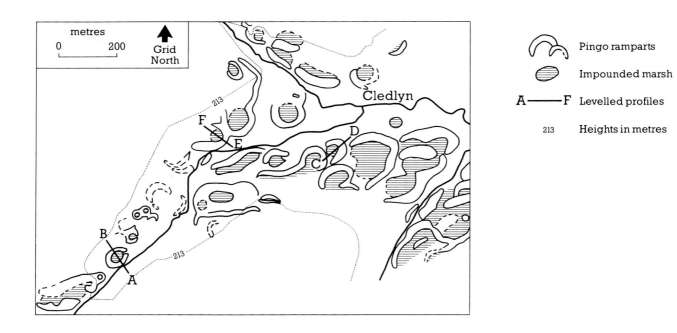

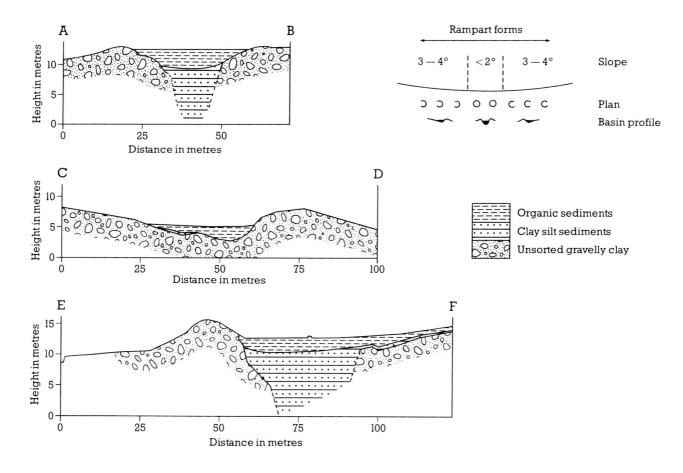

Figure 17 The Cledlyn Valley pingos (after Watson 1971; Watson and Watson 1972)

Moreover, other studies using radiometric techniques (for example, Handa and Moore 1976) indicate that the Cledlyn and Cletwr pingos formed at some time during the Devensian late-glacial. This has thrown considerable doubt on Watson's use of fossil pingos as indicators of glacier ice-free conditions in south-west Wales during the earlier Late Devensian. Moreover, open-system pingos have now been mapped in considerable densities *inside* the Late Wisconsinian limit in North America.

Radiocarbon dates are available for muds at the base of selected pingos from both the Cledlyn and Cletwr Valleys (Shotton and Williams 1973; Shotton *et al.* 1975). The small sample size resulted in large standard errors, but it appears that organic sedimentation commenced in the pingo basins between *c.* 10,300 and 9,000 BP (Handa and Moore 1976). These determinations show that the pingos had formed and that some sedimentation had occurred prior to the rise of *Juniperus* pollen at the close of Godwin's Pollen Zone III. Handa and Moore (1976) considered that this placed the date of pingo formation during the Younger Dryas. To some extent this is supported by Trotman's (1963) preliminary study of the Llangurig pingos which showed that organic sedimentation commenced at the boundary between Pollen Zones III and IV. Pollen studies from the East Walton pingos (Bell 1969; Sparks *et al.* 1972), however, suggest the presence of Older Dryas and Allerød deposits, indicating an even earlier phase of formation, perhaps at the close of the Older Dryas (Godwin's Pollen Zone I). Similar Allerød sediments have been recorded from pingos in Belgium (Pissart 1963). This led Watson (1971) to suggest that the Welsh pingos formed in Pollen Zone I or earlier. Evidence from the Cledlyn pingos, however, suggests that this is unlikely (Handa and Moore 1976): because the temperature threshold for ice melt in the pingo cores was lower than that for juniper flowering, it seems probable that the threshold would have been crossed in Pollen Zone I. Moore (1970) showed that *Juniperus* flowered even in upland Mid Wales during the Allerød, suggesting that the pingos' ice could not have survived this warm phase. Handa and Moore (1976) concluded, therefore, that the Cledlyn and Cletwr pingos both formed and collapsed during the cold Younger Dryas, showing that conditions were severe enough to provide at least discontinuous permafrost in the lowlands of west Wales at this time.

Handa and Moore's (1976) pollen study of the basal sediments in selected pingos from the Cledlyn and Cletwr sites permitted a reconstruction of regional and local vegetation succession during the transition from Late Devensian to Holocene times. The basal deposits show that sedimentation began before woodland invasion and prior to the initial expansion of *Juniperus* at the beginning of the Holocene. The early Holocene pollen spectra closely resemble those obtained from the upland valley site at the Elan Valley Bog (Moore 1970), although several important differences were noted

(Handa and Moore 1976). First, the pingo sites show very low frequencies of montane and arctic/alpine taxa in marked contrast to the record from the Elan Valley. Second, the records do not show the early rise of *Corylus* documented at other sites. Handa and Moore suggested that the invasion and spread of *Corylus* had probably been localised to what is now the Cardigan Bay area, and that although pollen from this area was carried to the exposed upland sites such as that at the Elan Valley, it did not penetrate south-east into the Teifi Valley area. The pollen evidence also indicated that *Pinus sylvestris* and *Alnus glutinosa* (L.) Gaertn became established in the Cledlyn Valley soon after the extinction of *Juniperus*.

Examples of fossil pingos are rare in Britain. Possible examples have been described from Cumbria (Bryant *et al.* 1985) and west Surrey (Carpenter and Woodcock 1981), but the classic areas for the study of such features are East Anglia and Wales. The Cledlyn Valley contains the best developed group in Wales. Organic sediments infilling the pingo basins provide an important record of vegetational changes in lowland west Wales during Devensian late-glacial to Holocene times. The pingos are most probably of the hydrostatic (open-system) type, having developed in an area of discontinuous permafrost; and pollen and radiocarbon evidence suggests that this development was probably during the Younger Dryas (Handa and Moore 1976). However, this should perhaps be regarded as a minimum age, since De Gans *et al.* (1979) have argued that pingo remnants on the Drenthe Plateau date from *c.* 18,000 BP, and Sparks *et al.* (1972) have suggested that there may have been two periods of formation in East Anglia; an initial period of development during the Late Devensian or early Devensian late-glacial (Pollen Zone I) and a subsequent phase during the Younger Dryas (Pollen Zone III). Borings in the Cledlyn pingos have not proved organic sediments dating from earlier than the Holocene. However, such deposits may exist, particularly in view of Watson's suggestion that the Cledlyn group comprises clusters of mutually interfering pingos of different ages. It follows that although the latest of these may have been formed during the Younger Dryas, others may prove to be older.

Together with comparable features at East Walton Common in East Anglia, the Cledlyn pingos are morphologically the best developed examples of these landforms in Britain. The clearly defined ramparts enclosing peat-filled basins are thought to be remains of open-system type pingos, formed by the collapse of melting ice lenses which had developed during permafrost conditions. Detailed stratigraphical, pollen and radiocarbon evidence shows that deposition in the basins began at the start of the Holocene (*c.* 10,000 BP), but the ramparts and basins may have formed during the Younger Dryas or even earlier. The basin deposits provide a valuable record of Holocene vegetational changes in lowland Dyfed.

Conclusions

The Cledlyn Valley contains the remains of pingos. Pingos are large circular mounds which contain a core of ice and are found in areas of permanently frozen ground (permafrost) in the Arctic today. The remains of such pingos consist of central depressions surrounded by ramparts. The Cledlyn pingos are some of the best developed examples of such landforms in the British Isles. Pollen and radiocarbon evidence shows that they were probably formed between 11,000 and 10,000 years ago. They are important because they show the former existence of permanently frozen ground in Wales at that time.

Cwm Llwch

Highlights

This site shows the finest glacial cirque and associated moraine in South Wales. The best of the Brecon Beacons cirques; it shows in addition to the final Devensian late-glacial moraine, possible evidence of pre-Younger Dryas ice occupying the cirque.

Introduction

Cwm Llwch in the Brecon Beacons (SO002220) is the finest example of a cirque and associated moraine in South Wales. The cirque is one of several on the Devonian (Old Red Sandstone) escarpment, and contains a semi-circular moraine of probable Younger Dryas age. The site has long attracted scientific interest being first described by Symonds in 1872. A description of the site was given by Reade (1894) and it has also been mentioned by Howard (1901), Richardson (1910), Robertson (1933), North (1955) and Thomas (1959). More recently, the significance and age of the morainic deposits at Cwm Llwch has been discussed by Lewis (1966a, 1966b, 1970a, 1970b) and Ellis-Gruffydd (1972, 1977).

Description

The valley head and cirque comprising Craig Cwm Llwch, Corn Dû and Pen-y-fan faces north-east, and contains a single broad arcuate moraine which encloses Llyn Cwm Llwch. The highest part of the moraine stands some 60 ft (18m) above the general level of the lake and valley floor. The feature has well developed lateral margins that climb the flanks of the back wall terminating 150 ft (46m) and 100 ft (30m) above the valley floor to the west and south-east, respectively (Ellis-Gruffydd 1972). Superimposed on the moraine are relatively minor ridges which run sub-parallel to its overall arcuate form. Towards the south-east end of the moraine two ridges are particularly conspicuous, and these are separated by a peat-flat from which a dry valley runs eastwards. A second peat-flat separates the back wall from the innermost ridge. The sides of

the moraine are generally steep (20°-30°) and a small exposure, near the present lake outlet, suggests a composition of angular blocks in a sandy-silt matrix (Ellis-Gruffydd 1972). Thomas (1959) and Lewis (1966a) suggested that the lake, some 6-7m deep (Howard 1901), did not occupy a rock basin. The lower slopes of the cirque back wall are scree-covered and the upper limit of the back wall is defined by an extensive plateau remnant in the Old Red Sandstone, and the twin highest peaks in the Brecon Beacons, Pen-y-fan (886m) and Corn Dû (873m). An area of hummocky terrain outside the moraine may represent older morainic material, in part soliflucted (Lewis 1970b).

Interpretation

The moraine impounding Llyn Cwm Llwch was first noted by Symonds in 1872 and subsequently described by Reade (1894). Lewis (1966a, 1966b), on the basis of morphological evidence, concluded that at many sites in the Brecon Beacons there was evidence for two phases of moraine and protalus rampart formation. Preliminary pollen evidence from peat deposits behind the 'fresh' inner moraine at Cwm Llwch indicated a probable Younger Dryas age for this moraine (Lewis 1970b). An early Devensian late-glacial (Pollen Zone Ic) age was favoured by Lewis for the degraded morainic sediments outside the 'fresh' moraine by analogy with palynological results elsewhere in the region (Trotman 1963). Lewis also identified up to five distinct ridges which he considered marked successive retreat stages of the Cwm Llwch glacier.

In contrast, Ellis-Gruffydd (1972, 1977) considered that, with the exception of Craig Cerrig-gleisiad, only one phase of moraine formation was represented in the Brecon Beacons. At other sites in the region, this period of moraine formation has since been relatively dated palynologically and by radiocarbon to the Younger Dryas (Walker 1980, 1982a, 1982b); it seems likely that the moraine at Cwm Llwch also dates from this part of the Devensian late-glacial. Ellis-Gruffydd noted that the compound nature of the moraine at Cwm Llwch probably reflected oscillations of the glacier margin, and that the channel at the south-east end of the moraine marked the former position of a proglacial stream. He considered, however, that there was insufficient morphological and sedimentological evidence to invoke the existence of extensive pre-Younger Dryas moraines at the site.

Conclusions

The sharply defined cirque and associated glacial moraine at Cwm Llwch are the finest examples in South Wales. It seems probable that the moraine enclosing Llyn Cwm Llwch dates from the time when glaciers last formed in the South Wales uplands, but the significance of apparently earlier degraded moraines has still to be resolved.

Mynydd Du (Black Mountain)

Highlights

This site includes the escarpment and associated cirques of the western Brecon Beacons. Its suite of probable Younger Dryas (Devensian late-glacial) erosional and depositional features affords outstanding evidence of the last cirque glaciation.

Introduction

The north and east-facing escarpment of Mynydd Du (Black Mountain) is important for a range of glacial and periglacial features of the Devensian late-glacial. Protalus ramparts and moraines occur at the foot of the escarpment and its associated cirques in an almost continuous landform assemblage. The site has been studied by Howard (1901), Robertson (1933), North (1955) and Thomas (1959). Detailed descriptions were provided by Ellis-Gruffydd (1972, 1977).

Description and interpretation

The north and east-facing Old Red Sandstone escarpment of Mynydd Du reaches 781m and runs from Llyn-y-Fan Fach in the west to beyond Fan Hir in the east. The principal features of the landform assemblage associated with the escarpment are shown in Figure 18. Along its northern edge, the escarpment is dissected by a number of cirques including that which houses Llyn-y-Fan Fach. Along its eastern margin, the cirque forms are less well developed and the complex depositional landforms at Llyn-y-Fan Fawr and Gwal y Cadno occupy small embayments in the escarpment – see Figure 18.

Fan Hir

The most striking of the depositional landforms is the large ridge running along the foot of Fan Hir (Figure 18), between c. SN833207 and SN836197 (Ellis-Gruffydd 1972). Little can be added to the description given by Robertson (1933) – "At the foot of Fan Hir there is a fine example of a snow-scree moraine. It runs as a lofty, rampart-like ridge of debris, three-quarters of a mile long, parallel to the scarp, and separated by a fosse-like gully". It reaches some 30m above the surrounding land and its sides slope at 30° (Ellis-Gruffydd 1972). The stream draining the gully between the ridge and escarpment shows the ridge to be composed of angular and subangular fragments of Devonian sandstones in a loose sandy matrix (Ellis-Gruffydd 1972). Robertson (1933) further noted that "...We may suppose that after the Tawe Valley ice had disappeared a snow-slope lingered for many years under the great escarpment, and that the scree material which otherwise would have accumulated at the foot of the latter, was shot down at some distance in advance to form the ridge". Although the ridge beneath Fan Hir has been regarded as a classic protalus feature (for example, Robertson 1933; Ellis-Gruffydd 1972, 1977), the possible influence of structural control has also been commented upon (Thomas 1959).

Llyn-y-Fan Fawr and Gwal y Cadno

The moraines enclosing Llyn-y-Fan Fawr were first described by Howard (1901) and later by Robertson (1933) and North (1955). A ridge comprising a series of low mounds separated by cols and two northerly trending channels can be traced around the northern, eastern and part of the southern lake shores – see Figure 18 (Ellis-Gruffydd 1972). These mounds are strewn with large boulders and are partly peat covered. Sections near the lake outlet suggest that the mounds are composed of angular material with a subordinate proportion of subangular and subrounded clasts set in a coarse matrix. It is not known if the lake itself occupies a rock basin (Howard 1901). The interest of this part of the site is enhanced by a prominent debris cone located at the foot of a bedrock chute in the escarpment face (Ellis-Gruffydd 1972).

Farther north at Gwal y Cadno, a moraine or protalus rampart was described by Howard (1901) and Robertson (1933). It consists of a single arcuate ridge enclosing a peat-flat, although at its north-west end it bifurcates and is separated from the back wall by a dry channel (Ellis-Gruffydd 1972). The ridge rises about 9m above the outlying terrain, although only 1m above the enclosed peat-flat (Ellis-Gruffydd 1972). Prominent avalanche chutes are incised into the back wall beneath Fan Foel – see Figure 18, and scree erosion continues to form prominent debris cones at the foot of the scree banks and onto the peat-flat behind the enclosing ridge. According to Ellis-Gruffydd (1972), there can be little doubt that the well developed arcuate ridge, which lies well in front of the cirque back wall, is a moraine.

Sychlwch, Pwll yr Henllyn and Llyn-y-Fan Fach

The cirques and embayments of the north-facing escarpment also contain a wide range of depositional landforms. Ridges were recorded in Cwm Sychlwch beneath Fan Foel and Bannau Sir Gaer by Howard (1901) and Robertson (1933) – see Figure 18. The northernmost ridge is situated close to the foot of the western face of Fan Foel – see Figure 18, and was interpreted by Ellis-Gruffydd (1972) as a protalus rampart. The principal ridge is arcuate and encloses a small peat-flat in its central portion, and bifurcates at its south end (Ellis-Gruffydd 1972). It is separated from a prominent linear ridge to the south which encloses a more substantial peat-flat and rises about six metres above the surrounding area. The features are interpreted as a moraine and a protalus rampart, respectively (Ellis-Gruffydd 1972).

North-west of Bannau Sir Gaer a prominent arcuate ridge occurs, its crest standing 6m to 12m above the surrounding ground surface. The ridge slopes outwards at 20-27° and encloses a peat-flat. Although arcuate in form, the lateral margins of the

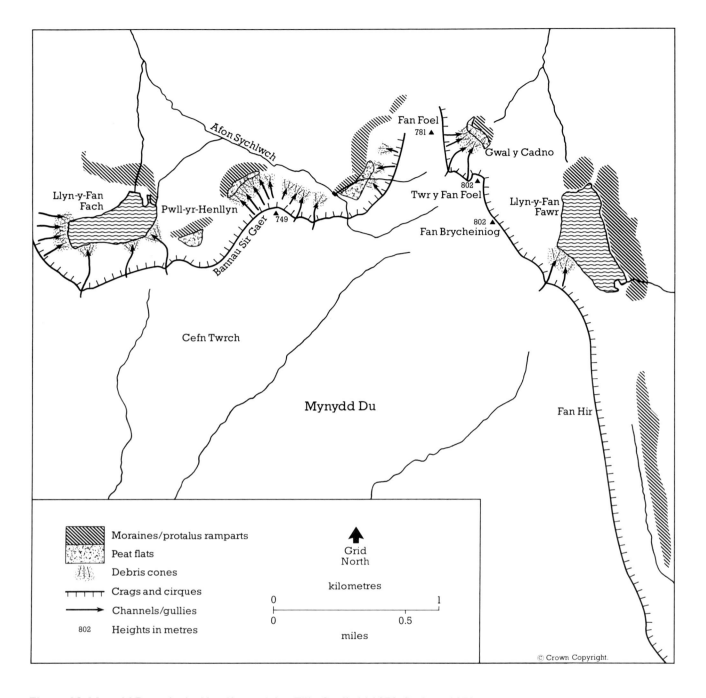

Figure 18 Mynydd Du: principal landforms (after Ellis-Gruffydd 1972; Statham 1976)

ridge are poorly developed and do not climb up-slope. Ellis-Gruffydd (1972) suggested that the feature was probably a protalus rampart, built at the foot of a circular snow-patch. Large gullies are incised into the scree behind the moraine (Statham 1976).

A further feature interpreted as a protalus rampart occurs beneath an embayment in the escarpment at Pwll yr Henllyn – see Figure 18, (Ellis-Gruffydd 1972). This single, slightly sinuous ridge abuts the back wall at its eastern end, but near the western end is separated from the back wall by a channel enclosing a peat-flat. The back wall is mantled with

scree which is extensively gullied.

Morainic accumulations have also been described around Llyn-y-Fan Fach (Howard 1901; Robertson 1933; Ellis-Gruffydd 1972) – see Figure 18. The feature is complex and is diversified by a series of smaller ridges, knolls and small enclosed depressions. Slope values along the length of the ridge vary between 15-25° and the form, extent and location of the ridge suggests that it is the product of glacial deposition (Ellis-Gruffydd 1972). To the south and south-west margins of Llyn-y-Fan Fach, the cirque back walls rise steeply by 160m. The lower slopes are extensively mantled with scree in which a number of spectacular gullies has been incised. Two particularly prominent chutes/avalanche couloirs cut the upper slopes of the back wall – see Figure 18, (Ellis-Gruffydd 1972).

Although cirque moraines and protalus ramparts have long been recognised in the Brecon Beacons (Symonds 1872; Reade 1894; Howard 1901; Richardson 1910; Robertson 1933), the first systematic interpretation of the features was made by Lewis (1966a, 1966b). He argued that the morphology of the moraines and protalus ramparts indicated two phases of formation during Pollen Zones Ic and III of the Devensian late-glacial. Preliminary pollen work in the region by Trotman (1963) was also used in support of this dating. Subsequent workers have, however, demonstrated sound evidence for only a single phase of moraine and protalus rampart formation in the South Wales uplands during the Devensian late-glacial (Ellis-Gruffydd 1972, 1977; Walker 1980, 1982a, 1982b).

Ellis-Gruffydd (1972, 1977) analysed the morphology, situation, aspect and altitude of moraines and protalus ramparts in the Brecon Beacons, including those of Mynydd Du. In total, 27 moraines and protalus ramparts of varying morphological complexity were identified at 23 locations along the escarpment. These included three moraines and five protalus ramparts around Mynydd Du. Morphological evidence indicated a single, synchronous phase of protalus rampart and moraine formation in the region (Ellis-Gruffydd 1977). The single exception to this rule was Craig Cerrig-gleisiad where, according to Ellis-Gruffydd (1977), possible evidence for more than one phase of moraine formation was present. Pollen, stratigraphic and radiocarbon evidence presented by Walker (1980, 1982a, 1982b) has since shown that a number of cirque moraines in the Brecon Beacons was formed during the Younger Dryas (c. 11,000-10,000 BP), and it is now widely held that the majority of cirque moraines and protalus features in the British Isles was formed at this time (for example, Ince 1981; Lowe 1981; Gray 1982a). Although the moraines and protalus ramparts around Mynydd Du have not been dated, it seems likely that they too were formed during the Younger Dryas.

Mynydd Du demonstrates a range of upland landforms with a significant bearing on attempts at reconstructing Devensian late-glacial palaeoenvironments. The relationship between the depositional landforms and the presence or absence of extensive plateaux surfaces in the Brecon Beacons is particularly striking, and is well illustrated around Mynydd Du: the cirques at Llyn-y-Fan Fach and Gwal y Cadno, for example, contain well developed moraines and lie at the north-east extremity of an extensive plateau. In these locations, specific meteorological conditions were conducive to the distribution and redistribution of snow, and ultimately the growth of glaciers. In contrast, an extensive plateau surface is absent west of the Fan Hir escarpment. In this location,

circumstances favoured only the accumulation of a perennial snowpatch, at the foot of which formed the large protalus rampart (Ellis-Gruffydd 1972).

The moraines and protalus ramparts which stretch around the foot of Mynydd Du escarpment form an almost continuous landform assemblage. This assemblage contrasts with other upland areas where individual landforms are more isolated. The fresh and distinctive morphology of the features strongly suggests that they were formed during the Younger Dryas. Mynydd Du also exhibits exceptional examples of Devensian late-glacial scree slopes and talus cones. These deposits have been extensively gullied in recent times, leaving spectacular scars and unvegetated debris flows.

Conclusions

The drift ridges of this site form one of the finest assemblages of such landforms in the British Isles. They were formed between 11,000 and 10,000 years ago at the foot of either small glaciers or large snow patches. Spectacular evidence of recent erosion also occurs throughout the area.

Traeth Mawr

Highlights

This site shows a unique pollen record which stretches through the Devensian late-glacial with evidence for marked climatic fluctuations during the Allerød. Its long record is important for the calibration of pollen records in the floors of the Brecon cirques.

Introduction

Traeth Mawr is a pollen site important for reconstructing environmental history since the Late Devensian glaciation in South Wales. The bog at Traeth Mawr occupies a critical location for establishing the age of moraines and protalus ramparts in the Brecon Beacons to the south. The pollen record shows that the deposits are of Devensian late-glacial and early Holocene age. The site has been studied by Walker (1980, 1982a, 1984), following a preliminary pollen study at the site by Moore (in Lewis 1970b).

Description

Traeth Mawr (SN967257) occupies an area of about 1km² in a large depression on the plateau of Mynydd Illtyd. Few areas of open-water still remain and the bog is drained by two streams flowing north-west into Cwm Camlais and finally into the Usk. Walker (1982a) recorded 5m of infill comprising –

8   Poorly humified sedge peat

7   Humified peat

6   Fine peat grading down into brown
    amorphous organic mud
5   Organic mud with silt and clay lenses
4   Clay mud
3   Red homogenous silt and clay
2   Very fine brown organic mud with occasional
    silt and clay bands
1   Red silt and clay with some rhythmic
    bedding

This sequence is shown in simplified form in Figure
19, with the identified pollen assemblage zones and
three radiocarbon dates.

Interpretation

Traeth Mawr was first investigated by J J Moore (*in*
Lewis 1970b). Moore produced a pollen zonation
which he interpreted as showing detailed evidence
for vegetation changes in Pollen Zone I. He
considered the data showed the presence of a
British analogue of the Bølling Interstadial and
claimed that at Traeth Mawr this event could further
be divided into three minor oscillations. The
interpretation and zonation of this diagram,
however, has since been questioned (Ellis-
Gruffydd 1972, 1977), and in view of the site's
critical position adjacent to the cirque moraines of
the Brecon Beacons, and because it is the only
known Devensian late-glacial site from this part of
South Wales, a re-investigation was carried out by
Walker (1980, 1982a).

Walker's (1982a) pollen and radiocarbon analyses
indicated the following sequence of
palaeoecological and inferred geomorphological
events. The lower red silts and clays (bed 1) are
virtually barren of pollen and, in counting the
rhythmites, Walker estimated that this inorganic
sedimentation could have taken as little as 100
years in a proglacial environment, during wastage
of the Late Devensian ice-sheet. Towards the end
of this phase, patches of grass, sedges, pioneer
herbs and dwarf shrubs probably existed around
the site. The overall palaeoecological
interpretation of this period, however, is a bleak
hostile landscape with an open, generally pioneer-
type vegetation, and perhaps disturbed soils.

The cessation of mineral inwash to the basin and
the start of organic sedimentation (bed 2) was
dated to 11,660 ± 140 BP (SRR-1562), a date which
Walker considered too young by approximately
1000 years, certainly in comparison with other sites
in upland Britain (for instance, Clogwynygarreg –
see Ince 1981). After the change, the pollen
indicates that the open-habitat conditions gave way
to a landscape with shrubs and copses, dominated
at first by juniper and willow, and later by birch.
These stands were interspersed with tall herb
communities and open-grassland. Thermophilous
taxa such as *Filipendula*, also indicate an
improvement in the thermal conditions. Improved
soil stability is reflected in a reduced number of
degraded pollen grains in the samples.

The remaining pollen assemblages representing
this phase of largely organic sedimentation,
however, pose problems of interpretation.
Variations in the pollen percentages and
concentration, and corresponding fluctuations in
lithology are also apparent, with clay bands present
in the organic sequence (bed 2). Walker
considered it unlikely that local variations in the
flowering of plants, or the influence of local site
factors could account for the observed fluctuations.
Rather, he suggested that they were probably
indicative of major landscape changes around the
basin caused by climatic conditions during the
Allerød (Devensian late-glacial interstadial). The
'interstadial' record was therefore seen as a
progression of three phases of vegetation
development interspersed with two periods of
climatic deterioration, in which woody taxa
declined and more open conditions prevailed.

The change from gyttja (bed 2) to silt and clay (bed
3) is isolated to 10,620 ± 100 BP (SRR-1561). The
latter phase of inorganic sedimentation represents
the Younger Dryas when glaciers and snow
patches occupied many cirques in upland Wales,
including a number in the Brecon Beacons (Walker
1982b). During this period, the landscape around
Traeth Mawr may well have resembled tundra; with
few woody plants, and an open-vegetation with
alpine communities and taxa characteristic of
disturbed soils. The evidence of soil instability is
consistent with the sediments of this phase having
been deposited by solifluction and inwashing from
a landscape with a reduced plant cover (Walker
1982a).

A reversion to organic sedimentation (bed 4
upwards), dated at 9,970 ± 115 BP (SRR-1560),
denotes the onset of milder conditions in the
Holocene. During this period, the tundra
communities of the Younger Dryas were gradually
displaced by more stable grassland with dwarf
shrubs and heathland communities, although some
soil instability may have persisted as witnessed by
occasional silt and clay bands in the basin deposits.
However, as thermal conditions improved, juniper
began to colonise rapidly, and copses of willow and
birch became established, culminating in the
formation of a predominantly birch woodland. This
latter development appears to have shaded out
juniper, which finally disappeared with the arrival
of *Corylus*. The later pollen zones reflect the
establishment of a birch-hazel woodland and the
arrival of the mixed forest genera with *Quercus
and Populus*. By this time, open-water conditions in
the basin may virtually have ended (Walker 1982a).

Traeth Mawr contains a record of Devensian late-
glacial and early Holocene environmental changes
in South Wales. Most Devensian late-glacial pollen
profiles from Wales show an early phase of open
habitats with pioneer vegetation, succeeded by
more stable conditions accompanied by a change
from inorganic to organic sedimentation. Renewed
inwash or solifluction of sediments, together with a
pollen record indicating more severe tundra-like

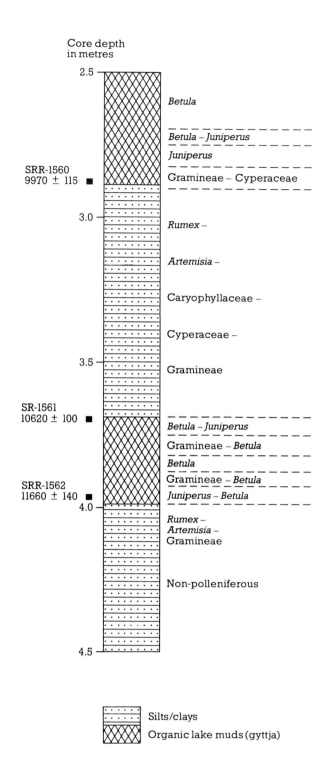

Figure 19 Traeth Mawr: a summary of pollen, lithological and radiocarbon evidence (from Walker 1984)

conditions, then characterise the change from interstadial conditions to the Younger Dryas. Both at Nant Ffrancon (Burrows 1974, 1975) and Cors Geuallt (Crabtree 1969, 1970, 1972) there is evidence for a more complex sequence, and at these sites it has been speculated that the equivalent of the Continental Bølling Interstadial may be present. However, Walker (1982a) observed that at Nant Ffrancon there were no pollen data to support Burrows' macrofossil evidence, and at Cors Geuallt there was also controversy about the status of the Bølling horizon (Moore 1975b). Traeth Mawr is therefore the only pollen profile so far described in Wales where there is unequivocal evidence for fluctuating climatic conditions within the Devensian late-glacial interstadial.

It is relevant to note that the radiocarbon dates for the Younger Dryas at Traeth Mawr are somewhat younger than at comparable sites in Scotland and North Wales. Walker speculated that this might have been caused by southward movement of the ocean surface water Polar Front, but further radiometric data are required to confirm this. Indeed, this situation appears paradoxical since it is logical that more southerly areas of Britain would have been free from Younger Dryas ice at an earlier stage.

The pollen record at Traeth Mawr contrasts with that obtained from the section at nearby Craig Cerrig-gleisiad which contains a moraine of Younger Dryas age and a pollen record commencing in the Holocene. The close geographical proximity of Traeth Mawr to the Brecon Beacons is significant: pollen analyses and radiocarbon dates from deposits within the Younger Dryas glacial limits (for instance, Craig Cerrig-gleisiad) and outside (Traeth Mawr) help to place the age of the final cirque glaciation of the Brecon Beacons.

Traeth Mawr is important for a sequence which contains a pollen record of Devensian late-glacial and Holocene vegetational changes. It is the only site in the Brecon Beacons with a radiocarbon dated Devensian late-glacial sequence. Its pollen record helps to establish the patterns of vegetation succession in the South Wales uplands since the wastage of the Late Devensian ice-sheet, and is particularly important in conjunction with pollen and radiocarbon evidence from nearby Craig Cerrig-gleisiad for establishing the age of the final cirque glaciation of the Brecon Beacons. The pollen evidence from Traeth Mawr is the most reliable from Wales to show fluctuating climatic conditions within the Late Devensian late-glacial interstadial.

Conclusions

Traeth Mawr contains a sequence of peat and clay deposits. Pollen analysis and radiocarbon dating of these have provided a record of climatic change which is applicable to the Brecon Beacons and the rest of south Wales for the period between about 14,000 years ago and the present.

Craig Cerrig-gleisiad

Highlights

This locality shows the best evidence, in the form of a pollen record and landforms, for the last cirque glaciation of the Brecon Beacons during the Younger Dryas (Late Devensian), and the climatic amelioration which followed in the early Holocene.

Introduction

Craig Cerrig-gleisiad, a fine example of a north-east facing cirque in the Brecon Beacons, contains

moraines and a pollen record significant in understanding and dating climatic and vegetational changes in upland South Wales since the Younger Dryas. The site contains the best example of an unequivocally dated moraine in the region. The cirque and its associated moraines have been described by Lewis (1970b) and Ellis-Gruffydd (1972, 1977), and more recently the pollen biostratigraphy by Walker (1980, 1982b, 1984).

Description

Craig Cerrig-gleisiad occurs on the north flank of the Old Red Sandstone escarpment of the Brecon Beacons (SN964220). The steep back wall of the north-east facing cirque reaches 622m OD, and it contains a complex of glacial depositional landforms that occupy an area of nearly 1 km^2 (Walker 1982b). These deposits extend beyond the cirque lip and comprise a series of undulating, subdued mounds. Nearer to the back wall a more prominent boulder-strewn ridge, up to 5m high, encloses a peat-filled depression (Walker 1982b).

The deepest part of the bog was sampled by Walker (1980, 1982b) who proved about 6m of deposits comprising the following sequence –

9	Poorly humified *Molinia* and *Eriophorum* peat
8	Fibrous peat
7	Amorphous sedge peat with wood layers
6	Telmatic (?) peat
5	Fine telmatic peat grading down into dark brown organic mud
4	Brown-green organic mud
3	Fine silt and clay (with some laminae)
2	Coarse silt and sand
1	Sand and gravel

This sequence is shown in simplified form together with identified pollen assemblage zones and a radiocarbon determination in Figure 20.

Interpretation

Whereas the glacial origin of the cirque and its deposits at Craig Cerrig-gleisiad has long been accepted, their precise dating and interpretation have been debated. Following pollen studies by Trotman (1963) and J J Moore (see Lewis 1970b), it was suggested that separate cirque glaciers had existed in the Brecon Beacons in both Pollen Zones Ic and III of the Devensian late-glacial (Lewis 1970b). Lewis considered the more diffuse mounds at Craig Cerrig-gleisiad to belong to an 'older series' of moraines formed during Pollen Zone Ic, and the fresher inner ridge he believed to belong to Pollen Zone III (Younger Dryas). Ellis-Gruffydd (1972, 1977), however, suggested that many of the more diffuse forms could date from wastage of the main Late Devensian ice-sheet.

Recently, more detailed pollen work by Walker (1980, 1982b) has provided evidence for the dating

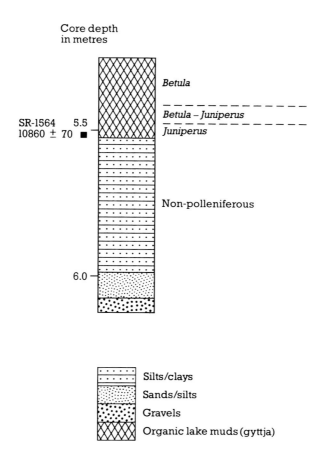

Core depth
in metres

SR-1564   5.5
10860 ± 70 ■

Betula

Betula – Juniperus

Juniperus

Non-polleniferous

6.0

Silts/clays
Sands/silts
Gravels
Organic lake muds (gyttja)

Figure 20 Craig Cerrig-gleisiad: a summary of pollen, lithological and radiocarbon evidence (from Walker 1984)

of the deposits at Craig Cerrig-gleisiad and for elucidating the environmental and vegetational history of the area during the early to middle Holocene.

During the Younger Dryas, a small glacier developed in the cirque at Craig Cerrig-gleisiad. The landscape of the surrounding area at this time was tundra, with pioneer herb communities and taxa indicating disturbed, unstable soils and extensive tracts of bare ground. Dwarf willow and occasional juniper and birch may also have been present in more sheltered locations. The deposits at this time reflect a severe periglacial environment, with solifluction and clastic inwash into the basin from poorly vegetated slopes. This phase of inorganic deposition (beds 1-3) is also recorded at Traeth Mawr, a few kilometres to the north, but at Craig Cerrig-gleisiad the renewed pulse of glacial activity during the Younger Dryas removed any evidence of earlier Allerød deposits. The radiocarbon date of 10,860 ± 70 BP (SRR-1564) marking the beginning of the Holocene (bottom of bed 4) at Craig Cerrig-gleisiad, has been considered (Walker 1982b) to be erroneously old, and the date of 10,030 ± 100 BP (SRR-1563) for the same boundary at nearby Craig-y-Fro to be more reasonable.

The transition from the Younger Dryas to the Holocene is marked at Craig Cerrig-gleisiad by a change to organic sedimentation (bed 4 upwards), and a marked rise in juniper pollen indicating improving climatic conditions. Such a peak of juniper is a common feature in early Holocene sections in north-west Britain and upland Wales. This rise cannot, however, be detected at certain lowland Welsh sites (for instance, Glanllynnau, Clarach, Esgyrn Bottom), and the behaviour of juniper in western Britain during the early Holocene is therefore not straightforward (Walker 1982b).

This early Holocene phase of *Juniperus* dominated scrub was followed by expansion of birch woodland over much of the area, and these forests were subsequently invaded by hazel *Corylus*. Mixed oak woodland then followed during the climatic optimum of the Holocene, with *Quercus* and *Pinus* on the hillsides and *Ulmus* in more sheltered base-rich sites on the valley floors (Walker 1982b, 1984). Increasing climatic wetness, commencing at *c.* 7,000 BP, was seen by Walker (1984) to have led to the decline of elm and birch, and the expansion of *Quercus* and *Alnus* throughout the woodlands of South Wales.

The interest of the site is enhanced by the apparent complexity of the depositional landforms. A Late

Devensian age for the diffuse outer mounds and ridges, and a Younger Dryas age for the inner ridge have been suggested, but Walker (1984) considered it plausible that the whole assemblage of landforms could have formed during the Younger Dryas alone. The outer more diffuse mounds might reflect an early ice build-up in the Younger Dryas in response to increased snowfall caused by southward movement of the ocean surface water Polar Front (Ruddiman and McIntyre 1981); their form being attributable to subsequent periglacial modification following a period of ice decay. The prominent inner ridge could then have developed later in the stadial, during a transient glacial pulse as the Polar Front moved northwards once again (Walker 1984). However, at present only the inner moraine at Craig Cerrig-gleisiad is dated with any certainty to the Younger Dryas.

Craig Cerrig-gleisiad contains a complex of glacial depositional landforms which extend beyond the lip of the cirque and which are of probable Late Devensian age. A small inner moraine occurs near the cirque back wall. The contrasting radiocarbon-calibrated pollen records from here and nearby Traeth Mawr provide the best evidence so far available for dating the last cirque glaciation of the Brecon Beacons to the Younger Dryas. The site also provides an important record of early to middle Holocene vegetation changes in the uplands of South Wales.

Conclusions

Craig Cerrig-gleisiad is a large cirque which was occupied by glacier ice during the last major ice age in Wales. The site's importance, however, stems from evidence which shows that the cirque was re-occupied by ice, certainly between 11,000 and 10,000 years ago, and possibly also somewhat earlier.

Cwm Nash

Highlights

This site uniquely shows screes of Devensian late-glacial age and tufas of Holocene age as well as contemporary tufa sedimentation. Its rock and land snail records allow insights into climatic change over at least the last 10,000 years.

Introduction

Cwm Nash (SS904700) is a unique site of great interest to the students of Devensian late-glacial and Holocene environmental history in South Wales. The common occurrence of land snails in a sequence of slope deposits comprising tufa, head and hillwash has allowed a detailed reconstruction of Devensian late-glacial and Holocene environmental change in South Wales that complements the available and more widespread pollen records. The site was first described by

Driscoll (1953) and was later studied by Bowen (1970a). More recently, Evans (1977a) and Evans *et al.* (1978) have provided detailed descriptions of the site and interpretations of its interest.

Description

Tufa deposits occupy much of the small valley at Cwm Nash which is cut in Lias limestones. The tufa occurs both upstream and downstream of Blaen-y-cwm (SS909703) and it appears to thicken considerably towards the coast where it has been cliffed by marine erosion. The critical exposures (at SS904700) allow examination of the full (*c.* 4m) thickness of the sequence, which extends for about 50m west of the Cwm Nash stream.

The following generalised succession can be recognised, although the five main stratigraphical units listed are not seen to be directly superimposed in any one section (Evans *et al.* 1978) –

5	Hillwash and modern soil
4	Buried soil
3	Tufa with several intercalated buried soils
2	'Buried soil weathered into scree'
1	Periglacial scree and intercalated clay bands

The site is also notable for tufa which is forming at the present time along much of the valley. The stream bed is crossed at numerous points by rims of tufa and cemented tree litter, causing local ponding and the formation of a series of stepped cascades. Small exposures through the tufa occur in the banks of the stream at several locations within the valley. Full details of the stratigraphy and molluscan fauna at Cwm Nash are provided by Evans (1977a) and Evans *et al.* (1978), and a simplified section is shown in Figure 21.

Interpretation

Tufa occurs in a number of small valleys cut into the cliffed Lias along the Glamorgan coastline between Cardiff and Southerndown (Strahan and Cantrill 1904). Driscoll (1953) interpreted the deposits at Cwm Nash as a series of marine and estuarine sediments, but a more detailed study by Bowen (1970a) showed that the sequence was more readily explicable as a series of slope deposits. A preliminary investigation of the molluscan fauna by Kerney (*in* Bowen 1970a) showed that the faunas were terrestrial and that the upper layers of slopewash material were Holocene in age. This is particularly significant since it suggests a Holocene age for hillwash deposits capping Pleistocene sequences elsewhere around the South Wales coast (Bowen 1970a).

The molluscan faunas of Cwm Nash have been investigated in detail by Evans (1977a) and Evans *et al.* (1978), who interpreted the following sequence of events. The virtual absence of marsh

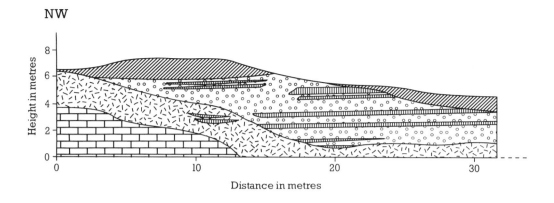

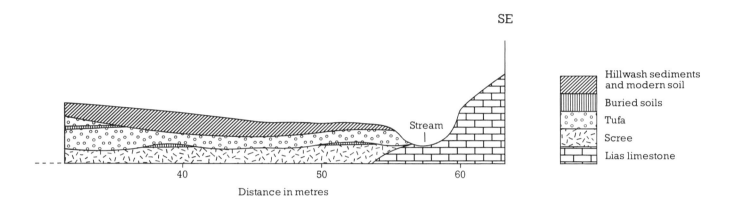

Figure 21 Quaternary sequence at Cwm Nash (after Evans *et al.* 1978)

snails indicated that the lower scree (bed 1) was deposited during fairly dry conditions, with the interstratified layers of finer material representing incipient soils. The restricted fauna suggested a Late Devensian age for these sediments, with the presence of *Helicella itala* (L.), in particular, implying a Pollen Zone II or Pollen Zone III age (Kerney 1963).

The overlying tufa (bed 3) marked a change from open-ground conditions in the Devensian late-glacial to shaded woodland with marshy conditions and perhaps pools of standing water, although true freshwater species were absent. Three distinct snail biozones have been recognised within the tufa (Evans *et al.* 1978), each reflecting an increase in the degree of tree cover, and being broadly equivalent to Pollen Zone IV, Pollen Zones V and VI combined, and Pollen Zone VIIa. Evans *et al.* (1978) stressed that this zonation was tentative. However, the extinction of *Discus ruderatus* (Férussac) and the appearance of a group of distinctively woodland snail species, probably mark a significant climatic change at the Boreal-Atlantic transition (Evans 1977a).
Soil layers within the tufa were considered by Evans *et al.* (1978) to represent periods of drier climate, including one possibly correlated with Pollen Zone VIc. A series of weakly developed soils within the upper layers of tufa was believed to mark oscillations within the Atlantic period,

perhaps reflecting temporary drier conditions (Evans 1977a).

The soil horizon (bed 4) towards the base of the hillwash sediments (bed 5) marked the reappearance of open-country snail species, a corresponding reduction in woodland cover and a cessation of tufa formation. Man was probably responsible for this phase of forest clearance, because the horizon contains charcoal, marine molluscs and angular stones, indicative of human activity. A lack of archaeological material has so far made it impossible to date this clearance phase. The upper hillwash saw the virtual extinction of woodland snail species.

Cwm Nash has yielded the most detailed molluscan record of Devensian late-glacial and Holocene environmental changes in South Wales. The lower scree, with its fauna indicative of a Devensian late-glacial age, demonstrates a period of open-country and probably periglacial conditions. Land snails from the overlying tufa show a range of environments varying from marsh, open-woodland to closed-woodland, and they record detailed changes that may mark the Boreal-Atlantic transition. Land clearance, perhaps during the Iron Age, is indicated by the fauna of the overlying sediments.

The site is also of considerable geomorphological

interest as one of the few places where it is possible to study tufa formation in progress. Cwm Nash therefore provides an important modern day analogue for the interpretation of lengthy ancient tufa sequences such as those at Caerwys and Ddol.

Conclusions

The sequence of deposits at Cwm Nash contains the fossils of snails which have allowed a reconstruction of the climate over the past 12,000 years or so. The tufa deposits (limestone precipitates) of Cwm Nash are important because of their comparative rarity. They contain evidence for possible land clearance by Iron Age peoples.

The Quaternary of Mid Wales

6

Introduction

In this account, Mid Wales is broadly defined as lying between a line running approximately west to east through the Barmouth Estuary and a line from the Cardigan Bay coast at Newquay to the northern escarpment of Mynydd Eppynt. The area includes the uplands of Cadair Idris, the Cambrian Mountains (Mynydd Elenydd) and the Welsh Borderlands. It excludes the coastlands of west Mid Wales which are dealt with separately – see Chapter 4. Although Late Pleistocene landforms and deposits are widespread in Mid Wales, these have received relatively scant attention. Two main themes, however, are of major significance to an understanding of the Welsh Quaternary as a whole. First, there has been considerable disagreement about whether landform and sedimentary evidence in the region indicates extensive glaciation of the uplands during the Late Devensian or is indicative of generally ice-free conditions and protracted periglacial activity throughout the Devensian Stage. Second, the region has become an important focus of attention in studies of Late Devensian late-glacial and Holocene environmental change and pollen biostratigraphy.

Extensive Late Devensian glaciation or a periglacial landscape?

Although aspects of the regional glacial history were discussed by Keeping (1882), Reade (1892, 1896), Dwerryhouse and Miller (1930), Jones and Pugh (1935), Miller (1946), Coster and Gerard (1947) and Howe and Yates (1953), these isolated studies have not led to any great elaboration of the Late Pleistocene history of Mid Wales, particularly the uplands. Miller (1946) concluded that Cadair Idris had formed a local centre for ice dispersal, with its own system of small glaciers feeding into and exploiting pre-existing valleys such as the fault-guided Tal-y-llyn Valley. The dominant regional direction of ice movement appears to have been NNE to SSW in this area. Although Cadair Idris nourished its own ice (Reade 1896; Miller 1946) and contributed westerly flows to the coast, this ice was subordinate to an ice cap, a larger dispersal centre, farther north. Working in the Harlech Dome, Foster (1968) demonstrated that this Merioneth ice cap deposited till as high as 427m on Aran Fawddwy, and that the ice escaped westwards through cols to provide felsite erratics for the tills of the Dyfi Estuary (Jones and Pugh 1935).

It was not until the work of Watson (1960, 1962, 1965a, 1965b, 1966, 1967, 1968, 1969, 1970, 1976, 1977a) and Potts (1968, 1971), however, that the landforms and deposits of these Mid Wales uplands were described in any detail. Watson provided substantive accounts of the glacial landforms around Cadair Idris (Watson 1960), the glacial morphology of the Tal-y-llyn Valley (Watson 1962), stratified screes in the area (Watson 1965a), nivation cirques in the Ystwyth Valley (Watson 1966), and slope deposits in the Nant Iago Valley near Aberstwyth (Watson 1969). He has used this evidence together with that derived from studies of local coastal sections (for example, Watson and Watson 1967; Watson 1982) to argue for a dominantly periglacial evolution of the west and Mid Wales landscapes during the Devensian Stage (Watson 1967, 1968, 1970, 1976, 1977a). Fundamental to Watson's views was the demonstration, by use of clast fabric analyses, that most Pleistocene deposits in the region were slope deposits and that any glacial deposits were not in their original position, having undergone extensive reworking and mixing with the slope deposits (Watson and Watson 1967; Watson 1969, 1982). In combination with studies of the distribution of fossil pingos (Watson 1971, 1972; Watson and Watson 1972, 1974), the Watsons argued for restricted Late Devensian glaciation in Wales, agreeing with the views of Mitchell (1960, 1962, 1972), Synge (1963, 1964) and Wirtz (1953). Mitchell and Synge envisaged that Irish Sea ice only reached as far south as the North Wales coast in the Late Devensian, being marked on Llŷn by the Bryncir-Clynnog moraine – see Chapter 7. Watson in fact argued that this ice had reached slightly farther south, to Sarn y Bwch. Wirtz (1953) envisaged that a lobe of Late Weichselian (Late Devensian) Irish Sea ice also impinged on south Ceredigion and Preseli but that Mid Wales remained largely ice-free. These argued that Welsh ice was only locally present in the uplands, but did not specify where in the region. Therefore, repeated cold pulses during the Devensian Stage, when the region was believed to have been largely ice-free, were considered to account for the thick accumulations of slope deposits and reworked glacial sediments – the latter presumably from a pre-Devensian glacial phase.

The widespread development of periglacial landforms and deposits in Mid Wales is not disputed, although the interpretations of the Watsons and others have been considerably modified by subsequent workers (for example, Potts 1968, 1971; Bowen 1974; Macklin and Lewin 1986). Four principal lines of evidence mitigate against the proposition that much of Mid Wales remained ice-free in the Late Devensian.

1   Considerable lithostratigraphic data from coastal sections around Wales (for example, Bowen 1970a, 1973a, 1973b, 1974, 1977a, 1977b; John 1970a) indicate extensive Late Devensian glaciation by Irish Sea and Welsh ice

to the limits proposed across South Wales by Bowen (1970a, 1981a, 1981b). This alone implies the presence of an extensive Late Devensian ice cover in the Mid Wales uplands (Bowen 1974).

2 The prominent *sarnau* present along the Cardigan Bay coast (Sarn Badrig, Sarn Cynfelyn, Sarn y Bwch) are thought to prove an extensive westward flow of Late Devensian Welsh ice from the uplands (Foster 1970b; Bowen 1974), which in places may have prevented contemporaneous Irish Sea ice from impinging onto the Welsh mainland over much of the present day Cardigan Bay coastline. Although Foster (1970b) proposed that the *sarnau* represented medial moraines between the Welsh and Irish Sea ice-sheets, Bowen (1974) argued that Sarn Badrig (near Mochras) was co-extensive with the upper till on eastern Llyn (Llanystumdwy Till), deposited when Irish Sea ice is thought to have been absent from western Llyn. Unfortunately the precise dating of the *sarnau* to either the main Late Devensian ice-sheet or to its possible subsequent readvance – see Chapter 7, and their correlation with stratigraphic sequences elsewhere, remains insecure.

3 The landform evidence from the Welsh Borderlands also shows an extensive development and a major easterly component of flow from Late Devensian ice in Mid Wales (Dwerryhouse and Miller 1930; Pocock 1940; Cross 1966, 1968; Luckman 1966, 1970). Ice nourished from central Wales is generally thought to have escaped eastwards into Herefordshire and Shropshire where it was unimpeded by other ice masses (Luckman 1970). The Clun, Teme, Lugg, Hindwell and Arrow Valleys are all believed to have contained glaciers fed by ice from the west (Luckman 1970). Similarly, farther south, the Wye glacier spread over the Hereford basin in a large piedmont lobe (Luckman 1970). The maximum extent of this Mid Wales ice is usually taken as the limit of continuous drift of an undissected nature (Bowen 1974), and it is marked in many areas by prominent morainic accumulations. Although absolute dates are unavailable, this morainic belt is thought to represent the maximum limit of the Late Devensian ice-sheet (Bowen 1974), and in this region the limit corresponds closely to the 'Newer Drift' limit drawn by Charlesworth (1929). Highly dissected drift and remanié deposits outside this limit are believed to date from a pre-Devensian glacial episode (Luckman 1970).

4 Landforms and sediments within this proposed Late Devensian maximum limit in Mid Wales are commensurate with a thoroughly glaciated landscape (Wood 1959; Potts 1971; Bowen 1974), but with a significant subsequent periglacial modification. Such evidence includes valley moraines, kettle holes and kame terraces in Radnorshire and Herefordshire (Luckman, 1966), and extensive lacustrine deposits around Wigmore and Presteigne where Cross (1968) estimated the thickness of Late Devensian ice to have been in the region of 240m, extensive outwash deposits in the Builth-Llanwrtyd lowland (Potts 1968; Lewis 1970b), and an extensive system of moraines and outwash terraces in the Wye Valley (Pocock 1940). Moreover, in the uplands proper Potts (1968) has mapped extensive areas of till and outwash in the major valleys, which he considered to be Late Devensian in age. Potts (1968, 1971) argued that extensive reworking of these glacial sediments by solifluction occurred during the Late Devensian late-glacial; and, where slope conditions and lithology were suitable, head, stratified screes, blockfields and tors formed.

More recently, Macklin and Lewin (1986) confirmed that a number of valleys in the region contain locally thick successions of glacial and alluvial sediments, and referred to local (Welsh) till mantling slopes and interfluves, for example, in the Rheidol Valley. In reply, S Watson (1987) maintained that nowhere was this till *in situ,* having been widely reworked and incorporated into slope deposits. In response, Macklin and Lewin (1987) concluded that till in the Rheidol Valley exhibited fabric properties entirely consistent with deposition by a westerly moving glacier.

It is within the context of this background that the selected GCR sites should be viewed. Those at Cadair Idris and Cwm Ystwyth provide some of the best evidence currently documented from Mid Wales for Late Pleistocene glacial and periglacial conditions. Cadair Idris and Tal-y-llyn demonstrate an excellent range of large-scale glacial erosional features, including the outstanding cirque of Cwm Cau (Watson 1960, 1977a) and the over-deepened valley of Tal-y-llyn (Watson 1962, 1977a). The interest of these sites is enhanced by landforms and deposits thought to have formed largely as the result of periglacial activity. These include the massive landslide impounding Tal-y-llyn, a number of alluvial fans and blockstreams, scree slopes and protalus ramparts. The cirque moraines and protalus features of this massif provide the best evidence for cirque glacier and snowpatch development in Mid Wales during the Devensian late-glacial. As such, the site provides complementary landform evidence to selected sites in northern Snowdonia and the Brecon Beacons. Cadair Idris also provides important exposures through stratified screes (Grèzes Litées). These deposits are a widespread feature in the Mid Wales uplands and they reflect the susceptibility of local geological strata, particularly mudstones and shales, to frost-assisted weathering processes under periglacial conditions (Watson 1965a, 1977a). It is likely that they formed in the Devensian late-glacial (Potts 1968).

Devensian late-glacial and Holocene environmental change

Although details of pre-Late Devensian late-glacial history are less well known in inland Mid Wales than in the coastal regions, the area is the most intensively studied in Wales for Devensian late-glacial and Holocene environmental history. Since Godwin and Mitchell's (1938) study at Tregaron, numerous profiles have been described and details of Devensian late-glacial and Holocene vegetational history established (for example, Moore 1966, 1968, 1970, 1972a, 1972b, 1973; Moore and Chater 1969a, 1969b; Smith and Taylor 1969; Hibbert and Switsur 1976; Lowe 1981; Lowe *et al.* 1988). Several studies have traced the course of vegetation development into historical and recent times (Turner 1964, 1965, 1977; Moore 1968, 1973; Moore and Chater 1969b), and Smith and Taylor (1969) have applied pollen biostratigraphic methods to soil profiles, enabling patterns of pedogenesis to be related to the established Holocene pollen zones, as well as documenting the influences of Bronze Age Man and his successors. Sites in the region have also featured in a number of nationwide studies which discuss aspects of regional floral diversity and diachroneity during major Devensian late-glacial and Holocene events (for example, Smith and Pilcher 1973; Taylor 1973; Deacon 1974; Birks *et al.* 1975). Sequences at Llyn Gwernan and the Elan Valley Bog provide the most extensive and complete Devensian late-glacial to Holocene sequences so far known in the region. Cors y Llyn (Llyn Mire), Tregaron Bog and the Elan Valley Bog represent the most detailed records of vegetation history during the Holocene for Mid Wales. Comprehensive radiocarbon calibration is available for the sequences at both Llyn Gwernan and Tregaron.

Cadair Idris

Highlights

This site provides one of the finest assemblages of large-scale glacial erosional features in Wales, showing a wide range of landforms formed by glacial and periglacial processes and mass-movement. This major dispersal centre for Welsh ice allows studies of cirque development in relation to substrate, aspect and relief.

Introduction

Cadair Idris and Tal-y-llyn are outstandingly important for glacial and periglacial landforms. Cadair Idris contains a number of glacial and nivation cirques, including Cwm Cau which was described by W V Lewis as the finest cirque in Britain. This shows a very clear relationship to geological structure and opens out on to the Tal-y-llyn Valley, a classic over-deepened valley developed along the line of the Bala Fault. In addition to large-scale features of glacial erosion, the area is also renowned for a range of depositional landforms associated with mass-movement and periglacial processes. Most spectacular of these is the bar impounding Tal-y-llyn, formed by a huge landslide from Graig Goch. The Tal-y-llyn Valley also contains very fine examples of stratified screes, well exposed near Maes-y-Pandy. Other periglacial interests include protalus ramparts, notably at Craig-y-llam, and a large debris fan or blockstream near Bwlch Llyn Bach. The glacial and periglacial geomorphology of the area has been described by Watson (1960, 1962, 1965a, 1967, 1968, 1970, 1976, 1977a), and has also been mentioned by Miller (1946), Lewis (1938, 1949), Howe and Yates (1953) and Cox (1983).

Description and interpretation

The main ridge of the Cadair Idris massif, which rises to *c.* 890m OD, runs south-west to north-east and is bounded to the south by the glaciated valley of Tal-y-llyn and to the north by the valley of the Mawddach. To the west is Cardigan Bay and to the east the Dulas Valley.

Despite the scale and range of Late Pleistocene geomorphological features around Cadair Idris and Tal-y-llyn, the area has received little attention from geomorphologists. Aspects of the regional glacial history were discussed by Reade (1896), Jones and Pugh (1935) and Miller (1946), and Cwm Cau was referred to in studies of cirque formation by Lewis (1938, 1949). A bathymetrical study of Llyn Cau was undertaken by Howe and Yates (1953). Miller (1946) concluded that the Cadair Idris massif acted as a centre of ice dispersal with its own system of small glaciers emanating from the cirques at, for example, Cwm Gadair and Cwm Cau. According to Miller, the regional direction of ice movement appears to have been from NNE to SSW exploiting pre-existing valleys developed along the lines of structural weakness such as that of Tal-y-llyn.

Cirques

The site contains a number of well developed glacial cirques and nivation cirques – see Figure 22. The Cadair Idris group of cirques is centred on Bwlch Cau to the south-west of the Cadair Idris summit. These demonstrate the relationship between cirque development and aspect and geological structure. In the group, magnificent cirques with precipitous head and side walls face north and east, with the more poorly developed south-facing Cwm Amarch (Watson 1960). The northern cirques are fashioned in a structural north-facing escarpment developed in a granophyre sill. Here, the steep back walls are formed by great joint blocks split from the sill: Cwm Gadair is a particularly fine example cut into this resistant igneous body. In contrast, the cirque of Cwm Amarch is cut in closely cleaved mudstones and acid volcanic rocks. The latter dip towards the cirque with the result that the back wall is much less precipitous.

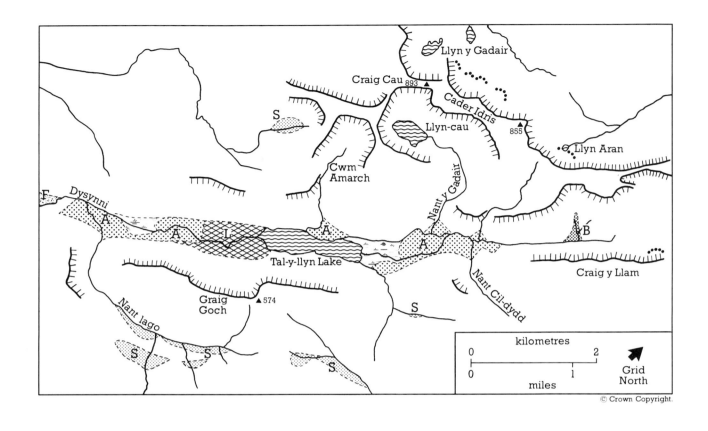

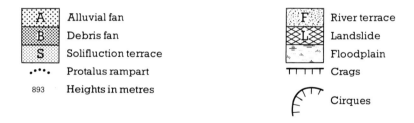

A	Alluvial fan		F	River terrace
B	Debris fan		L	Landslide
S	Solifluction terrace			Floodplain
·•••·	Protalus rampart		TTTTT	Crags
893	Heights in metres			Cirques

Figure 22 Cadair Idris: principal landforms (after Watson 1977a)

Of the Cadair group of cirques, Cwm Cau is undoubtedly the most impressive. It is surrounded on three sides by rock walls varying between 305-457m in height. The east-facing head wall and southern slopes are developed in highly resistant Ordovician igneous rocks, while softer mudstones occupy a line of weakness along which the cirque floor has been excavated. The head wall of Cwm Cau is exceptionally steep, rising c. 335m in a horizontal distance of some 200m. The present day lake is dammed by morainic material beyond which the valley floor falls in level via a series of roches moutonnées, many of which take the form of miniature steps (Cox 1983).

The Tal-y-llyn Valley

The glacial morphology of this valley was described in some detail by Watson (1962). It is a straight valley trending north-east to south-west. For most of its length it cuts through mudstones but nearer its head it is developed in volcanic rocks. The trough lacks spurs and has well developed cliffs below the valley shoulder. Tributary valleys all hang above the main trough, which their streams enter by spectacular falls (Watson 1960). The valley has many features, including an over-deepened profile, produced by glacial erosion (Watson 1962), and the pronounced straightness of the main valley is clearly a reflection of geological structure (Watson 1960). The Tal-y-llyn is a classic example of a glacial trough, but it has perhaps become better known for its wide range of depositional landforms associated with periglacial and mass-movement processes.

The Tal-y-llyn landslide

The bar impounding Tal-y-llyn lake is the most spectacular of the landforms in the valley. It is a massive feature some 24m above the level of the lake and it extends down the valley for almost 1 km.

Reade (1896) considered that this hummocky feature was a glacial moraine damming the lake; subsequent work (Watson 1960) showed that the feature was a rock bar. More detailed studies (Watson 1968, 1976, 1977a) have shown that the feature is a landslide of mudstones from the face of Graig Goch, where a scar demonstrates the source of the material. Watson (1977a) concluded that the landslide had occurred in several stages.

Stratified screes or Grèzes Litées

Much of the Tal-y-llyn Valley has been infilled with periglacial scree derived from the steep valley sides. The scree is stratified in places and consists of alternating thin beds of coarse and fine debris, the coarse beds generally being the thicker (Watson 1965a, 1977a). The finer beds are silty but the coarse beds frequently have an open texture (Watson 1965a). Classic examples of stratified screes or Grèzes Litées are well exposed in small quarries near Maes-y-Pandy in the southern part of the valley below the large landslide, and at the valley head where up to 18m of scree has been recorded (Watson 1968). A study of fourteen such sites in Mid Wales led Watson (1965a) to suggest that the stratified screes always rested on unsorted slope deposits. He considered that they had formed under periglacial conditions by freeze-thaw processes acting on the fine-grained mudstones of the region.

Moraines and protalus ramparts

Fine examples of cirque moraines and protalus ramparts occur within the area – see Figure 22. Watson (1960) demonstrated that the pattern of moraines within the cirques, as well as the cirques themselves, show the strong influence of aspect. For example, the relatively poorly developed western cirque has no recognisable moraines, but those in Cwm Cau and Cwm Gadair, the north and north-east facing cirques, are well developed. Those in Cwm Gadair are symmetrically arranged across the lower end of the lake which usually drains by seepage through the boulder moraine (Watson 1960). In Cwm Cau the moraines are hummocky and similarly impound the cirque lake. They are thickest and rise highest on its south side. In both cirques, the moraines occur at a considerable distance from the back walls.

Well developed examples of protalus ramparts also occur within the area, both in the Tal-y-llyn Valley, below Craig-y-Llam, and near Cadair Idris, at Llyn Aran and beneath Twr Du – see Figure 22. Watson (1967) considered that four protalus moraines occurred along the northern face of Cadair Idris, the easternmost forming the southern shore of Llyn Aran. He observed that, like the nivation cirque and protalus moraine described from Cwm Tinwen near Aberystwyth, none of the Cadair Idris examples occupied true glacial cirques. Rather, the protalus moraines occur in slight embayments or recessions within the steep ridge. Unlike the glacial moraines described at Cwm Cau and Cwm Gadair, these protalus features occur close against the ridge or back wall, indicating that they probably originated as rockfall accumulations downslope from perennial snow patches.

Perhaps the most impressive protalus rampart is that at Llyn Bach beneath Craig-y-Llam (Watson 1977a). Here, the rampart rises more than 20m above the surrounding surface, and its external width is some 200m. The rampart curves at both ends into the slight embayment within the steep valley side. The narrow basin which the rampart should typically enclose had been infilled with head.

The cirque moraines and protalus ramparts within the Cadair Idris area have not been dated precisely. However, in view of the detailed palynological and geomorphological evidence from northern Snowdonia (for example, Ince 1981, 1983; Gray 1982a), and from the Brecon Beacons, South Wales (for example, Walker 1980, 1982a, 1982b), a Younger Dryas age would seem probable. This interpretation is corroborated by palynological and radiocarbon evidence from Llyn Gwernan to the north of Cadair Idris where the Younger Dryas is represented (Lowe 1981).

Alluvial fans and blockstreams

Alluvial fans are a common feature of the Tal-y-llyn Valley, covering large areas of the valley floor at the discordant junctions of the tributary valleys – see Figure 22. Watson (1977a) noted that the fans which spread across the valley floor are composed of mudstone gravel bedded at low angles. On the other hand, fans of coarse blocky igneous rock debris stand at higher angles. Fine examples of such fans occur at the junction of the Tal-y-llyn Valley with the tributary Nant Iago, below Cwm Amarch and at the exit of Nant y Gadair from Llyn Cau. They are believed to be associated with a periglacial régime (Watson 1977a). Watson (1968, 1977a) also described what he called an avalanche fan or blockstream some 3.5 km north-east of Tal-y-llyn lake.

The Cadair Idris and Tal-y-llyn area contains an outstanding range of glacial and periglacial landforms which are important for reconstructing the Late Pleistocene history of the region. The area contains some of the finest glacial and nivation cirques in Wales and one of the most impressive glacial troughs. The landslide impounding Tal-y-llyn lake is also a remarkable geomorphological feature, as are the exposures of stratified scree in the Tal-y-llyn Valley. Together with the mountains of northern Snowdonia and the Brecon Beacons in South Wales, Cadair Idris provides an important example of large-scale glacial erosional features. The widespread development and range of periglacial landforms also makes the area of exceptional interest. The interpretation of this range of landforms is crucial to the understanding and reconstruction of Late Pleistocene events in the region as a whole.

The cirques of the Cadair massif demonstrate a

close relationship between cirque development, aspect and relief, and provide, in a compact area, the best range of glacial landforms associated with a dispersal centre for Welsh ice in the Mid Wales uplands. The area is also noted for the wide range and fine development of landforms formed by mass-movement and periglacial processes; of these, the large landslide which impounds Tal-y-llyn lake, and the stratified screes, which are a characteristic feature of the region, are particularly impressive. Well developed cirque moraines and protalus ramparts demonstrate important evidence for cirque glacier and snow patch development during the Devensian late-glacial. The glacial and periglacial landforms are central to the discussion over whether or not the region was extensively glaciated during the Late Devensian.

Conclusions

Cadair Idris contains one of the finest assemblages of landforms caused by glacial erosion anywhere in Wales. It includes the cirque described as the most perfectly formed in the British Isles. The area also contains a wide range of periglacial landforms and deposits. Together the glacial and periglacial features combine to form one of the best teaching areas in the British Isles.

Cwm Ystwyth

Highlights

Features occur here which have been interpreted as nivation cirques, formed by persistent snow patches during the Late Devensian. The features show little evidence of glacial erosion typical of cirques elsewhere in upland Wales.

Introduction

Cwm Ystwyth is an important site with two features interpreted by Watson as nivation cirques, Cwm Du (SN811740) and Cwm Tinwen (SN832748). These features occur at much lower altitudes than would normally be expected for glacial cirques in the area. They are not thought to be associated with glacial erosion and are believed to have originated from nivation processes during the Devensian Stage. The site was first described by Keeping (1882) and has been studied in some detail by Watson (1966, 1968, 1970, 1976) and Watson and Watson (1977).

Description

The two cirque forms, Cwm Du and Cwm Tinwen (Figure 23) are developed in the north-facing slope of the Ystwyth Valley. According to Watson and Watson (1977), they are smaller and lie c. 180m lower than typical glacial cirques in the area (for instance, Cwm Cau, Cadair Idris). They possess steep rocky back walls, but apparently show none of the features often associated with glacial erosion,

such as the typical rock basin with an enclosing rock lip.

Mapping at Cwm Tinwen (Watson 1966), showed a moraine-like ridge up to 17m thick, enclosing a boggy flat against the back wall. This ridge is highest in the centre, but west of a small gully that bisects the ridge, the drift accumulation becomes narrower. Where this narrowing occurs, there is some suggestion of a double ridge – a small ridge superimposed on a larger one. The material in the ridge is highly variable, comprising a mixture of loose yellow-grey head with lenses of sand, silt and gravel. Larger blocks up to 1.5m are also present (Watson 1966). The deposits show downslope stratification.

Cwm Du is larger than Cwm Tinwen, but in contrast is not simply occupied by just a 'moraine-like' ridge (Watson 1966). Instead, the basin is fronted by a steep bank of drift, some 18m high in the centre, which forms a smooth, generally concave, slope rising up to the back wall. This smooth slope is interrupted near the back wall by a small ridge of stony clay which fills the south-west corner of the cirque – see Figure 23. The main expanse of deposits at Cwm Du forms a fan that is stepped in profile. Gully exposures through the fan show that it consists of stony clays with bedded silts and gravels.

Interpretation

Keeping (1882) considered that the deposits at Cwm Du formed a terminal moraine "heaped up at the end of the melting glaciers". In contrast, Watson (1966, 1968, 1970, 1976) and Watson and Watson (1977) showed that the landform and its associated deposits may be the product of nivation rather than glacial processes. Watson proposed that Cwm Du and Cwm Tinwen had formed in response to the accumulation of two quite different types of perennial snow patch; one gently sloping, the other steeply sloping. At Cwm Tinwen, the steep moraine-like ridge located close to the back wall was interpreted by Watson (1966) as a protalus rampart formed at the foot of a steep perennial snow patch. He thought that the hollow enclosed by the ridge was narrow because the snow had been banked steeply against the valley side, giving a pronounced gradient down which frost-shattered debris could glissade eventually to accumate as a ridge at the foot. The curved back wall may have produced a convergence of debris towards the centre where the rampart is thickest. Where it shows a double ridge structure, a later rampart is probably resting on a larger, older one. The age of these features is uncertain, but Watson (1966) argued that they had probably formed during the Devensian late-glacial when ice is thought to have persisted in nearby but more elevated cirques such as Cwm Cau, Cadair Idris.

The debris fan at Cwm Du, however, was attributed (Watson 1966) to an entirely different set of circumstances and processes. It was thought to have accumulated beneath a large but gently

Cwm Tinwen

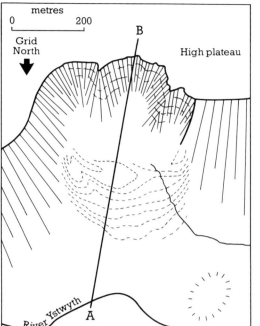

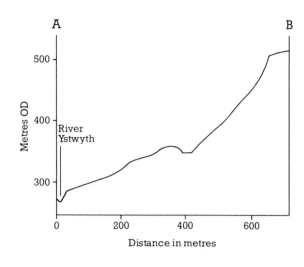

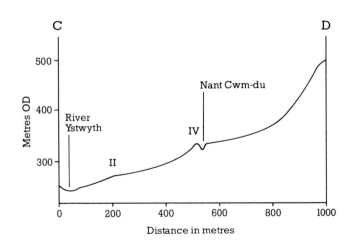

Cwm Du

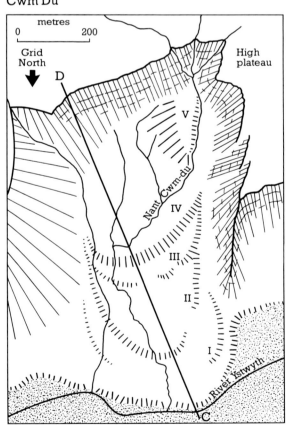

Figure 23 Cwm Ystwyth: principal landforms (after Watson 1966; Watson and Watson 1977)

sloping perennial snow patch as a series of solifluction deposits. Watson envisaged that the drift had been built up in a series of layers, in much the same manner as the mechanism described by Botch (1946), in the Ural Mountains, with solifluction debris accumulating beneath the lower part of the snow patch and moving subaerially downslope as a series of solifluction terraces. Watson noted that waterlain silts, sands and gravels capped more poorly sorted (head) deposits on a number of the terrace 'treads' in the stepped fan profile. He postulated that these deposits might have been laid down during a recessive phase of the snow patch when summer melting was pronounced. In turn, these waterlain deposits were then partly submerged beneath the solifluction deposits of the succeeding, more rigorous climatic phase. The small ridge in the south-west corner of the cirque was interpreted by Watson as a small protalus rampart, representing the final stages of nivation, when steeply sloping névé occupied this part of the cirque. As with Cwm Tinwen, a Devensian late-glacial age seems likely in view of evidence from other areas of Wales where significant glacier development is well documented, particularly during the Younger Dryas (c. 11,000-10,000 BP).

On the basis of the evidence then available, Watson (1966) suggested that the fan at Cwm Du had been entirely built up by solifluction and related slope processes. A new exposure in 1972 near the front of the gully, however, led to a modified interpretation (Watson and Watson 1977). The greater part of this exposure consisted of grey clay containing clasts in a tangential arrangement to the outer limit of the fan, indicating possible pressure along the fan axis. Further evidence for thrusting in the beds was also seen by Watson and Watson (1977) who concluded that the lower deposits were therefore the result of an initial ice advance from the cirque. This, they suggested, had been followed by a period of nivation responsible for the remainder of the fan form.

Cwm Ystwyth is important for a series of cirque landforms and associated deposits, the interpretation of which remains crucial to the understanding of Late Pleistocene events and processes in the area. Cwm Tinwen shows a fine example of a feature which is fairly common in upland Wales, a moraine-like ridge fronting a narrow basin elongated parallel to the ridge. Such features are found in strongly shaded positions and frequently below the level of more typical glacial cirques. The ridge at Cwm Tinwen is thought to be a protalus rampart developed at the base of a former, steeply sloping snow patch (Watson 1966). It contrasts with Cwm Du with its more open cirque-like basin floored by terraced superficial deposits. It has been proposed that this debris accumulated in Cwm Du as solifluction deposits beneath an inert mass of névé. Although there is also some evidence that glacier ice may have played a role in the formation of these deposits, the major part of the landform and sediment association is thought to have been derived from nivation processes beneath a relatively gently sloping snow

patch. It has been proposed therefore that these 'nivation' cirques were occupied by perennial snow patches, of demonstrably different character, not of sufficient thickness for plastic deformation and flow as glacier ice. The precise place of these features in the Late Pleistocene chronology of the region is not exactly determined, although it seems likely that considerable development probably occurred during the Devensian late-glacial. Watson, however, considered that the preponderance within the region of these nivation and other periglacial landforms, rather than true glacial features, was indicative of an extremely restricted Late Devensian Welsh ice mass; a view that has not been widely accepted.

Cwm Ystwyth displays cirque landforms and associated deposits which are significant for interpreting Late Pleistocene events. These cirque-like features occur at lower altitude than the true cirques in the region. They have been interpreted as nivational landforms; with Cwm Tinwen containing a well developed protalus rampart and Cwm Du containing extensive terraced deposits, formed largely by solifluction processes beneath a large, gently sloping snow patch. The evidence from Cwm Ystwyth has been taken to be consistent with generally ice-free conditions over much of Mid Wales during the Late Devensian. It is also possible that the cirque deposits were formed during the Devensian late-glacial.

Conclusions

Cwm Ystwyth contains two unique cirque landforms, together with their associated deposits. Cwm Tinwen and Cwm Du have been interpreted as nivation cirques (that is landforms resembling glacial cirque features, but which are thought to have been fashioned by periglacial or cold climate and snow accumulation processes). The cirques and their deposits have been compared with similar features in the Ural Mountains of Russia and as such they are important in showing important variations in geomorphological processes towards the end of the last ice age.

Llyn Gwernan

Highlights

A key site where new radiocarbon dating techniques have been used to calibrate the Devensian late-glacial and Holocene rock record. Such dating allows accurate dates to be given for the onset of the last, Younger Dryas, glaciation in the Cadair Idris area, as well as for the wastage of this ice and the commencement of the Holocene.

Introduction

Llyn Gwernan contains an exceptional thickness of Devensian late-glacial deposits. Their biostratigraphy and radiocarbon dating have

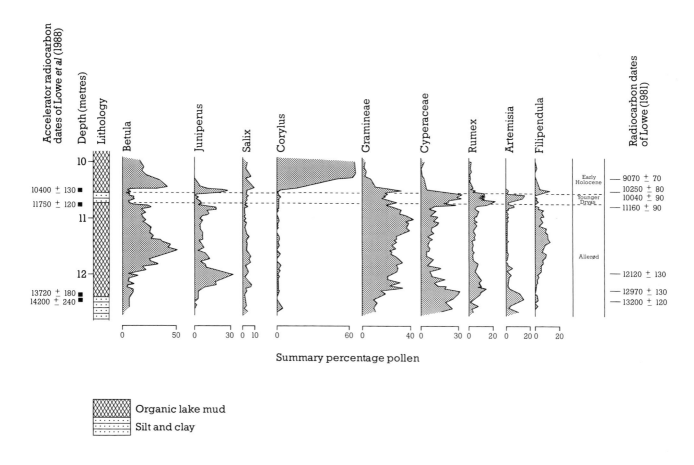

Figure 24 Llyn Gwernan: a summary of pollen, lithological and radiocarbon evidence (from Lowe *et al.* 1988)

allowed greater resolution of Devensian late-glacial environmental change than at other sites in Wales (Lowe 1981; Lowe *et al.* 1988). A preliminary investigation of the Holocene pollen biostratigraphy was undertaken by Laing (1980).

Description

Llyn Gwernan (SH703159) is a small freshwater lake on the northern flank of Cadair Idris. It occupies a steep-sided valley at *c.* 170m OD. Sediments, which include about 3.5m of Devensian late-glacial, and about 10m of Holocene deposits, have accumulated on the western edge of the lake, where a gradual succession of plant communities has raised the bog to a level higher than the adjacent lake. The following generalised late-glacial and early Holocene succession occurs (Lowe 1981; Lowe *et al.* 1988) –

4   Organic lake mud (0.75m)

3   Clay and silt with occasional stones (0.30m)

2   Organic lake mud (1.35m)

1   Clay and silt with some sand lenses and iron-rich (goethite) layers (>1.95m)

Organic material from comparable horizons was bulked from separate cores, and subjected to radiocarbon analyses. Eight dates were initially

obtained (Lowe 1981) and are shown in relationship to lithology and a summary pollen diagram in Figure 24. Lowe *et al.* (1988) obtained accelerator mass spectrometry measurements of radiocarbon activity for comparison with the earlier radiometric dates – see Figure 24. The original samples for dating were bulked to minimise standard deviations from the assays (Lowe 1981).

Interpretation

From detailed pollen and radiocarbon analyses, Lowe (1981) reconstructed a sequence of Devensian late-glacial and early Holocene events. Organic sedimentation in the basin began at *c.* 13,200 ± 120 BP (SRR-1705). The clay and silt (bed 1) contain pollen that suggests a generally open-grassland landscape prior to *c.* 13,200 BP. This date is thought to provide a minimum age for Late Devensian ice wastage at the site.

The rise of *Juniperus* (bed 2) is the first clear evidence at Llyn Gwernan of thermal improvement, and is dated to 12,970 ± 130 BP (SRR-1704). A date of 12,120 ± 130 BP (SRR-1703) from higher in bed 2 is believed to mark the beginning of climatic deterioration which eventually culminated in the Younger Dryas, about a thousand years later (Lowe 1981). At Llyn Gwernan, the onset of the Younger Dryas is marked by an abrupt lithological change from organic lake muds (bed 2) to clay-rich clastic sediments (bed 3). A radiocarbon date of 11,160 ± 90 BP (SRR-1701) from organic material at the top of bed 2 provides a maximum age for clastic sediments of bed 3 (Lowe 1981). The sharp lithological change is reflected in the differing pollen content of the two beds: the tree, shrub and thermophilous pollen found in bed 2, is replaced by an assemblage in bed 3 indicating open-habitats with herbs, notably Cyperaceae, *Rumex* and *Artemisia,* showing cooler, less favourable conditions (Lowe 1981). Radiocarbon dates of 10,040 ± 80 BP (SRR-1700) and 10,020 ± 130 BP (SRR-1702) mark the end of the Younger Dryas and the beginning of organic sedimentation (bed 4) in the Holocene. The expansion of *Corylus* during the Holocene was dated to 9,070 ± 70 BP (SRR-1698).

Lowe *et al.* (1988) examined the potential of accelerator mass spectrometry for assessing the reliability of radiocarbon dates obtained from Devensian late-glacial sediments: the thick late-glacial sequence at Llyn Gwernan was considered to provide suitable test material for such a study.

A core was taken close to that in Lowe's (1981) study. Pollen analyses were made (Lowe *et al.* 1988) in order to provide biostratigraphical correlation with the original diagram, and to provide a basis for comparing the cores and radiocarbon dates obtained from samples in them. The pollen analytical results compare well with those reported by Lowe (1981), and are shown in summary form in Figure 24. The overall pollen biostratigraphical sequence and the successive maxima and minima of *Betula, Juniperus, Rumex, Artemisia* and *Filipendula* match almost exactly, and make comparison of the accelerator and radiometric dates straightforward (Lowe *et al.* 1988).

An advantage of accelerator measurements is that residual radiocarbon can be determined from minute amounts of sample carbon, enabling various components of sedimentary organic matter, such as lipids, amino acids and humic acids to be assessed individually (Lowe *et al.* 1988). In theory, this aids the identification of contaminants such as older and younger compounds which may have been incorporated into the sediments through, for example, recycling of sediments, infiltration or sampling contamination.

Lowe *et al.* presented accelerator mass spectrometry data for four horizons which coincided with clearly defined lithostratigraphic boundaries. Three samples correspond directly with material dated by Lowe (1981), and an additional determination (OxA260) was presented from material at the base of bed 2 –

Accelerator dates (humic acid fraction)
(Lowe *et al.*1988)

OxA240	10,400 ± 130
OxA246	11,750 ± 120
OxA253	13,720 ± 180
OxA260	14,200 ± 240

Radiometric (decay) dates (Lowe 1981)

SRR-1700	10,040 ± 80
SRR-1702	10,020 ± 130
SRR-1701	11,160 ± 90
SRR-1705	13,200 ± 120

Note – all ages in years BP.

It should be noted that the age estimates (OxA 240, 246, 253, 260) are those derived from the humic acid component of the samples; these may provide the most reliable age estimates, since they are not subject to mineral carbon error (Lowe *et al.* 1988). In every case, the accelerator dates are older than the equivalent radiometric (decay) dates provided by Lowe (1981).

Although the studies by Laing (1980), Lowe (1981) and Lowe *et al.* (1988) provide an important record of Devensian late-glacial and Holocene environmental changes in Mid Wales, the pollen results so far presented are just enough to provide a biostratigraphic framework for interpreting the radiocarbon dates and for allowing correlations. More detailed presentations of the pollen results, together with palaeomagnetic data, will be published later (Lowe *et al.* 1988).

The relative advantages of the accelerator and standard radiocarbon dating techniques are discussed in detail by Lowe *et al.*, and although it is clear that the accelerator technique has certain clear advantages, such as pinpointing sources of error, it is not intended to replace the earlier method and dates. One of the main conclusions drawn in the study of Lowe *et al.* (1988), was that a degree of mineral carbon error appears to have affected all four of the stratigraphic horizons investigated. If the humic acid activity is compared with the earlier results, a systematic error of about 600 years is evident. The cause of this error is unclear: the fact that the two sets of dates (SRR and OxA) were obtained from different cores hampers direct comparisons. It is nonetheless clear that variations within the site in radiocarbon activity occur within contemporaneous sedimentary horizons (Lowe *et al.* 1988). Lowe *et al.* concluded that sediments will therefore vary in suitability for the application of accelerator radiocarbon techniques, and that, until the method has been more widely applied and evaluated, they recommend that radiometric measurements of bulk samples are still simultaneously undertaken for the same horizons.

A minimum age for Late Devensian ice-sheet wastage in the Cadair Idris region, and for the commencement of early late-glacial sedimentation is now indicated by a date of 14,200 ± 240 BP (OxA 260) from Llyn Gwernan. This date corresponds closely with dates from Glanllynnau and Clogwynygarreg of 14,468 ± 300 BP (Birm 212) and 13,670 ± 280 BP (Birm 884), respectively. Despite the inherent uncertainties associated with radiocarbon dates and their comparison, these dates probably confirm that the wastage of the Late Devensian ice-sheet was not uniform everywhere in Wales.

The accelerator measurements which date the Younger Dryas at Llyn Gwernan to between 11,750 ± 120 BP (OxA 246) and 10,400 ± 130 BP (OxA 240), differ significantly from Lowe's (1981) original estimates, which corresponded more closely with dates from other sites in Wales (Ince 1981; Seymour 1985). Paradoxically, the opening of Holocene sedimentation at Llyn Gwernan, the start of organic sedimentation and a major rise in *Juniperus* pollen, at 10,400 ± 130 BP (OxA 240) is now even earlier than at Traeth Mawr in the Brecon Beacons (Walker 1980, 1982a). This situation is the reverse of what might be expected; with areas of South Wales apparently being free from the grip of Younger Dryas ice later than sites farther to the north. Walker (1980, 1982a) speculated that this situation might have been caused by a southward shift of the ocean surface water Polar Front. It is also interesting to note that the palynological evidence from Llyn Gwernan does not show the Bølling oscillation interpreted from other sites such as Cors Geuallt (Crabtree 1969, 1970) and Nant Ffrancon (Burrows 1974, 1975).

Llyn Gwernan is a key site for pollen and radiocarbon studies of the Devensian late-glacial and early Holocene in Wales. The importance of the site lies in the considerable thickness of Devensian late-glacial organic deposits. These preserve a detailed pollen record that, together with radiocarbon dates, have allowed a far greater resolution of the Devensian late-glacial than elsewhere in Wales. The site is particularly important for the detailed radiocarbon timescale of Devensian late-glacial events: standard radiometric dates having recently been supplemented by accelerator derived dates. Llyn Gwernan is the first site in Wales where the newer method has been applied and is therefore important for methodological comparisons which have considerable implications for Devensian late-glacial and Holocene studies.

Conclusions

Llyn Gwernan contains an exceptional thickness of organic deposits which accumulated over the last 15,000 years or so. These contain fossil pollen grains and have been radiocarbon dated to give the most detailed timescale of climatic change over this period anywhere in Wales. This evidence has been recently supplemented by AMS (accelerator mass spectrometry) radiocarbon dates, the same technique as used to date the Turin Shroud.

The Elan Valley Bog

Highlights

The bog has provided a section with a vegetational record stretching through the Devensian late-glacial, including representative parts of the Older and Younger Dryas and the warmer interstadial Allerød, as well as the Holocene up to the point in the record where human activities became a significant factor.

Introduction

The Elan Valley Bog (Gors Llwyd) records detailed evidence for vegetational and environmental changes in Mid Wales during the Devensian late-glacial and Holocene. It is one of only two sites so far studied in Mid Wales with a pollen record extending back to the Devensian late-glacial. It has been studied and described by Moore and Chater (1969a) and Moore (1970), and has also been referred to by Moore and Chater (1969b), Smith and Taylor (1969), Taylor and Tucker (1970), Moore (1972b, 1977), Handa and Moore (1976), Taylor (1980) and Ince (1981).

Description

The Elan Valley Bog (SN857756) lies at 384m OD in Mynydd Elenydd. It occupies a relatively flat, shallow depression in till on the watershed between the rivers Elan and Ystwyth, which drain south-east and west, respectively. The bog has probably been drained by both rivers during its development (Moore 1970). Sections through the bog and underlying superficial sediments are exposed along Afon Elan.

A line of borings across the bog (from SN855753 to SN859754) was used to establish the stratigraphy of deposits within the basin (Moore and Chater 1969a). The detailed stratigraphy at SN858753 is –

6   Peats varying in composition and degree of humification (5.00m)
5   Brown organic gyttja (0.29m)
4   Grey silty gyttja (0.07m)
3   White soft clay gyttja (0.04m)
2   Grey silty gyttja (0.20m)
1   Stiff blue lake clay (bottom not seen)

A simplified stratigraphic section of the Elan Valley Bog deposits is shown in Figure 25. The sequence indicates initial occupation of the basin by a lake which became infilled with both organic and inorganic deposits. Later, the site was invaded by *Carex* and *Phragmites* and then by birch carr. This eventually gave way to ombrogenous bog, with *Eriophorum* and *Sphagnum*. No radiocarbon dates are available for the site.

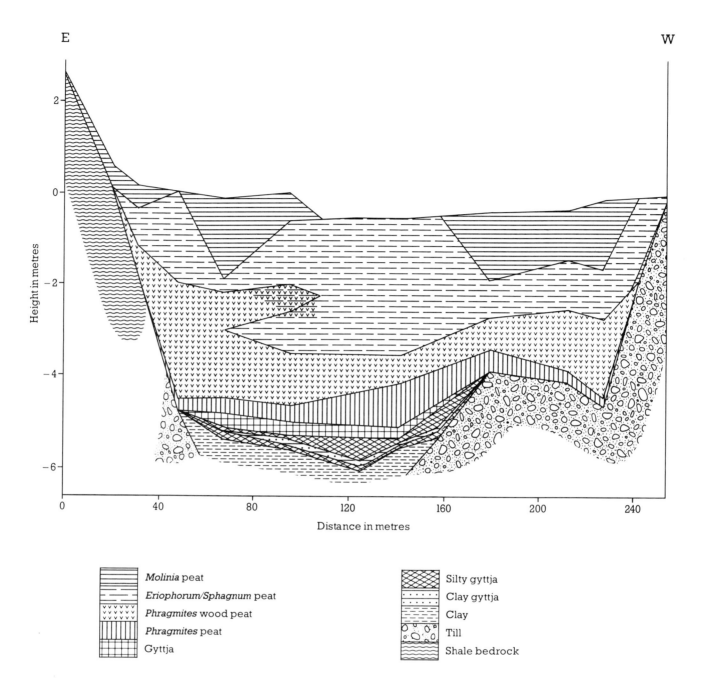

E   W

Height in metres

Distance in metres

	Molinia peat
	Eriophorum/Sphagnum peat
	Phragmites wood peat
	Phragmites peat
	Gyttja

	Silty gyttja
	Clay gyttja
	Clay
	Till
	Shale bedrock

Figure 25 Elan Valley Bog: Devensian late-glacial and Holocene sequence (from Moore and Chater 1969a)

Interpretation

The pollen biostratigraphic data of Moore and Chater (1969a) and Moore (1970) allow the following sequence of vegetational changes to be reconstructed. The Devensian late-glacial was divided into Pollen Zones I-III. Intermediate pollen zones were also recognised.

The basal blue lake clay (bed 1) contained pollen characteristic of Pollen Zone I (Moore 1970), indicating a vegetation of dwarf shrub heath (*Betula nana* L. and *Dryas*) with tall herb communities. The assemblage shows a period of unstable environmental conditions with disturbed

soils, and generally open-habitats. This phase was followed by increasingly shrubby vegetation in bed 2 (Pollen Zone I-II; Moore 1970) with birch carr and/or scrub birch. At this time, *Juniperus* also showed a marked rise. This period can be correlated with the change from periglacial conditions, following wastage of the Late Devensian ice-sheet, to warmer conditions associated with the Allerød.

The succeeding Pollen Zone II (bed 2), is characterised by a rise in tree birch pollen and a continued improvement in conditions, as demonstrated particularly by the occurrence of warmth-demanding taxa such as *Filipendula* and

Urtica. This assemblage was correlated with the Allerød represented at other sites in Britain and the Continent (Moore 1970).

A transitional zone (Pollen Zone II-III) was recognised by Moore (1970). During this period, birch declined but juniper was probably still present on local hillsides. Communities indicative of exposed montane grassland with some disturbed soils are present, and this transitional pollen zone appears to represent colder conditions than Pollen Zone II, but not cold enough to eliminate *Filipendula* and *Juniperus* (Moore 1970). A July mean of 10°C was estimated, on the basis that such a temperature would restrict *Betula* more severely than it would *Juniperus.*

During Pollen Zone III (upper bed 2 and bed 3) the exposed montane and alpine communities reached their greatest development. Taxa indicating disturbed soils and dwarf birch scrub became more prominent, and the assemblage indicates a return to colder conditions, with associated solifluction and the development of tundra vegetation. An accompanying change in lithology from largely organic to inorganic deposition (bed 2 to bed 3) also occurred at this time, and can be correlated with the Younger Dryas when glaciers occupied cirques in upland Wales (for example, Walker 1980; Ince 1981).

A further transitional pollen assemblage (Pollen Zone III-IV) represents a change from the cold Younger Dryas to milder conditions in the early Holocene. This pollen assemblage (bed 4) was marked by a return of *Filipendula* and the re-expansion of *Juniperus* scrub. Birch scrub and carr may also have begun to develop, but the succeeding Pollen Zone IV (bed 5) is marked by a much more rapid rise in birch pollen, although the presence of *Betula pubescens* Ehrh. fruits indicates that the local development of birch carr may have exaggerated this expansion. At this time, juniper probably gave way to birch. Later in Pollen Zone IV, juniper and dwarf birch virtually disappeared as birch woodland expanded. This pollen zone also records the arrival of *Corylus* and a decline in taxa which preferred open-ground.

The succeeding pollen zones all occur in bed 6 (peats). Pollen Zone V shows a sudden expansion of hazel which reaches its maximum in Pollen Zone VIa. This suggests that hazel favoured the maritime conditions of the west, and a similar expansion has been recorded at other sites in north and west Britain. Pine pollen increases sufficiently during this pollen zone, to indicate the local presence of pine trees.

Quercus and *Ulmus* pollen first occurs in Pollen Zone IV at Elan Valley, and it increases in Pollen Zone V and VIa. The latter pollen zone is associated with a decrease in *Betula.* Elm may initially have been more successful in colonising than oak, but by Pollen Zone VIb oak is dominant in the record, indicating the continued invasion of the shallow hillside soils by oak at the expense of hazel.

Pollen Zone VIa is characterised by a prominence of pine pollen (Moore and Chater 1969a). Oldfield (1965) suggested that *Pinus* invasion of upland deciduous woodland was in response to increased rainfall, but Moore and Chater suggested that locally at Elan Valley pine invaded the bog surface which was becoming progressively drier, prior to the beginning of Pollen Zone VIIa.

Pollen Zone VIIa is characterised by changes in the pollen curves and in stratigraphy. There is a sudden decline in pine, an increase in *Alnus* and *Quercus* pollen, and *Tilia* occurs for the first time. Birch declines still further from the preceding pollen zone. In addition, *Phragmites* (reed swamp) became dominant and *Phragmites* peat accumulated, perhaps indicating flooding of the bog surface. That this increased wetness was caused by climatic rather than local factors is suggested by an increase in alder. This period, as elsewhere in Britain, can be regarded as the time of maximum forest expansion (Moore and Chater 1969a).

The elm decline, frequently taken as denoting the onset of Pollen Zone VIIb, is well marked in the Elan Valley Bog pollen record, although the cause is not clear. Two distinct but conflicting lines of evidence can be deduced from the pollen spectra. First, there is evidence for climatic change involving an increase in the ratio of precipitation to evaporation. This is accompanied by a sudden increase in the rate of peat formation as shown by the stratigraphy and related pollen frequency index. This phase coincides with the initiation of blanket peat formation at several other sites in the area, and generally indicates wetter conditions (Moore 1966). Second, the pollen evidence suggests that human activity began to influence vegetation at the time of the elm decline: pollen of *Plantago lanceolata* L. (ribbed plantain) and an increase in *Pteridium* (fern) spores, suggests human interference by forest clearance and the grazing of domestic animals. Turner (1964) has suggested that *P. lanceolata* can be used as an indicator of grazing. Thus, although both climatic and human influences have been discerned in the record, it is not possible to attribute the changes to either of these mechanisms with certainty (Moore and Chater 1969a).

The Elan Valley Bog contains an important pollen biostratigraphic record of Devensian late-glacial and Holocene environmental and vegetational changes. The sub-division of the Devensian late-glacial sequence into a number of intermediate pollen assemblage zones as well as Pollen Zones I, II and III has allowed greater precision in interpreting the vegetational record (Moore 1970). The Devensian late-glacial record at Elan Valley shows that following the wastage of the Late Devensian ice-sheet a time of relatively severe conditions, dominated by broken, open-habitat vegetation with disturbed soils, occurred. This was followed by an improvement in conditions when birch and juniper flourished. A succeeding colder phase is then indicated, equivalent to the Younger

Dryas (c. 11,000-10,000 BP), when glaciers again occupied many cirques in upland Wales. At this time, large perennial snow patches and even glacier ice may have occupied the relatively low-level cirques at nearby Cwm Ystwyth (Watson 1966). The pattern of Devensian late-glacial events recorded at Elan Valley, closely follows the tripartite division comprising the Older Dryas, Allerød and Younger Dryas of the Continental Late Weichselian Stage (Late Devensian) – see Mangerud *et al.* 1974. It reflects a single warm phase equivalent to the period that Ince (1981) described at Clogwynygarreg as the 'late-glacial interstadial', preceded and followed by colder climatic phases. The site provides contrasting evidence, therefore, to sites at Nant Ffrancon and Cors Geuallt (Snowdonia) and Traeth Mawr (Brecon Beacons) which show evidence for a possibly more complex sequence of Devensian late-glacial events.

Conclusions

The Elan Valley Bog provides evidence for a continuous record of vegetational and environmental history for the last 14,000 years up until the time when human interference with the vegetation became a significant factor. It is an upland site for demonstrating important regional variations in the vegetational history of Wales.

Tregaron Bog (Cors Tregaron)

Highlights

This locality is one of the largest raised bogs in Britain. Its peats yield pollen making it possible to elucidate vegetational change through the Holocene. This, with close interval radiocarbon dating, has allowed the reconstruction of an accurate history of environmental change and later land use.

Introduction

Tregaron Bog is important for reconstructing Holocene environmental conditions in western Mid Wales. The stratigraphy and development of the raised bog at Tregaron were first studied in detail by Godwin and Mitchell (1938), and its ecology by Godwin and Conway (1939). The effect of human activity in the development of vegetation at the site, including forest clearance, was discussed by Turner (1964, 1965). Radiocarbon dates were given by Godwin and Willis (1960, 1962), Switsur and West (1972) and Hibbert and Switsur (1976). More general accounts of the Holocene history were given by Moore (1977) and Turner (1977), and the site has been widely discussed (for example, Turner 1962; Moore and Chater 1969b; Smith and Taylor 1969; George 1970; Moore 1972b; Deacon 1974; Taylor 1980; Walker 1980, 1982a, 1982b; Ince 1983).

Description

The site consists of three bogs known locally as Cors Goch Glan Teifi, developed upstream of a broad arcuate moraine near Tregaron. The moraine was regarded as the southern limit of Late Devensian ice in the Teifi Valley (Charlesworth 1929). The largest bog, usually referred to as the west bog (c. SN680630), lies on the west bank of the Teifi and is roughly oval in shape, measuring some 2,400m by 1,200m.

The other bogs lie to the east of the Teifi and are separated by a ridge of higher ground which runs towards the river from the valley side at Maes Llŷn. These bogs are referred to as the north-east and south-east bogs. Details of bog morphology and present vegetation are given by Godwin and Conway (1939). All three show marked raised profiles. The north-east bog has been extensively altered by drainage, but the west and south-east bogs are relatively intact, despite cutting at the margins.

The stratigraphy of the bogs at Tregaron was determined by Godwin and Mitchell (1938) and Hibbert and Switsur (1976), and consists over most of the valley centre of –

7   Fresh, light-coloured *Sphagnum* peat with remains of *Calluna* and *Eriophorum*

6   Thin (0.07-0.5m) highly humified peat, termed a retardation layer – see text

5   Light-coloured *Sphagnum* peat with remains of *Calluna* and *Eriophorum*

4   Highly humified *Sphagnum* peat with fibres and roots of *Eriophorum* and twigs of *Calluna*

3   *Phragmites* peat with scattered wood fragments, remains of *Cladium mariscus* (L.) Pohl and numerous seeds of *Menyanthes* and *Nuphar luta* (L.)

2   Pale brown mud with seeds of open-water plants and scattered fragments of wood

1   Stiff blue-grey (lacustrine) clay

Borings from the bog margins, however, show peats with a higher wood and silt content, overlying angular gravelly hillwash (Godwin and Mitchell 1938; Turner 1977).

The pollen biostratigraphy at Tregaron was first studied by Erdtman (1928), although a full pollen diagram was not published. Subsequently, the stratigraphy of the bogs was investigated by Godwin and Mitchell (1938) who described up to 5m of bog peat overlying *Phragmites* peat, mud peats and clays (beds 1-3). The bog peat was divided into a lower highly humified dark *Sphagnum* peat (bed 4) and an upper, light-coloured *Sphagnum* peat (beds 5 and 7). In all three bogs there is a well marked contact between the lower highly humified peat (bed 4) and the upper fresh peat (bed 5) termed the *Grenzhorizont* by Godwin and Mitchell (1938). A thin layer of

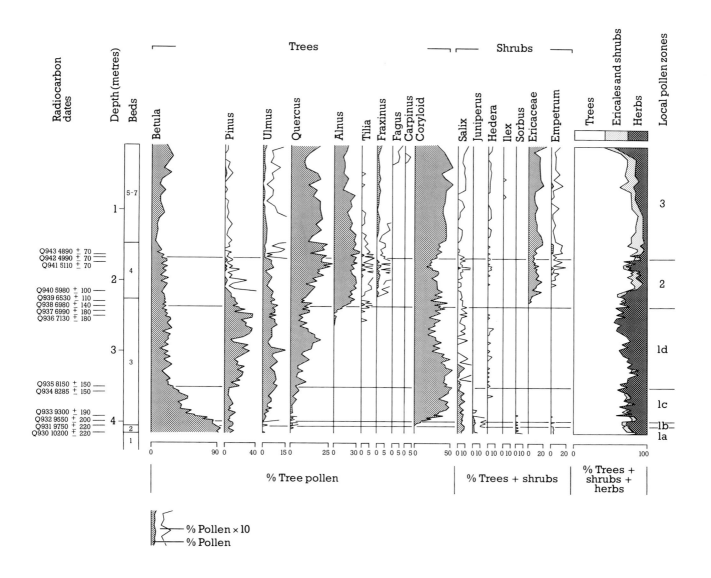

Figure 26 Tregaron Bog: a summary of pollen, lithological and radiocarbon evidence (from Hibbert and Switsur 1976)

highly humified peat (bed 6) occurs approximately mid-way between the *Grenzhorizont* and the upper surface of the fresh *Sphagnum* peat in bed 7; this was termed a 'retardation' layer (Godwin and Mitchell 1938).

In 1960, Godwin and Willis published radiocarbon dates from the south-east bog. These included dates of 760 ± 70 BP (Q-75) and 1,477 ± 90 BP (Q-391), between which the 'retardation' layer (bed 6) was believed to have formed. Dates of 2,954 ± 78 (Q-389) and 2,647 ± 78 BP (Q-388) were presented to show that the contact between beds 4 and 5 (the *Grenzhorizont*) represented a hiatus in deposition of about 300 years.

Interpretation

Godwin and Mitchell (1938) charted the course of vegetation development at Tregaron from the pre-Boreal to the sub-Atlantic using pollen analysis. Their interpretations were confirmed by Hibbert

and Switsur (1976) who presented a detailed analysis of the pollen biostratigraphy with radiocarbon dates – see Figure 26. They showed that deposition began in the Holocene at Tregaron at 10,200 ± 200 BP (Q-930), marked by an abrupt lithological change from blue-grey clay (bed 1) to organic mud (bed 2). The first pollen assemblage zone (bed 2) shows *Betula* to be the dominant tree pollen, with pollen of *Juniperus* and *Salix*. *Pinus* pollen is also present in relatively low, yet constant, frequencies. The start of the succeeding pollen zone (bed 3), dominated by *Betula, Pinus* and *Corylus,* was dated to 9,750 ± 220 BP (Q-931). This zone shows the first continuous representation of *Corylus* in the profile.

The following pollen zone (also in bed 3) began at 9,300 ± 190 BP (Q-933), and is dominated by *Corylus* and *Pinus. Corylus* increased sharply at the start of this zone and maintained high values – see Figure 26. At this time, *Juniperus* declined, probably indicating shading-out by other woodland taxa such as *Ulmus* and *Quercus,* which first become continuously represented (Hibbert and Switsur 1976). The following *Pinus-Corylus-Quercus* pollen zone (bed 3) begins at 8,150 ± 150 BP (Q-935) and is marked by a rise in *Pinus* frequencies. In this biozone, *Ulmus* reaches its acme, yet it is exceeded by values of *Quercus* pollen. The representation of shrub pollen was at its lowest during this period – see Figure 26; (Hibbert and Switsur 1976).

The *Quercus-Ulmus-Alnus* pollen zone (bed 4 and top of bed 3) opens at 6,990 ± 180 BP (Q-937). *Alnus* values rise markedly, and Ericaceae pollen and spores of *Sphagnum* are present for the first time. The following *Quercus-Alnus* pollen zone (in beds 4-7) begins at 4,990 ± 70 BP (Q-942) and is marked by a fall in *Ulmus, Tilia* and *Fraxinus* values at the beginning of the zone.

Although *Quercus* and *Alnus* dominate this later pollen zone, which encompasses beds 4 to 7, several significant events occur. These have been discussed both by Hibbert and Switsur (1976) and Turner (1964). First, the 'elm decline', widely documented at other British sites, is clearly seen at Tregaron within bed 4, although it is not as pronounced as in other Welsh Holocene profiles (Moore 1977); it has been radiocarbon dated at Tregaron to 4,890 ± 70 BP (Q-943). Second, the *Grenzhorizont,* or contact between beds 4 and 5, has been shown by radiocarbon dating to represent a break in sedimentation of some 300 years. It has been proposed that this hiatus represents a drier period; its ending marks the opening of Pollen Zone VIII (the Atlantic). Third, the highly humified peat layer (bed 6) within the *Sphagnum* peat sequence would also appear to mark a change in conditions during which peat grew only very slowly (Godwin and Mitchell 1938; Turner 1977).

Finally, Turner (1964, 1965, 1977) studied the pollen biostratigraphy of the upper 2m of Holocene deposits at Tregaron (beds 5-7 and the top of bed 4), and inferred human influences in the later Holocene vegetational history of the site. She concluded that the area was well wooded with only small clearings during the Bronze Age. At about 400 BC, most of the woodland was replaced by grassland, perhaps as part of the pastoral economy of the Iron Age peoples who built a fort to the north-east end of the bog near Pontrhydfendigaid. This economy appears to have continued until the twelfth century when Cistercian monks founded an abbey at nearby Strata Florida (Ystrad Fflur) and established arable farming on their granges (Turner 1964, 1965, 1977).

Tregaron, therefore, provides an exceptionally detailed record of Holocene vegetational changes. Open-water conditions existed at the site until early Holocene times. The course of vegetation development can then be traced as open-ground conditions were replaced by woodland of increasing diversity. At Tregaron, the early Holocene is marked by a rise in *Juniperus* pollen

followed closely by a rapid expansion of *Corylus.* A date of 9,750 ± 220 BP (Q-931) for the rise in *Corylus* is significant in being one of the earliest for the arrival of the genus in Britain (Deacon 1974; Taylor 1980; Walker 1982b). The relationship between the expansion of *Corylus* and *Juniperus* in western Britain is not straightforward, however, and varies with both altitude and latitude (Moore 1972b, 1977). The evidence from Tregaron suggests that *Corylus* may have expanded earlier in the west as the result of more favourable maritime conditions. Thus, the low lying area of Cardigan Bay may have acted as an area of early invasion for the genus *Corylus,* or may even have been a refugium for it during the Devensian late-glacial (Moore 1977).

Tregaron is also significant for the detailed record of later Holocene vegetational development. The *Grenzhorizont* or contact between the highly humified and fresh *Sphagnum* peats (beds 4 and 5) is a feature found elsewhere in Britain (for example, Borth Bog); at Tregaron, it has been dated between 2,954 ± 78 BP (Q-389) and 2,647 ± 78 BP (Q-388) and shows that the bog surface was drier for some 300 years at the beginning of the first millenium BC. A phase of renewed *Sphagnum* growth was then interrupted between 1,477 ± 90 BP (Q-391) and 760 ± 70 BP (Q-75) by very slow peat growth, which produced a thin layer of highly humified peat (bed 6). Subsequently, *Sphagnum* peat growth was renewed at an increased rate as the result of wetter conditions. The pollen record at Tregaron also allows a detailed pattern of vegetational changes in the local area, brought about by human influences, to be traced.

Tregaron Bog provides an important record of Holocene environmental conditions in Mid Wales. It forms part of a network of sites which demonstrates important trends and regional diversities in vegetational development during the Holocene. Its close interval radiocarbon timescale, together with pollen analysis and historical records have enabled a continuous pattern of changing environmental and land-use conditions to be reconstructed, from the early Holocene up to and beyond the establishment of the Forestry Commission in 1919.

Conclusions

Tregaron Bog is historically important because it was one of the earliest sites where pollen analysis was applied in the British Isles. It has yielded an important record of vegetational and environmental change over the past 10,000 years. These changes have been dated by radiocarbon methods and the detailed pollen evidence is sufficiently accurate to demonstrate the cereal growing activities of the Cistercian monks in the Middle Ages as well as the beginning of Forestry Commission activities in 1919. As such it is an exceptional example of the power of pollen analysis and radiocarbon dating in showing detailed climatic and other changes.

Cors y Llyn

Highlights

This locality provides one of the most detailed records of Holocene vegetational and environmental change in Mid Wales, and the only such record in the eastern Cambrian Mountains. The Holocene sequence lies above what is probably a full Devensian late-glacial sequence.

Introduction

Cors y Llyn (Llyn Mire) provides the most detailed record of Holocene vegetation and environmental changes in Mid Wales. The basin contains Late Devensian lake sediments overlain by Holocene organic muds, with swamp and carr vegetation on the north and west side. The south-east part of the site continued as a lake until about two hundred years ago when it was colonised by a floating raft of vegetation. The vegetational and historical development of Llyn Mire have been studied by Moore and Beckett (1971) and Moore (1978).

Description

Llyn Mire occupies a depression in the upper Wye Valley (SO016552) at 170m OD, about 6 km north-east of Builth Wells. The bog measures approximately 600m by 200m, and the present vegetation consists of four main groups – a peripheral carr of *Betula pubescens*; a *Sphagnum-Calluna* area with stunted trees of *Pinus sylvestris* in the south-east; an arc surrounding the south-east area with *Molinia caerulea* (L.), *Vaccinium oxycoccus* L. and *Pleurozina schreberi* (Brid.) Mitt.; and a northern area where extensive carpets of *Eriophorum angustifolium* Hoppe predominate and most of the species already mentioned are absent (Moore 1978).

A series of borings shows that the mire occupies three basins formed on an undulating surface of glacial sediments (Moore and Beckett 1971). The stratigraphy at the deepest point of the south-east basin (Moore 1978) showed a 10.5m thick sequence of –

10	*Sphagnum* peat
9	*Phragmites* and/or *Carex* peat
8	Water
7	Mud
6	Gravel
5	Silty mud
4	Clay
3	Silty mud
2	Clay
1	Till

The lower beds (1-4) were not analysed in detail by Moore (1978) but were believed to represent a Devensian late-glacial sequence. The upper part of the sequence, some 8m, was analysed in detail for both pollen and macrofossils by Moore (1978). No radiocarbon dates are available for the site.

Interpretation

Moore (1978) described six local pollen assemblage biozones representing Holocene vegetation development locally. The earliest assemblage (pollen zone LM-1) was dominated by *Betula*, *Juniperus* and Gramineae, and demonstrated the expansion of birch woodland into open-grassland with juniper scrub. Towards the end of this zone, many open-ground species were present, which show that woodland development was incomplete.

This pollen zone was succeeded by another (pollen zone LM-2) dominated by *Betula*, *Ulmus*, *Corylus* and *Myrica*. The changes in this pollen zone are best explained in terms of the invasion and displacement of the birch woodland, grassland and juniper scrub by elm, oak and hazel. Pine may also have invaded the area at this time. The layer of gravel within this pollen zone (bed 6) was not associated with any discernible change in the pollen assemblage. Moore (1978) suggested that the layer was, therefore, probably caused by local erosion followed by washing of sediment into the lake basin.

The major event of the following zone (pollen zone LM-3) is the development of *Quercus*, *Ulmus*, *Corylus* and *Myrica* woodland which increased at the expense of birch. Alder may also have been present in the latter part of this zone. The occurrence of juniper pollen suggests that some open areas may have survived locally, and the presence of ferns indicates the acidification of local soils (Moore 1978).

The succeeding pollen zone (pollen zone LM-4), dominated by *Quercus*, *Alnus*, *Ulmus*, *Betula*, *Corylus* and *Myrica*, records, in particular, the attainment of dominance by oak and alder. The upper part of this zone is marked by pronounced changes in the ratio of non-arboreal to arboreal pollen, and Moore (1978) has suggested that the presence of ribbed plantain *Plantago lanceolata* and fumitory *Fumaria* is particularly indicative of disturbance to the vegetation cover at this time, perhaps by human agencies. This short-lived event, however, precedes the very marked elm decline of the next zone.

The following *Quercus*, *Alnus*, *Corylus* and *Myrica* dominated zone (pollen zone LM-5) records evidence for vegetation disturbance in the form of a rapid decline in elm, pine and lime pollen. Moore considered that there was strong circumstantial evidence to relate these changes to forest clearance and the cultivation of cereals. The pollen record from the upland site at the Elan Valley Bog to the north-west, however, suggests that increased climatic wetness at this time may also have been an important factor (Moore and Chater 1969a).

The major changes of the last recorded Llyn Mire

pollen zone (pollen zone LM-6), characterised by *Pinus, Quercus* and Gramineae pollen, are best explained in terms of continued woodland clearance and the development of agriculture. At this time, *Betula* carr probably survived around the edge of the basin, and peat harvesting may have led to the invasion of *Pinus sylvestris* (Moore 1978).

Llyn Mire provides the only detailed record of Holocene vegetational and environmental changes from the upper Wye Valley. The site therefore provides information on the Holocene development of vegetation in a major valley on the eastern side of Mynydd Elenydd (Cambrian Mountains). In contrast, most other studies of vegetational changes in Mid Wales have been concerned with the ridge of Mynydd Elenydd itself and the land to the west (for instance, the Elan Valley Bog, Borth Bog, Tregaron Bog, Cledlyn Valley). The record from Llyn Mire shows vegetational development from the early Holocene *(c.* 10,000 BP) when birch woodland began to develop on the otherwise open-ground, grassland and juniper dominated landscape. The course of this development can be traced through the displacement of this early assemblage by elm, oak and hazel woodland, and the eventual attainment of dominance by oak and alder. The elm decline is very marked and is accompanied by evidence of cultivation; the first such evidence of cereal growing in early Neolithic times in Mid Wales (Moore 1978).

The lithological evidence shows that following the wastage of Late Devensian ice, sedimentation occurred in three basins on the till surface at Llyn Mire. A succession of clay, silty mud and clay (beds 2-4) was deposited on the surface of the till and is thought to be Devensian late-glacial in age; the threefold succession is characteristic of sequences elsewhere in Wales where the Older Dryas, Allerød and Younger Dryas are represented. The succeeding silty mud (bed 5) occurs in all three basins and shows deposition in open-water conditions in the early Holocene. The invasion of reed swamp and fen vegetation followed, and open-water conditions ceased in the northern and western basins. In the south-east basin the lake became enveloped by a floating mat of aquatic vegetation. This floating mat or *Schwingmoor* type of bog is rare in Britain, and Llyn Mire is an unusually fine example. The final vegetation invasion of the lake surface is believed to have occurred in historic times, during the post-Mediaeval period (Moore and Beckett 1971).

Llyn Mire contains an important Devensian late-glacial to Holocene sequence. Although the Devensian late-glacial sediments have not been studied in detail, the record of Holocene vegetational changes is one of the most detailed in Mid Wales, and the only such record on the eastern side of Mynydd Elenydd. The course of vegetation development can be traced from the early Holocene well into historic times. The pollen record shows clearly the 'elm decline' and provides the first evidence of cereal cultivation in early Neolithic times in Mid Wales. Part of the site was still a lake until two hundred years ago when it was colonised by floating vegetation.

Conclusions

Llyn Mire is the only site which provides a record of vegetational, environmental and climatic change on the eastern side of Mynydd Elenydd (Cambrian Mountains). It is important because it shows the first evidence of cereal cultivation in early Neolithic times in Mid Wales. Botanically, its floating vegetation *Schwingmoor* bog is one of the best examples in Britain.

Introduction

The coastal margins of north-west Wales are one of the key areas for the elaboration and interpretation of Late Pleistocene and Holocene events and processes. In common with Gower, the coasts of Anglesey and the Llŷn Peninsula exhibit complex sequences of glacial, periglacial and some interglacial sediments which show changing environmental conditions during the Late Pleistocene. In particular, these sediments provide evidence for the interaction of Irish Sea and Welsh ice masses, and they, in addition, record changes in relative sea-levels. A number of themes are important. First, the area figured prominently in the development of the Glacial Theory and attempts to sub-divide the Pleistocene. Second, recent studies have elaborated the provenance and directions of movement of various ice masses affecting the area. Third, attempts have been made to establish a chronology for the region, based largely on lithostratigraphy and radiocarbon dating. One sequence, at Glanllynnau, has been compared with modern glacial depositional systems. A comprehensive chronology for the region, however, has not been developed, a situation made worse by a general lack of interglacial indicators and the uncertain significance of a number of weathering horizons. The Late Pleistocene record in north-west Wales is particularly important for demonstrating possible evidence for a readvance of Late Devensian Stage ice.

Early sub-division

Historically, the area is important in two respects. It figured prominently in the development of the Glacial Theory; Trimmer's (1831) early account of the shelly sand and gravel deposits on Moel Tryfan marked an important milestone in glacial geomorphological research, because it began approximately seventy years of fierce debate centred on the contending theories of the 'glacialists' and 'diluvialists'. Moreover, the site continued to play a central role in the development and resolution of the debate.

The area is also notable for some of the earliest attempts in Britain to sub-divide the Pleistocene sequence. By the 1850s, enough was known about the glacial deposits in North Wales for Ramsay to postulate a threefold division – 1) a Lower Boulder Clay deposited by local Welsh glaciers, 2) the Middle Sands and Gravels and the shelly till of Moel Tryfan and 3) an Upper Boulder Clay deposited by a readvance of small valley glaciers (Davies 1969). Although Ramsay accepted a glacial origin for the boulder clays, he still found it necessary to invoke a period of marine submergence to account for the shelly drift deposits on Moel Tryfan. Thomas Belt's (1874) perceptive paper concerning the Moel Tryfan deposits, however, did much to advance the Glacial Theory, but even as late as 1910, Edward Hull, former director of the Irish Geological Survey, still regarded the shelly drift as evidence for marine submergence (Davies 1969).

Following these early pioneering studies in North Wales, Jehu (1909) and Greenly (1919) published detailed accounts of the Pleistocene deposits of the Llŷn Peninsula and Anglesey, respectively. Jehu (1909) considered that Llŷn had been glaciated twice by ice from northern Britain (Northern or Irish Sea ice). At many sites around the Llŷn coast he described Upper and Lower Boulder Clays separated by Intermediate Gravels and Sands; the latter he considered to have formed probably during interglacial melting of the first ice-sheet. Jehu assumed that similar advances of Welsh ice had also issued from Snowdonia. Above all, he established that the Pleistocene deposits in north-west Wales had resulted from the interaction of ice masses from the Irish Sea Basin and Snowdonia. Greenly (1919) produced a comprehensive account of the Pleistocene geology of Anglesey and established that the island had been overrun by Irish Sea ice on two occasions. Using glacial striae and erratics trains as indicators of former ice movement directions, Greenly was able to show that Anglesey had been glaciated by Irish Sea ice from the north-east while coeval ice from Snowdonia may have impinged upon the south-east coast of the island. Like Jehu (1909), Greenly (1919) suggested that the directions of movement of the Irish Sea ice-sheet had been similar during both glaciations. The tripartite sub-division of deposits on Llŷn by Jehu (1909) is particularly relevant, because many of the GCR stratigraphical sites in the region were originally described and interpreted using this classification. Both Gwydir Bay and Dinas Dinlle, for example, were regarded by Jehu as showing all three members of the tripartite scheme.

Recent approaches to Pleistocene problems

Although most studies agree that Llŷn and probably much of north-west Wales was affected by ice from two main sources during the Late Pleistocene, interest in the coastal sections in recent years has centred upon a) establishing a chronological framework for Late Pleistocene events and b) determining the characteristics and extent of the ice masses affecting the region. Consequently, the GCR site coverage in the coastlands of north-west Wales demonstrates the major sedimentary units and the most important themes that have featured in the emerging Pleistocene chronology.

Ice-sheets and ice movement directions

Studies of till fabric patterns and clast lithology at sites throughout Llŷn (Saunders 1963, 1968b, 1968d; Simpkins 1968) have helped to determine more clearly former patterns of ice movement directions. During the first inferred glaciation, Irish Sea ice is believed to have moved onto Llŷn from the north and north-west, while much of Arfon and south-east Llŷn was crossed by ice from the Snowdonian massif. During the second inferred advance, there is some evidence to suggest that the Irish Sea ice-sheet moved onto both the North Wales coast and the Llŷn Peninsula from the north and east, and that it was probably confluent with south-west moving Welsh ice in the Menai Straits region (Whittow and Ball 1970). During this second phase, it has been suggested that neither the Welsh nor Irish Sea ice masses was as extensive as previously, and certain parts of Llŷn may have remained ice-free. The GCR sites at Hen Borth, Red Wharf Bay and Lleiniog on Anglesey, show the dominant onshore and generally south-west movement of the Irish Sea ice, probably during the last of the inferred major glacial events. In the same context, coastal stratigraphical sites on Llŷn also demonstrate the movements of the Irish Sea and Welsh ice-sheets at different times. From fabric and clast lithology measurements (for example, Saunders 1963, 1968b, 1968d; Simpkins 1968), in combination with lithostratigraphic interpretations, three patterns of ice-movement have been identified. First, the coastal sections in northern Llŷn show evidence for a generally southward movement of Irish Sea ice. The evidence suggests that sites in the west, for example Porth Oer, were exclusively overrun by Irish Sea ice, whereas from Gwydir Bay northwards to Dinas Dinlle, the combined effects of Irish Sea and Welsh (Snowdonian) ice-sheets are evident. Second, on the southern coast of the peninsula, sites in the east such as Morannedd and Glanllynnau show evidence for glaciation by ice of Welsh provenance, from sources in Snowdonia. Third, exposures such as those at Porth Ceiriad and Porth Neigwl on the southern coast, show that the western part of the peninsula (in the area around St Tudwal's) may have been a zone of transition between Welsh and Irish Sea ice-sheets on one or more occasions.

The work of Saunders (1968b, 1968d), Simpkins (1968) and Whittow and Ball (1970) has also established that an upper till on Llŷn is found widely outside Synge's (1963, 1964) proposed maximum limit for Late Devensian (Late Weichselian) ice.

Chronology

While the broad pattern of Late Pleistocene ice movements is well established, their timing is less certain, as is the precise extent of each glaciation. In determining a chronology for the region, the well exposed coastal sites are important. In an investigation of the coastal stratigraphy around Llŷn, Synge (1963, 1964) suggested that ice of Late Devensian age only impinged on its northern coastal margins. More weathered and cryoturbated glacial sediments to the south of this limit at, for example, Criccieth (Morannedd) and Glanllynnau, were, therefore, considered to be older. Synge's classification was based on correlation with a stratigraphic model developed in Ireland, in which raised beach sediments such as those at Porth Oer in western Llŷn were ascribed to the Hoxnian Stage. Such a view, however, has not been widely accepted, and most workers including Saunders (1968a, 1968b, 1968c, 1968d) and Bowen (1973a, 1973b, 1974, 1977a, 1977b) considered the raised beach sediments at Porth Oer to be of Ipswichian age and the till on Llŷn to have been deposited during the Devensian Stage. These views have developed from three main lines of evidence outlined below.

Regional correlations

Bowen (1973a, 1973b, 1974, 1977a, 1977b) proposed a classifiction for the Pleistocene of Wales. In this, the widespread raised beaches of South Wales were ascribed to the Ipswichian Stage. Raised beach sediments in North Wales have been recorded only at Porth Oer, and at Red Wharf Bay in eastern Anglesey. Like Saunders (1968a), Bowen (1973a, 1973b, 1974, 1977a, 1977b) considered that the glacial and periglacial sediments which overlie the raised beach at Porth Oer and Red Wharf Bay were Devensian in age. Bowen also supported Saunders' contention that the Bryncir-Clynnog moraine as well as additional deposits to the south represented a readvance of a Late Devensian ice-sheet.

Weathering horizons

Weathering horizons described from a number of coastal sections in north-west Wales have had a major bearing on classification. Simpkins (1968) classified the Pleistocene deposits in central Caernarvonshire into formal lithostratigraphic units. These units have been applied over wider areas and they have been subsequently used in the individual accounts of the GCR sites. According to Simpkins (1968) the earliest glacial advance in Llŷn was shown by the Criccieth (Welsh) till found along the southern Llŷn coast at, for example, Criccieth and Glanllynnau. Weathering of the surface of the Criccieth Till suggested a possible pre-Devensian age to Simpkins, who like Synge (1963, 1964) believed the weathering to have occurred in an interglacial. The Criccieth Till is overlain by Welsh fluvioglacial sediments of the Afon Wen Formation and by the Llanystumdwy Till ascribed to the Devensian by Simpkins (1968). In contrast, Saunders (1968a, 1968d) partly on the basis of radiocarbon evidence (see below), suggested that the surface of the Criccieth Till had been weathered during an interstadial in the Devensian, a view upheld by Whittow and Ball (1970) and Bowen (1973a, 1973b, 1974, 1977a, 1977b).

On the northern coast of Llŷn, Simpkins described a similar threefold sequence to that of Jehu (1909) with a succession of – 1) lower Irish Sea till (Trevor

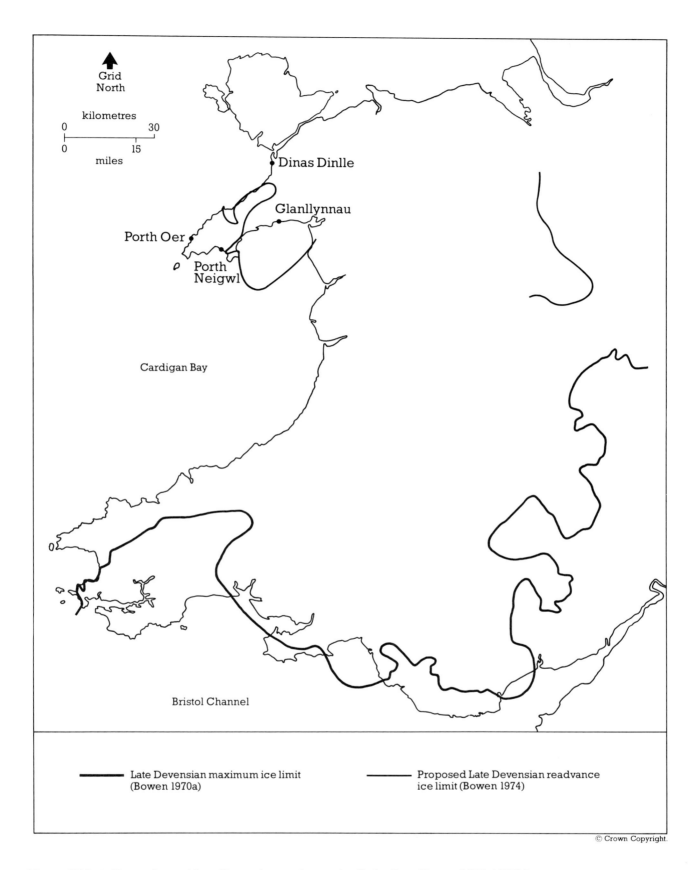

Figure 27 Late Devensian and Late Devensian readvance ice limits (from Bowen 1974, 1977b)

Till), 2) fluvioglacial sediments (Aberafon Formation), and 3) an upper Irish Sea till (Clynnog Till). No weathering horizon was seen by Simpkins (1968) in this sequence and the tills were, therefore, considered to have been deposited by two closely-spaced advances of the Late Devensian ice-sheet. Saunders (1968a, 1968b, 1968c, 1968d), however, recognised evidence for weathering

133

between deposition of the two till units at Gwydir Bay and interpreted the sediments in terms of two distinct glacial advances separated by an interstadial period with warmer conditions. The GCR sites reflect the importance of weathering horizons for establishing a Pleistocene classification for the region, especially at Glanllynnau and Morannedd, Gwydir Bay and Dinas Dinlle.

Radiocarbon dating

Saunders (1968a) obtained a radiocarbon date of 29,000 ± 1200 BP (I-3262) from shells in Irish Sea till at Porth Neigwl in southern Llŷn. He considered this bed to be equivalent in age to the lower of the Irish Sea tills found commonly along the northern Llŷn coast, and he suggested that this could be correlated with the Late Devensian. He presented evidence for a subsequent readvance of ice, namely the upper till on the north Llŷn coast. The southernmost limit for this later expansion of the Irish Sea ice is marked at Bryncir by what has been interpreted as a terminal moraine. This moraine was regarded by Synge (1963, 1964) as marking the southern maximum limit of the Late Devensian ice-sheet in this part of North Wales, but a radiocarbon date of 16,830 + 970 - 860 BP (I-2801) from possible organic material within the moraine (Foster 1968, 1970a) indicates that the feature was formed by a readvance of the Late Devensian ice-sheet. Despite the uncertainties based on single radiocarbon dates, and in particular the questionable nature of the sample (Bowen 1974), the chronology has largely been upheld by subsequent workers using this and other lines of evidence.

Multiple till sequences

The area as a whole, and the GCR site at Glanllynnau in particular, have gained prominence as a result of Boulton's (1972, 1977a, 1977b) work in interpreting complex Pleistocene sequences using modern Arctic glaciers as depositional analogues. His investigations at Glanllynnau may have considerable bearing on Pleistocene classification in north-west Wales, and indeed elsewhere in Britain. Boulton (1977a) demonstrated how a complex multiple drift sequence at Glanllynnau on the south Llŷn coast could have formed during a single Late Devensian glacial event. He suggested that similar complex sequences at Gwydir Bay and Porth Neigwl, and elsewhere in Llŷn could also be accounted for by this simple model, without recourse to further sub-division.

Evidence from Glanllynnau has been used to reconstruct a detailed record of Late Devensian late-glacial and Holocene environmental changes (Simpkins 1968, 1974; Coope and Brophy 1972). Radiocarbon, pollen and particularly fossil beetle evidence from the sequence have made the site a cornerstone for Late Devensian late-glacial studies in lowland North Wales, as well as giving the site national importance. Faulting structures in the late-glacial sequence provide crucial evidence to tie the glacial and late-glacial sequences together;

showing that buried glacier ice did not finally melt until well into the Devensian late-glacial (Boulton 1977a). It follows that this part of southern Llŷn, at least, was glaciated during the Late Devensian, this evidence, and other lithostratigraphic data from the region were used by Bowen (1974, 1977b) to estimate the limits of the Late Devensian and possible Late Devensian readvance ice-sheets in north-west Wales – see Figure 27.

Lleiniog

Highlights

An historical site where the tripartite (till-sand and gravel-till) Pleistocene sequence was recorded. Its glacigenic sediments record the wastage of Devensian ice and a subsequent advance of Irish Sea ice.

Introduction

Irish Sea till and fluvioglacial sediments exposed in coastal cliffs at Lleiniog (SH619787) form a complex sequence important to the understanding and elaboration of Late Pleistocene events both in Anglesey and North Wales. Indeed, Greenly (1919) remarked that the deposits at Lleiniog formed "..... the most complex and striking drift section on the island". The sequence is of particular importance in displaying possible evidence for sequential wasting of the Late Devensian ice-sheet (Helm and Roberts 1984). According to Greenly (1919), Lleiniog was also notable for the two largest erratic blocks found on Anglesey, one measuring 24 ft x 10 ft x 10 ft (7.3m x 3m x 3m). The site was described as early as 1831 by Trimmer, and it has since featured in studies by Edwards (1905), Greenly (1919), Embleton (1964c), Whittow and Ball (1970), Walsh et al. (1982) and Helm and Roberts (1984).

Description

The principal sections occur on the east coast of Anglesey, south of Lleiniog, and extend south from the mouth of Afon Lleiniog for about 500m, reaching a maximum height of about 12m. Exposures of Quaternary sediments form the low cliffs and foreshore at Trwyn y Penrhyn and can also be found on the foreshore near Gored-bach lifeboat station. The most extensively exposed sediments occur in cliff sections, and in plan on the foreshore, just to the south of the mouth of Afon Lleiniog. The succession consists of well stratified outwash (the Lleiniog Gravels of Greenly (1919)), overlain by a more homogenous, unstratified, red Irish Sea till.

Helm and Roberts (1984) divided the gravel and sand deposits at Lleiniog into two units; a lower Grey-brown Sand and Gravel Member (bed 1), and an upper Red-brown Sand and Gravel Member (bed 2). Bed 1 crops out only towards the base of the cliff, where it reaches a maximum thickness of about 2.5m, and also extensively in plan on the foreshore where the sediments are arranged in a series of ridges and troughs. These gravels are poorly sorted, sparsely cemented with calcite, and they contain a wide variety of rock types from two principal source areas. The first group includes granites from southern Scotland; Carboniferous limestones, sandstones, siltstones, shales and cherts; red millet-seed sandstones of Permian or Triassic age; pale chert and flint; and black, probably Tertiary, basalt. Such an assemblage indicates an origin from northern Britain and the Irish Sea Basin together with some local material from the immediate vicinity of Anglesey. A second group of rock types includes clasts of flow-banded devitrified rhyolite, welded tuff, extensively altered dolerite, altered microgranitoid, cleaved, plagioclase-rich greywacke and a few fragments of soft slate. The rhyolite fragments can be matched with those on Conway Mountain, and the rest of this Lower Palaeozoic assemblage is also consistent with derivation from the Conway hinterland (Helm and Roberts 1984).

The overlying sediments (bed 2) reach a maximum thickness of about 6m and rest on an irregular, undulating and channelled surface cut into bed 1. These infilled channels range from 1-60m in width and the largest extends to an estimated depth of about 2-3m below the modern beach at the base of the cliff. The fill of the channels is highly variable, from cobbly pebble gravels to very well sorted sand, and some channels, especially the smaller ones, have been modified by syn-depositional faulting. The most striking example of this faulting occurs immediately west of a large sea-stack, where the channel margins are bounded by faults which clearly post-date deposition of the infill. The clast assemblage from this bed is essentially similar to that in bed 1 beneath, and the very well sorted sands in this deposit consist mainly of iron-stained millet seed sand grains derived from Permian-Triassic (quartz) sandstones (Helm and Roberts 1984).

The overlying till (bed 3) reaches a maximum thickness of about 4.5m and overlies bed 1 directly in the northern part of the sections and bed 2 to the south. The till is generally poorly sorted although it contains a number of stratified lenses of silt and fine sand. The junction between the till and the gravels beneath is frequently marked by a boulder bed, interpreted by Helm and Roberts (1984) as washed, matrix-free till. Boulders up to 1.5m across occur in the till, and many larger boulders occur on the foreshore which have evidently been liberated from the till. The large limestone erratics recorded by Greenly (1919) and now perched on a low alluvial apron at the mouth of Afon Lleiniog, may also have originated from the till. Most boulders and cobbles in the till range from rounded to subangular in shape and comprise mostly Carboniferous rocks, mainly limestone, with a smaller proportion of farther-travelled rocks including the distinctive Ailsa Craig microgranite (Edwards 1905; Helm and Roberts 1984). Where the till directly overlies bed 1, but only there, the latter sometimes shows evidence of deformation to a depth of 1-2m, with recumbent and occasionally upright folds; although such disturbances are not found where the till overlies bed 2. Helm and Roberts (1984) noted that the till was sporadically overlain by a very fine sandy silt (bed 4) with vertical columnar joints and very few stones.

A sequence of Holocene marine sediments and submerged forest beds crops out towards the northern end of the cliff sections at Lleiniog, although these have not been studied in detail.

Interpretation

The coastal Pleistocene deposits in south-east Anglesey were described as early as 1831 by Trimmer who referred to broken shells occurring in the low coastal cliffs. Trimmer considered that, like the shelly sands and gravels of Moel Tryfan, these sediments were of 'diluvial' origin, and were deposited during a 'great flood'. The glacial origin of the beds at Lleiniog was, however, soon recognised (Edwards 1905). By 1919, Greenly had reconstructed a threefold sequence of Late Pleistocene events from lithostratigraphic evidence in Anglesey. At Lleiniog he recorded a sequence of blue till overlain by red sands and gravels, which in turn were succeeded by red till. He regarded the lower blue till as the product of Welsh ice which impinged on Anglesey only in the Menai Straits region.

This blue till has not been relocated at Lleiniog by subsequent workers, although similar deposits are known from other parts of eastern Anglesey (Whittow and Ball 1970). Greenly regarded the red sands and gravels as meltwater sediments deposited by currents flowing south-west between Welsh ice to the south-east and Irish Sea ice to the north-west. The upper red till was cited by Greenly as evidence of a readvance of the south-west moving Irish Sea ice-sheet. In contrast, Embleton (1964c) suggested that the sands and gravels were probably laid down beneath the decaying Irish Sea ice, but Whittow and Ball (1970) regarded the sediments as outwash belonging to their Liverpool Bay Phase of the Late Devensian ice-sheet. No part of the eastern Anglesey Pleistocene succession has been dated, although recently Whittow and Ball (1970), Bowen (1977a, 1977b) and Boulton (1977a) have regarded similar sequences in the region as Late Devensian in age. Alternatively, Thomas (1976) considered that Anglesey lay outside the maximum limit for Late Devensian Irish Sea ice, implying that the glacial sediments in Anglesey must be older.

Walsh et al. (1982) investigated the palynology and provenance of coal fragments contained in the Pleistocene sequence at Lleiniog. The coal occurs both as isolated fragments and more occasionally as hydraulic concentrates (Walsh et al. 1982) or 'seams' (Greenly 1919). The largest of the coal layers described by Walsh et al. (1982) measured about 4m long by 0.20m thick. Greenly (1919) recorded that the largest seam then exposed was

27 feet by 3 inches (8.2m x 0.076m). Walsh *et al.* (1982) established that coal clasts in the Lleiniog gravels contained a varied assemblage of early Westphalian spores. Directional data such as sedimentary structures, glacial striae and erratics trains in the local area showed the sediments had been derived from the north-east. Walsh *et al.* (1982) therefore considered, like Greenly (1919), that the coal clasts were probably derived from an, as yet, unidentified submarine coal outcrop located only a few kilometres to the north-east of Lleiniog. The possibility that the coal clasts had been derived from the breaking-up, locally, of far-travelled rafts of the Coal Measures was also discussed. Roundness studies of limestone clasts taken from the gravels showed that at the time of deposition the ice front probably lay across the eastern approaches of the Menai Straits, perhaps not more than 1 or 2 km from Lleiniog (Walsh *et al.* 1982).

In the most comprehensive account of the sections to date, Helm and Roberts (1984) reconstructed a detailed sequence of events and processes. They divided the sequence into four main members (as described earlier) which they interpreted as the sequential products of a single downwasting Irish Sea ice lobe of Late Devensian age. They believed that bed 1 (Grey-brown Sands and Gravels) formed when subglacial streams from the ice-front, just offshore, debouched into a proglacial lake. Bed 2 (Red-brown Sands and Gravels), a series of channel sands and gravels, was deposited by proglacial streams, while bed 3 (Red-brown Till) was interpreted as a melt-out till, deposited following a readvance of the ice-front. The last member of the sequence (bed 4 - Red-brown Sand) is wind-blown material deposited in temporary pools on the surface of the till. The composition of the sediments indicates that they have mostly originated from northern Britain, the Irish Sea Basin and Anglesey, in particular the north and north-east of the island. A small but persistent input of clasts, however, occurred from the Welsh mainland, probably from the Conway area. Two alternative explanations were put forward to account for this mixture of erratics. Most likely, the mixture of erratics probably indicated a confluence of Irish Sea and Welsh ice immediately north-east of Penmon during the Late Devensian; or the locally derived erratics may have been reworked from pre-existing Welsh glacial sediments offshore (Helm and Roberts 1984).

The exposures at Lleiniog are the finest through Pleistocene glacial and fluvioglacial deposits in Anglesey, and they provide one of the most complete Late Pleistocene to Holocene stratigraphical records in north-west Wales. The site first featured in a number of pioneering studies which were fundamental to the firm establishment of the Glacial Theory in Great Britain and to the early sub-division of the Pleistocene record. Continued reference to the site has reinforced its importance for Pleistocene palaeoenvironmental studies.

In particular, the thick red till at the site provides some of the clearest evidence for the incursion onto Anglesey of ice from the Irish Sea Basin. In combination with stratigraphic reference sites elsewhere in Anglesey and in Llŷn, Lleiniog is important for establishing a network of sites that can be used to determine patterns of ice movements across north-west Wales during the Late Pleistocene.

The site is one of very few in north-west Wales where a variety of detailed sedimentological techniques has been applied to reconstructing palaeoenvironments. Lithostratigraphical and sedimentological data from Lleiniog suggest that till was deposited as a melt-out product following a readvance of the Irish Sea ice-sheet over a thick sequence of earlier proglacial sediments. Analysis of the latter have shown them to be the product of sequential downwasting of Irish Sea ice. The sections at Lleiniog are therefore important in providing some of the most detailed evidence from Wales for former glacial and fluvioglacial processes at or near the margins of an oscillating ice-sheet.

Although a Late Devensian age is probable for the glacigenic sequence at Lleiniog, it is not clear whether the till can be correlated with the upper till found in north Llŷn, where it has been interpreted as a readvance feature of the Late Devensian ice-sheet. It is conceivable that the Lleiniog till represents an even later readvance or minor oscillation of the Late Devensian Irish Sea ice-sheet. Lleiniog is therefore significant in demonstrating possible climatic complexity during the Late Devensian.

The interest of the site is further enhanced by Holocene marine and submerged forest beds which have considerable potential for palaeoenvironmental and sea-level studies.

Lleiniog provides one of the finest sequences through glacigenic sediments in north-west Wales. It shows a detailed sequence of events during a cycle of deglaciation and subsequent readvance of the Late Devensian Irish Sea ice-sheet. The site demonstrates the onshore movement of the Irish Sea ice-sheet onto Anglesey.

Conclusions

The succession of ice age sediments at Lleiniog is one of the finest in north-west Wales. It shows evidence for the cycle of glaciation and subsequent ice wastage during the last major glacial phase.

Red Wharf Bay

Introduction

This locality provides rare evidence in North Wales of interglacial conditions. Its possible Ipswichian raised beach occurs beneath till deposited by Irish

Sea ice during the subsequent and last glacial phase.

Introduction

Red Wharf Bay (SH532816) and Porth Oer are the only two sites in northern Wales where raised beach sediments have been recorded. As such, they provide a basis for lithostratigraphical correlation with sequences in South Wales. Red Wharf Bay shows evidence for a sequence of environmental changes from temperate interglacial conditions, as inferred from the high sea-level shown by the raised beach, to colder, and then to fully glacial conditions. The Pleistocene sequence at Red Wharf Bay was first noted by Edwards (1905) and was later described by Greenly (1919). The site has been discussed by Whittow and Ball (1970), Bowen (1973a, 1973b, 1974, 1977b) and Peake et al. (1973).

Description and interpretation

Two separate exposures of Pleistocene sediments occur at Red Wharf Bay. At Trwyn Dwlban (SH532820) in the northernmost part of the bay, a low cliff consisting of up to about 4m of red Irish Sea till overlies a fine example of a grooved and striated Carboniferous Limestone shore platform. To the south, beneath Castell Mawr Quarry (SH532816), raised beach and head deposits overlie a raised shore platform of Carboniferous sandstone at about 3m OD. The lowest member of the Pleistocene succession is a calcite-cemented limestone head deposit up to 7m thick (Whittow and Ball 1970). A thin development of raised beach sediments occurs as a wedge within this limestone head; this is also cemented with secondary calcite. Occasionally, this deposit rests directly on the rock platform but mostly it occupies what Whittow and Ball described as a wave-cut notch in the head, some of which is incorporated into the raised beach wedge. The raised beach is composed entirely of local, Carboniferous rocks. Overlying the head is a red-brown Irish Sea till, much of which is disturbed and mixed with quarry spoil. The relationship of the head to the till is obscured by slumping, but in nearby sections red till clearly overlies the head (Whittow and Ball 1970).

A brief description of the site was given by Edwards (1905) who recorded the red till resting on an ice-scratched limestone surface. Indeed, it was the striated and furrowed bedrock surface at Red Wharf Bay rather than the overlying sediments that attracted most of the early interest in the site. Greenly (1919) referred to the "large glaciated floors of limestone" at Trwyn Dwlban with "the remarkable deflections and under-cuttings". Although striae on the pavement generally trend north-east to south-west, Greenly remarked on the deflected striae that occurred in the trumpet-shaped hollows (palaeokarstic pits) found on the platform. These large hollows up to 2m diameter are plugged with pipes of Carboniferous sandstone. Around the plug margins, where the edges of the pits are clearly visible, the striae can

be seen to curve into the pits resuming their normal direction where they emerge. Greenly described one particular example where the striae swept completely round the moat-like hollow surrounding a plug, until on its south-west side, the striae pointed 20° north of west, having therefore undergone a deflection of nearly 90° within the space of about 2m. Undercut furrows were also recorded, and Greenly noted that the ice "must have adapted itself as a practically plastic body to every irregularity in the surface of the rock". He also recorded about 4m of red till resting on the ice-worn limestone, with in places a little blue till visible beneath; the latter, however, has not been relocated.

Whittow and Ball (1970) also described the sequence at Red Wharf Bay and considered that the rock shore platform was representative of the most widespread geomorphological feature pre-dating the Pleistocene drifts in North Wales, although of uncertain age. The fact that the raised beach was separated from the platform by a limestone head indicated that the platform had been fashioned during an earlier period of high sea-level. The red till was assigned to their Liverpool Bay Phase of the Late Devensian (Whittow and Ball 1970).

Bowen (1973a) noted that exposures similar to those at Red Wharf Bay, with head in close association with the raised beach gravels, also occurred in south Pembrokeshire and Gower. It seemed likely that they represented cliff fall material which accumulated contemporaneously with the beach sediments, and were therefore broadly Ipswichian in age. By analogy with the Pleistocene deposits in Gower, it would appear likely that head overlying the raised beach at Red Wharf Bay was formed during some part of the Devensian Stage prior to the ice advance that deposited the red Irish Sea till. These chronostratigraphic assignments were also followed by Bowen (1973b, 1974, 1977b) and Peake et al. (1973).

From the foregoing, it is clear that Red Wharf Bay is an important site for a number of different reasons. It is only at one or two sites in North and north-west Wales that raised beach deposits are found; these not only provide a record of interglacial conditions during times of high sea-level, but allow lithostratigraphic correlation with sequences in South Wales. Although an Ipswichian age has been suggested for the raised beach at Red Wharf Bay, its precise age is uncertain. Amino acid geochronological studies in South Wales and south-west England have shown that a complicated sequence of raised beaches occurs. An Ipswichian age for the raised beach at Red Wharf Bay would help to constrain the age of the overlying Irish Sea till to some part of the Devensian Stage, but correlations are at present tentative.

The Irish Sea till at Red Wharf Bay demonstrates the incursion of ice from the Irish Sea Basin onto eastern Anglesey, and with GCR sites at Hen Borth and Lleiniog, and those in Llŷn, helps to establish regional patterns of ice movement by use of diagnostic clast lithology and till fabric measurements. Although a Late Devensian age for the till at Red Wharf Bay is likely, it is not clear if it is the product of the main thrust of Late Devensian ice or a later readvance.

The shore platform at Red Wharf Bay is an excellent example of a widespread geomorphological feature. It is very likely to be composite in age, having been fashioned during a number of high interglacial sea-levels. It is clear from the evidence at Red Wharf Bay that the shore platform and raised beach cannot date from the same high sea-level event because they are separated by head.

Red Wharf Bay demonstrates the finest example of a striated shore platform in north-west Wales. The clear relationship between the striated platform and the overlying glacigenic sediments at the site was important in establishing the Glacial Theory in North Wales. It also shows the close association between erosional and depositional processes in certain subglacial environments, and is therefore important for the study of glacier rock bed forms.

Finally, the sequence of head, raised beach, head and till resting on a striated shore platform at Red Wharf Bay, provides a level of sedimentary and palaeoenvironmental detail rarely found elsewhere in North and north-west Wales. The succession is therefore one of the most complete Pleistocene records in the region and allows a sequence of palaeoenvironmental changes to be reconstructed including the interglacial conditions and high sea-levels shown by the raised beach and the fully glacial conditions shown by the till.

The important stratigraphic reference site of Red Wharf Bay, records some of the best evidence currently available for the Late Pleistocene glacial and interglacial history of North Wales. The sequence contains three chief elements which make the site of special interest. Apart from raised beach deposits at Porth Oer in Llŷn, those at Red Wharf Bay are unique in North Wales and they provide an important record of high sea-levels probably during the Ipswichian Stage; and they enable a degree of stratigraphic correlation with reference sites in South Wales. The till at Red Wharf Bay provides a clear indication of the passage of Irish Sea ice onto the coast of eastern Anglesey. Finally, the shore platform here bears unusually fine deflected glacial striae important in studies of erosion in subglacial environments.

Conclusions

The sequence of deposits at Red Wharf Bay provides evidence for the last interglacial to glacial cycle from about 125,000 years ago. The last interglacial is recorded by a raised beach which provides evidence for a global sea-level higher than at present. Above it, scree deposits provide evidence for a cold (periglacial) climate. The glacial deposits at the site provide evidence for the movement of an Irish Sea ice-sheet onto eastern

Anglesey. Only two sites in North Wales provide detailed evidence of this kind.

Hen Borth

Highlights

An excellent example of a drumlin, a landform so well represented in Anglesey but more rare in mainland Wales. Formed beneath the ice-sheet of the last glaciation, this drumlin is shown in cross-section.

Introduction

In Hen Borth Bay (SH321931) on the northern coast of Anglesey, an excellent coastal exposure through a drumlin occurs. The prevailing coastal configuration and the alignment of the drumlin at Hen Borth have allowed marine erosion of the drumlin parallel to its long axis, clearly revealing its internal structure and composition. According to Greenly (1919) it is one of the three finest examples of a dissected drumlin on the island.

Description

Drumlins are common in Anglesey, and Greenly mapped over two hundred examples in the north and west of the island alone. The Hen Borth drumlin is one of a large swarm in the Cemlyn Bay area, which show a striking alignment from north-east to south-west. Such an orientation closely matches that of striae found on local bedrock surfaces; the two therefore provide evidence to show that northern Anglesey was glaciated by Irish Sea ice moving to the south-west (Greenly 1919).

The crest of the drumlin, which has an elliptical ground plan, reaches 13m OD and is dissected by the exposure, revealing a maximum depth of about 5m of sediment. Deposits exposed along the 300m long axis are mainly grey-brown, stony Irish Sea till, with weathering and cryoturbation features in the uppermost layers. In the northern part of the bay, where the solid strata of the headland crop out, the sequence of Pleistocene deposits is more complex. Here, a lower head is overlain and incorporated into the overlying till. Greenly (1919) also observed this incorporated material, referring to the "shattered rock worked up into the boulder-clay". The till is overlain by a thin development of what is probably redistributed till.

Interpretation

Exposures through drumlins are generally rare in Wales, and Hen Borth is an unusually fine example, showing sections end to end through an individual feature. Hen Borth is also representative of the drumlins of northern Anglesey, where such landforms are well developed and where they form important elements in the geomorphology of the island.

The drumlins of northern Anglesey are important

historically, as it was recognised at an early stage that debris deposited beneath moving ice was frequently streamlined in the direction of ice movement. Thus, using the orientation of drumlin long-axes together with other ice directional indicators such as striae, Greenly (1919) was able to chart the movement of the Irish Sea ice-sheet over Anglesey. Today, Hen Borth is still important in demonstrating patterns of ice movement across North and north-west Wales. In particular, it provides convincing evidence to show that northern Anglesey was last glaciated by south-westerly moving ice from the Irish Sea Basin. Since drumlins frequently occur in lowland areas where ice flow was probably radiative or dispersive, the swarms on northern Anglesey demonstrate that similar conditions pertained over the northern part of the island.

Despite numerous published studies, drumlin formation is still not fully understood (Menzies 1978), and Hen Borth is therefore important for studying the origin of drumlins and for testing theoretical models of drumlin formation. The site provides an unusual opportunity in Britain to study former glacier dynamics, including indications of basal ice pressures and the rates and type of glacier flow.

Conclusions

Hen Borth is an exceptional example of an exposure through a drumlin (a streamlined mound of glacial drift), a type of Pleistocene landform well developed in northern Anglesey, but relatively uncommon elsewhere in Wales. It demonstrates that the last glaciation of northern Anglesey was by Irish Sea ice moving from north-east to south-west, and is therefore important for reconstructing regional patterns of ice movement. It is also important for testing theoretical models of drumlin formation.

Moel Tryfan

Highlights

An historical site in the development of the Glacial Theory. It shows outstanding evidence for the Devensian glaciation of upland North Wales by Irish Sea ice, in the form of shelly sea-bed sediments transported to 400m above sea-level.

Introduction

Since their discovery by Trimmer in 1831, the shelly drifts of Moel Tryfan have formed a classic topic of study for glacial geologists. Indeed, as Reade (1893) stated, the site had become "a battleground of contending theories" between the "Diluvialists" and the "Glacialists". Although the theory that marine submergence accounted for the drifts was abandoned by the early twentieth century, the site has remained controversial where the origin and the dating of the sediments are concerned. The site provides unique and important evidence for Late Pleistocene events in north-west Wales, and forms a classic landmark in the development of glacial geology. The site has perhaps the longest history of research of any site in Wales, having been described and referred to by numerous workers in the last century (for example, Trimmer 1831; Buckland 1842; Ramsay 1852, 1881; Darbyshire 1863; Lyell 1873; Belt 1874; Jeffreys 1880; Mackintosh 1881, 1887; Blake 1893; Reade 1893; Greenly and Badger 1899; Hicks et al. 1899). More recently, the site was discussed by Foster (1968, 1970a), Whittow and Ball (1970) and Bowen (1977a). Amino acid ratios were provided by Davies (1988).

Description and interpretation

The shelly drift is located in the disused Alexandra slate quarry to the south-east of the Moel Tryfan summit at 426m OD. The exposures have always been endangered, particularly during the expansion of the quarry (Greenly and Badger 1899; Hicks et al. 1899; Greenly 1900), and the sequence of beds is far from clear. From Hicks et al's (1899) description of the stratigraphy, it appears that the shelly sands and gravels probably occurred as a large wedge between till deposits. They recorded about 7.6m of drift deposits lying on a slate floor at 390m OD on a small ridge between the then expanding Moel Tryfan and Alexandra slate quarries, and suggested that two main formations could be seen in the drifts – a shelly sand and gravel sequence occurring to the north-west and being replaced to the south-east by boulder clay. The sands and gravels were described as yellow, and containing pockets of gravel in which numerous marine shell fragments were present, and in which bedding was very irregular. The junction between the sands and gravels and the till was contorted into sharp folds. The till was described as a strong, unstratified deposit, dark grey in colour and full of stones, up to one metre in size. Most of the stones were subangular, many well striated, and most were of Welsh origin; the riebeckite microgranite of Mynydd Mawr being especially abundant (Hicks et al. 1899). The drift beds overlay slate bedrock and the lowest layers contained numerous angular slate fragments. The slate floor beneath the deposits showed terminal curvature towards the ESE. According to Hicks et al. (1899) and Greenly (1900) there was some suggestion that the sands and gravels were interdigitated with the till. Unfortunately, today there is little evidence for such a sequence although the till and shelly sand and gravel deposits are still visible in small exposures in separate parts of the quarry.

In contrast to many other classic Pleistocene sites in Wales, most of the references to Moel Tryfan were made during the latter part of the nineteenth century, and since that time the site has received relatively scant attention. This no doubt has been due to the destruction of key parts of the site, forecasted by earlier workers.

Trimmer (1831) was the first to record the high

level drifts of Moel Tryfan with their contained fauna. Importantly, he noted that these supposed "diluvial" or flood-formed sands and gravels were extensive in this part of Caernarvonshire, a fact also supported by Ramsay (1852) who traced the 'marine' drift to the height of 701m (2,300 ft) OD in the recesses of Carnedd Dafydd and Carnedd Llewellyn, and two miles west of Snowdon near Maenbras. At this early stage, most authors favoured a marine origin for the Moel Tryfan shelly sands and gravels, and the opinions then prevalent were summed up by Sir Charles Lyell in 1873 who believed that "these shells show that Snowdon and all the highest hills which are in the neighbourhood of Moel Tryfaen were mere islands in the sea at a comparatively late period" (Davies 1969). Such was the entrenchment of the belief that Trimmer (1831), in describing striae and furrows on slate bedrock in Snowdonia, concluded that they had been caused by the 'diluvial currents'.

Despite advancement of the Glacial Theory elsewhere in Europe, Buckland (1842) rectified Trimmer's mistake and cited striations in the Llanberis Pass as clear evidence of glaciation, but still invoked a period of marine submergence to account for the shelly sands and gravels on Moel Tryfan. Darwin (1842), while refuting the concept of a flood to account for the beds on Moel Tryfan, however, also concurred with the idea that the beds were emplaced beneath the sea. Such an origin, he argued, would help to account for the presence in the sections of erratic boulders (Trimmer 1831) which he considered had been transported by floating ice. The first detailed faunal analysis of the drift beds at Moel Tryfan was carried out by Darbyshire (1863) who recognised fifty six different species of molluscs. While the majority of these was considered to be Arctic in character, there was also an infusion of more temperate, British and Atlantic species. The list was updated by Jeffreys (1880) and collectively such faunal analyses helped to reinforce the idea that the beds were of marine origin.

A marine origin was also upheld by Mackintosh (1881, 1887) who noted that the sands and gravels were obliquely laminated in a manner similar to that seen on a modern beach. Similarly, Reade (1892, 1893) undertook a microscopic examination of sand grains from the Moel Tryfan beds and concluded that their extraordinary roundness and polish could only have resulted from marine agencies. Reade (1892) additionally showed that these 'marine' sands were overlain by till, probably of local derivation, whereas the sands and gravels were full of erratics from Scotland and the Lake District. However, like Darwin (1842), Reade (1893) envisaged that local glaciers had caused the submergence and consequent flooding of the land. It was during this marine submergence that the sea lapped against the Snowdonian hills depositing the shelly marine drift. Exotic, distantly derived erratics such as Shap Fell granite and Ailsa Craig microgranite in this deposit had, according to Reade, been rafted on floating ice. In contrast, Reade (1892) believed the overlying till to be a locally derived glacial deposit.

Against the tide of opinion, Thomas Belt (1874) published a perceptive paper in which he refuted the theory of marine submergence to account for the Moel Tryfan beds. He noted that "..... the shells are broken and worn ..... they are just where they ought to be found on the supposition that an immense body of ice coming down from Northern Ireland, Scotland and from Cumberland and Westmorland, filled the basin of the Irish Sea, scooped out the sand with the shells that had lived and died there, and thrust them far up amongst the Welsh hills that opposed its course southward....." (Belt 1874). He therefore concluded that there was no evidence for the submergence of Great Britain either during or since the 'Ice Age'.

Like Belt (1874), Blake (1893) favoured a glacial origin for the superficial deposits at Moel Tryfan. He foresaw no great difficulty in "getting the Irish Sea glacier to so great a height" and suggested that the shelly drifts of Moel Tryfan were the earliest of the glacial deposits in North Wales and that the shells themselves must have lived in pre-glacial times. However, even as late as 1910, the Moel Tryfan shelly sands were still regarded by Edward Hull, former director of the Irish Geological Survey, as evidence of marine submergence (Davies 1969).

Shortly before the turn of the century it became clear that expansion of the slate quarries on Moel Tryfan would result in the destruction of some of the key sections. A rescue operation to record and photograph the sections was therefore called for by Greenly and Badger (1899) and the results of the operation were later reported by Hicks *et al.* (1899) and by Greenly (1900). The latter two reports, which are identical, furnish what is perhaps the most detailed account of the sections, and since that time little detailed research has been undertaken.

The dating of the sediments at Moel Tryfan has proved difficult. Whittow and Ball (1970) suggested that the shelly sands represented the earliest glacial deposits in North Wales, perhaps being equivalent in age to the Criccieth Advance deposits (Simpkins 1968) in southern Llŷn and therefore of pre-Devensian age. They considered that the sands and gravels had been dredged from a pre-existing sea-floor at the onset of a glaciation, following their accumulation during a substantial interglacial period. Foster (1968, 1970a) undertook the radiocarbon dating of a bulk shell sample from the Moel Tryfan site. He obtained a date of 33,740 +2,100 -1,800 BP (I-2803) and concluded that because the shell material was derived, the glaciation responsible for its deposition must therefore post-date *c.* 34,000 BP. A Late Devensian age was therefore attributed by Foster to the beds. While a Late Devensian age would place the deposits firmly within the glacial succession established elsewhere in North Wales (for example, Saunders 1968a), such an age does little to explain the restricted and high-level occurrence of such deposits, which in fact may be explained more easily by an earlier glacial episode (Whittow and Ball 1970). Many doubts have also been expressed concerning the reliability of radiocarbon dates from bulked shell samples (for example, Shotton 1967, 1977a; Boulton 1968). Amino acid measurements on the fauna, notably on *Macoma,* suggest that the sediment is Late Devensian in age (Davies 1988).

The site, first and foremost, is a landmark in glacial geology and geomorphology. It has the longest and most detailed history of early research at any site in Wales and was paid significant attention by both the pioneers and the opponents of the Glacial Theory. In this respect, it has been important in the development of geomorphological and geological thought in Great Britain.

Moel Tryfan also provides an important lithological record of the high-level shelly drift widely recorded from other locations in the Snowdonian foothills. It is both representative, and the best exposed of these deposits.

Further, the shelly drift demonstrates a penetration of the Irish Sea ice-sheet a considerable distance inland, and a vertical movement of the ice-sheet amounting to *c.* 400m in just about 10 km (Flint 1971). This southward and onshore movement of Irish sea ice, as shown by discontinuous Irish Sea sediments in Snowdonia generally and at Moel Tryfan in particular, has major repercussions for the timing and interaction of Irish Sea and Welsh ice-sheet advances. The evidence at Moel Tryfan clearly implies that the shelly drift was deposited when Welsh ice was neither sufficiently developed nor powerful enough to deflect the Irish Sea ice in this area.

The age of the Moel Tryfan deposits has been a matter of debate. It is one of very few sites in Wales where a radiocarbon date has been obtained. Recent amino acid data from the fauna have, however, supported a Late Devensian age (Davies 1988).

This locality is important for having been one of the first and also one of the most controversial Pleistocene sites described in Britain. It has been a key site in the development of scientific thought and establishment of the Glacial Theory. It provides a unique lithostratigraphical record of the high-level, shelly Irish Sea deposits, which are important for determining the sequence and pattern of Late Pleistocene glacial events in north-west Wales.

Conclusions

Moel Tryfan is an internationally famous site. Its shelly glacial deposits figured prominently in the debate which led to the acceptance of the Glacial Theory in Britain. Before 1840 or so, the view was that these deposits represented the Biblical deluge. Acceptance that they were deposited by an ice-sheet was important for changing that opinion and led directly to the acceptance of the effect of glaciers on the landscape.

Dinas Dinlle

Highlights

A remarkable site showing spectacularly folded and faulted Devensian glacigenic sediments. Such effects have been attributed to the Late Devensian ice advance over previously deposited till and gravels.

Introduction

Dinas Dinlle (SH436563) is a coastal exposure through a complex drift sequence which provides possible evidence for a readvance of Late Devensian ice. It was first investigated by Reade (1893) and later in some detail by Jehu (1909). The site has also featured in studies by Synge (1963, 1964), Saunders (1963, 1968a, 1968b, 1968c, 1968d, 1973) and Whittow and Ball (1970).

Description

The sections at Dinas Dinlle are cut through two large drift mounds, the northernmost of which approaches 25m in height. The sequence extends laterally for about 900m and comprises a complex series of tills and associated fluvioglacial sediments. Below this sequence, a lower till of limited extent is sporadically exposed. This red to purple weathered till (blue to grey in its unweathered condition) is thought to extend beneath the foreshore. It is a tough, homogenous and highly calcareous deposit. The thick sequence of stratified sands and gravels above contains marine shell fragments. These deposits are often coarse with the upper horizons iron-stained. Well developed iron pans are displaced by faulting. These sands and gravels form almost the entire southern drift mound. Both the lower till and the sands and gravels are affected by isoclinal folds, accompanied by thrust and reverse faulting in the northern part of the section – see Figure 28. This steep bedding which approaches 80° is replaced to the south by more gentle folding and the beds are arranged in a low anticline. The sands and gravels are succeeded by a yellow-grey, stony upper till. A weathering horizon up to 0.5m thick and showing deep iron-staining, induration and frost-heaving has been described between the upper till and the underlying sands and gravels (Saunders 1968a, 1968c, 1968d), and this was considered to mark a stratigraphic break between these two units. The upper till is also cryoturbated in places and it is overlain by hillwash sediments and blown sand.

Interpretation

Major differences in interpreting the sediments at Dinas Dinlle have occurred. Reade (1893) first described the sections in detail and considered that the till deposits were conclusive evidence of former glacial conditions. The sands and gravels, however, had formed by marine submergence. In contrast, Jehu (1909) interpreted the same sequence in terms of the tripartite scheme, with two

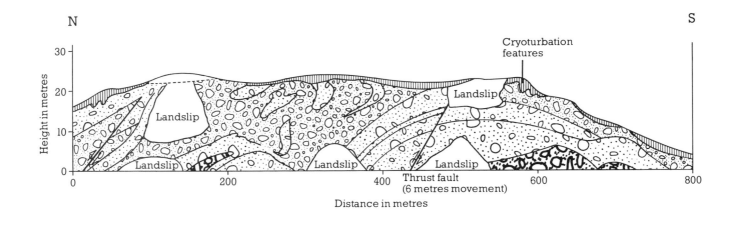

Hillwash and blown sand

Upper gravelly till (Clynnog Till)

Fluvioglacial sands and gravels (Aberafon Formation)

Lower argillaceous Irish Sea till (Trevor Till)

Figure 28 Quaternary sequence at Dinas Dinlle (from Whittow and Ball 1970)

major glacial episodes separated by a more temperate, possibly interglacial, period. The concept of marine submergence to account for the sand and gravel horizons was finally abandoned and the sediments were interpreted by Jehu (1909) as being fluvioglacial. The occurrence of marine shell fragments in the upper till, together with common Chalk flints, pebbles of Ailsa Craig microgranite, Goat Fell granite (Arran), Dalbeattie granite, and schists and serpentinites from Anglesey was taken by Jehu to indicate that the deposits had been derived from the Irish Sea Basin to the north.

Synge (1963, 1964) also recorded two tills separated by sands and gravels. He suggested the lower till and associated sediments were probably Saalian in age but that the upper till was Weichselian (Late Devensian) and was associated with the nearby Bryncir-Clynnog moraine; a moraine which he considered marked the maximum extent of Late Devensian ice in north-west Wales. Synge (1963, 1964), however, made no mention of the glaciotectonic structures at Dinas Dinlle.

Like previous workers, Saunders (1963, 1968a, 1968b, 1968c, 1968d, 1973) also recognised two tills at Dinas Dinlle separated by waterlain sands and gravels, but suggested these beds had been folded as a result of pressures exerted by the advancing ice which later deposited the upper till. Fabric analysis (Saunders 1963, 1968b, 1968d) showed that the lower till was deposited by ice

moving north-west to south-east and that the later advance was from north-east to south-west. A study of clast lithology by Saunders (1963, 1968d) also tended to confirm a generally northern (Irish Sea) origin for the sediments, many of the rock types being derived from Anglesey. Indeed, the disposition of the glaciotectonic structures themselves provided strong evidence that the second recorded ice advance came from the north-east. Of significance was Saunders' (1968a, 1968c, 1968d) recognition of a weathering horizon between the upper Irish Sea till and the underlying coarse outwash sands and gravels. This evidence together with radiocarbon dates from other Late Pleistocene sites on Llŷn suggested to Saunders that the lower till was Late Devensian in age, while the upper till could be attributed to a later readvance of Late Devensian ice, then correlated with the Scottish Readvance (Saunders 1968a). The Late Devensian readvance, according to Saunders, was therefore responsible for the upper till at Dinas Dinlle and for contorting the underlying fluvioglacial sediments and the lower till. This readvance was also considered to have produced the upper northern till found along much of the north Llŷn coast, for example at Gwydir Bay, and the Bryncir-Clynnog moraine.

Simpkins' (1968) work in central Caernarvonshire did not extend to Dinas Dinlle, but it is clear that the tripartite succession is broadly comparable to that at Gwydir Bay and elsewhere along the north Llŷn coast (Simpkins 1968). The lower till at Dinas Dinlle may be broadly equated to the Trevor Till, the sands and gravels to the Aberafon Formation and the upper till to the Clynnog Till. Simpkins (1968) suggested that this tripartite sequence was probably the result of an oscillating Late Devensian ice margin rather than the result of two distinct glacial episodes separated by interstadial conditions proposed by Saunders (1968a, 1968c, 1968d).

Whittow and Ball (1970) outlined a broadly comparable sequence of events at Dinas Dinlle to Saunders (1963, 1968a, 1968b, 1968c, 1968d), although they considered the upper till to be Welsh (from a Snowdonian ice stream) rather than of northern (Irish Sea) origin. They argued that the sections represented the northernmost occurrence of the Trevor Till, deposits of this advance being excluded from the remainder of Arfon due to the magnitude of the Welsh ice cap of the equivalent Criccieth Advance. Like Whittow and Ball (1970), Bowen (1974) cited the glaciotectonic structures at Dinas Dinlle as evidence for a Late Devensian readvance of ice in North Wales, although he disputed the validity of the sample used by Foster (1968) for radiocarbon dating from the Bryncir area.

Dinas Dinlle shows some of the most convincing evidence in north-west Wales for a readvance of the Late Devensian ice-sheet. Although sections characteristic of the tripartite sequence in northern Llŷn occur at Dinas Dinlle, the sequence is more completely exposed at nearby Gwydir Bay. It is the large-scale glaciotectonic structures which make Dinas Dinlle especially significant, because they have been used as evidence in support of a Late Devensian readvance. Work at Glanllynnau in southern Llŷn (Boulton 1977a, 1977b) and on contemporary glacial environments (Boulton 1972; Boulton and Paul 1976) has shown that multiple till sequences similar to that at Dinas Dinlle, with associated folded and faulted structures, are common features of supraglacial landforms and sediment associations – and need not therefore be the product of multiple glaciations. However, the glaciotectonic structures at Dinas Dinlle vary considerably from those at Glanllynnau, indicating that they were not formed in the same manner. In particular, the large thrust blocks of till, the steeply dipping gravels and sands and the overthrust structures at Dinas Dinlle are more easily explained as the result of stresses caused by a readvance of ice associated with the upper till. Boulton's simple model of ice wastage would not seem to be applicable to Dinas Dinlle. The site is therefore fundamentally important in demonstrating that the wastage of the Late Devensian ice-sheet in north-west Wales was not a uniform process, being interrupted by a readvance of the ice front.

Although clast lithology and fabric studies at Dinas Dinlle have not been conclusive, there is an indication that the lower till was deposited by Irish Sea ice moving north-west to south-east, while the upper till was probably deposited by confluent Irish Sea and Welsh ice moving south-westwards. Dinas Dinlle is the northernmost known occurrence

of the lower (Trevor) till, and the lithostratigraphic record therefore helps to delimit the patterns of ice movement during both of the glacial advances which occurred during the Late Devensian.

Glacigenic sediments here provide important evidence for the sequence and pattern of movements of Irish Sea and Welsh ice masses during the Late Pleistocene. Although evidence for renewed glacier activity following wastage of the Late Devensian ice-sheet has been shown to be equivocal in some areas of Great Britain, Dinas Dinlle is notable for the fine series of glaciotectonic structures which provide evidence for a possible readvance of the Late Devensian ice-sheet in north-west Wales.

Conclusions

The glacial sediments at Dinas Dinlle show evidence for major structural deformation. This was caused by some form of overriding by an ice-sheet. This may possibly have been caused by a marine-based ice-sheet grounding on the margins of the land.

Gwydir Bay

Highlights

This is a key site for the study of the glacial and fluvioglacial sediments deposited in Llŷn by Irish Sea and/or Welsh ice. It is a reference locality for Devensian glacigenic stratigraphy in North Wales.

Introduction

Glacial sediments derived from the Irish Sea Basin are commonly exposed along the north Llŷn coast. Sections at Gwydir Bay, however, provide an unusually complete and detailed sequence that can be used to reconstruct Late Pleistocene glacial events in north-west Wales. The site was studied by Reade (1893) and Jehu (1909), and more recently was described by Synge (1964), Saunders (1968a, 1968b, 1968c, 1968d, 1973), Simpkins (1968) and Whittow and Ball (1970).

Description

The sections at Gwydir Bay run from near Porth Trevor northwards to beyond Afon Hen. Three main units occur –1) a lower till, 2) intervening gravels and sands and, 3) an upper till. These typify the tripartite succession widely described in northern Llŷn by Jehu (1909). The sequence is shown in Figure 29 and the beds correspond to the Trevor Till, Aberafon Formation and Clynnog Till, respectively, of Simpkins (1968).

The Trevor Till is a homogenous Irish Sea till, the base of which is not seen in central Caernarvonshire (Simpkins 1968). It attains a maximum exposure height in Gwydir Bay of some

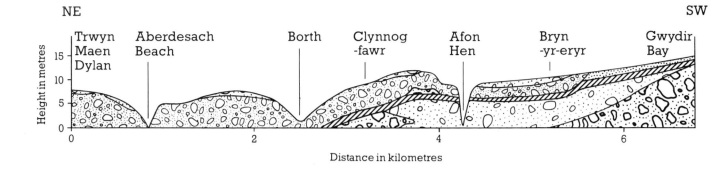

NE   SW

Sand
Upper gravelly till (Clynnog Till)
Weathering horizon
Fluvioglacial sand and gravel (Aberafon Formation)
Lower argillaceous Irish Sea till (Trevor Till)

Figure 29 Pleistocene sequence at Gwydir Bay (from Saunders 1968d)

30m. It is argillaceous and contains shell fragments and distantly derived erratics. The Trevor Till was, however, described as purple and stoneless by Synge (1964), although others have described it as red (Reade 1893), blue-grey (Jehu 1909) and dark grey-brown (Simpkins 1968). It is prone to slumping, and sections through it in Gwydir Bay are stepped, with individual exposures rarely amounting to more than 6m (Saunders 1968d). The Trevor Till is highly calcareous – up to 42.5% carbonate (Simpkins 1968).

The junction between the Trevor Till and the overlying sands, silts and gravels of the Aberafon Formation is not clearly exposed. The latter thickens to the north-east and comprises a series of almost horizontal beds of sorted, olive brown sands, silts and gravels. Near Afon Hen (Figure 29), the coastal cliff is cut almost entirely in these deposits, which average between 12 and 15m height. In places, the upper 2m of sand reveals elaborate convolution and festoon structures, a series of possible frost wedges, indurated zones and iron-pan formations. Collapse structures caused by the melting of buried ice have also been noted in the Aberafon Formation which, like the Trevor Till, contains Irish Sea erratics. Conversely, the sands and gravels are only slightly calcareous. Dislocated masses of Trevor Till occur within the sands and gravels of the Aberafon Formation (Simpkins 1968).

The Aberafon Formation is replaced laterally and vertically by a stony deposit, the Clynnog Till (Simpkins 1968). Towards Clynnog Fawr, the Clynnog Till forms most of the cliffline and the Trevor Till and Aberafon Formation are only seen

sporadically towards the base of the cliff. The texture of the Clynnog Till is variable and, in places, shows a degree of fluvial sorting. It is yellow-brown and slightly calcareous (up to 4.7%) and it contains a mixture of Irish Sea and Welsh rock types (Simpkins 1968). Where the surface of the till is exposed, it is cryoturbated to the same degree as the Aberafon Formation and leached to a depth of 1-2m (Simpkins 1968). A thin development of cryoturbated sands and gravels has been described overlying the Clynnog Till in places (Synge 1964; Saunders 1968d) – see Figure 29.

This tripartite sequence has been consistently recognised by successive workers (for example, Reade 1893; Jehu 1909; Saunders 1963, 1968a, 1968b, 1968c, 1968d, 1973; Simpkins 1968; Whittow and Ball 1970), but disagreement as to the presence or absence of a weathering horizon at the top of the Aberafon Formation at the site has led to radically different interpretations of the sequence of Late Pleistocene events in the area. Figure 29 illustrates the stratigraphic context of the weathering horizon described by Saunders (1968d).

Interpretation

Reade (1893) was the first to study the Pleistocene deposits of the north Llŷn coast in detail. He described a range of northern rock types from the Trevor Till, his Lower Boulder Clay, and established a source from the Irish Sea Basin. A microscopy study of sand grains from the overlying sands and gravels (Aberafon Formation) led Reade to suggest that the beds had been deposited, at least in part, by marine submergence.

144

Jehu (1909) identified two tills separated by fluvioglacial sands and gravels. He confirmed that the lower or Trevor Till contained rock types from sources in Anglesey and in the Irish Sea Basin, and interpreted the sequence in terms of two glacial events separated by warmer, possibly interglacial conditions.

More recent studies at Gwydir Bay fall into two main categories and have established the source and patterns of movement of the invading ice-sheets, and allowed a reconstruction of the sequence and chronology of Late Pleistocene events.

Early studies established an Irish Sea origin for the sediments at Gwydir Bay (Reade 1893; Jehu 1909), when a range of exotic rock types, including Ailsa Craig microgranite and porphyrites from the Dalbeattie area of Scotland, was described. Recent studies have applied pebble lithology measurements and till fabric analyses to try to determine the sediment provenance at Gwydir Bay (Saunders 1963, 1968b, 1968d; Simpkins 1968; Whittow and Ball 1970). Saunders confirmed that the Trevor Till contained a predominance of rocks from Anglesey and more northern (Irish Sea) sources, and showed that the Clynnog Till contained a more varied pebble lithology, with an assemblage indicating derivation from local sources in Anglesey and Snowdonia. Irish Sea pebble lithologies, however, were still common in the Clynnog Till. These findings were broadly confirmed by Simpkins (1968) who demonstrated that many pebbles in the Clynnog Till were relatively local in origin, including Cambrian grit, felsite, feldspar porphyry from Porth Trevor and slates and Ordovician volcanic rocks from Snowdonia. She suggested that the variable lithological and textural characteristics of the Clynnog Till indicated deposition as an end-moraine, whereas the more homogenous properties of the Trevor Till indicated deposition as ground-moraine or lodgement till.

Till fabric studies, however, proved less conclusive (Saunders 1963, 1968b, 1968d; Simpkins 1968). Although Saunders' measurements suggested that the Trevor Till was deposited by ice moving from north-west to south-east, and the Clynnog Till by ice moving almost due south, a considerable degree of fabric variability within units did not allow precise differentiation between the tills. However, the lithological and fabric evidence from Gwydir Bay have together been widely taken to indicate that the Trevor Till was deposited by Irish Sea ice which pushed across Anglesey before invading Llŷn. Comparable evidence from the Clynnog Till has also been used to suggest that during the second glacial advance, the area was invaded by confluent Irish Sea and Welsh ice moving almost due south (Saunders 1963, 1968b, 1968d; Synge 1964; Simpkins 1968; Whittow and Ball 1970).

Although the source of the invading ice-sheets at Gwydir Bay is reasonably well established, their age is poorly understood. Early attempts to integrate stratigraphic evidence from the north Llŷn coast into a chronology of Pleistocene events were made by Mitchell (1960) and Synge (1963, 1964), who used evidence from Gwydir Bay and elsewhere on Llŷn. Synge recognised Jehu's tripartite division of deposits along the north Llŷn coast and used Irish stratigraphic evidence to derive a framework for Pleistocene events. He suggested that raised beach gravels at Porth Oer (north-west Llŷn) were Hoxnian in age, and consequently that the two tills found along the north Llŷn coast including Gwydir Bay, belonged to the succeeding Saalian and Weichselian (Devensian) glaciations. The limited occurrence of the upper (Clynnog) till, between Clynnog Fawr and Bryncir, led Synge (1963, 1964) and Mitchell (1960, 1972) to regard this area as being at the limit for Late Devensian ice. Indeed, Mitchell (1960) suggested that his Late Devensian limit could be traced offshore, and extrapolated right across St George's Channel to Wexford. The Trevor Till and associated sands and gravels (Aberafon Formation) exhibited signs of weathering and cryoturbation according to Synge (1964), and this weathering was thought to have occurred during the Ipswichian Stage.

The views of Mitchell and Synge on Pleistocene events in north-west Wales have not been accepted by subsequent workers (for example, Saunders 1968a; Whittow and Ball 1970; Bowen 1974), who have suggested that the glacial succession at Gwydir Bay was deposited largely during the Late Devensian. Later workers have generally considered the limited occurrences of raised beach sediments, which occur at Porth Oer and Red Wharf Bay, to belong to the Ipswichian Stage, thereby fixing the glacigenic successions firmly in the Devensian Stage.

Saunders (1968a, 1968b, 1968d) reconstructed the following sequence of events from the evidence at Gwydir Bay and from other sites in north Llŷn. He suggested that the Trevor Till was deposited during the principal thrust of the Late Devensian Irish Sea ice-sheet. In support of this view he cited radiocarbon dates from the Trevor Till and associated Aberafon Formation deposits elsewhere in north and west Llŷn which, he believed, constrained the maximum age of the first recorded ice advance to around 30,000 BP. He argued that the sands and gravels of the Aberafon Formation overlying the Trevor Till at Gwydir Bay, were fluvioglacial in origin and that they were related to wastage of the Late Devensian ice. Saunders placed much emphasis on the weathering horizon which he reported affected the surfaces of both the Aberafon Formation and the Trevor Till – see Figure 29. Unlike Synge, Saunders (1968b, 1968d) attributed this weathering to interstadial conditions in the Devensian. He argued that a return to periglacial conditions should be inferred from the cryoturbation and frost-cracking of this weathered surface, and a return to fully glacial conditions was marked by deposition of the Clynnog Till at Gwydir Bay and northwards to Dinas Dinlle. The Clynnog

Till he suggested, was deposited by a later advance of the Irish Sea and Welsh ice-sheets which impinged on northern Llŷn, and extended as far south as Bryncir, where the maximum limit was marked by prominent moraines. At Bryncir, organic material disseminated within gravels of the moraine was dated by Foster (1968, 1970a) to 16,830 +970 -860 BP (I-2801). Saunders (1968a) tentatively correlated the later expansion of Late Devensian ice with the Scottish Readvance. Although Bowen (1974) disputed the validity of the radiocarbon date from Bryncir because he felt there was no evidence that the deposit sampled was in fact organic, he accepted the concept and other evidence for a Late Devensian readvance in this area.

Simpkins (1968) did not recognise a weathering horizon at Gwydir Bay and therefore defined an alternative sequence of events for the area. Some of the structures attributed to frost-action by Saunders (1968d, 1973) were instead interpreted by Simpkins as due to tectonic disturbances caused by the melting of buried ice. No significant time interval was therefore envisaged between deposition of the three main units at Gwydir Bay and she suggested that the whole sequence was Late Devensian in age with the Clynnog Till representing only a minor oscillation of the ice-sheet.

Gwydir Bay provides the most detailed and extensive exposure through the typical tripartite sequence of northern Llŷn. It can be regarded as a reference site for the Trevor Till, the Aberafon Formation and the Clynnog Till. Although individual members of this sequence are extensively exposed elsewhere in Llŷn, Gwydir Bay is particularly important for showing the stratigraphic relationship between these deposits in a single section. It is the type locality in northern Llŷn for the Trevor Till, which is much better exposed than at Dinas Dinlle to the north.

The sequence provides an important record of changing environmental conditions in north-west Wales during the Late Pleistocene, showing evidence for two separate glacial advances. It is widely held that the sequence is Late Devensian in age, and the stratigraphic detail at Gwydir Bay together with well developed glaciotectonic structures at nearby Dinas Dinlle, provide evidence for a possible readvance of the Late Devensian ice-sheet in north-west Wales.

Gwydir Bay is one of the most intensively studied sites in north-west Wales and has provided significant data for charting the patterns of movement and interaction of Irish Sea and Welsh ice masses. The Trevor Till was deposited by Irish Sea ice which moved across Anglesey before invading Llŷn, while the Clynnog Till may have been deposited by confluent Irish Sea and Welsh ice masses. The weathering horizon described at Gwydir Bay by Synge (1964) and Saunders (1968a, 1968d) is important for interpreting the sequence, particularly in determining a possible ice-free interval between deposition of the Trevor and Clynnog Tills.

This is a reference site for the three principal sedimentary units found along the northern Llŷn coast – the Trevor Till, the Aberafon Formation of sands and gravels and the Clynnog Till. The site demonstrates the stratigraphic relationships of these deposits and shows important evidence for the timing and interaction of the Irish Sea and Welsh ice masses which affected north-west Wales during the Late Pleistocene. The evidence suggests that the coastal margin was first invaded by Irish Sea ice which moved across Anglesey into Llŷn, and then by a confluent Irish Sea and Welsh ice stream. The detailed lithostratigraphic evidence at Gwydir Bay is complementary to the glaciotectonic structures at Dinas Dinlle which have been used as evidence for a readvance of the Late Devensian ice-sheet in north-west Wales.

Conclusions

Gwydir Bay is a reference site for three major units of glacial deposits. These are the Trevor Till (boulder clay), the Aberafon Formation consisting of sands and gravels, and the Clynnog Till. Their mutual relationships show how the Irish Sea ice-sheet and Welsh ice-sheet interacted on the margins of north-west Wales.

Porth Oer

Highlights

This locality shows unique Pleistocene evidence of a high shore platform, interglacial raised beach deposits, and till from the last glacial period. It therefore records rare evidence in North Wales of temperate high sea-levels during the last, Ipswichian, interglacial.

Introduction

Porth Oer (SH167301) is a unique site in the Llŷn Peninsula recording critical evidence for the interpretation of Late Pleistocene events which affected North and north-west Wales. The site is notable for being one of only two sites in the region where pre-Holocene raised beach sediments (presumed interglacial) have been recorded. The site was first described by Jehu (1909) and has since featured in studies by Whittow (1957, 1960, 1965), Mitchell (1960), Synge (1963, 1964, 1970), Saunders (1963, 1967, 1968a, 1968b, 1968c, 1968d, 1973), Whittow and Ball (1970), Bowen (1973a, 1973b, 1974, 1977b), and Peake et al. (1973). The most detailed accounts of the site were provided by Saunders (1963, 1968d, 1968d).

Description

The site comprises one of the finest examples of a raised shore platform in North Wales, cut across

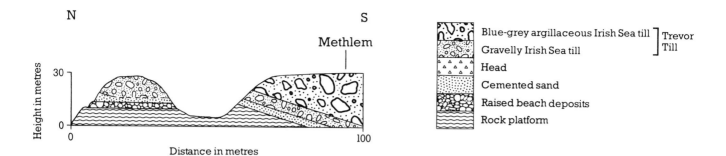

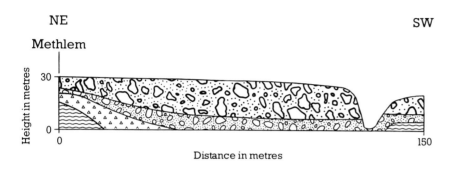

Figure 30 Pleistocene sequence at Porth Oer (from Saunders 1968d)

Precambrian rocks of complex structure at both the northern and southern headlands of the bay – see Figure 30. The most important part of the sedimentary sequence at Porth Oer occurs on a fossil sea stack towards the northern end of the bay – see Figure 30. Here, the platform at *c.* 7.5m OD (Whittow 1960; Bowen 1974) is overlain by up to 0.4m of locally derived head, and by raised beach gravel up to 1.2m thick. The raised beach is succeeded by up to 0.5m of current-bedded ferruginous cemented sand. The remainder of the succession at this location is, however, obscured by slumping and vegetation, although there is some suggestion that the cemented sand is succeeded by periglacial head and then glacial sediments. The latter crop out extensively between the north and south headlands of the bay where the steep cliffs are formed mostly in Irish Sea till up to 15m in thickness. The till is homogenous and relatively stoneless, but contains northern erratics and abundant marine shell fragments. Occasional lenses and layers of gravel and silt occur in the till, and towards the northern end of the bay the till becomes gravelly in character and merges downwards into head. The upper surface of the Irish Sea till is decalcified in places to depths of up to 4m.

Interpretation

The first description of the sections at Porth Oer was by Jehu (1909) who noted the beds of cemented sand and gravel which he regarded as a pre-glacial raised beach. He suggested that the underlying rock platform was succeeded in places by a rock rubble or head which was entirely local in origin and derived from adjacent Precambrian rocks. He suggested it had formed subaerially by freeze-thaw processes in pre-glacial (pre-Pleistocene) times. At the south-west end of the bay, this rock rubble formed a horizon about 0.3m thick on top of the shore platform and beneath thick blue-grey till. This till, which also formed most of the cliff at Porth Oer, belonged to his Lower Boulder Clay series and represented evidence of the earliest of the glacial advances in Llŷn (Jehu 1909). It contained irregular masses of marine sand, and occasionally some gravel in addition to numerous marine shell fragments from the floor of the Irish Sea (Jehu 1909).

Whittow (1957, 1960) originally doubted Jehu's evidence for the beach at Porth Oer, but later accepted it (Whittow 1965). He described the shore platform at Porth Oer, and suggested that the lack of raised beach deposits was not surprising since glacial striae on the platform indicated that it had been severely scoured by Irish Sea ice moving onshore from a northerly direction. He suggested that the age of the platform was uncertain but that it could be Hoxnian or even earlier. This was supported by Mitchell (1960) who correlated the raised beach at Porth Oer with the Fremington raised beach in north Devon, which he believed was Hoxnian in age. Similarly, Synge (1963, 1964) considered Porth Oer to be important because it was the sole locality in Llŷn where an interglacial raised beach deposit could be observed. He considered that a number of factors pointed towards the antiquity of the sequence at Porth Oer. First, the great age of the platform was attested by its highly weathered condition (Synge 1963). Second, the till at Porth Oer was weathered at its surface, a process that must have taken place under fully interglacial conditions. Therefore, a Saalian age was attributed to the till at Porth Oer, with the interglacial weathering of its surface attributed to the succeeding Ipswichian Stage (Synge 1964). The basal raised beach was Hoxnian in age and the underlying platform was ascribed to the Hoxnian or possibly earlier.

The sequence at Porth Oer described by Saunders (1963, 1967, 1968a, 1968b, 1968c, 1968d, 1973) was, essentially similar to that of Jehu. He believed Porth Oer was the most westerly drift-filled hollow in Llŷn, and considered that the pre-drift surface at the site provided conclusive evidence for a former high sea-level between 7.6 and 9.1m OD (25 ft and 30 ft) before deposition of the till. He argued that the shore platform represented a multi-cyclical feature of probable Ipswichian and pre-Ipswichian ages, while the raised beach gravels themselves belonged to the Ipswichian Stage. Saunders and other workers (for example, Whittow and Ball 1970; Peake et al. 1973; Bowen 1974) recognised foreign erratics in the raised beach at Porth Oer and alluded to the possibility that they had been derived by marine reworking of glacial deposits from an earlier glaciation. An Ipswichian age for the raised beach at Porth Oer was also proposed by Bowen (1973a, 1973b, 1974, 1977b).

On the basis of radiocarbon dates from till sites elsewhere in Llŷn, Saunders argued that the till at Porth Oer was deposited during the principal invasion of the Late Devensian Irish Sea ice-sheet. He correlated this till with the lower or Trevor Till (Simpkins 1968) of the north Llŷn coast and suggested that it could also be correlated with the lower or Criccieth Till exposed in southern Llŷn (at Criccieth and Glanllynnau), and was supported by Bowen (1973a, 1973b, 1974, 1977b). Deposits from the proposed later readvance of Late Devensian ice (the Clynnog Till of north Llŷn) found, for example, at Dinas Dinlle and Gwydir Bay, have not been recorded at Porth Oer. The weathered surface of the Trevor Till at Porth Oer was correlated with a comparable horizon at Gwydir Bay which affected both the Trevor Till and the sands and gravels of the Aberafon Formation, and pre-dated deposition of the Clynnog Till. Saunders suggested that the weathering at both sites therefore occurred during interstadial conditions in the Late Devensian.

Detailed pebble lithology and till fabric measurements have been undertaken at Porth Oer (Saunders 1963, 1968b, 1968d). Fabric properties have established that the Trevor Till was deposited by Irish Sea ice moving onshore from between the north and ENE, and a generally northern source was confirmed by high percentages of fine- and coarse-grained acid igneous rock types.

The broad sequence of Late Pleistocene events reconstructed from lithostratigraphic evidence at Porth Oer by Saunders, was also upheld by Whittow and Ball (1970) who suggested that the site was glaciated by Irish Sea ice of the first recorded (Devensian) advance in Llŷn, but not during the subsequent advance of the Irish Sea ice-sheet.

Porth Oer provides an important lithostratigrapic record of Late Pleistocene events in north-west Wales and in particular, evidence for a cycle of interglacial and glacial events. It displays the finest example of raised marine deposits anywhere in North or north-west Wales. It is the only such site in Llŷn, and together with Red Wharf Bay on Anglesey, provides rare evidence for former high relative sea-levels and probably interglacial conditions in the region. The presence of raised beach deposits at Porth Oer has resulted in the site having featured prominently in studies of Pleistocene correlations (for example, Mitchell 1960; Synge 1963, 1964; Bowen 1973a, 1973b, 1974, 1977b; Peake et al. 1973). In particular, the raised beach deposits formerly allowed correlation of the Pleistocene succession in Llŷn with that in the Gower Peninsula (for example, Bowen 1973a, 1973b, 1974, 1977b) where the raised beach fragments were regarded as Ipswichian in age and were used as a lithostratigraphic marker horizon. Although the age of the raised beach at Porth Oer has not been determined, the site provides rare evidence in North Wales, and the only sedimentary evidence in Llŷn, for former high sea-level, interglacial conditions.

The unusually fine development of a raised shore platform beneath the raised beach sediments at Porth Oer gives a rare opportunity to study earlier elements of the Late Pleistocene sequence. Although the age of this platform is unknown and probably composite, it is representative of the most widespread geomorphological feature pre-dating Late Pleistocene glaciation in Llŷn (Whittow and Ball 1970), and it provides evidence for former high sea-levels before the raised beach event.

The site is also important for establishing details of the glacial history of Llŷn. The till exposure has provided lithological and fabric evidence which indicates deposition by ice moving onshore from the Irish Sea Basin. Porth Oer therefore helps to establish regional patterns of ice movement. Saunders' studies have provided a firm foundation for correlating this till with the lower or Trevor Till found widely elsewhere along the north coast of Llŷn. The occurrence of this till here, on the western tip of Llŷn, helps to establish that virtually the whole northern coast was inundated by Irish Sea ice during this probably Late Devensian glacial episode. The upper or Clynnog Till which occurs in north Llŷn, for example at Dinas Dinlle and Gwydir Bay, is not present at Porth Oer. It follows that the sequences at these sites help to constrain the extent to which north Llŷn was affected by ice during the second recorded advance of Late Devensian ice – the proposed Late Devensian readvance. The site, therefore, helps to establish that parts of western Llŷn were not glaciated by the possibly confluent Irish sea and Welsh ice that affected the Menai Straits region and other parts of the north Llŷn coast.

Although the significance of the leached and weathered surface of the Trevor Till at Porth Oer is debatable, the implication is that this horizon, and comparable ones at Dinas Dinlle and Gwydir Bay, were formed during a period of weathering between the two recorded Late Devensian ice advances (for example, Saunders 1968a, 1968d).

This locality provides the only known sedimentary record in Llŷn of pre-Holocene high sea-levels associated with interglacial conditions. With Red Wharf Bay, the site provides the only evidence in north-west Wales for a cycle of interglacial and glacial events. The interest of the site is enhanced by the thick till (Trevor Till) sequence which overlies the raised beach. This till demonstrates the onshore movement of the Irish Sea ice-sheet onto north and west Llŷn during the principal invasion of the Late Devensian ice-sheet. Whereas depositional evidence from Dinas Dinlle and Gwydir Bay show that parts of northern Llŷn were affected by a subsequent readvance of Late Devensian ice, Porth Oer shows that this ice did not reach western Llŷn.

Conclusions

The raised beach at Porth Oer together with that at Red Wharf Bay in Anglesey, are the only known examples of their kind in North Wales. The overlying deposits show the events of the last glacial cycle, which followed the previous interglacial period when the raised beaches were formed.

Porth Neigwl

Highlights

An important site which records possible evidence for three glacial events in this part of North Wales: a pre-Devensian glacial event, a Late Devensian Irish Sea invasion of ice and a later Welsh ice advance moving in a different direction.

Introduction

Porth Neigwl provides evidence to suggest that southern Llŷn was inundated by southward moving ice from the Irish Sea Basin. The site has a long history of research commencing with the work of Jehu (1909). Porth Neigwl has also featured in studies by Nicholas (1915), Matley (1936), Synge (1963, 1964), Saunders (1963, 1968a, 1968b, 1968c, 1968d, 1973), Whittow (1960), Whittow and Ball (1970) and Boulton (1977a).

Description

Porth Neigwl or Hell's Mouth Bay is situated on the southern coast of Llŷn and opens out to the south-west. To the south-east, the bay is bounded by the high ground of Mynydd Cilan, a promontory of Cambrian rocks, and to the north-west, by Ordovician shales and basic intrusive rocks. Between these rock masses, the head of the bay is formed entirely of Late Pleistocene and Holocene sediments which extend for about four miles, giving one of the finest drift sections in north-west Wales. In the lowland plain behind Porth Neigwl, boreholes have proved a drift cover in excess of 110m (360 ft) (Saunders 1968b). The cliffed sequence comprises mostly thick, blue-grey to brown Irish Sea till, up to 30m in thickness, and the western part of Porth Neigwl Bay between Pen-yr-Allt (SH243286) and Trefollwyn (SH269274) is almost entirely composed of this thick, homogenous till. The area included within the GCR site, however, extends from near Pen-towyn Farm (SH283263) to just beyond Nant Farm (SH291255) in the east, where the drift stratigraphy is more complex and potentially more rewarding for elaborating Late Pleistocene and Holocene events – see Figure 31. Immediately south of Pen-towyn Farm, the Irish Sea till is well exposed and forms massive faces. To the south-east of this, Saunders (for example, 1963, 1968d) recorded a sequence showing –

9   Blown sand

8   Peat with birch and hazelnuts (Pollen Zone VII-VIII?)

7   Gravelly local till (Llanystumdwy Till)

6   Weathered horizon

5   Shelly outwash sands, gravels and laminated clays (Aberafon Formation)

4   Blue-grey, calcareous Irish Sea till (Trevor Till)

3   Soliflucted local till

2   Fine flaky head with pseudo-stratification

1   Coarse, blocky head

The chief elements of this succession are shown in Figure 31.

Interpretation

Jehu (1909) was the first to describe the deposits at Porth Neigwl, which he did as part of a comprehensive classification of drift deposits in western Caernarvonshire. As at Gwydir Bay in northern Llŷn, he described a tripartite sequence of two tills separated by sands and gravels, which, he argued, showed evidence for two glacial advances separated by possible interglacial conditions. He described a wide range of rock types from the lower till (bed 4) including Chalk flints, various granites from southern Scotland and Ailsa Craig microgranite, which he considered indicated derivation from the Irish Sea Basin. The lower till also contained pieces of wood and a comprehensive marine mollusc fauna, further proof that it was deposited by ice which moved south

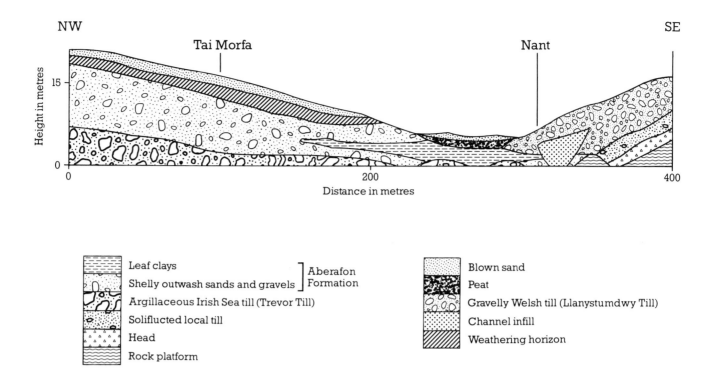

NW   SE

Tai Morfa   Nant

Figure 31 Quaternary sequence at Porth Neigwl (from Saunders 1968d)

over the floor of the Irish Sea. He demonstrated that the overlying sands and gravels (bed 5) also contained typical Irish Sea erratics and shells, and regarded them as sea-floor materials transported by ice and subsequently redeposited by fluvioglacial action. Jehu noted that the upper till (bed 7) was only present in the southern part of the bay; and, because it contained far-travelled erratics and marine shell fragments, argued that it too had been derived, at least in part, from the Irish Sea Basin. In contrast, Nicholas (1915) interpreted the upper till as the product of local Welsh (Snowdonian) ice which had invaded Llŷn following retreat of Irish Sea ice from St Tudwal's Peninsula.

Matley (1936) described the Pleistocene sequence at Porth Neigwl near Tyddyn-y-don Farm. He showed that Jehu's lower till was overlain by a series of laminated clays and sands (leaf-clays), which he argued had been deposited in a marine lagoon largely shut off from the sea by a barrier of ice. These sediments formed part of a 50 ft (15m) terrace which Matley traced at various locations in southern Llŷn, and which he judged to be of 'Late-glacial' age.

The Late Pleistocene and Holocene deposits at Porth Neigwl were also described by Synge (1963, 1964). He argued that the main calcareous shelly till (Jehu's lower till and Saunders' bed 4 – see Figure 31) was probably Saalian in age and that the soliflucted local till (bed 3) showed evidence for an even earlier local glacial phase. Evidence from coastal sections around Llŷn was used by Synge to

suggest that only the northern coastal margin had been affected by Devensian Stage ice. He suggested that during this glacial phase a rubbly head (equivalent to Saunders' bed 7 – gravelly local till) was formed at Porth Neigwl. Elsewhere along the south Llŷn coast, Saalian drifts were cryoturbated under periglacial conditions.

The most detailed work at Porth Neigwl was done by Saunders (1963, 1968a, 1968b, 1968c, 1968d, 1973) whose reconstructed succession is shown in Figure 31. He envisaged that before deposition of the Irish Sea till (bed 4), periglacial conditions were experienced in the area and resulted in formation of head deposits (beds 1 and 2) and the redistribution of existing Welsh glacial sediments (bed 3). Detailed pebble lithology and till fabric measurements showed that the till (bed 4) was deposited by Irish Sea ice moving onshore from NNW to SSE. The typical erratic assemblage, including limestones from the central plain of Ireland, metamorphic and fine-grained basic igneous types from Anglesey and northern Llŷn, provided strong evidence of an Irish Sea origin for the till. Saunders correlated the Irish Sea till at Porth Neigwl with the lower till or Trevor Till of the north Llŷn coast. He regarded the shelly sands and gravels (bed 5) overlying the Trevor Till as fluvioglacial deposits associated with decay of the Irish Sea ice and interpreted the laminated leaf-clays as lagoonal or lacustrine deposits probably associated with temporary still water conditions in the fluvioglacial environment. Although no correlation was made by Saunders, these sands,

150

gravels and clays are broadly equivalent to the sands and gravels of the Aberafon Formation (Simpkins 1968) along the north Llŷn coast.

The overlying gravelly till (bed 7) was, according to Saunders, clearly differentiated from the Irish Sea sediments beneath. Both Irish Sea and Welsh erratics were recorded from this till but Saunders emphasised that the preponderance of Welsh erratics, particularly those from southern Snowdonia, suggested a Welsh origin. These conclusions were also supported by fabric analyses which showed that the Welsh till had been deposited by ice moving from north-east to south-west. Because a zone of weathering (unit 6) separated the Welsh till from the Irish Sea sediments beneath, Saunders argued that the upper till represented an entirely separate and later advance of ice from Snowdonia, which in moving south-westwards incorporated Irish Sea erratics from the previous glacial episode.

Fundamental to Saunders' interpretation of the sequence was a radiocarbon date of 29,000 ± 1200 BP (I-3262) from marine shell fragments taken from the lower (Trevor) till. A comparable sample from Porth Dinllaen on the north Llŷn coast gave an age of 31,800 + 1,800 - 1,200 BP (I-3273). On the basis of these dates, Saunders referred the Trevor Till at Porth Neigwl and elsewhere in Llŷn to the Late Devensian. The gravelly upper till at Porth Neigwl he considered to represent a readvance of the Late Devensian Welsh ice-sheet, sometime after c. 17,000 BP, on the basis of Foster's (1968, 1970a) radiocarbon date from Bryncir. This readvance was tentatively correlated by Saunders with the Scottish Readvance.

Bowen (1973, 1977b) accepted this interpretation. The weathering horizon (unit 6) described by Saunders, he took to indicate interstadial weathering (Bowen 1973a, 1977b; Saunders 1968a, 1968d; Whittow and Ball 1970), and not fully interglacial conditions as proposed by Synge (1964). Bowen considered that Porth Neigwl represented the most westerly occurrence of the upper Welsh till in southern Llŷn, and correlated it with the gravelly Welsh till farther east at Glanllynnau and Criccieth, named locally the Llanystumdwy Till (Simpkins 1968). Such sedimentary data were used to reconstruct a maximum limit (Figure 27) for the proposed readvance of Late Devensian ice (Bowen 1974, 1977b) with the extreme parts of south-west Llŷn remaining ice-free. The Irish Sea till at Porth Neigwl was correlated with the Trevor Till on the north coast.

An alternative explanation for the sequence at Porth Neigwl was proposed by Boulton (1977a). He suggested that the sequence was similar to that at Glanllynnau where he had demonstrated that the sediments had formed in a supraglacial landform and sediment association, in a single Late Devensian glacial event. In this interpretation, the weathering horizon simply reflected a relatively short break in sedimentation and not a protracted period of deglaciation or interstadial conditions as had previously been suggested.

The age of the deposits at Porth Neigwl is controversial. Mitchell (1960, 1972) and Synge (1963, 1964) stressed the much-weathered and frost-heaved nature of the tills in southern Llŷn, and used the evidence to suggest that it was not glaciated during the Late Devensian, with ice restricted largely to the northern coastal margin. This view has not, however, been widely accepted and most workers (for example, Saunders 1968a, 1968b, 1968c, 1968d, 1973; Bowen 1973a, 1973b, 1974, 1977b; Whittow and Ball 1970) believed that all the till in Llŷn was deposited during the Late Devensian. Porth Neigwl is one of very few Pleistocene sites in North and north-west Wales to have yielded a radiocarbon date, which although potentially unreliable, may provide evidence to confirm that the area was glaciated during the Late Devensian.

Porth Neigwl is the finest exposure through the Irish Sea (Trevor) till in southern Llŷn. It demonstrates that the south-west tip of Llŷn was invaded by Irish Sea ice moving broadly north to south. Both the inferred direction of ice movement and the considerable thickness of the Trevor Till strongly suggest that during the principal invasion of the Late Devensian ice-sheet, Irish Sea ice was dominant on south-west Llŷn and at this time was unimpeded by Welsh ice. In this context, Porth Neigwl provides contrasting evidence to the sites at Porth Ceiriad, Glanllynnau and Morannedd (Criccieth) which display sediments of predominantly Welsh derivation.

The upper gravelly Welsh till at Porth Neigwl, of proposed Late Devensian readvance age, demonstrates a later incursion of ice moving broadly east to west into the area. Its limited exposure at Porth Neigwl has been used to demonstrate that Late Devensian readvance Welsh ice was here near to its most westerly limit. The site therefore provides important evidence to constrain the limit of Welsh ice on south-west Llŷn during the proposed Late Devensian readvance. Porth Neigwl further demonstrates that the area around St Tudwal's Peninsula was glaciated by both Welsh and Irish Sea ice masses during the Late Pleistocene.

The sequence at Porth Neigwl is also important for demonstrating a period of periglacial conditions before deposition of the thick Irish Sea till, when head was deposited and pre-existing glacial sediments redistributed by solifluction. The site provides sedimentary evidence in north-west Wales for a glacial event prior to deposition of the main Irish Sea (Trevor) till.

The site was once regarded as important for a Holocene raised beach which occurred at the base of the coastal cliffs near high water mark (Whittow 1960). West (1972) has since shown that this feature was merely part of the present day beach, cemented by inorganic calcite and providing no evidence for the height of a Holocene raised beach in north-west Wales. The Holocene peat and sand cliffed in the southern part of the bay provide additional interest.

Porth Neigwl is important for reconstructing the Late Pleistocene history of north-west Wales. It provides the finest sections in southern Llŷn through till of Irish Sea provenance (Trevor Till). A radiocarbon date on shell gives evidence to suggest that the Trevor Till was deposited by Late Devensian ice. The upper gravelly till at Porth Neigwl demonstrates a later incursion of Welsh ice into the area. The sequence helps to establish the directions of ice movement and the relative strength and interactions of the Irish Sea and Welsh ice masses during both recorded glacial episodes. The site also shows evidence for periglacial conditions prior to deposition of the Trevor Till. Redeposited Welsh erratics in the periglacial sediments record possible evidence for an even earlier glacial episode.

Conclusions

The extensive exposures of ice age sediments at Porth Neigwl are important for reconstructing the ice age history of north-west Wales. The Irish Sea ice-sheet deposit (Trevor Till) has been interpreted as a boulder clay: that is, the sedimentary product of a land-based ice-sheet. On the other hand, it could perhaps be a glacio-marine deposit representing deposition in a sea, adjacent to the Irish Sea ice-sheet.

Porth Ceiriad

Highlights

This locality with its periglacial sediments above and below glacial till may show that this part of Llŷn was glaciated by confluent Irish Sea and Welsh ice during the Late Devensian, but lay in a periglacial area beyond the western limit of a later advance of Welsh ice.

Introduction

Porth Ceiriad is an important coastal exposure which shows that the St Tudwal's Peninsula may have been a zone of transition between Irish Sea and Welsh ice masses during the Late Pleistocene. The sections were first noted by Ramsay (1881) and have since featured in studies by Jehu (1909), Saunders (1967, 1968a, 1968b, 1968c, 1973) and Whittow and Ball (1970).

Description

The sections at Porth Ceiriad extend laterally for about 700m, and they reach a maximum height of 30m. Whittow and Ball (1970) recorded the following generalised sequence, shown in Figure 32.

6	Hillwash
5	False-bedded shale head (cryoturbated)
4	Solifluction deposits
3	Grey-brown non-calcareous Welsh till
2	Fine shale head
1	Blocky head

Bed 4 contains a large lens of calcareous Irish Sea till, reworked Welsh till from bed 3 and beds of laminated clays and sands with gravel lenses.

Interpretation

Although Ramsay (1881) described the head deposits at Porth Ceiriad as an angular breccia of post-Tertiary age resting on slaty strata, Jehu (1909) was the first to describe the sections in detail. He noted that many of the boulders and pebbles in the till were of Welsh origin although other farther-travelled, probably Irish Sea, erratics were also recorded. He regarded the till at Porth Ceiriad as representing the Upper Boulder Clay of his tripartite succession, representing the most recent of two glacial advances in Llŷn.

The sections at Porth Ceiriad were next studied by Saunders (1967, 1968a, 1968b, 1968c, 1973). Using pebble lithology and till fabric measurements, he ascertained that the till at Porth Ceiriad (bed 3) had been deposited by Welsh ice moving from north-east to south-west. This suggested that when the Welsh till was deposited at Porth Ceiriad, the area to the west was probably free from Irish Sea ice, which otherwise would have caused a major southward deflection of the Welsh ice-sheet. The Welsh till was therefore considered younger than the main Irish Sea till (Trevor Till) at nearby Porth Neigwl, which Saunders ascribed to the main invasion of the Late Devensian ice-sheet in Llŷn. He correlated the Welsh till at Porth Ceiriad with the younger of the two Welsh tills exposed elsewhere along the south coast of Llŷn, (the Llanystumdwy Till of Simpkins (1968)), for example at Glanllynnau and Morannedd. Saunders suggested that the till at Porth Ceiriad had been deposited during the second glacial advance on Llŷn of proposed Late Devensian readvance age. The till at Porth Ceiriad was consequently seen to be equivalent in age to the gravelly Welsh till at Porth Neigwl.

These correlations were not, however, accepted by Whittow and Ball (1970) who suggested that the Welsh till at Porth Ceiriad belonged to the first of the recognised glacial advances in Llŷn and could therefore be correlated with the lower of the Welsh tills on the south Llŷn coast, at Criccieth (Morannedd) and Glanllynnau (the Criccieth Till of Simpkins (1968)). A lens of calcareous Irish Sea till (in bed 4) was noted by Whittow and Ball but was not considered to be *in situ*. It appeared to have been soliflucted from a nearby deposit of the Irish Sea till, and it was used as evidence to suggest that St Tudwal's Peninsula had been a zone of transition between the Welsh and Irish Sea ice masses during

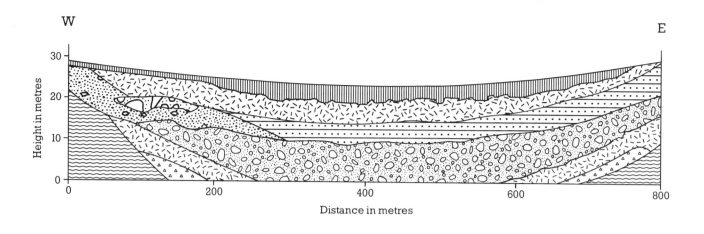

Figure 32 Quaternary sequence at Porth Ceiriad (from Whittow and Ball 1970)

this first glacial episode. The till and soliflucted till at Porth Ceiriad (beds 3 and 4) were succeeded by cryoturbated head deposits. The implication was that the head deposits and the structures were formed during a later glacial episode, when periglacial conditions were experienced at Porth Ceiriad and an upper till was deposited elsewhere in Llŷn. Saunders (1973) later accepted this interpretation.

Porth Ceiriad is particularly important for showing evidence for the interactions and movements of the Irish Sea and Welsh ice-sheets in south-west Llŷn during the Late Devensian.

Saunders originally presented lithological and fabric data to correlate the Welsh till at Porth Ceiriad with the upper of two tills found farther east along the south Llŷn coast, the Llanystumdwy Till – broadly equivalent to the Clynnog Till of north Llŷn and of postulated Late Devensian readvance age. This evidence was used to suggest that western Llŷn was free from Irish Sea ice during a later advance of the Late Devensian ice-sheet. However, most subsequent authors, including Saunders (1973), have correlated the Welsh till at Porth Ceiriad with the Irish Sea till at Porth Neigwl and the lower of the two tills found commonly elsewhere in Llŷn (the Trevor and Criccieth Tills of Irish Sea and Welsh provenance, respectively). Such a correlation together with the close association of soliflucted Irish Sea and Welsh glacial sediments at Porth Ceiriad has led to the proposal of an entirely different sequence of Late Pleistocene events in south-west Llŷn. In particular, this evidence has been used to suggest that St Tudwal's

Peninsula was a zone of transition between the Irish Sea and Welsh ice masses during the principal invasion of the Late Devensian ice-sheet. With lithological evidence from Porth Neigwl to the west and Glanllynnau and Criccieth to the east, the evidence from Porth Ceiriad suggests that south-west Llŷn was glaciated by a Late Devensian Irish Sea ice-sheet moving southwards, while southern Llŷn was invaded contemporaneously by an ice-stream moving north-east to south-west from Snowdonia. From the evidence at Porth Ceiriad it appears that both ice-streams were confluent in the St Tudwal's area.

The absence of an upper till at Porth Ceiriad that could be correlated with the Welsh Llanystumdwy Till, found eastwards along much of the south Llŷn coast, places an important constraint on the maximum westward limit of the subsequent expansion of the Late Devensian ice-sheet which deposited that till. It has been shown that a gravelly Welsh till of limited extent occurs to the west, at Porth Neigwl. This implies that only a tongue of Welsh ice impinged on the coast of south-west Llŷn in this area, leaving Porth Ceiriad in the glacier-free zone during the inferred Late Devensian readvance. The presence of head, solifluction deposits and cryoturbation structures in the sequence above the Welsh till, lends some support to the proposal that the site and its immediate environs were situated in the periglacial zone during the later expansion of the Late Devensian ice.

The stratigraphic record at Porth Ceiriad is difficult to interpret although it would appear that the sequence contains evidence for at least one phase of glacial activity which was both preceded and followed by periods of periglacial conditions, when the upper and lower heads were formed. Although the sections show some of the finest stratigraphical detail on the Llŷn Peninsula, it is the juxtaposition of Irish Sea and local Welsh glacial sediments which gives the site special significance. Such evidence contrasts with Porth Neigwl to the west where glacial deposits mainly from the Irish Sea Basin are found, and Glanllynnau and Morannedd (Criccieth) in the east where glacial deposits of exclusively Welsh provenance are recorded.

Conclusions

The succession of ice age and cold climate deposits at Porth Ceiriad is one of the most detailed on the Llŷn Peninsula. Of particular importance is the occurrence of the Irish Sea ice-sheet and local Welsh ice-sheet deposits, that is glacial sediments coming from different ice-sheets.

Glanllynnau

Highlights

A complex site showing evidence for a fluctuating Devensian ice front. Its sediments, pollen, beetles and absolute dates have afforded one of the most detailed records of climatic change and, in particular, glacial retreat in Wales.

Introduction

Glanllynnau is a site of considerable importance for understanding glacial and late-glacial events in Wales. The glacial sediments have been interpreted as the product of two separate ice advances, but may also be explained as the result of a single glaciation. The deposits at Glanllynnau were first studied by Jehu (1909), and then by Matley (1936), Saunders (1963, 1967, 1968a, 1968b, 1968c, 1968d, 1973), Synge (1964, 1970) and Whittow and Ball (1970). Accounts of the Devensian late-glacial and Holocene successions were provided by Simpkins (1968, 1974) and Coope and Brophy (1972). The lithostratigraphy of the site was recently re-examined by Boulton (1977a, 1977b), and the succession has been discussed in a wider area by Bowen (1973a, 1973b, 1974, 1977b). It has also been referred to by Moore (1970, 1977), Shotton and Williams (1971) and Coope (1977).

Description

The coastal cliffs at Glanllynnau (SH456372) reveal a sequence of tills and fluvioglacial sediments, the latter displaying well developed glaciotectonic structures. The area inland is studded with kettle holes, some of which have been breached by coastal erosion to reveal a succession of Devensian late-glacial silty clay, peat and sand horizons.

Whittow and Ball (1970) described the following succession at Glanllynnau – see Figure 33.

11 Hillwash
10 Peat
9 Grey silt with boulders
8 Organic pond clay
7 Lake mud
6 Stony solifluction clay
5 Brown stony till (Llanystumdwy Till)
4 Fluvioglacial sand and gravel (Afon Wen Formation)
3 Laminated stoneless clays, silts and sands (contorted)
2 Yellow-brown weathered surface of Criccieth Till
1 Blue-grey till disturbed by fossil ice-wedge casts (Criccieth Till)

Interpretation

The glacial sequence

When the exposures were described by Jehu in 1909, the lower till (bed 1) was not exposed. He recorded only one till (bed 5) lying above sands and gravels, and classified these as the upper two thirds of his tripartite sequence in Llŷn. He established that the deposits were of Welsh provenance. Matley (1936) suggested that the sequence had been trimmed into a terrace, which commonly occurred at about 50 feet (c. 15m) in southern Llŷn, formed either by marine agencies or at the margins of a glacially-impounded lake in 'Late-Glacial' times.

Saunders (1963, 1967) was the first to record the lower blue-grey till (bed 1) beneath the sand and gravel at Glanllynnau. Saunders (1968a, 1968b, 1968c, 1968d, 1973) also described additional lithological and till fabric evidence. He showed that the lower till was argillaceous with an erratic suite dominated by slate (over 85%) derived from the Nantlle-Bethesda slate belt; its fabric indicating deposition by ice moving from ENE to WSW. He suggested it was overlain by a thin band of weathered and soliflucted till (bed 2) of the same origin, which in places, filled well developed fossil ice-wedge casts in the surface of the lower till. The weathered horizon was succeeded by a thin bed of wavy laminated silts (bed 3), which sealed the top of the ice-wedge casts, and which he considered could have been caused by freeze-thaw activity or by subsequent overriding of the sediments by the ice of a later advance. The silts are overlain by the fluvioglacial sand and gravel (bed 4) described by earlier workers, and by the upper till (bed 5) which shows well developed cryoturbation structures. Saunders showed that, like the lower till, the upper till was also Welsh in origin and it contained erratics from the Vale of Ffestiniog, deposited by ice moving from east to west. On regional lithostratigraphic grounds he suggested that large

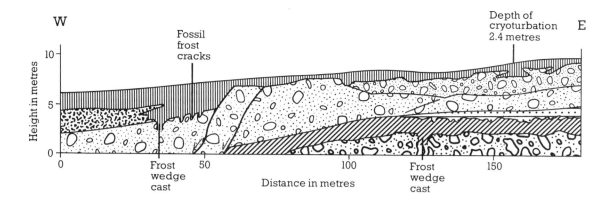

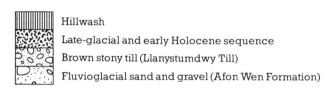

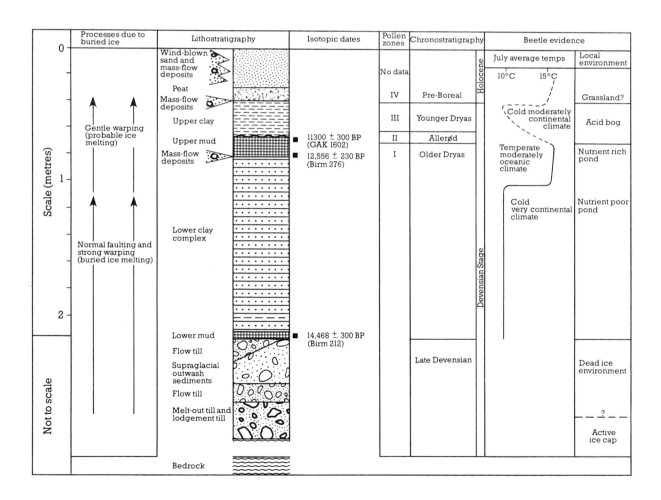

Figure 33 Quaternary sequence at Glanllynnau (after Whittow and Ball 1970; Boulton 1977a)

areas of western Llŷn were ice-free during the most recent glacial pulse (upper till at Glanllynnau). Saunders developed a framework for Late Pleistocene events in Llŷn using lithostratigraphical evidence supported by radiocarbon dating. He argued that the lower till (Criccieth Till) at Glanllynnau and elsewhere in southern Llŷn, for example at Morannedd, was deposited during the main pulse of the Late Devensian ice-sheet. He correlated it with the Trevor Till of northern Llŷn and Porth Neigwl. He suggested that the gravelly till (Llanystumdwy Till - Simpkins 1968) at Glanllynnau and at Morannedd had been deposited by a subsequent advance of Late Devensian Welsh ice. Saunders (1968a) reported a radiocarbon date of 11,740 ± 170 BP (I-3261) from peat collected at the base of a kettle hole developed in the fluvioglacial sands and gravels. Together with a determination of 16,830 + 970 - 860 BP (I-2801) (Foster 1968, 1970a) from material disseminated in sands and gravels of an equivalent formation at Bryncir, these dates were used by Saunders as upper and lower limits for the last phase of glacial activity in Llŷn. He correlated this with the Scottish Readvance glaciation.

Thus, Saunders established a Late Devensian age for the Criccieth and Llanystumdwy Tills at Glanllynnau, the latter ascribed to an ice readvance later in the Late Devensian. The zone of weathering and frost-cracking on the surface of the Criccieth Till was ascribed to the time between deposition of the two tills. This was supported by Whittow and Ball (1970) and Bowen (1973a, 1973b, 1974, 1977b). Earlier, Synge (1964), suggested that the weathered till surface elsewhere in Llŷn was sufficiently deep and well developed to have formed under fully interglacial conditions, probably during the Ipswichian Stage. The tills were therefore considered by him to be Saalian in age. This view was also supported by Simpkins (1968) who argued that the deeply weathered Criccieth Till of southern Llŷn was older than the Trevor Till of the north Llŷn coast. In an alternative explanation, Synge (1970) suggested that the horizon of weathering was an iron-pan effect and the fossil ice-wedge casts were loading structures.

In contrast to earlier workers, Boulton (1977a, 1977b) suggested that the multiple till sequence at Glanllynnau was the result of a single glacial episode. The local landscape and sediments were seen to be evidence for a supraglacial landform system and sediment association. This model was developed from his studies of modern Arctic glaciers and their depositional sequences (Boulton 1972; Boulton and Paul 1976). He considered that the lower blue-grey massive till at Glanllynnau had been deposited beneath a glacier which contained a thick sequence of englacial debris. This glacier had moved from east to west as shown by Saunders' (1968b) fabric analyses and Boulton's determinations of magnetic anisotropy susceptibility. During ice wastage, englacial debris melted out onto the glacier surface and protected underlying ice from further ablation,

when well defined ice-cored ridges developed. Flow till (released as a water-saturated fluid mass) accumulated on the surface of the dead ice, together with outwash from small streams and silts in surface ponds. Weathering of the exposed till and frost-cracking may also have occurred at this time. Any hiatus was only a brief interlude and not the result of protracted interstadial or even interglacial conditions as suggested by earlier workers. This was followed quickly by deposition of sands and gravels onto the lower till, the pattern being controlled by the positions of the ice-cored till ridges. The sands and gravels form large lenticular masses up to 15m in thickness and show low angle cross-stratification, and scour and fill structures. These features are typical of braided stream deposits, and Boulton estimated the mean palaeocurrent direction to have been approximately north to south along the troughs between the ice-cored ridges.

The sands and gravels are overlain intermittently by an upper till whose internal structure and position on the surface of the hummocky landscape suggested to Boulton an origin as a flow till following cessation of outwash sedimentation. Boulton suggested that deposition of flow till and outwash was mutually exclusive, there being no upper till where the outwash gravels completely cover the lower till.

As the buried ice in the ridges began to melt, there was a complete reversal in topography with a warping of the supraglacial sequence. Faulting occurred in the gravels as kettle holes were formed at the sites of the former ice-cored ridges. These faults are developed as normal faults with downthrows of up to 0.5m towards the kettle hole depressions. Grey silty clay, derived from the flow till, was then washed into the kettle holes to form the base of the Devensian late-glacial and early Holocene sequence described in detail by Simpkins (1968, 1974) and Coope and Brophy (1972).

Boulton's model serves also to explain observed textural and lithological differences between the two tills at Glanllynnau. Saunders (1968b) claimed that the lower till contained an erratic suite derived from the Nantlle-Bethesda slate belt but that the upper till contained erratics from the Vale of Ffestiniog. Boulton's work, however, showed that the change in erratic suite took place in the upper part of the lower till, rather than between the two tills. This, he considered, was likely to reflect vertical differentiation in the englacial debris content of the glacier: namely that the vertical sequence of englacial debris in a glacier often reflects in reverse order the lithologies over which the glacier has moved; giving a sequence in which the farther-travelled debris is at the top. Therefore, the lower, fine-grained till may have been derived subglacially, although the upper till may have originated from coarser-textured supraglacial material.

The Devensian late-glacial and early Holocene sequence

Above the glacial succession, Jehu (1909) recorded two peat beds containing *Sphagnum, Potamogeton* fruits, scraps of birch bark and wood and other floral remains, and separated from the glacial succession by a rootletted blue-grey clay. He did not discuss the significance of the peat beds. The detailed analysis of the late-glacial and early Holocene pollen sequence was by Simpkins (1968, 1974). Coope and Brophy (1972) dealt with coleopteran (beetle) faunas.

Description

Devensian late-glacial and early Holocene deposits were recorded by Simpkins from borings in an unbreached inland kettle hole at Glanllynnau Marsh and from a single kettle hole in Glanllynnau Cliff. This consisted of two basins of deposition linked behind the cliff, suggesting that the original plan of the kettle hole was kidney-shaped. Simpkins described the following sequence of deposits overlying iron-stained and cryoturbated fluvioglacial gravels of the Afon Wen Formation –

8 Modern soil developed on blown sand

7 Dark brown, highly humified and oxidised peat with some sand

6 Black, fibrous highly humified peat

5 Grey-brown clay-mud with leaves of *Salix herbacea* L.

4 Dark grey-brown mud with some clay

3 Dark brown fine mud with many *Potamogeton* fruitstones, *Menyanthes* seeds and *Carex* nutlets

2 Grey-brown clay-mud

1 Grey silty clay

Interpretation

Pollen

The palynology of the sequences shown in Glanllynnau Cliff and Marsh was used by Simpkins (1968, 1974) to divide the terrestrial vegetation history at Glanllynnau into four main pollen zones. Zone I was represented by pollen assemblages found in bed 1, and was termed the 'pre-interstadial' period, roughly equivalent to the Older Dryas. The grey silty clay contained a low overall pollen concentration comprising mainly species from environments of disturbed ground and open-habitats. A dominance of grass and sedge pollen, and pollen from plants which today have a mainly northern montane distribution, indicated that this was a dominantly cold period. Simpkins suggested that the dominance of *Artemisia* pollen probably reflected the importance of solifluction processes at this time. This early cold phase was succeeded by a warm 'interstadial' period represented in the rock record by beds 2-4. This phase was characterised by a dominance of *Rumex* and *Juniperus* pollen, and

was marked in the early interstadial period by a rapid change to biogenic sedimentation and a cessation of solifluction into the kettle holes. The latter part of this warm interstadial phase was characterised by a *Betula-Filipendula* assemblage. The 'post-interstadial' period (Pollen Zone III/Younger Dryas) was marked by an overall decline in pollen production. A decline in *Betula* and increased percentages of pollen from open and disturbed habitats – for example, *Artemisia* and *Rumex* – characterise this period and bear witness to a deterioration in climate and a return to solifluction in the kettle holes (bed 5). Macrofossil evidence shows that least willow *Salix herbacea* may have grown in close proximity to the cliff kettle hole at that time (Simpkins 1974).

The early Holocene (pre-Boreal) is represented at Glanllynnau by beds 6 and 7, and is characterised by a cessation of solifluction and a rapid increase in pollen concentration. During this period, thickets of juniper may have become quickly shaded out by the expansion of birch woodlands, although a number of herbs characteristic of the late-glacial were also slow to disappear. It is of interest that the expansion of *Juniperus* at Glanllynnau during the interstadial and at the beginning of the Holocene is not as marked as at other Welsh late-glacial and Holocene sites, for example, at Cors Geuallt (Crabtree 1972) and the Elan Valley (Moore 1970). It has been suggested that the lower juniper values cannot be explained in terms of simple altitudinal differences between these sites, and it is possible that peaks in juniper pollen may reflect localised stands of this shrub during these periods (Moore 1977).

Simpkins' palynological analysis also allowed reconstruction of the aquatic vegetation history and palaeoecology at Glanllynnau. Pollen Zone I (pre-interstadial) was dominated by the development of marginal reed swamp, while lacustrine conditions were experienced during the warmer interstadial. Towards the end of the late-glacial there is evidence that reed swamp and/or fen developed, while the diminution of all aquatics at the beginning of the Holocene, with the change to peat at Glanllynnau Cliff, marks the displacement of lacustrine conditions. The peat was colonised by *Sphagnum,* ferns, herbs and shrubs capable of growing in damp and boggy situations. At Glanllynnnau Marsh, the early Holocene is marked by the widespread accumulation of fine mud, which records the continued existence of pond conditions in this particular kettle hole.

A timescale was based on a number of radiocarbon determinations (Simpkins 1974). A date of 12,050 ± 250 BP (Gak-1603) was considered to mark the beginning of the interstadial, and a date of 11,300 ± 300 BP (Gak-1602) the end of purely organic deposition marked by the close of the *Rumex* pollen zone and the beginning of the *Betula-Filipendula* zone.

The Devensian late-glacial pollen diagrams from

Glanllynnau therefore indicate a continuous ecological succession from pre-interstadial time, where the pollen spectra represent local pioneer vegetation, through to the warm interstadial period beginning at about 12,000 BP, comprising the *Rumex, Juniperus* and *Betula-Filipendula* zones. This climatic amelioration is also indicated by a lithological change from dominantly clastic to organic sedimentation. Evidence for vegetational recession and renewed solifluction in the post-interstadial period is suggested, and the early Holocene is shown by the immigration of thermophilous tree species and forest development in response to rapid climatic improvement.

Coleoptera (beetles)

Coope and Brophy's (1972) study was designed to compare the environmental inferences made from fossil beetles with those from Simpkins' (1968, 1974) palynological data. The Devensian late-glacial and early Holocene sequence described at Glanllynnau by Coope and Brophy was similar to that described by Simpkins, and contained four distinctive faunal units.

The oldest fauna, from bed 1, indicates an environment of bare ground with a thin patchy vegetation cover, possibly of short grasses and moss. Coope and Brophy considered that bed 1 had probably accumulated in a pool of standing water. The outstanding feature of this fauna was a high proportion of species which today have an entirely arctic or montane habitat. There was little doubt that the fauna indicated a rigorously cold climate with thermal conditions at least as cold as those in the alpine zones of Scandinavia today. Coope and Brophy estimated the average July temperature at least as low as 10°C, and several species suggested that the climate at this time may have been distinctly continental. The constancy of specific composition suggests that there was no deviation from this arctic climate during deposition of the lower layers of bed 1.

A second fauna characterises the upper part of bed 1 and part of the more organic sequence above (beds 2-4). This fauna proves a gradual improvement in environmental conditions, although vegetation was still sparse until the uppermost sample of this bed. Near the top of the bed, species occur which suggest a meadow-like vegetation, with no evidence of trees. Many species lived in a pool which may also have supported *Potamogeton natans* L. The beetle specimens collected also provided evidence for a rich flora developed around the edges of the pool, where there may have been bush willows. Coope and Brophy suggested that there could be no doubt of the thermophilous character of this fauna; all the stenothermic species of the preceding fauna were absent. There was, however, no evidence for a gradual transition from fauna 1 to fauna 2, and the sharp faunal break occurred at a level in bed 1 where no lithological break could be detected. Chemical investigations by Coope and Brophy revealed that sedimentation had probably been

continuous and they concluded that the sharp faunal break was proof of a real change in climatic conditions. Average July temperatures during this warmer period were estimated at least as high as 17°C, and there was no evidence that the climate at that time was any more continental than today.

A third fauna occurred in the upper part of bed 4 and bed 5 and was characterised by a loss of thermophilous species and their replacement by species whose distributions today are predominantly northern. This change at Glanllynnau, however, was overshadowed by a profound change in local conditions. The habitat became decidedly more acidic and substantially colder, and the kettle hole pond became choked by *Sphagnum*. Although Coope and Brophy noted the difficulty in assessing the average July temperature for this fauna, the beetles clearly indicated a considerable deterioration in the thermal environment, and this drop must have been rapid. It was estimated that the average July temperature may have been in the region of 14°C, and the climate was probably still no more continental than today.

The fourth fauna (bed 5) shows no abrupt change from the preceding one. Rather, a series of faunal changes reflected a more or less continuous deterioration in the thermal environment. A precise figure for the average July temperature was not established, but it was clear that temperatures were low.

A further and final fossil beetle assemblage was discerned from the overlying beds 6 and 7, although remains were sparse, and poorly preserved, and inadequate to make any detailed observations; the fauna from these beds, however, was thought to indicate climatic amelioration.

Both the sequences of beetle assemblages and the pollen spectra at Glanllynnau were, therefore, interpreted in terms of a single Devensian late-glacial climatic oscillation, although the possibility was noted that the interstadial floras and faunas at Glanllynnau represented a combination of the Continental Bølling and Allerød Interstadials (Moore 1977). However, the climatic events inferred from these separate suites of data differ from one another, both in their timing and in their intensity. Whereas the pollen indicates that the thermal maximum of this warm oscillation occurred during Pollen Zone II, the beetles suggest that the episode of greatest warmth was earlier than this, occurring during Pollen Zone I. Despite the pollen evidence, the beetles show that by Pollen Zone II times, the environment had deteriorated considerably.

Coope and Brophy identified a visible increase in pollen in the profile where the organic content of the sediment was dominant. The lithology therefore mirrored the expansion of the local flora at this time. The beetles show, however, a sharp improvement in the thermal climate at a level 0.20-0.25m lower in the section, where no consistent lithological break can be discerned in the grey silty clay (bed 1). Chemical investigations of this bed showed there was no evidence for a break in sedimentation during deposition of bed 1. The change in the thermal environment indicated by the beetles cannot therefore be attributed to a hiatus in deposition. Thus, the evidence points to a real and sudden shift in climate in which the mean July temperature rose from about 10°C to about 17°C. Coope and Brophy explained the anomaly between the palynological and beetle evidence in terms of the differential rate of plant and animal responses to rapid changes of climate.

Their study also provided new radiocarbon dates. First, a date of 14,468 ± 300 BP (Birm 212) was obtained from moss towards the base of bed 1, at the start of the Late Devensian late-glacial sequence – see Figure 33. Second, dates of 12,050 ± 250 BP (Gak-1603) and 11,300 ± 300 (Gak-1602) were obtained by Simpkins (1974) from bulk samples from the basal 2cm and uppermost 2cm of bed 3. The possibility of contamination, however, was recognised in these samples, and a specially collected and prepared sample of seeds from the base of the mud was dated by Shotton and Williams (1971) to eliminate the possible sources of error. The date obtained, 12,556 ± 230 BP (Birm 276), was some 500 years older than the older of the two obtained by Simpkins. Third, samples were obtained from sparse plant remains from just above and just below the faunal break interpreted in bed 1. These samples yielded dates of 11,617 ± 270 BP (Birm 233) and 11,714 ± 255 BP (Birm 232), respectively (Shotton and Williams 1971). These samples, however, were obtained from plant debris made up largely of rootlets that penetrated the deposit from above. The dates, which are younger than those obtained 0.2-0.3m higher in the section, confirm the suspicion of rootlet contamination.

The estimated age of the faunal break, determined by calculations of average rates of sedimentation, and the onset of temperate conditions was placed at 12,850 ±250 BP (Coope and Brophy 1972). Further estimates suggest that the 5cm of grey silty clay (bed 1) during which the sudden climatic shift took place, must have accumulated in about 75 years. This indicates a dramatic rate of change in the average July temperature of about 1°C per decade. A summary of the beetle evidence from Glanllynnau and its significance was later given by Coope (1977).

Boulton (1977a) also made several observations about the Devensian late-glacial succession at Glanllynnau. First, faulting occurs in both the fluvioglacial gravels and in the lower part of the late-glacial succession. The basal silty clay has joints and faults throughout, while, in places, the overlying mud is also jointed and warped. This was considered as evidence for the melting of buried ice beneath the kettle hole after 14,468 ± 300 BP (Birm 212) – see Figure 33. There is evidence that the melting of buried ice continued at least until the end of the Older Dryas (12,556 ± 230 BP (Birm 276)) and possibly into the Allerød and Younger Dryas periods. Second, the intensity of faulting is greatest in the silty clay but is substantially reduced in the overlying beds, which suggests that the greatest rates of ice melting occurred towards the end of the period of deposition of these silty clays. Evidence for jointing in the upper clays and the pattern and distribution of the peat bed suggests, however, that the buried ice may have survived even longer, into the warm interstadial period inferred from the palynological and beetle evidence.

Glanllynnau displays a representative section through the tripartite sequence of southern Llŷn. Whereas Morannedd has come to be regarded as a reference site for the Criccieth and Llanystumdwy Tills, the fluvioglacial sands and gravels of the Afon Wen Formation are best developed at Glanllynnau. The sequence of Welsh sediments provides information for interpreting patterns of ice movement across southern Llŷn. Before Boulton's (1977a) interpretation, the sequence was interpreted as the product of two glacial advances separated by ice-free conditions.

From evidence at Glanllynnau, however, Boulton argued that the beds of the traditional tripartite sequence could be explained in an alternative manner. He suggested that much of the surface topography at Glanllynnau represented a foundered sediment surface let down by the melting of buried ice. He considered that the sequence of deposits was evidence for only a single Late Devensian glacial episode. This model of sedimentation has regional stratigraphic implications. Sequences essentially similar to that at Glanllynnau occur elsewhere in Llŷn, for example at Porth Neigwl and Gwydir Bay, where large lenticular masses of sand and gravel lie above dense tills with an undulating surface. These outwash deposits are also overlain sporadically by a thin upper till. Although Boulton's model explains a number of observed stratigraphic, textural and lithological changes in the sequence at Glanllynnau, it does not satisfactorily account for the deeply weathered surface of the Criccieth Till. Boulton argued that the Criccieth Till was subaerially weathered as the surface became transiently exposed in a supraglacial environment, prior to deposition of outwash and flow till. He concluded that the surface did not therefore mark a significant break in sedimentation. Others, including Bowen (1974, 1977b), have maintained that the scale of weathering at Glanllynnau, and particularly at Morannedd, indicates a protracted hiatus in deposition. The lack of an acceptable explanation for the weathering horizon in Boulton's sedimentation model is, therefore, a major impediment to applying the model to other sequences.

Whether the sequence at Glanllynnau was the product of one or two glacial advances, the composite age of the glacial sequence is clearly indicated by the evidence for melting of buried ice well into the Late Devensian late-glacial. This provides some of the strongest evidence in North and north-west Wales to confirm that widespread inundation of the region by ice occurred in the Late Devensian. The date of 14,468 ± 300 BP (Birm 212) from the base of the late-glacial succession is significant. It is one of the earliest radiocarbon dates for Late Devensian deglaciation in Wales. Glanllynnau also provides a record of late-glacial and early Holocene palaeoenvironmental conditions. It is the only sequence in Wales yielding both pollen and beetles that has been calibrated by radiocarbon methods. It gives one of the most detailed records of environmental changes in the late-glacial and early Holocene at any lowland site in North and north-west Wales. Together with sites in Snowdonia, the pollen record at Glanllynnau serves to demonstrate regional and altitudinal variations in vegetation history during these times.

Glanllynnau displays evidence for Late Pleistocene and early Holocene events in north-west Wales, and is perhaps the most intensively studied glacial to late-glacial sequence in Wales. Furthermore, it is the only late-glacial site in Wales where fossil beetle faunas have been investigated and is thus the only site where late-glacial palaeotemperature estimates have been possible. Although coastal erosion has removed part of the late-glacial and early Holocene sequence at Glanllynnau Cliff, the remaining kettle holes inland are likely to show comparable stratigraphic, pollen and faunal sequences, and this reference site therefore retains an outstanding potential for further research. Although some consider the glacigenic sequence

to represent two ice advances, Boulton's work has shown that the sequence may have formed during a single Late Devensian glaciation. The site may, therefore, provide an important model for re-evaluating multiple drift sequences elsewhere. Radiocarbon analysis and studies of pollen and beetles in the late-glacial sediments significantly enhance the interest for environmental reconstructions.

Conclusions

Glanllynnau is one of the most intensively studied glacial sites in the World. An on-going debate continues on the precise origin and age of the different deposits exposed here. Exposures also occur through the infill of kettle holes. These have provided evidence from pollen and fossil beetles which shows how the climate changed from the end of the ice age, to the present. A radiocarbon date of 14,468 years, obtained from the base of one of the kettle hole deposits, is one of the earliest known dates for the disappearance of the last major ice-sheet in Wales.

Morannedd

One of the best available sequences of Late Pleistocene glacial sediments in North Wales, this site provides evidence for two Welsh ice advances

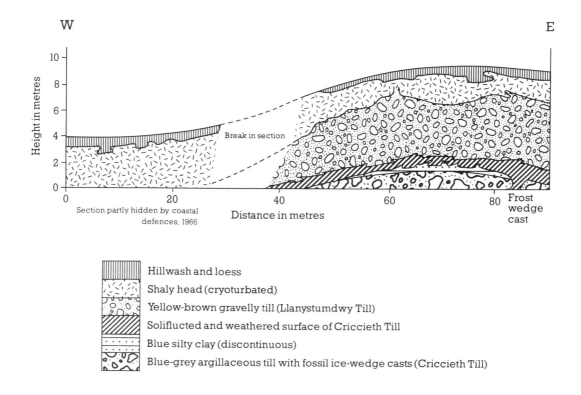

W   E

Break in section

Section partly hidden by coastal defences, 1966

Distance in metres

Frost wedge cast

Height in metres

Hillwash and loess

Shaly head (cryoturbated)

Yellow-brown gravelly till (Llanystumdwy Till)

Soliflucted and weathered surface of Criccieth Till

Blue silty clay (discontinuous)

Blue-grey argillaceous till with fossil ice-wedge casts (Criccieth Till)

Figure 34 Quaternary sequence at Morannedd (from Whittow and Ball 1970)

probably during the Late Devensian. Controversy has arisen over the time gap between these two events.

Introduction

Morannedd shows an important sequence through Pleistocene deposits in the eastern Llŷn Peninsula. Evidence from the site has been used to show that the area was glaciated by ice from the Welsh highlands on two separate occasions. Although the chronology of events at the site remains uncertain, the sections are amongst the finest in Llŷn that expose tills of local Welsh provenance. The site has a long history of research commencing with Jehu (1909). It has featured in studies by Fearnsides (1910), Synge (1963, 1964, 1970), Saunders (1963, 1967, 1968a, 1968b, 1968c, 1968d, 1973), Simpkins (1968), Whittow and Ball (1970) and Campbell (1985a). The site has been discussed in the context of the Irish Sea Basin and Wales by Bowen (1973a, 1973b, 1974, 1977b).

Description

The exposures at Morannedd (SH507381) extend along the coast for about 250m and attain a maximum height of about 9m. Whittow and Ball recorded the following generalised succession, shown in Figure 34.

6   Hillwash and loess
5   Shaly head (cryoturbated)
4   Yellow-brown gravelly till (Llanystumdwy Till)
3   Soliflucted and weathered surface of Criccieth Till
2   Blue silty clay (discontinuous)
1   Blue-grey argillaceous till (Criccieth Till) with fossil ice-wedge casts

Their sequence, however, has been debated and the interpretation of the sediments is controversial.

Interpretation

Jehu (1909) recognised only a single till at the site (probably bed 4), and established that it contained neither shell fragments nor far-travelled (Irish Sea) erratics. The common occurrence of greenstones in the till led him to suggest that it had been deposited by ice from Snowdonia. He regarded the till as representing the Upper Boulder Clay of his tripartite succession in Llŷn. However, according to Fearnsides (1910), the till also contained boulders from west Caernarvonshire and Anglesey.

The sections at Morannedd were also noted by Synge (1963, 1964) who correlated the drifts of North and north-west Wales with successions in Ireland. At that time, he recognised only a single Welsh till, derived from the east. He regarded the yellow-brown till (bed 4 -the Llanystumdwy Till of

Simpkins (1968)) as the weathered surface of the blue-grey till (bed 1) near the base of the section. He also noted that the upper surface of the weathered till was severely disturbed by frost-action, with many vertical stones. On the basis of the weathering and frost disturbance, Synge argued that the till had been deposited probably during the Saalian Stage. He suggested that its deep weathering occurred during the subsequent Ipswichian Stage, while cryoturbation of the upper layers had taken place during periglacial conditions in the Weichselian (Devensian) Stage.

Subsequent workers including Saunders (1963, 1967, 1968a, 1968b, 1968c, 1968d), Simpkins (1968), Whittow and Ball (1970) and Bowen (1974, 1977b) have recognised two tills at Morannedd. Simpkins (1968) termed the blue-grey argillaceous till and the yellow-brown gravelly till, the Criccieth and Llanystumdwy Tills, respectively. She considered that the surface of the Criccieth Till had been weathered during the Ipswichian Stage. The Criccieth Till was therefore taken to belong to the Saalian Stage, and the overlying Llanystumdwy Till, to the Late Devensian.

Saunders also noted the Criccieth Till and its badly weathered and frost-heaved surface, overlain by a gravelly upper till. He presented detailed pebble lithology and till fabric measurements to demonstrate that both tills were of Welsh origin, having been deposited by ice moving ENE to WSW, from the Vale of Ffestiniog. The close correspondence between till fabrics in both horizons was taken to indicate that the direction of ice movement had been substantially similar during both ice advances. It is, however, possible that the most recent of the ice movements caused a marked reorientation of pebbles in the lower till, and that this overprinting masks any original clast fabric patterns.

On the basis of a model developed from lithostratigraphical evidence elsewhere in Llŷn and supported by radiocarbon determinations, Saunders argued that the Criccieth Till had been deposited during the main invasion of the Late Devensian Welsh ice-sheet, and he correlated it with the lower, Irish Sea till of the north Llŷn coast and at Porth Neigwl (the Trevor Till). He suggested that the upper gravelly till at Morannedd had been deposited by a subsequent advance of Late Devensian Welsh ice, and that it could be correlated with the upper till of the north Llŷn coast (the Clynnog Till). Saunders believed that the frost-cracked and weathered surface of the lower till at Morannedd was critical to the interpretation of the sequence. He argued that it indicated a clear hiatus between deposition of the tills, reinforcing his argument that they were the product of two separate ice advances which crossed southern Llŷn during the Late Devensian.

Whittow and Ball (1970) accepted Saunders interpretation of the sequence at Morannedd and considered that the blue-grey till was the product of the first of the inferred glacial advances in Llŷn, and followed Simpkins' (1968) terminology and called it the Criccieth Till. They also noted tectonic structures in its upper layers which could have formed as slump structures during a phase of weathering or as drag features from an overriding ice mass. Whittow and Ball suggested that the upper Llanystumdwy Till (Simpkins 1968), represented a subsequent advance of Welsh ice. A final phase of periglacial conditions was interpreted from the cryoturbated shale head which capped the sequence.

In 1970, Synge likewise distinguished two tills at Morannedd, although he argued that there was no hiatus between deposition of the two. He suggested that the lower till had been deposited by Welsh ice moving in a slightly different direction to that which deposited the upper. The weathering horizon judged by Saunders and Whittow and Ball to have formed during interstadial conditions, and by Synge (1964) and Simpkins during fully interglacial conditions, was reinterpreted by Synge (1970) as an iron-pan effect, and the fossil ice-wedge casts as load structures.

The debate on the exposures at Morannedd is typical of many of the problems in interpreting Late Pleistocene successions in the region (Campbell 1985a). Two features make the site significant. First, Morannedd can be regarded as a reference site for the Criccieth and Llanystumdwy Tills of southern Llŷn. These glacigenic sediments provide evidence that southern Llŷn was glaciated by Welsh ice, probably on two occasions. The strongly preferred ENE to WSW trend of clasts in the Llanystumdwy Till shows that western Llŷn was free from Irish Sea ice during the second of these proposed glacial advances, which otherwise would have impeded and deflected the Welsh ice to a different course.

Second, the fine development of weathering and frost-crack features on the surface of the Criccieth Till provides evidence for a time separation between deposition of the Criccieth and Llanystumdwy Tills. This evidence, however, has proved controversial. Synge and Mitchell argued that the deep weathering at Morannedd and elsewhere in southern Llŷn indicated that only the northern coastal fringe of Llŷn was glaciated during the Late Devensian. They considered that drifts south of their reconstructed Late Devensian maximum limit, therefore, dated from the Saalian Stage and that they had been deeply weathered during the Ipswichian.

Whereas Boulton (1977a, 1977b) interpreted a similar sequence from Glanllynnau in southern Llŷn as the result of a single Late Devensian glacial episode, and suggested that the weathering horizon there did not represent a significant break in sedimentation, the evidence from Morannedd has been continually used as support for there having been two ice advances during the Late Devensian. Bowen (1973a, 1973b, 1974, 1977b) considered that the fine development of the weathering horizon and the fossil ice-wedge casts

at Morannedd was evidence for an interval between deposition of the Criccieth and the Llanystumdwy Tills.

Morannedd provides evidence for the glacial history of southern Llŷn. The sections are among the finest in the region through tills of local Welsh provenance. The site can be regarded as a reference site for the Criccieth and Llanystumdwy Tills. The status of the weathering horizon between these tills is critical to the interpretation of the sequence, but has proved controversial. The development of the weathered and frost-cracked surface of the Criccieth Till here could provide evidence for a time interval between the deposition of the Criccieth and Llanystumdwy Tills.

Conclusions

Morannedd is the type site for the main glacial deposits of the southern Llŷn peninsula. It is a reference site for the Criccieth and Llanystumdwy Tills (boulder clays). Between the two tills is a horizon of weathering. Its exact significance is still unknown but it continues to figure prominently in debates about the glacial history of North Wales.

The Quaternary of North Wales

Introduction

Except for the Quaternary sediments exposed around the coasts of Anglesey and north-west Wales – see Chapter 7, North Wales is best known for its upland glacial and periglacial landforms. The glacial landforms of Snowdonia were amongst the first in Britain to be investigated in relation to the Glacial Theory (for example, Bowman 1841; Buckland 1842; Darwin 1842) and they have since featured in a number of important geomorphological studies (for example, Davis 1909; Seddon 1957; Unwin 1970; Gray 1982a; Gemmell et al. 1986). There is also evidence for the Pleistocene evolution of the region.

Deposits pre-dating the Ipswichian Stage

Evidence for environmental conditions prior to the Late Devensian is sparse in North Wales apart from Pontnewydd Cave in the Elwy Valley, where deposits have yielded a molar of early Neanderthal Man dated to c. 200,000 BP (Green et al. 1981; Green 1984). This suggests occupation of the cave during Oxygen Isotope Stage 7. In addition to the oldest known human evidence from Wales, the sequence provides a Middle Pleistocene sedimentary record. Stratigraphic, faunal, and dating evidence from Pontnewydd provides an important Pleistocene record and the only known Lower Palaeolithic finds from a stratified context. Work by H S Green of the National Museum of Wales has resulted in detailed descriptions and an interpretation of the Pontnewydd sequence.

The Ipswichian Stage

Evidence for conditions during the Ipswichian Stage in North Wales is sparse. The only documented North Wales sites with evidence are the caves at Pontnewydd and Cefn. Although Sutcliffe regarded some of the mammal remains from Pontnewydd as representing a typical Ipswichian assemblage, recent excavations have not confirmed the age of the fauna as Ipswichian (Currant in Green 1984). Indeed, there is considerable evidence to suggest that the cave entrance at Pontnewydd may have been closed during the Ipswichian (Green 1984). The best evidence so far available for this time is from the nearby Cefn Caves where a fauna including hippopotamus and straight-tusked elephant has been recorded (Falconer 1868; Neaverson 1942). Although the precise stratigraphical context of these finds is unknown, they provide palaeontological information which may be useful for elaborating longer term aspects of regional Pleistocene evolution (Bowen 1973a, 1974; Peake et al. 1973).

The Devensian Stage

Late Devensian deposits are widespread in North Wales and their broad distribution has been known for some time (Bowen 1974). In common with the coastlands of north-west Wales, it has long been recognised that the North Wales coast was subjected to complex fluctuations and interactions between ice flows moving outwards from the Welsh uplands and Irish Sea ice moving generally southward. Evidence for the interplay of these ice masses, in the form of superimposed tills of Welsh and Irish Sea origin, is common along the North Wales coast, particularly around Llandudno and Conway (Whittow and Ball 1970; Fishwick 1977). Whittow and Ball (1970) suggested these tills were formed during separate glaciations, but Fishwick (1977) argued there is no evidence to suggest that glacial deposits beneath the Irish Sea till along the coast are older than Late Devensian. It was therefore envisaged that till deposits along the north coast were related principally to the onshore movement of Late Devensian Irish Sea ice which incorporated deposits from an earlier Welsh glaciation as it moved south. This Irish Sea glaciation was powerful enough to penetrate the Vale of Clwyd to deposit shelly drift at c. 300m on Halkyn Mountain near Wrexham (Strahan 1886) and at over 300m on Gloppa Hill near Oswestry (Wedd et al. 1929). At the same time, it is generally believed that Welsh ice covered most of the Welsh uplands: for example, the Arenig region (Rowlands 1970), the Berwyns (Travis 1944), Montgomeryshire (Brown 1971) and the south Shropshire hill country (Rowlands 1966; Brown 1971). Studies of ice wastage phenomena in the region have also been provided by Embleton (1957, 1961, 1964a, 1964b, 1964c) in north-east Wales, and by Brown and Cook (1977) and Thomas (1984) in the Wheeler Valley and Mold areas.

The broad distribution and provenance of the glacial sediments of the region is known (Bowen 1974). A relative lack of good exposures and interglacial indicators, including weathering and biostratigraphic horizons, has hampered correlation and interpretation in the region. In many respects the debates about the age of the drifts in North Wales are similar to those in the north-west Wales coastlands; namely, is there evidence for a readvance of Late Devensian ice? In this context the cave site at Tremeirchion in the Vale of Clwyd could be important. Here, Rowlands (1971) obtained a radiocarbon date of c. 18,000 BP, from material apparently sealed within the cave by Irish Sea till. If correct, the date provides evidence to show Irish Sea glaciation after 18,000 BP, when ice moved southwards into the Vale of Clwyd to the limit marked by the Bodfari-Trefnant moraine

(Rowlands 1955). Although correlation of this glacial phase with the Scottish Readvance (Pocock *et al.* 1938) is not now accepted, the evidence from Tremeirchion has been used to support a Late Devensian readvance (Bowen 1974), and it is consistent with evidence described from the Llŷn Peninsula (for example, Saunders 1968a, 1968b) – see Chapter 7. It is also interesting to note the close correspondence of the Tremeirchion date with those obtained from Dimlington in Yorkshire (Penny *et al.* 1969) which have been used to provide a maximum age for the principal advance of Late Devensian ice in eastern England, during the 'Dimlington Stadial' (Rose 1985).

North-east Wales is one of the potentially most rewarding areas for elaborating Late Pleistocene glacial history. This potential stems partly from its proximity to the Cheshire-Shropshire lowland, an area that has figured prominently in investigations of the Late Pleistocene. It is, however, beyond the scope of the present work to review such developments in that area, and reviews are available elsewhere (for example, Worsley 1970, 1977, 1985; Bowen 1974). It is important to note, however, that north-east Wales, and the Wrexham area in particular, forms an important link between the complex Cheshire-Shropshire lowland sequences and the more fragmentary records found elsewhere in North Wales. These important aspects of regional stratigraphy are more fully discussed in the introductory section to the GCR site at Vicarage Moss. Recent work in the Wrexham area (Dunkley 1981; Wilson *et al.* 1982; Thomas 1985) has demonstrated the complexity of the deposits there, with evidence for sequential wasting of Late Devensian ice, interrupted by brief ice advances at the margin of an oscillating ice-sheet (Thomas 1985). To some extent this evidence throws doubt on the more simplistic 'monoglacial' and 'tripartite' schemes erected by earlier workers in the area, and demonstrates a range of conditions at or near the margin of the Late Devensian ice-sheet – but see Chapter 2. Until better evidence is available to the contrary, it may be as well to regard multiple glacigenic sequences along the North Wales coastal margin in the same manner, namely as broadly Late Devensian in age, without sub-division.

The uplands

During the Late Devensian, local ice masses in Snowdonia and Arenig were subordinate to a major ice dispersal centre – the Merioneth ice cap (Greenly 1919; Foster 1968). This is believed to have contributed westerly and easterly flows from just east of Arenig Fawr and Rhobell Fawr (Foster 1968; Bowen 1974). Both Foster and Rowlands (1970) showed, as did Greenly, that the greatest thickness of ice occurred in the neighbourhood of Trawsfynydd. Foster (1968) demonstrated that the erratic content of tills in the Harlech Dome reflected deposition from different layers within the westerly moving limb of the Merioneth ice; with the upper portions of the ice crossing the Rhinog Mountains and entering Cardigan Bay, and the lower layers

entering the Vale of Trawsfynydd and Afon Eden. Similarly, it was established (Rowlands 1970) that an easterly extension of the Merioneth ice cap overrode lower lying parts of the north-east Wales massif, being sufficiently powerful for a time to obstruct southward moving Irish Sea ice and prevent it from entering the Vale of Clwyd.

Exposures in glacial deposits occur widely within the network of selected GCR sites in Snowdonia, and these have been chosen primarily to represent three main aspects of the Quaternary for which the area has become nationally important.

First, three sites – Snowdon (Yr Wyddfa), Y Glyderau, Y Carneddau, represent an outstanding range of large-scale glacial erosional features. These spectacular upland landforms include classic examples of cirques, arêtes and troughs, all modified by glacial and periglacial processes. These three principal upland sites demonstrate a range of landforms which have resulted from varying conditions controlled by such factors as altitude, aspect, geological composition and structure. Snowdon, for example, demonstrates a classic 'Alpine' arrangement of cirques radiating from a horn and separated by precipitous arêtes. One cirque complex within this erosional assemblage also demonstrates a classic example of a 'cirque stairway'. The adjacent massif of Y Glyderau is a departure from this pattern, with a series of cirques, including Cwm Idwal, showing a marked structural alignment. These cirques fed ice into the spectacular Nant Ffrancon trough. In contrast, the easternmost part of the main Snowdonian massif is represented by landforms in the Carneddau range. Although cirque forms are also well represented here, for example Cwm Dulyn and Cwm Melynllyn, the landscape is far less rugged in nature and contains many broad-shouldered ridges. Y Carneddau exhibits an outstanding assemblage of fossil and contemporary periglacial landforms, for which the site has primarily been selected.

Second, although small and medium-scale features formed by the agencies of glacial erosion, particularly striae and roches moutonnées, are well represented within these three large upland sites, they are exceptionally well developed within the Snowdon site at Llyn Llyddaw (Gray and Lowe 1982) and in the Llanberis Valley at Llyn Peris. The latter site demonstrates an unparalleled range of small-scale erosional features including striae, friction cracks and forms associated with subglacial meltwater erosion.

Third, the selected upland sites of Snowdon, Y Glyderau and Y Carneddau contain an outstanding range and diversity of depositional landforms, formed largely during the Late Devensian late-glacial. Cirque glaciation during Younger Dryas times is by no means limited to these north Snowdonian sites, and landforms belonging to this phase are widely documented elsewhere in Wales – in the Arenig Mountains (Rowlands 1970), around Cadair Idris (for example, Watson 1977a); and in the Brecon Beacons (for example, Lewis 1970b; Ellis-Gruffydd 1972; Walker 1980, 1982a, 1982b).

The principal features of this late-glacial landform assemblage, the cirque moraines and protalus ramparts, however, are among the finest examples of their kind in Britain, and are well represented within the three main Snowdonian sites. These depositional landforms have long been known from the region (for example, Darwin 1842; Ramsay 1860; Daykins 1900), with Kendall's (1893) treatise *On a moraine-like mound near Snowdon* representing one of the first descriptions of a protalus rampart in Britain. The presence of both inner and outer moraine arcs in many of the Snowdonian cirques, and a mixture of 'sharp' and 'diffuse' moraine forms was noted by workers mapping their distribution (Seddon 1957; Unwin 1970). They concluded from this distribution and the morphology of the features that both protalus ramparts and moraines dated from two separate events. Analysis of pollen bearing sequences by Godwin (1955) and Seddon (1957, 1962) was fundamental in establishing this sequence of Late Devensian late-glacial vegetational events. This led to the suggestion that the outer and generally 'diffuse' moraines and protalus features might date from Pollen Zone I or to a recessive stage of the Late Devensian ice-sheet, with the inner 'fresh' features dating to the Younger Dryas (Pollen Zone III) (Seddon 1957, 1962; Unwin 1970).

More recently, Gray (1982a) has remapped these features, and provided evidence for thirty five Younger Dryas cirque glaciers in northern Snowdonia. Gray demonstrated that many of these small glaciers left complex depositional evidence to mark their maximum limits, including not only end-moraines but boulder limits and the down-valley extent of hummocky moraine – the Snowdon, Y Glyderau and Y Carneddau sites have, in part, been chosen to reflect the considerable variety of these depositional landforms. Gray further suggested that the highly variable evidence marking these glacier limits threw doubt on the widespread existence in the region of pre-Younger Dryas moraines (the 'Older Series' of Unwin (1970)). Palynological and radiocarbon dating evidence (Burrows 1974, 1975; Crabtree 1969, 1972; Ince 1981, 1983) from the region has also helped to place tighter constraints on the age of the final cirque glaciation of the uplands, and the majority of cirque moraines and protalus ramparts are now widely held to date from the short Younger Dryas, between *c.* 11,000-10,000 BP.

At Cwm Dwythwch, however, just north of the main Snowdon massif, Seddon (1962) described a typical full Late Devensian late-glacial sequence behind a large cirque moraine. This site, therefore, displays the only reliable relatively dated evidence from Wales for a cirque moraine of demonstrably pre-Younger Dryas age.

Late Devensian late-glacial and Holocene environmental history

Pollen analysis has been used in North Wales to reconstruct vegetational and environmental history during the Late Devensian late-glacial and Holocene. The network of selected pollen sites, some with radiocarbon calibration, provides evidence for conditions across North Wales from the wastage of the Late Devensian ice-sheet. In terms of the diversity of topography and climate in North Wales, both past and present, the range of sites illustrates both the broad patterns of environmental change and regional variations.

Evidence for palaeoenvironmental conditions during the late-glacial of the Late Devensian is recorded in the major upland GCR site at Nant Ffrancon in the Glyderau (Seddon 1962; Burrows 1974, 1975). It is supplemented by the sequences at Cwm Dwythwch, Clogwynygarreg and Cors Geuallt. Cwm Dwythwch provides evidence for ascribing a cirque moraine to a pre-Younger Dryas episode. Clogwynygarreg and Cors Geuallt also lie outside the mapped Younger Dryas limits of Gray (1982a), and place further limits on the possible age of the final cirque glaciation in the uplands. Clogwynygarreg records a near complete late-glacial sequence, including what appears, on the basis of the sediments, to be a single interstadial – the 'late-glacial interstadial' (Ince 1981). A minimum age for Late Devensian deglaciation in the area is indicated by a radiocarbon determination of 13,670 ± 280 BP (Birm 884) (Ince 1981). The pollen record shows a gradual improvement in conditions associated with the 'late-glacial interstadial'. A change from organic to clastic sedimentation, and a decline in *Juniperus* pollen mark the onset of the Younger Dryas (*c.* 11,000 BP) – a brief cold pulse when glaciers again occupied many of the upland cirques (Ince 1981).

This simple threefold lithology may represent the division of the pre-Allerød, Allerød and post-Allerød episodes of the Continental late-glacial (Moore 1977), which shows a single warm phase preceded and followed by colder climatic ones – but see Chapter 1. This is not recorded everywhere, which shows the need for a range of sites to reconstruct late-glacial conditions. At Glanllynnau – Chapter 7, for example, both Coope and Brophy (1972) and Simpkins (1974) suggested that what appeared to be a single 'late-glacial interstadial' might represent a combination of the Continental Bølling and Allerød Interstadials (Moore 1977). In Snowdonia, similar complexity has been recorded at Nant Ffrancon (Y Glyderau), where Burrows (1974, 1975) described what he interpreted as the Bølling 'oscillation'. A similar pre-Allerød climatic oscillation, possibly equivalent to the Bølling, has also been recorded from Cors Geuallt (Crabtree 1969, 1972). Moore (1975b, 1977) and Ince (1981), however, have questioned the validity of this evidence, particularly the radiocarbon dates from Nant Ffrancon. The network of GCR late-glacial sites represents these aspects of regional floral and environmental diversity which establish the relative timing of late-glacial climatic and environmental changes in Wales.

Within the principal upland sites of Snowdon, Y Glyderau and Y Carneddau, a number of pollen analytical sites with sequences from the beginning of the Holocene have been studied, which are the basis for environmental reconstruction in the uplands. These include the radiocarbon dated Holocene profiles at Cwm Cywion and Llyn Llyddaw (Ince 1981, 1983), and those at Cwm Idwal (Godwin 1955), Cwm Clyd (Evans and Walker 1977) and Cwm Melynllyn (Walker 1978). The last two sites also record detailed diatom evidence for changing Holocene environmental conditions.

The Holocene vegetation succession in North Wales reflects the development of temperate deciduous forest in response to climatic amelioration after the Younger Dryas. The early Holocene, c. 10,000 BP, is usually marked by expansion in *Juniperus* and *Betula* (Moore 1977) with a rise in *Corylus* very shortly after, although Moore (1972b) noted that the precise relationship between these rises varies both with altitude and latitude across western Britain. The mid Holocene sees a sharp expansion in *Betula* which at most Welsh sites declines again rapidly with the invasion of other trees. At Cwm Idwal, however, this *Betula* peak is more protracted. The birch and hazel woodlands are replaced eventually by forests of birch, oak, elm and alder (Ince 1983) and *Alnus* assumes a major, if not dominant, role in the pollen records of many Snowdonian profiles (Moore 1977). Deteriorating environmental conditions and human interference from about 5,000 years BP onwards resulted in the gradual decline of upland forests and the development of open-grassland and heathland which characterises the area today (Moore 1977; Ince 1981, 1983). The Holocene pollen profiles within the large upland GCR sites of Snowdon, Y Glyderau and Y Carneddau, and those from the selected pollen sites at Cwm Dwythwch, Cors Geuallt and Clogwynygarreg are important in establishing the timing of regional variations in these major vegetational and environmental changes.

Tufa

Tufa deposits in North Wales were mapped and described at an early stage (Maw 1866; Strahan 1890; Wedd and King 1924) and their potential for palaeoenvironmental reconstruction recognised (for example, Jackson 1922; McMillan 1947; Millot 1951; Bathurst 1956). A number of tufa localities has been recorded in the region, around Prestatyn and the Wheeler Valley (Neaverson 1941; McMillan 1947). Those at Caerwys and Ddol provide contrasting records: Caerwys represents the only known example of tufa formation from the Late Devensian late-glacial in Wales. The tufa and buried soils at these sites provide an exceptional

biostratigraphic record (molluscs, leaf-beds and vertebrate faunas) recently re-examined by Preece (1978), Preece *et al.* (1982), McMillan and Zeissler (1985) and Pedley (1987). These accounts of the biostratigraphy and carbonate sedimentology of the tufa are complemented by radiocarbon calibration, and provide one of the most extensive and detailed records of environmental changes in Wales since the wastage of the Late Devensian ice-sheet.

Periglacial landforms

Upland North Wales is a classic area for periglacial landforms and processes. Many landforms, such as solifluction terraces and scree slopes, are widespread (Ball 1966; Ball and Goodier 1970), but other indicators of periglacial action, for example, patterned ground, are also well developed, although they are limited in extent. The network of GCR sites in the region reflects the considerable importance of non-glacial, cold-climate processes for landform evolution in North Wales during the Late Pleistocene and Holocene, even in historical and modern times. Although the major upland landform sites of Snowdon and Y Glyderau contain an impressive assemblage of periglacial features, including scree slopes, block scree (Pont-y-Gromlech), frost-shattered summits and tors (Y Glyderau) and a fine series of vegetated stripes (Y Garn), the scale and diversity of forms does not generally match that developed in the adjacent Carneddau massif. Many of the periglacial landforms in the Carneddau, including well developed screes, blockfields, tors and solifluction lobes and terraces, are classic examples of their kind. Although dating evidence is not yet available, it is believed that many features were formed during periglacial conditions following wastage of the Late Devensian ice-sheet and during the Younger Dryas (Ball 1966; Ball and Goodier 1970; Scoates 1973). Some features (patterned ground at Waun-y-Garnedd) are currently active and provide evidence for contemporary frost-assisted processes (Pearsall 1950; Tallis and Kershaw 1959; Ball and Goodier 1970; Scoates 1973). The factors influencing the distribution and maintenance of a range of landforms in the Carneddau associated with periglacial activity, have been discussed in detail by Scoates (1973).

Although the Carneddau provide a range of fossil and contemporary frost-assisted features in a compact area probably unparalleled elsewhere in Wales, three further sites in North Wales, at Moelwyn Mawr, Rhinog Fawr and Y Llethr, add a contrasting range of landforms, including for example, the only known occurrence in Wales of a fossil rock glacier (Lowe and Rose *in* Gray *et al.* 1981), and a fine series of unsorted vegetated stripes (Taylor 1975).

Sites in the Rhinog Mountains at Y Llethr and Rhinog Fawr also provide landform evidence for periglacial conditions and frost-assisted activity on a number of different occasions. Sorted stone stripes at Rhinog Fawr, thought to date from the

Late Devensian late-glacial (Ball and Goodier 1968, 1970), are the finest examples in Wales, and they are developed at a larger-scale than similar features elsewhere in Britain. In contrast, landforms at nearby Y Llethr may provide unique evidence in Wales for formation during a later cold period in historical times (Goodier and Ball 1969; Ball and Goodier 1970), perhaps during the climatic deterioration of the 'Little Ice Age' between c. 1550 and 1750 A.D. (Manley 1964; Lamb 1967).

This selected network of sites therefore provides substantial evidence for a wide range of landforms associated with periglacial conditions and frost-assisted processes from the Late Devensian late-glacial to the present day.

Pontnewydd Cave

Highlights

This is a site with a long Pleistocene rock and fossil record which has yielded the oldest human remains in Wales, artefacts and an associated 'warm' mammal fauna. This dated evidence indicates a pre-Ipswichian temperate interglacial.

Introduction

Pontnewydd Cave (SJ015710) contains a sequence of deposits with faunal, artefact and human remains important for reconstructing late Middle and Late Pleistocene events in North Wales. Pontnewydd has yielded the oldest known human remains from Wales, at about 200,000 years old. The site was first mentioned by Stanley in 1832 and was studied by Dawkins (1871, 1874, 1880), Hughes and Thomas (1874), Mackintosh (1876) and Hughes (1885, 1887). More recently the site was studied by Kelly (1967), Valdemar (1970) and Molleson (1976). Excavations by the National Museum of Wales since 1978 have led to a number of detailed reports (Green 1981a, 1984; Green et al. 1981; Green and Currant 1982).

Description

Pontnewydd Cave is formed in the Carboniferous Limestone of the Elwy Valley, and it lies at c. 90m OD. The difference in level between the cave and the present day River Elwy is 50m, and the valley contains both glacial sediments and recent alluvium (Embleton 1984; Livingston 1986).

The cave comprises one major east-west trending chamber, with a west-facing entrance. This chamber terminates at the East Passage and is made up of a number of smaller, generally north-south trending subsidiary chambers – the North Passage, the North-East Fissure, the South Fissure, the Back Passage, South Passage and South-East Fissure (Green 1984).

Outside the main entrance lies a large spoil heap from Dawkins' excavations in the nineteenth century, overlain by waste from World War Two activities at the cave. Recent excavations by Green and his colleagues have been at a number of different locations within the cave, and details of the sediments and stratigraphy for these sites are given by Collcutt (1984). Although no reference section representing the whole of this sequence is available at any one point, the following

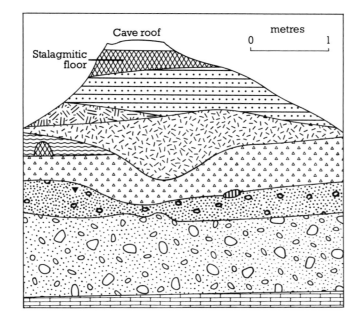
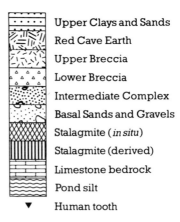

Figure 35 Quaternary sequence at Pontnewydd (after Green et al. 1981)

generalised sequence has been interpreted (Collcutt 1984), and is shown in Figure 35 –

11   Earthy unit*

10   Laminated Travertine*

9   Upper Clay and Sands*

8   Red Cave Earth*

7   Upper Breccia*

6   Silt*

5   Stalagmite*

4   Lower Breccia*

3   Intermediate Complex*

2   Upper Sands and Gravels**

1   Lower Sands and Gravels**

*Calcareous Member
**Siliceous Member (basal sands and gravels)

Interpretation

Pontnewydd Cave was first recorded by Stanley in 1832, who was then also working in nearby Cefn Caves. He noted that Pontnewydd Cave appeared choked with deposits and virtually unexplored. It seems that the cave remained in this condition until an excavation by Williams and Dawkins (Dawkins 1871, 1874, 1880) when only faunal remains were recovered. By the time the cave was next explored by Hughes and Thomas (1874) it was apparent that the earlier excavations had removed substantial deposits. Hughes and Thomas recorded a sequence of gravel, limestone breccia and cave earth beds in the main cave passage. Their investigation yielded both fauna and artefacts including a large human tooth (now lost). They noted that the implements were crude and made from 'felstone', the raw materials for which they suggested were the glacial deposits of the local area. The artefacts were compared with finds from Le Moustier and St Acheul, and, before excavations at Pontnewydd in 1978, it was generally held that these finds represented a Mousterian or Acheulian industry (Green 1984).

The fauna described by Hughes and Thomas comprised the following – *Homo sapiens* L., *Crocuta crocuta, Canis lupus, Vulpes vulpes, Ursus spelaeus, 'Ursus ferox', Meles meles, Dicerorhinus hemitoechus, Equus ferus, Cervus elaphus, Capreolus capreolus* (L.), and the same species list was also recorded by Hughes (1885, 1887). Hughes (1880), however, mentioned that *Palaeoloxodon antiquus, Hippopotamus* sp. and *Rangifer tarandus* were also present, although some doubt has been expressed as to the reliability of these latter records (Currant 1984). Mackintosh (1876) suggested that the sequence in Pontnewydd Cave comprised beds of marine, fluvial and glacial origin, and he attempted, admittedly unsuccessfully, to correlate the beds with the

Pleistocene deposits of the local area. A summary of the earlier findings from Pontnewydd was given by Neaverson (1942). More recently, the cave was mentioned by Kelly (1967) who recovered only a few bones, supposedly of wolf and hare (Green 1984), and brief reviews of the earlier work have been given by Valdemar (1970) and Molleson (1976).

Green (1984) divided the sequence into eleven beds – see site description. These consist of two main elements, a basal siliceous member comprising beds 1 and 2, and a calcareous member consisting of the overlying beds. The basal siliceous member was interpreted as a mixture of fluvial and debris flow deposits (Bull 1984; Collcutt 1984) and it yielded neither artefacts nor fauna. Scanning Electron Microscopy (Bull 1984) and petrological analysis (Bevins 1984) revealed that the basal layers contained elements of redeposited till with erratics from north-west Wales and the Lake District. The sediments were deposited in a harsh environment when surface vegetation was locally absent. Selective cementation of these sediments may reflect, however, a milder climatic event during this phase of deposition.

Interpretation of the succeeding sediments which make up the Intermediate Complex and Upper and Lower Breccias, however, is more straightforward. These deposits have yielded not only artefacts and fauna, but human remains including a molar. The presence of limestone fragments in all these beds probably reflects the inclusion of typical cave entrance weathering products. The beds appear largely to be the product of debris flows, as shown by the apparent reworking of faunal elements through the sequence. Debris flow may have been interrupted by stalagmite growth on a number of occasions and ages for stalagmite fragments, both derived and *in situ*, provide a geochronological framework for this part of the sequence. A burnt flint found close to the human molar in the Intermediate Complex has been dated by thermoluminescence to 200,000 ± 25,000 BP (Huxtable 1984). It seems likely that this flint core was burnt in a domestic fire, and it offers the best date for the human occupation of the cave (Green 1984). Uranium-series dates on speleothem have shown that the Lower Breccia (bed 4) formed at sometime between 225,000-160,000 BP, and a period of renewed stalagmite growth is indicated between 95,000-80,000 BP. A long period thus separates the Lower and Upper Breccias. In places, the Upper Breccia (bed 7) is succeeded by the Red Cave Earth (bed 8) and by current bedded clays and sands (bed 9). The sequence is capped by a stalagmitic floor (bed 10) – see Figure 35, dated at *c.* 20,000 BP, suggesting that the underlying sediments date from no later than the Late Devensian late-glacial or early Holocene.

Currant (1984) recognised three mammal faunas of different ages from beds in the calcareous member. Most of the faunal material is not *in situ*; it has been substantially reworked by debris flows. Under such conditions, an increasingly derived faunal content could be expected in successive debris flows. Bones were grouped on the basis of their preservation: three different preservational states were identified and material assigned to these. The first occurs in the Intermediate Complex, and also as a derived component in the Lower Breccia. It is a 'warm' fauna and it includes beaver *Castor fiber* L., wood mouse *Apodemus* cf. *sylvaticus*, bear *Ursus* sp., roe deer and horse *Equus* sp., indicative of an open-woodland habitat. There is some evidence that the cave may have been used as a bear den during this period. According to Currant, this assemblage is probably post-Cromerian and has certain Hoxnian affinities. An Ipswichian age is ruled out on both faunal and stratigraphic grounds.

The second preservation group occurs mainly in the Lower Breccia, is dominated by bear *Ursus* sp., horse *Equus* sp. and extinct rhinoceros *Dicerorhinus hemitoechus*, and generally indicates an open-steppe environment. This second fauna appears close in age to the first, with only minor changes in species composition (Currant 1984).

The third mammal group occurs in the Silt (bed 6) and the Upper Breccia. It is a classic 'cold' fauna characteristic of the Arctic tundra today; it is the most readily placed of the faunal groups identified from Pontnewydd. A harsh environment with open, treeless vegetation and extensive seasonal snow cover is indicated. Much of the bone material is interpreted as the debris of a wolf den. This third fauna is readily assigned to the Late Devensian and Devensian late-glacial. It includes wolf *Canis lupus*, red fox *Vulpes vulpes*, reindeer *Rangifer tarandus*, arctic hare *Lepus* cf. *timidus* and brown bear *Ursus* cf. *arctos*, and entirely lacks extinct forms. Similar well dated faunas are known from numerous British cave sites.

Currant noted that elements of a classic Ipswichian type fauna, with *Palaeoloxodon antiquus* and *Hippopotamus* sp. described by early workers at the site, could not be confirmed. These records may have come from deposits now destroyed at Pontnewydd or may have been confused with faunal records from nearby Cefn Caves. Indeed, there is evidence to suggest that during the Ipswichian Stage, the cave entrance at Pontnewydd was blocked (Green 1984).

Seven human bone and tooth fragments have so far been recovered from Pontnewydd. The first, a human molar, was discovered during the last century but it was subsequently lost. Stringer (1984) has described the human remains from the recent excavations. These include the molar of an adult, found in the Intermediate Complex close to the burnt flint core with a thermoluminescence date of 200,000 ± 25,000 BP. Near this find, in the Upper Breccia, were recovered fragments of a juvenile upper jaw with two teeth. From an unknown bed within the cave have come further fragments of a child's mandible and a vertebra, and the 1983

season also yielded two pre-molars in the Lower Breccia. The two permanent upper molars are of great interest since they resemble early Neanderthal teeth and they compare closely with finds from Krapina in Yugoslavia (Stringer 1984).

Some 300 artefacts were recovered during the National Museum of Wales' excavations, mainly from the Intermediate Complex and the Lower and Upper Breccias. No evidence of settlement within the cave was found; all the artefacts appear to have been transported into the cave by mass-movement. The principal tools are handaxes of Acheulian types and Levallois tradition. The nature of these artefacts and the small size of the cave entrance suggests that Pontnewydd was probably used only as a temporary butchering site (Green 1981a, 1984).

The combination of stratigraphic, sedimentological, faunal, human and dating evidence from Pontnewydd provides the most extensive terrestrial Pleistocene record so far known in Wales. The earliest event recorded is deposition of the Lower and Upper Sands and Gravels, probably in a cold environment. These sediments contain erratics, presumably derived from an earlier glacial event. The succeeding Intermediate Complex contains mammal bones, artefacts and human remains. The recognition of a 'warm' mammal fauna (interglacial or interstadial) from these sediments (bed 3), together with a human tooth dated to *c*. 200,000 BP, provides evidence to suggest human activity at Pontnewydd during the temperate conditions in Oxygen Isotope Stage 7 (Green 1984). The earliest certain growth of stalagmite within the cave has been correlated with Oxygen Isotope Sub-stage 7c (*c*. 250,000-230,000 BP) and it seems reasonable that the human finds and associated artefacts could, in part, belong to this time. The evidence suggests that the succeeding Lower Breccia was also formed in Oxygen Isoptope Stage 7, probably during Sub-stage 7b (Andrews 1983) which is consistent with the 'cool temperate' fauna (Green 1984). Overlying the Lower Breccia, in places, are deposits of stalagmite (bed 5) *in situ* that range in age between *c*. 215,000 and 83,000 BP, indicating no clastic sedimentation during this extended period, which covers much of Oxygen Isotope Stage 6 (cold) and Sub-stage 5e (temperate). Stable isotope data from the youngest of these *in situ* stalagmite deposits confirms that the cave was sealed, during a cool episode towards the end of the Ipswichian Stage.

Renewed deposition, during the Devensian Stage, is marked by the succeeding Silt and Upper Breccia. The latter contains a typical 'cold' Late Devensian and Devensian late-glacial fauna. The overlying Red Cave Earth formed as a mass debris flow towards the end of the latter period, channelling into and incorporating older sediments. The Upper Clays and Sands and Laminated Travertine are complex waterlain deposits, containing the bones of modern mammals, and extending the record at Pontnewydd into the

Holocene.

Pontnewydd Cave contains the most extensive Pleistocene sequence in Wales and the only record of Middle Pleistocene conditions in North Wales. The sequence has been dated and correlated with the deep-sea oxygen isotope record. The human tooth is the earliest such find in Wales, and except for the Swanscombe fossil, the earliest in the British record. This probable early Neanderthal was associated with over 300 artefacts of Acheulian type. These are the only finds of Lower Palaeolithic antiquity from a stratified sequence in Wales, and they provide strong evidence for human activity probably in Oxygen Isotope Stage 7.

Conclusions

Pontnewydd Cave contains some of the oldest ice age rocks known in Wales. The latest methods of dating such rocks have been applied and they are known to be at least 200,000 years old. The human tooth dated to this time is the earliest evidence for Man in Wales.

Cefn and Galltfaenan Caves

Highlights

This is an important site yielding the only known 'warm' Ipswichian mammal fauna from North Wales, as well as a 'cold' mammal fauna from the rocks of the succeeding Devensian Stage.

Introduction

Cefn and Galltfaenan Caves (the Cefn Caves) are important for reconstructing the Late Pleistocene history of North Wales. Unlike South Wales, evidence for Pleistocene interglacial conditions in North Wales is strictly limited and a 'warm' mammal fauna from Cefn Caves, including hippopotamus and straight-tusked elephant, provides an important record of environmental conditions during the Ipswichian Stage. A 'cold' fauna associated with the Devensian Stage, is also present. The site has a long history of research commencing with Stanley (1832) and has also been described by Trimmer (1841), Falconer (1868), Mackintosh (1876), Hughes (1885, 1887) and Neaverson (1942). The place of the site with regard to the Late Pleistocene history of the region has been discussed by Bowen (1973a, 1974) and Peake et al. (1973). A more detailed account of its faunas and artefacts was given by Valdemar (1970), and the faunal evidence was also discussed by Currant (in Green 1984).

Description

Cefn Cave (SJ021705) occurs at approximately 76m OD in Carboniferous Limestone above the Elwy Valley, and consists of a number of interconnecting passages with multiple entrances. Galltfaenan Cave (SJ023702) is situated in a small ravine about 400m to the south-east. Reliable

details of the stratigraphic sequences in these caves are not available, although Trimmer's (1841) account of Cefn Cave would appear to offer the best description thus far available. Trimmer recorded a sequence of –

4   Sand and silt containing marine shells

3   Calcareous loam containing bones and fragments of limestone

2   Stalagmite floor

1   Sediment containing smooth pebbles, bones and wood fragments

Unfortunately, the position of the faunas and artefacts within this sequence is not known, making dating and interpretation difficult. Significant deposits are thought to remain *in situ* at both caves.

Interpretation

A mammalian fauna was first discovered in the Cefn Caves by Stanley (1832). He gave an account of the caves and their contents, which included the remains of hyaena and rhinoceros. Trimmer (1841) interpreted beds 2 and 3 as terrestrial cave deposits and bed 1 as fluvial in origin. The overlying sand and silt with marine shells (bed 4) was considered to be a marine deposit formed during 'glacial submergence' of the land. This interpretation was largely followed by Mackintosh (1876).

In 1866, Moore excavated for a short time at Cefn; specimens from this time were placed in the Liverpool City Museum (Neaverson 1942). The site was also described by Hughes (1885, 1887), who unlike Trimmer and Mackintosh, believed that the 'shelly marl' (bed 4) had been washed in from the overlying boulder clay via fissures, and was not marine in origin.

The first detailed faunal list from the site was given by Falconer (1868) and later updated by Neaverson (1942), and now revised as follows –

Straight-tusked elephant *Palaeoloxodon antiquus*

Extinct rhinoceros *Dicerorhinus hemitoechus?*

Hippopotamus *Hippopotamus amphibius L.*

Horse *Equus ferus*

Reindeer *Rangifer tarandus*

Giant deer *Megaceros giganteus*

Red deer *Cervus elaphus*

Extinct bison *Bison priscus*

Lion *Panthera leo*

Spotted hyaena *Crocuta crocuta*

Cave bear *Ursus spelaeus*

Wolf *Canis lupus*

Red fox *Vulpes vulpes*

Brown bear *Ursus arctos*

Badger *Meles meles*

Human bones and artefacts were also recovered during early excavations at the site (Dawkins 1874). Both the human remains and tools were described as being of Neolithic type and they were apparently intermixed with the mammalian fauna. Dawkins (1871) also recorded finds of reindeer, bear and hyaena from Galltfaenan Cave.

More recently, Valdemar (1970) reassessed the faunas and artefacts from Cefn Cave, and discussed these in relation to those from Pontnewydd. He showed that the flint artefacts described by Dawkins as Neolithic, were probably Upper Palaeolithic in age, belonging to a Creswellian or Cheddarian culture. The stratigraphic context of these finds, however, was uncertain. Dawkins had identified the human remains as belonging to a brachycephalic race usually attributable to the Neolithic (Foulkes 1872). Valdemar therefore suggested that there must have been at least two phases of human occupation. He noted that, since Cefn Cave had yielded Upper Palaeolithic artefacts as well as human remains, it is possible that other caves excavated by Dawkins and earlier excavators also contained evidence from both the Upper Palaeolithic and Neolithic periods.

Elements of both a 'temperate' interglacial type mammal fauna, including hippotamus and straight-tusked elephant, and a 'cold' glacial type fauna, with woolly rhinoceros, mammoth and reindeer, have been described from the Cefn Caves. These records have been discussed by Bowen (1973a, 1974), Peake *et al.* (1973) and Stuart (1982) who have emphasised the difficulties of interpreting the assemblages without precise stratigraphic details. It has also been noted that early workers may even have confused faunal material from Cefn with specimens from Pontnewydd Cave (Currant 1984). Nevertheless, the fauna from Cefn Caves is of considerable importance in reconstructing Late Pleistocene events in North Wales, and it has been suggested that the 'temperate' fauna can be assigned to the Ipswichian Stage and the 'cold' fauna to the Devensian Stage (Bowen 1973a, 1974; Peake *et al.* 1973; Stuart 1982).

The fauna of proposed Ipswichian age at Cefn assumes considerable importance in view of the lack of evidence in North Wales for Pleistocene interglacial conditions. Cefn Caves, therefore, provide a contrasting record to nearby Pontnewydd where, although an extensive Middle Pleistocene sequence is present, sediments and fauna from the Ipswichian Stage are absent (Green 1984). Together they form important elements in a network of cave sites that demonstrates evidence for changing environmental conditions in North Wales in the Pleistocene.

The Cefn Caves have yielded the only mammalian fauna known in North Wales from the Ipswichian Stage. They also provide an important Devensian 'cold' fauna. Although the stratigraphic context of these finds has not been established, substantial deposits remain *in situ*, giving the site considerable potential for elaborating Late Pleistocene conditions in North Wales. Human and artefact evidence from here strongly suggests occupation during both the Upper Palaeolithic and Neolithic periods.

Conclusions

The Cefn Caves contain rocks which have yielded a prolific assemblage of fossils, including hippopotamus, which can be dated to some 125,000 years ago. This is important because it was the last time that Britain enjoyed conditions similar to the present. Evidence of this kind when assembled over a wide area may provide information on how interglacials like the present come to an end. The Cefn Caves were also occupied by Man during the Palaeolithic and Neolithic periods.

Tremeirchion (Cae Gwyn and Ffynnon Beuno) Caves

Highlights

Bone and human Palaeolithic implement-bearing deposits are found here beneath glacial sediments laid down during the last major Pleistocene cold phase in the Late Devensian. The 'cold' mammal fauna from the cave has been dated to about 18,000 BP, immediately before this glacial episode.

Introduction

Tremeirchion comprises the caves of Cae Gwyn and Ffynnon Beuno. These have yielded rich mammalian faunas including the remains of mammoth, woolly rhinoceros, spotted hyaena, lion and reindeer, and they have provided some of the earliest clear evidence for the association of man-made stone tools with the remains of extinct mammals. The site is particularly significant in providing evidence that the last glaciation of the Vale of Clwyd took place during the Late Devensian. The site was first investigated by Hicks (1884, 1886a, 1887, 1888), and the evidence from these early excavations has been reviewed by Garrod (1926), Boswell (1932), Neaverson (1942), Embleton (1970) and Synge (1970). A radiocarbon date obtained from faunal material at the site (Rowlands 1971) has been discussed within the wider context of the Pleistocene history of North

Wales (Oakley 1971; Bowen 1973a, 1973b, 1974; Peake *et al.* 1973; Campbell 1977; Green 1984).

Description

Ffynnon Beuno and Cae Gwyn Caves (SJ085724) are situated close together at the base of the Carboniferous Limestone escarpment on the eastern side of the Vale of Clwyd. Cae Gwyn Cave consists of two entrances connected by a narrow single passage. One entrance faces south at *c.* 19m above the floor of the Ffynnon Beuno Valley. The other entrance faces west and was completely buried prior to its excavation (Campbell 1977). Ffynnon Beuno Cave, which lies at a slightly lower level, comprises three galleries and has two openings to the south (Garrod 1926).

The sequence found at the southern entrance to Cae Gwyn and inside the cave was as follows (Hicks 1886a) –

5   Reddish recent loam (0.60m)

4   Laminated clay with thin ferruginous and stalagmitic lenses (0.20m)

3   Reddish sandy clay with pebbles of felsite, granite, gneiss, quartz, quartzite, sandstone and limestone, with an early Upper Palaeolithic tool – partially disturbed (0.60m)

2   Unfossiliferous gravel mostly of local rock types (0.30m)

1   Carboniferous Limestone bedrock

Following a partial collapse in a field above the cave, a second section and entrance to the cave was exposed, showing the following sequence (Hicks 1886a; Garrod 1926; Campbell 1977) –

12   Surface soil (0.15m)

11   Brown till (0.85m)

10   Yellow clay with silt and sand (0.18m)

9   Stiff red till (0.70m)

8   Sand (0.05m)

7   Purple clay (0.25m)

6   Sand with boulders (0.50m)

5   Gravelly sand with boulders and lenses of purple clay (0.65m)

4   Sandy gravel (0.60m)

3   Sand lenses (0.40m)

2   Red laminated clay and 'bone earth' with angular limestone fragments and a few boulders (0.80m)

1   Carboniferous Limestone bedrock

From Ffynnon Beuno Cave, the following sequence was recognised (Hicks 1886a; Garrod 1926) –

6   Surface soil

5   Cemented breccia with charcoal

4   Red cave earth with bones and implements

3   Yellow band (ancient floor?)

2   Gravel with angular blocks of limestone

1   Carboniferous Limestone bedrock?

Cae Gwyn and Ffynnon Beuno Caves were first excavated by Hicks and Luxmoore between 1883-1887 (Hicks 1884, 1886a, 1887, 1888). Both contained a considerable mammalian fauna (Hicks 1886a; Garrod 1926) –

Lion *Panthera leo*
Wild cat *Felis sylvestris*
Spotted hyaena *Crocuta crocuta*
Wolf *Canis lupus*
Fox *Vulpes vulpes*
Bear *Ursus* sp.
Badger *Meles meles*
Wild boar *Sus scrofa*
Bovine *Bos*?
Giant deer *Megaceros giganteus*
Red deer *Cervus elaphus*
Roe deer *Capreolus capreolus*
Reindeer *Rangifer tarandus*
Horse *Equus* sp.
Woolly rhinoceros *Coelodonta antiquitatis*
Mammoth *Mammuthus primigenius*

Interpretation

Hicks considered that this fauna showed that the cave had been a hyaena den during the Pleistocene, and he noted that amongst the remains, the teeth of horse, rhinoceros, hyaena and reindeer were most numerous. Both caves also yielded human artefacts. He suggested that the evidence furnished from the bones and artefacts showed that Man had been contemporaneous with the mammals. His most significant claim, however, was that the caves had been sealed by undisturbed till. In places, the till contained marine shell fragments and erratics, indicative of a northern or Irish Sea origin. The sealing of the caves was considered by Hicks to demonstrate that the bones and artefacts were 'pre-glacial' age. This suggestion was strongly refuted, especially by Hughes (1887) who argued that the glacial deposits were not *in situ*. Hughes was convinced that the Tremeirchion Cave deposits were 'post-glacial' in age. In the discussion (Hughes 1887), debate occurred concerning the antiquity of Man in relationship to the deposits, and it was noted that "......the interest attaching to the cave depends on the light which it throws on the relation of Palaeolithic Man to the glacial period". Hicks' view that the caves were sealed by till and that the fossiliferous remains pre-dated glaciation of the local area, however, prevailed (Garrod 1926; Boswell 1932; McBurney 1965; Embleton 1970; Synge 1970).

Garrod (1926) reviewed the earlier work at Tremeirchion and considered that the artefacts from the caves were of two principal types; Middle Aurignacian and Proto-Solutrean. Indeed, on the basis that the Irish Sea till at Tremeirchion post-dated the Aurignacian tools, Charlesworth (1929) established a Magdalenian (Creswellian-Cheddarian) age for the 'Newer Drift' (Devensian) glaciation of Wales and adjoining regions. Campbell (1977), however, observed that Garrod's sub-division of the artefacts was probably arbitrary, and assigned the finds more broadly to the Upper Palaeolithic. Neaverson (1942) also reviewed the early excavations at the site, providing useful details of the museums and establishments to which the finds had been dispersed.

Rowlands (1971) submitted a mammoth carpal collected by Hicks for radiocarbon dating. A date of 18,000 +1,400 -1,200 BP was obtained on the collagen, and this was used by Rowlands to demonstrate that the last glaciation of the area was Late Devensian in age, after c. 18,000 BP. He considered the date too young to provide an age for the Palaeolithic industry at the site. Oakley (1971), however, pointed out that although the dates of similar industries in France were in the region of 10,000 years older, a radiocarbon date on human bones at Paviland Cave in Gower, South Wales, showed a very close correspondence to Rowlands' Tremeirchion date. This indicated that human occupation may have occurred close to the peak of the Late Devensian glaciation.

The radiocarbon date from Tremeirchion demonstrates that the glacial deposits of the local area post-date c. 18,000 BP and are, therefore, Late Devensian in age. The exact significance of the date is, however, less clear: in discussing the evidence from Tremeirchion, Bowen (1973a, 1973b, 1974) suggested two main possibilities for interpreting the radiocarbon date. Either, the date indicates that the main thrust of Late Devensian Irish Sea ice in the region post-dated c. 18,000 BP, and a close similarity was noted between the Tremeirchion date and a radiocarbon date from Dimlington in Holderness (Penny et al. 1969) or, the date provides a maximum age for a readvance of the Late Devensian ice-sheet, rather than the main pulse of the glaciation. Although this remains unresolved, the Tremeirchion date shows that the fauna and human industries pre-date the last, Late Devensian, glaciation of the area (Peake et al. 1973; Campbell 1977; Green 1984). Historically, the site also provides some of the earliest evidence for the association of man-made stone tools with the remains of Pleistocene mammals. Although contemporary assessment of the mammal fauna from Tremeirchion is not available, it represents a generally 'cold' assemblage, and would appear to date, at least in part, from immediately before the Late Devensian glaciation.

Tremeirchion Caves provide an important record of Late Pleistocene conditions in North Wales, with a unique combination of faunal, archaeological, sedimentary and radiocarbon dating evidence. They provide a reference point for Late Pleistocene/Upper Palaeolithic tools which were apparently overlain by till from the last glaciation. The radiocarbon date from the site has shown that the glacial deposits post-date c. 18,000 BP and are, therefore, Late Devensian in age. Radiocarbon dates from Tremeirchion and Dimlington indicate that a substantial area of Britain was covered by glacier ice sometime after 18,000 BP.

Conclusions

The Tremeirchion Caves are among the most important archaeological sites in Europe. Because they contain a rich sequence of archaeological remains which are dated broadly to the period between 20,000 and 40,000 years ago, and because these were sealed inside the cave by glacial deposits of the last ice-sheet, they provide an important limiting date for that glaciation. A radiocarbon date of 18,000 years ago from a mammoth bone is one of only a few age determinations from this time in the British Isles.

Vicarage Moss

Highlights

This site shows one of the best developed kettle hole complexes in Wales. These depressions, formed by the melting of glacier ice caught up in glacial and fluvioglacial sediments, are typical of many developed towards the end of the Late Devensian glaciation in north-east Wales.

Introduction

Vicarage Moss is one of the best developed examples of a kettle hole complex in Wales. The features here are representative of many developed throughout the Wrexham area on the landform known as the 'Wrexham delta terrace'; they were probably formed towards the close of the Late Devensian glaciation by the melting of buried ice. The features have been described in numerous publications (for example, Wedd et al. 1928; Peake 1961; Poole and Whiteman 1961; Francis 1978; Dunkley 1981; Wilson et al., 1982; Thomas 1985). The features have been mapped and described in relationship to soil development in the Wrexham area by Lea and Thompson (1978).

Description

Kettle holes are depressions formed by the melting of ice masses which were formerly buried within glacial sediments. Those at Vicarage Moss (SJ360540) lie in the eastern part of the Wrexham delta terrace, an extensive area composed largely of sands, gravels and fine-grained diamicts. The site comprises one very large and two subsidiary kettle holes. The largest forms a deep basin occupied by mire vegetation and open-water which extend across the floor of the kettle hole for some 200m. Of the smaller subsidiary kettle holes, one contains a boggy floor but the other has no appreciable sediment infill. Other, even smaller, hollows with intervening ridges and mounds occur within the site. The main basin mire is exceptionally well defined by the junction of the surrounding steep, well drained gravel slopes. The vegetation of the main moss is dominated by bog moss, cotton grass and cranberry.

Interpretation

Wedd *et al.* (1928) showed that the Wrexham area had been affected by two major ice streams, one coming from the west (Welsh ice) and one from the north (Irish Sea ice). They divided the drift succession of the area into a tripartite sequence of Lower Boulder Clay, Middle Sands and Upper Boulder Clay. They argued that this sequence was formed in a single ice advance and retreat episode, during which the Middle Sands had been deposited by meltwater from the retreating Welsh ice draining eastwards into a large lake impounded by the Irish Sea ice to the north. According to Wedd *et al.*, this built the Wrexham delta terrace, and they noted that the complex kame and kettle topography on parts of its surface had been produced during the waning phase of the glacial episode, during 'Late-Glacial' conditions.

Peake (1961) argued that the terrace was built up by meltwater draining south from both the retreating Welsh ice and Irish sea ice margins, to form a 'composite prograding delta', on the edge of a lake occupying the Cheshire lowlands. She noted that the prominent series of large kettle holes and mounds south of Gresford, including Vicarage Moss, could represent a previous ice-stand. Peake (1961, 1979, 1981) has also argued that Irish Sea till overlying sands and gravels in the terrace in the Llay area of north-east Wrexham was distinct from the Upper Boulder Clay described by Wedd *et al.* (1928). This till, she suggested represented a separate ice advance, termed the Llay readvance.

Other workers, however, have suggested that the terrace was not in fact produced by deltaic processes. Poole and Whiteman (1961), for example, considered that the feature represented part of an end-moraine extending from Wrexham across the Cheshire-Shropshire lowland towards Ellesmere. The outer edge of the terrace was therefore seen as an ice-contact slope to the rear of Irish Sea outwash spreading westwards. This view has also been supported by Worsley (1970). Poole and Whiteman further suggested that the 'billowy, hummocky topography with occasional kettle-holes' was extremely characteristic of such morainic drift.

Similarly, Francis (1978) has suggested that the 'delta terrace' was not formed by deltaic processes, but as a subaerial fan supplied by glacial outwash. The well developed kettle-holed surface was believed to imply deposition in contact with ice; a view upheld by Dunkley (1981) and Wilson *et al.* (1982).

Most recently, however, Thomas (1985) has argued that the previous models do not explain adequately the variety of depositional conditions observed in the area in boreholes and in more recently exposed gravel workings such as those at Marford and Singret quarries. Thus, he considered that the Wrexham delta terrace could not be regarded as either a simple 'lake-delta' or as a simple 'alluvial fan', but rather as a much more complex and diachronous feature showing evidence for a variety of sedimentary environments, including ice-front, debris-flow, alluvial fan, sandur and proglacial and ice-contact lakes formed at the margin of the stagnating Irish Sea ice-sheet (Thomas 1985). He envisaged that the kettle holes south of Gresford and at Vicarage Moss had formed part of a complex dead ice topography at the retreating ice margin.

In demonstrating that considerable lateral and vertical variation occurs in the deposits of the terrace, Thomas concluded that the complexity was consistent with a period of oscillating ice-marginal conditions during the Late Devensian accompanied by the formation of ice-front outwash fans and short-lived lake basins.

Viewed against the extremely complex Late Pleistocene evolution of north-east Wales, the kettle holes at Vicarage Moss and elsewhere on the surface of the Wrexham delta terrace (see also Chapter 2) assume considerable importance in elaborating the nature and sequence of Late Pleistocene events in the area. The features at Vicarage Moss are representative of many developed in the sands and gravels of the Wrexham area and were probably formed towards the close of the Late Devensian glaciation by the melting of buried ice. They are classic examples of the kettle hole landform.

Conclusions

Vicarage Moss shows outstanding examples of kettle hole landforms. These are representative of numerous similar features in the Wrexham area. They contain peat deposits which can provide important information about climatic change at the end of the last ice age.

Snowdon (Yr Wyddfa)

Highlights

One of the first areas studied for its glacial features, this site shows numerous classic large, medium and small-scale examples of erosional and depositional landforms associated with glacial conditions, particularly in the Devensian Stage. Many moraines and protalus ramparts date from the last, Younger Dryas, cirque glaciation of Snowdonia.

Introduction

The mountain area of Snowdon contains a wide range of glacial and periglacial landforms of exceptional interest. The large spectacular features of glacial erosion (cirques, arêtes and troughs) were among the first in Britain to be described, and they have few parallels in Wales. Numerous fine examples of medium-scale, ice-sculptured features include rock steps and roches moutonnées. Further enhancing the interest of the area, particular around Llyn Llydaw, are many well developed, small-scale erosional features such as glacial striae and friction cracks. This assemblage of erosional forms is also accompanied by depositional landforms, particularly moraines and protalus ramparts. Although many of the latter have been assigned to the Younger Dryas, others may relate to wastage of the Late Devensian ice-sheet. Therefore, in addition to providing classic landform examples, the Snowdon area is important for interpreting patterns of mountain glaciation and deglaciation in north Wales.

The area was one of the first in Britain to be investigated with respect to the Glacial Theory, with studies by Bowman (1841), Buckland (1842), Darwin (1842) and Mackintosh (1845). It was not, however, until the work of Ramsay (1860, 1866, 1881) that the impact of glaciation in the area gained general acceptance (for example, Kidson 1888, 1890; Kendall 1893; Marr and Adie 1898; Daykins 1900; Jehu 1902; Davis 1909, 1920; Dewey 1918; and Carr and Lister 1948). Since these early studies, the area has become a classic ground for geomorphologists, with major studies by Seddon (1957), Embleton (1962, 1964a), Unwin (1970, 1973, 1975), Gray (1982a), Gray and Lowe (1982) and Gemmell *et al.* (1986). The area has also been described in texts by Williams (1927), Smith and George (1961), Johnson (1962) Ball *et al.* (1969) and Addison (1983, 1987). Ball and Goodier (1970) described the distribution of features associated with periglacial activity in Snowdonia, and Ince (1981, 1983) has reconstructed the late-glacial and Holocene vegetational history of the area using pollen analytical methods.

Description and interpretation

The Snowdon GCR site comprises a series of cirques radiating from the summit of Snowdon and representative sections of the spectacular glacial troughs in the Llanberis and Gwynant Valleys – see Figure 36.

Large-scale features of glacial erosion

Processes of glacial erosion have cut the Snowdon massif into a horn with large cirques radiating from a central point. The Crib Goch and Crib-y-ddysgl and Yr Wyddfa to Y Lliwedd arêtes are fine examples of the precipitous slopes developed in glaciated uplands. Indeed, probably only the broad-shouldered ridge extending north from Snowdon remains to give any impression of a pre-glacial land surface – see Figure 36.

The cirques within the site are generally complex in plan, with the concept of a cirque stairway clearly exemplified in Cwm Dyli (Embleton and King 1968). Here, the 'Snowdon Horseshoe' defines the eastern basin of the Snowdon massif; the arêtes of Crib Goch and Y Lliwedd encircling the largest glacial excavation of the massif (Addison 1983). Unwin (1970) recorded twenty five cirques in the Snowdon area, including Cwm Dwythwch to the north, although problems of definition may have led to an over-estimate of the total number. Many of the cirques are illustrative of the continuum of features described as cirque troughs and complexes (Gordon 1977). Little lithological control has been identified, although there is a significant orientation, probably climatically controlled, of secondary cirques (Unwin 1973).

Early in the development of the Glacial Theory, the Llanberis Pass was identified as a major glacial trough cut through the Snowdonian massif. Buckland (1842) described this as one of the finest examples of glacial erosion he had seen, comparable to landforms in the Alps. The GCR site includes part of the narrow trough extending from Pen-y-Pass to Llyn Peris GCR site, although the landform as a whole extends north-west as an 8 km long rock basin containing Llyn Peris and Llyn Padarn. The breaching of the Snowdonian uplands at Pen-y-Pass, the modern-day watershed, shows that the dispersal centres of North Wales ice-sheets, at various times in the Pleistocene, lay south of the Snowdon and Glyderau massifs (for example, Greenly 1919; Addison 1983).

The Gwynant Valley is a spectacular U-shaped trough (Johnson 1962), into which ice from the Snowdon Horseshoe flowed. This valley is separated from Cwm Dyli by an impressive rock lip, leaving what is perhaps best described as a 'hanging cwm' (Embleton 1962). The precipitous slopes of Gallt-y-Wenallt make this one of the most impressive features of glacial erosion in North Wales.

Small-scale features of glacial erosion

Small-scale features of glacial erosion are developed within the Snowdon massif. The widespread development of striated bedrock surfaces, particularly within the Llanberis Valley, led to Ramsay's (1860) early study of ice movement directions within the area. More recently, similar features have allowed a large-scale reconstruction of patterns of such movement over Snowdonia (Gemmell *et al.* 1986).

Small-scale glacial erosional features are, however,

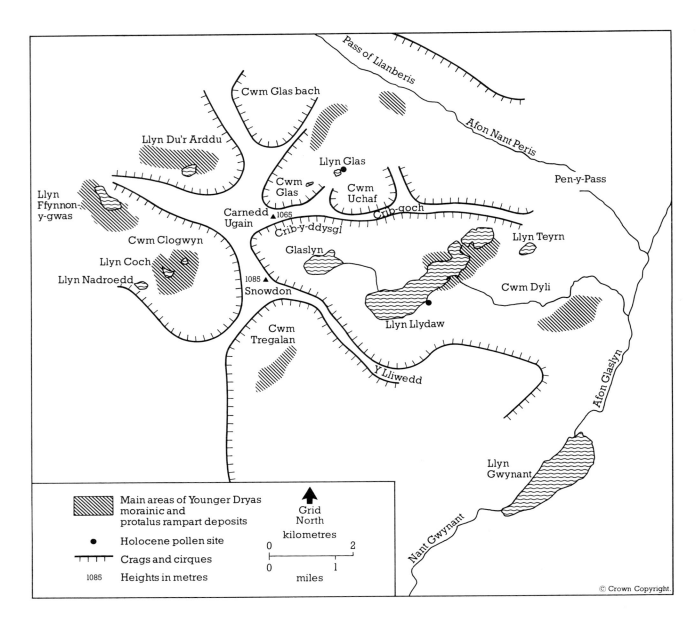

Figure 36 Snowdon (Yr Wyddfa): principal landforms

particularly well preserved in areas where bedrock surfaces have been protected from Holocene weathering, beneath for example, lake waters. Reductions in lake levels at Llyn Llydaw have revealed exceptionally fresh examples on the bedrock of ice erosion (Gray and Lowe 1982); excellent examples of abrasion and smoothing, with streamlined and striated bosses indicating a general easterly direction of former ice movement, can be examined. Roches moutonnées with clearly plucked facets are also visible. The importance of this particular area, however, lies in the small-scale features of subglacial erosion, including plastically-moulded forms (p-forms), well known from Scandinavia (Dahl 1965; Gjessing 1965) and North America (Gilbert 1906; Bernard 1971a, 1971b, 1972), but whose formation has yet to be adequately explained (Embleton and King 1975a). Other small-scale erosional features were noted

(Gray and Lowe 1982), including grooves and channels and sichelwannen, possibly formed by subglacial meltwater, as well as friction cracks, gouges and striae. Gray *et al.* (1981) and Gray and Lowe (1982) have suggested that two dominant sets of crossing striae measured in Cwm Llydaw and adjacent areas can be related to different directions of ice movement: one set related to ice flow during the last recorded ice advance, during the Younger Dryas, the other to an earlier glacial event.

Depositional landforms

Glacial depositional landforms are well known (for example, Darwin 1842; Ramsay 1860; Kidson 1890; Kendall 1893; Marr and Adie 1898; Daykins 1900; Jehu 1902; Williams 1927). Recent work has elaborated the distribution of these landforms but it has also raised questions concerning the processes responsible for their formation.

The first systematic mapping of moraines in Snowdonia was by Seddon (1957) who examined the palaeoclimatic factors responsible for their distribution. Pollen analyses made from cores in peat bogs both inside and outside the moraine arcs (Godwin 1955; Seddon 1962), led Seddon to argue that the moraines had formed during two separate phases – at some stage during the retreat of the Late Devensian ice-sheet and again during the Younger Dryas (c. 11,000 -10,000 BP). Unwin (1970) subsequently studied the distribution of cirques and cirque moraines using multi-variate analysis. He grouped the moraines into an older series of diffuse forms and a younger series of fresh forms; he further sub-divided both groups into glacial moraines and protalus ramparts. Unwin considered the older series features to have been formed during a readvance of ice in Pollen Zone I or during a recessive stage of the Late Devensian ice-sheet, and the younger series features during the Younger Dryas.

More recently, the depositional landforms of Snowdonia, including the Snowdon massif, were remapped and described in detail by Gray (1982a). In all, he mapped evidence for thirty five cirque glaciers, with glacial limits based on the distribution of end-moraines, boulder and drift limits and the down-valley extent of hummocky moraine. Detailed mapping in the region also indicated the presence of sixteen protalus ramparts, reflecting the former presence of semi-permanent snowbeds down to altitudes of 150m OD. Within the main Snowdon massif, Gray inferred the presence of six former cirque glaciers which he believed had formed during the Loch Lomond Stadial (Younger Dryas). Many of the landforms mapped by Gray cannot be classified simply as 'moraine' or 'protalus rampart'. Many limits are marked by diffuse bouldery or hummocky terrain, and several features are of complex origin; for example, the outer part of the large arcuate ridge in Cwm Tregalen (Figure 36) may be glacial in origin but the inner rim accumulated as a protalus feature by gravity sliding of debris (Gray 1982a).

Dating of moraines and protalus features

Relatively few of the glacial limits thus far identified (Unwin 1970; Gray 1982a) have been dated by radiocarbon and/or pollen analysis. Gray (1982a) suggested that a Loch Lomond Stadial age (Younger Dryas) is likely for the mapped cirque moraines in Snowdonia on the basis of stratigraphic and pollen investigations from the general area (for example, Godwin 1955; Seddon 1962; Burrows 1974, 1975; Crabtree 1970, 1972). However, only Ince's (1981, 1983) study from Cwm Llydaw provides confirmatory dating for moraines actually within the Snowdon GCR site. Radiocarbon dates and pollen analyses of basal samples inside the mapped cirque glacier limits at Cwm Llydaw (Gray 1982a) show that organic sedimentation commenced at c. 10,000 BP. This contrasts with

sites at Clogwynygarreg and Llyn Goddionduon (Ince 1981) outside the mapped cirque glacier limit, where organic sedimentation began earlier, in the Devensian late-glacial. Collectively, these data provide strong constraints on the dating and extent of the last cirque glaciation of the uplands which occurred during the Younger Dryas. Such evidence is entirely consistent with recent studies in Scotland (for example, Sissons 1976, 1979; Gray and Lowe 1977).

Gray (1982a) generally doubted the widespread existence of pre-Loch Lomond Stadial (Younger Dryas) moraines (the older series of Unwin) in Snowdonia, but the nearby GCR site at Cwm Dwythwch provides evidence for such an 'older', large cirque moraine (Seddon 1962), with a typical late-glacial sequence behind.

Holocene environmental and vegetational history

Pollen studies at Cwm Llydaw (Ince 1981, 1983) provide a detailed record of vegetational and environmental changes during the Holocene. The record shows that after c. 10,000 BP the recently deglaciated uplands were colonised by grassland and open-habitat plant taxa. These early herbaceous communities were then invaded by juniper and birch, which were in turn replaced by birch and hazel woodland and, eventually, by forests of birch, pine, oak, elm and alder (Ince 1983). Altitudinal factors ensured the survival of many open-habitat taxa in the uplands throughout the Holocene. Deteriorating environmental conditions and human interference during mid to late Holocene times resulted in the gradual decline of forests in the uplands and the development of the open-grassland and heathland communities which characterise the area today (Ince 1981, 1983).

Periglacial landforms and features

Periglacial processes have been of major importance in shaping the Snowdonian landscape. Many landforms, types of patterned ground and other features attributable to frost-action, occur within the region. The range and scale of such features in the Snowdon site is not so great as in the Carneddau, but individual landforms and features are discussed by Ball and Goodier (1970) who mapped their morphology and distribution. These include widespread scree slopes of suggested late-glacial age (Ball 1966), a solifluction terrace and an indurated till horizon in Cwm y Llan (Fitzpatrick 1956; Ball and Goodier 1970), and impressive block screes in the Llanberis Valley near Pont-y-Gromlech where individual boulders the size of a small house occur.

Snowdon is important for a wide range of glacial and periglacial landforms. In particular, the site shows the best examples in Wales of large-scale landforms of glacial erosion, including a classic central horn surrounded by a group of radiating cirques abruptly divided by arêtes. This assemblage comprises some of the most

177

spectacular glaciated topography in Wales, and indeed Britain, ranking favourably with parts of the Scottish Highlands in terms of intensity of erosion. In this respect, Snowdon contrasts markedly with the adjacent massif of Y Glyderau where the cirques show pronounced structural alignment, and to the Carneddau massif farther east where classic features of glaciation are less sharply defined and where the generally broad-shouldered landscape shows an unparalleled range of periglacial landforms and features. Of the Snowdon cirques, Cwm Dyli (the Snowdon Horseshoe) is a particularly fine example of a complex cirque with steep rock walls enclosing a series of lake basins and a varied assemblage of Younger Dryas moraines. These moraines indicate that the whole staircase from Glaslyn to the lip of Cwm Dyli was probably occupied by a single glacier – the largest Younger Dryas glacier in Snowdonia. The moraines also clearly demonstrate a recessional phase of this glacier as it retreated from Cwm Dyli towards Cwm Llydaw. Organic deposits from the site have helped in dating the moraines to the Younger Dryas, and the deposits also preserve an important record of vegetational changes in upland Wales during the Holocene. Cwm Dyli is also important for a wide range of well developed small-scale features of subglacial erosion, which help in determining the former directions of ice movement within the cirque during various glacial advances.

The spectacular large-scale landforms of glacial erosion here are some of the finest in Wales and were important for establishing the Glacial Theory in Great Britain. The site is also noted for a wide range of medium and small-scale glacial erosional forms as well as extremely varied depositional landforms. In particular, the site displays an outstanding assemblage of Younger Dryas moraines. The geomorphological interest of the site is enhanced by well developed periglacial landforms and by deposits which preserve important records of Holocene vegetational and environmental changes in upland North Wales.

Conclusions

Yr Wyddfa (Snowdon) displays internationally important landforms of glacial erosion and glacial deposition. These figured prominently in the debate and ultimate acceptance of the Glacial Theory in the British Isles a century and a half ago. Evidence for a glacier advance which only lasted for a thousand years, between 11,000 and 10,000 years ago, is important because it was caused by changes in the circulation in the North Atlantic Ocean. This information, together with cold-climate landforms and deposits, and evidence from pollen which shows climatic change, is important for reconstructing changes in climate over a wide area, and contributes to theories about future changes in climate.

Y Glyderau

Highlights

This major site shows outstanding examples of glacial landforms. Structurally controlled cirques, moraines and protalus ramparts combine to form some of the most spectacular glaciated scenery in Wales. Cwm Idwal, in particular, shows a diverse assemblage of features attributable to the final corrie glaciation of the region.

Introduction

Y Glyderau (the Glyders) are important for their assemblage of well developed glacial and periglacial landforms. The principal features include a series of impressive cirques, notably Cwm Idwal, and the classic glacial trough of Nant Ffrancon. Moraines are present in most of the cirques and some have been assigned on the basis of pollen analysis to the Younger Dryas. A number of the depositional landforms, for example in Cwm Idwal, are controversial in origin. The interest of the site is enhanced by well developed periglacial features, including a massive protalus rampart along the eastern flank of Nant Ffrancon, a fine series of vegetated periglacial stripes below Y Garn, numerous scree slopes, and the summit tors of Y Glyderau. The area was one of the first to be studied in Wales (for example, Darwin 1842; Mackintosh 1845; Ramsay 1860; Kidson 1888, 1890; Jehu 1902; Davis 1909) and has since featured in many geomorphological studies (Seddon 1957; Smith and George 1961; Embleton 1962, 1964a; Unwin 1970, 1973, 1975; Escritt 1971; Addison 1977, 1978, 1983, 1986, 1988; Watson 1977a; Gray et al. 1981; Campbell 1985b; Gemmell et al. 1986). Features in the area attributable to the Younger Dryas were recently described by Gray (1982a). The periglacial landforms of the site have been discussed by Ball and Goodier (1970). The area has featured in a number of studies of Devensian late-glacial and Holocene vegetational and environmental changes (Woodhead and Hodgson 1935; Godwin 1955; Seddon 1962; Switsur and West 1973; Burrows 1974, 1975; Evans and Walker 1977; Ince 1981, 1983).

Description and interpretation

The Glyderau lie east of the main Snowdon massif and west of the Carneddau. Bearing a similar range of large-scale features of glacial erosion to the Snowdon area (for example, cirques, arêtes, troughs), the Glyderau differ because the cirques show marked structural alignments (Unwin 1970, 1973): they show a preferred north-east orientation and open onto the trough of the Nant Ffrancon Valley. This striking glacial trough is enclosed at its upper end by a 'trough end', where a belt of grits and rhyolite crosses the valley (Watson 1977a). Examples of ice-smoothed bedrock and roches moutonnées are found in the area, especially to the north and east of Llyn Idwal. The Glyderau cirques and Nant Ffrancon were probably scoured by

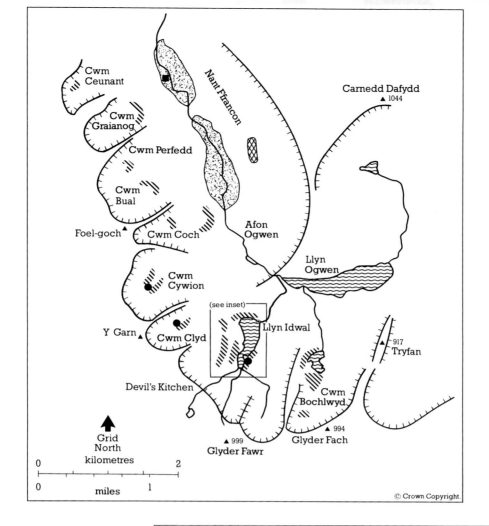

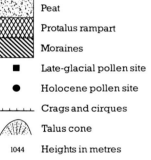

Peat

Protalus rampart

Moraines

■ Late-glacial pollen site

● Holocene pollen site

┴┴┴┴┴ Crags and cirques

Talus cone

1044 Heights in metres

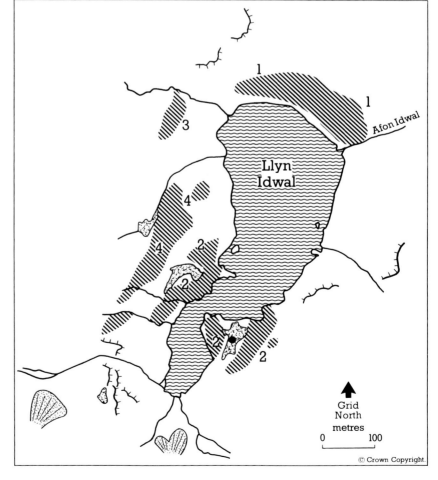

Figure 37 Y Glyderau: principal landforms (after Campbell 1985b)

179

glacier ice on several occasions during the Pleistocene, but the principal depositional features of the area consist of a number of small cirque moraines formed during the Devensian late-glacial. These depositional landforms, although common in most of the cirques, are frequently of contentious origin, none more so than those in Cwm Idwal. The depositional landforms of the area have been mapped and described by Seddon (1957), Unwin (1970, 1973, 1975), Escritt (1971), Gray (1982a) and Addison (1986, 1988).

Cwm Idwal

Cwm Idwal is one of the best developed glacial erosional features in Wales and as such is notable as one of the first to be described (Darwin 1842). The site is a large, north-east facing cirque occupied by Llyn Idwal. This lake is surrounded by a complex of glacial and possibly periglacial depositional landforms which are the subject of continuing controversy – see Figure 37. Darwin (1842) observed that the appearance of these landforms was fresh even in comparison with those he had seen in South America and remarked – "It is, I think, impossible ... to stand on these mounds and for an instant to doubt that they are ancient moraines."

Four principal series of deposits have been recognised within the cirque (Escritt 1971; Gray 1982a; Campbell 1985b) – see Figure 37 –

1 A diffuse outer moraine at the north end of Cwm Idwal

2 Morainic mounds on either side of the constriction in Llyn Idwal which have been interpreted by some authors as marking a glacial limit (Godwin 1955; Seddon 1962)

3 A group of landforms that curves away from the lake at its north-eastern end and which may represent moraine deposited by ice from nearby Cwm Clyd (Escritt 1971)

4 A contentious group of landforms on the west bank of Llyn Idwal that comprises a series of elongated mounds parallel to the western wall of the cirque

These features have been interpreted variously as lateral moraines (Jehu 1902; Godwin 1955), nivation ridges or protalus ramparts (Unwin 1970) or fluted moraine ridges (Gray et al. 1981). More recently, Addison (1986) mapped three further groups of features.

Dating the moraines

The traditional interpretation of landforms in Cwm Idwal is simply of an older series moraine at the lip of Cwm Idwal, and a younger series moraine (Younger Dryas) at the constriction half-way along Llyn Idwal (Seddon 1957, 1962; Unwin 1970, 1975). Despite pollen analyses and radiocarbon dating at a number of sites, the sequence of events is still unresolved.

Following Woodhead and Hodgson's (1935) pioneering work on the peats of Snowdonia, the first detailed pollen analytical study in the Glyderau by Godwin (1955) described a Holocene sequence from a small peat bog situated between the morainic mounds at the constriction of Llyn Idwal – see Figure 37. He tentatively suggested that this group of moraines had formed during the Younger Dryas (Pollen Zone III). In 1962, Seddon described a sequence of deposits extending back to Pollen Zone I of the Devensian late-glacial from a site in the Nant Ffrancon Valley – see Figure 37. There, the pollen and lithostratigraphic records revealed a period of cold tundra conditions in Pollen Zone III. Seddon suggested that during this phase moraine and nivation ridges were formed in adjacent cirques such as Cwm Idwal. Radiocarbon dates from the Nant Ffrancon site (Burrows 1975) and at Cwm Cywion in the Glyderau (Ince 1981, 1983) provide strong evidence that a short-lived glacial pulse, between about 11,000 and 10,000 BP was responsible for many of the cirque moraines in the area. This is the case elsewhere in Britain.

Seddon (1962), however, provided evidence to suggest that not all of the cirque moraines were formed during this Younger Dryas event. At Cwm Dwythwch in Snowdonia, he described a late-glacial pollen sequence behind a 'diffuse' cirque moraine. This, therefore, precluded a Younger Dryas age for the moraine and indicated that 'diffuse' cirque moraines elsewhere might also be earlier in the Devensian than the Younger Dryas. Gray (1982a) has suggested that the moraine groups in Cwm Idwal all belong to the Younger Dryas, some perhaps being recessional or even fluted moraine features, but a pre-Younger Dryas age cannot at present be ruled out for the 'diffuse' outer features (for example, Addison 1986).

Devensian late-glacial and Holocene environmental and vegetational history

Seddon (1962) described a sequence of deposits extending back to Pollen Zone I of the late-glacial from a site (SH632633) in the Nant Ffrancon Valley. The basal sediment was a layer of stiff blue clay, which he interpreted as solifluction inwash. Pollen analysis showed that this bed belonged to Pollen Zone I, when low scrub and open-herb vegetation indicative of tundra conditions was present. This clay is overlain by organic mud (averaging 1.40m thick), containing pollen indicating a change to open-birch woodland in Pollen Zone II. Above is a second solifluction clay in which a rapid decline in tree pollen shows a return to tundra conditions in Pollen Zone III. During this cold phase, moraine and nivation ridges (protalus ramparts) were formed in adjacent cirques. Overlying beds at Nant Ffrancon are wholly organic passing up into a modern raised Sphagnum and Eriophorum bog.

The Nant Ffrancon site was also investigated by Burrows (1974, 1975) who examined plant macrofossils and provided radiocarbon dates from the late-glacial sequence. Burrows revealed the occurrence of what he considered to be a pre-

Allerød interstadial, apparently equivalent to the Bølling (Pollen Zone Ib). He also suggested that at Nant Ffrancon there was evidence for a period of cooling between the Bølling and Allerød. The beginning of Pollen Zone II was dated at 11,900 ± 500 BP (Q-1124) and the deteriorating climate associated with the recrudescence of ice in local cirques was dated at 11,000 ± 400 BP (Q-1123). Moore (1975b), however, questioned the validity of this interpretation of the sequence, in particular throwing doubt on the occurrence of the Bølling oscillation. Switsur and West (1973) provided a comprehensive framework of radiocarbon dates from the Holocene sequence at Nant Ffrancon.

At Llyn Clyd, Evans and Walker (1977) studied a Holocene sequence containing pollen and diatoms from the small lake situated behind a moraine – see Figure 37. More recently, Ince (1981, 1983) used pollen analysis and radiocarbon dating of basal samples from behind the moraine at Cwm Cywion to show that organic sedimentation commenced in the early Holocene at around 10,000 BP. Ince's studies place an age limit on the final cirque glaciation of the area.

Periglacial landforms and features

The geomorphological interest of the Glyderau is enhanced by well developed periglacial landforms which include a large protalus rampart on the eastern edge of the Nant Ffrancon Valley (Gray 1982a), a fine series of vegetated periglacial stripes beneath the summit of Y Garn (Ball and Goodier 1970), numerous scree slopes (Ball 1966), and the frost-shattered summits of the Glyderau themselves. Although impressive, and an integral part of the overall landform assemblage, the periglacial landforms and features of the Snowdon and Glyderau massifs do not match the scale and variety of those developed in the Carneddau.

The Glyderau are important for some of the most spectacular glaciated scenery in Wales, especially large-scale features of glacial erosion, such as the cirques which overhang the Nant Ffrancon Valley. In contrast to the cirques of the Snowdon massif, those in the Glyderau show very marked structural alignment and many contain fine examples of depositional landforms (moraines and protalus ramparts) associated with the final cirque glaciation of the region. Cwm Idwal contains a particularly diverse assemblage of landforms attributable to the Younger Dryas. The controversial nature and age of some of these landforms make the site of considerable interest.

The Glyderau also contain important Devensian late-glacial and Holocene deposits which not only help to constrain the ages of moraines in the area, but also provide detailed records of vegetational and environmental changes in upland Wales. Many of these changes have been calibrated with radiocarbon dating.

The large-scale features of glacial erosion within Y Glyderau are some of the finest in Wales, and

unlike those of Yr Wyddfa (Snowdon), demonstrate very clearly the influence of geological structure on cirque development. Like Snowdon, the Glyderau demonstrated important evidence for establishing the Glacial Theory in Great Britain. Although glacial deposits are widespread in the cirques of the Glyderau massif, Cwm Idwal, in particular, has long been noted for its diversity of depositional landforms, the age and interpretation of which are still controversial. The geomorphological interest of the site is enhanced by well developed periglacial landforms and by pollen bearing deposits which record detailed changes in vegetational history from the Devensian late-glacial to modern times.

Conclusions

Y Glyderau are important for the same reasons as Yr Wyddfa (Snowdon). In addition, however, they contain Cwm Idwal which has figured in scientific investigations since the 17th century. The detailed information now available from Cwm Idwal is of outstanding importance for reconstructing climatic change.

Y Carneddau

Highlights

Classic ground in early studies of glacial and periglacial phenomena, this site shows some of the finest patterned ground in Wales. Many periglacial landforms had their origins in the Late Devensian but others are still active. Late-glacial depositional features include perhaps the most complex suite of Younger Dryas, final cirque glaciation, moraines in Wales.

Introduction

The Carneddau are important for their range of glacial and periglacial landforms including well developed cirques and Devensian late-glacial moraines, for example at Ffynnon Llugwy and Melynllyn. The Carneddau are noted for periglacial landforms formed by frost-action both during the Late Pleistocene and at the present day (Pearsall 1950; Tallis and Kershaw 1959; Ball 1966; Ball and Goodier 1970; Scoates 1973). Like Snowdon and the Glyderau, the area was one of the first to be studied with respect to the Glacial Theory (for example, Buckland 1842; Mackintosh 1845; Ramsay 1860, 1881; Kidson 1898; Marr and Adie 1898; Jehu 1902). It has featured in geomorphological studies by Seddon (1957), Embleton (1962, 1964a), Unwin (1970, 1973, 1975) and Gray (1982a), and evidence from selected sites within the area provides the basis for reconstructing environmental and vegetational history (Woodhead and Hodgson 1935; Thomas 1972; Walker 1978).

Description and interpretation

The Carneddau lie east of the Glyderau and Snowdon massifs and form the largest area of upland Wales over 900m OD. To the west the range is bounded by the Nant Ffrancon trough, to the east by the Conway Valley and to the north by the coastal plain. The character of the landscape is markedly different to the Glyderau and Snowdon groups of the northern Snowdonian massif, being less highly dissected by large-scale features of glacial erosion. Nonetheless, Unwin (1975) recognised nineteen cirques within the Carneddau, including several examples such as Cwm Lloer and Cwm Ffynnon Llugwy with a convincing staircase of forms. Morphologically the cirques of this range vary considerably from large, semi-circular and over-deepened forms such as those at Dulyn and Melynllyn, to rounded and shallow hollows such as those at Moch and Bychans (Unwin 1975). In contrast to the Glyderau where the dominant cirque orientation is along the strike with the cirque floors excavated in less resistant strata, the Carneddau cirques show considerable variation in relationship to structure. The over-deepened form at Dulyn (Figure 38) is particularly exaggerated, with Jehu's (1902) soundings showing the cirque lake to be 57m deep.

The massif was probably occupied by ice and acted as a dispersal centre on a number of occasions during the Pleistocene, and it also displays significant evidence for a late phase of cirque glacier development. The cirque moraines of the area have been mapped and discussed by Seddon (1957), Unwin (1970, 1973, 1975) and Gray (1982a), and most are believed to have formed during the Younger Dryas (between c. 11,000-10,000 BP).

Of the cirque forms included within the GCR site, those at Melynllyn, Dulyn and Cwm Ffynnon Llugwy (Figure 38) are particularly notable, both as erosional forms, and for their unusually diverse range of associated depositional landforms of Younger Dryas age. A particularly fine example of a drift and boulder limit with several recessional moraines behind occurs in Cwm Ffynnon Llugwy (Gray 1982a). Here, Gray traced the limit of a former glacier for about 900m on the west side of the valley, although comparable evidence from the eastern side was absent. At c. 630m OD a lateral moraine complex, covered with boulders, occurs south of Craig-y-Llyn cliffs. Below about 530m OD the extent of the former glacier is marked by drift and boulders that run across the valley floor to reach Afon Llugwy. The river at this point is incised into what Gray interpreted as a small marginal glacial meltwater channel. Inside the glacial limit the ground appears to be a chaos of morainic undulations and boulder spreads. However, Gray was able to trace at least five ridges marking successive stages in ice recession. A sequence of recessional features associated with the retreating ice mass also occurs north of the reservoir. The depositional landforms in Cwm Ffynnon Llugwy were formed by the largest glacier of Younger Dryas age in the Carneddau range (Gray 1982a).

In contrast, the ice limit in the nearby Melynllyn cirque is marked by an unusual, straight and virtually boulder-free moraine (Gray 1982a). At Cwm Dulyn, however, the drift limit is again complex; there is a striking contrast between the mass of blocks and boulders inside the northern limit and the smooth, peat-covered slopes outside (Gray 1982a). Southwards, the limit grades into a series of low (<1m), boulder-covered, end-moraine ridges, from which at least three recessional positions can be recognised (Gray 1982a).

Periglacial landforms and features

The Carneddau Mountains contain a range of periglacial landforms and features probably unparalleled elsewhere in Wales, although the inaccessibility of the area has meant that relatively few studies have been carried out (Pearsall 1950; Tallis and Kershaw 1959; Ball 1966; Ball and Goodier 1970; Scoates 1973). The distribution of the main features is shown in Figure 38.

Pearsall (1950) was the first to record patterned ground in the Carneddau; on the broad saddle (Waun-y-Garnedd) connecting Foel Grach with Carnedd Llewellyn, where he described a series of stone polygons and stripes. These were later studied by Tallis and Kershaw (1959) who concluded that the polygonal patterns were unstable, showing rapid rearrangements because of fluctuating climatic conditions, particularly the erosive influence of wind and rain. Ball and Goodier (1970) recorded a graduated sequence of features ranging from well defined polygons, through elongated polygons to rather sinuous sorted stripes, in each case with a repeat distance of some 0.30-0.45m. They showed that over a number of seasons the patterns were less active than when observed by Tallis and Kershaw (1959). They also noted that such features were absent at lower altitudes in Snowdonia, and concluded that the present climate could only sustain patterned ground at the highest altitudes (that is above 900m). This was supported by a study of periglacial features throughout the Carneddau which confirmed that all polygons were found, without exception, above altitudes of 913m (3,000 ft), on volcanic rocks, and always in groups on flat or nearly flat areas (<2° of slope) (Scoates 1973).

Scoates also described sorted nets (patterned ground transitional between circles and polygons) on a number of other flat summit tops (for instance, Drosgl and Llwydmor) and low angle slopes (for instance, Foel Fras) at high altitude. Patterned ground in the form of stone stripes was also recorded, with good examples at Foel Fras and on the back wall of Cwm Ffynnon Llugwy. No conclusions were drawn about the distribution of these features with regard to altitude and aspect, although most of the stripes showed a north-west aspect above 770m (2,500 ft).

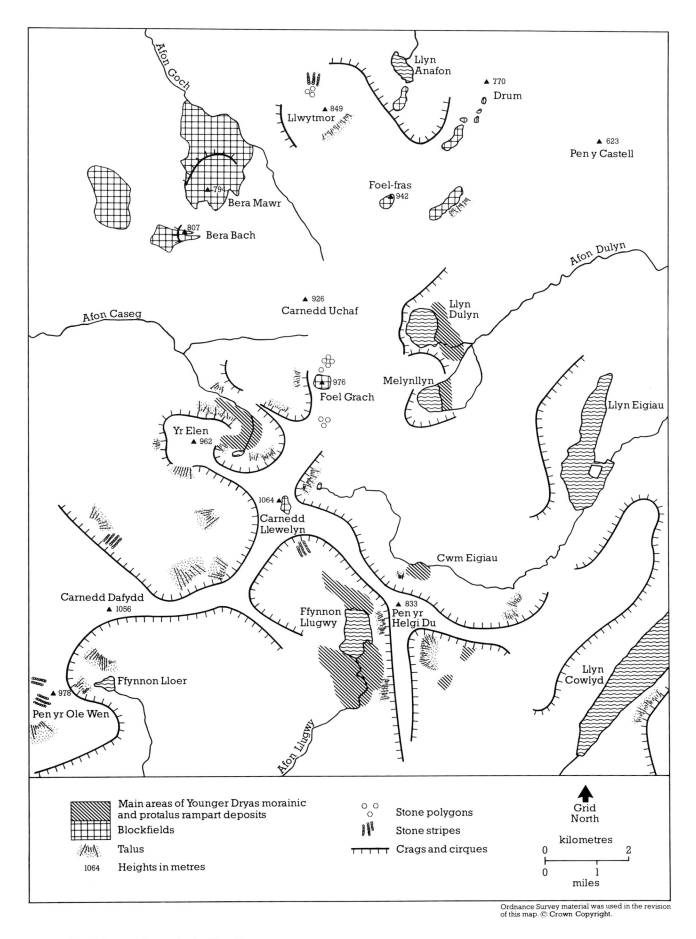

Figure 38 Y Carneddau: principal landforms

Ordnance Survey material was used in the revision of this map. © Crown Copyright.

A wide range of other features associated with frost-action have been recorded in the Carneddau (Ball and Goodier 1970; Scoates 1973). Blockfields are widespread and conspicuous, being especially well developed at Foel Fras (SH696683) at 942m (3,092 ft), Garnedd Uchaf (SH687668) at 904m (2,970 ft), and Bera Bach (SH673678) at 780m (2,560 ft) (Scoates 1973). These blockfields, felsenmeer or areas of 'mountain-top detritus' were considered to have formed by shattering of bedrock, the size of the accumulated material being highly dependent on lithology, temperature and the duration and rate of weathering. The age of the features is not known, but their large-scale development probably precludes a Holocene age, and it would appear that major gelifractive activity has now ceased (Scoates 1973).

Frequently associated with the blockfields are a number of well developed tors. These have been divided into upland tors, including degraded tors on crests, ridges and summit plains (Scoates 1973), and these are equivalent to the tor-like summits (Ball and Goodier 1970), and valley side or buttress tors (Scoates 1973). Examples of the summit tors include those at Foel Grach, Garnedd Uchaf, Bera Bach and Bera Mawr. The origin of tors occupies a substantial literature and is more fully discussed elsewhere (see Trefgarn and Preseli reports) and a wide variety of mechanisms has been proposed. Linton (1955) suggested a non-periglacial origin; with tors formed at depth under warm humid conditions, followed by a period of exhumation. However, Palmer and Nielson (1962) in discussing the origin of granitic tors on Dartmoor, proposed that formation was due to periglacial conditions. Angular clitters and the lack of clay in the disintegrated residue led Scoates to argue a periglacial origin for features in the Carneddau. However, it is likely that weathering products from any chemical weathering phase would have been removed from the exposed watershed locations, although Ball (1964) described the weathering product gibbsite, a clay mineral from the feldspars of the microporphyritic granite on Y Llymllwyd (SH631609) in the Glyderau. Other workers (for example, Jahn 1962), however, have stressed the importance of rock structure rather than climatic factors in tor formation, and in this context Scoates (1973) noted that jointing had played an important role in the formation of the tors at Bera Mawr and Bera Bach.

One of the most extensive landforms associated with frost-action in the Carneddau is scree. Particularly extensive and well developed examples are found in Cwm Ffynnon Llugwy and around the slopes of Yr Elen. The characteristics of these features have been described in detail by Ball (1966), Ball and Goodier (1970) and Scoates (1973). Ball (1966) suggested that the Carneddau screes, in common with those elsewhere in Mid and North Wales, dated from Pollen Zones I and III of the Devensian late-glacial, and that re-sorting, rather than accretion of freshly shattered rock, was the dominant contemporary process.

The Carneddau also contain a wide range of other features attributable to frost-action. These include widespread solifluction deposits and terraces, stone or turf-banked lobes, terracettes, earth-hummocks and gliding blocks; the morphology and distribution of these features are discussed by Ball and Goodier (1970) and Scoates (1973), but they have not been investigated in detail.

Many factors have contributed to the development and range of periglacial landforms seen in the Carneddau massif. In a detailed study of similar features in the Cairngorms, King (1968) pinpointed five controls of overriding importance, namely lithology, slope angle, altitude, vegetation and aspect. Scoates assessed the range and distribution of periglacial features within the Carneddau with respect to these parameters and she concluded that lithology was of overriding importance in tor and blockfield formation and, to a lesser degree, in scree development. Patterned ground, however, occurred irrespective of underlying lithology.

As regards angles of slope, Scoates considered an almost flat, plateau-like surface to be a prerequisite for blockfields and to a lesser extent tors. Similarly, patterned ground in the area was clearly related to changes in slope angle, with nets, polygons and circles occurring on slopes of <3°, and stone stripes occurring in areas where slopes exceeded 5°.

Altitude was seen by Scoates as being the most significant factor in limiting the distribution of features, particularly patterned ground which occurs over a small range and always around 900m in the Carneddau. She concluded that the available evidence did not emphasise any particular correlation of periglacial features with aspect, save for the lack of westerly-facing phenomena. The effect of vegetation was also similarly difficult to assess.

Holocene environmental and vegetation history

With the exception of Woodhead and Hodgson's (1935) preliminary study of selected peats and Thomas' (1972) inventory of diatomaceous deposits, the Carneddau have received surprisingly scant attention in studies of vegetational change. Walker's (1978) study of diatoms and pollen from a sediment profile at Melynllyn provides the only detailed record of such changes in the Carneddau. She obtained pollen and diatoms from two cores from the bottom deposits of Cwm Melynllyn, situated behind the moraine. Also obtained from the profile were materials yielding six radiocarbon dates. The stratigraphy of the sediments at Melynllyn compares closely with a profile described by Evans and Walker (1977) from Llyn Glas, in the Snowdon massif: at both sites the lowest deposit sampled is a clay with a typical post-Allerød (post Devensian late-glacial interstadial) pollen assemblage. The apparent absence of any earlier deposits within these basins was used by Walker (1978) as evidence to support Seddon's (1957) claim that the moraines at Cwm Melynllyn and Cwm Glas were formed during the post-Allerød climatic recession, during the Younger Dryas. This is consistent with dated, pollen and geomorphological evidence from elsewhere in Snowdonia (Ince 1981, 1983; Gray 1982a).

The diatom succession at Melynllyn indicates that in early Holocene times a change from alkaline to approximately neutral conditions took place. Diatoms characteristic of acidic, oligotrophic waters have been well established in the lake from mid Holocene times to the present day (Walker 1978). The pollen data from the site show a fairly typical Holocene vegetation succession for upland North Wales, and permit correlation of deposits with other sites in Snowdonia (Walker 1978).

The Carneddau demonstrate a wide range of glacial and periglacial landforms. The cirques at Cwm Ffynnon Llugwy, Melynllyn and Dulyn are noteworthy both as large-scale erosional forms and for the contrasting depositional features contained within them: Cwm Ffynnon Llugwy displays one of the most extensive and complex suites of Younger Dryas moraines in Wales, and the features at Dulyn and Melynllyn further serve to show the diversity of landforms associated with glacial limits of the Younger Dryas. The features at Cwm Ffynnon Llugwy, in particular, provide a graphic demonstration of recessional phases and limits associated with the wasting of Younger Dryas ice. Organic deposits behind the moraine at Melynllyn have provided confirmatory radiocarbon and pollen evidence for the dating of this last glacial phase in the area. The deposits at Melynllyn also provide an important record of vegetational changes in this part of upland Wales during the Holocene.

The Carneddau are perhaps of the greatest interest for the wide range and fine development of landforms associated with frost-action and former periglacial conditions. Stone polygons developed at Waen-y-Garnedd are the finest features of their kind in Wales. Blockfields, tors, scree slopes, and a variety of patterned ground and related forms are also well developed, providing an unparalleled assemblage in Wales. Their dating, however, is problematical and although many may have formed during the Devensian late-glacial, others, such as stone polygons, are still active. The site provides a complementary range of features to those described in the Rhinog Mountains and at Moelwyn Mawr.

Cwm Ffynnon Llugwy contains one of the most impressive and diverse assemblages of landform features and moraines formed in the Younger Dryas. However, the Carneddau area is most important for a wide range of periglacial landforms unparalleled elsewhere in Wales. Small sorted stone polygons at the site are one of the finest examples in Great Britain. Although many of the periglacial landforms were probably formed

during the Devensian late-glacial, others provide evidence for formation, or at least maintenance, by contemporary processes. The Carneddau therefore provide an outstanding opportunity to demonstrate a wide range of periglacial phenomena, and to study their relationships within a relatively compact area.

Conclusions

Y Carneddau contain a range of glacial and periglacial features without equal elsewhere in Wales. Some of the small-scale periglacial (cold-climate) features are the finest examples in the British Isles and show evidence that they are still forming today. Many of the features were formed between 11,000 and 10,000 years ago during the minor glaciation at the end of the last ice age.

Llyn Peris

Highlights

This is a classic site for the study of small-scale glacial and fluvioglacial erosional features. Glaciated striated pavements hereabouts have been studied since the earliest Victorian workers realised the significance of such phenomena in relation to the action of glacier ice.

Introduction

The shores of Llyn Peris are important for exceptionally fine examples of glaciated bedrock surfaces and small-scale forms of glacial erosion. Although it is some 13,000 years at least since the area was last glaciated, features including glacial striae, friction cracks, sichelwannen and sinuous grooves and channels have been remarkably well preserved from subaerial weathering beneath the lake waters. Glacial striae were first described in the Llanberis Valley by Ramsay (1860, 1881), and the late-glacial and Holocene deposits of the Peris-Padarn area were described by Tinsley and Derbyshire (1976) and Derbyshire (1977). A detailed account of the glacial erosional forms at Llyn Peris was given by Gray (1982b) and similar features in adjacent areas were described by Gray and Lowe (1982). The site was mentioned by Addison (1983) in an account of the classic glacial landforms of Snowdonia, and has also featured in a study of ice movement directions (Gemmell et al. 1986).

Description

The existence of well developed glacial erosional features, including roches moutonnées and glacial striae, has long been known from the Llanberis Pass in Snowdonia. As long ago as 1860, Ramsay described the distribution of striae in the Llanberis Valley and interpreted the former directions of ice movement. Recent construction of the Dinorwic hydro-electric power scheme has afforded a rare opportunity to study unweathered glaciated bedrock. During construction work, the lake levels were lowered both in the upper lake of the storage scheme (Marchlyn Mawr) and in the lower reservoir at Llyn Peris. The small-scale erosional features exposed at these sites have been described by Gray and Lowe (1982) and Gray (1982b).

Llyn Peris and Llyn Padarn occupy an over-deepened basin towards the lower end of the Llanberis glacial trough. There was once one lake but this was divided by an alluvial fan near Pont-y-Bala. At both ends of Llyn Peris, boreholes reveal considerable depths of sediment – lake rhythmites, sands, gravels, organic lake muds, wood debris and peat (Tinsley and Derbyshire 1976; Derbyshire 1977). Cambrian slate and sandstone bedrock, preserving a wide range of glacial erosional features is exposed along the lake margins. Gray's (1982b) description of the site pertains to the low lake levels experienced during construction of the HEP scheme, although substantial areas of glaciated bedrock are still visible even at relatively high lake levels.

Three chief areas of exposed bedrock bear significant evidence for glacial and fluvioglacial erosion processes. The first lies on the north shore of Llyn Peris at the eastern end of the lake (SH599591); the only stretch of the north shore not obscured by slate spoil. The bedrock surface here is heavily abraded and striated. Large, steeply sloping slabs of slate up to 10m high show that ice moved upwards against these obstacles at angles of 5-10°, and abraded lee slopes in this area frequently show a conspicuously stepped appearance as a result of rapid changes in lithological composition. Smoothed cavities on lee slopes can also be seen, and these bear witness to fluvioglacial smoothing in cavities beneath the ice. The unusual feature of a trench following an igneous dyke occurs at this site. The trench, 1-1.5m deep, runs transverse to the valley and the main down-valley trend of the striae. The trench also carries striae parallel to its trend.

The second main glaciated bedrock area, bearing a similar range of features, stretches along the southern shore between SH597589 and SH589594, and a smaller area carrying comparable features occurs on the shores below Dolbadarn Castle (SH588597 to SH586599).

Interpretation

The Llanberis trough was probably last glaciated during the Late Devensian, and a series of radiocarbon dates from deposits at Pont-y-Bala and East Peris (Shotton *et al.* 1975; Tinsley and Derbyshire 1976) dates the thick sediment sequence to the Devensian late-glacial and the Holocene. The basin could not therefore have been glaciated during the Younger Dryas, and the erosional features described by Gray (1982b) from

Llyn Peris were most probably caused by Late Devensian ice.

Gray (1982b) considered that abraded bedrock was the most striking feature of the floor of Llyn Peris, noting that the homogenous fine-grained slate was particularly susceptible to subglacial scratching and polishing. He measured the orientations of striae at a number of locations on flat bedrock surfaces, confirming the expected down-valley trend of ice movement. However, small deviations of movement were also recorded, showing that the ice had changed direction as it moved north-west along the trough. In particular, once the ice had passed the steep confining slopes below Gweithdy (SH593590), it appears to have swung into the bay on the south-west shore as it became less constricted, moving into the wider valley where Llanberis is now situated. Other smaller-scale features influencing striae trends were also noted, including the trench running transverse to the main trend of the striae (with striae in the trench running parallel to the orientation of the trench), and several linear joint-controlled grooves bearing curved striae. These features appear to have controlled locally the streaming of basal ice and debris layers. Differential erosion had occurred as a result of lithological changes and jointing, as well as in response to the local occurrence of iron pyrite crystals which had caused small-scale 'crag and tail' forms (Gray 1982b).

Gray also described irregularly-shaped transverse marks at Llyn Peris, which had given the rock surface at many localities a rough appearance perpendicular to ice movement, probably as the result of bedrock fracture or crushing. Other locations were described where fracturing and plucking had been facilitated by cleavage and jointing in the slate.

The role of meltwater in eroding the bedrock surface was discussed by Gray: many sharp edges had been rounded off, and smoothed 'lee' faces with small shallow bowls were also commonly displayed. Because such features resembled meltwater-produced forms observed in cavities beneath the glacier d'Argentière in the French Alps (Vivian and Bocquet 1973), Gray considered this was also probably the most likely mechanism for widespread smoothing of lee slopes at Llyn Peris.

Other erosional forms including features resembling sichelwannen (Sugden and John 1976, Figure 15.1) and sinuous channels and grooves with striated floors were described by Gray from Llyn Peris. The latter were likened to 'p-forms' studied by Gray (1981) on Mull, which he considered had resulted from meltwater corrasion and/or cavitation, with active ice later moving through the channels to striate them. The processes of till squeezing, the movement of till as a semi-saturated mass under pressure beneath the ice (Gjessing 1965), or direct glacial abrasion (Boulton 1974) were also considered as alternative explanations.

Llyn Peris shows some of the finest glaciated bedrock surfaces in Britain. Examples of abrasion, bedrock fracture, plucking and meltwater erosion are found at the site, including a great diversity of typical small-scale erosional features such as striae and friction cracks. The interest of the site is enhanced by the presence of possible sichelwannen features and sinuous grooves and channels, perhaps formed by subglacial meltwater. Recent studies of the assemblage of features at Llyn Peris have shown that the standard view of glacial bedrock erosion occurring by the twin processes of 'abrasion' and 'plucking' is an over-simplification. From evidence at Llyn Peris, it is clear that bedrock fracture, particularly in highly-cleaved rocks, and meltwater erosion are also important processes. The process of erosion by the squeezing of subglacial till may also have contributed to the formation of some features.

Conclusions

The wide range of small-scale erosional features displayed at Llyn Peris and their remarkable state of preservation, make the site probably the finest of its kind in Britain and of exceptional interest to geomorphologists. The site provides a unique opportunity, in a country that has no present-day glaciers, to study former glacial and fluvioglacial erosion processes and resultant bedrock forms.

Cwm Dwythwch

Highlights

A key site that provides evidence of Late Devensian glaciation prior to the last, Younger Dryas, glacial event; either during a readvance of the dwindling Devensian ice-sheet or as part of a separate glacial pulse.

Introduction

Cwm Dwythwch (SH570580) is a unique site in North Wales with evidence for a possible stadial early in the Devensian late-glacial. It is the most northerly cirque in the Snowdon (Yr Wyddfa) massif and is occupied by a large lake impounded behind an impressive moraine. The moraine is more subdued (rounded and indistinct) in appearance than many of the typically steep-sided Younger Dryas moraines in the region. Pollen analysis from an infilled part of the lake has revealed a late-glacial profile dating back to Pollen Zone I. This is the only moraine in Wales that has been shown, by pollen analysis, to date from the early part of the Devensian late-glacial. The site has been mapped and described by Seddon (1957) and Unwin (1970), and a detailed study of the

pollen biostratigraphy was carried out by Seddon (1962).

Description

Cwm Dwythwch is a massive compound cirque with four subsidiary cirques, and a lake, Llyn Dwythwch, situated at about 280m OD (Seddon 1957). The subsidiary cirques with floors at approximately 450m OD, also contain possible morainic accumulations (Gray 1982a). The main and the subsidiary cirque forms show a strong orientation to the north-east, towards the Llanberis Valley. The compound cirque back wall is cut into the peaks of Moel Eilio (726m), Foel Gron (593m) and Foel Goch (605m). A broad tract of alluvium covered by *Sphagnum-Polytrichum* bog extends from the west side of the lake to the head of the cirque. Boulder strewn areas surround the lake, except on its east side, where the base of the massive terminal moraine impounds the lake (Seddon 1962).

From a borehole core, Seddon (1962) described an 8.4m thick sequence (at SH568580), commencing with a basal layer of stiff blue clay, overlain by the friable grey-buff mud, succeeded by a further clay layer; making up the three-fold sequence that Seddon suggested was typical of late-glacial sites elsewhere in North-West Europe. The upper clay was succeeded by a sequence of wholly organic muds derived from successive phases in the development of aquatic vegetation (Seddon 1962).

Interpretation

Seddon (1962) interpreted the basal blue clay at Cwm Dwythwch as material solifluxed from surrounding slopes during a relatively cold climatic phase. Pollen from this bed shows a dominance of herb vegetation with few trees, with sea buckthorn, juniper and dwarf birch forming a low scrub in the otherwise open swards of herbs. Seddon correlated this assemblage with conditions characteristic of Pollen Zone I of the Late Devensian late-glacial.

The succeeding highly organic muds showed pollen characteristic of climatic improvement in the Allerød (Pollen Zone II). The Cwm Dwythwch pollen shows a marked increase of tree birches at that time, perhaps to a state best described as 'park-tundra' rather than true birch woodland; with herb vegetation still predominant but with a notable increase in meadowsweet *Filipendula*, indicating warmer conditions.

The beginning of Pollen Zone III is marked by a rapid decline of *Betula* pollen and of the ratio of arboreal pollen to non-arboreal pollen. Seddon considered this indicated the onset of less favourable climatic conditions and a tundra environment, with trees perhaps surviving only in the most sheltered locations. The end of this zone is terminated abruptly by almost pollen-barren clastic sediments, reworked by solifluction into the lake. Seddon argued that it was at this time that a recrudescence of glacier ice occurred in many of the cirques in Snowdonia. Pollen in the succeeding sediments shows an amelioration of climate and demonstrates the course of forest development through the Holocene (Seddon 1962).

The interpretation and relative dating of the landforms at Cwm Dwythwch are based entirely on pollen biostratigraphic and geomorphological evidence. No radiocarbon calibration is yet available for the sequence.

Although pollen analysis has revealed a detailed record of Devensian late-glacial and Holocene environmental changes in upland Wales, it is the geomorphological implications of these data that make the site particularly important. The palynological and stratigraphical evidence shows that the vegetation of the Devensian late-glacial first formed in a tundra environment (Pollen Zone I), with arctic-alpines, notably dwarf birch. This is followed by a period of park-tundra associated with warmer conditions in the Allerød. No evidence exists at Cwm Dwythwch in the late-glacial profile for the Bølling oscillation described from some Continental and British sites. A deterioration of climate in Pollen Zone III is clearly marked in the section.

The climatic deterioration associated with Pollen Zone III has been widely documented as a period of limited cirque glacier and perennial snow patch development in parts of upland Britain (c. 11,000-10,000 BP – Younger Dryas), and several cirque moraines in North Wales have been dated, both palynologically and by radiocarbon techniques, to this time (for example, Seddon 1962; Ince 1981, 1983). The full late-glacial succession accumulated at Cwm Dwythwch within the confines of the large outer moraine, and therefore provides evidence for a cirque moraine of pre-Younger Dryas age. A similar age cannot therefore be ruled out at other sites where large 'diffuse' cirque moraines also occur, for example, the outer moraine at Cwm Idwal (Campbell 1985b). Whether such moraines belong to a readvance of cirque ice in Devensian late-glacial Pollen Zone I, or simply to a recessive stage of the main Late Devensian ice-sheet, remains to be determined. The smaller morainic or nivational accumulations within the higher subsidiary cirques at Cwm Dwythwch, in all probability, date from Pollen Zone III, the Younger Dryas (Gray 1982a).

Cwm Dwythwch provides an important pollen biostratigraphic record of Late Devensian late-glacial and Holocene conditions in upland North Wales. The pollen record, which extends back to Pollen Zone I, clearly post-dates deposition of the large 'diffuse' cirque moraine at the site. It therefore shows important evidence to suggest that active glaciers possibly existed earlier in the Devensian late-glacial than the well documented Younger Dryas cirque glaciation at around 11,000-10,000 BP, when the majority of cirque moraines in the region was formed.

Conclusions

Cwm Dwythwch is one of only two sites in Wales which provide evidence for events between the disappearance of the last ice-sheet and the onset of the minor glaciation between 11,000 and 10,000 years ago. It is an important site for research on climatic change.

Clogwynygarreg

Highlights

A key site that provides a rare record of Late Devensian pollen, and thus vegetation changes, with independent radiocarbon dates. These confine precisely the dating of the wastage of the main Devensian ice-sheet and the onset of the last, Younger Dryas, glacial event.

Introduction

Clogwynygarreg (SH560538) is an important palynological site which yields evidence from the Late Devensian late-glacial and the Holocene. The site is one of very few in Wales where a detailed late-glacial pollen sequence has been calibrated with a radiocarbon timescale (Ince 1981).

Description

The site lies west of the main Snowdon (Yr Wyddfa) massif, in the lowlands to the east of the rocky outcrop of Clogwynygarreg, and immediately north of Llyn Dywarchen. It consists of an infilled lake basin covering approximately 4ha and occupies what has been interpreted as a glacial meltwater channel (Ince 1981). The site lies at an altitude of 235m, and is about 2 km outside the Younger Dryas ice limit mapped by Gray (1982a).

The following succession was recorded by Ince (1981) at SH560538 –

8	Peat and organic deposits (too wet to sample with piston corer)
7	Dark brown, wet peaty gyttja
6	Dark brown, coarse clastic gyttja
5	Compact, fine clastic gyttja
4	Compact grey clay with angular slate gravel
3	Compact, fine, clastic, grey-brown mottled gyttja with sporadic small angular stones
2	Dark grey lake mud, coarse sand fraction towards base
1	Compact grey clay with angular slate gravels

Detailed pollen analyses together with counts of deteriorated pollen and spores were carried out by Ince (1981), and four radiocarbon assays were provided for significant levels in the sequence. The results provide the basis for detailed interpretations of vegetational change in the Snowdonian foothills during the Late Devensian late-glacial and early Holocene. Ince (1981) also provided comparable data from a late-glacial to early Holocene sequence at Llyn Goddionduon (SH753583) and at two sites, Llyn Llydaw (SH632543) and Cwm Cywion (SH632604), with early to mid Holocene sequences – see Snowdon and Y Glyderau site reports respectively for details of these last two sites.

Interpretation

Prior to 13,670 ± 280 BP (Birm 884), clays and silts (with occasional small stones) were deposited at Clogwynygarreg as the Late Devensian ice-sheet wasted. Pollen assemblages from the basal clastic deposits show that sedimentation occurred in a sparsely vegetated landscape characterised by areas of unstable ground and perhaps stagnant ice wastage. The Late Devensian late-glacial at Clogwynygarreg was then characterised by a prolonged period of vegetation development commencing with pioneer herbaceous communities and culminating in the establishment of *Juniperus* scrub. During this development, the trend towards soil stability is marked by sedimentation of an increasingly organic character, with pollen spectra indicating changes from a mosaic of pioneer herbaceous communities to a dominantly grassland community. Further diversification of the pollen spectra and the establishment of juniper scrub, reflect a marked climatic improvement in this part of the sequence. Birch was also present at this time, but the evidence for establishment of birch woodland is doubtful (Ince 1981).

The succession of plant communities proved by the pollen record at Clogwynygarreg was taken by Ince to indicate a response to climatic amelioration following disappearance of the Late Devensian ice-sheet. This period, he termed the 'late-glacial interstadial'.

By *c.* 11,020 ± 150 BP (Birm 886), a marked decline in juniper pollen in the succeeding local pollen zone and a change in lithology, commencing with deposition of a stone layer, mark a regression in environmental conditions and vegetational development. This is correlated with the Younger Dryas, when glaciers reoccupied many of the highland cirques of Snowdonia (Gray 1982a). At that time, widespread solifluction and increasingly severe conditions led to the break up of existing plant communities and the proliferation of open-habitat and disturbed ground taxa; and the renewed inwashing of clays and silts containing an increase in degraded pollen grains (Ince 1981)

The vegetation of the Younger Dryas and early Holocene transition at Clogwynygarreg is marked by a change in lithology from clastic to organic sediment, accompanied by a sudden rise in *Juniperus* pollen. These changes mark the transition from periglacial conditions to the milder

climate of the early Holocene. An early radiocarbon date of 10,760 ± 140 BP (Birm 887) at this lithological transition is believed to be too old because of hardwater error (Ince 1981).

Following development of an open-grassland community during the period of transition, tree birches became established, and extensive woodland developed around the site. A fall in juniper pollen, which has been interpreted as marking its shading out by larger trees such as birch, was followed by a sudden expansion of *Corylus* and *Myrica* pollen, which denotes the arrival and dispersal of hazel in the local woodlands. These taxa also displaced birch. Continued diversification of the woodland taxa marks progressive vegetational development through the Holocene (Ince 1981).

Subsequent to this stage of woodland development, Ince noted a change in the arboreal and non-arboreal pollen ratio, with an increase in degraded pollen grains showing changes in the vegetation resulting from disturbance or a change in hydrological conditions in the lake basin. At this time, *Ulmus* and *Betula* pollen declined and Ince speculated that this may have been caused by local human activity. The age of these sediments, however, is unknown and it is not possible to correlate the elm decline with Neolithic activities discussed widely elsewhere. Woodland recovery, however, was rapid with *Pinus* and *Quercus* becoming important elements. Continued changes in the woodland community are also reflected by the local arrival of *Alnus* and the development of damp woodland in which *Alnus, Corylus* and *Betula* formed the dominant components (Ince 1981).

Clogwynygarreg provides an important radiocarbon calibrated pollen record of late-glacial and early Holocene environmental changes in the Snowdonian foothills. Organic sedimentation began after about 13,670 BP, a date which provides a minimum age for wastage of Late Devensian ice in the area. The pollen record shows a gradual improvement in thermal and environmental conditions associated with the 'late-glacial interstadial'.

A later decline, particularly in *Juniperus* pollen, is thought to mark deteriorating conditions culminating in the Younger Dryas. During this period, small glaciers again occupied cirques in the Snowdon massif, and Clogwynygarreg lay in the periglacial zone. A change to organic sedimentation and a rapid expansion of *Juniperus* pollen marks the transition from this cold stadial period to milder environmental conditions in the early Holocene. The site provides a contrasting record to that of nearby upland cirques at Llyn Llydaw and Cwm Cywion, and thereby helps to place limits on the age of the final cirque glaciation of North Wales. Clogwynygarreg shows no evidence of the Bølling 'oscillation' which has been recorded at some Welsh sites in the early part of the late-glacial sections (for instance, Cors Geuallt and Nant Ffrancon).

The radiocarbon dated pollen sequence at Clogwynygarreg is one of the most extensive and detailed in Wales, and it provides important evidence for changing Late Devensian late-glacial and Holocene environmental conditions in North Wales. The site yielded radiocarbon dates which provide a minimum age for the wastage of the Late Devensian ice-sheet and for the onset of cold conditions in the Younger Dryas. Together with adjacent sites in the uplands which provide radiocarbon dates for the cessation of cold conditions in the Younger Dryas, Clogwynygarreg helps to constrain the duration and timing of the final cirque glaciation of North Wales.

Conclusions

The Clogwynygarreg site is important because it shows a sequence of climatic changes over the last 14,000 years which have been dated by radiocarbon. It is an important site in a network of complementary ones throughout the British Isles and Europe which demonstrate vegetation and climatic change.

Cors Geuallt

Highlights

A unique site showing controversial evidence of climatic fluctuations during the early Devensian late-glacial, a warmer interstadial oscillation, the Bølling Interstadial, during the otherwise cold Older Dryas.

Introduction

Cors Geuallt is an important pollen site recording detailed vegetational changes in North Wales during the Devensian late-glacial and Holocene. It

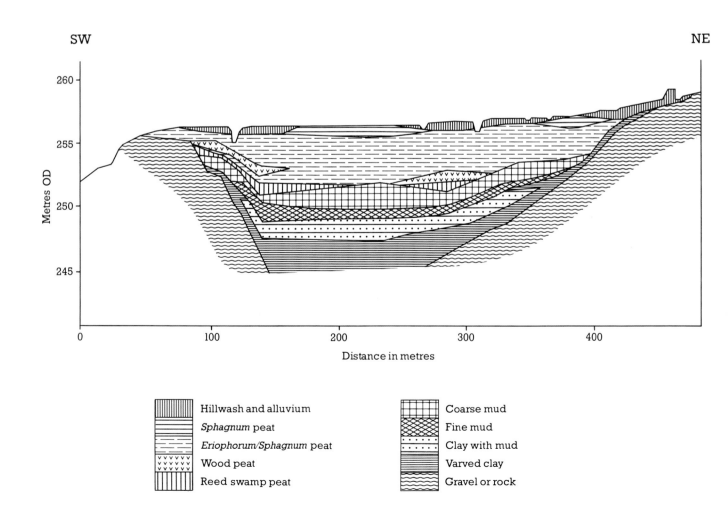

Figure 39 Devensian late-glacial and Holocene sequence at Cors Geuallt (after Crabtree 1972)

is one of a few sites in Britain that provide possible evidence for a pre-Allerød climatic oscillation during the Late Devensian, possibly equivalent to the Bølling Interstadial. Cors Geuallt is also the only site in Wales where a detailed record of diatoms extending back into the late-glacial has been studied. Detailed accounts of the pollen biostratigraphy and diatoms at the site have been provided by Crabtree (1969, 1970, 1972). The possible record of the Bølling Interstadial has also been discussed by Moore (1975b) and Ince (1981). Thomas (1972) referred to the site in a survey of diatomaceous deposits in Snowdonia.

Description

Cors Geuallt (SH734596) lies north-east of Capel Curig, in the foothills of the Carneddau. With dimensions of about 400m by 250m and lying at a height of some 255m OD, this former lake basin is now a mire. It has an irregular rocky floor generally not deeper than 4m, although in the central southern area, through which Nant-y-Geuallt flows, there is a deeper region (about 275m by 110m) which could not be bottomed with a 7.6m auger (Thomas 1972). Here, the mire is floating on a layer of water, and augering in this deeper area suggests the presence of a saucer-like deposit of mud, up to 2m thick, over an area of some 27,000 m^2 (Thomas 1972). The site lies well outside the ice limits of the last cirque glaciation in Snowdonia (Seddon 1957; Gray 1982a).

Levelling and boring was carried out at Cors Geuallt by Crabtree (1970, 1972) to determine the stratigraphy of the superficial deposits within the basin. The generalised sequence consists of –

6	Hillwash and alluvium
5	Reed swamp, wood, *Eriophorum* and *Sphagnum* peats
4	Coarse mud
3	Fine mud
2	Coarse mud and clay
1	Varved clays

The distribution and relative thicknesses of the beds are shown in Figure 39.

Two cores, referred to as the 1964 and 1969 cores, were taken by Crabtree (1969, 1970, 1972). These were analysed for their chemical, diatom and pollen characteristics. Crabtree (1970, 1972) zoned the pollen spectra in the standard manner (Pollen Zones I –VIII) but used additional local pollen sub-zones where appropriate. Detailed pollen diagrams for the two cores were presented, although these have no radiocarbon calibration.

Interpretation

Based on the relative frequency of *Betula* and herbaceous pollen types in the 1964 core, Crabtree (1970) assigned the lower pollen assemblages to the Late Devensian late-glacial, and the upper ones to the Holocene. Values of juniper pollen peak at the end of Pollen Zone II and again at the end of Pollen Zone III. Importantly, beneath sediments with a Pollen Zone II assemblage, Crabtree recorded a single organic band within the clastic, varved basal clays (bed 1). This band contained both rich pollen and diatom assemblages, which were tentatively ascribed to Pollen Zone Ib, with the implication that the bed had formed during the 'warm' Bølling Interstadial described from sites elsewhere in North-West Europe.

Pollen collected from the 1969 core made it possible to recognise a similar full Devensian late-glacial sequence, with a clearly defined Pollen Zone II flora (Allerød) and Pollen Zone I flora (pre-Allerød). Crabtree (1970) suggested that the pollen diagram constructed from work on the 1969 core showed the salient features proved in Devensian late-glacial sequences elsewhere in upland Britain. He noted that there was no correlative of the Pollen Zone Ib that had been identified in the other core. The core indicated a normal progression of vegetation without any such indication of a climatic oscillation. Crabtree (1972) suggested that the earlier identified Ib pollen assemblages might have been produced from a contaminated sample, although at the time there was every indication that the thin organic band, with its well developed pollen and diatom flora, was *in situ*.

With the pollen diagram constructed from work on the 1969 core largely in mind, Crabtree charted the following sequence of vegetational and environmental changes from the deposits at Cors Geuallt. First, the varved clays (bed 1) were deposited following wastage of the Late Devensian ice-sheet. The pollen spectra indicate development of open-grassland with many herb taxa, giving the overall impression of a restricted pioneer flora with a general absence of thermophilous taxa. Towards the end of this period, a gradual rise in *Juniperus* pollen occurs, indicating that juniper may have occupied areas with snow patches or formed an incomplete shrub cover.

The second main pollen zone (Pollen Zone II) was correlated by Crabtree with the Allerød, widely recognised in Britain and elsewhere in North-West Europe by a sequence of a juniper pollen maximum followed by a rise in birch, including tree birches. At this time, there is also an increase in thermophilous herb pollen types, such as *Filipendula,* and a decrease in shade intolerant taxa. The pollen spectra generally indicate an improvement over the preceding period: and this phase can be correlated with the phase described by Ince (1981) at nearby Clogwynygarreg as the 'late-glacial interstadial'.

Towards the end of Pollen Zone II at Cors Geuallt, *Betula* and *Filipendula* percentages fall markedly and a corresponding increase in taxa characteristic of open and disturbed ground habitats is also noted. These changes are accompanied by the change from organic sedimentation to deposition of clays. Both pollen and sedimentary evidence point to a period of intense cold with soil instability during Pollen Zone III, which may be correlated with the recrudescence of glacier ice in many of the upland cirques (Ince 1981; Gray 1982a). Towards the end of this event, the rapid decline in open and disturbed ground taxa suggests a very rapid change to the milder conditions of the Holocene (Crabtree 1972). However, many herb taxa persist into the early Holocene despite the increase in *Betula* pollen, and it is only with the rise of *Corylus*, in Pollen Zone V, that many of these heliophytic taxa disappear from the record.

The remaining record provides a clear picture of the infilling of the lake basin at Cors Geuallt. The pollen evidence shows a large amount of wood peat dating to the sub-Boreal and suggests that upland forest destruction began at this time. By the beginning of the sub-Atlantic, much of the uplands at this altitude had developed blanket or hill peat (Crabtree 1970).

Diatom counts were also made from samples taken from the Devensian late-glacial and Holocene deposits at Cors Geuallt, with samples chosen to cover the pollen zones already identified (Crabtree 1969, 1970). Peak diatom frequencies occurred in Pollen Zones II-III and in the Holocene. The organic band within the basal clays in the 1964 core also contained a well developed diatom flora (Crabtree 1970). The sequence shows rapidly changing diatom communities, both in terms of total numbers and in floral composition, during the late-glacial. The early Holocene is characterised by a period of *Fragilaria* dominance, and of peak diatom productivity. This peak was accompanied by a decline in base tolerant species, leading to a final stage where acid tolerant species dominate, but during which there was an overall decline in diatom numbers.

Cors Geuallt provides a pollen record of Late Devensian late-glacial and Holocene vegetational changes in North Wales. The site has also yielded a record of diatom floras extending back into late-glacial time, and, in this respect, the site is unique in Wales. The controversial organic band described from the early part of the late-glacial sequence may provide important evidence for a climatic oscillation, perhaps equivalent to the Bølling Interstadial. Indeed, Burrows (1974, 1975) published radiocarbon and fossil plant evidence from a nearby late-glacial site in the Nant Ffrancon Valley, which he also claimed indicated a climatic oscillation at this time. Moore (1975b) and Ince (1981), however, believe these data to be equivocal and see no evidence for a Bølling Interstadial in these profiles. Cors Geuallt, therefore, may prove to be an important site for establishing a framework for early Late Devensian late-glacial events in Britain, and for the presence of an interstadial before the Allerød.

The sequence of Late Devensian late-glacial and Holocene deposits at Cors Geuallt preserves important pollen and diatom assemblages that record changing environmental conditions in upland North Wales. The site is important in establishing regional variations in Devensian late-glacial conditions, and in particular, demonstrates controversial evidence for a climatic oscillation in the early late-glacial, that has been correlated with the Bølling Interstadial. The pollen record therefore contrasts with other sites in Wales which show evidence for only one warm episode in late-glacial times.

Conclusions

Cors Geuallt is important because not only does it contain evidence for climatic change from pollen but also from diatom fossils in sediments dating from the end of the last ice age. As such it has unique qualities particularly because the evidence suggests a climatic variation (warming) not generally detected elsewhere in the Welsh upland.

Y Llethr

Highlights

A unique site showing periglacial features which are evidence of the 16th to 18th Century 'Little Ice Age'.

Introduction

Y Llethr is a unique geomorphological site in the Rhinog Mountains which exhibits an unusual range of periglacial landforms, some of which may be associated with the climatic deterioration of the 'Little Ice Age', *c.* 1550-1750 AD (Lamb 1967). Detailed accounts of the features at the site have been provided by Goodier and Ball (1969) and Ball and Goodier (1970).

Description

The site occurs on the north-facing slopes of Y Llethr (SH659261) between 600m and 754m OD, and the features, which include striped ground, terraced slopes, gliding blocks and stone-banked lobes, cover a total area of some 25ha. The generally smooth relief of the summit and flanks of Y Llethr is controlled by the underlying shales of Cambrian age. There is very little drift in the immediate area.

The partially-sorted stripes are of a small-scale pattern and occur on slopes between 15° and 30°; they comprise a series of prominent vegetated ridges and troughs orientated perpendicular to the local contours, with a repeat distance of *c.* 0.7-1.0m and an amplitude of *c.* 0.1-0.2 m (Goodier and Ball 1969). On the steeper slopes below, the stripes merge with well developed terracettes. Fine examples of 'gliding blocks' also occur, with frontal soil 'bow-waves' and pronounced upslope furrows, indicating movements of up to 13m. The most significant feature of the site, however, is an old stone wall built before 1815 (and possibly Mediaeval in age), which has become disrupted into a series of 'stone-banked lobes' by gelifluction processes (Goodier and Ball 1969).

Interpretation

Goodier and Ball considered that the displaced wall was important for assessing the period of formation for the features seen at Y Llethr. This wall runs along the northern slopes of the site at altitudes between 600m and 700m OD. It is a dry-stone wall and its independence from the later nineteenth century boundary system in the area, and its comparative state of collapse, indicate that it is of great age: local records indicate a probable Mediaeval age. The wall is down-thrown along its entire length, and its component boulders, which range in size from 30-50cm, have been rearranged differentially, so that stones occur in a lobate pattern towards the steeper slopes. An estimated maximum movement of some 9m downslope is indicated by the lobes; although, where the wall has become totally disrupted, downslope movement may have been as much as 30-40m (Goodier and Ball 1969).

Goodier and Ball considered that gelifluction and cryoturbation had played an important role in forming the stone lobes, and it seems extremely likely that frost-action was also involved in the formation of the adjacent stripes. There is little evidence to suggest that the features at Y Llethr are the result of contemporary frost-action: both the fossil stripes and gliding blocks appear stable at the present time and the stones in the wall show no signs of contemporary movement. Historical records confirm the presence of 'old' walls in the area during construction of newer walls in the nineteenth century, and there is no evidence that these later walls have in any way been disturbed by solifluction. This suggested to Goodier and Ball that the old wall had been disrupted by a period of gelifluction sometime between Mediaeval and nineteenth century times.

Both Manley (1964) and Lamb (1967) have shown that a period of extreme cold, the coldest in Britain in historic times, occurred between c. 1550 and 1750 AD - a period referred to by Lamb as the 'Little Ice Age'. It has been demonstrated that land and sea-ice in Britain during that period was at its most extensive since the end of the Younger Dryas at around 10,000 BP. Goodier and Ball (1969) considered that the historically dated evidence showed that periglacial conditions had probably formed all the Y Llethr features, and noted that stripes of a similar scale elsewhere in North Wales at Moelwyn Mawr, Yr Aran (Snowdon) and Y Garn (Y Glyderau) may also have been formed during the same 'Little Ice Age'.

Y Llethr provides the only documented occurrence of periglacial landforms in Wales that date from the 'Little Ice Age', and the site therefore provides contrasting evidence to that at nearby Rhinog Fawr, where large-scale stone stripes have been ascribed to the end of the Late Devensian, prior to the Younger Dryas. The features at Y Llethr also contrast with contemporary cold-climate landforms described from the Carneddau (Tallis and Kershaw 1959) and Moelwyn Mawr (Taylor 1975). These sites are important for demonstrating considerable diversity in the ages of periglacial landforms in the uplands of North Wales. In particular, the stone-banked lobes formed by collapse of the Mediaeval wall, may have important implications for interpreting small-scale periglacial features of unknown age found elsewhere. Although Goodier and Ball (1969) argued a strong case for ascribing the stone-banked lobes to the 'Little Ice Age', there is no clear evidence which dates the other periglacial features at the site to the same period.

Y Llethr is important for exhibiting an unusual range of periglacial landforms, including partially-sorted stone stripes, terracettes, 'gliding' (ploughing) blocks with prominent bow waves and furrows, and a stone wall deformed by gelifluction. Documentary records provide evidence to suggest that this wall is Mediaeval in age and that its collapse probably occurred in the climatic deterioration of the 'Little Ice Age' between c. 1550-1750 AD. This is the only known occurrence of periglacial activity in Wales from this period.

Conclusions

Y Llethr is a site of outstanding importance because it contains evidence for cold-climate processes during the 'Little Ice Age'. One of the most interesting features is the disturbance of a Mediaeval wall by periglacial slope processes. This site may well be the standard for similar, but as yet undiscovered, examples elsewhere in Britain.

Rhinog Fawr

Highlights

A key locality showing the largest stone stripes in Britain, evidence of periglacial activity on a large-scale during the Late Pleistocene.

Introduction

Rhinog Fawr (SH643286) is an important geomorphological site for a series of well developed large-scale stone stripes. The stripes are thought to be well preserved relics of Late Pleistocene periglacial conditions, and they occur at a larger-scale than sorted stone stripes described elsewhere in Britain. They were first noted by Ball and Goodier (1968), and their age and geomorphological significance was discussed by Foster (1970a). The site has also been mentioned in studies by Foster (1968), Goodier and Ball (1969), Ball and Goodier (1970), Whittow and Ball (1970) and Allen and Jackson (1985).

Description

Rhinog Fawr, in the Harlech Dome, consists of outcrops of Lower Cambrian Rhinog Grit (Matley and Wilson 1946) which reach 720m OD. The stripes occur on the south-west facing slopes at an altitude of 425-490m OD, lying at the margins of a drift-filled basin near the head of Cwm Nantcol. The stripes are visible over an area of about 10ha, occurring on slopes between 12° and 18° (Ball and Goodier 1968). There are two main elements in the stripe morphology –1) exposed stripes composed of sandstone and conglomerate (Rhinog Grit) boulders of a general size range between 0.60m and 1.50m, and a repeat distance between crests of 5-8m, 2) intervening vegetated zones composed largely of small shrubs dominated by *Calluna vulgaris* (L.) Hull. A trench across a typical pattern showed that the sub-surface boulder zone, was wider than that exposed on the surface, and that in the centre of the vegetated zone, fine earth was present to a depth of about 1m. At about 1.5m from the centre of the vegetated/fine earth zone, an area of large boulders occurred with a fine earth matrix, and in turn this was succeeded at a further 0.75m distance towards the exposed boulder stripe, by a change of matrix from fine earth to a non-stratified peaty humus. This zone extends for a further metre until the unvegetated, matrix-less stripe is reached. Dip and orientation measurements showed that only boulders in the central, unvegetated part of the stripes had a strongly preferred fabric, with steep dips and a marked downslope orientation between 213° and 252° – coincident with the direction of the ground slope at about 218° (Ball and Goodier 1968).

Interpretation

It is generally held that the processes of sorting by freeze and thaw coupled with solifluction movement on gentle or moderate slopes, can produce stone stripes (Ball and Goodier 1968; Washburn 1979). Patterned ground in Britain has been recorded from a number of localities, and it has been interpreted either as a relic of Pleistocene periglacial conditions or as the result of contemporary formation. Sorted stripes of *c*.2m pattern width, for example, were recorded by Galloway (1961) at 950m on Ben Wyvis, Scotland, and smaller contemporary stripe patterns of less than 1m repeat width have been described from Tinto Hill, Lanarkshire by Miller *et al.* (1954). In Wales the occurrence of small active polygons at 940m in the Carneddau (Snowdonia) was noted by Pearsall (1950) and Tallis and Kershaw (1959), and larger-scale, fossil sorted stone stripes (repeat width up to 6m) were described from the Stiperstones in Shropshire by Goudie and Piggott (1981). The features described by Ball and Goodier (1968) at Rhinog Fawr, however, are of a larger-scale than any of those previously reported in upland Britain, although similar scale features have been described in the Arctic (Sharp 1942) and in the Appalachians (Rapp 1967).

Ball and Goodier (1968) interpreted the Rhinog Fawr examples as 'fossil' features for the following reasons –1) the present climate of the area is too temperate to allow contemporary formation of the features at such altitudes, 2) the central vegetated zones are developed over mature podzols, 3) the exposed boulders possess weathered rinds and are covered by lichens, and finally, 4) nineteenth century walls beneath which the features pass are undisturbed. Ball and Goodier, however, suggested that a lack of detailed knowledge of the glacial history of the area prevented precise dating of the features. Although it has been shown that periglacial processes were important in the region during the Devensian late-glacial, especially during the Younger Dryas (for example, Seddon 1962; Ball 1966; Ince 1981; Gray 1982a), Ball and Goodier thought that the location, low altitude and large-scale of the Rhinog Fawr stripes indicated that they were formed at an earlier stage of ice retreat from the region. They further suggested that the drift cover in the higher areas of the Rhinog Mountains had been largely removed, probably by intense solifluction following glaciation, and that preservation of the stripes was due to an unusual combination of circumstances: the aspect of the south-facing hollow was conducive to producing numerous freeze-thaw cycles and the drift contained a suitable size range of frost-resistant boulders to allow sorting. They noted that indistinct patterning was present beneath the entire drift-filled basin, suggesting that the stripes were covered by peat and colluvium. They concluded that most of the Rhinog site had been similarly covered for much of the Holocene, with exhumation of the boulder stripes only occurring subsequent to woodland clearance, grazing and burning in the area. A series of post-Neolithic vegetation changes in the western Rhinogau has been confirmed by pollen analyses made by Walker and Taylor (1976).

Foster (1970a) suggested that the large, sorted stone stripes were formed during periglacial conditions after the last major Late Devensian glaciation of the area, probably during the readvance of ice that formed the Bryncir-Clynnog moraine in northern Llŷn. This readvance has been radiocarbon dated at sometime after 16,830 +970 - 860 BP (Foster 1968), although doubt has been expressed concerning the validity of this particular date (Simpkins 1968; Bowen 1974). Indeed, there is no firm evidence to confirm the association between this readvance of the ice and the formation of the Rhinog Fawr stripes, and a later Devensian, Younger Dryas age is equally, if not more, likely.

The sorted stone stripes at Rhinog Fawr are some of the finest in Wales, and are larger-scale examples than those elsewhere in Britain. Although the scale of the features makes them unique in Britain, they cannot be dated exactly. The features, however, are an important record of Late Devensian periglacial conditions and the site contrasts with those at Moelwyn Mawr and Y Carneddau, where there are periglacial landforms associated with contemporary processes of formation. In particular, the Rhinog Fawr examples contrast to the largely unsorted, vegetated and much smaller-scale stripes that are found elsewhere in Wales (for instance, Y Garn and Y Llethr).

Conclusions

Rhinog Fawr displays a series of well developed stone stripes. They are notable both as an uncommon landform and because their scale is greater than comparable features elsewhere in Britain. The age of the stripes is not known although they are believed to have formed during a periglacial phase in the last ice age, by sorting processes under exceptionally cold conditions.

Moelwyn Mawr

Highlights

Here are associated a probable Devensian late-glacial rock glacier and periglacial patterned ground. The latter is regarded as being still active.

Introduction

There are two controversial landforms at Moelwyn Mawr (SH660450). At Cwm Croesor a series of transverse boulder ridges and debris spreads have been interpreted as a fossil 'rock glacier'. Nearby, on the north-east flanks of Moelwyn Mawr, a series of well developed, apparently unsorted vegetated stripes occurs; some of the finest examples of their kind in Wales. The stripes have been studied by Taylor (1975), and preliminary studies of the fossil rock glacier were made by Lowe and Rose (*in* Gray *et al.* 1981)

Description

Patterned ground in the form of small-scale vegetated stripes occurs between 550m and 720m on Moelwyn Mawr (SH662452). The stripes occur on slopes between 15° and 30° and they cover an area of about 20ha. They overlie parent material of Ordovician Croesor Slate (Fearnsides and Davies 1944; Beavon 1963; Taylor 1975). The surface vegetation is a grassland community with a scattering of some heather. The patterned ground consists of a series of ridges and furrows, the corrugations having a wavelength of *c.* 0.8m and an amplitude of 0.2m. The stripes are completely vegetated, and there is little differentiation in vegetation type between the ridges and furrows. Some lineation downslope of large unvegetated stones was noted by Taylor (1975).

A feature interpreted as a fossil rock glacier has been described by Lowe and Rose (Gray *et al.* 1981) on the north face of Moelwyn Mawr (SH656453). The feature comprises a series of transverse boulder ridges with a steep scarp front

and areas of pitted boulder strewn terrain. Well developed lateral ridges occur at the margins of the transverse ridges. The whole rock and morainic debris complex extends for about 300-400m NNW into Cwm Croesor from a small north-facing cirque-like feature. A shallow depression separates the rock accumulation from the head wall (Gray *et al.* 1981).

Interpretation

Patterned ground

Patterned ground was first described on the flanks of Moelwyn Mawr by Goodier and Ball (1969) and Ball and Goodier (1970). They noted that the stripes were on a similar scale to those found in the Rhinog Mountains at Y Llethr and at several other localities in Snowdonia. No dating or interpretation of the features were given, but it was suggested that the features were active, and were maintained by seasonal needle-ice (pipkrake) formation (Ball and Goodier 1970).

The stripes on Moelwyn Mawr were studied in greater detail by Taylor (1975). He described the vegetation and morphology of the features and constructed a map of a sample area of the stripes. Both mechanical and structural analyses of the soil were undertaken which showed particle sorting within the stripe pattern, but only within an extremely narrow size fraction (Taylor 1975). The high water content and low structural strength of the ridges was taken as evidence that they were probably maintained by active contemporary frost-assisted processes. He considered that in the absence of such processes, the ridges would probably have collapsed in response to heavy grazing and subaerial compaction. Taylor showed that although the stripes appeared superficially unsorted, mechanical analysis had proved there to be some sorting; and it seemed likely that wherever patterned ground occurs some sorting had taken place, even if this is not reflected in preferential growth of vegetation.
Together with sorted polygons in the Carneddau and similar scale vegetated stripes elsewhere in North Wales (Y Garn and Y Llethr), the stripes at Moelwyn Mawr provide evidence for formation, or at least maintenance, by contemporary frost-assisted processes. These features provide contrasting evidence to the larger-scale stripes at Rhinog Fawr and the Stiperstones which are believed to be fossil periglacial features.

Fossil rock glacier

Preliminary observations of this feature were made by Lowe and Rose – see Gray *et al.* (1981). The debris tongue extends into the Croesor Valley, well outside the confines of the cirque, and it appears to be flanked by distinctive lateral accumulations of postulated morainic material. This is the only documented occurrence of a fossil rock glacier in Wales, and little is known about its precise age and origin.

A possible analogue is the tongue-shaped postulated rock glacier described at Beinn Alligin, on the north side of Loch Torridon in Scotland (Sissons 1975, 1976). This is the largest such feature in Scotland, for which a variety of modes of formation has been suggested. Sissons (1975) considered that the feature had probably formed towards the end of the Loch Lomond Stadial (Younger Dryas) when a small decaying glacier was submerged by rockslide debris, which was subsequently reactivated as a rock glacier. In contrast, Whalley (1976) suggested that the feature was simply a rockslide. Further work at Moelwyn Mawr could provide a variety of hypotheses to explain the formation of the feature. At present it could be postulated that the so-called rock glacier was formed by unusually heavy rockfalls that submerged a small cirque glacier of Younger Dryas age; detailed pollen analytical and geomorphological studies elsewhere in Snowdonia have shown that this period was significant for widespread glacier growth within the region's cirques. As a result, numerous moraines and boulder limits of an extremely varied nature were developed, and it might be that specific local geomorphological and geological controls led to development of a rock glacier at Moelwyn Mawr.

Conclusions

The fossil rock glacier at Moelwyn Mawr is important as the only such feature so far described from Wales. As yet, its age and mode of formation are indeterminate. The well developed vegetated stripes enhance the interest of the site. They are some of the finest examples in Wales and provide important evidence for formation, or at least maintenance, by contemporary frost-assisted processes. These features may provide important evidence about climatic change and processes in upland regions.

Caerwys and Ddol

Highlights

One of the thickest and most complex tufa deposits in Britain occurs here. These limestones and their contained fossils record a history of sedimentary, hydrological and climatic change through the latest Devensian and the Holocene.

Introduction

Caerwys and Ddol provide some of the finest tufa deposits in Britain. The site contains buried soils and an exceptional fossil record (molluscs, leaf-beds and vertebrate faunas) recording environmental changes in the late-glacial and Holocene. The tufa at Ddol incorporates fossil groups including beetles and plant macrofossils not represented at Caerwys. The Wheeler Valley tufas were first described by Maw (1866) and some additional work was carried out by Hughes (1885) and Strahan (1890). Jackson (1922) provided a comprehensive list of molluscs from the site. Since then, Wedd and King (1924), McMillan (1947), Millott (1951) and Bathurst (1956) have all added data on the tufa, its flora and fauna. Detailed accounts of the tufas were given by Preece (1978), Preece et al. (1982), McMillan and Zeissler (1985) and Pedley (1987).

Description

The tufas at Caerwys (SJ129719) and Ddol (SJ142714) in the Wheeler Valley are the most extensive in Britain, occupying an estimated 80ha (Maw 1866). They occur in two small tributary valleys that enter the Wheeler Valley from the north. The tufa deposits contain leaf, twig, moss, liverwort and cyanobacterial tufas (Pedley 1987) and they overlie red sands and gravels – probably Late Devensian fluvioglacial deposits (Brown and Cooke 1977).

The Caerwys deposit extends downslope into the Wheeler Valley as a delta-shaped fan (Pedley 1987). The tufa is well exposed in both current and abandoned quarry sections. In the main quarried deposit, the tufa reaches a maximum depth of about 12m (Pedley 1987). In the centre of the quarry, a basal dark grey peat passes up into a transition zone of organic-rich carbonates overlain by reworked tufa (Pedley 1987). Away from the axis of the valley, however, the succession is more complex; the peat is absent and the tufa is interdigitated with red sands and gravels. This is well illustrated in the old disused quarry (SJ129717) where only a thin tufa layer is interbedded with substantial thicknesses of red sand. For the most part, the Caerwys succession can be generalised as follows (Preece 1978; Preece et al. 1982) –

6	Modern soil
5	Hillwash sediments
4	Main tufa deposit, devoid of organic material
3	Tufa with peat and soil horizons
2	Sandy tufa with two thin soil horizons
1	Fluvioglacial sands

However, it must be stressed that the sequence is highly variable both laterally and vertically. The distinction between each bed is not sharp, with beds grading imperceptibly into one another. The beds are frequently lenticular and sometimes interleaved. This complexity led Pedley (1987) to distinguish a number of lithological types, rather than to draw a stratigraphical sequence. He recognised five principal lithologies at Caerwys –

1	Tufa build-ups or encrustations on reeds, grass, mosses (phytoherms)
2	Oncoids (accretionary carbonate bodies, often oblate spheroids associated with pond sediments and frequently found in basal,

fluvial channel fills)

3   Wackestones and lime mudstones (often reworked deposits believed to have accumulated in relatively shallow ponds between raised tufa build-ups)

4   Subaerial slopewash

5   Palaeosols

The Ddol tufas (SJ142714) are less extensive and less well exposed; the formerly extensive quarry exposures are now overgrown, and the tufa is less than 6m thick (Pedley 1987). Small sections, however, are visible along Afon Pant-gwyn and in small ditch exposures near the old workings at Felin-gonglog. The deposits at Ddol are richer in organic horizons than those at Caerwys (Preece *et. al.* 1982), and consist largely of brown organic tufaceous silts alternating with white nodular tufa, and beds intermediate in character and composition between these two.

Interpretation

The Wheeler Valley tufas were first examined by Maw (1866) who established the distribution and broad sequence of deposits. He noted the impressions of marsh plants in the tufa and recorded 19 species of land snail. He considered that the tufa was deposited by carbonate-rich streams emanating from the Carboniferous Limestone to the north. Brief accounts of the deposits were also given by Hughes (1885) and Strahan (1890). Strahan commented that the land snail fauna appeared to be entirely modern.

Jackson (1922) recorded 43 species of non-marine mollusc at Caerwys. A variety of other finds, including the tusks of wild boar, ox molars, horse and human remains was noted (Jackson 1922), although their precise stratigraphical context is unknown. Jackson considered the tufas to be Holocene in age, and he emphasised the similarities of the deposits with those of Neolithic age at Blashenwell, Dorset. The human remains recovered by Jackson (1922) have since been radiocarbon dated (Barker *et al.* 1971). A date of 2,100 ± 140 BP (BM-255) confirms that the burial was recent and intrusive. The tufas of the Wheeler Valley were also mentioned briefly by Wedd and King (1924) and by McMillan (1947) and Millott (1951).

A preliminary study showed pollen from lime, alder, oak, pine and hazel to be present in one of the peat beds at Caerwys (Bathurst 1956). He concluded that such an assemblage of trees was not present in the British flora until early Pollen Zone VI (Holocene) (Godwin 1941). He also described the numerous tree leaf impressions in the tufa. These included hazel, willow, elm, oak, poplar, ivy and beech; the latter, he suggested, did not enter the British flora until the Holocene climatic optimum (Pollen Zone VII/early Neolithic times).

McMillan and Zeissler (1985) analysed the land snail fauna from the Caerwys tufa, recording a total of 54 species. Their study classified the molluscan assemblage in terms of environmental preferences (there were 22 woodland species, 11 catholic, 4 characteristic of short-turf grassland, 8 marsh species and 9 freshwater), and showed that most of the assemblage was therefore terrestrial with many obligatory marsh dwellers and species preferring marshy habitats. The snail fauna was used to demonstrate that freshwater habitats in the succession were restricted to only small bodies of water (McMillan and Zeissler 1985).

Recent investigations have attempted to interpret a sequence of palaeoenvironmental events and conditions from the molluscan evidence (Preece 1978; Preece *et al.* 1982) and the sedimentary evidence (Pedley 1987).

Preece (1978) and Preece *et al.* (1982) emphasised the difficulties of relating particular molluscan assemblages to individual beds within the highly complex and laterally and vertically changeable sequences at Caerwys and Ddol. However, detailed analysis of molluscs sampled from the beds at both sites allowed a number of molluscan assemblages to be recognised and the tufa to be zoned. The definition of the biozones was based principally on molluscan evidence from Holywell Combe, Kent (Kerney *et al.* 1980; Preece *et al.* 1982), where six molluscan biozones were recognised from the Holocene sequence. These principal zones were also recognised at Caerwys and Ddol, and although they cannot be related to specific beds, and traced throughout the quarries, the zones A, B and C broadly correspond with bed 3 at Caerwys, zone D with bed 4, and zones E and F with beds 5 and 6, respectively.

At Caerwys, molluscan zone A is dominated by terrestrial species. There is also an open-ground fauna, and a few species suggesting bare soil conditions. The assemblage indicates improving conditions in the early Holocene, following the cold conditions of the Younger Dryas. A radiocarbon date of 9,780 ± 200 (Q-2343), from organic material associated with a molluscan zone A type fauna at Ddol, supports the ascription of this molluscan assemblage to the early Holocene, and allows its correlation with Pollen Zone IV (Preece *et al.* 1982).

Molluscan zone B is characterised by a woodland fauna, demonstrating the development of woodland in the area. It is correlated with Pollen Zone V and the early part of Pollen Zone VI (Preece *et al.* 1982). Molluscan zone C also has a woodland assemblage and occurs largely within a prominent soil layer developed immediately above an erosion surface in the tufa succession (bed 3). The faunal boundary therefore corresponds with a change in lithology; there followed drier conditions in which the soil formed, and tufa formation temporarily ceased. The soil horizon has been radiocarbon dated to 7,880 ± 160 BP (BM 1736) (Preece *et al.* 1982).

The succeeding molluscan zone D is also

dominated by woodland species, and is thought to correlate with the later part of Pollen Zone VI and Pollen Zone VIIa. The implication is clearly that the bulk of the tufa deposit (bed 4) at Caerwys formed at this time. A radiocarbon date of 6,260 ± 120 BP (Q-1533) was obtained from sediments associated with a molluscan zone D fauna at Ddol, but this does little to establish the duration and timing of the phase as a whole.

Molluscan zones E and F at Caerwys show a clear change to open-ground conditions, with a decline in shade demanding species and an increase in grassland species (beds 5 and 6). In bed 5, horizontally bedded tufa has been weathered into small slabs and incorporated into a rubbly colluvium or hillwash. These hillwash sediments and the modern soil (beds 5 and 6) were correlated with Pollen Zones VIIb and VIII, respectively. The abrupt change in which woodland species of the tufa are replaced by open-country forms in the colluvium, is thought to have resulted from woodland clearance (Preece 1978; Preece *et al.* 1982).

In addition to the molluscan zones associated with Holocene tufa development at Caerwys, an additional trench cut into the floor of the main quarry (Preece 1978; Preece *et al.* 1982) revealed a thin lower sequence of tufa and soil horizons (bed 2) overlying fluvioglacial sand (bed 1). Molluscan analyses from bed 2 show a restricted fauna composed mainly of ecologically tolerant species, many of which have modern ranges that extend well into the Arctic Circle (Preece *et al.* 1982). Also, several Arctic-Alpine species were recorded which no longer live in Britain. The soil horizons within the bed were not marked by any faunal changes. The beds are devoid of identifiable pollen and their precise age is unknown. The molluscan evidence would appear, however, to indicate a Late Devensian late-glacial rather than a Holocene age (Preece 1978; Preece *et al.* 1982).

At Ddol, the entire exposed section of tufa and interbedded organic deposits contains a molluscan fauna of zone D type. Analyses of core samples show, however, that zone A, B and C type assemblages are also present in the sequence below. The exposed tufa is dominated by woodland species and by a freshwater fauna indicating a flooding event. In contrast with Caerwys, a heavily shaded stream environment is suggested, where local conditions favoured the preservation of much organic debris. Both at Caerwys and Ddol, pollen grains and ostracods were recorded (Preece 1978; Preece *et al.* 1982). Although certain pollen assemblages were recognised, there had been a very marked differential destruction of pollen grains in the strongly alkaline environment; the results are of little use for palaeoenvironmental reconstruction. Similarly, the limited ostracod fauna has proved extremely difficult to interpret (Preece 1978).

Pedley analysed the carbonate sedimentology of the tufa deposits at Caerwys, and recognised five main lithologies – see site description. In tracing the complex distribution of these elements, he was able to reconstruct the following sequence of events. Initially, the entire tributary valley at Caerwys formed the site of braided stream deposition, with oncoid and clastic tufa being formed, derived from upstream carbonate areas. Subsequently, ponding occurred as two tufa phytoherm barrages developed. Later, a single larger tufa barrier became established downstream causing ponding and flooding of the earlier tufa constructions. Ultimately, this led to the development of a single tufa marsh complex, upstream from the barrier. According to Pedley the phytoherms were sub-parallel, forming downstream-convex porous dams. The barrage-dammed ponds functioned as efficient sediment traps, perhaps even maintaining high upstream water-tables, while palaeosols developed in other downstream areas. Pedley envisaged that water from narrow ponds seeped through and trickled over the barrages sustaining the surficial colonies of mosses and liverworts. In doing so, the water descended via a series of plant-colonised gutters and micro-terraces and the principal barrage, and onto the clastic tufa facies. This promoted braided stream activity as well as the development of small reed phytoherms. Pedley noted that palaeosols and humus-rich levels are restricted to the downstream part of the Caerwys sequence. Finally, the last episode of the tufa succession was the breaching of the deposits by the River Wheeler tributary stream with a resultant lowering of the water-table. No tufa deposits are forming at Caerwys today.

An important characteristic of the Caerwys and Ddol deposits is their considerable vertical and lateral variability; the floral and faunal remains described in many of the earlier studies were thus not assigned to any particular bed or even lithology. The level of palaeoenvironmental reconstruction achieved was, therefore, limited. Recent studies at the site have redressed this situation, although the nature of the deposits has mitigated against a detailed stratigraphic interpretation of the sequence in the accepted sense.

The work of Preece (1978), Preece *et al.* (1982) and Pedley (1987), in particular, has helped to establish a clearer pattern of events. It has been shown that springs and seepages emanating from the Carboniferous Limestone, led to tufa formation over large areas of marsh. Calcium carbonate was precipitated around the stems and leaves of marsh and tree vegetation. In places at Caerwys, large encrustations of tufa (phytoherms) formed 'rims' and ponded back water in a series of small and larger barrages. The complex series of cascades, standing pools, marshes, and the drier land towards the margins, provided varied environments, each supporting a molluscan fauna. Evidence of the constantly changing pattern of tufa formation, as ponds developed, braided streams changed course and tufa was eroded and redeposited, is superimposed on the environmental framework of the Late Devensian late-glacial and Holocene. The Caerwys tufa, in particular, demonstrates the interrelationships between constructional and clastic sediments in an ancient barrage tufa complex.

Despite the problems outlined of correlating the beds and their fossil contents throughout the quarries, an environmental sequence has been detected from the land snail evidence (Preece 1978; Preece *et al.* 1982). The open-country assemblages of the late-glacial are replaced by more shade-demanding, woodland species in the early and middle Holocene. Eventually, a return to open-ground conditions with grassland communities is shown in the upper colluvial and soil horizons, and this is thought to be in direct response to Man's activities and his clearance of woodland from the local slopes. This record demonstrates that the tufa-forming ecosystem was extremely fragile; with increased run-off, the streams began to cut down, rather than trickle and seep through and over the vegetation, and tufa formation ceased (Preece *et al.* 1982).

It has not yet been possible to correlate the various organic horizons at Caerwys and Ddol precisely with the established record of Holocene vegetational changes in Britain. Nonetheless, a broad pattern of environmental changes based on molluscan zones has been established from the sites, and from a small number of tufa sites in Dorset, Somerset, Northamptonshire, Lincolnshire and Kent. The records from North Wales form an important element in this range of localities that have helped to establish regional patterns and variations in Holocene environmental conditions based on mollusc zonation.

The sequences at Caerwys and Ddol are also important for understanding the mechanisms and conditions required for tufa formation. There has been debate as to whether calcium carbonate precipitation is the result of biochemical reactions involving micro-organisms, algae and even mosses, or whether it is a straightforward chemical process in which plants play an indirect role. Lengthy ancient sequences such as those at Caerwys and Ddol, and sites where there is contemporary tufa formation (Cwm Nash and Matlock Bath), offer scope for elaborating the possible processes and mechanisms involved.

Studies of the leaf impressions and beetle faunas recovered offer considerable scope for further elaborating the nature and sequence of events at this site.

Conclusions

The Wheeler Valley tufas are the best exposed and most extensive of the documented tufas in the British Isles. The land snails in the tufa provide an important record of environmental and climatic changes over the past 14,000 years. Caerwys is the only accessible example of tufa formation in Britain from towards the end of the last ice age.

References

ADAMS, T.D. & HAYNES, J. 1965. Foraminifera in Holocene marsh cycles at Borth, Cardiganshire (Wales). *Palaeontology, 8,* 27-38.

ADDISON, K. 1977. The influence of structural geology on glacial erosion in Snowdonia, North Wales. Tenth INQUA Congress, Birmingham, Abstracts 5.

ADDISON, K. 1978. Magnificent Nant Ffrancon on the Holyhead Road. *Geographical Magazine, London, 40,* 315-319.

ADDISON, K. 1983. *Classic glacial landforms of Snowdonia.* The Geographical Association, Landform Guide, 3, 48pp.

ADDISON, K. 1986. *The Ice Age in Cwm Idwal.* K and M.K. Addison, Shropshire, 16pp.

ADDISON, K. 1987. *Snowdon in the Ice Age.* K. and M.K. Addison, Shropshire, 28pp.

ADDISON, K. 1988. *The Ice Age in Y Glyderau and Nant Ffrancon.* K. and M.K. Addison, Shropshire, 28pp.

ALCOCK, L. 1958. Post-Roman sherds from Longbury Bank Cave, Penally (Pembrokeshire). *Bulletin of the Board of Celtic Studies, 18,* 77-79.

ALLEN, E.E. & RUTTER, J.G. 1944. A survey of the Gower Caves with an account of recent excavations. Part I. *Proceedings of the Swansea Scientific field naturalists' Society, 2,* 221-246.

ALLEN, E.E. & RUTTER, J.G. 1948. *Gower Caves.* Thomas, Swansea.

ALLEN, J.R.L. 1982. Late Pleistocene (Devensian) glaciofluvial outwash at Banc-y-Warren, near Cardigan (West Wales). *Geological Journal, 17,* 31-47.

ALLEN, P.M. & JACKSON, A.A. 1985. *Geology of the country around Harlech.* Memoir for 1:50,000 geological sheet 135 with part of sheet 149. British Geological Survey, H.M.S.O. London, 90-102.

AL-SAADI, R. & BROOKS, M. 1973. A geophysical study of Pleistocene buried valleys in the Lower Swansea Valley, Vale of Neath and Swansea Bay. *Proceedings of the Geologists' Association, 84,* 135-153.

ANDERSON, J.G.C. 1977. Glais moraine. In: Bowen, D.Q. (ed.) *Wales and the Cheshire-Shropshire lowland.* INQUA X Congress. Guidebook A8 and C8. Geo Abstracts, Norwich, 19.

ANDERSON, J.G.C. & OWEN, T.R. 1979. The late Quaternary history of the Neath and Afan Valleys, South Wales. *Proceedings of the Geologists' Association, 90,* 203-211.

ANDREWS, J.T. 1983. Short ice age 230,000 years ago. *Nature, 303,* 21-22.

ANDREWS, J.T., BOWEN, D.Q. & KIDSON, C. 1979. Amino acid ratios and the correlation of raised beach deposits in south-west England and Wales. *Nature, 281,* 556-559.

ANDREWS, J.T., GILBERTSON, D.D. & HAWKINS, A.B. 1984. The Pleistocene succession of the Severn Estuary: a revised model based on amino acid racemization studies. *Journal of the Geological Society of London, 141,* 967-974.

ApSIMON, A. 1976. A view of the early prehistory of Wales. In: Boon, G.C. & Lewis, J.M. (eds) *Welsh Antiquity.* Cardiff.

BADEN-POWELL, D.F.W. 1933. Raised beaches in Gower. *Geological Magazine, 70,* 239-432.

BALL, D.F. 1960. Relic-soil on limestone in South Wales. *Nature, 187,* 497-498.

BALL, D.F. 1964. Gibbsite in altered granitic rock in North Wales. *Nature, 204,* 673-674.

BALL, D.F. 1966. Late-glacial scree in Wales. *Biuletyn peryglacjalny, 15,* 151-161.

BALL, D.F. & GOODIER, R. 1968. Large sorted stone stripes in the Rhinog Mountains, North Wales. *Geografiska Annaler, 50,* 54-59.

BALL, D.F. & GOODIER, R. 1970. Morphology and distribution of features resulting from frost-action in Snowdonia. *Field Studies, 3,* 193-217.

BALL, D.F., MEW, G. & MACPHEE, W.S.G. 1969. Soils of Snowdon. *Field Studies, 3,* 69-107.

BARKER, H., BURLEIGH, R. & MEEKS, N. 1971. British Museum natural radiocarbon measurements. *Radiocarbon, 7,* 157-188.

BARTLEY, D.D. 1960a. Rhosgoch Common, Radnorshire: stratigraphy and pollen analysis. *New Phytologist, 59,* 238-262.

BARTLEY, D.D. 1960b. Ecological studies on Rhosgoch Common, Radnorshire. *Journal of Ecology, 48,* 205-214.

BATEMAN, J.A. 1973. Faunal remains from Ogof-yr-Ychen, Caldey Island. *Nature, 245*, 454-455.

BATHURST, R.G.C. 1956. The Caerwys tufa. *Liverpool and Manchester Geological Journal, 1*, 24-28.

BATTIAU-QUENEY, Y. 1980. *Contribution à l'étude géomorphologique du massif Gallois.* Atelier reproduction des thèses, Université de Lille III, Lille. Ph.D. thesis, University of Western Britanny 1978, 797pp.

BATTIAU-QUENEY, Y. 1984. The pre-glacial evolution of Wales. *Earth Surface Processes and Landforms, 9*, 229-252.

BEAVON, R.V. 1963. The succession and structure east of the Glaslyn River, North Wales. *Quarterly Journal of the Geological Society of London, 119*, 479-512.

BEHRE, K.E. 1989. Biostratigraphy of the last glacial period in Europe. *Quaternary Science Reviews, 8*, 25-44.

BELL, F.G. 1969. *Weichselian glacial floras in Britain.* Unpublished Ph.D. thesis, University of Cambridge.

BELT, T. 1874. The glacial period. *Nature, 10*, 25-26.

BENSON, S. 1852. An account of the cave deposit at Bacon Hole. *Annual Report of the Swansea Literary and Scientific Society*, for 1851, 10-19.

BERNARD, C. 1971(a). Les marques sous-glaciaires d'aspect plastique sur la roche en place (p-forms): observation sur la bordure du bouclier Canadien et examen de la question (I). *Revue Géographique Montreal, 25*, 111-27.

BERNARD, C. 1971(b). Les marques sous-glaciaires d'aspect plastique sur la roche en place (p-forms): leur rapport avec l'environnement et avec certaines marques de corrasion (II). *Revue Géographique Montreal, 25*, 265-279.

BERNARD, C. 1972. Les marques sous-glaciaires d'aspect plastique sur la roche en place (p-forms): interpretation genetique (III). *Revue Géographique Montreal, 26*, 177-191.

BEVINS, R.E. 1984. Petrological investigations. In: Green, H.S. (ed.) *Pontnewydd Cave. A Lower Palaeolithic hominid site in Wales.* The first report. National Museum of Wales, Cardiff, 192-199.

BIRKS, H.J.B., DEACON, J. & PEGLAR, S. 1975. Pollen maps for the British Isles 5000 years ago. *Proceedings of the Royal Society of London, 189 B*, 87-105.

BLAKE, J.F. 1893. The shell beds of Moel Tryfaen. *Geological Magazine, 10*, 267-270.

BOSWELL, P.G.H. 1932. The contacts of geology: the Ice Age and early Man in Britain. *Report of the British Association for the Advancement of Science* (York, 1932), 57-88.

BOTCH, S.G. 1946. Snejniki i snejnaya eroziya v severnykh tchastyakh Urala. (Translation by C.E.D.P. Paris; Les névés et l'érosion par la neige dans la partie Nord de l'Oural). *Bulletin of the Geographical Society of the USSR, 78*, 207-222.

BOULTON, G.S. 1968. A Middle Würm interstadial in south-west Wales. *Geological Magazine, 105*, 190-191.

BOULTON, G.S. 1972. Modern Arctic glaciers as depositional models for former ice-sheets. *Quarterly Journal of the Geological Society of London, 128*, 361-393.

BOULTON, G.S. 1974. Processes and patterns of glacial erosion. In: Coates, D.R. (ed) *Glacial geomorphology.* Publications in Geomorphology, State University of New York, Binghampton, 41-87.

BOULTON, G.S. 1977(a). A multiple till sequence formed by a Late Devensian Welsh ice-cap: Glanllynnau, Gwynedd. *Cambria, 4*, 10-31.

BOULTON, G.S. 1977(b). Glanllynnau. In: Bowen D.Q. (ed.) *Wales and the Cheshire- Shropshire lowland.* INQUA X Congress. Guidebook A8 & C8. Geo Abstracts, Norwich, 40-46.

BOULTON, G.S. & PAUL, M.A. 1976. The influence of genetic processes on some geotechnical properties of glacial tills. *Quarterly Journal of Engineering Geology, 9*, 159-194.

BOWEN, D.Q. 1965. *Contributions to the geomorphology of central South Wales.* Unpublished Ph.D. thesis, University of London.

BOWEN, D.Q. 1966. Dating Pleistocene events in south-west Wales. *Nature, 211*, 475-476.

BOWEN, D.Q. 1967. On the supposed ice-dammed lakes of South Wales. *Transactions of the Cardiff Naturalists' Society, 93*, 4-17.

BOWEN, D.Q. 1969(a). Port-Eynon Bay north side : Horton to Western Slade to Eastern Slade. In: *Coastal Pleistocene deposits in Wales.* Quaternary Research Association Field Guide 1969, 12-15.

BOWEN, D.Q. 1969(b). A new interpretation of the Pleistocene succession in the Bristol Channel area. *Proceedings of the Ussher Society, 2*, 86.

BOWEN, D.Q. 1970(a). South-east and central South Wales. In: Lewis, C.A. (ed.) *The glaciations of Wales and adjoining regions.* Longman, London, 197-228.

BOWEN, D.Q. 1970(b). The palaeoenvironment of the 'Red Lady' of Paviland. *Antiquity, 44*, 134-136.

BOWEN, D.Q. 1971(a). The Quaternary succession of south Gower. In: Bassett, D.A. & Bassett, M.G. (eds) *Geological excursions in South Wales and the Forest of Dean*. Geologists' Association, South Wales Group, Cardiff, 135-142.

BOWEN, D.Q. 1971(b). The Pleistocene succession and related landforms in north Pembrokeshire and south Cardiganshire. In: Bassett, D.A. & Bassett, M.G.(eds) *Geological excursions in South Wales and the Forest of Dean*. Geologists' Association, South Wales Group, Cardiff, 260-266.

BOWEN, D.Q. 1973(a). The Pleistocene history of Wales and the borderland. *Geological Journal, 8*, 207-224.

BOWEN, D.Q. 1973(b). The Pleistocene succession of the Irish Sea. *Proceedings of the Geologists' Association, 84*, 249-272.

BOWEN, D.Q. 1973(c). The Excavation at Minchin Hole 1973. *Journal of the Gower Society, 24*, 12-18.

BOWEN, D.Q. 1973(d). Time and place on the British Coast. *Geography, 58*, 207-216.

BOWEN, D.Q. 1974. The Quaternary of Wales. In: Owen, T.R. (ed.) *The Upper Palaeozoic and post-Palaeozoic rocks of Wales*. University of Wales Press, Cardiff, 373-426.

BOWEN, D.Q. 1977(a). *Wales and the Cheshire-Shropshire Lowland*. INQUA X Congress. Guidebook for excursions A8 & C8. Geo Abstracts, Norwich, 64pp.

BOWEN, D.Q. 1977(b). The coast of Wales In: Kidson, C. & Tooley, M.J. (eds) *The Quaternary history of the Irish Sea*. Geological Journal Special Issue No. 7, Seel House Press, Liverpool, 223-256.

BOWEN, D.Q. 1977(c). Studies in the Welsh Quaternary: retrospect and prospect. *Cambria, 4*, 2-9.

BOWEN, D.Q. 1977(d). Hot and cold climates in pre-historic Britain. *Geographical Magazine, 49*, 685-698.

BOWEN, D.Q. 1977(e). The land of Wales. In: Thomas, D. (ed.) *Wales: A New Study*. Newton Abbot, 11-35.

BOWEN, D.Q., 1978. *Quaternary geology*. Oxford, 237pp.

BOWEN, D.Q. 1980(a). The Pleistocene scenario of Palaeolithic Wales. In: Taylor, J.A. (ed.) *Culture and environment in Palaeolithic Wales*. British Archaeological Report, 76, 1-14.

BOWEN, D.Q. 1980(b). *The Llanelli landscape*. Salesbury Press, Llandybie, 280pp.

BOWEN, D.Q. 1981(a). The 'South Wales end-moraine': fifty years after. In: Neale, J. & Flenley, J. (eds) *The Quaternary of Britain*. Pergamon Press, Oxford, 60-67.

BOWEN, D.Q. 1981(b). Sheet 1.3. In: Carter, H. & Griffiths, H.M. (eds) *National Atlas of Wales*. University of Wales Press, Cardiff.

BOWEN, D.Q. 1981(c). Polarised views of Quaternary ice-sheets, *Nature*, 293-319.

BOWEN, D.Q. 1982(a). Pleistocene deposits and fluvioglacial landforms of north Preseli. In: Bassett, M.G. (ed.) *Geological Excursions in Dyfed, south-west Wales*, 289-295.

BOWEN, D.Q. 1982(b). Surface Morphology. In: Carter, H. & Griffiths, H.M. (eds) *National Atlas of Wales*. University of Wales Press, Cardiff.

BOWEN, D.Q. 1984. Introduction, Western Slade and Eastern Slade, Langland Bay, Abermawr, Fishguard-Newport-Cardigan. In: Bowen, D.Q. & Henry, A. (eds) *Wales : Gower, Preseli, Fforest Fawr*. Quaternary Research Assocation Field Guide, April 1984, 102pp.

BOWEN, D.Q. 1989(a). The Welsh landform. In: Owen, H. (ed.). *Settlement and society*. University of Wales Press, Cardiff.

BOWEN, D.Q. 1989(b). Time and space in glacial sediment systems in the British Isles. In: Ehlers, J., Gibbard, P.L. & Rose, J. (eds) *Glacial deposits of the British Isles*. Balkema, Rotterdam.

BOWEN, D.Q., ANDREWS, J.T., DAVIES, K.H. & HENRY, A. 1984. Bacon Hole Cave amino acid ratios. In: Bowen, D.Q. & Henry, A. (eds) *Wales: Gower, Preseli, Fforest Fawr*. Quaternary Research Association Field Guide, April 1984, 46.

BOWEN, D.Q & GREGORY, K.J. 1965. A glacial drainage system near Fishguard, Pembrokeshire. *Proceedings of the Geologists' Association, 74*, 275-281.

BOWEN, D.Q. & HENRY, A. (eds) 1984. *Wales: Gower, Preseli, Fforest Fawr*. Quaternary Research Association Field Guide, April 1984, 102pp.

BOWEN, D.Q., HUGHES, S.A., SYKES, G.A. & MILLER, G.M. 1989 (in press). Land-sea correlations in the Pleistocene based on Isoleucine epimerization in non-marine molluscs.

BOWEN, D.Q. & LEAR, D.L. 1982. The Quaternary geology of the lower Teifi Valley. In: Bassett, M.G. (ed.) *Geological excursions in Dyfed, south-west Wales*. National Museum of Wales, Cardiff, 297-302.

BOWEN, D.Q., REEVES, A. & SYKES, G.A. 1986. Age of the Broughton Bay till, Gower, South Wales: comments on the note by S. Campbell and R. A. Shakesby. *Quaternary Newsletter, 47*, 33-36.

BOWEN, D.Q., SYKES, G.A., REEVES, A., MILLER, G.H., ANDREWS, J.T., BREW, J.S. & HARE, P.E. 1985. Amino acid geochronology of raised beaches in south-west Britain. *Quaternary Science Reviews, 4,* 279-318.

BOWEN, D.Q. & SYKES, G.A. 1988. Correlation of marine events and glaciations on the north-east Atlantic margin. *Philosophical Transactions of the Royal Society of London,* Series B, 318, 619-635.

BOWMAN, J.E. 1841. On the question, whether there are any evidences of the former existence of glaciers in North Wales. *London, Edinburgh and Dublin Philosophical Magazine, 19,* 469-479.

BRAMWELL, D. 1977. Bird faunas from Cathole, 1968 and Robin Hood's Cave, 1969. In: Campbell, J.B. *The Upper Palaeolithic of Britain. A study of Man and nature in the late Ice Age.* Clarendon Press, Oxford (2 vols), 216-217.

BRIDGES, E.M. 1985. Gower: the Ice Age limit. *Journal of the Gower Society, 36,* 71-79.

BROWN, E.H. 1960. *The relief and drainage of Wales.* Cardiff.

BROWN, E.H. & COOKE, R.U. 1977. Landforms and related glacial deposits in the Wheeler Valley area, Clwyd. *Cambria, 4,* 32-45.

BROWN, M.J.F. 1971. *Glacial geomorphology of Montgomeryshire and west Shropshire.* Unpublished Ph.D. thesis, University of London.

BROWN, M.J.F., ELLIS-GRUFFYDD, I.D., FOSTER, H.D. & UNWIN, D.J. 1967. A new radiocarbon date for Wales. *Nature,* 213, 1220-1221.

BRYANT, R.H., CARPENTER, C.R. & RIDGE, T.S. 1985. Pingo scars and related features in the Whicham Valley, Cumbria. In: Boardman, J. (ed.) *Field Guide to the periglacial landforms of northern England.* Quaternary Research Association, 47-53.

BUCKLAND, W. 1842. On the glacial-diluvial phenomena in Snowdonia and the adjacent parts of North Wales. *Proceedings of the Geologists' Association, 3,* 579-584.

BULL, P.A. 1975. *An electron microscope study of clastic cave sediments from Agen Allwedd, Powys.* Unpublished M.Sc. thesis, University of Wales.

BULL, P.A. 1976. *Contributions to the study of clastic cave sediments with particular reference to Agen Allwedd, Powys.* Unpublished Ph.D. thesis, University of Wales.

BULL, P.A. 1984. Scanning Electron Microscope studies of sediments. In: Green, H.S. (ed.) *Pontnewydd Cave. A Lower Palaeolithic hominid site in Wales.* The first report. National Museum of Wales, Cardiff, 77-89.

BURROWS, C.J. 1974. Plant macrofossils from Late Devensian deposits at Nant Ffrancon, Caernarvonshire. *New Phytologist, 73,* 1003-1033.

BURROWS, C.J. 1975. Radiocarbon dates from Late Devensian deposits, Nant Ffrancon, Caernarvonshire. *New Phytologist, 75,* 167-171.

CAMPBELL, J.A. & BAXTER, M.S. 1979. Radiocarbon measurements on submerged forest floating chronologies. *Nature, 278,* 409-413.

CAMPBELL, J.B. 1977. *The Upper Palaeolithic of Britain. A study of Man and nature in the late Ice Age.* Clarendon Press, Oxford, 264pp & 376pp, (2 vols).

CAMPBELL, S. 1984. *The nature and origin of the Pleistocene deposits around Cross Hands and on west Gower, South Wales.* Unpublished Ph.D. thesis, University of Wales.

CAMPBELL, S. 1985a. Coastal Pleistocene sediments at Criccieth, Llŷn Peninsula, north-west Wales. In: Shakesby, R.A. & Walsh, R.P.D. (eds) *Guide to field study excursion in Wales.* First International Conference on Geomorphology 10-15th September 1985, Swansea, 60-64.

CAMPBELL, S. 1985b. Quaternary geomorphological features in Snowdonia. In: Shakesby, R.A. & Walsh , R.P.D. (eds) *Guide to field study excursion in Wales.* First International Conference on Geomorphology 10th-15th September 1985, Swansea, 65-69.

CAMPBELL, S., ANDREWS, J.T. & SHAKESBY, R.A. 1982. Amino acid evidence for Devensian ice, west Gower, South Wales. *Nature, 300,* 249-251.

CAMPBELL, S. & SHAKESBY, R.A. 1982. A preliminary report on new evidence for the glaciation of west Gower. *Journal of the Gower Society, 33,* 60-68.

CAMPBELL, S. & SHAKESBY, R.A. 1983. *Quaternary stratigraphy at Broughton Bay.* B.G.R.G. Spring Meeting, May 13-15th. Field excursion handbook. Swansea, 30-35.

CAMPBELL, S. & SHAKESBY, R.A. 1985. Wood fragments of possible Chelford Interstadial age from till at Broughton Bay, Gower, South Wales. *Quaternary Newsletter, 47,* 33-36.

CAMPBELL, S. & SHAKESBY, R.A. 1986(a). Comments on the note by D.Q. Bowen, A. Reeves, and G.A. Sykes. *Quaternary Newsletter, 49,* 14-16.

CAMPBELL, S. & SHAKESBY, R.A. 1986(b). Comments on the note by P. Worsley. *Quaternary Newsletter, 49,* 19-20.

CANTRILL, T.C., DIXON, E.E.L., THOMAS, H.H. & JONES, O.T. 1916. *The geology of the South Wales Coalfield, Part 7. The country around Milford.* Memoir of the Geological Survey of Great Britain. H.M.S.O., London.

CARPENTER, C.P. & WOODCOCK, M.P. 1981. A detailed investigation of a pingo remnant in western Surrey. *Quaternary Studies, 1*, 1-26.

CARR, H.R.C. & LISTER, G.A. 1948. *The Mountains of Snowdon*. Crosby Lockwood, London.

CASE, D.J. 1977. Horton (loess). In: Bowen, D.Q. (ed.) *Wales and the Cheshire-Shropshire lowland*. INQUA X Congress. Guidebook for excursions A8 and C8, Geo Abstracts, Norwich, 26-29.

CASE, D.J. 1983. *Quaternary airfall deposits in South Wales: loess and coversands*. Unpublished Ph.D. thesis, University of Wales.

CASE, D.J. 1984. Port-Eynon Silt (loess). In: Bowen, D.Q. & Henry A. (eds) *Wales: Gower, Preseli, Fforest Fawr*. Quaternary Research Assocation Field Guide, April 1984, 51-54.

CHAMBERS, F.M. 1981. Date of blanket peat initiation in upland South Wales. *Quaternary Newsletter, 35*, 24-26.

CHAMBERS, F.M. 1982(a). Environmental history of Cefn Gwernffrwd, near Rhandirmwyn, Mid Wales. *New Phytologist, 92*, 607-615.

CHAMBERS, F.M. 1982(b). Two radiocarbon dated pollen diagrams from high altitude blanket peats in South Wales. *Journal of Ecology, 70*, 445-459.

CHAMBERS, F.M. 1983. Three radiocarbon dated pollen diagrams from upland peats north-west of Merthyr Tydfil, South Wales. *Journal of Ecology, 71*, 475-487.

CHARLESWORTH, J.K. 1929. The South Wales end-moraine. *Quarterly Journal of the Geological Society of London, 85*, 335-358.

CHURCHILL, D.M. 1965. The displacement of deposits formed at sea-level, 6,500 years ago in southern Britain. *Quaternaria, 7*, 239-249.

CLAYDEN, B. 1977(a). Hunts Bay plateau. In: Bowen, D.Q. (ed.) *Wales and the Cheshire-Shropshire lowlands*. INQUA X Congress. Guidebook for excursions A8 and C8. Geo Abstracts, Norwich, 25-26.

CLAYDEN, B. 1977(b). Palaeosols. *Cambria, 4*, 84-97.

CLEGG, J. 1969. Excavations at Coygan Cave near Laugharne. *Carmarthen Antiquary, 5*, 13-20.

COLLCUTT, S.N. 1984. The sediments. In: Green, H.S. (ed.) *Pontnewydd Cave. A Lower Palaeolithic hominid site in Wales*. The first report. National Museum of Wales, Cardiff, 31-77.

COOPE, G.R. 1975. Climatic fluctuations in North-West Europe since the last interglacial indicated by fossil assemblages of coleoptera. *Geological Journal Special Issue, 6*, 153-168.

COOPE, G.R. 1977. Coleoptera as clues to the understanding of climatic changes in North Wales towards the end of the last (Devensian) glaciation. *Cambria, 4*, 65-72.

COOPE, G.R. & BROPHY, J.A. 1972. Late-glacial environmental changes indicated by a coleopteran succession from North Wales. *Boreas, 1*, 97-142.

COOPE, G.R. & PENNINGTON, W. 1977. The Windermere Interstadial of the Late Devensian. *Philosophical Transactions of the Royal Society, Series, B, 208*.

COSTER, H.P. & GERARD, J.A.F. 1947. A seismic investigation of the history of the River Rheidol in Cardiganshire. *Geological Magazine, 84*, 360-368.

COX, A.H., GREEN, J.F.N., JONES, O.T. & PRINGLE, J. 1930. The geology of the St David's district, Pembrokeshire. *Proceedings of the Geologists' Association, 41*, 241-273.

COX, M. 1983. Cadair Idris National Nature Reserve, Gwynedd. *Nature in Wales, 2*, 21-28.

CRABTREE, K. 1969. Post-glacial diatom zonation of limnic deposits in North Wales. *Mitteilungen Internationale Vereinigung fur theoretische und angewandte Limnologie, 17*, 165-171.

CRABTREE, K. 1970. Late Quaternary deposits in North Wales. In: *Etudes sur le Quaternaire dans le Monde*. INQUA Congress (8[e], Paris, 1969), 2 volumes, 1053pp.

CRABTREE, K. 1972. Late-glacial deposits near Capel Curig, Caernarvonshire. *New Phytologist, 71*, 1233-1243.

CRAMPTON, C.B. 1960. Analysis of heavy minerals in the Carboniferous Limestone, Millstone Grit and soils derived from certain glacial gravels of Glamorgan and Monmouth. *Transactions of the Cardiff Naturalists' Society, 87*, 13-22.

CRAMPTON, C.B. 1961. An interpretation of the micromineralogy of certain Glamorgan soils, the influence of ice and wind. *Journal of Soil Science, 12*, 158-171.

CRAMPTON, C.B. 1964. Certain aspects of soils developed on calcareous parent materials in South Wales. *Transactions of the Cardiff Naturalists' Society, 91*, 4-16.

CRAMPTON, C.B. 1966(a). Analysis of pollen in soils on the peaks of South Wales. *Scottish Geographical Magazine, 82*, 46-52.

CRAMPTON, C.B. 1966(b). An interpretation of the pollen and soils in cross-ridge dykes of Glamorgan. *Bulletin of the Board of Celtic Studies, 21*, 376-390.

CRAMPTON, C.B. 1966(c). Certain effects of glacial events in the Vale of Glamorgan, South Wales. *Journal of Geology, 6*, 261-266.

CROSS, P. 1966. *The glacial geomorphology of the Wigmore and Presteigne basins and some adjacent areas.* Unpublished M.Sc. thesis, University of London.

CROSS, P. 1968. Aspects of the glacial geomorphology of the Wigmore and Presteigne districts. *Transactions of the Woolhope Naturalists' Field Club, 39,* 198-220.

CULVER, S.J. 1976. The development of the Swansea Bay area during the past 20,000 years. *Journal of the Gower Society, 27,* 58-62.

CULVER, S.J. & BULL, P.A. 1979. Late Pleistocene rock basin lakes in South Wales. *Geological Journal, 14,* 107-116.

CURRANT, A.P. 1984. The mammalian remains. In: Green, H.S. (ed.) *Pontnewydd Cave. A Lower Palaeolithic Hominid site in Wales.* The first report. National Museum of Wales, Cardiff, 171-180.

CURRANT, A.P., STRINGER, C.B. & COLLCUTT, S.N. 1984. Bacon Hole Cave. In: Bowen, D.Q. & Henry, A. (eds) *Wales: Gower, Preseli, Fforest Fawr.* Quaternary Research Association Field Guide, April 1984, 38-44.

DAHL, R. 1965. Plastically sculptured detail forms on rock surfaces in northern Nordland, Norway. *Geografiska Annaler, 47A,* 83-140.

DARBYSHIRE, R.D. 1863. On marine shells in stratified drift at high levels on Moel Tryfan in Caernarvonshire. *Proceedings of the Manchester Literary and Philosophical Society, 2,* 177-181.

DARWIN, C. 1842. Notes on the effects produced by the ancient glaciers of Caernarvonshire, and on the boulders transported by floating ice. *Philosophical Magazine, 21,* 180-188.

DAVID, J.E. 1883. On the evidence of glacial action in south Brecknockshire and east Glamorganshire. *Quarterly Journal of the Geological Society of London, 39,* 39-54.

DAVIES, D.C. 1988. *The amino-stratigraphy of British Pleistocene glacio-deposits.* Unpublished Ph.D. thesis, University of Wales.

DAVIES, G.L. 1969. *The earth in decay: a history of British geomorphology, 1578-1878.* MacDonald, London.

DAVIES, K.H. 1983. Amino acid analysis of Pleistocene marine molluscs from the Gower Peninsula. *Nature, 302,* 137-139.

DAVIS, W.M. 1909. Glacial erosion in North Wales. *Quarterly Journal of the Geological Society of London, 65,* 281-350.

DAVIS, W.M. 1920. Glacial erosion of Snowdon –correspondence. *Geological Magazine, 57,* 381-382.

DAWKINS, W.B. 1871. Discovery of the glutton *Gulo iuscus* in Britain. *Quarterly Journal of the Geological Society of London, 27,* 406-410.

DAWKINS, W.B. 1874. *Cave Hunting.* McMillan, London.

DAWKINS, W.B. 1880. *Early Man in Britain and his place in the Tertiary Period.* London.

DAYKINS, J.R. 1900. Some Snowdon tarns. *Geological Magazine, 4,* 58-61.

DEACON, J. 1974. The location of refugia of *Corylus avellana* L. during the Weichselian glaciation. *New Phytologist, 73,* 1055-1063.

DE GANS, W., CLEVERINGA, P. & PARIS, F.P. 1979. The Stokersdobbe: geology and palynology of a deep pingo remnant in Friesland (the Netherlands). *Geologie en Mijnbouw, 58,* 33-38.

DENTON, G.H. and HUGHES, T.J. (eds) 1981. *The last great ice-sheets.* Wiley, New York and London.

DERBYSHIRE, E. 1962. Late-glacial drainage in part of north-east Wales: an alternative hypothesis. *Proceedings of the Geologists' Association, 73,* 327-334.

DERBYSHIRE, E. 1977. *Water level control of late-glacial and post-glacial sedimentation in the Llŷn Peris basin, North Wales.* Abstracts of the INQUA Congress X, Birmingham, 1977, 110.

DEWEY, H. 1918. On the origin of some landforms in Caernarvonshire, North Wales. *Geological Magazine, 5,* 145-157.

DIXON, E.E.L. 1921. *The geology of the South Wales Coalfield, Part 8. The country around Pembroke and Tenby.* Memoir of the Geological Survey of Great Britain. H.M.S.O., London.

DONNELLY, R. 1988. *Glacial sediments at sites of opencast coal extraction in South Wales.* Unpublished Ph.D. thesis, University of Wales.

DRISCOLL, E.M. 1953. *Some aspects of the geomorphology of the Vale of Glamorgan.* Unpublished M.Sc. thesis, University of London.

DUNKLEY, P.N. 1981. Description of 1:25,000 resource sheet SJ35 and part of SJ25. *The sand and gravel resources of the country north of Wrexham, Clwyd.* Mineral Assessment Report, Institute of Geological Sciences, 61, 1-13.

DWERRYHOUSE, A.R. & MILLER, A.A. 1930. The glaciation of Clun Forest, Radnor Forest and some adjoining districts. *Quarterly Journal of the Geological Society of London, 86,* 96-129.

EDWARDS, W. 1905. The glacial geology of Anglesey. *Proceedings of the Liverpool Geological Society, 10,* 26-37.

EINARSSON, T. & ALBERTSON, K.J. 1988. The glacial history of Iceland during the past three million years. *Philosophical Transaction of the Royal Society of London, Series B*, 318, 637-644.

ELLIS-GRUFFYDD, I.D. 1972. *The glacial geomorphology of the upper Usk basin (South Wales) and its right bank tributaries.* Unpublished Ph.D. thesis, University of London.

ELLIS-GRUFFYDD, I.D. 1977. Late Devensian glaciation in the upper Usk basin. *Cambria, 4*, 46-55.

EMBLETON, C. 1957. Some stages in the drainage evolution of part of north-east Wales. *Transactions of the Institute of British Geographers, 23*, 19-35.

EMBLETON, C. 1961. The geomorphology of the Vale of Conway, North Wales, with particular reference to its deglaciation. *Transactions of the Institute of British Geographers, 29*, 47-70.

EMBLETON, C. 1962. A description of the Ordnance Survey one inch sheet 107: Snowdon. *British landscapes through maps 5. Snowdonia.* Geographical Association, Sheffield, 28pp.

EMBLETON, C. 1964(a). The geomorphology of Snowdonia and adjacent districts of North Wales. In: Steers, J.A. (ed.) *Field studies in the British Isles.* Nelson, London, 294-313.

EMBLETON, C. 1964(b). Subglacial drainage and supposed ice-dammed lakes in north-east Wales. *Proceedings of the Geologists' Assocation, 75*, 31-38.

EMBLETON, C. 1964(c). The deglaciation of Arfon and southern Anglesey and the origin of the Menai Straits. *Proceedings of the Geologists' Association, 75*, 407-430.

EMBLETON, C. 1964(d). The planation surfaces of Arfon and adjacent parts of Anglesey, a re-examination of their age and origin. *Transactions of the Institute of British Geographers*, 17-26.

EMBLETON, C. 1970. North-eastern Wales. In: Lewis, C.A. (ed.) *The glaciations of Wales and adjoining regions.* Longman, London, 59-82.

EMBLETON, C. 1984. Location, setting and geomorphology. In: Green, H.S. (ed.) *Pontnewydd Cave. A Lower Palaeolithic hominid site in Wales.* The first report. National Museum of Wales, Cardiff, 23-30.

EMBLETON, C. & KING C.A.M. 1968. *Glacial and periglacial geomorphology.* Arnold, London.

EMBLETON, C. & KING, C.A.M. 1975a. *Glacial geomorphology.* Arnold, London.

EMBLETON, C. & KING, C.A.M. 1975b. *Periglacial geomorphology.* Arnold, London.

ERDTMAN, G. 1928. Studies in the post-arctic history of the forests of north-western Europe. *Geologiska föreningens : Stockholm föfhandlingar, 50*, 123-192.

ESCRITT, E.A. 1971. Plumbing the depths of Idwal's moraines. *Geographical Magazine, 44*, 52-55.

EVANS, G.H. & WALKER, R. 1977. The late Quaternary history of the diatom flora of Llyn Clyd and Llyn Glas, two small oligotrophic high mountain tarns in Snowdonia (Wales). *New Phytologist, 78*, 221-236.

EVANS, J.G. 1977(a). Cwm Nash. In: Bowen, D.Q. (ed.) *Wales and the Cheshire- Shropshire lowland.* INQUA X Congress. Guidebook for excursions A8 & C8. Geo Abstracts, Norwich, 11-13.

EVANS, J.G. 1977(b). Land snail faunas from Cathole, 1968 and Longhole, 1969. In: Campbell, J.B. *The Upper Palaeolithic of Britain. A study of Man and nature in the late Ice Age.* Clarendon Press, Oxford, 208-210, (2 vols).

EVANS, J.G., FRENCH, C. & LEIGHTON, D. 1978. Habitat change in two late-glacial and post-glacial sites in southern Britain. In: Limbrey, S. & Evans, J.G. (eds) *The effect of Man on the landscape: the lowland zone.* Research Report of the Council for British Archaeology, 21, 63-75.

EVANS, W.D. 1945. The geology of the Prescelly Hills, north Pembrokeshire. *Quarterly Journal of the Geological Society of London, 101*, 89-110.

EYLES, C.H. & EYLES, N. 1984. Glaciomarine sediments of the Isle of Man as a key to Late Pleistocene stratigraphic investigations in the Irish Sea Basin. *Geology, 12*, 359-364.

EYLES, N. & McCABE, A.M. 1989. The Late Devensian Irish Sea Basin: the sedimentary record of a collapsed ice-sheet margin. *Quaternary Science Reviews, 8*.

FALCONER, H. 1860. On the ossiferous caves of the peninsula of Gower, in Glamorganshire, South Wales. With an appendix, on a raised beach in Mewslade Bay, and the occurrence of the boulder-clay on Cefn-y-bryn. *Quarterly Journal of the Geological Society of London, 16*, 487-491.

FALCONER, H. 1868. Ossiferous caves of Gower. In: Murchison, C. (ed) *Palaeontological memoirs and notes of the Late Hugh Falconer, A.M., M.D. Vol. II.* Hardwicke, London, 498-540.

FEARNSIDES, W.G. 1910. The Tremadoc Slates and associated rocks of south-east Caernarvonshire. *Quarterly Journal of the Geological Society of London, 56*, 142-188.

FEARNSIDES, W.G. & DAVIES, W. 1944. The geology of Deudraeth. The country between Traeth Mawr and Traeth Bach, Merioneth.

Quarterly Journal of the Geological Society of London, 99, 247-276.

FIELD, E. 1968. Unpublished undergraduate dissertation, University of Durham (Botany Department).

FISHWICK, A. 1977. The Conway Basin. *Cambria, 4*, 56-64.

FITZPATRICK, E.A. 1956. An indurated soil horizon formed by permafrost. *Journal of Soil Science, 7*, 248-254.

FLINT, R.F. 1929. Stagnation and dissipation of the last ice-sheet. *Geographical Review, 19*, 256-289.

FLINT, R.F. 1942. Glacier thinning during deglaciation. *American Journal of Science*, 240, 1B.

FLINT, R.F. 1943. Growth of the North American ice-sheet during the Wisconsin age. *Bulletin of the Geological Society of America, 54*, 325-362.

FLINT, 1971. *Glacial and Quaternary geology.* Wiley, New York and London.

FOSTER, R.F., H.D. 1968. *The glaciation of the Harlech Dome.* Unpublished Ph.D. thesis, University of London.

FOSTER, H.D. 1970(a). Establishing the age and geomorphological significance of sorted stone stripes in the Rhinog Mountains, North Wales. *Geografiska Annaler, 52A*, 96-102.

FOSTER, H.D. 1970b. Sarn Badrig, a sub-marine moraine in Cardigan Bay, North Wales. *Zeitschrift für Geomorphologie, 14*, 475-486.

FOULKES, W.W. 1872. On the discovery of Platycnemic Men in Denbighshire, and notes on their remains. *Archaeologica Cambrenesis*, for 1872, 22-32.

FRANCIS, E.A. 1978. (ed.) *Annual field meeting Keele, 1978.* Quaternary Research Association Field Guide, 101pp.

GALLOWAY, R.W. 1961. Ice wedges and involutions in Scotland. *Biuletyn Peryglacjalny, 10*, 169-193.

GARRARD, R.A. 1977. The sediments of the south Irish Sea and Nymphe Bank area of the Celtic Sea. In: Kidson, C. & Tooley, M.J. (eds) *The Quaternary history of the Irish Sea.* Geological Journal Special Issue No. 7, Seel House Press, Liverpool, 69-92.

GARRARD, R.A. & DOBSON, M.R. 1974. The nature and maximum extent of glacial sediments off the west coast of Wales. *Marine Geology, 16*, 31-44.

GARROD, D.A.E. 1926. *The Upper Palaeolithic Age in Britain.* Clarendon Press, Oxford, 211pp.

GEMMELL, C., SMART, D. & SUGDEN, D. 1986.

Striae and former ice flow directions in Snowdonia, North Wales. *Geographical Journal, 152*, 19-29.

GEORGE, T.N. 1932. The Quaternary beaches of Gower. *Proceedings of the Geologists' Association, 43*, 291-324.

GEORGE, T.N. 1933(a). The glacial deposits of Gower. *Geological Magazine, 70*, 208-232.

GEORGE, T.N. 1933(b). The coast of Gower. *Proceedings of the Swansea Scientific and field naturalists' Society, 1*, 192-206.

GEORGE, T.N. 1936. The geology of the Swansea main drainage excavations. *Proceedings of the Swansea Scientific and field naturalists' Society, 2*, 23-48.

GEORGE, T.N. 1938. Shoreline evolution in the Swansea district. *Proceedings of the Swansea Scientific and field naturalists' Society, 2*, 23-49.

GEORGE, T.N. 1970. *British regional geology. South Wales* (third edition). H.M.S.O., London, 152pp.

GEORGE, T.N. 1974. The Cenozoic evolution of Wales. In: Owen, T.R. (ed.) *The Upper Palaeozoic and post-Palaeozoic rocks of Wales.* University of Wales Press, Cardiff, 341-371.

GEORGE, T.N. & GRIFFITHS, J.C. 1938. The superficial deposits at the mouth of the River Tawe. *Proceedings of the Swansea Scientific and field naturalists' Society, 2*, (1 + 2) 63-71.

GJESSING, J. 1965. On "plastic scouring" and "subglacial erosion". *Norges geologisk tidsskrift, 20*, 1-37.

GILBERT, G.K. 1906. Crescentic gouges on glacial surfaces. *Geological Society of America Bulletin, 17*, 303-314.

GODWIN, H. 1940(a). Pollen analysis and forest history of England and Wales. *New Phytologist, 39*, 370-400.

GODWIN, H. 1940(b). A boreal transgression of the sea in Swansea Bay. *Data for the study of post-glacial history. VI. New Phytologist, 39*, 308-321.

GODWIN, H. 1941. Pollen analysis and Quaternary geology. *Proceedings of the Geologists' Association, 52*, 328-361.

GODWIN, H. 1943. Coastal peat beds of the British Isles and North Sea. *Journal of Ecology, 31*, 199-247.

GODWIN, H. 1955. Vegetational history at Cwm Idwal, a Welsh plant refuge. *Svensk botanisk tidsskrift, 49*, 35-43.

GODWIN, H. & CONWAY, V.M. 1939. The ecology

of a raised bog near Tregaron, Cardiganshire. *Journal of Ecology, 27*, 313-359.

GODWIN, H. & MITCHELL, G.F. 1938. Stratigraphy and development of two raised bogs near Tregaron, Cardiganshire. *New Phytologist, 37*, 425-454.

GODWIN, H. & NEWTON, F.N. 1938. The submerged forest at Borth and Ynyslas, Cardiganshire. *New Phytologist, 37*, 333-344.

GODWIN, H. & WILLIS, E.H. 1960. Cambridge University natural radiocarbon measurements II. *Radiocarbon, 2*, 62-72.

GODWIN, H. & WILLIS, E.H. 1961. Cambridge University natural radiocarbon measurements III. *Radiocarbon, 3*, 60-76.

GODWIN, H. & WILLIS, E.H. 1962. Cambridge University natural radiocarbon measurements V. *Radiocarbon, 4*, 57-70.

GODWIN, H. & WILLIS, E.H. 1964. Cambridge University natural radiocarbon measurements VI. *Radiocarbon, 6*, 116-137.

GOODIER, R. & BALL, D.F. 1969. Recent ground pattern phenomena in the Rhinog Mountains, North Wales. *Geografiska Annaler, 51*, 121-126.

GORDON, J.E. 1977. Morphometry of cirques in the Kintail –Affria –Cannish area of North Scotland. *Geografiska Annaler*, 177-194.

GOUDIE, A.S. & PIGGOTT, N.R. 1981. Quartzite tors, stone stripes and slopes at the Stiperstones, Shropshire, England. *Biuletyn peryglacjalny, 28*, 47-56.

GRAY, J.M. 1981. P-forms from the Isle of Mull. *Scottish Journal of Geology, 17*, 39-47.

GRAY, J.M. 1982(a). The last glaciers (Loch Lomond Advance) in Snowdonia, North Wales. *Geological Journal, 17*, 111-133.

GRAY, J.M. 1982(b). Unweathered, glaciated bedrock on an exposed lake bed in Wales. *Journal of Glaciology, 28*, 483-497.

GRAY, J.M., INCE, J. & LOWE, S. 1981. Report on a short field meeting in North Wales. *Quaternary Newsletter, 35*, 40-44.

GRAY, J.M. & LOWE, J.J. 1977. The Scottish late-glacial environment, a synthesis. In: Gray, J.M. & Lowe, J.J. (eds) *Studies in the Scottish late-glacial environment*. Pergamon, Oxford, 163-187.

GRAY, J.M. & LOWE, J.J. 1982. Problems in the interpretation of small-scale erosional forms on glaciated bedrock surfaces, examples from Snowdonia, North Wales. *Proceedings of the Geologists' Association, 93*, 403-414.

GREEN, H.S. 1981(a). The first Welshman: excavations at Pontnewydd. *Antiquity, 55*, 184-195.

GREEN, H.S. 1981(b). A Palaeolithic flint handaxe from Rhosili, Gower. *Bulletin of the Board of Celtic Studies, 29*, 337-339.

GREEN, H.S. 1984. *Pontnewydd Cave. A Lower Palaeolithic hominid site in Wales*: the first report. National Museum of Wales, Cardiff, 227pp.

GREEN, H.S., BULL, P.A., CAMPBELL, E., COLES, G. & CURRANT, A. 1986. Excavations at Little Hoyle (Longbury Bank), Wales in 1984. In: Roe, D.A. (ed.) *Studies in the Upper Palaeolithic of Britain and North-West Europe*. British Archaeological Report, 296, (International Series), 99-119.

GREEN, H.S. & CURRANT, AP. 1982. Early Man in Wales: Pontnewydd Cave (Clwyd) and its Pleistocene fauna. *Nature in Wales, 1*, 40-43.

GREEN, H.S., STRINGER, C.B., COLLCUTT, S.N., CURRANT, A.P., HUXTABLE, J., SCHWARCZ, H.P., DEBENHAM, N., EMBLETON, C., BULL, P., MOLLESON, T.I. & BEVINS, R.E. 1981. Pontnewydd Cave in Wales – a new Middle Pleistocene hominid site. *Nature, 294*, 707-713.

GREENLY, E. 1900. Report on the drift at Moel Tryfaen. With notes by Chairman and members, T.M. Reade and a list of foraminifera of Pleistocene beds of Moel Tryfaen by J. Wright. *Geological Magazine, 4*, 115-123.

GREENLY, E. 1919. *The geology of Anglesey*. Memoirs of the Geological Survey of Great Britain. H.M.S.O., London, 980pp., (2 vols).

GREENLY, E. & BADGER, A.B. 1899. The glacial sections at Moel Trifaen. *Report of the British Association for the Advancement of Science* (Bristol, 1898), 882.

GREGORY, K.J. & BOWEN, D.Q. 1966. Fluvioglacial deposits between Newport (Pembrokeshire) and Cardigan. In: Price, R.J. (ed.) *Deglaciation*. Occasional Publication of the British Geomorphological Research Group, 2, 25-8.

GRIFFITHS, A.P. 1972. Recent work at Bacon Hole. *Journal of the Gower Society, 23*, 76-77.

GRIFFITHS, J.C. 1937. *The glacial deposits between the River Tawe and the River Towy*. Unpublished Ph.D. thesis, University of Wales.

GRIFFITHS, J.C. 1939. The mineralogy of the glacial deposits of the region between the rivers Neath and Towy, South Wales. *Proceedings of the Geologists' Association, 50*, 433-462.

GRIFFITHS, J.C. 1940. *The glacial deposits west of the Taff*. Unpublished Ph.D. thesis, University of London.

GRINDLEY, H.E. 1905. Glacial dam at Llanvihangel. *Transactions of the Woolhope Naturalists' Field Club* (for 1905), 194-196.

GROOM, G.E. 1971. Geomorphology. In: Balchin W.G.V. (ed.) *Swansea and its region.* British Association for the Advancement of Science, Swansea, 29-40.

HAMMEN, T. VAN DER & VOGEL, J.C. 1966. The Susuca Interstadial and the sub-division of the late-glacial. *Geologie en Mijnbouw, 45,* 33-35.

HANDA, S. & MOORE, P.D. 1976. Studies in the vegetational history of Mid Wales IV. Pollen analysis of some pingo basins. *New Phytologist, 77,* 205-225.

HARRIS, C. 1973. The Ice Age in Gower, as illustrated by coastal landforms and deposits, Heatherslade to Hunts Bay. *Journal of the Gower Society, 24,* 74-79.

HARRIS, C. & WRIGHT, M.D. 1980. Some last glaciation drift deposits near Pontypridd, South Wales. *Geological Journal, 15,* 7-20.

HARRISON, C.J.O. 1977. Non-passerine birds of the Ipswichian Interglacial from the Gower Caves. *Transactions of the British Cave Research Association, 4,* 441-442.

HAWKINS, A.B. & KELLAWAY, G.A., 1971. Field meeting at Bristol and Bath with special reference to new evidence of glaciation. *Proceedings of the Geologists' Association, 82,* 267-292.

HAYES, J.D., IMBRIE, J. & SHACKLETON N.J. 1976. Variations in the Earth's orbit, pacemaker of the Ice Ages. *Science, 194,* 1121-1132.

HAYNES, J.R. & DOBSON, M.R. 1969. Physiography, foraminifera and sedimentation in the Dovey Estuary (Wales). *Geological Journal, 6,* 217-256.

HEDBURG, H.D. 1976. *International stratigraphic guide.* New York.

HELM, D.G. & ROBERTS, B. 1975. A reinterpretation of the origin of sands and gravels around Banc-y-Warren, near Cardigan, west Wales. *Geological Journal, 10,* 131-146.

HELM, D.G. & ROBERTS, B. 1984. The origin of Late Devensian sands and gravels, south-east Anglesey, North Wales. *Geological Journal, 19,* 33-55.

HENRY, A. 1984(a). *The lithostratigraphy, biostratigraphy and chronostratigraphy of coastal Pleistocene deposits in Gower, South Wales.* Unpublished Ph.D. thesis, University of Wales.

HENRY, A. 1984(b). Horton. In: Bowen, D.Q. & Henry, A. (eds) *Wales: Gower, Preseli, Fforest Fawr.* Quaternary Research Association Field Guide, April 1984, 48-51.

HEYWORTH, A. & KIDSON, C. 1982. Sea-level changes in south-west England and Wales. *Proceedings of the Geologists' Association, 93,* 91-111.

HEYWORTH, A., KIDSON, C. & WILKS, P. 1985. Late-glacial and Holocene sediments at Clarach Bay, near Aberystwyth. *Journal of Ecology, 73,* 459-480.

HIBBERT, F.A. & SWITSUR, V.R. 1976. Radiocarbon dating of Flandrian pollen zones in Wales and northern England. *New Phytologist, 77,* 793-807.

HICKS, H. 1884. On some recent researches in bone caves in Wales. *Proceedings of the Geologists' Association, 9,* 1-42.

HICKS, H. 1886a. Results of recent researches in some bone caves in North Wales (Ffynnon Beuno and Cae Gwyn) with a note on the animal remains by W. Davies. *Quarterly Journal of the Geological Society of London, 42,* 3-19.

HICKS, H. 1886b. Evidence of Man and Pleistocene animals in North Wales prior to glacial deposits. *Nature, 34,* 216.

HICKS, H. 1887. On some further researches in bone caves in North Wales. *Proceedings of the Geologists' Association, 10,* 14-18.

HICKS, H. 1888. On the Cae Gwyn Cave, North Wales. *Quarterly Journal of the Geological Society of London, 44,* 561-577.

HICKS, H. 1894. The evidences of ice-action in north-west Pembrokeshire. *Glacialists' Magazine, 1,* 191-196.

HICKS, H., GREENLY, E., BLAKE, J.F., KENDALL, P., LAMPLUGH, G.W., LOMAS, J., READE, M.T., SHONE, W. & STRAHAN, A. 1899. Drift at Moel Tryfaen. *British Association for the Advancement of Science Report for 1899,* 414-423..

HOLMES, G.W., HOPKINS, D.M. & FOSTER, H.L. 1968. Pingos in central Alaska. *United States Geological Survey Bulletin,* 1241-H, 40pp.

HOPPE, G. 1950. Några exempel på glacifluvial dränering fran det Inre Norrbotten. *Geografiska Annaler, 32,* 37-59.

HOPPE, G. 1957. Problems of glacial morphology and the ice age. *Geografriska Annaler, 39,* 1-18.

HOULDER, C.H. 1977. Man in the Welsh Quaternary. *Cambria, 4,* 98-104.

HOWARD, F.T. 1901. Observations on the lakes and tarns of South Wales. *Transactions of the Cardiff Naturalists' Society, 32,* 29-43.

HOWARD, F.T. & SMALL, E.W. 1901. Notes on ice-action in South Wales. *Transactions of the Cardiff Naturalists' Society, 32,* 44-48.

HOWE, G.M. & YATES, R.A. 1953. A bathymetrical study of Llyn Cau, Cader Idris. *Geography, 38*, 124-131.

HUGHES, K.J. 1974. *The nature and origin of Pleistocene deposits in the Avan Basin, south-west Glamorganshire.* Unpublished Ph.D. thesis, University of Wales.

HUGHES, S. 1984. Amino acid ratios of *Cepaea nemoralis.* In: Bowen, D.Q. & Henry,?10?A. (eds) *Wales: Gower, Preseli, Fforest Fawr.* Quaternary Research Association Field Guide, April 1984, 47.

HUGHES, T McK. 1885. Notes on the geology of the Vale of Clwyd. *Proceedings of the Chester Society for Natural Science, 3*, 5-37.

HUGHES, T. McK. 1887. On the drifts of the Vale of Clwyd and their relation to the caves and cave deposits. *Quarterly Journal of the Geological Society of London, 43*, 73-120.

HUGHES, T. McK & THOMAS, D.R. 1874. On the occurrence of felstone implements of the Le Moustier type in Pontnewydd Cave, near Cefn, St Asaph. *Journal of the Royal Anthropological Institute, 3*, 387-392.

HUXTABLE, J. 1984. Thermoluminescence studies on burnt flint and stones. In: Green, H.S. (ed.) *Pontnewydd Cave. A Lower Palaeolithic hominid site in Wales.* The First Report. National Museum of Wales, Cardiff, 106-107.

HYDE, H.A. 1936. On a peat bed at the East Moors, Cardiff. *Transactions of the Cardiff Naturalists' Society, 69*, 39-48.

HYDE, H.A. 1940. On a peat bog at Craig-y-Llyn, Glamorgan. Data for the study of post-glacial history IV. *New Phytologist, 39*, 226-233.

IMBRIE, J., HAYES, J.D., MARTINSON, D.G., McINTYRE, A., MIX, A.C., MORLEY, J.J., PISIAS, N.J., PRELL, W.L., SHACKLETON, N.J. 1984. The orbital theory of Pleistocene climate: support from a revised chronology of the marine record. In: Burger, A.L., Imbrie, J., Hayes, J., Kukla, G. and Saltzman, B. (eds) *Milankovitch and climate.*

IMBRIE, J. & IMBRIE, K.P. 1979. *Ice Ages: solving the mystery.* McMillan, London and Basingstoke.

INCE, J. 1981. *Pollen analysis and radiocarbon dating of late-glacial and early Flandrian deposits in Snowdonia, North Wales.* Unpublished Ph.D. thesis, City of London Polytechnic, 307pp.

INCE, J. 1983. Two post-glacial pollen profiles from the uplands of Snowdonia, Gwynedd, North Wales. *New Phytologist, 95*, 159-172.

IVES, J.D., ANDREWS, J.T. & BARRY, R.G. 1975. Growth and decay of the Laurentide ice-sheet and comparisons with Fenno-Scandinavia. *Die Naturwissenschaften, 62*, 118-125.

JACKSON, J.W. 1922. On the tufaceous deposits of Caerwys, Flintshire and the mollusca contained therein. *Lancashire and Cheshire Naturalist, 14*, 147-158.

JAHN, A. 1962. Origin and development of patterned ground in Spitsbergen. *Proceedings of the International Conference on Permafrost* (1963), 140-145.

JEFFRIES, J.G. 1880. On the occurrence of marine shells of existing species at different heights above the present level of the sea. *Quarterly Journal of the Geological Society of London, 36*, 351-355.

JEHU, T.J. 1902. A bathymetrical and geological study of the lakes of Snowdonia and eastern Caernarvonshire. *Transactions of the Royal Society of Edinburgh, 40*, 419-467.

JEHU, T.J. 1904. The glacial deposits of northern Pembrokeshire. *Transactions of the Royal Society of Edinburgh, 41*, 53-87.

JEHU, T.J. 1909. The glacial deposits of western Caernarvonshire. *Transactions of the Royal Society of Edinburgh, 47*, 17-56.

JENKINS, G.D., BOWEN, D.Q., ADAMS, C.G., SHACKLETON, N.J. & BRASSEL, S.C. 1985. The Neogene: Part 1. In: Snelling, N.J. (ed.) The chronology of the geological record. *Geological Society of London Memoir, 10*, 199-260.

JOHN, B.S. 1965(a). *Aspects of the glaciation and superficial deposits of Pembrokeshire.* Unpublished D.Phil. thesis, Oxford University (2 vols).

JOHN, B.S. 1965(b). A possible Main Würm glaciation in west Pembrokeshire. *Nature, 207*, 622-623.

JOHN, B.S. 1967. Further evidence for a Middle Würm Interstadial and a Main Würm glaciation of south-west Wales. *Geological Magazine, 104*, 630-633.

JOHN, B.S. 1968(a). Age of raised beach deposits of south-western Britain. *Nature, 218*, 665-667.

JOHN, B.S. 1968(b). Directions of ice movement in the southern Irish Sea Basin during the last major glaciation, an hypothesis. *Journal of Glaciology, 7*, 507-510.

JOHN, B.S. 1968(c). A Middle Würm Interstadial in south-west Wales. A reply to G.S. Boulton. *Geological Magazine, 105, 398-400.*

JOHN, B.S. 1969. Pembrokeshire and south Cardiganshire. In: *Coastal Pleistocene deposits in Wales.* Quaternary Research Association Field Guide 1969, 18-26.

JOHN, B.S. 1970(a). Pembrokeshire. In: Lewis, C.A. (ed.) *The glaciations of Wales and adjoining regions.* Longman, London, 229-265.

JOHN, B.S. 1970(b). The Pleistocene drift succession at Porth Clais, Pembrokeshire. *Geological Magazine, 107,* 439-457.

JOHN, B.S. 1971(a). Glaciation and the west Wales landscape. *Nature in Wales, 12,* 138-155.

JOHN, B.S. 1971(b). The 'Red Lady' of Paviland, a comment. *Antiquity, 45,* 141-144.

JOHN, B.S. 1972. The Fishguard and Pembroke area. A description of the Ordnance Survey one inch sheet 138/151: Fishguard and Pembroke. In: Edwards, K.C. (ed.) *British landscapes through maps, 16,* 35pp.

JOHN, B.S. 1973. Vistulian periglacial phenomena in south-west Wales. *Biuletyn Peryglacjalny, 22,* 185-212.

JOHN, B.S. 1974. Ice Age events in south Pembrokeshire. *Nature in Wales, 15,* 66-68.

JOHN, B.S. 1976. *Pembrokeshire.* David and Charles, Newton Abbot.

JOHN, B.S. & ELLIS-GRUFFYDD, I.D. 1970. Weichselian stratigraphy and radiocarbon dating in South Wales. *Geologie en Mijnbouw, 49,* 285-296.

JOHNSON, R.H. 1962. Some observations on the glaciation of the Aber-Glaslyn Nant Gwynant Valley, North Wales. *Journal of the Manchester Geographical Society, 58,* 41-51.

JONES, A. & KEIGWIN, L.D. 1988. Evidence from Fram Straight (78°N) for early deglaciation. *Nature, 336,* 56-59.

JONES, E.L. 1882. On the exploration of two caves in the neighbourhood of Tenby. *Quarterly Journal of the Geological Society of London, 38,* 282-288.

JONES, M. 1946. *The development of the Teifi drainage system.* Unpublished M.Sc. thesis, University of Wales.

JONES, O.T. 1942. The buried channel of the Tawe Valley near Ynystawe, Glamorganshire. *Quarterly Journal of the Geological Society of London, 98,* 61-88.

JONES, O.T. 1965. The glacial and post-glacial history of the lower Teifi Valley. *Quarterly Journal of the Geological Society of London, 121,* 247-281.

JONES, O.T. & PUGH, W.J. 1935. The geology of the district around Machynlleth and Aberystwyth. *Proceedings of the Geologists' Association, 46,* 247-300.

JONES, R.O. 1931(a). Note on a supposed terrace in the Tawe Valley. *Proceedings of the Swansea Scientific and field naturalists' Society, 1,* 145.

JONES, R.O. 1931(b). The development of the Tawe drainage. *Proceedings of the Geologists' Association, 52,* 305-321.

JUDD, J.W. 1901. Note on the nature and origin of the rock-fragments found in the excavations made at Stonehenge by Mr Gowland in 1901. *Archaeologia, 58,* 70.

KEEPING, W. 1878. Geology of Aberystwyth. *Geological Magazine, 5,* 532-547.

KEEPING, W. 1882. The glacial geology of central Wales. *Geological Magazine, 9,* 251-257.

KELLAWAY, G.A. 1971. Glaciation and the stones of Stonehenge. *Nature, 233,* 30-35.

KELLAWAY, G.A., REDDING, J.H., SHEPHARD-THORN, E.R. & DESTOMBES, J.P. 1975. The Quaternary history of the English Channel. *Philosophical Transactions of the Royal Society of London, 279,* 189-218.

KELLY, S.F. 1967. As good as new. *The Speleologist, 2,* 20-21.

KENDALL, P.F. 1893. On a moraine-like mound near Snowdon. *The Glacialists' Magazine, 1,* 68-70.

KENDALL, P.F. 1902. A system of glacier-lakes in the Cleveland Hills. *Quarterly Journal of the Geological Society of London, 58,* 471-571.

KERNEY, M.P. 1963. Late-glacial deposits on the chalk of south-east England. *Philosophical Transactions of the Royal Society of London,* B, 246, 203-254.

KERNEY, M.P., PREECE, R.C. & TURNER, C. 1980. Molluscan and plant biostratigraphy of some Late Devensian and Flandrian deposits in Kent. *Philosophical Transactions of the Royal Society of London,* B, 291, 1-43.

KIDSON, C., BOWEN, D.Q. 1976. Some comments on the history of the English Channel. *Quaternary Newsletter, 18,* 8-10.

KIDSON, E. 1888. Evidences of glacial action in Snowdonia. *Report of the Transactions of the Nottinghamshire Naturalists' Society, 36,* 14-19.

KIDSON, E. 1890. Further evidences of glacial action in Snowdonia. *Report of the Transactions of the Nottinghamshire Naturalists' Society,* 37 (for 1889), 14-20.

KING, R.B. 1968. Periglacial features in the Cairngorm Mountains, Scotland. *Journal of Glaciology, 10,* 375-386.

KUKLA, G.J. 1977. Pleistocene land-sea correlations. I. Europe. *Earth Science Reviews, 13,* 307-374.

KUKLA, G.J. 1987. Loess stratigraphy in central China and correlation with an extended Oxygen Isotope Stage scale. *Quaternary Science Reviews, 6,* 191-220.

LACAILLE, A.D. & GRIMES, W.F. 1955. The prehistory of Caldey. *Archaeologica Cambrenesis, 104*, 85-165.

LAING, F. 1980. *Pollen analysis of early Flandrian peat deposits at Llyn Gwernan, Gwynedd, Wales.* Unpublished M.Sc. thesis, City of London Polytechnic.

LAMB, H.H. 1967. Britain's changing climate. *Geographical Journal, 133*, 445-468.

LAUTRIDOU, J.P. 1982. Quaternary excursion in Normandy, IGCP24, *Quaternary glaciations in the Northern Hemisphere* 88pp. Caen.

LAWS, E. 1878. On a "kitchen midden" found in a cave near Tenby, Pembrokeshire, and explored by Wilmot Power. *Journal of the Anthroplogical Institute, 7*, 84-89.

LAWS, E. 1888. *The history of Little England beyond Wales and the non-Kymric colony settled in Pembrokeshire.* George Bell & Sons, London.

LEA, J.W. & THOMPSON, T.R.E. 1978. *Soils in Clwyd I. Sheet SJ 35 (Wrexham North).* Soil Survey Record No. 48.

LEACH, A.L. 1910. On a glacial drift at Marros near Amroth. *Geological Magazine, 5*, 278-279.

LEACH, A.L. 1911. On the relation of the glacial drift to the raised beach near Porth Clais, St Davids. *Geological Magazine, 5*, 462-466.

LEACH, A.L. 1913. Stone implements from soil drifts and chipping floors in south Pembrokeshire. *Archaeologica Cambrenesis, 13*, 391-432.

LEACH, A.L. 1918(a). Flint-working sites on the submerged land (submerged forest) bordering the Pembrokeshire coast. *Proceedings of the Geologists' Association, 29*, 46-67.

LEACH, A.L. 1918(b). *Some prehistoric remains in the Tenby museum.* 8 vol., Tenby.

LEACH, A.L. 1931. *Some prehistoric remains in the Tenby Museum.* (2nd. ed.) 8 vol., Tenby.

LEACH, A.L. 1933. The geology and scenery of Tenby and the south Pembrokeshire coast. *Proceedings of the Geologists' Association, 44*, 187-216.

LEACH, A.L. 1945. The Rev. G.N. Smith: A Pembrokeshire antiquary. *Archaeologica Cambrenesis, 98 (1944-45)*, 248-254.

LEAR, D.L. 1986. *The Quaternary deposits of the lower Teifi Valley.* Unpublished Ph.D. thesis, University of Wales.

LEES, D.J. 1982. The evolution of Gower coasts. In: Humphrys, G. (ed.) *Geographical excursions from Swansea. Vol I: physical environment.* Publication of the Department of Geography, University College, Swansea, 15-32.

LEES, D.J. 1983. *Post-glacial sand dune history and archaeology at Broughton Bay, Gower.* B.G.R.G. Spring Meeting, May 13th-15th. Field excursion handbook. Swansea, 27-29.

LEWIS, C.A. 1966(a). *The periglacial landforms of the Brecon Beacons, Wales.* Unpublished Ph.D. thesis, University of London.

LEWIS, C.A. 1966(b). The Breconshire end-moraine. *Nature, 212* 1559-1561.

LEWIS, C.A. 1970(a). (ed.) *The glaciations of Wales and adjoining regions.* Longman, London.

LEWIS, C.A. 1970(b). The Upper Wye and Usk regions. In: Lewis, C.A. (ed.) *The glaciations of Wales and adjoining regions.* Longman, London, 147-173.

LEWIS, C.A. 1970(c). The glaciations of the Brecknock Beacons, Wales. *Brycheiniog, 14*, 97-120.

LEWIS, H.C. 1894. *Glacial geology of Great Britain and Ireland.* Longman.

LEWIS, W.V. 1938. A meltwater hypothesis of cirque formation. *Geological Magazine, 75*, 249-265.

LEWIS, W.V. 1949. The function of meltwater in cirque formation, a reply. *Geographical Review, 39*, 110-128.

LINTON, D .L. 1955. The problem of tors. *Geological Journal, 121*, 470-487.

LISTER, A.M.1984. The fossil record of Elk *Alces alces* (L.) in Britain. *Quaternary Newsletter, 44*, 1-7.

LIVINGSTON, H. 1986. *Quaternary geomorphology of part of the Elwy Valley and Vale of Clwyd, north-east Wales.* Unpublished Ph.D. thesis, University of London.

LOWE, J.J. & WALKER, M.J.C. 1984. *Reconstructing Quaternary environments.* Longman, London and New York.

LOWE, J.J., LOWE, S., FOWLER, A.J., HEDGES, R.E.M. & AUSTIN, T.J.F. 1988. Comparison of accelerator and radiometric radiocarbon measurements obtained from Late Devensian late-glacial lake sediments from Llyn Gwernan, North Wales, UK. *Boreas, 17*, 355-369.

LOWE, S. 1981. Radiocarbon dating and stratigraphic resolution in Welsh late-glacial chronology. *Nature, 293*, 210-212.

LUCKMAN, B.H. 1966. *Some aspects of the geomorphology of the Lugg and Arrow Valleys.* Unpublished M.A. thesis, Manchester University.

LUCKMAN, B.H. 1970. The Hereford Basin. In: Lewis C.A. (ed.) *The glaciations of Wales and adjoining regions.* Longman, London, 175-196.

LYELL, C. 1873. *The geological evidences of the antiquity of Man with an outline of the glacial and post-Tertiary geology and remarks on the origin of species.* John Murray, London.

MacDONALD, H.A. 1961. Some erratics from the Teifi Estuary western Cardiganshire. *Geological Magazine, 98,* 81-84.

MACKINTOSH, A.F. 1845. On the supposed evidences of the former existence of glaciers in North Wales. *Quarterly Journal of the Geological Society of London, 1,* 460-467.

MACKINTOSH, D. 1876. On the correlation of the deposits in Cefn and Pontnewydd Caves with the drifts of the north-west of England and Wales. *Quarterly Journal of the Geological Society of London, 32,* 91-94.

MACKINTOSH, D. 1881. On the precise mode of accumulation and derivation of the Moel-Tryfaen shelly deposits; on the discovery of similar high-level deposits along the eastern slopes of the Welsh mountains; and on the existence of drift-zones showing probable variations in the rate of submergence. *Quarterly Journal of the Geological Society of London, 37,* 351-369.

MACKINTOSH, D. 1887. Additional discoveries of high-level marine drifts in North Wales with remarks on driftless areas. *Quarterly Journal of the Geological Society of London, 38,* 184-196.

MACKLIN, M.G. & LEWIN, J. 1986. Terraced fills of Pleistocene and Holocene age in the Rheidol Valley, Wales. *Journal of Quaternary Science, 1,* 21-34.

MACKLIN, M.G. & LEWIN, J. 1987. Terraced fills in the Rheidol Valley, Wales. Reply to Mrs S. Watson. *Journal of Quaternary Science, 2,* 166.

MANGERUD, J., ANDERSEN, S.Th., BERGLUND, B.E. & DONNER, J.J. 1974. Quaternary stratigraphy of Norden, a proposal for terminology and classification. *Boreas, 3,* 109-126.

MANLEY, G. 1964. The evolution of the climatic environment. In: Watson, J.W. (ed.) *The British Isles: a systematic geography.* Nelson, London, 452pp.

MANNERFELT, C.M. 1945. Några glacialmorfologiska formelement. *Geografiska Annaler, 27, 1-239.*

MARR, J.E. & ADIE, R.H. 1898. The lakes of Snowdon. *Geological Magazine, 5,* 51-61.

MARTINSON, D.G., PISIAS, N.J., HAYES, J.D., IMBRIE, J., MOORE, T.C. & SHACKLETON, N.J. 1987. Age dating and the Orbital Theory of the Ice Ages, development of a high resolution nought to 300,000 year chronostratigraphy. *Quaternary Research, 27,* 1-29.

MATLEY, C.A. 1936. A 50-foot coastal terrace and other late-glacial phenomena in the Lleyn Peninsula. *Proceedings of the Geologists' Association, 47,* 221-233.

MATLEY, C.A. & WILSON, T.S. 1946. The Harlech Dome, north of the Barmouth Estuary. *Quarterly Journal of the Geological Society of London, 102,* 1-40.

MAW, G. 1866. On the occurrence of extensive deposits of tufa in Flintshire. *Geological Magazine, 3,* 253-256.

McBURNEY, C.B.M. 1959. Report on the first season's work on British Upper Palaeolithic cave deposits. *Proceedings of the Prehistoric Society, 25,* 260-269.

McBURNEY, C.B.M. 1965. The Old Stone Age in Wales. In: Foster, I.L. & Daniel, G. (eds) *Prehistoric and early Wales.* Routledge & Kegan Paul, London, 244pp.

McCABE, A.M. 1987 Quaternary deposits and glacial stratigraphy in Ireland. *Quaternary Science Reviews, 6,* 259-299.

McMILLAN, N.F. 1947. The molluscan faunas of some tufas in Cheshire and Flintshire. *Proceedings of the Liverpool Geological Society, 19,* 240-248.

McMILLAN, N.F. & ZEISSLER, H. 1985. The tufa deposit at Caerwys, North Wales, and its molluscan fauna. *Amateur Geologist, 11,* 3-11.

MENZIES, J. 1978. A review of the literature on the formation and location of drumlins. *Earth Science Reviews, 14,* 315-350.

MILLER, A.A. 1946. Some physical features related to the river development in the Dolgelly district. *Proceedings of the Geologists' Association, 57,* 174-203.

MILLER, G.H. 1985. Aminostratigraphy of Baffin Island shell bearing deposits. In: Andrews, J.T. (ed.) *Quaternary environments, eastern Canadian Arctic Baffin Bay, and western Greenland,* 394-427.

MILLER, R., COMMON, R. & GALLOWAY, R.W. 1954. Stone stripes and other surface features of Tinto Hill. *Geographical Journal, 120,* 216-219.

MILLOTT, J. 1951. The non-marine mollusca of the Caerwys tufa deposit. *Proceedings of the Chester Society for Natural Science, Literature and Art, 4,* (for 1950), 138-142.

MITCHELL, G.F. 1960. The Pleistocene history of the Irish Sea. *British Association for the Advancement of Science, 17,* 313-325.

MITCHELL, G.F. 1962. Summer field meeting in Wales and Ireland. *Proceedings of the Geologists' Association, 73*, 197-213.

MITCHELL, G.F. 1971. Fossil pingos in the south of Ireland. *Nature, 230*, 43-44.

MITCHELL, G.F. 1972. The Pleistocene history of the Irish Sea: second approximation. *Scientific Proceedings of the Royal Dublin Society*, Series A, 4, 181-199.

MITCHELL, G.F. 1973. Fossil pingos at Camaross Townland, County Wexford. *Proceedings of the Royal Irish Academy, 73*, 269-282.

MITCHELL, G.F., PENNY, L.F., SHOTTON, F.W. & WEST, R.G. 1973. A correlation of Quaternary deposits in the British Isles. *Special Report of the Geological Society of London, 4*, 99pp.

MOLLESSON, T. 1976. Remains of Pleistocene Man in Paviland and Pontnewydd Caves, Wales. *Transactions of the British Cave Research Association, 3*, 112-116.

MOLLESON, T. & BURLEIGH, R. 1978. A new date for Goat's Hole Cave. *Antiquity, 52*, 143-145.

MOORE, P.D. 1963. Unpublished B.Sc. thesis.

MOORE, P.D. 1966. *Investigations of peats in central Wales.* Unpublished Ph.D. thesis, University of Wales.

MOORE, P.D. 1968. Human influence upon vegetational history in north Cardiganshire. *Nature, 217*, 1006-1009.

MOORE, P.D. 1970. Studies in the vegetational history of Mid Wales II. The late-glacial period in Cardiganshire. *New Phytologist, 69*, 363-375.

MOORE, P.D. 1972(a). Studies in the vegetational history of Mid Wales III. Early Flandrian pollen data from west Cardiganshire. *New Phytologist, 71*, 947-959.

MOORE, P.D. 1972(b). The influence of post-Weichselian climatic fluctuations upon forest composition and development in Mid Wales. In: Taylor, J.A. (ed.) *Research papers in forest meteorology.* Cambrian News, Aberystwyth, 20-30.

MOORE, P.D. 1973. The influence of prehistoric cultures upon the initiation and spread of blanket bog in upland Wales. *Nature, 241*, 350-353.

MOORE, P.D. 1975(a). Origin of blanket mires. *Nature, 256*, 267-269.

MOORE, P.D. 1975(b). Bølling Interstadial in Britain. *Nature, 257*, 356-357.

MOORE, P.D. 1977. Vegetational history. *Cambria, 4*, 73-83.

MOORE, P.D. 1978. Studies in the vegetational history of Mid Wales V. Stratigraphy and pollen analysis of Llyn Mire in the Wye Valley. *New Phytologist, 80*, 281,302.

MOORE, P.D. & BECKETT, P.J. 1971. Vegetation and development of Llyn, a Welsh mire. *Nature, 231*, 363-365.

MOORE, P.D. & CHATER, E.H. 1969(a). Studies in the vegetational history of Mid Wales I, the post-glacial period in Cardiganshire. *New Phytologist, 68*, 183-196.

MOORE, P.D. & CHATER, E.H. 1969(b). The changing vegetation of west-central Wales in the light of human history. *Journal of Ecology, 57*, 361-379.

MOORE, T.J. 1865. The source of the stones of Stonehenge. *Antiquaries Journal, 3*, 239-261.

MORGAN, R.E. 1913. Bacon Hole. In: *the 78th Annual Report of the Council 1912- 1913. Report of the Royal Institute of South Wales.* Wright & Co., Swansea.

MORGAN, W.L. 1913. Bacon Hole, Gower. *Archaeologica Cambrenesis, 13*, 173-180.

MORGAN, W.L. 1919. *Report of the Royal Institute of South Wales.* Swansea, 14-15.

MULLER, F. 1959. Beobachtungen über pingos. *Meddelelser om Grønland, 153*.

NEAVERSON, E. 1941. The extent of the tufa deposit at Prestatyn. *Proceedings of the Liverpool Geological Society, 18*, 49-56.

NEAVERSON, E. 1942. A summary of the records of Pleistocene and post-glacial mammalia from North Wales and Merseyside. *Proceedings of the Liverpool Geological Society*, 70-85.

NEDERVELDE van, J., DAVIES, M. & JOHN, B.S. 1973. Radiocarbon dating from Ogof-yr-Ychen, a new Pleistocene site in west Wales. *Nature, 245*, 453-454.

NICHOLAS, T.C. 1915. The geology of the St Tudwal's Peninsula (Caernarvonshire). *Quarterly Journal of the Geological Society of London, 71*, 83-143.

NORTH, F.J. 1943. Centenary of the glacial theory. *Proceedings of the Geologists' Association, 54*, 1-28.

NORTH, F.J. 1955. The geological history of Brecknock. *Brycheiniog, 1*, 9-77.

NUNN, K.R. & BOZTAS, M. 1977. Shallow seismic reflection profiling on land use and controlled source. *Geoexploration, 15*, 87-97.

OAKLEY, K.P. 1968. The date of the 'Red Lady' of Paviland. *Antiquity, 42*, 306-307.

OAKLEY, K.P. 1971. Radiocarbon dating of Proto-Solutrean in Wales. *Nature, 231,* 112.

OLDFIELD, F. 1965. Problems of mid post-glacial pollen zonation in part of north-west England. *Journal of Ecology, 53,* 247-260.

PALMER, J. & NIELSON, R.A. 1962. The origin of granite tors on Dartmoor, Devonshire. *Proceedings of the Yorkshire Geological Society, 33,* 315-340.

PALMER, J. & RADLEY, J. 1961. Gritstone tors of the English Pennines. *Zeitschrift für Geomorphologie, 5,* 37-52.

PEAKE, D.S. 1961. Glacial changes in the Alyn river system and their significance on the glaciology of the North Welsh Border. *Quarterly Journal of the Geological Society of London, 117,* 335-363.

PEAKE, D.S. 1979. The limit of the Devensian Irish Sea ice-sheet on the North Welsh Border. *Quaternary Newsletter, 27,* 1-4.

PEAKE, D.S. 1981. The Devensian glaciation on the North Welsh Border. In: Neale, J. & Flenley, J. (eds) *The Quaternary of Britain.* Pergamon, Oxford, 49-59.

PEAKE, D.S., BOWEN, D.Q., HAINS, B.A. & SEDDON, B. 1973. Wales. In: Mitchell, G.F. *et al.* (1973) Correlation of Quaternary deposits in the British Isles. *Special Report of the Geological Society of London, 4,* 59-99.

PEARSALL, W.H. 1950. *Mountains and moorlands.* Collins, London.

PEDLEY, H.M. 1987. The Flandrian (Quaternary) Caerwys tufa, North Wales: an ancient barrage tufa deposit. *Proceedings of the Yorkshire Geological Society, 46,* 141-152.

PENNINGTON, W. 1977. The Late Devensian flora and vegetation of Britain. *Philosophical Transactions of the Royal Society of London, 280B,* 247-271.

PENNY, L.F., COOPE, G.R. & CATT, J.A. 1969. Age and insect fauna of the Dimlington Silts, east Yorkshire. *Nature, 244,* 65-67.

PISSART, A. 1963. Les traces de 'pingos' du Pays de Galles (Grande-Bretagne) et du Plateau des Hautes Fagnes (Belgique). *Zeitschrift für Geomorphologie, 7,* 147-165.

PISSART, A. 1965. Les pingos des Hautes Fagnes: les problèmes de leur gènese. *Annales de la Société géologique de Belgique, 88,* 277-289.

POCOCK, R.W., WHITEHEAD, T.H., WEDD, C.B. & ROBERTSON, T. 1938. *Shrewsbury district including the Hanwood Coalfield.* Memoir of the Geological Survey of Great Britain. H.M.S.O., London.

POCOCK, T.I. 1940. Glacial drift and river terraces of the Hereford Wye. *Zeitschrift für Gletscherkunde, für Eiszeitforschung und Geschichte des Kilmas, 27,* 98-117.

POOLE, E.G. & WHITEMAN, A.J. 1961. The glacial drifts of the southern part of the Shropshire-Cheshire basin. *Quarterly Journal of the Geological Society of London, 117,* 91-123.

PORSLID, A.E. 1938. Earth mounds in unglaciated arctic north-west America. *Geographical Review, 28,* 46-58.

POST von, L. 1933. A Gothiglacial transgression of the sea in south Sweden. *Geografiska Annaler, 15,* 21-36.

POTTS, A.S. 1968. *The glacial and periglacial geomorphology of central Wales.* Unpublished Ph.D. thesis, University of Wales.

POTTS, A.S. 1971. Fossil cryonival features in central Wales. *Geografiska Annaler, 53A,* 39-51.

PREECE, R.C. 1978. *The biostratigraphy of the Flandrian tufas in southern Britain.* Unpublished Ph.D. thesis, University of London.

PREECE, R.C., TURNER, C. & GREEN, H.S. 1982. *Field excursion to the tufas of the Wheeler Valley and to Pontnewydd and Cefn Caves.* Quaternary Research Association Field Guide, 1-9.

PRENTICE, J.E. & MORRIS, P.G. 1959. Cemented screes in the Manifold Valley. *East Midland Geographer, 2,* 16-19.

PRESTWICH, J. 1892. The raised beaches and head or rubble drift of the south of England. *Quarterly Journal of the Geological Society of London, 48,* 263-343.

PRINGLE, J. & GEORGE, T.N. 1948. *South Wales: British Regional Geology.* H.M.S.O., London.

RAE, A.M., IVANOVICH, M., GREEN, H.S., HEAD, M.J. & KIMBER, R.W.L. 1987. A comparative dating study of bones from Little Hoyle Cave, South Wales, U.K. *Journal of Archaeological Science, 14,* 243-250.

RAMSAY, A.C. 1852. On the superficial accumulations and surface markings of North Wales. *Quarterly Journal of the Geological Society of London, 8,* 371-376.

RAMSAY, A.C. 1858. *Geology of parts of Wiltshire and Gloucestershire.* Memoir of the Geological Survey of Great Britain (Sheet 34). H.M.S.O., London.

RAMSAY, A.C. 1860. *The old glaciers of Switzerland and North Wales.* Longman, Green, Longman and Roberts, London, 116pp.

RAMSAY, A.C. 1866. *The geology of North Wales* (Volume III). Memoir of the Geological Survey of Great Britain. H.M.S.O., London.

RAMSAY, A.C. 1881. *The geology of North Wales* (Volume III –2nd edition). Memoir of the Geological Survey of Great Britain. H.M.S.O., London.

RAPP, A. 1967. Pleistocene activity and Holocene stability of hillslopes, with examples from Scandinavia and Pennsylvania. *Congress of the University of Liege, 40*, 229-244.

READE, T.M. 1892. The drift beds of the North Wales and Mid Wales coast. *Quarterly Journal of the Geological Society of London, 48*, 181-182.

READE, T.M. 1893. The drift beds of the Moel Tryfaen area of North Wales. *Proceedings of the Liverpool Geological Society, 7*, 36-79.

READE, T.M. 1894. The moraine of Llŷn Cwm Llwch, on the Beacons of Brecon. *Proceedings of the Liverpool Geological Society, 7*, 270-276.

READE, T.M. 1896. Notes on the drift of the Mid Wales coast. *Proceedings of the Liverpool Geological Society, 7*, 410-419.

READE, T.M. 1898. High-level marine drift at Colwyn Bay. *Quarterly Journal of the Geological Society of London, 54*, 582-584.

RICHARDSON, L. 1910. Some glacial features in Wales and probably in the Cotteswold Hills. *Cotteswold Naturalists' Club, 17*, 37-39.

ROBERTS, J. 1887-8. Cats Hole Cave. *Annual Report and Transactions of the Swansea Scientific Society, 1887-8*, 15-23.

ROBERTSON, T. 1933. *The geology of the South Wales Coalfield, Part V. The country around Merthyr Tydfil.* Memoir of the Geological Survey of Great Britain. H.M.S.O., London, 176-192.

ROLLESTON, G., LANE FOX, A., BUSK, G., DAWKINS, W.B., EVANS, J. & HILTON-PRICE, F.G. 1878. Report of a committee ... appointed for the purpose of examining two caves containing human remains, in the neighbourhood of Tenby. *Report of the British Association for the Advancement of Science (Dublin), 48*, 207-217.

ROSE J. 1985. The Dimlington Stadial/Dimlington Chronozone, a proposal for naming the main glacial episode of the Late Devensian in Britain. *Boreas, 14*, 225-230.

ROWLANDS, B.M. 1955. *The glacial and post-glacial evolution of the landforms of the Vale of Clwyd.* Unpublished M.A. thesis, University of Liverpool.

ROWLANDS, B.M. 1970. *The glaciation of the Arenig region.* Unpublished Ph.D. thesis, University of Liverpool.

ROWLANDS, B.M. 1971. Radiocarbon evidence of the age of an Irish Sea glaciation in the Vale of Clwyd. *Nature, 230*, 9-11.

ROWLANDS, P.H. 1966. *Pleistocene stratigraphy and palynological investigation in the Marston, Church Stoke and Church Stretton Valleys, west of Shropshire.* Unpublished Ph.D. thesis, University of Birmingham.

ROWLANDS, P.H. & SHOTTON, F.W. 1971. Pleistocene deposits of Church Stretton (Shropshire) and its neighbourhood. *Journal of the Geological Society of London, 127*, 599-622.

RUDDIMAN W.F. 1987. Synthesis: The ocean/ice-sheet record. In: Ruddiman, W.F. & Wright, H.E.J. (eds) *North America and adjacent oceans during the last deglaciation.* The Geology of North America, Vol. K-3, 463-478.

RUDDIMAN, W.F. & McINTIRE, A. 1981. The North Atlantic during the last deglaciation. *Palaeogeography, Palaeoclimatology, Palaeoecology, 35*, 145-214.

RUDDIMAN, W.F. & RAYMO, M.E. 1988. Northern hemisphere climate regimes during the past three million years, possible tectonic connections. *Philosophical Transactions of the Royal Society of London*, Series B, 318, 637-644.

RUDEFORTH, C.C. 1970. *Soils of north Cardiganshire.* Memoir of the Soil Survey of Great Britain.

RUTTER, J.G. 1948. Minchin Hole – recent excavations. *Journal of the Gower Society, 1*, 22-23.

RUTTER, J.G. 1949. Archaeology of Gower 1949. *Journal of the Gower Society, 2*, 11-13.

RUTTER, J.G. 1950. Excavations at Minchin Hole, 1950. *Journal of the Gower Society, 3*, 46.

RUTTER, J.G. 1952. Minchin Hole excavations 1952. *Journal of the Gower Society, 5*, 34.

RUTTER, J.G. 1953. The Minchin Hole excavations, 1953. *Journal of the Gower Society, 6*, 42.

RUTTER, J.G. 1955. *Minchin Hole excavations 1955. Journal of the Gower Society, 8*, 52.

RUTTER, J.G. 1956. Minchin Hole, 1956. *Journal of the Gower Society, 9*, 26-27.

RUTTER, J.G. 1957. Minchin Hole excavation, 1957. *Journal of the Gower Society, 10*, 57.

SAUNDERS, G.E. 1963. *The glacial deposits and associated features of the Lleyn Peninsula of south-west Caernarvonshire.* Unpublished M.Sc. thesis, University of Bristol. 275pp.

SAUNDERS, G.E. 1967. Written contribution to the discussion of a paper previously taken as read: 3 April 1964. With a reply by the author, F.M. Synge. *Proceedings of the Geologists' Association, 78*, 347-350.

SAUNDERS, G.E. 1968(a). Glaciation of possible Scottish Re-advance age in north-west Wales. *Nature, 218*, 76-78.

SAUNDERS, G.E. 1968(b). A fabric analysis of the ground moraine deposits of the Lleyn Peninsula of south-west Caernarvonshire. *Geological Journal, 6*, 105-118.

SAUNDERS, G.E. 1968(c). A reappraisal of glacial drainage phenomena in the Lleyn Peninsula. *Proceedings of the Geologists' Association, 79*, 305-324.

SAUNDERS, G.E. 1968(d). *The glacial and post-glacial evolution of landforms in the Lleyn Peninsula.* Unpublished Ph.D. thesis, University of London.

SAUNDERS, G.E. 1969 Caernarvonshire. In: *Coastal Pleistocene deposits in Wales.* Quaternary Research Association Field Guide 1969, 40-44.

SAUNDERS, G.E. 1973. Vistulian periglacial environments in the Lleyn Peninsula. *Biuletyn Peryglacjalny, 22*, 257-269.

SAVORY, H.N. 1973. Excavations at the Hoyle, Tenby, in 1968. *Archaeologica Cambrenesis, 122*, 18-34.

SCOATES, E.A. 1973. *Cold climate processes in North Wales.* M. Phil. thesis, University of Reading.

SEDDON,B. 1957. Late-glacial cwm glaciers in Wales. *Journal of Glaciology, 3*, 94-99.

SEDDON, B. 1962. Late-glacial deposits at Llyn Dwythwch and Nant Ffrancon, Caernarvonshire. *Philosophical Transactions of the Royal Society of London*, Series B, 244, 459-481.

SEYMOUR, E.J. 1973. *A stratigraphical and palynological investigation of a raised bog in Pembrokeshire.* B.Sc. thesis, University of Wales (Botany Department, U.C.W., Aberstwyth).

SEYMOUR, W.P. 1985. *The environmental history of the Preseli region of south-west Wales over the past 12,000 years.* Unpublished Ph.D. thesis, University of Wales.

SHACKLETON, N.J. 1987. Oxygen isotopes, ice volume and sea-level. *Quaternary Science Reviews, 6*, 183-190.

SHACKLETON, N.J., HALL, M.A., LINE, J. & CANG SHUXI, 1983. Carbon isotope data in Core V19-30 confirm reduced carbon dioxide concentration in the Ice Age atmosphere. *Nature, 306*, 319-322.

SHACKLETON, N.J. *et al.* 1984. Oxygen isotope calibration of the onset of ice rafting and history of glaciation in the North Atlantic region. *Nature,* 216-219.

SHACKLETON, N.J., DUPLESSY, J.C., ARNOLD, M., MAURICE, P., HALL, M.A. & CARTLIDGE, J. 1988. Radiocarbon age of last glacial Pacific deep water, *Nature, 335*, 708-711.

SHACKLETON, N.J. & OPDYKE, N.D. 1973. Oxygen isotope and palaeomagnetic stratigraphy of equatorial Pacific core V28-238: oxygen isotope temperatures and ice volumes on a 105 and 106 year scale. *Quaternary Research, 3*, 39-55.

SHAKESBY, R.A. & CAMPBELL, S. 1985. Gower Peninsula. In: Shakesby, R.A. & Walsh, R.P.D. (eds) *Guide to field study excursion in Wales.* First International Conference on Geomorphology 10-15th September 1985, Swansea, 11-25.

SHARP, R.P. 1942. Soil structures in the St Elias Range, Yukon Territory. *Journal of Geomorphology, 5*, 274-301.

SHENNAN, I. 1982. Interpretation of Flandrian sea-level data from Fenland, England. *Proceedings of the Geologists' Association, 93*, 56-63.

SHENNAN, I. 1983. A problem of definition in sea-level research methods. *Quaternary Newsletter, 39*, 17-19.

SHOTTON, F.W. 1967. The problems and contributions of methods of absolute dating within the Pleistocene Period. *Quarterly Journal of the Geological Society of London, 122*, 357-383.

SHOTTON, F.W. 1977(a). The Devensian Stage; its development, limits and sub-stages. In: Mitchell, G.F. & West, R.G. The changing environmental conditions in Great Britain and Ireland during the Devensian (last) cold stage. *Philosophical Transactions of the Royal Society of London, Series B, 280*, 107-374.

SHOTTON, F.W. 1977(b). *British Quaternary studies. Recent advances.* Clarendon Press, Oxford, 298pp.

SHOTTON, F.W. & WILLIAMS, R.E.G. 1971. Birmingham University radiocarbon dates V. *Radiocarbon, 13*, 141-156.

SHOTTON, F.W. & WILLIAMS, R.E.G. 1973. Birmingham University radiocarbon dates VII. *Radiocarbon, 15*, 451-468.

SHOTTON, F.W., WILLIAMS, R.E.G. & JOHNSON, A.S. 1975. Birmingham University radiocarbon dates IX. *Radiocarbon, 17*, 255-275.

SIBRAVA, V., BOWEN, D.Q. & RICHMOND, G.M. (eds) 1986. Quaternary glaciations in the Northern Hemisphere. *Quaternary Science Reviews, 5*, 510pp.

SIMPKINS, K. 1968. *Aspects of the Quaternary history in central Caernarvonshire, Wales.* Unpublished Ph.D. thesis, University of Reading.

SIMPKINS, K. 1974. The late-glacial deposits at Glanllynnau, Caernarvonshire. *New Phytologist, 73*, 605-618.

SINCLAIR, D.A. 1963. *Observations on Pingos.* English translation of Müller, 1959. National Research Council Canada, Technical Translation 1073.

SISSONS, J.B. 1975. A fossil rock glacier in Wester Ross. *Scottish Journal of Geology, 11,* 83-86.

SISSONS, J.B. 1976. A fossil rock glacier in Wester Ross. Reply to W.B. Whalley. *Scottish Journal of Geology, 12,* 178-179.

SISSONS, J.B. 1979. Palaeoclimatic inferences from former glaciers in Scotland and the Lake District. *Nature, 278,* 518-521.

SLATER, F.M. & SEYMOUR, E.J. 1977. Esgyrn Bottom – the most westerly raised bog in Wales. *Proceedings of the Birmingham Natural History Society, 23,* 193-205.

SMITH, A.G. & CLOUTMAN, E.W. 1984. Waun-Fignen-Felen. In: Bowen, D.Q., & Henry, A. (eds) *Wales: Gower, Preseli, Fforest Fawr.* Quaternary Research Association Field Guide, April 1984, 83-90.

SMITH, A.G. & PILCHER, J.R. 1973. Radiocarbon dates and vegetational history of the British Isles. *New Phytologist, 72,* 903-914.

SMITH, B. & GEORGE, T.N. 1961. *North Wales: British regional geology (third edition).* H.M.S.O., London.

SMITH, G.N. 1860. On three undescribed bone caves near Tenby. *Report of the British Association (Oxford), 30,* 101-102.

SMITH, G.N. 1862. On a successful search for flint implements in a cave called 'The Oyle', near Tenby, South Wales. *Report of the British Association (Cambridge), 32,* 95.

SMITH, G.N. 1864. The Pembrokeshire bone and flint-knife caves in regard to the antiquity of Man. *Archaeologica Cambrensis,* for 1864, 342-345.

SMITH, G.N. 1866. Recent researches in a bone cave .... near Tenby. *Proceedings of the Bristol Naturalists' Society, 1,* 10-17.

SMITH, R.T. & TAYLOR, J.A. 1969. The post-glacial development of vegetation and soils in northern Cardiganshire. *Transactions of the Institute of British Geographers, 48,* 75-96.

SOLLAS, W.J. 1913. Paviland Cave, an Aurignacian station in Wales. *Journal of the Royal Anthropological Institute, 43,* 1-50.

SOLLAS, W.J. 1924. *Ancient hunters and their modern representatives.* London.

SOLLAS, W.J. & BREUIL, A.M. 1912. Letter to the Times.

SPARKS, B.W., WILLIAMS, R.B.G. & BELL, F.G. 1972. Presumed ground-ice depressions in East Anglia. *Proceedings of the Royal Society of London,* A, 327, 329-343.

STANLEY, E. 1832. Memoir on a cave at Cefn, Denbighshire. *Edinburgh New Philosophical Journal, 14,* 40-53.

STATHAM, I. 1976. Debris flows on vegetated screes in the Black Mountain, Carmarthenshire. *Earth Surface Processes, 1,* 173-180.

STEPHENS, N. & SHAKESBY, R.A. 1982. Quaternary evidence in south Gower. In: Humphrys, G. (ed.) *Geographical excursions from Swansea, Vol. I: physical environment.* Publication of the Department of Geography, University College, Swansea, 33-50.

STEVENSON, A.C. & MOORE, P.D. 1982. Pollen analysis of an interglacial deposit at West Angle, Dyfed, Wales. *New Phytologist, 90,* 327-338.

STEWART, V.I. 1961. A perma-frost horizon in the soils of Cardiganshire. *Welsh Soils Discussion Group Report, 2,* 19-22.

STRAHAN, A. 1886. On the glaciation of south Lancashire, Cheshire and the Welsh Border. *Quarterly Journal of the Geological Society of London, 42,* 369-391.

STRAHAN, A. 1890. *The geology of the neighbourhoods of Flint, Mold and Ruthin.* Memoir of the Geological Survey of Great Britain. H.M.S.O., London.

STRAHAN, A. 1896. On submerged land surfaces at Barry, Glamorganshire. With notes on the fauna and flora by Clement Reid and an appendix on the microzoa by Professor T.R. Jones and F. Chapman. *Quarterly Journal of the Geological Society of London, 52,* 474-489.

STRAHAN, A. 1907(a). *The geology of the South Wales Coalfield, Part VIII. The country around Swansea.* Memoir of the Geological Survey of Great Britain. H.M.S.O., London.

STRAHAN, A. 1907(b). *The geology of the South Wales Coalfield, Part IX. West Gower and the country around Pembrey.* Memoir of the Geological Survey of Great Britain. H.M.S.O., London.

STRAHAN, A. 1909. *The geology of the South Wales Coalfield, Part I. The country around Newport* (2nd edition). Memoir of the Geological Survey of Great Britain. H.M.S.O., London.

STRAHAN, A. & CANTRILL, T.C. 1904. *The geology of the South Wales Coalfield, Part VI. The country around Bridgend.* Memoir of the Geological Survey of Great Britain. H.M.S.O., London.

STRAHAN, A., CANTRILL, T.C., DIXON, E.E.L. & THOMAS, H.H. 1907. *The geology of the South*

Wales Coalfield, Part VII. The country around Ammanford. Memoir of the Geological Survey of Great Britain. H.M.S.O., London.

STRAHAN, A., CANTRILL, T.C., DIXON, E.E.L. & THOMAS, H.H., 1909. *The geology of the South Wales Coalfield, Part X. The country around Carmarthen.* Memoir of the Geological Survey of Great Britain. H.M.S.O., London.

STRAHAN, A., CANTRILL, T.C., DIXON, E.E.L., THOMAS, H.H. & JONES, O.T. 1914. *The geology of the South Wales Coalfield, Part XI. The country around Haverfordwest.* Memoir of the Geological Survey of Great Britain. H.M.S.O., London.

STRAHAN, A. & GIBSON, W. 1900. *The geology of the South Wales Coalfield, Part II. Abergavenny.* Memoir of the Geological Survey of Great Britain. H.M.S.O., London.

STRINGER, C.B. 1975. A preliminary report on new excavations at Bacon Hole Cave. *Journal of the Gower Society, 26*, 32-37.

STRINGER, C.B. 1977(a). Tenth INQUA Congress, Birmingham, Abstracts, 44.

STRINGER, C.B. 1977(b). Evidence of climatic change and human occupation during the last interglacial at Bacon Hole Cave, Gower. *Journal of the Gower Society, 28*, 36-44.

STRINGER, C.B. 1984. The hominid finds. In: Green, H.S. (ed.) *Pontnewydd Cave. A Lower Palaeolithic hominid site in Wales.* The first report. National Museum of Wales, Cardiff, 159-177.

STRINGER, C.B. & CURRANT, A.P. 1981. Comment on "Ipswichian mammal faunas ....." -Turner (1981). *Quaternary Newsletter, 34*, 27-29.

STRINGER, C.B., CURRANT, A.P., SCHWARCZ, H.P. & COLLCUTT, S.N. 1986. Age of Pleistocene faunas from Bacon Hole, Wales. *Nature, 320*, 59-62.

STUART, A.J. 1977(a). British Quaternary vertebrates. In: Shotton, F.W. (ed.) *British Quaternary Studies. Recent advances.* Clarendon Press, Oxford, 298pp.

STUART, A.J. 1977(b). The vertebrates of the last cold stage in Britain and Ireland. *Philosophical Transactions of the Royal Society of London, Series B, 280*, 295-312.

STUART, A.J. 1982. *Pleistocene vertebrates in the British Isles.* Longman, London and New York.

SUGDEN, D. & JOHN, B.S. 1976. *Glaciers and landscape: a geomorphological approach.* Arnold, London.

SUTCLIFFE, A.J. 1976. The British glacial-interglacial sequence. *Quaternary Newsletter, 18*, 1-7.

SUTCLIFFE, A.J. 1981. Progress report on excavations in Minchin Hole, Gower. *Quaternary Newsletter, 3*, 1-17.

SUTCLIFFE, A.J. & BOWEN, D.Q. 1973. Preliminary report on excavations in Minchin Hole, April-May, 1973. *Newsletter of the William Pengelly Cave Studies Trust, 21*, 12-25.

SUTCLIFFE, A.J. & CURRANT, A.P. 1984. Minchin Hole Cave. In: Bowen, D.Q. & Henry A. (eds) *Wales: Gower, Preseli, Fforest Fawr.* Quaternary Research Association Field Guide, April 1984, 33-37.

SWITSUR, V.R. & WEST, R.G. 1972. University of Cambridge natural radiocarbon measurements X. *Radiocarbon, 14*, 239-246.

SWITSUR, V.R. & WEST, R.G. 1973. University of Cambridge natural radiocarbon measurements XI. *Radiocarbon, 15*, 156-164.

SYMONDS, W.S. 1872. *Records of the rocks; or, notes on the geology, natural history and antiquities of North and South Wales, Devon and Cornwall.* John Murray, London.

SYNGE, F.M. 1963. A correlation between the drifts of south-east Ireland with those of west Wales. *Irish Geographer, 4*, 360-366.

SYNGE, F.M. 1964. The glacial succession in west Caernarvonshire. *Proceedings of the Geologists' Association, 75*, 431-444.

SYNGE, F.M. 1969. North cliff, Abermawr, Pembrokeshire. In: *Coastal Pleistocene deposits in Wales.* Quaternary Research Association Field Guide 1969, 26a.

SYNGE, F.M. 1970. The Pleistocene Period in Wales. In: Lewis, C.A. (ed.) *The glaciations of Wales and adjoining regions.* Longman, London, 315-350.

SYNGE, F.M. 1973. The glaciation of south Wicklow and the adjoining parts of the neighbouring counties. *Irish Geographer, 6*, 561-569.

TALLIS, J.H. & KERSHAW, K.A. 1959. Stability of stone polygons in North Wales. *Nature, 183*, 485-486.

TAYLOR, J.A. 1973. Chronometers and chronicles. A study of palaeo-environments in west central Wales. *Progress in Geography, 5*, 247-334.

TAYLOR, J.A. 1975. *An investigation of patterned ground on Moelwyn Mawr, North Wales.* Unpublished report.

TAYLOR, J.A. 1980. Environmental changes in Wales during the Holocene period. In: Taylor, J.A. (ed.) *Culture and environment in prehistoric Wales.* British Archaeological Report, 76, Oxford, 101-130.

TAYLOR, J.A. 1984. A pictorial reconstruction of the lower Dyfi Estuary in 6,700 BP. *Nature in Wales, 3*, 107-108.

TAYLOR, J.A. & TUCKER, R.B. 1970. The peat deposits of Wales, an inventory and interpretation. *Proceedings of the Third International Peat Conference, Ottowa, 163-173*.

THOMAS, D. 1972. Diatomaceous deposits in Snowdonia. *Report of the Institute of Geological Science, 72*, 1-9.

THOMAS, G.S.P. 1976. The Quaternary stratigraphy of the Isle of Man. *Proceedings of the Geologists' Association, 87*, 307-323.

THOMAS, G.S.P. 1984. A Late Devensian glacio-lacustrine fan-delta at Rhosesmor, Clwyd, North Wales. *Geological Journal, 19*, 125-141.

THOMAS, G.S.P. 1985. The Late Devensian glaciation along the border of north-east Wales. *Geological Journal, 20*, 319-340.

THOMAS, H.H. 1923. The source of the stones of Stonehenge. *Antiquaries Journal, 3*, 239-261.

THOMAS, K.W. 1965. The stratigraphy and pollen analysis of a raised peat bog at Llanllwch near Carmarthen. *New Phytologist, 64*, 101-117.

THOMAS, T.M. 1959. The geomorphology of Brecknock. *Brycheiniog, 5*, 55-156.

THORPE, P.M., HOLYOAK, D.T., PREECE, R.C. & WILLING, M.J. 1987. Validity of corrected ^{14}C dates from calcareous tufa. Actes du Colloque de l'A.G.F. *Formations carbontées extrêmes, tufs et travertins*. Paris.

TIDDEMAN, R.H. 1900. On the age of the raised beach of southern Britain as seen in Gower. *Geological Magazine, 7*, 441-443.

TINDALL, S.J., 1983. *The nature of drift deposits at Rhosili and their bearing on the last glacial limit*. Unpublished undergraduate dissertation, Department of Geography, University College, Swansea.

TINSLEY, H.M. & DERBYSHIRE, E. 1976. Late-glacial and post-glacial sedimentation in the Peris-Padarn rock basin, North Wales. *Nature, 260*, 234-238.

TOOLEY, M.J. 1974. Sea-level changes during the last 9,000 years in north-west England. *Geographical Journal, 140*, 18-42.

TRAVIS, C.B. 1944. The glacial history of the Berwyn Hills, North Wales. *Proceedings of the Liverpool Geological Society, 19*, 14-28.

TRIMMER, J. 1831. On the diluvial deposits of Caernarvonshire between the Snowdon chain of hills and the Menai Strait, and on the discovery of marine shells in diluvial sand and gravel on the summit of Moel Tryfane near Caernarvon, 1000' above the level of the sea. *Proceedings of the Geologists' Association, 1*, 331-332.

TRIMMER, J. 1841. *Practical geology and mineralogy*. Parker and Son, London.

TROTMAN, D.M. 1963. *Data for late-glacial and post-glacial history in South Wales*. Unpublished Ph.D. thesis, University of Wales.

TRUEMAN, A.E. 1924. The geology of the Swansea district. *Proceedings of the Geologists' Association, 35*, 283-308.

TURNER, A. 1981(a). Ipswichian mammal faunas, cave deposits and hyaena. *Quaternary Newsletter, 33*, 17-22.

TURNER, A. 1981(b). Ipswichian mammal faunas – a reply to Stringer and Currant. *Quaternary Newsletter, 35*, 32-37.

TURNER, J. 1962. The *Tilia* decline, an anthropogenic interpretation. *New Phytologist, 61*, 328-341.

TURNER, J. 1964. The anthropogenic factor in vegetational history I. Tregaron and Whixhall Mosses. *New Phytologist, 63*, 73-90.

TURNER, J. 1965. A contribution to the history of forest clearance. *Proceedings of the Royal Society of London, 161B*, 353-354.

TURNER, J. 1977. Tregaron Bog and the Dyfi Estuary: Ynyslas and Borth. In: Bowen, D.Q. (ed.) *Wales and the Cheshire-Shropshire lowland*. INQUA X Congress. Guidebook for excursions A8 and C8. Geo Abstracts, Norwich, 34-37.

UNWIN, D.J. 1969. Banc-y-Warren. In: *Coastal Pleistocene deposits in Wales*. Quaternary Research Assocation Field Guide 1969, 29.

UNWIN, D.J. 1970. *Some aspects of the glacial geomorphology of Snowdonia, North Wales*. Unpublished M. Phil. thesis, University of London.

UNWIN, D.J. 1973. The distribution and orientation of corries in northern Snowdonia, Wales. *Transactions of the Institute of British Geographers, 58*, 85-97.

UNWIN, D.J. 1975. The nature and origin of the corrie moraines of Snowdonia. *Cambria, 2*, 20-33.

VALDEMAR, A.E. 1970. A new assessment of the occupation of the Cefn Cave in relation to the Bont Newydd Cave. *Transactions of the Cave Research Group of Great Britain, 12*, 109-112.

VINCENT, P.J. 1976. Some periglacial deposits near Aberystwyth, Wales, as seen with a scanning electron microscope. *Biuletyn Peryglacjalny, 25*, 59-64.

VIVIAN, H.H. 1887. Parc Cwm tumulus. *Archaeologica Cambrenesis*, for 1887, 200-201.

VIVIAN, R.A. & BOCQUET, G. 1973. Subglacial cavitation phenomena under the glacier d'Argentiere, Mont Blanc, France. *Journal of Glaciology, 12*, 439-451.

WALKER, M.F. & TAYLOR, J.A. 1976. Post-Neolithic vegetation changes in the western Rhinogau, Gwynedd, north-west Wales. *Transactions of the Institute of British Geographers, 1*, 323-345.

WALKER, M.J.C. 1980. Late-glacial history of the Brecon Beacons, South Wales. *Nature, 287*, 133-135.

WALKER, M.J.C. 1982(a). The late-glacial and early Flandrian deposits at Traeth Mawr, Brecon Beacons, South Wales. *New Phytologist, 90*, 177-194.

WALKER, M.J.C. 1982(b). Early and mid-Flandrian environmental history of the Brecon Beacons, South Wales. *New Phytologist, 91*, 147-165.

WALKER, M.J.C. 1984. Craig-y-fro and Craig Cerrig-gleisiad, Brecon Beacons/Fforest Fawr. In: Bowen, D.Q. & Henry, A. (eds) *Wales: Gower, Preseli, Fforest Fawr*. Quaternary Research Association Field Guide, April 1984, 91-96.

WALKER, R. 1978. Diatom and pollen studies of a sediment profile from Melynllyn, a mountain tarn in Snowdonia, North Wales. *New Phytologist, 81*, 791-804.

WALSH, P.T., BUTTERWORTH, M.A. & WRIGHT, K. 1982. The palynology and provenance of the coal fragments contained in the Late Pleistocene Lleiniog gravels, of Anglesey, North Wales. *Geological Journal, 17*, 23-30.

WASHBURN, A.L. 1979. *Geocryology: a survey of periglacial processes and environments*. (2nd ed.) Edward Arnold, London, 406pp.

WATSON, E. 1960. Glacial landforms in the Cader Idris area. *Geography, 45*, 27-38.

WATSON, E. 1962. The glacial morphology of the Tal-y-llyn Valley, Merionethshire. *Transactions of the Institute of British Geographers, 30*, 15-31.

WATSON, E. 1965(a). Grèzes litées ou eboulis ordonnés tardiglaciaires dans la région d'Aberystwyth, au centre du Pays de Galles. *Bulletin of the Association of French Geographers, 338*, 16-25.

WATSON, E. 1965(b). Periglacial structures in the Aberystwyth region of central Wales. *Proceedings of the Geologists' Association, 76*, 443-462.

WATSON, E. 1966. Two nivation cirques near Aberystwyth, Wales. *Biuletyn Peryglacjalny, 15*, 79-101.

WATSON, E. 1967. *The periglacial element in the landscape of the Aberystwyth region*. Unpublished Ph.D. thesis, University of Wales (Aberystwyth).

WATSON, E. 1968. The periglacial landscape of the Aberystwyth region. In: Bowen, E.G., Carter, H. & Taylor, J.A. (eds) *Geography at Aberystwyth*. University of Wales Press, Cardiff, 35-49.

WATSON, E. 1969. The slope deposits in the Nant Iago Valley, near Cader Idris, Wales. *Biuletyn Peryglacjalny, 18*, 95-113.

WATSON, E. 1970. The Cardigan Bay area. In: Lewis, C.A. (ed.) *The glaciations of Wales and adjoining regions*. Longman, London, 125-145.

WATSON, E. 1971. Remains of pingos in Wales and the Isle of Man. *Geological Journal, 7*, 381-392.

WATSON, E. 1972. Pingos of Cardiganshire and the latest ice limit. *Nature, 236*, 343-344.

WATSON, E. 1976. Field excursions in the Aberystwyth region. *Biuletyn Peryglacjalny, 26*, 79-112.

WATSON, E. 1977(a). *Mid and North Wales*. INQUA X Congress. Guidebook for excursion C9, Geo Abstracts, Norwich, 48pp.

WATSON, E. 1977(b). The periglacial environment of Great Britain during the Devensian. In: Mitchell, G.F. & West, R.G. The changing environmental conditions in Great Britain and Ireland during the Devensian (last) cold stage. *Philosophical Transactions of the Royal Society of London*, Series B, 280, 183-198.

WATSON, E. 1977(c). A section through a fossil pingo rampart in Mid Wales. Tenth INQUA Congress, Birmingham, Abstracts, p.494.

WATSON, E. 1982. Periglacial slope deposits at Morfa-bychan, near Aberystwyth. In: Bassett, M.G. (ed.) *Geological excursions in Dyfed, south-west Wales*. National Museum of Wales, Cardiff, 313-325.

WATSON, E. & WATSON, S. 1967. The periglacial origin of the drifts at Morfa-bychan, near Aberystwyth. *Geological Journal, 5*, 419-440.

WATSON, E. & WATSON, S. 1970. The coastal periglacial slope deposits of the Cotentin Peninsula. *Transactions of the Institute of British Geographers, 49*, 125-144.

WATSON, E. & WATSON, S. 1971. Vertical stones and analogous structures. *Geografiska Annaler, 53*, 107-114.

WATSON, E. & WATSON, S. 1972. Investigations of some pingo basins near Aberystwyth, Wales. *Report of the 24th International Geological Congress, Montreal*, Section 12, 212-223.

WATSON, E. & WATSON, S. 1974. Remains of pingos in the Cletwr basin, south-west Wales. *Geografiska Annaler, 56A*, 213-225.

WATSON, E. & WATSON, S. 1977. Nivation forms and deposits in Cwm Ystwyth. In: Watson, E. (ed.) *Mid and North Wales*. INQUA X Congress, Guidebook for excursion C9, Geo Abstracts, Norwich, 24-27.

WATSON, S. 1987. Terraced fills in the Rheidol Valley, Wales. *Journal of Quaternary Science, 2*, 165-166.

WATTS, W.A. 1980. Regional variations in the response of vegetation to late-glacial climatic events in Europe. In: Lowe, J.J., Gray, J.M. & Robinson, J.E. (eds) *The late-glacial of North-West Europe*. Oxford.

WEDD, C.B. & KING, W.B.R. 1924. *The geology of the country around Flint, Hawarden and Caergwrle*. Memoir of the Geological Survey of Great Britain. H.M.S.O., London.

WEDD, C.B., SMITH, B., KING, W.B.R. & WRAY, D.A., 1929. *The geology of the country around Oswestry*. Memoir of the Geological Survey of Great Britain, H.M.S.O., London.

WEDD, C.B., SMITH, B. & WILLS, L.J. 1928. *The geology of the country around Wrexham, Part 2. Coal Measures and newer formations*. Memoir of the Geological Survey of Great Britain, H.M.S.O., London.

WELCH, F.B.A. & TROTTER, F.M. 1961. *Geology of the country around Monmouth and Chepstow*. Memoir of the Geological Survey of Great Britain, H.M.S.O., London.

WEST, I.M. 1972. The origin of the supposed raised beach at Porth Neigwl, North Wales. *Proceedings of the Geologists' Association, 83*, 191-195.

WEST, R.G. 1968. *Pleistocene geology and biology*. Longman, London.

WEST, R.G. 1977. Early and Middle Devensian flora and vegetation. In: Mitchell, G.F. & West, R.G. The changing environmental conditions in Great Britain and Ireland during the Devensian (last) cold stage. *Philosophical Transactions of the Royal Society of London*, Series B, 280, 229-246.

WHALLEY, W.B. 1976. A fossil rock glacier in Wester Ross. *Scottish Journal of Geology, 12*, 175-178.

WHEELER, R.E.M. 1925. *Prehistoric and Roman Wales*. Clarendon Press, Oxford.

WHITTOW, J.B. 1957. *The Lleyn Peninsula, North Wales. A geomorphological study*. Unpublished Ph.D. thesis, University of Reading.

WHITTOW, J.B. 1960. Some comments on the raised beach platform of south-west Caernarvonshire and on unrecorded raised beach at Porth Neigwl, North Wales. *Proceedings of the Geologists' Association, 71*, 31-39.

WHITTOW, J.B. 1965. The interglacial and post-glacial strandlines of North Wales. In: Whittow, J.B. & Wood, P.D. (eds) *Essays in geography for Austin Miller*. University of Reading, 337pp.

WHITTOW, J.B. & BALL, D.F. 1970. North-west Wales. In: Lewis, C.A. (ed.) *The glaciations of Wales and adjoining regions*. Longman, London, 21-58.

WILKS, P.J. 1977. *Holocene sea-level change in the Cardigan Bay area*. Unpublished Ph.D. thesis, University of Wales (Aberystwyth).

WILKS, P.J. 1979. Mid-Holocene sea-level and sedimentation interactions in the Dovey Estuary area, Wales. *Palaeogeography, Palaeoclimatology, Palaeoecology, 26*, 17-36.

WILLIAMS, A. 1939. Prehistoric and Roman pottery in the Museum of the Royal Institution of South Wales, Swansea. *Archaeologica Cambrensis, 94*, 21-29.

WILLIAMS, A. 1941. Local archaeology 1939-1941. *Proceedings of the Swansea Scientific and field naturalists' Society, 2*, 130-132.

WILLIAMS, G.J. 1968(a). The buried channel and superficial deposits of the lower Usk and their correlation with similar features in the lower Severn. *Proceedings of the Geologists' Association, 79*, 325-348.

WILLIAMS, G.J. 1968(b). *Contributions to the Pleistocene geomorphology of the middle and lower Usk*. Unpublished Ph.D. thesis, University of Wales.

WILLIAMS, K.E. 1927. The glacial drifts of western Cardiganshire. *Geological Magazine, 64*, 205-227.

WILSON, A.C., MATHERS, S.J. & CANNELL, B. 1982. The Middle Sands, a prograding sandur succession; and its significance in the glacial evolution of the Wrexham-Shrewsbury region. *Report of the Institute of Geological Science, 82*, 30-35.

WINWOOD, H.H. 1865. Exploration of the Hoyle's Mouth Cave, near Tenby. *Geological Magazine, 2*, 471-473.

WIRTZ, D. 1953. Zur Stratigraphie des Pleistocäns in westen der Britischen Inseln. *Neues Jahrbuch für Geologie und Paläontologie, 96*, 267-303.

WOOD, A. 1959. The erosional history of the cliffs around Aberystwyth. *Geological Journal, 2*, 271-279.

WOODHEAD, N. & HODGSON, L.M. 1935. A preliminary study of some Snowdonian peats. *New Phytologist, 34*, 263-282.

WOODLAND, A.W. & EVANS, W.B. 1964. *The geology of the South Wales Coalfield, Part 4. The country around Pontypridd and Maesteg.* Memoir of the Geological Survey of Great Britain. H.M.S.O., London.

WORSLEY, P. 1970. The Cheshire-Shropshire lowlands. In: Lewis, C.A. (ed.) *The glaciations of Wales and adjoining regions.* Longman, London, 83-106.

WORSLEY, P. 1977. Periglaciation. In: Shotton, F.W. (ed.) *British Quaternary studies: recent advances.* Oxford University Press, 205-220.

WORSLEY, P. 1980. Problems in radiocarbon dating the Chelford Interstadial of England. In: Cullingford, R.A., Davidson, D.A. & Lewin, J. (eds) *Timescales in geomorphology.* Wiley, New York, 360pp.

WORSLEY, P. 1984. Banc-y-Warren. In: Bowen, D.Q. & Henry, A. (eds). *Wales: Gower, Preseli, Fforest Fawr.* Quaternary Research Association Field Guide, April 1984, 68-76.

WORSLEY, P. 1985. Pleistocene history of the Cheshire-Shropshire plain. In: Johnson, R.H. (ed.). *The geomorphology of north-west England.* Manchester University Press, Manchester, 201-221.

WORSLEY, P. 1986. On the age of wood in till at Broughton Bay. *Quaternary Newsletter, 49*, 17-19.

WRIGHT, W.B. 1914. *The Quaternary Ice Age.* Macmillan, London.

YAPP, R.H., JOHNS, D. & JONES, O.T. 1916. The salt marshes of the Dovey Estuary, Part I. *Journal of Ecology, 4*, 27-42.

YAPP, R.H., JOHNS, D., JONES, O.T. 1917. The salt marshes of the Dovey Estuary, Part II. *Journal of Ecology, 5*, 65-103.

ZAGWIJN, W.H. 1974. The Pliocene-Pleistocene boundary in western and southern Europe. *Boreas, 3*. 75-97.

ZEUNER, F.E. 1945. *The Pleistocene Period.* Hutchinson, London.

ZEUNER, F.E. 1959. *The Pleistocene Period.* (2nd ed.) Hutchinson, London.

ZITTEL, K. von 1901. *History of geology and palaeontology to the end of the nineteenth century.* Walker Scott, London, pp. 562.

Index

The Nature Conservancy Council is the body responsible for advising Government on nature conservation in Great Britain. Its work includes the selection, establishment and management of National Nature Reserves; the selection and management of Marine Nature Reserves; the identification and notification of Sites of Special Scientific Interest; the provision of advice and dissemination of knowledge about nature conservation; and the support and conduct of research relevant to these functions.

This is one of the range of publications produced by Publicity Services Branch.
A catalogue listing current titles is available from Dept GCR
Nature Conservancy Council, Northminster House, Peterborough PE1 1UA.

NATURE CONSERVANCY COUNCIL

ISBN 0 86139 570 0 © NCC 1989
Designed by Meridian Creative. Typesetting by Apple Pie (DTP) Ltd. Printed by BAS Printers Ltd. 1M